Commentary on the American Prayer Book

COMMENTARY ON THE AMERICAN PRAYER BOOK

MARION J. HATCHETT

The Seabury Press / New York

Page references to The Book of Common Prayer appearing in this book are to the standard edition of 1979.

Citations of scripture (except for the psalms) are to the Revised Standard Version of the Bible, copyright © 1946, 1952 by the Division of Christian Education of the National Council of the Churches of Christ in the U.S.A.

Citations of psalms are to the psalter of The Book of Common Prayer, 1979.

Quotations from the *Oxford American Prayer Book Commentary* by Massey Hamilton Shepherd, Jr., New York: Oxford University Press, 1950, are used with permission.

Excerpts from the English translation of *The Roman Missal* copyright © 1973, International Committee on English in the Liturgy, Inc. All rights reserved.

References are also made to *The Book of Occasional Services,* copyright © 1979 by the Church Pension Fund, New York.

1981
The Seabury Press / 815 Second Avenue / New York, N.Y. 10017

Second Printing

Library of Congress Cataloging in Publication Data

Hatchett, Marion J
Commentary on the American prayer book.

Bibliography: p. 595
Includes index.
1. Protestant Episcopal Church in the U.S.A.
Book of common prayer. I. Title.
BX5945.H37   264'.03   80-20719
ISBN 0-8164-0206-X

To my wife, Carolyn,
and to my three children,
Martha, Ann, and John

Contents

Foreword

"Anamnesis is the antithesis of amnesia." This is the principle on which the Reverend Marion J. Hatchett, author of this commentary on the Book of Common Prayer, 1979, bases his scholarly work. "A person with amnesia has lost identity and purpose. To know who you are, to whom you belong, and where you are headed, you must remember . . . . A Christian is one for whom, through anamnesis, the death and resurrection of Jesus Christ is a present reality, and one who has already entered the Kingdom, though it is not yet realized in its fullness." This commentary helps us to recall our Christian heritage, and to be more Christian.

For a person claiming no expertise in liturgical scholarship the general introductions to each rite bring to mind the principles, texts, and development of Christian worship from the earliest times until now—with illuminating insights on prayer, theology, ministry, mission, and much else.

The serious scholar will place this book alongside the Book of Common Prayer, and will be led to re-read many a document, from Hippolytus, through the several sacramentaries, and on into the formularies and rites in the English language since the sixteenth century. The references are well documented to make such detailed study possible.

The commentary takes advantage of the "explosion of knowledge of the history and basic structures of the liturgy; and a growing awareness of its anthropological, sociological, psychological, and pastoral dimensions." *Recall* includes the recovery of the baptismal and paschal imagery of the early church, a deepened awareness of the tides of church history, of the influence of Vatican II, of the Lambeth Conferences of the Anglican Communion, of the annual meetings of the House of Bishops of the Episcopal Church, of the many revisions in progress in other Anglican churches, and of the processes of Trial Use in this church. The author gives due recognition to scholars in every age, as well as to the many other persons who had a share in this latest revision of the Book of Common Prayer.

It had been the stated purpose of the Standing Liturgical Commission of the Episcopal Church to compile an authoritative study of the sources of the various liturgical formularies included in the 1979 Prayer Book. When, however, the Commission learned that one of its leading members was already engaged in the preparation of a detailed commentary, it decided to forego any possible duplication and to entrust the project to Dr. Hatchett. Thus, the present work incorporates what the Commission had intended and, at the same time, provides a detailed commentary. It should be stressed, however, that the work is entirely that of Dr. Hatchett.

Dr. Hatchett is eminently suited to this task. He is the author of what is fast becoming a classic study of liturgy, *Sanctifying Life, Time, and Space* (Seabury Press, New York, 1976). As a member of the Standing Liturgical Commission since 1976, he chaired the Committee which produced *The Book of Occasional Services,* 1979. He was also the Chairman of the ecumenical sub-committee which produced the Common Eucharistic Prayer (Prayer D in Rite Two of the Prayer Book).

In the course of our close association in the work of Prayer Book revision, I have come to admire Dr. Hatchett's thoroughness, the breadth and depth of his knowledge, and his devotion to all that is best in our Anglican heritage.

It is a signal honor to commend this outstanding work to all members of the Episcopal Church, and to all other Christians who would like to know more about the rich spiritual resources of our Prayer Book.

(The Rt. Rev.) Chilton Powell,
Chairman of the Standing Liturgical
Commission from 1966 to 1979

Preface

The *Oxford American Prayer Book Commentary* by Massey
Hamilton Shepherd, Jr., which was first published in 1950,
made available the latest liturgical knowledge of that time. That book
served the church well in terms of the liturgical and theological
background and interpretation of the 1928 American revision of the
Prayer Book. It also introduced its readers to further liturgical developments and to advances in liturgical knowledge, and thereby
helped to pave the way for liturgical revision. This commentary upon
the 1979 American Prayer Book is heavily indebted to the work of Dr.
Shepherd. In the same year in which that commentary was published
the first of the Prayer Book Studies with specific recommendations
for revision came into print.

Because of various complications in layout, and in order to keep
the volume within a manageable size, the text of the 1979 Prayer
Book is not included within this volume. Page references to the
Prayer Book are provided instead. In addition to detailed commentary, this volume includes background information on each of the
rites. Quotations from Prayer Books prior to the revision of 1662 have
been modernized in spelling and punctuation. References to the
Scriptures are to the Revised Standard Version, except for the psalms
which are cited in the version of this Prayer Book.

I am indebted to more sources and authorities than it is possible to
acknowledge. The selected bibliography contains some of the principal secondary sources. Many primary sources are noted within the
text. I would not have embarked upon the project had I not been
approached by the Rev. F. Reid Isaac of the Seabury Press and encouraged to pursue it by the Rev. Dr. Thomas J. Talley and my
long-suffering wife and children. A student, John M. Gibson, con-

scientiously put in long hours throughout a long hot summer as a research assistant. Several persons who have been most heavily involved throughout much of the revision process have given generously of their time and knowledge in answering my queries, tracing elusive sources, and reading and checking substantial portions of the manuscript. For such help I owe special debts of gratitude to Captain Howard E. Galley, formerly of the Prayer Book Revision Office, and to a number of members of the Standing Liturgical Commission and its drafting committees, especially Otis Charles, Robert H. Greenfield, Charles M. Guilbert, Anne LeCroy, Leonel L. Mitchell, H. Boone Porter, Chilton Powell, and Charles P. Price, and to the Commission's Coordinator, Leo Malania. The Rev. Edward Meeks Gregory has contributed greatly by reading the manuscript and making many valuable recommendations. I wish to thank a colleague, the Rev. Dr. Donald S. Armentrout, for checking a substantial portion of the manuscript. A number of students have given generously of their time to help with the tedious task of proof reading, especially Charles D. Cooper, Edwin M. Cox, Beverly Davis, Carl P. Daw, Richard G. Elliott, John M. Gibson, Edward E. Godden, Maurice L. Goldsmith, J. Hunter Isaacs, John S. Liebler, W. William Melnyk, J. Blaney Pridgen, Marcus B. Robertson, Melissa Rundlett, John R. Throop, J. Scott Turner, William D. Wieland, and Wayne P. Wright. I am indebted to Lyn Kelly who typed a portion of the manuscript, and to Bettie Lou Grayson who took over when school started and worked conscientiously and enthusiastically on the major portion. Howard E. Galley with his experience as editorial assistant in the Prayer Book Revision Office, and Dr. Anne LeCroy, professor of English and member of the Standing Liturgical Commission, brought unique qualifications to their tasks as editors of this work. Finally, I wish to thank my wife, Carolyn, and my children, Martha, Ann, and John, who have exhibited unusual patience and understanding throughout the process and have been encouraging and helpful in many ways.

M.J.H.
The Baptism of Our Lord Jesus Christ, 1980

Introduction

The first Christians had no explicitly liturgical books. Apparently they continued the ritual pattern of Judaism, but interpreted and remodeled it in accordance with the Christian gospel. Once the church moved further from its Jewish roots and sought to adapt itself to the languages, culture, and thought of the Gentile world, there developed a type of book, the church order, which contained descriptions of various liturgies, models for prayers, and directions for the conduct of rites. The most important of these orders still extant are: the Didache, an Eastern document probably dating from the second century; the Apostolic Tradition of Hippolytus, usually considered a Roman document, dating about A.D. 215; the Didascalia, a third century Syrian document; and the Apostolic Constitutions, a Syrian document of the late fourth century which used the three earlier church orders as sources.

Early in the fourth century, Christianity was officially recognized by the Roman State. The monastic movement and the theological controversies of the period led to elaboration of the liturgy, more theological definition within the rites, strict regulation of the functions of various orders of ministers, and the establishment of fixed, written texts. During the fourth and fifth centuries the church orders were supplemented or replaced by *libelli* (booklets) which were eventually put together to form books for those responsible for various parts of the rites. The celebrant, for example, had a sacramentary which contained the prayers to be read by him. The reader's parts were written or indicated in a lectionary which might have been in any of three forms: (1) a table which indicated the beginnings and endings of the readings; (2) a marked Bible; (3) a collection of

1

pericopes or selections. In another book were the litanies and any other portions of the rites for which a deacon might be responsible. The cantor and choir had antiphonary, psalter, gradual, or hymnal as might be appropriate. Fixed portions of the rites were said from memory. A gathering of participants was necessary at the celebration of a eucharist, daily office, baptism, marriage, or burial.

As liturgies developed in various parts of the empire, they acquired different characteristics. Eastern forms retained ancient practices and structures, with a highly developed ceremonial and hymnody, and texts rich in biblical and homiletic content. In theory, the rite has always been in the vernacular, with litanies and icons having a prominent place in the liturgy. The theology is centered on the resurrection (eschaton) and retains more tension between "chronos," chronological time, and "kairos," the fulfillment of time, than that of the West.

Western liturgies are of two principal kinds, the Gallican and the Roman. Until late in the eighth century, the Roman rite was limited to Western North Africa, Roman missionary outposts, and the city of Rome. The Gallican was the rite of Western Europe until the Roman gradually superseded it. In contrast to the Eastern and Gallican rites, the Roman was characterized by simplicity, brevity, and a somber quality. It contained little popular hymnody or vocal participation by the congregation. At a relatively early date, the number of readings was reduced, and preaching and the prayers of the people were dropped.

Gallican rites, largely suppressed between the eighth and twelfth centuries, differ from the Roman in certain general characteristics. They were characterized by a multiplicity of texts and elaborate ceremonial; like the Eastern liturgies, Gallican liturgies were basically conservative in structure (for example, they retained the custom of three readings and the prayers of the people after these had been dropped from the Roman rite). Within a fixed framework there was a variety of elaboration drawn from both Eastern and Western sources, allowing much vocal participation by the congregation. Homiletic material was extensive, and the rites as a whole had a highly poetic quality.

Some prayers and formularies in the 1979 Prayer Book have been derived from, or strongly influenced by, ancient church orders and the Eastern liturgies. Numerous prayers and formularies come from early Roman and Gallican sacramentaries. (In the text these are identified by number in the current scholarly, critical editions.) Most important among the Roman sacramentaries are the Leonine, the Gelasian, and the Gregorian.[1]

The alliance of the papacy with the Holy Roman Empire stimulated a concerted effort to suppress the Gallican rites, making the Roman rite a symbol of unity. The ninth century was a time of illiteracy and superstition; few of the laity could understand the Latin of the rites, and many of the clergy were poorly educated, unable to preach competently, unskilled in the words and actions of the Mass. Monks occupied the more prominent positions in the church and, as the parochial system expanded rapidly, bishops were no longer able to function in the role of *pater familias* to the people. Presbyters often took on many of the responsibilities formerly belonging to the episcopate. The eleventh century brought massive reorganization and revision of liturgical books; further efforts were made to suppress the Gallican rites. The Fourth Lateran council in 1215, in company with the papal court and the Franciscan Order, supported further revision and moves toward uniformity.

Romanizing of the Gallican rites had begun even before the days of Charlemagne, as Roman commemorations and texts gradually replaced or supplemented Gallican forms. In the Bobbio missal, for example, is a eucharistic rite that is Gallican through the Sanctus, then Roman to the close of the rite. The Celtic Stowe missal contains a Roman canon in its Eucharist, but the canon has all the elements of a Gallican eucharistic prayer: a Gallican post-Sanctus, Gallican expansion of the institution narrative, and a normal Gallican post-institution supplication. Even the essentially Gallican Missale Gothicum and Missale Gallicanum vetus contain some Roman forms.

Some evidence of Gallicization in the Roman rite appears in the Gelasian sacramentary, but the Gallicizing process was greatly accelerated by efforts to suppress the Gallican rites. A Gallican supplement, probably by Benedict of Aniane, was added to the Gregorian sacramentary, providing propers, rites, and ceremonies which were important in the liturgical life of the Gallican people. Many such incorporations into the Roman rite eventually affected the books used in Rome itself and then spread elsewhere. For example, in the eleventh century the Gloria in excelsis came into normal use and the Nicene Creed was included in the eucharistic rite.

From the eleventh century on, the Roman rite was the rite of Western Europe, except in the area around Milan and some places in

---

[1] See page 14 for the list of major texts.

Spain. Various late medieval uses, mistakenly called rites, were variants of the Roman rite characteristic of a particular location or monastic order. These uses were marked by Gallican elements or innovations, or by resistance to particular revisions or innovations. In England, just before the Reformation, the most popular uses were those of Sarum, York, and Hereford. By far the most popular was the Sarum, the use of Salisbury Cathedral. Its codification was probably begun with the founding of the new cathedral at Salisbury when Richard la Poore was bishop (1217–1228).

The inconvenience of having a number of booklets for the Mass apparently was felt as early as the ninth century, as a few manuscripts indicate, but liturgical books were not reorganized to any extent until the eleventh century. At that time all things necessary for conduct of the eucharist were gathered into one book—the missal; material for the daily offices into the breviary, litanies into the processional, pastoral offices into the manuale (agenda or rituale), episcopal rites into the pontifical or benedictional. Rules for the conduct of the rites were collected in the ordinale (customary, or pie). No longer was it necessary to have a group of ministers to conduct services; one priest could celebrate the eucharist, say the daily office, baptize, marry, or bury. The saying of daily offices, and even the celebration of the eucharist became the individual duty of those in holy orders. Portable breviaries (portiforia) and a portable missal (missale itinerarium) were provided for clergy on journeys.

Since a single officiant could conduct the various rites without requiring the help of other ministers, services soon came to be celebrated for the people rather than by them. A system of stipends developed so that the individual performing the rite could be paid by the person or persons for whom it was conducted. These changes were in part the result of the laity's increasing inability to understand ecclesiastical Latin, particularly where the unfamiliar Roman rite had replaced the Gallican; in part they resulted from the spread of individual, nonparticipatory worship. The liturgy became a spectator sport, or, as often happened, rites became the private devotions of the priest and the setting for nonliturgical devotions of the people. In the later middle ages Peter Lombard, Hugh of St. Victor, and Thomas Aquinas, like other theologians of the period, provided definitions, rationales, and allegorical interpretations for the rites; theologians of earlier periods had, in contrast, found in the rites themselves the foundations and sources of theology—lex orandi, lex credendi ("the law of prayer, the law of faith").

4

In his *Babylonian Captivity*, Luther attacked certain sacramental teachings and practices of the Roman church. Carlstadt and other reformers began to revise the liturgy. Luther's own work of revision began in 1523: he provided forms for the Mass, the daily offices, baptism, marriage, ordination, and the litany; wrote a catechism, and composed a number of hymns. His work was conservative in comparison with other forms appearing among continental reformers. A flood of church orders was produced by various impatient persons; Luther adhered more closely to medieval forms than did the others.

Several of the orders are especially important in the history of the Prayer Book. One, published by Johann Brenz and Andreas Osiander for Brandenburg-Nürnberg in 1533, came to the attention of Thomas Cranmer in 1532. He was boarding with Osiander, while on a mission for Henry VIII, at the time Osiander was preparing the order. Another German church order which contributed heavily to the Prayer Book was that of Electoral Brandenburg, published in 1540. Possibly the most important of all was the Consultation of Archbishop Herman von Wied of Cologne, the liturgical portion of which was written by Martin Bucer, of Strassburg. It was first published in Germany in 1543; two printings in English were soon after made in London, the first in 1547, and a second revised version in 1548.

The conservative attempt at revision had not satisfied the radical reformers. Zwingli, in 1525, proposed a German liturgy which was more didactic, rationalistic, and subjective than the Lutheran liturgies. Calvin found at Geneva rites similar to those of Zwingli in Zurich; from his exile in Strassburg he brought rites influenced by the liturgy he found there. The rites, he stated, should be based on warrant of scripture and the custom of the early church. Exiles in England in the sixteenth century used Calvin's rites which were published by Pullain in 1551. During the reign of Mary Tudor, English exiles on the continent used a service book which became the basis for the Scottish Book of Common Order in 1562.

Shortly after Henry's break with the papacy, efforts toward reform in England gained strength as numerous publications appeared: "Marshall's Primer," the Ten Articles, the royal injunctions, *The Bishops' Book*, the Thirteen Articles, Hilsey's Primer, the Six Articles, *The King's Book*, the Rationale of Ceremonial, the reform of the Sarum breviary, Cranmer's drafts for the Daily Office, the English Litany, Henry's Primer, the book of homilies, the Edwardian injunctions, the English editions of Hermann's Consultation, the Order of the Communion of 1548, and Cranmer's Catechism. Each of these helped to pave the way for the Act of Uniformity requiring exclusive use of the Book of Common Prayer by Whitsunday, June 9, 1549.

Varied works contributed to the content of the 1549 Book. Writings of the early church fathers, German church orders, the proposed breviary of the Spanish Cardinal Francisco Quiñones, Eastern liturgies, Gallican rites, and various uses of the medieval Roman rite provided rich sources of material.

The act recalling the old service books, and the Act of Uniformity attached to the first revision, set forth the principles controlling the composition of the new Book. The Prayer Book was said to be: (1) "grounded upon the holy scripture"; (2) "agreeable to the order of the primitive church"; (3) unifying to the realm; and (4) "edifying" to the people. (See the preface of the first Prayer Book, pp. 866–867 of the 1979 Book, and the commentary in this volume, pp. 585–586.)

The 1549 Book was too radical for the Devonshire rebels, for various conservative bishops, such as Bonner, Thirlby, and Gardiner, and for priests who continued to use the old service books or who "counterfeited Masses." On the other hand, its revisions were not radical enough to satisfy the Norfolk rebels, or the continental reformers, including Martin Bucer and Peter Martyr, who had come to positions of importance in England. The Anabaptists and some of the clergy and bishops, John Hooper and John Knox among them, were also displeased by the Book's conservatism.

The Act of Uniformity which enforced the use of a revision of the Prayer Book on All Saints' Day 1552 called the 1549 Book a "godly order" which needed reform only because of misinterpretations and because of doubts about the manner of ministrations. In the revision of 1552, rubrics were tightened and teachings more explicitly asserted than in the 1549 Book. It also restored some of the "black letter" days, some relics of octaves, and the obligation that all clergy say daily offices. Generally it made explicit what had been implicit in the 1549 version, but may also have introduced elements from Calvinistic liturgies.

The Roman rite was officially restored in England during Mary Tudor's reign. Some of the refugees to the continent continued use of the 1552 Book; those who went to Frankfurt revised it; those in Geneva substituted a liturgy based on that of Calvin.

In 1559 Elizabeth restored the 1552 Book, moderately revised. A Latin version, with some changes, was published in 1560 for use in the universities. A number of "black letter" days were added to the calendar in 1561. Despite Elizabeth's official imposition of the Book on all of England, however, Puritan versions or revisions of the Book of Common Prayer were published and used surreptitiously. The Scots established the Book of Common Order, based on Knox's Genevan service book, as their manual for worship. Near the end of Elizabeth's reign, in response to this activity, Richard Hooker wrote in the fifth book of his *Ecclesiastical Polity* a systematic defense of the Prayer Book.

Hoping for reform, the Puritans presented the "Millenary Petition" to James I when he became king of England. This work consisted mainly of protests against features of the 1559 Book. The Hampton Court Conference held shortly afterward authorized both the preparation of the King James Version of the Scriptures and a slightly revised edition of the Prayer Book (1604) which made a few concessions to the Puritans. During the reigns of both James I and Charles I, however, a number of "anti-Calvinistic" clergy came to positions of power and authority. These men, among them John Overall, Lancelot Andrewes, William Laud, Matthew Wren, and John Cosin, were concerned for "decency and order" in worship. Their reactions toward certain aspects of Roman, Lutheran, and Eastern theology and liturgical practice were, furthermore, much less negative than the attitudes of the Puritans.

Under James I the episcopacy was established in Scotland and efforts were made to bring Scottish liturgy more into harmony with that of the Book of Common Prayer. Charles I and Archbishop Laud attempted to enforce in Scotland the use of the Prayer Book of 1637, which incorporated some of the elements of Scottish tradition, some principles of "Laudian" churchmanship, and some parts of the 1549 Book. Contention over this move brought a temporary end to episcopacy in Scotland.

Further struggle arose over the new Laudian canons of 1640 which legislated matters previously left to the individual conscience. In 1641 a committee of the House of Lords criticized certain Laudian innovations and recommended concessions which it hoped would appease the Puritans, but the move was too late and the concessions too few. By 1645 use of the Book of Common Prayer had been forbidden and a Directory for the Publique Worship of God replaced it.

The Directory was the result of compromise among several groups—Scots and English of presbyterian persuasion, some who adhered to free church principles, and some with moderate episcopal principles. The book provided rubrics and models rather than fixed texts and was fleshed out by different people with different forms: extemporaneous prayers, materials from the Scottish Calvinistic tradition, forms "in Scripture words," forms taken largely from or modeled after those of the Book of Common Prayer (for example, those of Robert Sanderson), or even material from Eastern liturgies (for example, the rites of Jeremy Taylor). In a few remote areas, in private chaplaincies, among exiles abroad, and in Virginia, the Book of Common Prayer continued in use. During the interregnum, Anthony Sparrow and Hamon L'Estrange published the first systematic commentaries on the Prayer Book.

With the return of the monarchy in 1660 certain revisions and freedoms were promised. The Puritans presented their "Exceptions" and Richard Baxter's alternative liturgy at the Savoy Conference, but the Laudians were once again in power both in Convocation and Parliament. Cosin prepared a draft for revision, "The Durham Book," which made some concessions to the Puritans but was largely based on notes he and Wren had made earlier. Convocation accepted many of the recommendations of the Durham Book, made relatively few concessions to the Puritans, and, through the Act of Uniformity, enforced the use of the 1662 revision. As a result, over seventeen hundred clergy were ejected from their livings.

The revision process continued in various forms. Two significant attempts at reconciliation were made in the proposals of 1668 and 1689. Edward Stephens, William Whiston, John Henley, and others published, for the use of small groups, liturgies based on Eastern liturgies and on material from the 1549 and 1637 Books. Early in the seventeenth century some Anglicans had begun to have high respect for these materials. Particularly influential among Eastern rites was the Apostolic Constitutions, which had become available in 1563. Early in the eighteenth century, Prayer Books printed for use in Ireland were supplemented by additional rites. In 1718 some of the Non-jurors, who were unable to hold positions in the Church of England because of their adherence to the Stuart monarchy, printed and used forms revised along Eastern lines. Thomas Deacon published his *Compleat Collection of Devotions* in 1734, and later used it with his splinter group of Non-jurors. Scots Non-juring Episcopalians in 1722 issued the first of a series of "Wee Bookies," editions of the 1637 eucharistic rite, modified in subsequent editions. Bishop Thomas Rattray's reconstruction of the Jerusalem Liturgy of St. James, along with English Non-juror rites, had the most significant influence on the "Bookies."

At the beginning of the eighteenth century, sentiment for revision grew among those of Latitudinarian sympathies (those tolerant of variations respecting church government and doctrine); numerous proposed revisions and arguments for revisions were published. Most significant among these were *Free and Candid Disquisitions,* a collection of anonymous essays by different authors, edited by John Jones of Alconbury and published in 1749, and another anonymous 1749 publication, *The Expediency and Necessity of Revising and Improving the Publick Liturgy,* to which was appended a proposal, *A New Liturgy.* A third influential work, *Reasons Humbly Offered for Composing A New Set of Articles of Religion,* published anonymously in 1751, contained twenty-one specimen articles. A series of proposals by "Arians" (eighteenth century forerunners of Unitarians) was also set forth. Several of these took as a starting point the Prayer Book as amended by Samuel Clarke. Theophilus Lindsey, who left the Church of England over the issue of subscription to the Articles of Religion, edited probably the most influential of these "Arian" proposals—a prayer book intended for use in the chapel he set up in London. Benjamin Franklin collaborated with Sir Francis Dashwood in a proposed revision published in London in 1773. Soon after the end of the American Revolution, John Wesley published a revised liturgy for the use of American Methodists, and King's Chapel in Boston adopted a liturgy based on the revision of Theophilus Lindsey. Those who were to exercise leadership in preparing liturgies for the American church were interested in and influenced by these various revisions.

The possibility of making a revision which would find general acceptance in the newly independent United States was complicated not only by liturgical and theological issues but also by political and personal enmities. As the only hope of unity seemed to lie in making just the changes necessitated by political independence, the first interstate convention adopted this stance as a "fundamental principle." In 1785 Bishop Samuel Seabury and a committee appointed by him proposed revisions for Connecticut that followed Latitudinarian lines; these were then sent on to Boston for a convention of other New England states. This convention in turn added proposals to be considered by a convention of states south of New England, meeting in Philadelphia. Various additional proposals were sent to Philadelphia by the Virginia convention as well as by a number of individuals. As a result, the states meeting in Philadelphia set aside the "fundamental principle" and authorized a revision for trial use.

Seabury, motivated by the liturgically and politically conservative Tories in his diocese, did a sudden about-face and set himself against the Proposed Book. When it came off the presses in 1786, however, all the states represented at the Philadelphia and New England conventions, with the exception of New Jersey and Connecticut, authorized use of the book. It was to serve as the basis for the book set forth by the first General Convention in 1789.

In addition to the Proposed Book of 1786, the revisers in 1789 used certain materials from the 1662 English Book, some proposals from the state conventions, and other materials from *Free and Candid Disquisitions* and *The Expediency and Necessity of Revising*, both of which had contributed to the Proposed Book. Jeremy Taylor's popular devotional manual, *Holy Dying*, Bishop Edmund Gibson's *Family Devotions*, and a notebook in which Seabury had written various forms from sources such as the work of Thomas Wilson, Bishop of Sodor and Man, the Scottish eucharistic rite of 1764, and the liturgy of King's Chapel, also contributed materials to the revision. A motion to use the 1662 Book as the basis for the deliberations of the convention of 1789 was defeated, and a copy of the Proposed Book was sent to the printers along with some sheets of instructions on changes to be made from the 1786 edition in the printing of the new Prayer Book.

In 1792 the General Convention adopted revised ordination rites; in 1799, a rite for the consecration of a church; in 1801, a slightly revised version of the Articles of Religion. The convention of 1804 added a rite for the institution of ministers, and a prayer for conventions was officially added among the occasional prayers in 1835. The metrical psalter, listed in the contents of the book, was revised in 1832, and additional hymns were added to the "Prayer Book Collection" in 1808, 1826, and 1865. The psalter and hymns were revised again and published as a separate book in 1871. Other minor changes were made in 1808, 1832, 1835, 1838, 1841, and 1868.

In 1877 the Prayer Book for Ireland was revised, with concessions to evangelical feelings and restrictions against the growing "ritualism" (ceremonialism) of the period as well as against "advanced" interpretations of the rites. In England, despite many proposals for revision, the political controversies and the strife within the church were such that the only successful revision was that of the lectionary for the daily offices in 1871.

William Reed Huntington was the leading figure in a movement toward Prayer Book revision in America, intended especially to provide "liturgical enrichment and increased flexibility of use," which resulted in the very conservative revision of 1892. Some of the proposals not accepted for that revision, however, were incorporated in the revision of 1928.

Supplementary material was added to the English Book for use in

10

Scotland in 1912; there was Prayer Book revision in Canada in 1922, in Ireland in 1926, in England in 1928, and in Scotland in 1929. These revisions, like the American revision of 1928, were primarily directed toward "enrichment" and "flexibility."

During the early decades of the twentieth century there arose renewed interest in biblical theology, patristics, and ecumenism; an explosion of knowledge of the history and basic structures of the liturgy; and a growing awareness of its anthropological, sociological, psychological, and pastoral dimensions. Lay participation·increased steadily, with a rediscovery of the corporate nature of the church and the roles of various orders—lay persons, bishops, priests, and deacons.

In the period after World War I a "liturgical movement," incorporating some of these renewed insights, gained significant following in Germany, France, Belgium, Austria, and Holland. In America the progress of the movement can be traced to the founding of the periodical *Orate Fratres* (now titled *Worship*) by the Benedictines of St. John's Abbey, Collegeville, Minnesota, in 1926. The Roman Catholic Church in the 1950's made some changes inspired by the liturgical movement: the Easter Vigil was restored, the rites of Holy Week reformed, and rubrics simplified. Regulations concerning the eucharistic fast became less strict, and congregations were encouraged to participate in musical portions of the rite. In the Constitution on the Sacred Liturgy, Vatican II emphasized the fact that the liturgy demands "full, conscious, and active participation." It called for a return to the sources of liturgy and for the adaptation of liturgy to modern conditions. Thus began a thorough revision of the liturgical books of the Roman Catholic Church.

Following the lead of the Roman Church, continental Protestants and Eastern Orthodox churches gradually recognized the importance of the liturgical movement and began to respond to it. The Protestant monastery at Taizé has become a center for liturgical renewal and a place of pilgrimage for people from all over the world. There has been in this period a sharing of knowledge and a growing consensus. A concrete result of this consensus can be seen in the present rites of the Church of South India, which incorporated fruits of new knowledge into rites adapted to the particular culture and to the pastoral needs of its people. That liturgy contributed in turn to later Protestant and Catholic revisions. At the present time most of the major Protestant churches throughout the world are actively involved in revision of their liturgical books.

Not until the 1930's did the liturgical movement begin to have some effect on the Anglican Communion, encouraged by the works of

Father A. G. Hebert, Dean William Palmer Ladd, and Walter Lowrie. The first results were the establishment of "parish communions" in some places, the restoration of baptisms to public services, and the return to the congregation of parts of the rites formerly reserved for choirs. Many of the recent discoveries of liturgical scholarship and insights of the liturgical movement were included in *The Oxford American Prayer Book Commentary,* written by Massey H. Shepherd, Jr. (1950). The Anglican Church observed the new directions taken by the Roman Catholic Church, by continental Protestant churches, and by the new rites of the Church of South India. The Lambeth Conference of 1958 acknowledged that the time for more drastic Prayer Book revision had arrived and set forth guidelines which were more fully developed by the Anglican Congress of 1963. Most of the provinces of Anglicanism are currently engaged in revision, employing the method of trial use, pioneered in America in 1786–1789, which allows both clergy and laity to respond after extensive use of trial rites.

The General Convention of 1928 had approved the establishment of a Standing Liturgical Commission. One of its major duties was to prepare for revision of the American Prayer Book. A revised lectionary for the daily offices was approved in 1943; beginning in 1950 the Commission published a series of Prayer Book Studies. The General Convention of 1964 charged the Commission to come to the next convention with concrete proposals for revision. As a result, the Liturgy of the Lord's Supper, a revision of the eucharistic rite, was presented to the convention of 1967 and approved for trial use. Reactions and suggestions of laity and clergy to this service affected the content and form of a series of rites published as *Services for Trial Use* and authorized by the General Convention of 1970. Three years later the convention authorized additional rites. The revised rites of initiation, the eucharistic rites and the daily office, and a complete revision of the Psalter were published as *Authorized Services 1973.* Small booklets containing alternative texts for certain of the rites, and revisions of the marriage rite and of the rites for baptism and confirmation, became available in 1975.

During the process of revision, the Standing Liturgical Commission sought the help of numerous drafting committees, asked for reactions and suggestions from several hundred consultants appointed in various dioceses, and attempted to gather responses from as broad a spectrum as possible of the laity and clergy. The full report of the Commission, known as the *Draft Proposed Book of Common Prayer,* won the majority approval of both houses at the General Convention in 1976. As the *Proposed Book of Common Prayer* it was voted through both houses of General Convention in 1979, and has become the present Standard Book.

Most forms in the 1928 Book have been retained in the 1979 Book; many have been condensed and revised, and some have been used in different ways. The principles which the first Prayer Book (1549) followed also guided this revision: fidelity to the Scriptures and the liturgy of the early church, the unifying of the realm (i.e. the church), the edification of the people. The revisers have drawn from the Scriptures, the church fathers, and the historic liturgies. They have brought together the results of liturgical scholarship with adaptations made to fit present conditions, as well as to meet missionary and pastoral needs. The language has been made contemporary and accords with standard modern English usage. Social concerns of the present have a place in prayers and litanies. There is additional flexibility in rubrics and forms to meet the needs of particular groups and worshiping communities. During the revision period, the Commission kept in contact with other denominations and other churches of Anglicanism so that, in revising, the various Christian communities might be drawn closer to each other rather than being pushed further apart.

Throughout the period from 1964, when the work of revision began, until the approval of the Book at the General Convention of 1976, Bishop Chilton Powell served as Chairman of the Standing Liturgical Commission, and the Rev. Dr. Massey H. Shepherd, Jr., as Vice-Chairman. Other bishops who served as members or consultants of the Commission during all or part of this time were Stanley H. Atkins, E. Otis Charles, A. Donald Davies, William A. Dimmick, William C. Frey, Joseph M. Harte, Arthur C. Lichtenberger, James W. Montgomery, Morgan Porteus, Jonathan G. Sherman, and Albert R. Stuart. Other presbyters, in addition to Dr. Shepherd and the Rev. Dr. Charles M. Guilbert, Custodian of the Standard Book of Common Prayer, were Harold Bassage, Lee M. Benefee, Lloyd S. Casson, Robert W. Estill, David R. Forbes, Donald L. Garfield, Robert H. Greenfield, Louis B. Keiter, Paul E. Langpaap, H. Boone Porter, Jr., Charles P. Price, Charles W. F. Smith, Bonnell Spencer, O. H. C., Preston Wiles, and Richard C. Winn. Lay persons who served during this period were John W. Ashton, Dupuy Bateman, Jr., Frank S. Cellier, James D. Dunning, Virginia Harbour (Mrs. Richard L.), Vivian Kingsley (Mrs. Donald), Anne LeCroy, and Harrison Tillman. Throughout the period, the Rev. Leo Malania served as Coordinator for Prayer Book Revision, and Captain Howard Galley as Assistant.

13

The Major Texts

Roman Sacramentaries

The Leonine or Verona sacramentary (actually a collection of *libelli* containing prayers for various Masses): this exists in a manuscript dated about A.D. 600. The material contained is largely from the sixth century with some sections from the fifth. Edited by L. C. Mohlberg as *Sacramentum Veronense* (Rome: Herder, 1956).

The Gelasian sacramentary: this exists in an eighth century manuscript and represents uses of a period slightly later than the Leonine. Edited by L. C. Mohlberg as *Liber Sacramentorum Romanae Aeclesiae Ordinis Anni Circuli* (Rome: Herder, 1968).

The Gregorian sacramentary: this exists in a manuscript from late in the eighth century; it purports to be the liturgy of the time of Gregory the Great. This copy was sent by Pope Hadrian I (c. 784–791) to Charlemagne as a standard for use in providing Roman books to replace the Gallican books. To meet the needs of the Gallican churches a supplement was added, once thought to be the work of Alcuin, but now considered probably to have been done by Benedict of Aniane early in the ninth century. Both sacramentary and supplement were later adopted in Rome itself and became the source for later Roman editions of the liturgical books. Edited by J. Deschusses as *Le Sacramentaire Grégorien* (Fribourg, 1971).

Gallican Sacramentaries

The principal codices are *Missale Gallicanum vetus*, edited by L. C. Mohlberg (Rome: Herder, 1958), and the *Missale Gothicum* also edited by Mohlberg (Rome: Herder, 1961). Two hybrid documents also include substantial material: *The Bobbio Missal*, edited by E. A. Lowe (London, 1920), and the *Missale Francorum*, edited by L. C. Mohlberg (Rome: Herder, 1957). These are generally considered seventh or eighth century documents.

The Title Page

The title page for the 1549 Prayer Book read "The Book of Common Prayer and Administration of the Sacraments and Other Rites and Ceremonies of the Church After the Use of the Church of England." The term "common prayer" has been used to define regular or cyclic services of the church (the Daily Office, the Litany, and the Eucharist) in contrast to the occasional sacraments and other rites associated with particular points in the life of a Christian. The term may refer, also, just to the Daily Office, or, as Cranmer put it, to Divine Service. In this case the Eucharist would be under the heading "sacraments." "Common Prayer" may have been used, however, in the title of the first Book as a deliberate contrast to the customs of the late medieval period when the daily office was a private obligation of the clergy and monastics, and a typical Eucharist was "Low Mass" performed by a priest, with the assistance of a clerk or cleric, for persons who paid a stipend. The Mass would be said for their "intentions," often without their presence or participation (except possibly at the time when the Sacrament was elevated).

Services in the 1549 Prayer Book assumed the active presence of laity throughout the rites: their personal participation as they joined in certain responses and received communion, and their vicarious participation in portions of the rites said or sung on their behalf by the clerks or other representatives of the people.

For the 1552 Prayer Book the title became "The Book of Common Prayer and Administration of the Sacraments and Other Rites and Ceremonies in the Church of England." In 1662, "according to the use of the Church" replaced "in the Church." By this time the Psalter and the ordination rites were part of the Book, and the title was expanded to read "Together with the Psalter or Psalms of David,

Pointed as They Are To Be Sung Or Said in Churches: And the Form or Manner of Making, Ordaining, and Consecrating of Bishops, Priests, and Deacons."

Ordination rites were not included in the first edition of the American Book, for which the title was simply "The Book of Common Prayer and Administration of the Sacraments and Other Rites and Ceremonies of the Church According to the Use of the Protestant Episcopal Church in the United States of America: Together with the Psalter or Psalms of David." The present revision has an abbreviated title: "The Book of Common Prayer and Administration of the Sacraments and Other Rites and Ceremonies of the Church Together with The Psalter or Psalms of David According to the Use of The Episcopal Church." Not until the eighteenth century were the words "The Book of Common Prayer" normally printed in larger letters than the remainder of the title.

In liturgical use the word "rites" usually refers to the texts of services and the word "ceremonies" to the actions. The title indicates that the services of this Book are those of the Church, that is, of the one, holy, catholic, and apostolic church. Throughout church history various national churches, provinces, or dioceses have adapted the tradition in terms of local "uses;" this edition of the Book of Common Prayer is "According to the Use of The Episcopal Church." An eloquent exposition of this principle is set forth in the preface of the Prayer Book (pp. 9–11). It was composed by the Rev. Dr. William Smith for the Proposed Book of 1786 and has been included, in abbreviated form, in every edition of the Book since that time.

Previous American editions named the church "The Protestant Episcopal Church in the United States of America," the name first adopted at the state convention of Maryland in 1780. It was accepted and incorporated in the constitution of the church at the first General Convention. The word "Protestant" distinguished this branch of the church from the Roman Catholic and Eastern Orthodox churches; the word "Episcopal" distinguished it from various nonconformist denominations. Because the church now includes dioceses not within the continental United States of America, and because the word "Protestant" is sometimes misunderstood in connotation, the General Convention of 1967 voted a constitutional change which provided for alternative use of "The Episcopal Church" to define this province of Anglicanism. Therefore the title of the church for the present Book is "The Episcopal Church."

Certificate

A merican revisions of the Book of Common Prayer have never been under copyright. Anyone may publish all or part of the Book; it can be amended or enlarged upon without penalty. Books used for services, however, must conform to the Standard Book.

At the General Convention of 1792 a committee was appointed to compare the printed edition of the Prayer Book with the acts of the Convention of 1789, "and to prepare a mode of authenticating the book by some certain standard." From this came the printing of the "Standard Book" by Hugh Gaine of New York in 1793. At the Convention of 1801 a canon was passed empowering the Ordinary in any state to compare new editions with the Standard Book, "and a certificate of their having been so compared and corrected shall be published with said books." Revisions and additions made by subsequent General Conventions necessitated the establishment of new Standard Books in 1823, 1832, 1838, 1844, and 1871. The Standard Book of the 1892 and 1928 revisions has not been a corrected edition of the previous Standard, however, but a certified copy of the Prayer Book as revised, authenticated by the signatures of the officers and secretaries of both houses of General Convention.

A Custodian was first appointed in 1868 to keep the plates and a copy of the Standard Book for General Convention. In 1871 the Custodian was given responsibility for making in the Prayer Book the alterations authorized by General Convention. Editions intended for official use must conform to the Standard Book and must contain a certificate from the Custodian. The following have been Custodians of the Standard Book of Common Prayer: Benjamin Isaac Haight, 1868–1879; Francis Harison, 1880–1885; Samuel Hart, 1886–1917; Lucien Moore Robinson, 1917–1932; John Wallace Suter, 1932–

1942; John Wallace Suter, Jr., 1942–1962; Charles Mortimer Guilbert, 1963–.

The Design of the Book

Nelson Gruppo of New York designed the Book in consultation with James Bradbury Thompson of New Haven. The single type face used throughout is Sabon, a rare German face based on original fonts designed by Claude Garamond in the sixteenth century. So that the shape of the rites would be apparent, and in order to make the services easier to follow, headings are provided for important elements in each rite. In earlier editions some of the basic elements—for example the psalms and the lessons of the Daily Offices and the lessons and sermon of the Eucharist—were not marked by a heading but mentioned only in the fine print of the rubrics.

Previous editions of the Prayer Book used extra capital letters within a line to indicate breathing points for the convenience of the people in passages to be read in unison. In this edition the psalms and canticles and the texts that are said in unison, for example, the Creed, the General Confession, the Lord's Prayer, are printed in sense lines.

The Table of Contents

The Prayer Book of 1549 had a table of contents that corresponded roughly to the three books most frequently used by parish priests in the last centuries of the medieval period. Corresponding to the breviary was a table of psalms and lessons for the Daily Office and the texts for Matins and Evensong. The texts of Introits, Collects, Epistles, and Gospels for the church year, and the Eucharist itself were comparable to the missal. To this was appended a slightly revised form of the English Litany of 1544 which, at an earlier stage of the Reformation, had replaced the book of litanies and processions. Then followed a section with the services used in the course of an individual's life: Baptism, Confirmation, Marriage, the Visitation and Communion of the Sick, and Burial of the Dead. This portion corresponded to the earlier priests' manuals. Two other offices—"The Purification of Women" and "A Declaration of Scripture, with certain Prayers to be used on the first Day of Lent, commonly called Ash Wednesday"—may have been last-minute additions. The Ordinal (ordination rites) was printed as a separate book in 1550 and not usually bound with the Book until the revision of 1662.

In the 1552 revision the Litany was moved forward to a place following the Daily Offices, since it was to be used after Morning Prayer every Wednesday, Friday, and Sunday, not just as an introduction to the Sunday Eucharists.

"Godly Prayers" for individual or family devotions were frequently bound with printings of the 1559 and 1604 Prayer Books.

The revision of 1662 included further additions: forms of prayer to be used at sea, special forms for state occasions, and the Articles of Religion. The Catechism was separated from the rite of Confirmation and given its own listing preceding that rite.

The first American Book of 1789 listed prayers and thanksgivings in the table of contents. The Thanksgiving of Women after Childbirth immediately preceded the forms of prayer to be used at sea. Additions were an office for Visitation of Prisoners (taken from the Irish Prayer Book), a service for Thanksgiving Day, "Forms of Prayers to be used in Families," "Selections of Psalms" which might replace the Psalms of the day at the discretion of the Minister, the Psalter, the Metrical Psalter of Tate and Brady, and twenty-seven hymns. A colophon "End of the Prayer Book" was printed after the last hymn.

When the revised ordination rites, the Articles of Religion, and new forms for the consecration of a church and the institution of ministers were added, they were inserted near the end of the Book, prior to the metrical Psalter. In 1871 a new edition of the Hymnal was printed as a separate book.

In the 1892 revision "A Penitential Office for Ash Wednesday" was inserted before the Collects, Epistles, and Gospels.

The order of the Litany and Occasional Prayers was reversed in 1928, and the Eucharist was placed before the Proper for the Church Year. Two "Offices of Instruction" supplanted the Catechism of earlier editions. Thanksgiving after Childbirth was placed immediately after the marriage rite and the Psalter moved to a position following the Burial Office. Rites for Ordination, Consecration of a Church, and the Institution of Ministers followed the Psalter. The older Catechism, forms of prayer to be used in families, and the Articles of Religion were printed as appendices.

In the present edition the table for finding holy days and the lectionaries, matters of concern principally to the clergy and to makers of commercial church calendars, have been moved to the end of the Book. The first section of the Book contains the daily services, including daily devotions for individuals and families. The Collects come between the Daily Offices and the Eucharist, a position they occupied in all editions except that of 1928. One very important aspect of this edition is the provision of "Proper Liturgies for Special Days," arranged in order from Ash Wednesday through the Easter Vigil and leading appropriately into the rite of Holy Baptism. Since Baptism is an initiation to the Eucharist, the eucharistic rite, the principal service of Sundays and other major feasts, follows immediately, restored to its pre-1928 position at the center of the Book. The Pastoral Offices follow in an order related to the critical stages of life. Episcopal Services and the Psalter are next. A large number of prayers and thanksgivings, many of them printed at various places in earlier editions, are gathered into one place for the convenience of clergy and people. Many new forms have been added to this section. "An Outline of the Faith, or Catechism" replaces both the Catechism of older editions and the Offices of Instruction of the 1928 Prayer Book. Included with the Articles of Religion in a section "Historical Documents of the Church" are other pivotal documents.

The Ratification of the
Book of Common Prayer 1789 (p. 8)

E ach revised publication of the English Prayer Books was accompanied by an Act of Uniformity which established the new edition as the liturgy to be used from a certain date "and none other." In America the first interstate convention, which met in New York on October 6–7, 1784, proposed certain alterations in the liturgy. A convention of states south of New England, meeting in Philadelphia on September 27–October 7, 1785, made substantial recommendations for a revision of the Prayer Book and appointed a committee to publish the Proposed Book. This work was issued in April of 1786 and received three years of trial use.

At the first General Convention, which met in Philadelphia in 1789 (September 29), the Proposed Book was revised. A number of changes reverted to the 1662 Book and additional material was brought in from other sources. On October 16, 1789, the new revision was ratified, for use throughout the church "from and after" October 1, 1790. Successive conventions authorized various additions and alterations. Two major revisions, those of 1892 and 1928, precede this present edition. It has not been considered legally necessary to print a new ratification in succeeding revisions.

The Preface (*pp.* 9-11)

This preface has been printed in every edition of the American Book of Common Prayer. It is a condensation of the preface written by the Rev. Dr. William Smith for the Proposed Book of 1786. The preface was heavily dependent upon an anonymous volume published in 1749, *Free and Candid Disquisitions*. Arguments for particular changes which had been part of the lengthier preface to that Book were omitted in 1789. The second and third paragraphs and a portion of the fourth are largely a paraphrase of the preface to the English revision of 1662.

The preface states the principle that the worship of the church may be altered for the edification of the people, "provided the substance of the Faith be kept entire." In the alterations of the Prayer Book there should be an effort to keep "the happy mean between too much stiffness in refusing, and too much easiness in admitting variations in things once advisedly established." The aims of Prayer Book revision are presented: the preservation of peace and unity in the church, the procuring of reverence, the exciting of piety and devotion, and the elimination of elements which provide the occasion for "cavil or quarrel" against the Prayer Book liturgy.

Revision was a necessary result of the changed political situation in this country. Further amendments and alterations were deemed expedient, yet an essential unity with the Church of England in basic points of doctrine, discipline, and worship was maintained. The preface ends with a brief commendation of the Book to "every true member of our church, and every sincere Christian."

23

Concerning the Service
of the Church (*pp. 13-14*)

T his section first appeared in the 1892 revision. It brings together certain regulations which had previously been governed by canon or custom, or implied in the rubrics of the Prayer Book. The section was revised for the 1928 revision and again for the present edition.

The Prayer Book Pattern of Regular Services (p. 13)

The first direction makes explicit the pattern of worship implicit in all previous editions of the Prayer Book: the Eucharist is the principal act of worship on the Lord's Day and other major feasts. Morning and Evening Prayer are regular daily services for public worship.

Early in the Christian era the church emphasized Sundays by celebration of the Eucharist. Both the day and the rite spoke of creation, resurrection, the outpouring of the Holy Spirit, and the coming of the Kingdom. The day and the rite reinforced each other. The weekdays—times in between—were marked by daily devotions at sunrise and sunset as the day was offered up to God in prayer and praise. In some areas there were also weekday liturgies of the word at which the Scriptures were read and commented upon. From the middle of the second century the Eucharist was also celebrated on certain weekdays in commemoration of local martyrs. By the third century the Great Fifty Days from Easter to Pentecost were thought of as the Great Sunday, a time when the Eucharist could be celebrated on weekdays.

During the middle ages the multiplication of saints' days, and other

24

factors, caused a lessening of the tension between Sunday and week-day, feast and fast. In the West, especially, elaborate monastic daily offices eventually displaced the earlier congregational or "cathedral" offices. The custom of receiving communion from the reserved Sacrament and the eventual practice of celebrating the Eucharist after None (3 P.M.) marked the end of the fast on fast days. Late in the middle ages, Mass became an individual obligation of the clergy; no lay congregation need be present to share the worship.

The Prayer Book of 1549 represented an attempt to return to the pattern of the early church. Once again the congregation was to participate in the daily offices which included reading of the Scripture, psalmody, and offering up the day to God in prayer and praise. Clergy in charge of congregations were to say the office publicly in church. The Book assumed that there might be daily Eucharist in "Cathedral churches or other places," but it forbade the priest to celebrate unless there were at least "three or two" others to share and communicate with him. To assure a celebration of Eucharist on Sundays, with communicants, those whose turn it was to offer the charges for bread and wine (the various households which made up the parish were to do this on a rota basis) should receive communion along with any others disposed to receive.

The 1552 revision made even more explicit the relationship between Sunday and the Eucharist. All reference to daily communion was deleted, though provisions were made for celebrations on weekdays in weeks immediately after the principal feasts for the convenience of those unable to receive on the day itself. This is indicated by the appointment of proper prefaces for every day of the week following those feasts. Even when Eucharist could not be celebrated on Sunday, for lack of communicants, the priest was still to read the initial portion of the eucharistic rite immediately following Morning Prayer and the Litany. This principle, which emphasized the Eucharist as a regular part of the Sunday rite, was maintained until the American revision of 1892. Even in that edition the rubrics continued to assume the traditional Anglican pattern. But concern for the shortening of the Sunday service prompted the insertion of a statement in the Book: "The Order for Morning Prayer, the Litany, and the Order for the Administration of the Lord's Supper or Holy Communion, are distinct services, and may be used either separately or together; *Provided,* that no one of these services be habitually disused."

The present revision reasserts the pattern of the early church and of the Prayer Books before the revision of 1892.

Extra Prayer Book Services (p. 13)

The first paragraph is a second revision of a direction first printed in the Prayer Book of 1892:

> On any day when Morning and Evening Prayer shall have been said or are to be said in Church, the Minister may, at any other Service for which no form is provided, use such devotions as he shall at his discretion select from this Book, subject to the direction of the Ordinary.

The 1928 form, after speaking of Morning and Evening Prayer as regular services, went on to say:

> *Provided,* that in addition to these Services, the Minister, in his discretion, subject to the direction of the Ordinary, may use other devotions taken from this Book or set forth by lawful authority within this Church, or from Holy Scripture; and *Provided further,* that, subject to the direction of the Ordinary, in Mission Churches or Chapels, and also, when expressly authorized by the Ordinary in Cathedral or Parish Churches or other places, such other devotions as aforesaid may be used, when the edification of the Congregation so requires, in place of the Order for Morning Prayer, or the Order for Evening Prayer.

Since the Daily Offices themselves are much more flexible in this revision, there is no longer permission to substitute other orders in their place. There is permission to use, in addition to Morning and Evening Prayer, the Holy Eucharist, and other rites contained in this Book, "other forms set forth by authority within this Church:" forms such as those contained in the Book of Occasional Services authorized by the General Convention. Permission is also given to use, besides Prayer Book rites, special devotions constructed from the Book or from the Scriptures "when the needs of the congregation so require," and "subject to the direction of the bishop."

The next paragraph dates essentially to the 1892 Prayer Book. In addition to special services and prayers, this direction permits bishops to set forth eucharistic propers for days which are important in the life or history of the diocese, and for which no provision is made either in the Prayer Book or in Lesser Feasts and Fasts.

The Various Liturgical Ministries (pp. 13–14)

In the early church the various orders performed, within the liturgy, roles which signified their functions within the community of

Christians. The bishop presided at the Eucharist, opening the liturgy of the word with a salutation, preaching on the lections, and saying the eucharistic prayer. The presbyters sat with the bishop during the liturgy of the word and stood with him about the eucharistic table during the thanksgiving, thus signifying their role as elders of the community and advisers to the bishop. The deacons, the first professional clergy, served the church and the bishop: they bade the people to pray for the needs of the church and the world, prepared the table, collected the offerings of the people, and administered communion both to those in the congregation and those unable to be present. Lectors read the lessons and were responsible for protecting the valued books of scripture, a duty which meant great risk to themselves in times of persecution. Cantors sang the texts of the psalms. Later, when hymns and psalms were used for the entrance, offertory, and communion processions, choirs sang these. Other members of the congregation joined in the antiphons (refrains) used with the psalmody, participated in hymnody, in responses, and in Amens. They offered money and other gifts, and shared in the communion. In the opening responses and the Great Amen, they gave their assent to the eucharistic prayer, and eventually joined in the Sanctus and the memorial acclamations which became a normal part of that prayer.

As the church grew, and because of a reluctance to continue subdividing dioceses, presbyters functioned more and more in the place of bishops. Eventually they were designated "priests," a title which had earlier been reserved for the priestly people or for the bishop as "high priest" of the people of God. By the end of the fourth century the deacons read the Gospel, previously a function of the lectors; but the deacons also lost more and more of their functions to the priests. Choirs usurped portions of the rite which had earlier belonged to the cantor or to the congregation.

Late in the middle ages the "low Mass" developed in the West. In this rite the priest performed all the functions previously belonging to the deacon, the lector, the cantor, and the choir. He said alone many texts which the congregation would have said with him at an earlier stage. A server, generally a cleric in training, took other portions which had once been congregational. When some of the continental reformers sought to involve the people again in various aspects of the rite, they were often resisted. The people were accustomed to services being done for them rather than with their active participation, in action or in word.

The 1549 Prayer Book made a strong effort to return portions of the rites to the people. Certain responses were to be said by the congregation. Other texts were to be said or sung by clerks, or by some individual other than the celebrant, on behalf of the congregation. Succeeding revisions designated additional texts for the people. The first American Prayer Book substituted the word "Minister" for "Priest" in the rubric prior to the Epistle and in other places to allow more participation by lay readers.

The present revision designates the liturgical functions of the various orders—lay persons, bishops, priests, and deacons—in the directions printed here and in rubrics of the various rites. There is explicit direction that lay persons read the lections, other than the eucharistic Gospel; that a deacon or lay person lead the Prayers of the People; and that representatives of the congregation bring forward the offerings of the people, including the eucharistic elements. Certain texts are reserved to the whole congregation. Participation by instrumentalists and choir is given more recognition than in any previous edition of the Book. The bishop is clearly the chief minister of the Word and Sacraments, while the priest is concelebrant and colleague of the bishop, acting as episcopal representative in the absence of the bishop. Once again the deacon has traditional functions: reader of the Gospel, leader of the Prayers of the People, preparer of the table, minister of the Sacrament (in either kind), performer of ablutions, dismisser of the people, and conveyer of the Sacrament to those unable to be present at the public celebration. These functions are extended, as in earlier editions of the Prayer Book, to allow the deacon, within certain limitations, to preside at the liturgy of the word and at other rites.

The Language of the Rites (p. 14).

The rites of this edition represent both a continuity with Prayer Books since 1549 and an intimate relationship with the world of the present. Both aspects are inextricably linked in the worship of God. To signify the relationship between the rites of the church and the life of the world, to provide a commentary on the forms retained in traditional language, and to meet needs of the immediate world, the rites of this edition of the Prayer Book are provided in contemporary language. To signify continuity with earlier editions of the Book and to meet pastoral needs on various occasions, Morning and Evening Prayer, the Eucharist, and the Burial rite are also printed in traditional language, and the vocabulary of the revised version of the Psalter is limited for the most part to that used by Coverdale in the sixteenth century. The direction on page 14 permits the Proper

28

Liturgies for Special Days and the Pastoral Offices and Episcopal Services, when celebrated in the context of Holy Eucharist: Rite One, to be conformed to traditional language.

For rites in contemporary language the last revision of *Prayers We Have in Common: Agreed Liturgical Texts Prepared by the International Consultation on English Texts* [ICET][1] is used for common texts, with a few exceptions. It is not used for the Nunc dimittis; in the Te Deum the word "shun" is substituted for "spurn." The word "men" has been deleted from a phrase in the Nicene Creed. "Lord, keep us from all sin today" replaces "Keep us today, Lord, from all sin" in the suffrages of Morning Prayer. The most controversial of the text forms, that of the Lord's Prayer, is presented in parallel columns, for alternative use, with the revision which dates to the 1789 Prayer Book.

In the sixteenth century "thou" in English was equivalent to "tu" in French or "du" in German—the familiar second person singular form used to address one person, intimates, children, servants, and God. It was appropriately used by those who knew themselves to be children in intimate relation to God rather than slaves of God. The use of "you" as a form of address in the rites and collects in contemporary language is the modern expression of intimacy linguistically equivalent to the usage of "thou" in earlier editions of the Prayer Book.

The Music of the Church (p. 14)

The next four paragraphs in the Book replace the rubric of the 1892 and 1928 editions of the Prayer Book: "Hymns set forth and allowed by the authority of this Church, and Anthems in the words of Holy Scripture or of the Book of Common Prayer, may be sung before and after any Office in this Book, and also before and after sermons." This general permission has been deliberately withdrawn; the use of hymns before or after some rites and before and after sermons is often inappropriate in relation to the text or movement of the rite. The points at which hymns may be suitably used are designated in the rubrics of the individual rites or in the additional directions appended to these rites.

Hymns

The word "hymn" used in the rubrics of this Book designates hymns currently authorized. In almost all of the rites the rubrics use

---

[1] Second edition, revised; Philadelphia: Fortress Press, 1975.

this word consistently, except in An Order for Celebrating the Holy Eucharist (pp. 400–401) where the word "song" appears in place of "hymn." This allows more freedom of choice for this Order than is found in other rites.

In the Psalter we have the hymnbook of Judaism, but services in the temple and synagogue also contained other musical elements, acclamations, responses, and refrains. New Testament writers refer to the use of psalms and hymns, and provide us with several examples of Christian hymnody, including hymns now used as canticles in the Daily Offices: Magnificat, Benedictus Dominus Deus, Nunc dimittis, Dignus es, and Magna et mirabilia. Other canticles originate in hymns dating from the early centuries of the church: Phos hilaron, Gloria in excelsis, and Te Deum laudamus. With the legalization of Christianity under Constantine and the move to larger buildings with larger congregations, more music was added to the services as accompaniment for the processional entrance of the clergy, the offertory procession, and the communion procession of the people. The Roman rite generally confined this music to psalmody, but other rites used hymns for the various processions. Hymns reflecting the season or the time of day became part of the daily office. Late in the middle ages a sequence, a hymn between the Epistle and the Gospel, was a normal part of the Eucharist in much of the Western church.

The continental reformers rejected most of the medieval sequences because of their content, although Luther brought popular folk hymnody into the liturgy. In the Reformed churches, metrical psalmody had an important place in the services.

Miles Coverdale published *Ghostly Psalms and Spiritual Songs* (1539), based upon the Wittenberg hymns; ten years later Thomas Sternhold issued a small collection of metrical psalms which was later enlarged by John Hopkins. Not until the reign of Elizabeth, however, was the use of metrical psalmody and hymnody allowed in the services of the Prayer Book. At this time the most popular of the metrical psalters was the Sternhold and Hopkins version, further enlarged, to which were appended a few hymns and metrical versions of the Creed, the Decalogue, the Lord's Prayer, and some of the canticles. One metrical psalm from that version remains popular, "All people that on earth do dwell" (Psalm 100).

A new metrical psalter was published by Nahum Tate and Nicholas Brady in 1696 and was soon after provided with a small appendix of hymns, including "While shepherds watched their flocks by night." The Tate and Brady version gained in popularity, replacing Sternhold and Hopkins in many places. In the American colonies it was the most popular version throughout the eighteenth century. Christianized versions of the Psalms (especially those by Isaac Watts) and hymns (especially those of Watts, Doddridge, Addison, and the Wesleys) won acceptance in the nonconformist churches of England and America and the beginnings of a wary acceptance in Anglicanism. By the middle of the eighteenth century some parishes were using small parochial collections of additional hymns which relied heavily on these sources.

The American revision of the Prayer Book in 1789 included the whole of the Tate and Brady Psalter and twenty-seven hymns, giving hymnody a more positive recognition than Anglicanism had previously accorded it. This psalter was replaced in 1832 by one that drew on other metrical versions as well as Tate and Brady; the "Prayer Book Collection" of hymns was enlarged, also, in 1808, 1826, and 1865. Hymnody made rapid advances in the mid-nineteenth century: there were many translations of Greek, Latin, and German hymns; new hymns were written and rapidly adopted. Metrical psalmody and scriptural paraphrases fell from favor, by contrast. The General Convention of 1871 authorized a hymnal twice the size of its predecessor, incorporating only a few metrical psalms, but drawing heavily on new hymns and translations. This hymnal, separate from the Prayer Book, was revised in 1874, 1892, 1916, and 1940. Two supplementary collections, *More Hymns and Spiritual Songs* and *Hymns III*, have been published by the Standing Commission on Church Music upon authorization of the General Convention.

Hymns, chosen carefully, provide a valuable enrichment for Prayer Book rites. They highlight liturgical seasons, the lections, or the various movements within the rites. Perhaps even more important, hymns sing themselves into people's souls and so become primary influences in the theology and spirituality of the worshiping congregation.

Anthems

In various editions of the Prayer Book, the word "anthem" has been used to refer to music sung by a choir rather than by the congregation. Perhaps as early as the fifth century, choirs sang the texts of psalms at the entrance, offertory, and communion processions. The congregation participated by singing the antiphon, much as it participated in the Gradual and Alleluia sung by a cantor. Later in the medieval period choirs also took some parts of the rites previously done by the people. Congregational participation was often prevented by the people's growing unfamiliarity with Latin as well as by

31

the elaboration of music and the increased professionalism of the choirs.

The 1549 Prayer Book directed clerks to sing texts which corresponded to the old processional songs of the choir in the Eucharist, and at marriages and burials. Clerks also sang some portions of the rite which historically had belonged to the people, such as the Kyrie, Gloria in excelsis, and Sanctus.

The 1552 revision did away with the Introit psalm and the Communion verse, and replaced the Kyrie with the Decalogue, its responses designated as responses of the people. The priest was to say the Offertory verse. The Sanctus and Gloria in excelsis were to be said or sung, but it is not stated who was to do this. Only in the burial rite were the clerks mentioned in connection with the anthems.

A place for an anthem was designated between the fixed collects and other prayers at Morning and Evening Prayer in the 1662 revision. This was not carried over into the American Book of 1789, but that revision did designate the Sanctus as a song of the people. The 1892 revision restored permission to sing an anthem at Evening Prayer and to sing "a Hymn, or an Offertory Anthem in the words of Holy Scripture or of the Book of Common Prayer . . . when the Alms and Oblations are presented." In the 1928 Book this statement was altered to read "when the Alms and Oblations are being received and presented." That revision also gave permission to sing "a Hymn or an Anthem" between the Epistle and the Gospel.

The present revision provides far more opportunity for use of anthems than any previous edition. The order of listing "psalm, hymn, or anthem" as alternatives is generally intentional, representing long historic tradition. In Morning and Evening Prayer a "hymn or anthem" may be sung between the collects and intercessions. "A hymn, psalm, or anthem" may be sung at the beginning of the Eucharist; a "Psalm, hymn, or anthem" may follow the first two readings. "During the Offertory, a hymn, psalm, or anthem may be sung." An "anthem" may be sung at the breaking of the bread. "During the ministration of Communion, hymns, psalms, or anthems may be sung." As a general rule, the principle of the early liturgies is maintained: anthems may be sung at times when the attention of the congregation is directed to the action: the entrance; the Gospel procession; during the offertory; during the preparation of the table; at the breaking of the bread; during the communion of the people. The Sanctus, the memorial acclamation, the Lord's Prayer, and a number of responses are reserved to the people by rubric. On the other hand, the rubrics are purposely vague in designating who shall sing the canticles of the Daily Office, the Creed in the Eucharist, the opening anthems of the burial rite, and certain other portions of various services. The principles which underlie the eucharistic rite are applicable to other rites as well.

Rubrics of earlier editions of the Prayer Book had limited the texts of anthems strictly to material from scripture or from the Prayer Book; this version permits use of other texts "congruent" with the Scriptures and Prayer Book.

Instrumental Music

This is the first edition of the Prayer Book to mention the use of instrumental music in the rites of the church. In the middle ages, instruments added interest or a festal note to singing or helped the singers to keep on pitch. Once the organ was perfected to the point that it could lead or accompany the singing of congregation and choir, it was generally used for that purpose. Where there was no organ, barrel-organs, or whatever instruments were available, accompanied the singing. Sometimes instrumental "voluntaries" were used within the rites, in Anglicanism normally after the psalms of the Daily Office as a preparation for the readings to follow. Eventually, instrumental music was played as a "prelude" to the service and as accompaniment for the exit of the people.

This edition of the Prayer Book states explicitly that instrumental music may be substituted "On occasion, and as appropriate" for a hymn or anthem. It is suggested as an alternative at the entrance and exit of the wedding party in the marriage rite (pp. 423 and 432), and during the procession and after the dedication of a musical instrument in the consecration of a church (pp. 567 and 572). Instrumental music is suitable on occasion at those points where an anthem might normally be desirable: at the entrance of the ministers; during the Gospel procession; at the preparation of the table and the placing of gifts upon it; at the breaking of bread; and during the communion of the people.

To Say or Sing?

This is an explicit statement that any part of a service may be either said or sung. The 1928 revision put this direction subtly: "NOTE, that in the directions for the several Services in this Book, it is not intended, by the use of any particular word denoting vocal utterance, to prescribe the tone or manner of their recitation." From a very early period, possibly from the beginning as a heritage of Judaism, the prayers and readings from the Scriptures were sung. In the Eastern rite today the entire liturgy is sung. After the distinction was made, during the late medieval period in the West, between the "low Mass" and "high Mass," the entire text heard by the congregation at "high Mass" was sung.

The 1549 edition makes clear that the equivalents of certain texts, which had been said secretly by the priest while the choir or people were singing their parts in the late medieval "high Mass," were again to be said aloud; Merbecke's *Book of Common Prayer Noted* (1550) indicates that they were to be sung. The prayer for the church and the eucharistic prayer were included among these. A rubric in the 1549 Book states: "And, to the end the people may better hear, in such places where they do sing, there shall the lessons be sung in a plain tune after the manner of distinct reading; and likewise the epistle and gospel." The late Victorian idea that certain texts are properly sung and others properly said has no historic basis.

What should be said and what sung depends upon the acoustics of the building, the ability of the various participants, the taste of the congregation, and the relative importance of the day or occasion—not upon canons of proper procedure.

Previously Authorized Texts

The last of the directions concerning music gives explicit permission to use certain previously authorized texts in place of the corresponding liturgical texts in this Book, when there is a desire to use music composed for them. Since 1789, the texts of the Te Deum laudamus and the Benedicite, omnia opera Domini have varied from those of the English Book of 1662. This direction allows the use of musical settings composed for English versions of the texts of these canticles or of any other forms. An earlier version of the text may be preferable because it is in the hands of the congregation or choir, or because the nature of the music does not lend itself to updating of the text. This direction also allows the use of texts in traditional language within rites in contemporary language when it seems desirable to use music composed for such traditional versions.

Translations of the Scriptures (p. 14)

This paragraph is important for clergy and lectors. Any translation of the Scriptures authorized by the canons of the church may be used in the rites, but the lectionaries and listings of scriptural passages in the various rites are all based upon the chapter and verse divisions of the Revised Standard Version of the Bible. Before making use of

34

another translation the reader should refer to the RSV to be sure of the proper beginning and ending for the lection; the divisions are not identical in all translations. In the Jerusalem Bible, for example, the order of verses is at times rearranged in a manner which might easily result in the reading of a different selection of verses.

As of the General Convention of 1976 the authorized versions for public reading in the services of the church are: the King James Version of 1611, with the Marginal Readings of 1901; the English Revised Version of 1881; the American Revised Version of 1901; the Revised Standard Version of 1952; the Jerusalem Bible of 1966; the New English Bible of 1970; the Good News Bible of 1976; the New American Bible of 1970; and the RSV Common Bible of 1973.

References to the Psalms, both in the lectionaries and in the listing in the various rites, are based upon the Psalter printed within the Book (pp. 581–808). The verse divisions differ in many places from those in other editions of the Psalter and the numbering of the Psalms, from Psalm 9 through Psalm 147, differs from that of many Roman Catholic versions.

35

The Calendar of the Church Year

In almost every culture, certain religious rituals are periodically repeated, some in relation to the cycle of the seasons, some to reinforce community relations in particular "crisis" situations that occur in the lives of individuals (birth, initiation, marriage, death). Some rites are performed daily, some weekly, some at wider intervals of once a month or once a year.

In Judaism the day was marked liturgically in the temple at Jerusalem with morning and evening sacrifices, and with services of psalms and prayers at 9 A.M. and 3 P.M. Devout Jews also marked the time of day with private prayers. Sabbath services in the synagogue centered on the reading and exposition of the Scriptures; by the first century of our era synagogue liturgies were conducted on some weekdays as well as before the Sabbath meal.

The basic unit of time in the Jewish ritual pattern was the seven-day week. The first chapter of Genesis indicates a ritual significance associated with each of the days of a week. Mondays and Thursdays were for private, and sometimes public, fasts. Among some groups of Jews, Sundays, Wednesdays, and Fridays were of particular liturgical significance; the priestly documents of the Old Testament seem to link these days to special types of events. In temple liturgy certain psalms were associated with certain days of the week. The Sabbath was basic to the liturgical week as the day of rest, the day which symbolized the covenant. To be a Jew was to be one who kept the Sabbath, and the high point of the week was the Sabbath meal in the home, following the synagogue liturgy of the word.

Basic to the Jewish year were three pilgrimage feasts, the origins of which may have been agricultural: Passover (probably associated with the new flock), Pentecost (the wheat harvest), and Tabernacles (the new wine). The Passover commemorated the slaying of the first born, the exodus from Egypt, and the entry into the Promised Land. High points of this celebration were the slaying of the Passover lamb, the use of unleavened bread, and the special Passover cup. The offering of barley after Passover inaugurated the seven weeks of harvest culminating in the feast of Pentecost, which commemorated the giving of the law and the covenant with Israel. The feast of Tabernacles (or Booths) celebrated the ingathering of the new wine, the time of dwelling in huts or booths in the wilderness, the choice of the House of David, the choice of Jerusalem as God's dwelling place, and the dedication of the temple. Dancing and the carrying of palm branches and torches were parts of the celebration.

The early Christians continued the practice of marking periods of the day with private prayer. At first they apparently attended and participated in synagogue services. When they were no longer permitted to attend, they imitated the services with liturgies of the word. Like the Jews they kept the seven-day week as the basic unit of time in the ritual pattern. Although Jesus had warned against the possible abuse of fasting, he himself fasted, and the practice was continued in the early church. The Didache, a document probably from the second century, indicates a change to Wednesdays and Fridays: "Be not as the hypocrites who fast on Monday and Thursday, but when you fast, fast on Wednesday and Friday." The fast days were called "station days," using a military term for days of keeping watch, and soon became associated with the betrayal and the crucifixion. Just as the Jewish week was organized around the Sabbath, so the Christian week was structured around the first day of the week—the day of creation, of light, of Pentecost. The first day was also known as "The Lord's Day," a phrase with eschatological implications from Old Testament times, the day of the resurrection of Jesus Christ and of the outpouring of the Holy Spirit. Yet another name for it was the "Eighth Day." Eight is the number which transcends seven, representing the break in the closed cycle symbolized by seven. Eight symbolizes redemption, baptism, the New Age, the *kairos*, the fulfillment of time, the Eschaton. The liturgical week looked backward to the First Day and forward to the Eighth Day.

The liturgies of the word and private devotions during weekday rites of *chronos* (chronological time) prepared for the rite which expressed the meaning of Sunday, the ritual of *kairos*—the eucharistic feast. The Christian week, very early in Christian history, was organized around the Sunday Eucharist.

In almost every language except English the same word is used to designate the Jewish Passover and the Christian Easter. Some authors find the feast (reinterpreted) celebrated within New Testament times and associated with baptisms. All the imagery of the Jewish Passover was brought into the rite—the Exodus, the Passover, and the entrance into the Promised Land.

The second chapter of Acts associates with the Jewish feast of Pentecost the outpouring of the Holy Spirit, baptism, and the mission of the new community to all nations. Some commentators have found correspondence between the Jewish feast of Tabernacles and the early chapters of the Gospel according to John. They have also seen a continuation of this feast in the Advent-Epiphany cycle of the church year. Certainly, what the booths, the city of Jerusalem, the House of David, and the temple meant in the life of Judaism was fulfilled in the incarnation. Jewish feasts and lectionaries indeed made some contributions to the development of the church year.

In one sense, however, the church year at an early stage was a dramatization of the more basic weekly cycle. The Great Fifty Days ("the Great Sunday"—seven squared), as a seventh of the year, related the Passover-Pentecost cycle to the year just as Sunday was related to the days of the week.

The greatest influence on the development of the Christian year, however, was the liturgy of Christian initiation. The Great Fifty Days, which began with the baptismal vigil, were days for special celebration, days when kneeling and fasting were outlawed, and when the Eucharist could be celebrated during the week. All persons, including the candidates for baptism, prepared for the Easter Vigil by rigorous fasting on the preceding Friday and Saturday, or on Saturday only; at a later stage, they prepared also by a less intense fast from Monday through Thursday before the vigil. Some degree of fasting seems to have been practiced by the candidates for baptism during their several weeks of preparation. Probably the combination of these two types of fasts developed into the Lenten fast of forty days, a tithe of the year. Sundays (and Sabbaths in some areas) were exempted from the fast.

About the middle of the second century the liturgical year also was marked by annual commemorations of local martyrs, often at the place of their burial. The earliest known example is that of Polycarp, the Bishop of Smyrna, martyred in 156. The book which tells of his martyrdom gives the reason for such a commemoration: ". . . both in memory of those who have already contested, and for the practice and training of those whose fate it shall be."[1] During the first centuries of the church's life such commemorations seem to have been celebrated just for local witnesses to the faith.

With Constantine's legalization of Christianity and the rise of monasticism, the daily office became more highly developed. In addition to the rites which corresponded to the morning and evening services of the earlier period, the monks developed "little offices" to mark the times formerly set for private devotions among Jews and early Christians. The liturgical week continued to center on the Sunday Eucharist. Prior to Constantine's fiat, Sunday had been a work day for most Christians who had to rise long before dawn for the weekly eucharistic celebration, but it was declared a day of rest by Constantine in 321.

The liturgical year was greatly affected by changes which followed the establishment of Christianity and the influx of those only partly converted from paganism. The feasts of Christmas and Epiphany developed as means to oppose or Christianize pagan festivals related to the winter solstice. The birthday of the Unconquerable Sun (Saturn), the dies natalis Solis Invicti, was celebrated at Rome beginning about December 21 and lasting for something more than a week. Probably by A.D. 336 Christians had appropriated December 25 as the day to celebrate the incarnation. In Egypt, January 6 was celebrated as the winter solstice when the sun god made his appearance (epiphany) and was honored with light, water, and wine. The Christians chose this time as the feast of the incarnation and connected it with three Gospel stories: the coming of the Magi, the baptism of Jesus, and the wedding at Cana. Of these the baptism was the primary event. Eventually both Christmas and Epiphany were celebrated throughout the Christian world. During the following centuries, an anticipatory element appeared in the Ambrosian and Roman rites for the weeks immediately before Christmas. In Gallican ritual, as in the East, Epiphany became a time for baptism, preceded by a forty-day season of preparation. Some churches knew this as "St. Martin's Lent" since it began near November 11, St. Martin's Day. The season of Advent resulted from the joining of these two traditions, hence its mixed notes of penitence and joy.

Once Christianity was established in the Roman world there was a great multiplication of saints' days, probably in part to combat the

---

[1] Martyrdom of Polycarp, 18.

celebration of days sacred to various pagan gods, protectors, or heroes. Churches with no local martyr to commemorate sought relics of saints or of the "true cross" in order to institute their own commemorative days. In various areas there was set aside a day to celebrate All Martyrs or All Saints. The saints came to represent intercessors or protectors rather than witnesses for the faith, and that note is strong in the later propers for those days.

Constantine was responsible for the building of churches in Jerusalem at sites traditionally associated with events in the life of Christ. These soon became places of pilgrimage and, late in the fourth century, it was customary to commemorate the principal events in the last week of our Lord's life on earth with services in appropriate churches. Primitive Sunday and primitive Easter-Pentecost services had celebrated all the mighty acts of God; these newer services in Jerusalem commemorated particular historical events and provided the prototype for the historical treatment of Holy Week which eventually spread throughout the church.

The historical approach to the liturgies of Holy Week was also applied to the Great Fifty Days, the Pentecost. The fiftieth day came to be understood not as the climax of a season but as a day for recalling the event of the outpouring of the Spirit. The Ascension was commemorated on the fortieth day after Easter, and other days also were assigned to recall events in the life of our Lord: the Annunciation (March 25), the presentation of Christ in the temple (February 2), and the birth of John the Baptist (June 24). Gallican custom celebrated January 1 as the feast of the circumcision of our Lord, and the three days before Ascension were set apart as rogation days, days of special prayers for the crops. In Rome began the observance of a pre-penitential season before Lent. Rome also developed the use of seasonal ember days which probably began as quarterly periods for renewal, but which also took on agricultural associations and became times for ordinations as well. The propers in liturgical books were often separated into two groups: those which centered on Easter or Christmas (the *temporale*); those which occupied the fixed dates of the calendar (the *sanctorale*).

Late in the middle ages Lent had become a time of penance for all and Advent a semi-penitential period of preparation for Christ's coming again as judge. The missals contain commemorations of over twice as many saints' days as were in the old Gregorian sacramentary, several times as many as in the old Gallican books. Not only had saints' days multiplied by the addition of propers from other churches where the commemorations had originated, but additional feasts of Christ (for example, the Transfiguration and the Name of Jesus), of Mary (the Visitation), and of New Testament saints not previously given a day (Matthias, among others) were added to the calendar. Trinity, All Souls' Day, and Corpus Christi were other significant new feasts. In England and northern Europe, Sundays were numbered from Trinity Sunday rather than from Pentecost. The general increase of the number of feast days tended to obscure the older structure of the liturgical week, the distinction between feast and fast, and the integral connection of Sunday with the Eucharist. A growing sabbatarianism in some areas, however, did continue to provide a pattern for the week as did the linking of particular votives to particular days of the week. The increasing popularity of infant baptism meant that the vigils of Easter, Pentecost, and Epiphany ceased to be special times for baptism, lessening the sense of the baptismal nature of the church year.

The continental reformers sought to restore the primacy of Sunday in the liturgical week. Luther, Zwingli, Bucer, and Calvin tried to establish the Eucharist with communions as the primary Sunday service, and many reformers attempted to provide public offices for weekdays. Some German churches designated Wednesdays and Fridays as days for the litany and otherwise retained the general structure of the church year. Reformed (but not Lutheran) churches typically rejected holy days and some even eliminated the celebration of Easter, Pentecost, and Christmas. In the Lutheran orders holy days were restricted to feasts of our Lord, the days of apostles and evangelists, St. Stephen the protomartyr, the Holy Innocents, St. John the Baptist, St. Michael the Archangel, and All Saints.

The Prayer Book of 1549 took steps to restore both the primacy of Sunday in the liturgical week and its connection with the Eucharist. Eucharist with communions was to follow Matins on Sundays. The Sunday service was always to include what later came to be called Ante-Communion: the eucharistic rite through the offertory, and (after 1552) through the Prayer for the Whole State of Christ's Church, ending with a collect and a blessing. This rite was mandated even when there was no one who desired to receive communion. On Fridays and Wednesdays, the Litany and Ante-Communion followed Matins, but use of the Ante-Communion was dropped on those days in the 1552 revision. A table of fasts, which designated Fridays as days for fasting, was included in the 1662 edition.

The Prayer Book retained the general structure of the church year but reduced the holy days to those retained in the German church orders. The 1552 Book restored four "black letter days": St. George,

41

Lammas Day (St. Peter in Chains), St. Laurence, and St. Clement. The popular term "black letter days" originated in the custom of printing the name beside these dates in black on many calendars; those for which a proper was provided were printed in red. In the Latin edition of the Prayer Book (1560) nearly every day was a black letter day, including a number of saints, among them some Eastern saints, who had not been in the medieval English calendars. Conspicuously absent were some of the days considered most important in the late medieval books, such as the Feast of the Assumption and All Souls' Day. A new calendar issued in 1561 contained more than sixty black letter days. The 1604 edition added Evurtius and the 1662 edition, Alban and Bede. The Prayer Book, however, took no further notice of these days. Perhaps they were listed in the calendar to identify old dates in pre-Reformation documents or names used to designate school terms or court days.

The first American revision eliminated all of the black letter days and replaced the propers for the four national days of the 1662 Book with one set of propers for Thanksgiving Day. The Feast of the Transfiguration with Collect, Epistle, and Gospel was added to the calendar in the revision of 1892. The 1928 revision provided propers for a saint's day, the feast of the dedication of a church, the ember days, the rogation days, and Independence Day. Wednesday was no longer continued as a day for the Litany; Friday, however, was still marked by the requirement that the Litany or General Confession be used at daily Morning Prayer.

The present Book attempts absolutely to restore the primacy of Sunday within the liturgical week; it provides proper prefaces for the Lord's Day stressing this as the day of creation, of resurrection, and of the outpouring of the Spirit. It gives Sundays precedence over saints' days. Within the Daily Office suitable collects are provided for Fridays, Saturdays, and Sundays. A table of canticles suggests those suitable for various days of the week. Fridays, except for those within the Easter and Christmas seasons and those on which major feasts of our Lord occur, are to be observed "by special acts of discipline and self-denial."

The Book emphasizes the baptismal nature of the church year, the central position of the Great Fifty Days, and the primacy of the proper of time over the proper of the saints. A baptismal vigil inaugurates the Great Fifty Days and a similar shorter vigil precedes Pentecost. The Pascha nostrum ("Christ our Passover") may be used as an invitatory at Daily Offices from Easter until the Day of Pentecost. Easter, Pentecost, the feast of the Baptism of our Lord, and All

Saints' Day are especially recommended for baptisms. Special liturgies for Ash Wednesday, Palm Sunday, Maundy Thursday, Good Friday, and Holy Saturday enrich the communal reenactment of Lenten preparation and, even more, of our Lord's Holy Week.

The number of red letter days is increased with the addition of the Confession of Saint Peter (January 18), Saint Joseph (March 19), the Visitation of the Blessed Virgin Mary (May 31), Saint Mary Magdalene (July 22), Saint Mary the Virgin (August 15), Holy Cross Day (September 14), and Saint James of Jerusalem (October 23). Over one hundred black letter days are in the calendar, with appropriate collects, psalms, and lessons provided under the title "Common of Saints." These include saints both Eastern and Western from the early centuries, and a number of British or Anglican worthies. Although it has undergone several minor revisions, the list is essentially that of Lesser Feasts and Fasts, a supplementary volume for optional use, first authorized in 1964.

The Calendar of the Church Year (pp. 15–30)

These pages list the days to be observed as feasts or holy days and those to be observed as days of special devotion. If two holy days fall on the same date, these pages also make clear which takes precedence.

Fixed holy days of the church year are listed in the calendar at the end of the section. The first Sunday of Advent, the beginning of the church year, always falls on the fourth Sunday before Christmas Day. The church year progresses through Advent season, the twelve days of Christmas, and into the Epiphany season. The Epiphany season may have a number of Sundays varying from four to nine since the seventh Sunday before Easter is always celebrated as the last Sunday after the Epiphany.

In the first Prayer Book (1549) was a calendar listing the fixed days, the Dominical (Sunday) letter, and the days of the month of the old Roman calendar. "An Almanac for Nineteen Years" was prefixed to the daily lectionary and the calendar of fixed holy days in the 1552 revision. It contained, for the years 1552–1570, the Golden Number, the epact (the number of days by which the solar year exceeds the lunar year), the cycle of the sun, the Dominical letter, and the date of Easter Day. This table was updated in 1559 and 1604, and a table "to find Easter forever" added in 1604. John Cosin in *A Collection of Private Devotions* (1627) added to the calendar of fixed holy days "A Table of Moveable Feasts," "Rules to know when the Moveable

43

Feasts and Holy Days Begin," and a listing of "The Fasting Days of the Church, or Days of Special Abstinence and Devotion." These were the basis for the tables added to the 1662 revision. After the change from the Julian to the Gregorian calendar in 1751, the table of moveable feasts and the table for finding the date of Easter were replaced by much fuller tables. These tables have been substantially simplified in this revision and moved to the end of the Book (pp. 879–885).

The first American revision of 1789 drew its tables and rules for fixed and moveable feasts from the 1662 Book, but revised the table "Of the Vigils, Fasts, and Days of Abstinence." In the 1928 revision "Tables of Precedence" were added. Before that time only custom had determined precedence; for example, if the fourth Sunday in Advent fell on December 21, only custom would determine whether the service should commemorate Saint Thomas or be that of the fourth Sunday in Advent. If the decision was to use the proper of the fourth Sunday in Advent, nothing in the Prayer Book indicated whether Saint Thomas should be ignored, celebrated on the day before, or on the day after. The 1928 revision made clear that precedence over any other Sunday or holy day was given to the Sundays of Advent, Christmas Day, Epiphany, the Sundays of Pre-Lent, Ash Wednesday, the Sundays of Lent, all of the days of Holy Week and the Easter octave, Ascension Day, the Sundays before and after it, the week of Pentecost, and Trinity Sunday. The Book advised that the observance of any other holy day falling upon one of these days "shall be transferred to the first convenient open day." The traditional red letter days were given precedence over any other days. Thanksgiving Day and days for which propers were provided for the first time in the 1928 Book (the ember and rogation days, "A Saint's Day," and the feast of the dedication of a church) were simply listed among those "days or occasions for which collect, epistle, and gospel are provided in this Book." Though a proper was provided for Independence Day, it was not listed in the tables of precedence.

1. Principal Feasts (p. 15)

In the present revision seven days are listed as the principal feasts: Easter Day, Ascension Day, the Day of Pentecost, Trinity Sunday, All Saints' Day, Christmas Day, and the Epiphany. These take precedence over any other days or observances including eucharists celebrated at weddings or funerals.

44

2. Sundays (p. 16)

Only three other feasts of our Lord—Holy Name, Presentation, and Transfiguration—in addition to the principal feasts, normally take precedence over Sunday. Exceptions are made for the feast of the dedication of a church, and the feast of its patron or title, which may be observed on a Sunday or transferred to a Sunday except in the seasons of Advent, Lent, and Easter. These days are provided with lections for their eves as well as with proper lections for the day (pp. 1000–1001).

Other red letter days, whether feasts of our Lord or other major feasts, when they occur on a Sunday, are to be transferred to the first convenient open day within the following week. If one of these days falls on a Sunday between the first and last Sundays after the Epiphany or between Trinity Sunday and the last Sunday after Pentecost, the feast may be honored on the Sunday by the substitution of the collect, the preface, and one or more of the lections for those of the Sunday. Such substitutions may not be made from the last Sunday after Pentecost through the First Sunday after the Epiphany or from the last Sunday after the Epiphany through Trinity Sunday. Only with the express permission of the bishop may any other occasion be observed on a Sunday.

3. Holy Days (pp. 16–17)

Other holy days which are to be observed in addition to the principal feasts and the Sundays of the year are listed under the titles "Other Feasts of our Lord" and "Other Major Feasts." The Visitation and Holy Cross Day, two feasts for which the 1928 Book provided no propers, are here included among other feasts of our Lord; additional major feasts are the Confession of Saint Peter, Saint Joseph, Saint Mary Magdalene, Saint Mary the Virgin, and Saint James of Jerusalem. Independence Day and Thanksgiving Day, given no measure of precedence in the 1928 Book, are listed among the other major feasts. The present revision permits the celebration of feasts listed in these two tables on any open day of the week within which they may fall.

Ash Wednesday and Good Friday are listed as "Fasts." Fixed days which fall within the two-week period of Holy Week and Easter Week are transferred to the week following the second Sunday of Easter and are observed within that week in the order of their occurrence. For example, Saint Mark's Day would be observed before the

45

day of Saints Philip and James in the years in which Easter falls on April 25.

4. Days of Special Devotion (p. 17)

No days of fasting or abstinence were listed in Prayer Books before 1662, although the minister, from the time of the 1552 revision, was after the sermon to "declare unto the people whether there be any holy days or fasting days the week following." The 1662 Book listed sixteen feasts as days before which a vigil was to be observed, and noted as "days of Fasting, or Abstinence" the forty days of Lent, the ember and rogation days, and all the Fridays of the year except Christmas Day.

In the 1789 revision only Ash Wednesday and Good Friday were under the title "A Table of Fasts." The days of fasting or abstinence of the 1662 Book were listed under a heading "Other Days of Fasting, on which the church requires such a measure of abstinence as is more especially suited to extraordinary acts and exercises of devotion." The 1928 revision added a phrase exempting Epiphany and any Friday between Christmas and Epiphany from the rule of abstinence.

The present revision lists Ash Wednesday and Good Friday among the holy days as "Fasts." The weekdays of Lent and Fridays of the year, with certain exceptions, are days to be observed "by special acts of discipline and self denial." The table of precedence in the 1928 Book did not specify whether the Lenten abstinence was to be observed on a saint's day which fell during Lent. This revision states explicitly that the only exception is the feast of the Annunciation. Though the early church considered fasting an offense during the Great Fifty Days, the Prayer Books required abstinence on Fridays of the Easter season. The present revision exempts Fridays during both Christmas and Easter seasons, as well as any Friday on which a feast of our Lord may occur. The Sundays in Lent are not included in the forty days of Lent, for all Sundays are feasts which commemorate the creation, the resurrection, and the outpouring of the Holy Spirit, and which anticipate the eschaton, the messianic banquet.

5. Days of Optional Observance (pp. 18–19)

Certain other days may be observed with duly authorized propers, so long as there is no conflict with the rules governing the precedence of the principal feasts or of the Sundays or holy days which are to be observed. There are the black letter days listed in the calendar for

46

which propers are published in a separate volume authorized by the General Convention,[1] the days of commemoration of other saints making use of the "Common of Saints" (pp. 195–199 or 246–250 and 925–927), ember and rogation days, and the various occasions for which propers are provided (pp. 199–210 or 251–261 and 927–931). Ember days were traditionally observed on the Wednesdays, Fridays, and Saturdays after the first Sunday in Lent, Pentecost, Holy Cross Day, and December 13. Since ordinations no longer necessarily take place on the Sundays following ember days, this revision makes it possible to observe the ember days at times related to local or diocesan custom for ordination. Propers for the ember days are among those for various occasions (pp. 205–206 or 256–257 and 929). Traditionally the rogation days were set for Monday, Tuesday, and Wednesday before Ascension Day, but there are many areas and many industries for which these days do not occur at the critical period of the year. This revision makes it possible to observe rogation days at times more vitally related to local concerns.

Fixed Days of the Calendar (pp. 19–30)

Each date except February 29 is followed by the Sunday Letter. Dates between March 22 and April 18 are prefaced by the Golden Number. For explanations see pp. 880–881 of the Prayer Book.

January (p. 19)

January 1: The Holy Name of Our Lord Jesus Christ

In previous editions of the Prayer Book January 1 had been observed as the feast of the Circumcision. This commemoration, of Gallican origin, antedated the council of Tours (567) which enacted a canon that speaks of it as a fast day set in a position counter to a pagan New Year's carnival. In the Roman rite, January 1 had been celebrated as the octave of Christmas, devoted especially to Mary. Holy Name originated about the middle of the fourteenth century as a cult devoted to the Name of Jesus, which means "Savior" or "Deliverer" (Joshua in Hebrew). A votive mass which developed from this cult was accepted in the calendar late in the fifteenth century. The feast was introduced in Canterbury and York on August 7, 1489, and restored as a black letter day in the Elizabethan calendar of 1561. The change from a commemoration of circumcision to that of the Holy

---

[1] *Lesser Feasts and Fasts* (third edition), New York: The Church Pension Fund, 1980.

47

Name in the present revision represents a more accurate understanding of the significance of the gospel passage traditionally associated with the day.

January 6: The Epiphany of Our Lord Jesus Christ
The word "epiphany" means "manifestation" or "appearance." Its origin dates at least to the end of the second century when it was celebrated in Egypt as a feast of our Lord's baptism. The date had been sacred to the winter solstice and was marked as the day of Osiris, to be celebrated with light, water, and wine. The Christians appropriated the day as a feast of the incarnation, and connected it with the gospel stories of the Magi, the baptism of Jesus, and the wedding feast at Cana. The translation of the supposed relics of the Magi from Constantinople to Milan may have introduced the feast to the West. Until the 1928 revision the commemoration of the baptism of our Lord at this season had been limited in the Prayer Book to the daily offices. In 1928 the story of the baptism was made the Gospel for the second Sunday after Epiphany. The present revision commemorates the baptism on the first Sunday, as does the recent Roman Catholic revision and the revisions by other churches. The story of the wedding feast at Cana is the Gospel for the second Sunday after the Epiphany in Year C.

January 10: William Laud, Archbishop of Canterbury, 1645
Archbishop under Charles I from 1633, the scholarly William Laud vigorously opposed both Roman Catholicism and Puritanism. He was impeached and imprisoned by the Commonwealth in 1641 and beheaded on a charge of treason in 1645. Many consider him a Christian martyr. One of his legacies is the prayer for the church (page 816).

January 13: Hilary, Bishop of Poitiers, 367
Hilary was elected bishop between A.D. 350 and 354. His refusal to give in to the emperor Constantius' attempt to force the western bishops to accept a creedal formula not consistent with Nicea caused him to be banished to the East for four years. Upon his return to Gaul, Hilary worked for the acceptance of the Nicene Creed in western Europe. His name is listed beside this date in the Elizabethan calendar of 1561.

January 17: Antony, Abbot in Egypt, 356
Antony, known as the father of monasticism, was born about A.D. 250 in Egypt. Although a hermit he attracted many disciples and

48

followers, and participated in the controversies which racked the church in his day. He was a friend and supporter of Athanasius of Alexandria (May 2) who wrote his biography.

January 18: The Confession of Saint Peter the Apostle
This liturgical celebration is new to the Prayer Book. The date is that of an ancient Gallican feast of the Chair of Saint Peter. The confession of Peter, "You are the Christ, the Son of the living God" (Mt. 16:13–19), is set at Caesarea Philippi, the site of representations of many pagan deities. The celebration of the feast within the Epiphany season is particularly appropriate since it marks the beginning of the Week of Prayer for Christian Unity. The martyrdom of Peter is commemorated along with that of Saint Paul on June 29.

January 19: Wulfstan, Bishop of Worcester, 1095
Wulfstan declined the call to be bishop of Worcester in order to enter a monastery. Twenty-five years later the call was again extended and he accepted. He was noted for his tireless work for the poor and the oppressed. He earned the respect of both William I and William II, whom he supported in their work for the reform of government.

January 20: Fabian, Bishop and Martyr of Rome, 250
Fabian was elected bishop of Rome on January 10, 236, just after the persecution under Maximinus. According to legend he was a layman who had come to Rome to witness the election; a dove lighted on his head, which was taken for a heavenly omen. He was responsible for many reforms, including development of the parochial structure of the Roman church and veneration of the martyrs. He himself was martyred in the persecution under Decius (A.D. 249–250). His name was restored among the black letter days in 1561.

January 21: Agnes, Martyr at Rome, 304
In the persecution under Diocletian (A.D. 304), Agnes, a child of twelve, was tortured publicly and finally killed with a sword. After Christianity was legalized, Constantine built a shrine in her honor at the site of her tomb. Her name was among the black letter days in the calendar of 1561.

January 22: Vincent, Deacon of Saragossa, and Martyr, 304
Because of his organizational abilities, the deacon Vincent was sought out by Datian, the Spanish governor under Diocletian. In an

effort to break him, Datian had the deacon beaten, stretched, roasted, and forced to walk and sleep on broken glass. One tradition says that Vincent was released and died shortly thereafter. According to another, he was burned. His was one of the black letter days restored in 1561.

January 23: Phillips Brooks, Bishop of Massachusetts, 1893
Phillips Brooks was born in Boston and educated at Harvard and at the Virginia Theological Seminary. After serving a parish in Philadelphia, he became rector of Trinity Church, Boston, in 1869, where he served until elected bishop of Massachusetts fifteen months before his death. He was internationally known for his preaching. His sermons are still studied, but he is best known for his hymn "O little town of Bethlehem."

January 25: The Conversion of Saint Paul the Apostle
This feast seems to date at least to the sixth century in books of the Gallican rite. Paul's dramatic conversion (Acts 9:1–22 and Acts 26) occurred when he was traveling to Damascus in order to persecute the Christians there. After his conversion he was the most instrumental in bringing the gospel to the Gentiles, through indefatigable missionary labors and through letters. It is particularly appropriate that his conversion is celebrated in the Epiphany season one week after the commemoration of the confession of Peter. According to tradition, he was martyred outside the city of Rome during the persecution under Nero in A.D. 64.

January 26: Timothy and Titus, Companions of Saint Paul
Timothy, son of a Gentile father and a Jewish mother, helped establish churches in Asia Minor and Greece, and served as an emissary for Paul on various occasions (Acts 16:1–3; Rom. 16:21; 1 Cor. 16:10; 2 Cor. 1:1, 19; Phil. 2:19; 1 Thess. 3:2; 1 Tim. 1:2; 2 Tim. 1:2; Heb. 13:12). Eusebius claims that Timothy was beaten to death by a mob of pagans at Ephesus. Titus accompanied Paul and Barnabas to the Jerusalem council where the decision was made to accept Gentiles as full members of the church (Gal. 2:1–3; see also 2 Cor. 2:13; 7:6, 13–14; 8:6, 16, 23; 12:18; 2 Tim. 4:10). According to tradition he founded the church on the island of Crete.

January 27: John Chrysostom, Bishop of Constantinople, 407
John, "the golden mouthed," born in Antioch about A.D. 350, was reputedly the greatest preacher in the history of the church. His

50

name is associated with the Liturgy of Saint Chrysostom. In 398 he was elected bishop of Constantinople, but his stern preaching led to his exile in 404. He died while still a prisoner in exile. On January 27, 438, his remains were returned in honor to Constantinople.

January 28: Thomas Aquinas, Priest and Friar, 1274

Thomas Aquinas is ranked as the foremost of the medieval theologians for his reconciliation of the philosophy of Aristotle with Christian doctrine. His greatest work was the *Summa Theologica*. Three centuries after his death he was declared "Universal Teacher" to the church. Aquinas was born in 1225 in southern Italy and joined the Dominican Order of Preachers in 1244. In addition to his theological works he is remembered for his prayers and hymns on the eucharist. He is the author of the collect used in the votive "Of the Holy Eucharist" (pp. 201 and 252).

February (p. 20)

February 2: The Presentation of Our Lord Jesus Christ in the Temple

This feast originated late in the fourth century in Jerusalem, where it was celebrated on February 14, forty days after the Epiphany. When December 25 was accepted in the East as the feast of the Nativity, the Presentation was moved to February 2. Eventually it spread to the West. Late in the seventh century Pope Sergius (687–701), a native of Syria, introduced in Rome a procession with candles and the singing of the Nunc dimittis. Hence the day came to be known as "Candlemas." Earlier editions of the Prayer Book titled it "The Purification of Saint Mary the Virgin," but the 1662 revision, restoring the ancient tradition, changed the title to "The Presentation of Christ in the Temple, commonly called, The Purification of Saint Mary the Virgin." Lev. 12 tells the Old Testament background for the gospel story (Lk. 2:22–40). (See *The Book of Occasional Services*, pp. 51—53, for provisions for a Candlemas procession.)

February 3: Anskar, Archbishop of Hamburg, Missionary
to Denmark and Sweden, 865

Anskar was born in 801 near the famous monastery at Corbie in France, where he was educated and professed as a monk. After several attempts to found Christian schools and missions in Denmark and Sweden, he was consecrated archbishop of Hamburg in 831. Pope Gregory IV made him papal legate to work among the Danes, Swedes, and Slavs. By training others in Germany he laid the founda-

51

tion for conversion of the Scandinavian countries, which consider him their apostle.

February 4: Cornelius the Centurion
According to Acts 10:1—11:18, Cornelius was the first Gentile converted to the Christian faith. He was a citizen of Rome, a soldier in charge of a hundred men. His conversion and his baptism by Peter set an important precedent for the admission of Gentiles to the church. Nothing else is known of him except the legend that he became the second bishop of Caesarea.

February 5: The Martyrs of Japan, 1597
Christianity was first carried to Japan in the sixteenth century by a Jesuit missionary, Francis Xavier, who was followed by Franciscans. When the government became suspicious that the church was a cloak for subversive activities, Christianity was declared illegal. On February 5, 1597, six Franciscan friars and twenty of their followers were publicly crucified in Nagasaki. When the ban against Christianity in Japan was lifted in the nineteenth century, the missionaries who entered the country found secret communities in which the faith was still alive.

February 13: Absalom Jones, Priest, 1818
Absalom Jones was born a slave on a Delaware plantation. When he was sixteen his family was sold and Jones went to Philadelphia. In 1784 he purchased his freedom. In 1787 he helped organize a "free African society" which in 1794 built a church, "St. Thomas African Episcopal Church of Philadelphia." Jones was ordained deacon in 1795 and priest in 1804, the first black person ordained in the American Episcopal Church.

February 14: Cyril, Monk, and Methodius, Bishop,
Missionaries to the Slavs, 869, 885
Cyril and Methodius were brothers sent to Moravia in 863 in response to a request from Prince Rotislav. Cyril developed an alphabet so that scriptures and liturgy could be translated into the native tongue. Methodius became archbishop of Sirmium in what is now Yugoslavia. By their work as missionaries and teachers the two brothers laid the foundation for the church in the Balkans.

February 15: Thomas Bray, Priest and Missionary, 1730
Thomas Bray was sent by Bishop Henry Compton of London as

commissary to Maryland in 1696. Although he spent only two and one-half months in the colony, upon his return to England he founded two notable societies: the Society for the Promoting of Christian Knowledge (SPCK) and the Society for the Propagation of the Gospel (SPG). In addition he fought vigorously for the relief of prisoners, the needs of slaves, and the education of children.

February 23: Polycarp, Bishop and Martyr of Smyrna, 156
According to his pupil Irenaeus (June 28), Polycarp was a pupil of John, "the disciple of the Lord," and was appointed bishop by "apostles in Asia." The Martyrdom of Polycarp gives an account of his death. Given a chance to recant, he replied, "For eighty-six years I have been His servant, and He has done me no wrong. How can I blaspheme my King who saved me?" Immediately after his death, a day was observed annually in commemoration of his martyrdom, possibly the first such commemoration.

February 24: Saint Matthias the Apostle
The feast of Matthias is found in liturgical books from the eleventh century. According to tradition he ministered in Judea and was killed by stoning. Acts 1:15–26 tells how he and one other, "Joseph called Barsabbas, who was surnamed Justus," were nominated from among those who had been followers of Jesus and witnesses of his resurrection to take the place of Judas. Matthias was chosen by a casting of lots, and numbered as an apostle with the other eleven.

February 27: George Herbert, Priest, 1633
George Herbert was born April 3, 1593. He was an accomplished musician, scholar, and orator, who gave up a career in public life to become a priest in the small village of Bremerton. His book of poems, *The Temple,* and his manual, *A Priest to the Temple, or The Country Parson, His Character, and Rule of Life,* are classics of devotional literature. Three of his poems are used as hymns: "Come, my Way, my Truth, my Life," "Let all the world in every corner sing," and "Teach me, my God and King."

March (p. 21)

March 1: David, Bishop of Menevia, Wales, c. 544
After the Romans withdrew their troops from Britain early in the fifth century, many British Christians moved to Wales. David rose as an effective leader, founding monasteries as refuges for the homeless

53

and as centers of learning. Many Irish monks came to his monastery in Menevia, to take advantage of his teaching. David is the patron saint of Wales. His name was restored to the Prayer Book calendar in 1561.

March 2: Chad, Bishop of Lichfield, 672
Trained by Aidan (August 31), Chad in 664 succeeded his brother as abbot at Lastingham, but was soon made bishop of Northumbria during the absence of Wilfrid. When Theodore (September 19) came as archbishop of Canterbury he removed Chad as an intruder. The humility with which he stepped down so impressed Theodore that he made him bishop of Lichfield. Chad was restored to the calendar in 1561.

March 3: John and Charles Wesley, Priests, 1791, 1788
John and Charles Wesley were the children of Samuel Wesley, the rector at Epworth. Both were educated at Oxford where, because of their methodical observances, they were called "Methodists." They spent some time in the colony of Georgia, then returned to England where both underwent conversion experiences and became leaders in the evangelical movement. John was particularly noted for his preaching. Charles is best remembered for his hymns. Though many of the Methodists later separated from the Church of England, John and Charles Wesley did not.

March 7: Perpetua and her Companions, Martyrs at Carthage, 202
Vibia Perpetua, a widow and the young mother of a nursing son, was imprisoned in Carthage during the persecution of A.D. 202. She, her slave Felicitas, and three men, Saturus, Saturninus, and Revocatus, all of whom were catechumens, were thrown into the amphitheater to be mangled by beasts. They were then killed by the sword, being baptized in their own blood. This commemoration was restored in the revision of the calendar in 1561.

March 9: Gregory, Bishop of Nyssa, c. 394
Gregory, who was born about A.D. 334, was the younger brother of Basil the Great (June 14). After a period as a professor of rhetoric, he entered his brother's monastery at Pontus. When Basil became bishop of Caesarea, he made his brother bishop of Nyssa, a small town in his jurisdiction. Gregory was a firm opponent of the Arian

heresy and wrote many dogmatic, ascetic, and exegetical works to strengthen the orthodox position. His mysticism has had a profound influence upon the Eastern churches.

March 12: Gregory the Great, Bishop of Rome, 604

Gregory, prefect of Rome, retired to a monastic life in a community which he organized in his home. In 579 Pope Pelagius II sent him as ambassador to Constantinople. Gregory was elected bishop of Rome in 590. He organized the defense of the city against the Lombards, reordered the church's liturgy and music, and produced a number of writings, most noted of which is his *Pastoral Care.* He fostered the mission of Augustine (May 26) to the Anglo-Saxons. The Venerable Bede (May 25) called him the "Apostle of the English." In the Elizabethan revision his name was restored to the calendar.

March 17: Patrick, Bishop and Missionary of Ireland, 461

Patrick, the child of British Christian parents, was captured at the age of sixteen and carried to Ireland, where he was forced to work for six years as a swineherd. He fulfilled his vow to return as a missionary and was ordained bishop in 432. From his see at Armagh, Patrick worked at evangelizing among the Irish and organizing the church. An ancient Irish hymn of uncertain authorship, "I bind unto myself today," is known as "St. Patrick's Breastplate."

March 18: Cyril, Bishop of Jerusalem, 386

Cyril became bishop of Jerusalem in 348. Because of the Arian heresy he had a stormy episcopate. He is best remembered for the catechetical lectures generally attributed to him and for the services he developed at various holy places. His services for Palm Sunday and Holy Week were spread throughout the church by pilgrims to Jerusalem and had a revolutionary effect upon the organization of the church year.

March 19: Saint Joseph

As early as the fourth century the Copts of Egypt kept a day in commemoration of Saint Joseph. There is some evidence of its observance in the West in the ninth and tenth centuries. The Dominican and Franciscan Orders added it to their calendars in the fourteenth century. Under the pontificate of Sixtus IV (1471–1484) March 19 was set aside in the Roman calendar for the commemoration of Saint Joseph. Little is known about the foster father of our Lord, other than that he was a just man, a carpenter by trade. It is generally assumed that he died a natural death before the beginning of our Lord's public ministry. (See Mt. 1:18–25 and Lk. 2:41–52.)

March 20: Cuthbert, Bishop of Lindisfarne, 687
Cuthbert was an Anglo-Saxon but trained in the rigorous tradition of Celtic monastic life. He became the prior at Lindisfarne in 664. After the council of Whitby, 664, he sought to reconcile the Celtic and Roman factions of the church in England. He spent eight years in seclusion on the Isle of Farne, then accepted the call of Theodore (September 19) to become bishop of Hexham in 684.

March 21: Thomas Ken, Bishop of Bath and Wells, 1711
Thomas Ken is best known for his hymns, especially for the doxology, "Praise God from whom all blessings flow." Though he rebuked Charles II for certain aspects of his private life, Charles made him a royal chaplain, and in 1685 appointed him the bishop of Bath and Wells. For refusing to subscribe to the Declaration of Indulgence of James II, Ken was sent to the Tower, though finally acquitted. He refused to swear fealty to William and Mary; along with other "Nonjurors" he was deprived of his living.

March 22: James De Koven, Priest, 1879
James De Koven, after being tutor in ecclesiastical history at Nashotah House, became warden of Racine College in 1859. At a time of partisan strife within the American church, he persuaded the Episcopal Church to comprehend its Catholic heritage of doctrine, worship, and spirituality.

March 23: Gregory the Illuminator, Bishop and
Missionary of Armenia, c. 332
Gregory is credited with the first conversion of a country to Christianity. Because of political unrest in Armenia he was taken to Cappadocia as a child. He returned to Armenia as an adult and converted the king to Christianity. With the help of the king the country was converted. Armenia lost her independence in 430, but the Armenian church and culture, though dispersed throughout the world and often severely persecuted, continue to exist.

*March 25: The Annunciation of Our Lord Jesus Christ
to the Blessed Virgin Mary*
The association of March 25 with the annunciation can be found as

early as the third century, and a feast of the annunciation can be traced to the fifth century in the East. Jesus was believed to have died on March 25. It was assumed that his earthly years must have been even and therefore that the annunciation must have taken place on this date. Probably this had something to do with the decision, in the fourth century, to establish December 25 as the date of the nativity. In the seventh century, the Mozarabic rite set December 18 as the date of the annunciation. In 692, at the council known as *in Trullo*, the Eastern churches settled on March 25 as the date for this commemoration, and forbade any festival to be observed in Lent other than Sabbaths, Sundays, and the feast of the Annunciation. Pope Sergius I (687–701), a Syrian by birth, instituted the feast at Rome.

March 27: Charles Henry Brent, Bishop of the Philippines, and of Western New York, 1929

Brent was a Canadian who worked in Boston with the Cowley Fathers, and in the slums, before his election as the first bishop of the Philippines. He worked among the Igorots and the Moros as well as among the English and the Chinese-speaking people. Brent was responsible for the call for a World Conference on Faith and Order in 1927. He is considered one of the founders of the modern ecumenical movement.

March 29: John Keble, Priest, 1866

John Keble was the author of a book of poems, *The Christian Year*, published anonymously in 1827. Excerpts from several of his poems continue to be printed in many hymnals. In 1833 Keble preached at Oxford a sermon entitled "National Apostasy" which set in motion the Oxford (Tractarian) Movement. Among other works, he edited an important collection of the works of Richard Hooker (November 3).

March 31: John Donne, Priest, 1631

John Donne was born in London to a Roman Catholic family in 1573. He trained for a career in law, but, after years of struggle, was ordained to the ministry of the Church of England in 1615. In 1622 he became dean of St. Paul's Cathedral and the best-known preacher of his day. His sermons, meditations, and poetry continue to be studied as classics of both artistry and devotion.

April (p. 22)

April 1: Frederick Denison Maurice, Priest, 1872

In 1837 Maurice published *The Kingdom of Christ*, the first and best known of his many books. He was a member of the faculty of King's College, Cambridge, from 1840 to 1853, but he was dismissed in 1853 for his theory of "Christian Socialism." He founded the Working Men's College in 1854. The last years of his life were spent as professor of moral philosophy at Cambridge and as rector of St. Edward's Church.

April 2: James Lloyd Breck, Priest, 1876

Breck was among the founders of Nashotah House which was to be a seminary, a monastic community, and a center for missionary work. He moved to Minnesota in 1850 to found schools for boys and girls and the Seabury Divinity School. He also began work among the Chippewa Indians. In 1867 he traveled on to California, there to found schools, a seminary, and many new parishes.

April 3: Richard, Bishop of Chichester, 1253

Richard, former chancellor at Oxford, while in exile for his opposition to the policies of Henry III, was elected bishop of Chichester. After he and the king were reconciled, Richard entered into an episcopate marked with concern for the poor and the oppressed, and for higher educational standards among the clergy. His name was restored among black letter days in 1561.

April 8: William Augustus Muhlenberg, Priest, 1877

Muhlenberg founded an academy in Flushing, New York; the free Church of the Holy Communion in New York City; St. Luke's Hospital; and the first order of sisters in the American church. At the General Convention of 1853 he sponsored a "memorial" which sought to encourage a commitment to liturgical renewal, ecumenism, and missionary outreach. His last years were spent in developing St. Johnland, a home for the handicapped and elderly.

April 9: William Law, Priest, 1761

Unable to function as a clergyman in the Church of England because he could not swear fealty to George I, William Law served for a while as a tutor in the home of Edward Gibbon. In 1740 he established a household notable for its discipline of prayer and meditation, and for its charitable works. Law was a defender of orthodoxy against

58

the Deists, but is best known for his devotional work, *A Serious Call to the Devout and Holy Life.*

April 11: George Augustus Selwyn, Bishop of New Zealand, and of Lichfield, 1878
Elected bishop in 1841, Selwyn established Christianity in New Zealand and Melanesia. During a tragic ten-year war between British colonists and the Maoris, he ministered to both sides, and finally helped to bring a peaceful settlement. The last ten years of his life were spent as bishop of Lichfield in England.

April 19: Alphege, Archbishop of Canterbury, and Martyr, 1012
While archbishop of Canterbury, Alphege was captured by Danish invaders, who demanded a ransom for his return. Alphege refused to allow his poor and overburdened people to pay; as a result he was beaten to death by his drunken captors. Some of the Danes were so impressed by his courage and faith, however, that they were later baptized. His name was restored to the calendar in 1561.

April 21: Anselm, Archbishop of Canterbury, 1109
Anselm was exiled by the king for his strong championship of the rights of the church. He is probably less known for his episcopal activity than for his scholarship. A pioneer in applying the scholastic method to theology, Anselm's works on the existence of God, the *Proslogium* and *Monologium,* and *Cur Deus Homo?*, his study of the incarnation and the atonement, stand as classics of medieval theological thought.

April 25: Saint Mark the Evangelist
According to tradition Mark was the boy who escaped capture by leaving his sheet behind him and running off naked when Jesus was taken prisoner in the Garden of Gethsemane (Mk. 14:51). He accompanied Paul and Barnabas on their first missionary journey, but turned back at Perga. Paul refused to take him on the second journey and Mark went instead with Barnabas to Cyprus (Acts 12:25; 13:13; 15:36–41). Eventually he and Paul were reconciled (Col. 4:10). Later he was associated with Peter (1 Pet. 5:13). Papias writing about A.D. 140 said that Mark was the interpreter of Peter. Tradition has it that he is the author of the Gospel according to Mark. Eusebius states that Mark carried the Gospel to Egypt where he was martyred. April 25 was not designated as a commemoration of Mark until the twelfth century. From the time of the Gregorian sacramentary this date was

the day of the Major Litany, the Roman counterpart of the rogation days of the Gallican churches.

April 29: Catherine of Siena, 1380
At the age of seven Catherine had a vision of Christ which marked the beginning of her life of dedication. After a later vision of herself as "the Bride of Christ," she formed a religious household to minister to the sick and the poor. Hoping to persuade the pope to return to Rome, she journeyed to Avignon in 1376. She wrote voluminous letters and a mystical work, *The Dialogue.*

May (p. 23)

May 1: Saint Philip and Saint James, Apostles
This feast dates from the pontificate of John III (561–574) when the Basilica of the Apostles was dedicated in Rome. Tradition holds that the relics of the two apostles were deposited there. Philip came from Bethsaida, the home of Peter and Andrew. He was one of the first of the disciples and introduced Nathanael to Jesus (Jn. 1:43–51). It was also Philip who mentioned the need for food for the multitude which had gathered to hear Jesus (Jn. 6:1–14). When certain Greeks wanted to see Jesus they came to Philip (Jn. 12:20–22). Philip made the request "Show us the Father," to which Jesus answered "He who has seen me has seen the Father" (Jn. 14:8–11). According to tradition he preached the gospel in Phrygia and died a martyr. We know nothing about James other than that in the lists of the twelve he is designated as the son of Alphaeus, so that he would not be confused with James the son of Zebedee and brother of John (July 25), or James who was the leader of the church in Jerusalem (October 23).

May 2: Athanasius, Bishop of Alexandria, 373
As a deacon, Athanasius accompanied the bishop of Alexandria to the council of Nicea at which the Arian heresy was condemned. Three years later he was elected bishop of Alexandria and spent a long episcopate, which included five periods of exile, combatting Arianism. His most famous work is *De Incarnatione.* The so-called Athanasian creed (Prayer Book, pp. 864–865), though it was composed after his death, expresses his faith in the divinity and the eternal existence of the Son.

May 4: Monnica, Mother of Augustine of Hippo, 387
We know of Monnica through the writings of her son, Augustine of

Hippo (August 28). She was born in North Africa and married a minor government official who was eventually converted to her Christian faith. Though at an earlier stage she was overly ambitious for the worldly success of her son, she became a woman of prayer, passionately concerned for his conversion. She died shortly after his baptism, while they were returning to Africa.

May 8: Dame Julian of Norwich, c. 1417

Dame Julian, on May 8, 1373, received a series of sixteen "showings" which are recorded in her *Revelations of Divine Love.* Following this experience she retired with a servant to a hermitage on the grounds of the Church of St. Julian, Conisford, Norwich. About twenty years later she expanded her writing, as a result of "inward teaching." It has become a devotional classic.

May 9: Gregory of Nazianzus, Bishop of Constantinople, 389

Gregory, son of the bishop of Nazianzus, was baptized as an adult in 357. He hoped to join his friend Basil (June 14) in the monastic life, but was ordained presbyter by his father. He later succeeded his father as bishop and in 379 was elected bishop of Constantinople where he played a leading role in the Second Ecumenical Council of 381. He, Basil, and Basil's brother, Gregory of Nyssa (March 9) are known as the "Cappadocian Fathers."

May 19: Dunstan, Archbishop of Canterbury, 988

Dunstan is noted for his work in the reform of monasticism and in the revival of learning and arts in England following the Scandinavian invasions. His monastic reform was influenced by the movement in process among the Benedictines on the continent. In addition, it stressed the involvement of the monastery with the life of the people. The present British coronation rite derives from that compiled by Dunstan for King Edgar in 973. His name was restored to the calendar in 1561.

May 20: Alcuin, Deacon and Abbot of Tours, 804

Charlemagne called Alcuin from his position as head of the cathedral school at York to serve as chief adviser in matters of religion and education in the Frankish kingdom. He was chiefly responsible for the revival and preservation of learning in the age of Charlemagne. He also played a part in the replacing of Gallican rites by Roman rites in the Frankish territory, although some of the work formerly attributed to him is now thought to be the work of Benedict of Aniane (c. 750–821).

May 24: Jackson Kemper, First Missionary Bishop in the United States, 1870

In 1835 the General Convention declared all baptized Episcopalians members of the Domestic and Foreign Missionary Society, and provided for the election of bishops and the organization of dioceses on the frontier and in foreign countries. Jackson Kemper was elected bishop at that convention. He initiated the establishment of the church in the midwest and played a part in the founding of Nashotah House.

May 25: Bede, the Venerable, Priest, and Monk of Jarrow, 735

The foremost scholar of his time, Bede wrote commentaries and homilies on the Scriptures, and textbooks on chronology, orthography, and poetic meter which were studied in medieval classrooms. He is best remembered for his *Ecclesiastical History of the English People*. Though not restored among the black letter days in the 1561 revision of the calendar, his name was added in 1662.

May 27: Augustine, First Archbishop of Canterbury, 605

Pope Gregory the Great (March 12) sent Augustine to convert the English. He established his see at Canterbury and founded two other sees, London and Rochester. Augustine's attempts to establish authority over the Christians of Wales and southwest England were unsuccessful. In the *Ecclesiastical History,* Bede includes the answers traditionally attributed to Pope Gregory when Augustine asked his advice in governing the see. His name was restored among the black letter days in 1561.

May 31: The Visitation of the Blessed Virgin Mary

Most feasts seem to originate as local observances which later spread throughout the church. The feast of the Visitation of the Blessed Virgin Mary to her cousin Elizabeth, a short time before the birth of John the Baptist, however, seems to have been established by a decree of Pope Urban VI on April 6, 1389. Nearly a hundred years passed before the feast was observed throughout the Western church. Propers for the feast were first printed in the Sarum breviary of 1494. In the calendar of 1561, the feast was listed among the black letter days on July 2, the date of its observance during the late medieval period. The Roman sacramentary of Paul VI shifted the date to May 31, replacing the feast of the Queenship of the Blessed Virgin Mary which had been instituted by Pius XII in 1954. The present revision of the Prayer Book is the first American edition in which the feast has been included. Propers have also been provided for the feast in various recent revisions for other provinces of Anglicanism.

The visitation is portrayed in the Gospel according to Luke as the occasion for Elizabeth's greeting, "Blessed are you among women, and blessed is the fruit of your womb." In the late medieval period this text became an important part of private devotions and one of the three texts which godparents were instructed to teach their godchildren. It is also the occasion for the Song of Mary, the Magnificat.

A note on the bottom of page 23 indicates that there may be a commemoration of the first Book of Common Prayer (1549) on a weekday following the Day of Pentecost, since it was on the feast of Pentecost in 1549 that use of the Prayer Book was first required throughout the realm.

June (p. 24)

June 1: Justin, Martyr at Rome, c. 167

Justin was born in Samaria of Greek parents. Having studied one philosophy after another, he finally came to Christianity by way of Platonism. He is one of the most important of the Christian "apologists" of the second century. His two *Apologies* addressed to pagans and his *Dialogue with Trypho*, addressed to Jews, are valuable for their presentation of the Christian faith, worship, and practice of the period. Accused of atheism, he was beheaded about 167.

June 2: The Martyrs of Lyons, 177

One of the most brutal persecutions in the early years of the church took place at Lyons where a colony of Christians from Asia Minor had settled. Among those killed were the bishop Pothinus, over ninety years of age, who died in prison from injuries, and a slave girl named Blandina who, with a youth of fifteen named Ponticus, was thrown to the wild beasts in the amphitheater on a pagan festal day.

June 3: The Martyrs of Uganda, 1886

Mission work began in Uganda in the 1870's when Mutesa was king. His son Mwanga, who succeeded him in 1884, feared white penetration of his country. Emissaries sent by him murdered Bishop James Hannington and his companions (October 29) on their way to Uganda. Ugandan Christians were also martyred. The first to die was Joseph Mkasa Bilikuddembe, who rebuked the king for his debauchery and for the murder of Hannington. Others killed included thirty-two Roman Catholic and Anglican boys and young men who were martyred on June 3, 1886.

June 5: Boniface, Archbishop of Mainz, Missionary to Germany, and Martyr, 754

After years as a monk in England, Boniface (Winfred) went as a missionary to Frisia where he met with little success in his efforts. Commissioned and named Boniface—"good deeds"—by Pope Gregory II, he then went to Germany and helped to establish the church in Hesse, Bavaria, Westphalia, Thuringia, and Württemburg. It was he who anointed Pippin king of the Franks. He returned to Frisia when he was over seventy, to be martyred soon afterward.

June 9: Columba, Abbot of Iona, 597

Columba, born and educated in Ireland, founded monasteries there at Derry and Durrow. About 561 he left Ireland to found a monastery at Iona, an island off the west coast of Scotland. It became the center for his missionary work among the Irish who had settled in Scotland and among the Picts of the Highlands. From this monastery came some of the best missionaries to the English, including Aidan (August 31).

June 10: Ephrem of Edessa, Syria, Deacon, 373

Ephrem moved from his native city of Nisibis to Edessa when Nisibis was captured by the Persians in 363. There he became head of the Christian school. His writings include commentaries, homilies, and hymns, many of which are used in the Syrian liturgy.

June 11: Saint Barnabas the Apostle

Although he was not one of the twelve, Barnabas, a Jew from Cyprus, was considered an apostle (Acts 14:4 and 14; 1 Cor. 9:6). According to Clement of Alexandria he was one of the seventy (Lk. 10:1). The first mention of him in the book of Acts tells that he sold a field and gave money to the infant church (Acts 4:36–37). He vouched for Paul before the leaders of the church in Jerusalem (Acts 9:27). The church in Jerusalem sent him to Antioch and brought Paul to be there with him (Acts 11:19–30; 12:25). He later went with Paul on his first missionary journey (Acts 13:1—15:35) and accompanied Paul to the council at Jerusalem (Acts 15 and Gal. 2). When Paul left on his second journey and did not wish to take Mark, Barnabas took Mark, who was his cousin, with him to Cyprus (Acts 15:36–41). This feast was celebrated in the East as early as the fifty century, but was not observed in Rome until after the eleventh.

June 14: Basil the Great, Bishop of Caesarea, 379

Basil was born to Christian parents in 329. After his baptism about 357, he founded a monastery on a family estate in Pontus, near a convent begun by his mother and his sister Macrina. His ascetic writings provided the primary basis for the rules and ideals of Eastern monasticism. He was probably the author or reviser of the eucharistic prayer of the Liturgy of Saint Basil, which is the source for Eucharistic Prayer D in Rite Two (pp. 372–375).

June 16: Joseph Butler, Bishop of Durham, 1752

Joseph Butler was noted for his sermons, but best known for his work *The Analogy of Religion, Natural and Revealed, to the Constitution and Course of Nature.* In this work he defends orthodoxy against the Deism prevalent in his day using as his basis the "reasonable probability" of Christianity. He declined an offer of the see of Canterbury.

June 18: Bernard Mizeki, Catechist and Martyr in Rhodesia, 1896

Mizeki escaped from his native Portuguese East Africa to Capetown, where he was converted by an Anglican missionary. In 1891 he volunteered to serve as catechist in Rhodesia. During an uprising against the Europeans and their friends he was warned to flee but would not desert his converts. He remained at the mission station and was brutally murdered.

June 22: Alban, First Martyr of Britain, c. 304

According to tradition, Alban was a Roman soldier during the persecution under Diocletian. He gave refuge to a fleeing Christian and exchanged clothes with his guest when a search was made. Both were captured. Alban's identity was discovered, he confessed the Christian faith, and was beheaded along with his guest and the executioner who had refused to kill him because of certain natural signs. The vivid account is in Bede's *Ecclesiastical History.* Alban's name was restored among the black letter days in 1662.

June 24: The Nativity of Saint John the Baptist

According to the Lukan account, John the Baptist was born under remarkable circumstances to the priest Zechariah and his elderly wife Elizabeth, a kinswoman of the Virgin Mary (Lk. 1:5–25 and 39–80). After a period as a hermit in the wilderness he appeared preaching a gospel of repentance and baptizing in the Jordan River. Jesus was baptized by John and called some of his disciples from among the followers of John (Mt. 3; Mk. 1:1–11; Lk. 3:1–22; Jn. 1). For rebuking Herod Antipas, John was imprisoned, but was able to learn of the ministry of Jesus. He was beheaded at the wish of Herodias, wife of Herod Antipas (Lk. 7:18–35; Mt. 14:1–12).

In the Eastern church John is ranked second only to the Virgin Mary among the saints. The Gallican Missale Gothicum contains propers for both the nativity (nos. 368–373) and the "passion" (nos. 384–388) of John the Baptist, as does the Bobbio missal (nos. 313–326). The Leonine sacramentary contains several sets of propers for the nativity (nos. 232–256). Propers for both the vigil and the feast of the nativity, and for the passion are in the Gelasian sacramentary (nos. 896–906 and 1009–1012). The Gregorian provides for both the vigil and the feast of the nativity (nos. 568–573). The feast of the beheading of John the Baptist was listed in the Sarum missal for August 29, but not retained in the Prayer Book, possibly because Cranmer did not consider him a Christian martyr. The feast of John's nativity was kept, however, as part of the cycle of the feasts of our Lord.

June 28: Irenaeus, Bishop of Lyons, c. 202

Irenaeus, a native of Smyrna, was strongly influenced by Polycarp (February 23). He went from Asia Minor to Lyons where he succeeded the martyred bishop Pothinus (June 2). He is best known for his treatise against the Gnostics, *Adversus haereses.* Tradition sets his martyrdom on June 28.

June 29: Saint Peter and Saint Paul, Apostles

In 258, during the persecution under Valerian, the church in Rome instituted a joint commemoration of their traditional founders, Peter and Paul, on June 29. Twenty-eight sets of propers for this day have been collected in the Leonine sacramentary (nos. 280–379). Propers are provided for a joint commemoration in the Gallican Missale Gothicum (nos. 374–379) and the Bobbio missal (nos. 327–333). The Gelasian sacramentary provides for both joint and separate commemorations on that day (nos. 915–938). In the Gregorian, as in the Sarum missal, the feast of Peter and Paul on June 29 (nos. 589–603) is followed by a commemoration of Paul on June 30 (nos. 604–606).

In the 1549 Prayer Book, Paul was commemorated with the feast of his conversion (January 25) and June 29 was given over to a commemoration of the martyrdom of Peter. Following revisions in other provinces of Anglicanism, June 29 has been restored in this present edition as a commemoration of the martyrdom of both Peter and Paul. The traditional account is that Peter and Paul were martyred at Rome during the persecution under Nero (A.D. 64)—Paul, as a Roman citizen, being beheaded, and Peter being crucified head downward at his own request. He did not feel worthy to be crucified in the same manner as his Lord.

July (p. 25)

July 4: Independence Day

Propers for both Morning Prayer and Eucharist were adopted by the interstate convention of 1785 with a resolution "That the said form of prayer be used in this Church, on the fourth of July, for ever." The propers were included in the Proposed Book of 1786. Despite his support of the American Revolution, William White considered this an unwise move because so many of the clergy had been loyalists. Soon after it was issued, Samuel Provoost wrote from New York of opposition to the Book: "The Thanksgiving for the Fourth of July is in all probability the one principal cause of the opposition." The service was not brought over into the 1789 revision, but was reprinted and used on occasion in the nineteenth century. The first evidence of reprinting of the rite dates from 1826 for use in the diocese of New York under the sponsorship of Bishop John Henry Hobart (September 12). Propers for the Daily Office and the Eucharist were inserted in the 1928 revision. In that Book Independence Day was treated as a votive; in this revision it is made a major feast.

July 11: Benedict of Nursia, Abbot of Monte Cassino, c. 540

Benedict is considered the father of Western monasticism. After a time as a solitary monk at Subiaco, he established his monastery at Monte Cassino. His *Rule*, which drew on earlier monastic rules, set forth a pattern of worship and work which became the basis for Benedictine monasticism. It was a Benedictine monk, Augustine (May 26), who came as a missionary to Canterbury.

July 17: William White, Bishop of Pennsylvania, 1836

William White was the first bishop of Pennsylvania and the first Presiding Bishop of the Episcopal Church. More than any other person he helped to reconcile competing factions, to organize the church in this country, and to encourage the adoption of the first American Prayer Book. He was also instrumental in the founding of various groups for the relief of the poor and the oppressed. In time, he was declared "first citizen" of Philadelphia.

July 22: Saint Mary Magdalene

In the Gospels Mary Magdalene is the woman who followed Jesus after He had cast out seven devils (Lk. 8:1-2). She was present at the crucifixion (Mt. 27:55-56; Mk. 15:40-41; Lk. 23:49 and 24:10; Jn. 19:25). She was also one of those who went on the first day of the week to anoint the body of Jesus (Mt. 28:1-10; Mk. 16:1-11; Lk. 23:55-24:12; Jn. 20:1-18). According to the accounts of Mark and John, Mary Magdalene was the first one to whom Jesus appeared after the resurrection; according to the Johannine account Jesus gave her a message to deliver to the brethren. From the time of Gregory the Great (March 12) she has often been identified in the Western church with the woman who was a sinner (Lk. 7:36-50), and with Mary, the sister of Martha and Lazarus (Lk. 10:38-42; Jn. 11:1-12:11). In the Eastern church these are treated as three different women. According to tradition, she retired to Ephesus with the Virgin Mary and John. In the Eastern church she is treated as the equal of an apostle, since she was the first to see the risen Lord.

The feast can be traced as far back as the council of Oxford in 1222 which made it a day of obligation. It was retained with a proper for the day in the 1549 Prayer Book, deleted in the revision of 1552, and restored as a black letter day in the revised calendar of 1561. Some recent Prayer Book revisions have restored it as a red letter day, but this is the first American edition which includes it.

July 24: Thomas a Kempis, Priest, 1471

Thomas is best known for his devotional classic, *The Imitation of Christ*, which is said to have been translated into more languages than any book other than the Bible. He was a member of the Brethren of the Common Life, an order founded by Gerald Groote (1340-1384), whose "modern devotion" has had great influence on both Catholic and Protestant spirituality.

July 25: Saint James the Apostle

James, the son of Zebedee and brother of John, was among the first to be called (Mt. 4:18-22; Mk. 1:16-20). With John and Peter he witnessed the healing of the daughter of Jairus, the transfiguration, and the agony in the garden (Mt. 17:1-8; Mk. 5:35-43, 9:2-8, and 14:32-42; Lk. 8:40-56). The first of the apostles to suffer martyrdom, James is the only one whose martyrdom is recorded in the Scriptures (Acts 12:1-2). He was put to death by the sword on the orders of Herod Agrippa. Tradition runs that his accuser repented and suffered execution with him. According to Spanish legend, James had visited

Spain and preached there; his body was brought from Jerusalem to Compostela, one of the most popular pilgrimage centers late in the middle ages. His feast is celebrated near Easter in the Eastern churches and was kept along with that of his brother John on December 27 in the Gallican rites. By the time of the supplement to the Gregorian sacramentary (no. 1640), July 25 had been adopted as his day in the Western church. The reason for this is obscure.

July 26: The Parents of the Blessed Virgin Mary
The Gospels tell us nothing about the parentage of the Blessed Virgin, but the *Protoevangelium of James*, an apocryphal writing of the second century, purports to give an account of the birth of Mary to Anne and Joachim. The story bears strong resemblance to the biblical accounts of the births of Isaac and Samuel. The name "Anne" is a derivative of Hannah, the name of Samuel's mother. In the East, the feast of Anne is observed on July 25. Pope Urban VI in 1378 set her date as July 26. The commemoration of Joachim joined that of Anne in the 1969 Roman calendar; prior to that it had been observed on March 20 or August 16. Anne was restored among the black letter days in 1561.

July 27: William Reed Huntington, Priest, 1909
Huntington was possibly the most influential presbyter in the House of Deputies in the late nineteenth century. He was the original proponent of the Chicago-Lambeth Quadrilateral (pages 876–878) and the leader in the Prayer Book revision of 1892. Certain elements in his work *Materia Ritualis* which were not incorporated in the 1892 revision contributed to that of 1928. He also revived the order of deaconesses in the Episcopal Church.

July 29: Mary and Martha of Bethany
All that we know of Mary and Martha is found in Lk. 10:38–42 and Jn. 11:1—12:11. They have been portrayed as representatives of the active and the contemplative life. In Eastern calendars they are commemorated on different dates, but in the West, because of the confusion of this Mary with Mary Magdalene, Martha's feast was placed on the octave day, July 29.

July 30: William Wilberforce, 1833
Wilberforce was one of the most noted laymen in the history of the church. He served in parliament most of his adult life, working for overseas missions, education, raising of moral standards, parliamen-

69

tary reform, Catholic emancipation, and most of all for the abolition of the slave trade. The bill which put an end to the slave trade was passed one month after his death.

July 31: Joseph of Arimathaea
All that the Gospels tell us about Joseph of Arimathaea is that he was a member of the Sanhedrin, a secret disciple, that he did not consent to the death of Jesus, and that he buried Jesus in his garden tomb (Mt. 27:57–61; Mk. 15:42–47; Lk. 23:50–56; Jn. 19:38–42). In the thirteenth century there appeared a legend that he founded the church at Glastonbury and planted there a thorn from the crown of thorns. He was also associated with the romance of the holy grail and King Arthur.

August (p. 26)

August 6: The Transfiguration of Our Lord Jesus Christ
The feast of the Transfiguration was celebrated in the East in the latter part of the fourth century. In the West it was observed after the ninth century in certain monastic liturgies. Pope Callistus III declared it a universal feast of the Western church in 1457, a decree ratified by provincial synods late in the fifteenth century. It is found in the late Sarum missal, but its observance was not carried over into the Prayer Book until the revision of the calendar in 1561 when it was restored among the black letter days. The American revision of 1892 restored it as a red letter day with propers, largely through the efforts of William Reed Huntington (July 27) who wrote the collect for the day. Since then it has been restored in Prayer Book revisions of other provinces.

August 7: John Mason Neale, Priest, 1866
An early convert to Tractarianism, Neale was one of the founders of the Camden, or Ecclesiological, Society. He spent most of his ministry as warden of Sackville College and chaplain to the Sisterhood of St. Margaret, which he had founded. He is best known for the hymns he wrote and those he translated from Latin and Greek.

August 8: Dominic, Priest and Friar, 1221
Following his experiences on a mission to the Albigensians, Dominic founded the Order of Preachers, later known as Dominicans, with an emphasis on learning, preaching, and teaching. Pope

Honorius III approved the order on December 22, 1216. By the time of Dominic's death it had spread to all parts of Europe and its members were beginning to occupy places in university centers.

August 10: Laurence, Deacon, and Martyr at Rome, 258
During the persecution under Valerian, Sixtus II, bishop of Rome, and six of his deacons were executed on August 6, 258. The execution of the seventh, Laurence the archdeacon, was postponed for four days in an effort to force him to surrender the church's treasures. Legend tells that he was roasted on a gridiron. His was one of the four black letter days restored to the calendar in the revision of 1552.

August 11: Clare, Abbess at Assissi, 1253
Impressed by Francis of Assissi (October 4) and his rule of life, Clare donned the habit of the Franciscans and observed their rule. In 1215 she founded the first Franciscan community for women. She was later joined by her sister and her widowed mother. The order is now known as the "Poor Clares."

August 13: Jeremy Taylor, Bishop of Down, Connor, and Dromore, 1667
Taylor, who had been chaplain to Charles I and Archbishop Laud (January 10), served as a private chaplain in Wales during the Commonwealth. In 1661 he was made bishop of Down and Connor in Ireland. He left many important scholarly works, but is best known for his two devotional classics, *Holy Living* and *Holy Dying.* The prayer "O God, whose days are without end" (pp. 489 and 504) is adapted from *Holy Dying;* the prayer "For a child not yet baptized" (p. 444) is from his *Collection of Offices.*

August 15: Saint Mary the Virgin, Mother of Our Lord Jesus Christ
In addition to the stories about the nativity (Mt. 1:1—2:23, Lk. 1:5—2:52), Mary is mentioned as present at the wedding in Cana (Jn. 2:1–12) and at the crucifixion (Jn. 19:25–27). She was also with the disciples in the upper room during the time between the Ascension and the outpouring of the Spirit (Acts 1:12–14). Other feasts associated with Mary, such as the Presentation in the Temple and the Annunciation, are feasts of our Lord. In the East, however, since the fourth century a day has been celebrated as the feast of the "dormition" of Mary and devoted to her commemoration. The feast of Saint Mary appears in the West in the Gelasian (nos. 993–996) and the

Gregorian (nos. 658–664) sacramentaries. The feast has been restored in some recent revisions of the Prayer Book for other provinces; in this present revision it is given red letter status.

August 18: William Porcher DuBose, Priest, 1918
A native of South Carolina, DuBose went to the University of the South as professor and was the person most instrumental in founding the School of Theology there. His perceptive scholarly writings have caused some to claim that he is the most important theologian that the Episcopal Church has produced. He combined evangelical fervor with Anglo-Catholic modernism effectively and forcefully.

August 20: Bernard, Abbot of Clairvaux, 1153
Bernard, a Benedictine monk, engaged in a remarkable variety of activities. He founded the house at Clairvaux, preached powerful sermons which drew many to the monastic life and to the Second Crusade, defended the faith against Abelard and the Albigensians. He wrote mystical works and biblical commentary, and was arbitrator of a papal schism. Possibly he is now best known for his hymns.

August 24: Saint Bartholomew the Apostle
All we know of Bartholomew is that he is listed among the twelve disciples. Some have identified him with Nathanael (Jn. 1:43–51 and 21:1–14), but this is speculation. Later writers associate him with India and with Armenia, where he was supposedly martyred by being flayed alive. His commemoration first appeared in the East, where it is associated with that of Barnabas (June 11). In the West it first appeared in the supplement to the Gregorian sacramentary (no. 1656).

August 25: Louis, King of France, 1270
Louis was crowned king of France in 1226, at the age of twelve. Throughout his life he was noted for piety, impartial administration of justice, charities, interest in theological issues of his day, and concern for the faith and its moral demands. Having led one Crusade, he died soon after embarking on another. He was considered the ideal medieval ruler.

August 28: Augustine, Bishop of Hippo, 430
Augustine, a native of North Africa, was the son of a Christian mother and a pagan father. After years of searching for a faith he became a convert and was baptized a Christian by Ambrose (De-

cember 7) at the Easter Vigil in 387. He was one of the most creative theologians in the history of the church. Of his voluminous writings probably the most important are his *Confessions, On the Trinity,* and *The City of God.*

August 31: Aidan, Bishop of Lindisfarne, 651
King Oswald called Aidan from the Celtic monastery on Iona to help reestablish Christianity in Northumbria. Following the pattern at Iona, he centered his work at a monastery on Lindisfarne, an island off the northeast coast of England. It became a center for learning and evangelizing. Aidan traveled on foot, gave generously to the poor, and worked for the manumission of slaves.

September (p. 27)

September 2: The Martyrs of New Guinea, 1942
When the Japanese invaded New Guinea in 1942, many European missionaries had been withdrawn, but the Anglican bishop challenged his clergy to stay and continue to minister to their people. Eight missionaries and two Papuan lay persons were betrayed to the invaders and martyred.

September 12: John Henry Hobart, Bishop of New York, 1830
Hobart was a forceful leader, instrumental in establishing new churches and beginning missionary work among the Oneida Indians. He founded General Theological Seminary, revived Geneva College (now Hobart College), and established the Bible and Common Prayer Book Society of New York. He was the first American churchman to produce a substantial number of theological and devotional manuals for the laity.

September 13: Cyprian, Bishop and Martyr of Carthage, 258
Cyprian, formerly a lawyer and a teacher of rhetoric, was elected bishop of Carthage only two or three years after his baptism. Of his many extant writings the most notable is *On the Unity of the Church,* in which he argues that the unity of the church is maintained collegially through its bishops, who are the guardians of the faith. He was beheaded during the persecution under Valerian. Cyprian was restored to the calendar as a black letter day in 1561.

September 14: Holy Cross Day
This feast is called "The Exaltation of the Holy Cross" in the East-

73

ern churches and in the Western sacramentaries and missals. It commemorates the dedication of the Church of the Holy Sepulchre in Jerusalem, which was built over the sites of the crucifixion and the tomb. In the Byzantine liturgy it is one of the twelve great feasts. At an early date the feast spread to the West and is included in the Gelasian (nos. 1023–1025) and Gregorian (nos. 690–692) sacramentaries. It was among the black letter days restored to the calendar in 1561 and has been made a red letter day in recent revisions of the Prayer Book for other provinces. This is the first edition of the American Prayer Book in which the feast has been included, although the date had been used to determine the fall ember days.

September 16: Ninian, Bishop in Galloway, c. 430

Ninian was born in southern Scotland. The most important influence on his life was Martin of Tours (November 11) for whom he named the monastery he founded in Galloway. Ninian did extensive work among the Picts, and his monastery also exercised considerable influence among the Celtic-speaking Christians of the British Isles.

September 18: Edward Bouverie Pusey, Priest, 1882

Pusey, professor of Hebrew at Oxford, was a leader in the Tractarian Movement. He founded a sisterhood, defended the practice of private confessions, and edited editions of the church fathers. He was a patristics scholar and a noted preacher.

September 19: Theodore of Tarsus, Archbishop of Canterbury, 690

In 668 Pope Vitalian ordained an elderly learned Eastern monk, Theodore, as archbishop of Canterbury. Theodore established an outstanding school at Canterbury, laid the foundations for the diocesan and parochial structures of the church in England, and presided over the council of Hertford which brought together the British and Celtic strains of Christianity. He found England an unorganized body of warring factions; he left it an organized province of the Catholic church.

September 20: John Coleridge Patteson, Bishop of Melanesia,
and his Companions, Martyrs, 1871

Patteson, an English cleric, responded to a call from Bishop George Augustus Selwyn (April 11) for helpers in New Zealand. He established a school and is said to have learned twenty-three of the Melanesian languages. In 1861 he was consecrated bishop of

Melanesia. He and several companions were killed by natives on the island of Nakapu in retaliation for the actions of slave traders.

September 21: Saint Matthew, Apostle and Evangelist
The only story in the New Testament which concerns Matthew is the account of his being called to follow Jesus (Mt. 9:9–13). He is identified as Levi in the parallel accounts in Mark (Mk. 2:14–17) and Luke (Lk. 5:27–32). A second century tradition says that he arranged the "oracles." These may be special Matthean material combined with the Gospel according to Mark to form the first Gospel. It is unlikely that Matthew himself wrote the Gospel that bears his name. According to Eusebius, Matthew proclaimed the gospel to his fellow Jews. Various legends place his ministry and martyrdom in Ethiopia, in Persia, or in other countries. In the East his feast is observed on November 16. When it spread to the West as early as the supplement to the Gregorian sacramentary (no. 1671) the date was shifted to September 21.

September 25: Sergius, Abbot of Holy Trinity, Moscow, 1392
Sergius grew up in a time of civil war in Russia. He founded several monasteries, but is particularly noted for the monastery of the Holy Trinity, which became the center for the revival of Christianity in Russia. He is also famed for his support of Prince Dimitri against the Tartar overlords. He refused the see of Moscow in 1378.

September 26: Lancelot Andrewes, Bishop of Winchester, 1626
Andrewes was a noted preacher whose sermons are still studied. His other writings present able apologies for Anglicanism, but he is principally remembered for his *Private Prayers*, published after his death, and for his role in the preparation of the King James Version of the Scriptures. His work is particularly important in the Pentateuch and the historical books of the Old Testament. The first of the two prayers on page 113 is taken from his *Private Prayers*.

September 29: Saint Michael and All Angels
The observance of a day to honor Saint Michael dates to the fifth century when a church near Rome was dedicated to the archangel. The Leonine sacramentary contains a proper for St. Michael's Day (nos. 844–859). In the Eastern churches other angels have been so honored, but the feasts of Gabriel and Raphael did not enter the Roman calendar until this century.

75

In the 1549 Book the title was expanded to include all angels. Michael is mentioned in Jude 9 and Rev. 12:7 (see also Dan. 10:13, 21 and 12:1). On the basis of these passages he has been honored as the "captain of the heavenly hosts." Gabriel was the messenger of God at the annunciation to Zechariah (Lk. 1:19) and to Mary (Lk. 1:26). He is also mentioned in Dan. 8:16 and 9:21. Raphael is named in the Old Testament Apocrypha (Tobit 3:16–17 and 5:5 ff.). The word "angel" literally means "messenger."

September 30: Jerome, Priest, and Monk of Bethlehem, 420

Jerome was born in northern Italy. After a period of study in the East and two years as secretary to Damasus, the bishop of Rome, he founded a monastery in Bethlehem. There he translated the Scriptures from Hebrew and Greek into Latin, the version which later came to be known as the "Vulgate." He is also noted for his commentaries and for his involvement, often bitter, in many of the theological controversies of his day.

October (p. 28)

October 1: Remigius, Bishop of Rhiems, c. 530

Remigius, or Remi, was elected bishop of Rheims at the age of twenty-two. He is chiefly remembered for having baptized Clovis, king of the Franks, on Christmas Day in 496, an event which changed the history of Europe. He is commemorated in Rheims on January 13, possibly the date of his death, but his day was transferred to October 1 in Western calendars as a result of the placing of his relics in a new abbey church in 1409. His name was restored in the calendar of 1561.

October 4: Francis of Assisi, Friar, 1226

The life of Saint Francis has possibly caught the imagination of more people than that of any other saint. The son of a wealthy merchant, Francis renounced all material possessions to preach Christ and minister to the poor. He founded the Friars Minor, authorized in 1210. Among the few writings he left is the "Canticle of the Sun," which is well known in the translations "All creatures of our God and King" and "Most High, omnipotent, good Lord." It is said as a daily canticle by the Order of the Companions of the Holy Cross.

October 6: William Tyndale, Priest, 1536

Meeting legal resistance in his efforts to translate the Scriptures into English, Tyndale fled to Germany. He was finally captured and executed in Brussels in 1536. By that time he had translated the New Testament, the Pentateuch, Jonah, and the historical books through 2 Chronicles. Much of his work was incorporated in later versions of the Bible.

October 9: Robert Grosseteste, Bishop of Lincoln, 1253
Before he became bishop of Lincoln, Grosseteste was head of the Oxford schools. An outstanding scholar in many fields, he translated into Latin the works of Aristotle, John of Damascus, and Dionysius the Areopagite. His zeal for reform brought him into conflict, as bishop, with the cathedral chapter, the king, and the pope.

October 15: Samuel Isaac Joseph Schereschewsky, Bishop of Shanghai, 1906
During his studies for the rabbinate in Germany, Schereschewsky was converted to Christianity. He came to the United States and at first studied for the Presbyterian ministry, then was confirmed as an Episcopalian and transferred to General Theological Seminary. As a missionary to China he established St. John's University and translated the Bible and parts of the Prayer Book into Mandarin. Because of paralysis he resigned his see in 1883. Although able to type with only one finger, he completed a translation of the Bible into Wenli.

October 16: Hugh Latimer and Nicholas Ridley, Bishops, 1555, and Thomas Cranmer, Archbishop of Canterbury, 1556
At an early stage of the English Reformation Hugh Latimer was one of the most outspoken advocates of reform. Nicholas Ridley, bishop of Rochester and later bishop of London, was an able administrator and supporter of Reformation principles. These men were burned together at the stake on October 16, 1555. Latimer's last words to the younger Ridley were, "Be of good comfort, Master Ridley, and play the man; we shall this day light such a candle by God's grace in England as, I trust, shall never be put out."
Cranmer was archbishop from 1533 through the reign of Edward VI. His principal legacy is the Book of Common Prayer, of which he was chief architect, author, and translator. He was burned at the stake on March 21, 1556.

October 17: Ignatius, Bishop of Antioch, and Martyr, c. 115
What we know of Ignatius comes from seven letters which he wrote while on his way to Rome to face death by wild beasts in the

Colosseum. In his letters he urges Christians to maintain unity under the presidency of the bishop, defends the faith against the Gnostic heresy, and expresses his devotion to the ideal of martyrdom in imitation of our Lord.

October 18: Saint Luke the Evangelist

According to Colossians 4:14, Luke was a physician. Since the second century he has been credited with authorship of the third Gospel and its continuation, the Acts of the Apostles. Certain passages in Acts may indicate that Luke was with Paul on parts of the second and third missionary journeys and on the trip to Rome (Acts 16:10–17; 20:5–15; 21:1–18; 27:1—28:16). The Gospel according to Luke is based on Mark, but it contains a substantial amount of material not included in the other Gospels, including infancy narratives (Lk. 1–2) and a number of parables (Lk. 10:30–36; 11:5–8; 14:8–11; 14:28–32; 15:1–32; 16:1–9; 16:19–31; 18:1–8; 18:10–14).

Luke is thought by many to have been a Gentile. One legend states that he was an artist, though a picture of the Virgin Mary said to have been painted by him is of a much later date. One early writer reports that Luke died a natural death in Greece at the age of eighty-four; other traditions claim that he was martyred. His supposed relics were buried in Constantinople with those of Andrew in 357. Both East and West observe his feast on October 18. It appears in Western calendars as early as the supplement to the Gregorian sacramentary (no. 1681).

October 19: Henry Martyn, Priest, and Missionary to India and Persia, 1812

Soon after his ordination Martyn went to India in 1806 as chaplain to the East India Company. During the six remaining years of his life he translated the New Testament into Hindi, the New Testament and Psalter into Persian, and the Prayer Book into Hindustani. He also revised an Arabic version of the New Testament.

October 23: Saint James of Jerusalem, Brother of Our Lord Jesus Christ, and Martyr, c. 62

This date is observed in the Eastern churches as a commemoration of James the brother of our Lord and first head of the church in Jerusalem. It has also been adopted in some recent revisions of the Prayer Book for other provinces. It was not adopted in the Roman calendar because, at least from the time of Gregory the Great, in the Roman tradition this James was identified with James the Less (May

78

1). New Testament scholars are almost unanimous in rejecting that identification.

There is no evidence in the Gospels that James was a disciple before he witnessed the resurrection (Mt. 13:55; Mk. 6:3; 1 Cor. 15:3–8). Acts and Paul attest his preeminence in the Jerusalem church and his part in dealing with the problem of the relationship between Jew and Gentile (Acts 12:17; 15; Gal. 1). Although he was traditionally considered the author of the Epistle of James, modern New Testament scholars seriously doubt this identification. The Jewish historian Josephus records that James was stoned to death. Hegesippus, a converted Jew writing a century later, said that James was first taken to the pinnacle of the temple and asked to dissuade the people from belief in Christ. When, instead, he boldly proclaimed the gospel, he was thrown from the pinnacle and stoned and clubbed to death.

October 26: Alfred the Great, King of the West Saxons, 899

Alfred became king in 871, following the death of his father and the short reigns of his older brothers. He halted the Danish invasions and gained control of southern England and a part of the midland regions. Seeking to revive culture and learning he sponsored the translation into Old English (West Saxon) of important theological and historical works, including the writings of Gregory the Great (March 12), Augustine of Hippo (August 28), and the Venerable Bede (May 25).

October 28: Saint Simon and Saint Jude, Apostles

All that we know of these two men from the New Testament comes from the four lists of the twelve apostles (Mt. 10:2–4; Mk. 3:14–19; Lk. 6:13–16; Acts 1:13). The only incident in which either appears is the scene in which Jude asked our Lord a question on the night before the crucifixion: "Lord, how is it that you will manifest yourself to us, and not to the world?" (Jn. 14:22). In Matthew and Mark, Simon is identified as "the Cananean," suggesting that he was from Cana. In Luke and Acts he is called "the Zealot," which must mean the "zealous" since the Zealot party did not form until shortly before the Jewish revolt of A.D. 66. In Luke and Acts, Jude is identified as the son of James; his name does not appear in the lists of Matthew and Mark. Its place is taken by Thaddeus. He has in the past been identified with the author of the Epistle of Jude, but New Testament scholars now dispute this. Tradition claims that Simon and Jude preached the gospel in Persia and were martyred together there on July 1, the date of their commemoration in the Eastern churches. The feast first appears in the West in the supplement to the Gregorian sacramentary (no. 1684). The date October 28 may commemorate a translation of their relics to an altar in St. Peter's Basilica.

October 29: James Hannington, Bishop of
Eastern Equatorial Africa, and his Companions, Martyrs, 1885
Hannington had served for a brief period in Africa before he was made bishop in 1884. On a trip to Uganda he and his companions were captured by emissaries of King Mwanga, who feared white penetration into his territory. After a week of torture Hannington and his companions were martyred. His martyrdom was followed by that of a number of native Ugandan Christians (June 3).

November (p. 29)

November 1: All Saints
All Saints is one of the seven principal feasts of the church (see page 15). Some authorities believe that the November 1 feast of All Saints originated in Ireland and spread from there to England and the continent. The first evidence of its observance in Rome is contained in the letter from Pope Gregory IV (828–844) to Louis the Pious, the Holy Roman Emperor, urging him to adopt the feast in his realm. This was done in 835. Some of the Eastern churches observe the Sunday after Pentecost as the Sunday of All Saints, a custom which dates back to the time of Saint Chrysostom according to a reference in his writings. The East Syrians observe the Friday of Easter Week, a celebration that dates to the early part of the fifth century. Saint Ephrem of Edessa (June 10), who died in 373, refers to May 13 as a feast of All Martyrs; on that date, about 610, the Roman Pantheon was dedicated as the Church of Saint Mary and All Martyrs. In a sermon by Gregory the Wonder Worker, who died about 270, there is mention of a feast of All Martyrs, but no date is given. Following the precedent of earlier German church orders, the only saints' days retained in the 1549 Book were those commemorating persons mentioned in the New Testament and this one feast of All Saints.

November 2: Commemoration of All Faithful Departed
Following the precedent of recent revisions of the Prayer Book for other provinces of Anglicanism, November 2 has been designated a day for the commemoration of all the faithful departed. In 998 at the famous monastery of Cluny the commemoration of All Souls was instituted. The custom spread to other places.

All Souls was eliminated from the calendars of the reformed churches on the continent and from the first Prayer Book. This was partly the result of abuses connected with Masses for the departed and partly because of the recognition that in the New Testament the word "saint" is applied to all baptized Christians, not to a special class of believers, or to those who have maintained higher moral standards. Such distinctions developed with the growth of the cult of martyrs. As stated in Prayer Book Studies 19: The Church Year:

Many requests have been received by the Liturgical Commission to include All Souls' Day on November 2. The reluctance of the Commission to accede to this popular memorial has been due to the fact that in the Prayer Book tradition All Saints' Day is essentially a celebration of Christ in his whole Mystical Body—the "elect" and the "saints" in the New Testament sense of these terms. On the other hand, popular piety has felt a real need for distinguishing between those saints who have been distinguished, and those who, while belonging no less to the body of the redeemed, are unknown in the wider fellowship of the faithful, but remembered in the more intimate circles of family and friends. We have therefore introduced on November 2 the entry "Commemoration of All Faithful Departed" as an extension of the feast of All Saints.

November 3: Richard Hooker, Priest, 1600

Hooker died at the age of forty-seven after having served several obscure parishes for brief terms, but he is accounted the foremost Anglican theologian and apologist because of his work *Laws of Ecclesiastical Polity.* It is a masterful defense of the "via media" between Roman Catholicism and Puritanism, based on scripture, tradition, reason, and experience.

November 7: Willibrord, Archbishop of Utrecht, Missionary to Frisia, 739

We know of Willibrord from the *Ecclesiastical History* of Bede (May 25) and from a biography of Alcuin (May 20). A native of Northumbria, Willibrord went as missionary to Frisia (Holland). He was consecrated bishop of the Frisians in 695 and established his see in Utrecht. He also made missionary journeys into Denmark and perhaps into Thuringia.

November 10: Leo the Great, Bishop of Rome, 461

Leo was elected bishop of Rome in 440. His letter to Flavian of

Constantinople in 449, known as the *Tome*, influenced the definition of the council of Chalcedon of 451 (see page 864). In 452 Leo persuaded Attila and the Huns to withdraw beyond the Danube. He extended the authority of the bishop of Rome and is considered by some to be the founder of the papacy.

November 11: Martin, Bishop of Tours, 397
Martin was converted to Christianity while serving in the Roman army. He founded the first monastery in Gaul. After his election as bishop of Tours he continued in the monastic life and, through Ninian (September 16), influenced Celtic monasticism. He opposed the bloody repression of the Priscillian heretics, and was known as a defender of the poor and helpless. Martin was one of the first persons not a martyr to be commemorated in the church calendar. His name was restored among the black letter days in 1561.

November 12: Charles Simeon, Priest, 1836
When Simeon entered King's College, Cambridge, he learned that he was required to receive communion. His conscientious preparation for this act changed his life. For fifty-three years he was vicar of Holy Trinity, Cambridge, and a leader among the Evangelicals. He founded the Church Missionary Society and had a strong influence upon William Wilberforce (July 30).

November 14: Consecration of Samuel Seabury, First American Bishop, 1784
A meeting of some Episcopal clergy of Connecticut resulted in the pilgrimage of Samuel Seabury to England and then to Scotland where he was consecrated by Non-juring Episcopalians. On August 3, 1785, the clergy of the Connecticut convocation elected him their bishop. He not only brought the Scottish line to the American episcopacy but also made several contributions to the first American revision of the Prayer Book. (See below, pp. 9–10, 359–360, 468, 567.)

November 16: Margaret, Queen of Scotland, 1093
Margaret, granddaughter of Edmund Ironside, king of the English, married in 1070 the Scottish king, Malcolm III. She was the mother of eight children. She used her influence to bring the church in Scotland more into line with the rest of the Western church. She was noted for her personal ascetisicm, and for her solicitude for the poor and for orphans.

November 17: Hugh, Bishop of Lincoln, 1200

Hugh was brought from Burgundy to direct a new Christian foundation in England. In 1186 he became bishop of Lincoln, the largest diocese at the time, and there laid the foundation for a cathedral. Noted for his championship of the poor and oppressed, he supported the common people against the forest laws, stood alone against mobs rioting against Jews, and refused to tax his needy parishes to raise money for King Richard's wars. He was perhaps unique in his concern for the care and treatment of lepers. His name was restored to the calendar in 1561.

November 18: Hilda, Abbess of Whitby, 680

Hilda was baptized at the age of thirteen when her great-uncle, the king of Northumbria, was converted to Christianity. She founded and presided over a double monastery for men and women at Whitby where, in 664, the council was held to decide whether the church in England should adhere to Celtic or Roman church customs. Though a protégé of Aidan (August 31), she accepted the decision of the council in the interest of unity and order in the church.

November 19: Elizabeth, Princess of Hungary, 1231

Elizabeth, the daughter of the king of Hungary, at fourteen married the landgrave of Thuringia, Ludwig IV. She used her dowry for the poor and sold her jewels to build a hospital. After her husband's death in 1227, she made provision for her three children, joined the Third Order of the Friars Minor, and devoted herself to the care of the poor and sick at Marburg.

November 23: Clement, Bishop of Rome, c. 100

According to a tradition reported by Irenaeus (June 28) Clement was a disciple of the apostles and the third bishop of Rome. He has been identified with the Clement who was possibly one of Caesar's household (Phil. 4:3 and 22). His epistle to the Corinthians was in some places ranked for a time with the books of the New Testament. He was martyred, tradition has it, by being lashed to an anchor and cast into the sea. His was one of four names restored to the calendar in 1552.

Thanksgiving Day

Many of the earliest liturgical celebrations seem to have been associated with harvest times. Among the Jews the three principal feasts were associated with harvests: Passover (the new flock), Pentecost (grain), and Tabernacles (wine). During the middle ages certain harvests were presented and blessed at the Mass, but these practices were not carried over into the first Prayer Book. The English "harvest-home" originated in the nineteenth century. Early American colonists in Virginia and Massachusetts observed days of thanksgiving in the fall. The Continental Congress initiated a custom of proclamation by civil authority of a national Thanksgiving Day. The Proposed Book of 1786 contained "A Form of Prayer and Thanksgiving to Almighty God, for the Fruits of the Earth, and all the other Blessings of his merciful Providence," which was patterned on the "state services" of the 1662 Book. In the 1928 revision the day was given the status of a votive and the materials proper to the day were placed among the other propers. The present Book lists Thanksgiving Day as a major feast.

November 30: Saint Andrew the Apostle

According to the Johannine account Andrew was a disciple of John the Baptist, who pointed out Jesus, "the Lamb of God," to him and another unnamed disciple. Andrew stayed with Jesus for a day and then sought out his brother Peter, saying, "We have found the Messiah" (Jn. 1:35–42). The parallel accounts in Mark and Matthew state that Andrew and Peter were called by Jesus while they were engaged in their work as fishermen (Mt. 4:18–20; Mk. 1:16–18). In both accounts Andrew is one of the first two to become a disciple. He is mentioned in several of the biblical stories, figuring as one of an inner circle of four in one of the accounts (Mk. 13:3ff; Jn. 6:8ff; 13:20–22). Late traditions associate Andrew with Scythia, Epirus, Constantinople, and Achaia where it is said that he was martyred on an x-shaped cross from which he preached for two or three days. He is commemorated in both the East and the West on November 30. Propers for Saint Andrew's Day are in the early Gallican and Roman sacramentaries. His cult began in Rome under Pope Simplicius (468–483) and he later became the patron saint of Scotland and of Russia.

December (p. 30)

December 1: Nicholas Ferrar, Deacon, 1637

Nicholas Ferrar, who had served as a member of Parliament and of the Virginia Company, retired to an estate at Little Gidding in Huntingtonshire to found a semi-monastic community which he served as chaplain. Living under strict discipline, he and his family and others founded a free school and a hospital for the area. After Ferrar's death, his mother was particularly influential in keeping alive the spirit of the community. The Puritans dispersed the colony ten years after Ferrar's death.

December 2: Channing Moore Williams, Missionary Bishop in China and Japan, 1910

After several years of missionary work in China, Williams entered Japan in 1859, the first Anglican missionary to set foot in that country. He did not baptize his first convert until 1866. He was the founder of a divinity school which became St. Paul's University, and an organizer of the Nippon Sei Ko Kai, the Holy Catholic Church of Japan.

December 4: John of Damascus, Priest, c. 760

John succeeded his father as an official in the court of the caliph of Damascus. In the midst of the iconoclastic controversy he wrote a defense of images and then entered a monastery where he devoted his time to theological works and hymnody. His work is highly regarded in the Eastern churches. Two of his hymns are popular in the West: "Come, ye faithful, raise the strain" and "The day of resurrection."

December 5: Clement of Alexandria, Priest, c. 210

About 180 Clement succeeded Pantaenus, the founder of the catechetical school in Alexandria, as head of the school. He labored to demonstrate the compatability of Christianity and philosophy, preparing the way for his famous pupil Origen, the most eminent of the early Eastern theologians. Clement's extant works are *An Exhortation to the Greeks* and *Instruction in Christian Living.* He is noted for his allegorical interpretation of the Scriptures.

December 6: Nicholas, Bishop of Myra, c. 342

Little is known about this fourth century bishop but legends abound. The tradition is that he suffered as a confessor during the persecution under Diocletian. He is the patron saint of sailors and children, and plays various heroic roles in medieval French carols. The name Santa Claus is derived, through the Dutch, from his name. Nicholas was restored to the calendar in the revision of 1561.

December 7: Ambrose, Bishop of Milan, 397

Ambrose was a catechumen when, as governor of the province, he presided over the election of a bishop of Milan in order to keep peace between Arians and orthodox Christians. His skill in this action led to his being elected bishop. His catechetical and mystagogical lectures are important sources for the doctrine, discipline, and worship of this period; a number of hymns have also been attributed to him. His preaching was an important factor in the conversion of Augustine (August 28). Ambrose was restored to the calendar in the revision of 1561.

December 21: Saint Thomas the Apostle

The fourth Gospel portrays Thomas as a man ready to die for his Master (Jn. 11:16), and as drawing from Jesus the declaration, "I am the way, and the truth, and the life" (14:5-7). Thomas is also skeptical about the resurrection, but when confronted by the risen Christ he makes the most profound statement of belief in the Gospels: "My Lord and my God" (20:24-29). The tradition is that he did missionary work in Persia and in India where he suffered martyrdom.[1] (The St. Thomas Christians of India are probably an offshoot of the Nestorian church and do not go back to Thomas as they claim.) His feast day, which apparently originated in East Syria and spread to the West, is found in the Gelasian sacramentary (nos. 1088-1090) but not in the earlier versions of the Gregorian.

December 25: The Nativity of Our Lord Jesus Christ

This title was new in the 1662 revision of the Prayer Book. In earlier books it had been "Christmas Day." The name "Christmas" is an English term traceable to the twelfth century "Christ's Mass." The feast originated in Rome about the year 336. The earlier Romans had celebrated December 25 and several days following at the winter solstice as the birthday of the Unconquerable Sun (Saturn, bringer of the Golden Age). Christians countered with a celebration of the incarnation on this day. The feast spread throughout the West and was accepted by most of the Eastern churches, as well.

December 26: Saint Stephen, Deacon and Martyr

What we know of Stephen is recorded in Acts 6-7. He is named first among the seven "deacons" chosen to care for the needs of Greek-speaking widows among the Jerusalem Christians. He himself was probably a Hellenistic Jew. Stephen boldly proclaimed the gos-

---

[1] The third century *Acts of Thomas* is one of the most interesting of the Christian apocryphal works.

pel before the council and was martyred for his outspokenness. It is possible that Paul's witnessing of the stoning of Stephen played a part in his own conversion. The feast probably originated in Jerusalem in the fourth century and soon spread to other churches. It was observed in Rome by the time of Pope Simplicius (468–483) who dedicated a church to Saint Stephen. In the West the feast is in the early Roman and Gallican sacramentaries. Probably the day was celebrated in Jerusalem before the observance of Christmas there. Soon, however, popular piety felt it suitable to remember, immediately after the feast of the Nativity, the first martyr to lay down his life for his Savior.

December 27: Saint John, Apostle and Evangelist

Traditionally, John has been identified as "the beloved disciple" who leaned on Jesus' breast at the Last Supper, to whom Jesus committed the care of his mother, who outran Peter on the way to the tomb, and was first to recognize the risen Lord by the Sea of Tiberias. John was a fisherman, the brother of James and the son of Zebedee. He was among the first to be called (Mt. 4:18–22; Mk. 1:16–20). With James and Peter, he witnessed the healing of the daughter of Jairus, the transfiguration, and the agony in the garden (Mt. 17:1–8; Mk. 5:35–43; 9:2–8, and 14:32–42; Lk. 8:40–53). He was, according to tradition, the youngest of the disciples and the only one to die a natural death. He is associated with Ephesus. For many centuries he was thought to have written the "Johannine literature"—the Gospel and the Epistles of John and the Book of Revelation—but this view is now disputed among biblical scholars. The Eastern churches celebrated his day from very early times. In the Gallican sacramentaries December 27 was the day of the commemoration of both John and James. In the earliest Roman sacramentaries the date was set apart for commemoration of John, though not of James, to whom July 25 was assigned at a later date.

December 28: The Holy Innocents

Some scholars find evidence that the holy innocents, the children killed by Herod in his effort to eliminate the Christ Child (Mt. 2:1–18), were commemorated in May in Bethlehem in the fourth century. Augustine of Hippo (d. 430) mentions a commemoration in North Africa. By the end of the fifth century this day seems to have been observed in Rome and other parts of the West; it appears in the early Roman and Gallican sacramentaries. In Spain the Innocents were commemorated in the Epiphany season.

The Titles of the Seasons, Sundays, and Major Holy Days observed in this Church throughout the Year (pp. 31–33)

The full proper title is given for each of the seasons and for each of the principal feasts, Sundays and other feasts of our Lord, other major feasts, fasts, and national days which are to be observed.

First are listed in order the Sundays and other feasts which are determined by the fixed date of Christmas and the moveable date of Easter. These are followed by a list of other fixed red letter days. The two national days for which propers are given are also listed. With one exception these days are all in the order in which collects and lections are to be found (pp. 159–194 or 211–246 and 889–1000). The exception is Independence Day which is listed at the end with Thanksgiving under "National Days."

The Daily Office

Two elements basic to the daily office, the setting apart of certain times of the day for prayer, and frequent repetition of the songs and traditions of the community, can be traced to primitive societies.

In Judaism the day was marked in the temple at Jerusalem with morning and evening sacrifices and with services of psalms and prayers at 9 A.M. and 3 P.M. Devout Jews also marked the times of the day with private prayers, "in the evening, in the morning, and at noonday" (Ps. 55:18). The services in the synagogue consisted principally of prayer and (at least on the Sabbath) the reading and exposition of the Scriptures. By the time of Christ the synagogue liturgy of the word was conducted on at least some weekdays as well as immediately before the Sabbath meal. Some believe that synagogues in the larger towns had daily morning and evening services.

As early as the second century, in some places, Christians marked the day liturgically with morning and evening services. The morning service consisted of psalmody, canticles, and prayers, and (in some areas) it included or was followed by scripture reading and instruction. Possibly it included the laying on of hands and exchange of the peace. Clergy and those laity who could manage it were expected to be present. Laity who could not be present were to study the Scriptures and pray at home at this time. The evening service, which included psalmody, prayers, and (on occasion) readings, was often introduced by a blessing of light (lucernarium) and sometimes associated with an agapé meal.

In addition to these public services or private devotions, other times of day were marked by private prayer. The third, sixth, and ninth hours (9 A.M., 12 Noon, and 3 P.M.) had been associated with private prayer in Judaism and also marked the divisions of the Roman day: these times were linked to the events of the Passion. The third hour was also associated with the descent of the Spirit. Two other times were added to these, midnight and cockcrow. Midnight celebrated the praise of God by all creation and the expectation of Christ's return. Cockcrow was associated with the denial of Christ and the hope of resurrection.

Following the recognition of Christianity under Constantine the weekday services spread more widely and became more formal. The principal morning and evening services, Lauds and Vespers, opened in a congregational or cathedral setting with selected psalms (Pss. 51, 63, 95, and 148–150 were typical for the beginning of Lauds). The evening service was preceded by the lucernarium and generally included Psalm 141. On occasion, lections and sometimes a homily or instruction followed the psalmody. The people participated in a responsory following the readings, when they occurred, and with hymns. Intercessions (or the Kyrie, remnant of an earlier use of intercessions) concluded the office, followed by the Lord's Prayer or a variable prayer and, possibly, a blessing.

The monastic office developed at the same time as the congregational or cathedral form of office. Monks based their devotional life on the reading of the Scriptures and the praying of the whole psalter. "In course" use of psalms and sequential readings from the Scriptures became related to traditional times for public and private daily worship. Some Eastern monks prayed the psalter daily, Roman monks weekly, Gallican monks fortnightly. Hymnody and prayers concluded such offices for various times of the day.

Offices said "in choir," i.e. in the chapel or church, were Matins (midnight or cockcrow devotions), Lauds (the public morning service), Terce (the third hour), Sext (the sixth hour), None (the ninth hour), and Vespers (the public evening service). Two other services were added to this daily regimen: Prime (the first hour), said in the chapter house at the commencement of daily duties, and Compline, said in the dormitories at bedtime.[1]

The two systems of daily offices, the congregational or cathedral and the monastic, coexisted or were combined for several centuries in situations where the monks worshiped in the cathedral or church, or where the clergy, monastic or "secular," were bound by rule to the use of the monastic offices. The pilgrim Egeria described the office of the church in Jerusalem late in the fourth century. The monks

---

[1] Important sources for study of the development of monastic hours are John Cassian's *Institutes* and the *Rule* of Benedict of Nursia.

gathered at various times of the day to say their office. The clergy and laity assembled to participate with the monks at the principal morning and evening services. Egeria notes that two groups of psalms were sung, before and after the entrance of bishop and clergy. After the monastic office became prefixed to the congregational morning and evening services, the elongated offices were cut. The first elements abbreviated or eliminated were the lections and instruction which earlier writers such as Gregory of Tours had considered essential to the offices. In Western usage, however, for monastics and clergy bound to say the office daily, this loss was compensated for by the inclusion of substantial readings from the Scriptures and from the sermons of the fathers in the office of Matins.

Late in the middle ages the daily office became the individual duty of monks and clergy, and was further removed from the people. Two revisions, one in the twelfth century made for the papal court, and one by Haymo of Faversham in the thirteenth century for the Franciscans, adopted by the papal court and used through much of Europe, resulted in a tremendous increase in the commemorations of saints and in octaves. The Lord's Prayer and the Ave Maria were prefixed to some offices; a creed, collects, and a confession of sin were added to some, and lections were reduced to make room for these additions. Proper psalms, lections, and readings from the lives of the saints replaced the orderly "in course" use of psalms and readings. In the Sarum offices for Advent, for example, only two days remained immune from commemorations and less than two chapters were left of the old course reading in the Book of Isaiah. Offices were so grouped that Matins, Lauds, and Prime were often said as one service, sometimes known as "Matins," Vespers and Compline were said together in a service sometimes called "Evensong." The Office of Our Lady and the Office of the Dead, two brief series, were added to the daily offices. During this period the literate laity had a simplified breviary, the "Book of Hours" or "Primer," based on these offices arranged for a daily or weekly cycle.

The weekday Masses which had become normal during the late medieval period were eliminated at the time of the Reformation; some German reformers sought to reestablish congregational morning and evening daily offices. Psalms and lections read in course and interpreted were followed by the Te Deum or one of the Gospel canticles (the Benedictus, the Magnificat, or the Nunc dimittis), the Lord's Prayer, other prayers, and a dismissal. Weekday services emphasizing a lecture, preaching, or prophesying were common among the Reformed churches. Within the Roman tradition, Quiñones pro-

The Daily Office

SARUM (typical late medieval rite)	1549 PRAYER BOOK
Matins	*Matins*
Lord's Prayer & Ave Maria (silently)	Lord's Prayer (aloud)
Opening Preces	Opening Preces
Venite with Antiphon	Venite
Hymn	
Psalms (1-109 with antiphons divided among the seven days of the week)	Psalms (1-150 at Matins or Evensong each month)
Lesson—divided into three portions with Responsory after each part	Lesson—one chapter from the Old Testament or Apocrypha in course
Te Deum on Sundays except in Advent, Pre-Lent & Lent	Te Deum—daily except in Lent
Lauds	
Opening Preces	
Psalms 93, 100, 63 & 67 with Antiphons	
Benedicite (shortened form) with Antiphon on Sundays	Benedicite (full Biblical text) in Lent
Psalms 148-150	
"Chapter" (typically one verse of Scripture)	Lesson—one chapter from the New Testament in course
Hymn	
Benedictus with Antiphon	Benedictus
Kyrie, Lord's Prayer & Preces	
Collect of the Day	
Marian Antiphon	
Variable Memorial Collect	
Prime	
Lord's Prayer & Ave Maria (silently)	
Preces	
Hymn	
Psalms (22-26, 54, 118, 119:1-32) with Antiphon	
Athanasian Creed on Sundays	Athanasian Creed—six times a year
"Chapter" (typically a verse of Scripture)	
Responsory	
Kyrie	Kyrie
Lord's Prayer	Apostles' Creed
Apostles' Creed	Lord's Prayer
Preces	Preces
Confiteor	
Preces	
	Collect of the Day
	Collect for Peace
Collect for Grace	Collect for Grace
Terce	
Opening Preces	
Hymn	
Psalm 119:33-80 with Antiphon	
"Chapter" (Scripture verse)	
Responsory	
Collect of the Day	

Sext
Opening Preces
Hymn
Psalm 119:81-128 with Antiphon
"Chapter" (Scripture verse)
Responsory
Collect of the Day
None
Opening Preces
Hymn
Psalm 119:129-176 with Antiphon
"Chapter" (Scripture verse)
Responsory
Collect of the Day

Vespers
Opening Preces
Psalms (110-147 with antiphons divided
    among the seven days of the week)
"Chapter" (Scripture verse)

Responsory
Hymn
Magnificat with Antiphon
Kyrie, Lord's Prayer & Preces
Collect of the Day
Marian Antiphon
Variable Memorial Collect
Compline
Lord's Prayer & Ave Maria (silently)
Opening Preces
Psalms (4, 31:1-6, 91, 134) with Antiphon
"Chapter" (Scripture verse)
Hymn
Nunc dimittis with Antiphon
Kyrie
Lord's Prayer
Apostles' Creed
Preces
Confiteor
Preces

Collect for Aid against Perils

Evensong
Lord's Prayer & Opening Preces
Psalms (1-150 at Matins or Evensong each
    month)
Lesson—one chapter from the Old
    Testament or Apocrypha in course

Magnificat

Lesson—one chapter from the New
    Testament in course
Nunc dimittis
Kyrie
Apostles' Creed
Lord's Prayer
Preces

Collect of the Day
Collect for Peace
Collect for Aid against Perils

Most of the fixed parts of Cranmer's Daily Office come from Sarum. The choice of what was retained from the medieval breviary system has affinities with various German Church Orders and with the reformed breviary of Cardinal Quiñones. The basic principle underlying the reforms of the Germans, of Quiñones, and of Cranmer was the restoration of a fuller lectionary. In all of these systems the reading of Scripture in the Temporal Cycle was greatly increased, and the extent to which the Sanctoral Cycle would interrupt the course readings was minimized.

duced a revised breviary in 1535 and a second edition in 1536 which went through more than one hundred printings. Each office had three psalms, saints' days were curtailed, and course readings restored. The Te Deum was said daily except in Advent and Lent. The Office of the Virgin was restricted to Saturdays and the Office of the Dead to All Souls' Day. This breviary was suppressed in 1568, but an official revised breviary was published in 1570, reducing the number of saints' commemorations.

Cranmer prepared two drafts for a revised daily office some years before the publication of the 1549 Book: one of these depended on the work of Quiñones, the other upon German church orders. Both contributed to the daily office of the first Prayer Book. The psalter was to be read monthly in the morning and evening offices of the book and there were to be two "lessons" at each office with "the most part" of the Old Testament and Apocrypha read yearly and the New Testament (except for the book of Revelation) three times each year. This "in course" reading was seldom to be interrupted. Only four days had proper psalms appointed; only twelve fixed days and ten moveable feasts were provided with even one proper lesson.

Cranmer set psalmody and lections within the framework of the late medieval rites. "Matins" was introduced by the Lord's Prayer, versicles and responses, the Gloria Patri, Alleluia, and the Venite from the medieval office of Matins. The Old Testament lesson, except in Lent, was followed by the Te Deum, which had been sung at the conclusion of Matins on Sundays. In Lent it was followed by the Benedicite, which had been the Old Testament canticle for use on Sundays at Lauds, and which was appointed for daily use in Primers. The New Testament lesson preceded the Benedictus, the Gospel canticle used daily at Lauds. Then followed the Kyrie, the Apostles' Creed, and the Lord's Prayer, which had been used at Prime, and a set of suffrages some of which had been used at Prime. The office ended with three collects: the collect of the day from Lauds, a collect for peace from the Little Office of Our Lady at Lauds, and a collect for Grace from the office of Prime.

"Evensong" began with the Lord's Prayer and with the versicle and response and the Gloria Patri which had introduced all the offices of the medieval breviary. The Magnificat, the Gospel canticle at Vespers, followed the Old Testament reading; the Nunc dimittis, the Gospel canticle of Compline, followed the New Testament lesson. After the Nunc dimittis the officiant was to say "the suffrages before assigned at Matins," followed by three collects. The first of these was to be the collect for the day, as at Vespers, the second the collect for peace from the Office of the Virgin at Vespers, and the third "for aid against all perils" from Compline.

These rites did not draw on the brief offices of Terce, Sext, and None, except that the psalms which had formed their basic content were included within the course of psalms for "Matins" and "Evensong."

As a part of the effort to make the offices generally available to the laity, the antiphons, responsories, and hymns which had enriched but also complicated the medieval offices were eliminated. Clergy in charge of congregations were to say the daily offices publicly "in the church, in the English tongue, to the end that the congregation may be thereby edified."

The 1552 revision required that a bell be rung to call the people together and that all clergy say the daily offices, not just those serving congregations. The titles of the offices were changed to Morning Prayer and Evening Prayer. A penitential introduction, analogous to that which came at the end of Prime and Compline in the late medieval books and that which preceded the Eucharist in the late middle ages and in the new continental Protestant liturgies, was added both morning and evening. A psalm was provided for use as an alternative to each of the Gospel canticles, because of objection to the general use of canticles thought to belong peculiarly to Zechariah, Mary, and Simeon.

The principal change in the 1662 revision was the addition of a series of prayers to be read after the fixed collects, except when the Litany was read. These were prayers for the king, for the royal family, for the clergy and people, and for "all sorts and conditions of men," "A Prayer of Saint Chrysostom," and the Grace.

During the reigns of Henry VIII, Edward VI, and Elizabeth, primers for private use appeared. Those of Henry VIII and Elizabeth included the little offices as well as the principal morning and evening services. The 1559 and 1604 editions of the Prayer Book often had bound with them a series of "Godly Prayers" for private or family use. John Cosin, later to be a leader in the revision of 1662, published *A Collection of Private Devotions* (1627) after the model of earlier Anglican primers.

The American Book of 1789 printed additional general opening sentences and provided the absolution taken from the eucharistic rite as an alternative form of absolution. The wording of the Lord's Prayer and of many other forms was updated. The revision deleted the second of the opening versicles and its response, substituted two verses from Psalm 96 for the last four verses of the Venite, and provided alternatives for the Venite for several major days. The requirement to say the Gloria Patri after several of the canticles and after each psalm and each section of Psalm 119 was replaced by a requirement to say it among the opening preces, and to say either the Gloria Patri or the Gloria in excelsis at the end of the day's psalmody. "Selections of Psalms" were provided as alternatives to the psalmody of the day. The daily office lectionary omitted readings from the Apocrypha and so rearranged readings from the four Gospels that they would be read twice rather than three times each year. Only the first four verses of the Benedictus were retained; psalms substituted for the Magnificat and the Nunc dimittis. The churches of a state convention might omit the phrase "he descended into hell" from the Apostles' Creed or substitute "He went into the Place of departed Spirits." The Athanasian Creed, the Kyrie, and the second use of the Lord's Prayer were omitted. Only the first and last of the suffrages were retained. The book included forms for daily morning and evening prayer for families.

The 1892 revision provided proper opening sentences. It omitted the anthems provided in 1789 for use in place of the Venite on special days and withdrew the permission to omit the "descent" clause from the Creed. A revised version of the suffrages of the English Prayer Book was restored to Evening, but not to Morning Prayer. This revision also restored the Magnificat, the Nunc dimittis and the full text of the Benedictus.

In the mid-nineteenth century many places had begun to use simplified forms of the daily offices called "Mission Services" or "Third Services." The General Convention of 1856 authorized bishops to provide simplified services for congregations not "capable" of using the daily offices of the Prayer Book. The 1892 Book allowed a third daily service, constructed from the contents of the Prayer Book, to be used subject to the discretion of the diocesan bishop. In 1928 the revisers incorporated both provisions within the directions "Concerning the Service of the Church" and also provided invitatory anthems for certain days and seasons. They added shorter alternative forms for family prayer as well as a number of "Additional Prayers" for use within that office.

The present edition of the Prayer Book includes daily offices for morning and evening, in both traditional and contemporary language, which provide for abbreviation, variety, and enrichment while holding to the basic structure of the rites in earlier Prayer Books. Several new options are provided: silence is permitted after each reading; a reading from non-biblical Christian literature may follow the biblical readings; a sermon may be preached and an offering received. Because many communities have felt the need for other daily rites, at least on certain occasions, two brief optional services, An Order of Service for Noonday and An Order for Compline are provided. The Book also has An Order of Worship for the Evening—a form of lucernarium or service of light based on the symbolism of light and the ceremonial lighting of candles. The verbose eighteenth century forms for family prayer included in the 1789 Book fell into disuse some time ago; the short alternatives provided in the 1928 revision seemed too brief and too rigid, however. The 1979 Book includes fuller and more flexible forms for morning, noon, early evening, and the close of day for use by individuals and families.

Concerning the Service (p. 36 or 74)

There is no clear tradition defining which order of ministers is to perform which functions in the daily office. The officiant may be a lay reader, bishop, priest, or deacon, but one person should function as officiant. It is appropriate for that person to be assisted by others who will read lessons and lead other parts of the rite which are not assigned by the rubrics to the officiant. It is also appropriate that a bishop, when present, conclude the rite with a blessing.

Morning or Evening Prayer, in conformity with the directions on page 142, may be substituted for all that precedes the offertory at the eucharistic rite.

Daily Morning Prayer (pp. 37–60 and 75–102)

In the 1549 Prayer Book the title of the morning office is "An Order for Matins Daily through the Year." The revision of 1552 altered the heading to read "An Order for Morning Prayer Daily throughout the Year," the word "prayer" being frequently used as a synonym for a daily office. The first American revision simplified the title: "The Order for Daily Morning Prayer." The present revision has dropped the word "order" since, strictly speaking, the provisions are not an outline or order, as for example, "An Order for Celebrating the Holy Eucharist" (pp. 400–401), but a rite with appointed texts.

The intention of the 1549 Prayer Book is clearly that both Morning and Evening Prayer be corporate services: the preface binds only those clergy serving congregations to read the daily office. The 1552 book binds all priests and deacons, either corporately or privately, to say both offices unless prevented by some "urgent cause." Though the preface of the American Prayer Books is not so explicit, the principle of daily office has continued to underlie the arrangement of the psalter and the lectionary, and the word "daily" has been retained. The 1979 Book, in the section "Concerning the Service of the Church," terms Daily Morning and Evening Prayer "regular services appointed for public worship in this Church." In the 1979 Book the word "daily" is used only in the titles of these rites.

The rubric permits Morning Prayer to begin either with a confession of sin, which must be preceded by an opening sentence of scripture or, in the ancient manner, with the versicle beseeching the Lord to open our lips that we may praise Him. If the confession of sin is omitted the opening sentence may still be used.

The Opening Sentences of Scripture (pp. 37–41 and 75–78)

No confession of sin nor any opening sentences of scripture were in the 1549 Book. When the confession was added in 1552 it was preceded by eleven sentences, eight from the Old Testament and three from the New, all of a penitential character:

Ezekiel 18:27	Matthew 3:2
Psalm 51:3, 9, 17	Luke 15:18–19
Joel 2:13	Psalm 143:2
Daniel 9:9–10	1 John 1:8
Jeremiah 10:24	

Those from the Old Testament (except Dan. 9:9–10) were from among the short lessons read during Lent in the medieval daily office or from the penitential psalms. The revisers of 1662 added a verse (1 Jn. 1:9) to the last sentence, thus ending on a more hopeful note.

The American revision of 1789 introduced the series with three sentences of a more general nature (Hab. 2:20; Mal. 1:11; and Ps. 19:14). The first two of these had appeared in the Proposed Book of 1786. The 1789 revision was the first Prayer Book to provide general sentences introducing the rite rather than restricting them to penitential ones introducing the confession of sin.

The revisers in 1892 increased the number of general sentences and appointed sentences appropriate to the various seasons. Hab. 2:20, Ps. 122:1, Ps. 19:14, and Phil. 1:2 were provided for general use. The sentences for Advent were Mt. 3:2 and Is. 40:3; for Christmas, Lk. 2:10–11; for Epiphany, Mal. 1:11 and Is. 52:1; for Good Friday, Lam. 1:12; for Easter, a sentence found in both Mk. 16:6 and

Lk. 24:34, and Ps. 118:24; for Ascension, Heb. 4:14,16; for Whitsunday, Gal. 4:6, Ps. 46:4, and Jn. 4:23; and for Trinity Sunday, Rev. 4:8. Ten of the original eleven sentences, with the 1662 addition, were retained as a block printed just before the exhortation. The idea of opening sentences appropriate for a particular day goes back to the special services for Thanksgiving Day and Independence Day of the American Proposed Book; the 1789 Book retained Thanksgiving. General sentences for Evening Prayer included three not in the morning series (Ps. 26:6; Ps. 141:2; and Ps. 96:9). The seasonal sentences for evening also included Mk. 13:35–36 for Advent; Rev. 21:3 for Christmas; Is. 2:5 and 3 for Epiphany; 2 Cor. 5:21 and Eph. 1:7 for Good Friday; Col. 3:1 for Easter; Heb. 9:24 for Ascension; and Rev. 22:17 and Ps. 43:3 for Whitsunday.

The 1928 revision moved two sentences (Ps. 43:3 and Jn. 4:23) from Whitsunday to general use, and added another general sentence (Is. 57:15). It transferred Eph. 1:7 from Evening to Morning Prayer. Acts 1:8 replaced Ps. 46:4 for Whitsunday; Is. 2:5,3 and 2 Cor. 5:21 were dropped from among the seasonal sentences. Pr. 3:9–10 and 3:19–20, the first two of the opening sentences from the special service for Thanksgiving Day (1789 and 1892 Books), were included among the opening sentences. Sentences from among the original penitential series were printed for use morning or evening, except four which were dropped (Ezek. 18:27; Ps. 51:9; Jer. 10:24; and Ps. 143:2).

The present revision gives proper sentences for use on All Saints' and other major saints' days, and the sentences for Thanksgiving Day are replaced by a general sentence suitable for any special thanksgiving. Some sentences have dropped from both offices: Is. 52:1; Ps. 51:17; Eph. 1:7; Heb. 4:14 and 16: Pr. 3:9–10 and 3:19–20; Ps. 26:8; Ps. 46:4; and Rev. 22:17. New sentences added to Morning Prayer are Is. 40:5; Is. 49:66; Mk. 8:34; Col. 1:12; Eph. 2:19; Ps. 19:4; and Ps. 105:1. Additions to Evening Prayer are Ps. 74:15–16; Ps. 16:7–8; Am. 5:8; Ps. 139:10–11; and Jn. 8:12.

Confession of Sin (pp. 41–42 and 79–80)

Late medieval breviaries usually inserted a mutual confession and absolution between minister and congregation near the end of Prime and Compline. Moving this to the beginning of the rite, as was done in the 1552 Book, may have been suggested by the reformed breviary of Cardinal Quiñones in which the office of Matins begins with the Lord's Prayer and a confession and absolution prior to the opening vesicle. Or it may have been suggested by the general confession and absolution which introduced many of the eucharistic rites or Sunday liturgies of the continental Reformed churches. The precedent for this preliminary confession was the mutual confession and absolution of priest and server at Mass which had developed in the late medieval period.

The American revision of 1892 allowed the confession to be omitted on any day when Holy Communion was to follow immediately. The 1928 Book allowed omission on any day not a day of fasting or abstinence and on any day when the Litany or Holy Communion was to follow immediately. The present edition never requires the use of the confession, though it may suitably be used to mark Fridays which are days of fasting, or on both of the old station days, Wednesday and Friday.

The Exhortation (pp. 41 and 79)

The exhortation is based on that in the 1552 Prayer Book. It begins by enumerating the purposes of the daily office: we assemble to set forth God's praise, to hear His Word, and to pray, "for ourselves and on behalf of others," for things necessary to life and salvation. The congregation is then to kneel in silence and prepare themselves to worship God by a confession of their sins. The full form of the 1552 exhortation reads:

> Dearly beloved brethren, the Scripture moveth us in sundry places, to acknowledge and confess our manifold sins and wickedness, and that we should not dissemble nor cloak them before the face of almighty God our heavenly Father, but confess them with an humble, lowly, penitent and obedient heart; to the end that we may obtain forgiveness of the same by his infinite goodness and mercy. And although we ought at all times humbly to knowledge our sins before God; yet ought we most chiefly so to do, when we assemble and meet together to render thanks for the great benefits we have received at his hands, to set forth his most worthy praise, to hear his most holy Word, and to ask those things which be requisite and necessary, as well for the body as the soul. Wherefore I pray and beseech you, as many as be here present, to accompany me with a pure heart and humble voice, unto the throne of the heavenly grace, saying after me.

The passage on the purpose of the daily office is derived from the explication of the fourth commandment in *The Bishops' Book* and *The King's Book*.

100

The short alternative to the exhortation, inserted in 1892, could be substituted for the exhortation on any day but Sunday. The 1928 Book permitted use of the shorter form on Sundays as well.

The rubric "silence may be kept" has been inserted in this revision. Earlier Prayer Books ordered a period of silence in one place only, before the Veni Creator Spiritus in the rite for ordination to the priesthood. The 1979 Book recommends silence at many points where a period of recollection or reflection is appropriate. It is fitting that a period of silence for recollection should precede a general confession. The exhortation makes it mandatory when the longer form is used as an invitation to confession.

The rubric of the 1928 edition, originating in the 1552 Book, reads "To be said by the whole Congregation, after the Minister." The intention of that rubric and the general practice for many years was for the minister to say the prayer phrase by phrase, and for the congregation to repeat each phrase after him. This practice was designed to aid the illiterate and those who did not own books, and to provide each person with an opportunity for self-examination and reflection. The rubric preceding the general confession in Forms of Prayer to be Used at Sea (in the Prayer Books of 1662, 1789, and 1892) reads, "Every one ought seriously to reflect upon those particular sins of which his conscience shall accuse him."

This Prayer Book requires the general confession to be said by officiant and people together, all kneeling. Although various editions of the Prayer Book have specified kneeling for very few prayers, it has been the standard posture for both ministers and people during prayers of confession from the time of the 1549 Book.

The General Confession (pp. 41–42 and 79)

In the general confession we should be aware not only of our individual sins but also of our failures as a community. The form provided in Rite One dates to the 1552 Prayer Book and is based upon Rom. 7:8–25. Scriptural allusions include Is. 53:6; Ps. 119:176; 1 Pet. 2:25; Ps. 51:13; Rom. 15:8; 1 Jn. 2:12; Tit. 2:11–12; and Jn. 14:13. Two phrases which tended often to be misunderstood, the omission of which had been proposed for over two hundred years, have been dropped: "And there is no health in us," and "miserable offenders." The form provided in Rite Two is the same as that used in the Holy Eucharist: Rite Two, and provided as an alternative for use in the Holy Eucharist: Rite One. In this form we confess not only our sins of omission and commission but also our lack of love for God and

101

neighbor. Not only do we ask that we may walk in God's ways but also that we may delight in God's will. (See below, pp. 343–344, for the sources of this form.)

The Absolution (pp. 42 and 80)

The absolution of Rite One was proposed for inclusion in the 1892 revision, as an alternative to the long declaration in Prayer Books since 1552. That revision did not admit it but the 1928 Book added the form as an alternative for use at Evening Prayer. It is the absolution from the confession said near the end of Prime and Compline in the late medieval period and at a mutual confession between priest and server at Mass.

The absolution in Rite Two also derives from the late medieval confession, where it was pronounced by priest and server to each other. This form is used in the Holy Eucharist: Rite Two (page 360) and in Ministration to the Sick (page 455). The equivalent Sarum form reads: "Almighty God have mercy on you, and forgive you all your sins, preserve and strengthen you in goodness, and bring you to everlasting life." The longer form of absolution from earlier Prayer Books is retained in this edition for the proper liturgy of Ash Wednesday. Both forms of absolution state what is provided for us in God's gift of forgiveness: pardon for the offenses of the past, and amendment of life, strength, grace, and consolation for the present and the future.

The rubric preceding the absolution in the 1552 Prayer Book reads, "The absolution to be pronounced by the minister alone;" in the 1662 Book the rubric was changed to read, "The Absolution, or Remission of sins, to be pronounced by the Priest alone, standing; the people still kneeling." Until the present revision, no equivalent form was provided to be used in the absence of a priest or bishop. The new rubric allows a deacon or lay reader, kneeling, to make use of the preceding form, substituting the first person plural for the second person forms of the pronouns.

The Invitatory and Psalter (pp. 42 and 80)

The earliest detailed accounts which are available indicate that the morning office in the Western church began with the use of Psalm 51:16 as a versicle. In the Eastern church today the whole of Psalm 51 is often sung at the opening of morning office.

The versicle is followed by the Gloria Patri which introduces the psalmody of the day. The 1549 Book directed that the priest say these verses. From 1662 until this present revision the last half was to be said by the people as a response. The present edition directs that the Gloria Patri is said by officiant and people together, a return to earlier Western practice. The exact form has varied in different ages and places. The form as we have it, except for the sixth century Western addition, "As it was in the beginning," to combat Arianism, is the one which has commonly been used since the fourth century. The translation of the Gloria Patri, as of many of the common forms, is the final revision of the International Consultation on English Texts (ICET), an official group representing most of the major English-speaking Christian denominations.

Cranmer inserted the phrase "Praise ye the Lord," in 1549, with "Alleluia," from Easter to Trinity Sunday, in place of the variable antiphon to the Venite of the medieval office. In 1552 the redundant Alleluia, which means "Praise ye the Lord," was dropped. The 1662 revisers, following the Scottish Book of 1637, added a response, "The Lord's Name be praised." The present revision eliminates these phrases and restores the Alleluia except during Lent.

The Antiphons (pp. 42–44 and 80–82)

The sixth century rule of Saint Benedict of Nursia prescribed that Psalm 95, Venite, should be sung with an antiphon as the first psalm of Matins every day. This continued as a custom in the medieval breviaries. The antiphon, generally a verse of scripture appropriate to the season, relieves the tediousness of constant repetition of the Venite, emphasizes the season, and provides opportunity for congregational participation when the musical setting might be too difficult to encourage participation in the singing of the text of the Venite itself. To simplify the services the variable antiphons were omitted from the rites in the 1549 Book. The 1928 revision included nine antiphons for optional use immediately before the Venite. They were provided for the Sundays in Advent; the twelve days of Christmas; the Epiphany octave and the feast of the Transfiguration; the Easter season; the Ascension season; the Pentecost octave; Trinity Sunday; the feasts of the Purification and the Annunciation; and saints' days.

The present revision includes all of the antiphons of the 1928 Book. Since octaves are not maintained, the antiphon for Pentecost is for that day only, and the Epiphany antiphon for use from Epiphany through the Baptism of Christ, and on the feast of the Transfiguration, and the feast of the Holy Cross. That for Advent may now be used on any day in Advent. Additional antiphons have been provided for

Sundays or weekdays which have no proper antiphon. The use of antiphons is more flexible in this revision so that by repetition they may more effectively state the seasonal theme and provide opportunity for congregational participation. In accordance with ancient tradition they may be sung after each verse or each section of the invitatory psalm, Venite or Jubilate, or simply before and after the psalm (after the Gloria Patri if that is said or sung).

Venite (pp. 44–45 and 82)

The earliest detailed accounts of the daily office in the Western church indicate that Psalm 95 introduced the psalmody of Matins except on certain special days. The 1549 Prayer Book made no exception to this custom. The 1552 Book provided for the use of two anthems (which are now paragraphs two and three of the canticle "Pascha nostrum") to replace Psalm 95 on Easter Day. (The "Pascha nostrum" was placed prior to the beginning of Matins on that day in the 1549 Book.) In the decades before the American Revolution there had been many proposals to strike the concluding verses (8–11) of Psalm 95. The 1789 revision substituted verses nine and thirteen of Psalm 96 for that section, although Psalm 95 was still to be read in its entirety in the course of psalms on the nineteenth day of each month. That edition also retained (from the Proposed Book of 1786) centos from the psalms for optional use in place of the Venite on Christmas Day, Ash Wednesday, Good Friday, Ascension Day, Whitsunday, and Thanksgiving Day. The 1892 and 1928 revisions included only the one for Thanksgiving Day. The 1928 edition gave permission to substitute the whole of Psalm 95 for the Venite at any time, to omit the Venite on Ash Wednesday and Good Friday, and to use the Pascha nostrum in place of the Venite throughout the Easter octave. The 1943 revision of the lectionary for the daily office appointed Psalm 95 in place of the Venite on the first six Fridays in Lent.

The present revision retains the 1789 version in Rite One, but the verses added at that time are removed and Psalm 95:7b is restored to the Venite in Rite Two. Psalm 100, Jubilate, may be an alternative. Psalm 95 in its entirety may be substituted at any time and is appointed in the Lectionary in place of the Venite on Ash Wednesday, Holy Saturday, and all of the Fridays in Lent including Good Friday.[1] The Pascha nostrum is to be used in its place throughout Easter Week and may be substituted until the Day of Pentecost.

---

[1] The Coverdale translation of Psalm 95 is printed on page 146 for use with Rite One.

104

The 1545 Primer of Henry VIII calls the Venite a "song stirring to the praise of God." The first two verses are a call to praise God with psalms; the next verses give the reasons: He is our sovereign, our provider, our creator.

Jubilate (pp. 45 and 82–83)

Psalm 100, Jubilate, was used among the opening psalms in the medieval office of Lauds on Sundays and festivals and was used daily in Prime. The 1552 revision provided it as an alternative to the Benedictus, the only canticle used after the second lesson in the 1549 Book. This was a concession to the prejudice against Gospel canticles, since many felt that the songs of Zechariah, of Mary, and of Simeon were not appropriate for general use. The 1662 revision qualified the use of the Jubilate as an alternative to the Benedictus. The Benedictus was to be used "except when that shall happen to be read in the chapter [that is, the second lesson] for the day, or for the Gospel on Saint John Baptist's Day." The first American revision dropped the qualification and printed the Jubilate before an abbreviated version of the Benedictus which was given as an alternative. The 1892 revision returned the Benedictus to primacy of place.

In the 1979 edition the Jubilate is restored as an invitatory psalm, a function it served both in the temple in Jerusalem and in the medieval office of Lauds. It is also allowed as an alternative to the Venite in the Roman breviary of 1970. The psalm invites us to come before God's presence with a song, for He has created us, He has chosen us, He is gracious, He is faithful, and His truth endures for ever.

Christ our Passover (pp. 46 and 83)

Books prior to 1928 limited the use of the Easter Anthems to Easter Day. The 1928 edition continued to require the use of this cento in place of the Venite on Easter Day but also permitted its use throughout the octave. The rubric preceding the title in the present edition requires its use throughout Easter Week and permits it daily until the Day of Pentecost.

The 1549 Prayer Book provided for the use of two "anthems" (Romans 6:9–11, two Alleluias, and 1 Corinthians 15:20–22 with one Alleluia) prior to Morning Prayer on Easter. A versicle and response and a collect followed. The structure of this preface, the first two verses of the first anthem, and a large part of the collect, derived from the order for the procession to the Easter sepulcher which had preceded the Sarum Mass for Easter Day. The 1552 revision deleted the

Alleluias, and the anthems were appointed for use in place of the Venite at Morning Prayer on Easter Day. The 1662 revision preceded these anthems with another (1 Corinthians 5:7-8) and the Gloria Patri was added at the end. The Gloria Patri was removed in 1789 but restored in 1892. The 1979 Book again removes the Gloria Patri (though it may be added), and restores Alleluia at the beginning and after each section.

The first of the anthems, 1 Corinthians 5:7-8, portrays the death and resurrection of Jesus Christ as the Christian Passover. The use of unleavened bread, sign of a new start, was for the Jew a reminder of deliverance from bondage in Egypt. The old leaven is used here as a sign of defilement and sin. The second anthem, Romans 6:9-11, comes from a setting within which Paul talks of baptism. In baptism we have died and been raised through Christ our Lord. The third anthem, 1 Corinthians 15:20-22, asserts that what was lost to humanity by the sin of the first Adam has been regained by the triumph of Christ, "the second Adam." This canticle is among those suggested for use as the initial song of praise at the Easter Vigil (p. 294) and as the body is borne from the church at a burial (pp. 484 and 500).

The Psalm or Psalms Appointed (pp. 46 and 84)

In the old cathedral or congregational daily offices a selective use was made of the psalms, which was the manner in which they had been used in the worship of the temple and the synagogue. Within monastic communities, however, systems were developed by which the whole of the psalter was recited within a fixed period of time. Some Eastern monks recited the psalter daily, Roman monks weekly, Gallican monks fortnightly. In the weekly Roman system which prevailed in the late medieval period certain psalms were said regularly at certain offices. The other psalms were distributed throughout the week. The multitudinous saints' days which called for the use of a few proper psalms, however, so interrupted the system that in actuality many psalms were frequently displaced and a few were used over and over again.

In reaction, Cranmer in the 1549 Prayer Book distributed the psalms over the course of the month in strict canonical order according to a system he had worked out some years before for the revision of the daily office. He appointed proper psalms for only four days of the church year—Christmas, Easter, Ascension, and Whitsunday. In 1662, Ash Wednesday and Good Friday were also given proper psalms.

106

The 1789 revision printed ten groups of selections from the psalms "to be used instead of the psalms for the day, at the discretion of the minister." The 1892 revision printed a table of twenty selections from the psalms; it also appointed proper psalms for several additional days: First Sunday in Advent, Circumcision, Epiphany, Purification, Annunciation, Easter Even, Trinity Sunday, Transfiguration, Saint Michael and All Angels, and All Saints' Day.

The 1928 revision further enlarged the table of proper psalms, and tables of psalms were provided for Sundays and for special occasions. The minister was allowed freedom to use one or more from among the psalms for the day or from the appropriate table.

The Daily Office Lectionary, revised in 1943, took a fresh approach to the division of the psalter. Every day of the church year was provided with proper psalms. Those for Sundays and holy days were integrated when possible with the lections of the day. On other days psalms were read fairly much in course. Some psalms were favored, eight were omitted, and the suitability of psalms for morning or evening was taken into account. The traditional Anglican monthly system was retained as an alternative except for the eleven holy days when there were special psalms appointed.

In this revision the psalter is in a seven week pattern (except for the period from the Fourth Sunday in Advent until the First Sunday after the Epiphany and from Palm Sunday to the Second Sunday of Easter). The whole of the psalter is appointed, although alternatives are provided for certain psalms. The revision has given special attention to the appropriateness of a psalm to the time of day, the day of the week, and the season of the church year. Creation and paschal deliverance psalms are scheduled for Saturday evenings and Sundays, and Lent and Easter are distinguished by certain variations in the patterns. The traditional Anglican monthly system is retained as an alternative.

A new option is the use of antiphons with the psalms of the office (see additional directions, p. 141; also p. 935). These may be taken from the psalms themselves, or from the opening sentences of the office, or from other passages of scripture. (See *The Prayer Book Office*, compiled and edited by Howard Galley, New York: The Seabury Press, 1980.) Directions are given for various ways to recite the psalms (p. 582).

Gloria Patri (pp. 46 and 84)

The Gloria Patri which follows the opening versicle introduces the psalmody of the day. It is also to be used after the last of the psalms, so that the psalmody is given a Christian reference and intention through this exclamation of praise to the Holy Trinity. In the Western church it was customary to sing the Gloria Patri after each psalm and after each section of Psalm 119; in the Eastern church, after each group of psalms. Cranmer retained the Western practice, except that the Gloria Patri was not to be repeated after each section of Psalm 119. The 1662 Book restored that custom even though sixteenth century Anglicans had objected to this repetitiveness and objections increased with each revision.

The first American revisers allowed the omission of all repetitions except the one printed after the opening versicle and that at the end of the psalmody of the day. The Gloria in excelsis was also provided as an alternative for use at the end of the psalmody. The 1928 revision eliminated the option to use Gloria in excelsis in Morning Prayer, though not in Evening Prayer. The present Book assumes the use of the Gloria Patri at the end of the psalmody, but additional directions (p. 141) permit its use after each psalm and after each section of Psalm 119.

The Lessons (pp. 47 and 84)

The Sabbath services of the Jewish synagogue centered on the reading and exposition of readings from the Law (the Pentateuch) and the Prophets (historical and prophetic books of the Old Testament). There may also have been readings from the wisdom literature in some places. One or another of three systems may have guided the choice of lections: (1) the discretion of the synagogue ruler; (2) "in course" reading (once a book was begun, it was read in consecutive sections to the end); or (3) a fixed lectionary. The early Christians modeled their services after those of the synagogue, with liturgies of the word which included the reading of Christian writings as well as the Old Testament lections. As a New Testament canon gradually developed, made up of books which had come into general use in worship, a systematic pattern for the selection of readings for the various days and seasons emerged.

Lessons appropriate to principal days and seasons of the church year were used on those occasions; readings in course filled the remainder of the year. No later than the ninth century there was a fully structured system for reading the Bible in its entirety at Matins. Genesis through Judges was read from Septuagesima, the beginning of pre-Lent, to Palm Sunday; Jeremiah was read in Lent; Isaiah and Lamentations in Holy Week; Epistles, Acts, and Revelation in the

Easter season; historical books, wisdom literature and the Apocrypha from Pentecost to Advent; Isaiah, Jeremiah, and Daniel from Advent to Epiphany; Ezekiel, the minor prophets and Job in the Epiphany season. The Gospels and Pauline Epistles were read throughout the year. Late in the middle ages, however, with the vast increase in the number of saints' days and their octaves, and the reading of many portions of the saints' lives, the orderly sequence was seriously affected. Only two days in the Sarum offices for Advent were free from commemorations, for example, and less than two chapters were left from the old course reading in Isaiah.

The preface of the 1549 Prayer Book (printed on pp. 866–867 of this revision) is dependent on the preface of the proposed revision of the Roman breviary by Cardinal Quiñones. It states the principle followed in the 1549 Lectionary: "the reading of holy Scripture is so set forth, that all things shall be done in order, without breaking one piece thereof from another." That lectionary followed the civil calendar. The Old Testament (except for Isaiah) including the Apocrypha was read from the beginning of January through November 27. Isaiah, the only book read out of course, was begun on November 28 to coincide with the season of Advent. Omitted from the cycle were the books of Chronicles, the material of which was largely covered in the books of Kings, the books of the Maccabees, and portions of the apocalyptic material in Ezekiel. The entire New Testament with the exception of Revelation was read three times within a year, the Gospels and Acts in the morning and the Epistles in the evening. Only twelve fixed days and ten moveable days (the last four days of Holy Week, Easter, and the two days following, Ascension, Whitsunday, and Trinity Sunday) had even one proper lesson.

The Elizabethan revision increased the number of proper lessons for the fixed holy days, and proper lessons from the Old Testament were provided for each Sunday. Important passages from Isaiah were read from Advent through Epiphany; selections from the Old Testament in order began with Genesis 1 on Septuagesima.

Following the Proposed Book of 1786, the American revision of 1789 rearranged the order of lections, dropping some to make more room for readings from the Prophets. It also, following the Proposed Book, provided proper New Testament lessons for Sundays and proper lections for Ash Wednesday. The Apocrypha was dropped from the weekday lectionary, and the New Testament so arranged that the Gospels and Acts would be read only twice each year in the mornings. The Epistles were still read three times through the year in the evenings. The new lectionary of the 1892 revision had many features of the lectionary adopted by the General Convention of 1877 which, in turn, depended upon the new Church of England lectionary adopted in 1871. The number of lessons from the Apocrypha for fixed holy days was reduced to three. A table was provided with optional proper lessons for the forty days of Lent, the rogation days, and the ember days. The New Testament (except for Revelation) was read through once each year at both daily offices. When the Gospel was read at one service, Acts or Epistles were to be read at the other. Alternate chapters of Revelation were assigned to the two services during the last part of December.

Following the lead of other twentieth century revisions, the 1928 Book abandoned Cranmer's principle of using the civil calendar as the basis for the lectionary. The 1928 lectionary began on the Monday after the first Sunday in Advent with Genesis 1 and 1 Kings 11 as Old Testament lessons. It restored more than thirty readings from the Apocrypha to the daily lectionary. Narrative material from the Pentateuch, the historical books, and the Gospels largely composed the Sunday cycle, at the expense of readings from the prophets, wisdom literature, and the epistles.

The 1928 lectionary had a poor reception, and work was soon begun which resulted in eight years of trial use and the adoption of a new lectionary by the General Convention of 1943. The Sunday two-year office lectionary was related to the eucharistic lectionary, and a fuller table of lections for special occasions as well as lessons for the eves of the fixed holy days was provided.

Instead of a straight course reading that had little relationship to the church year, this 1943 revision displayed a sensitivity to the ways in which certain books suited certain seasons. Much more flexibility was present in the directions for the use of the lectionary.

The present revision has a lectionary arranged in a two-year cycle so that the New Testament can be read through twice in a two-year cycle and the Old Testament once. Further efforts have been made to provide for the readings of books at suitable and traditional times. The Eucharistic Lectionary, however, is to be used at the principal Sunday service, whether that is a liturgy of the word or a daily office. The daily office lectionary is designed for those who say the office each day. Because there are few saints' days for which lessons can be provided which add to our knowledge of the saint, and since these lessons interrupt the course reading at daily office, no proper lessons are provided for the eves of saints' days, although there is one set of lections which is intended primarily for the eve of an apostle who is patron of a parish. A general permission is given: "When a Major Feast interrupts the sequence of Readings, they may be re-ordered by lengthening, combining, or omitting some of them, to secure continuity or avoid repetition." This direction includes permission to omit any or all of the lections appointed for a saint's day in order to avoid interruption of a sequence if that seems preferable.

Until the 1928 revision two lessons had been required at both daily offices. That edition allowed the omission of one lesson at Evening Prayer. In the present revision an Old Testament Lesson, an Epistle, and a Gospel are listed for each day. Normally the Old Testament Lesson would be used in the morning and one of the New Testament readings—the Epistle in Year One and the Gospel in Year Two—used in the morning and the other in the evening. There is provision for postponing the Old Testament reading to the evening when it is desirable to have only one lesson in the morning. If there is but one office in a day all three readings may be used. If a daily office is the principal service of a Sunday or other major Holy Day, the readings are to be from the Eucharistic Lectionary.

The Announcement of a Lesson (pp. 47 and 84)

Earlier Prayer Books required the reader to announce the chapter and verse as well as the name of the book. This is now optional, for it is meaningful only in situations where people follow the lessons in the version used or in another translation or language, or in situations where the level of biblical scholarship is such that the citation puts the lection into context for members of a congregation. The new order (first the book, then the chapter, then the verse) is more logical than the order of the announcement in earlier Prayer Books.

The Response (pp. 47 and 84)

The medieval offices contained responses after the readings which were omitted from the 1549 Book. At the end of each lesson the reader simply said "Here endeth such a chapter of such a book." The 1662 revision changed this to read "Here endeth the first, or the second lesson." The present revision gives two forms for announcing the end of the lesson, the first of which elicits from the people the response "Thanks be to God."

It is fitting that there be a period of silence for reflection after each reading; a rubric to this effect is in the present revision.

111

Canticles (pp. 47–53 and 85–96)

The 1549 Prayer Book provided only three canticles for use in Matins: the Te Deum laudamus to be used after the first lesson except in Lent; the Benedicite for Lent; the Benedictus to be used after the second lesson. Two canticles were provided for Evensong: the Magnificat after the first lesson, the Nunc dimittis after the second lesson. The 1552 revision removed the directions concerning use of the Te Deum and the Benedicite. There were objections to the general use of New Testament canticles; the Jubilate (Psalm 100) was provided as an alternative to the Benedictus; Psalm 98, Cantate Domino, for the Magnificat; Psalm 67, Deus misereatur, for the Nunc dimittis. The 1662 revision restricted the use of the Jubilate to those times when the Benedictus would be read in one of the daily lections or as the Gospel of the day. The American revision of 1789 abbreviated the Benedictus to four verses, printed after rather than before the Jubilate. Bonum est confiteri (Ps. 92:1–4) substituted for the Magnificat, and Benedic, anima mea (Ps. 103:1–4, 20–22) for the Nunc dimittis. The 1892 revision restored the Magnificat, the Nunc dimittis, and the full text of the Benedictus, though the use of this full text was required only on the Sundays of Advent. The 1928 revision provided another alternative, Benedictus es, Domine, for use after the first lesson in Morning Prayer.

The 1979 Book moves the Jubilate to a more suitable place as an alternative to the Venite. The other psalms, which faded in popularity as substitutes for canticles, are replaced by eight additional canticle texts: The Song of Moses; the First, Second, and Third Songs of Isaiah; A Song of Penitence; A Song to the Lamb; The Song of the Redeemed; and Gloria in excelsis. These new canticles, though printed with Rite Two, may be used with Rite One as well. Canticles particularly appropriate for Lent and for Easter season are provided. A table (pp. 144–145) suggests a distribution of the canticles related to the days of the week, and suggests that certain canticles are more suitable after readings from the Old Testament and certain others after readings from the New Testament. No longer are some canticles limited to morning and some to evening use. The additional directions (pp. 141–142) provide for the use of antiphons with the canticles, for the use of metrical versions of the canticles, and for the substitution of a hymn for a canticle in special circumstances. The Gloria Patri is printed at the end of certain canticles, but the permission to omit it, rubricated in the American revision of 1789, still remains.

Canticle 1 or 12: A Song of Creation: Benedicite,
omnia opera Domini (pp. 47–49 and 88–90)

The Benedicite is a continuation of the Benedictus es, Domine (Canticle 2 or 13). Together they form an expanded paraphrase of Psalm 148. The first portion summons all the hosts of heaven and all the physical elements of earth to praise God; the second summons the earth and all its creatures, including humanity; the last portion summons the people of the covenant, living and departed. This hymn, probably the composition of an Alexandrian Jew, is in the book of Daniel in the Septuagint, though not in the Hebrew Old Testament. The Apocrypha includes it as the Song of the Three Young Men. From late in the fourth century this canticle was among the psalms of the morning office. In the Eastern rites it is used daily at morning office. The Mozarabic rite used it on Sundays and festival days and daily during the first four weeks of Lent and during Easter week. It was also used every Sunday at the Eucharist before the Epistle. The medieval breviaries of the Roman rite appointed it as the Old Testament canticle at Lauds on Sundays, and at festivals. The Gallican rite used it between the Epistle and Gospel at the Eucharist in certain seasons. The refrain, repeated after each verse in the Septuagint version, was in the late Roman breviaries repeated only at the beginning of each of the three sections, after the final verse of the last section, after the Trinitarian doxology, and after a concluding antiphon from the Benedictus es, "Blessed are you, Lord, in the firmament of heaven."

The 1549 Prayer Book appointed this canticle for use after the first lesson in Lent (in place of the Te Deum), using the translation from the Great Bible, with the refrain repeated after each verse. Cranmer replaced the Trinitarian doxology and the antiphon with the Gloria Patri. The 1552 version removed restrictions for use.

The American Proposed Book of 1786 printed a revised version of the canticle for permissive use on the thirty-first day of the month as the psalmody of the day. (The English books had appointed for that day the repetition of the psalms of the thirtieth day.) The last verse, "O Ananias, Azarias, and Misael, bless ye the Lord," was omitted. The 1789 Book restored the version of the Proposed Book to its traditional Anglican use as an alternative to the Te Deum. The 1928 Book added the doxology which had been used with the canticle in the medieval breviaries.

The 1979 Book deletes some of the repetitions of the refrain and gives permission to omit one or two of the sections of the canticle. The concluding antiphon is also restored in the version printed in Rite Two, which was translated by the Rev. Dr. Charles M. Guilbert. In the table of suggested canticles (pp. 144–145) it is recommended for Saturday mornings and Wednesday evenings.

Canticle 2 or 13: A Song of Praise: Benedictus es, Domine (pp. 49 and 90)

This canticle entered the Prayer Book with the 1928 revision, as an alternative for the Te Deum and the Benedicite after the first lesson of Morning Prayer. The present revision allows it for either Morning or Evening Prayer. The canticle has been used in morning offices in Eastern churches and it was sung in the Mozarabic rite of Spain along with the Benedicite at Lauds on Sundays and festivals and daily in the first four weeks of Lent and Easter week. The Gallican Eucharist used it on occasion. In recent Roman breviaries it alternates with the Benedicite as the Old Testament canticle at Lauds on Sundays and festivals. It is the first portion of a hymn of which the Benedicite is the continuation. Some believe that this canticle was a hymn of praise for the restoration of temple worship. The table of suggested canticles (pp. 144–145) recommends its use on Tuesday mornings and Friday evenings. The translation in Rite Two is by the Rev. Dr. Charles M. Guilbert.

Canticle 3 or 15: The Song of Mary: Magnificat (pp. 50 and 91–92)

The Gospel according to Luke attributes this hymn to Mary at the time of her visit to Elizabeth, the mother of John the Baptist (Lk. 1:39–56). Modeled after the song of Hannah (1 Sam. 2:1–10), it is a mosaic of phrases from the Old Testament. The latter part is eschatological, summing up the hopes of the lowly, the hungry, and the poor for the fulfillment of God's promises to Israel. As the song of Mary it is the song of the church.

In the Eastern churches the Magnificat is sung in the morning office. Gallican churches used it in the morning offices as well. The sixth century Rule of Benedict of Nursia called for a Gospel canticle at Vespers, almost certainly the Magnificat, for it was the canticle of the evening offices in medieval breviaries of the Roman rite. As the climactic canticle of the rite, leading into the prayers, it was on occasion accompanied by incense. In the Mozarabic breviary it was appointed for Incarnational and Marian feasts.

114

The 1549 Prayer Book appointed it as the only canticle for use after the first lesson at Evensong, in the translation from the Great Bible. Psalm 98, Cantate Domino, was provided as an alternative in the 1552 revision, because of the prejudice against use of Gospel canticles, of this one particularly. The first American revision (1789) substituted Psalm 92:1–4, Bonus est confiteri. The 1892 revision restored the Magnificat, and the 1928 Book provided for its use in the climactic position at Evening Prayer. When only one lesson was read at Evening Prayer the Magnificat could be the canticle after that lesson. The present revision permits its use at both morning and evening office. The translation printed in Rite Two is that of the International Consultation on English Texts (hereafter ICET).

Canticle 4 or 16: The Song of Zechariah: Benedictus Dominus Deus (pp. 50–51 and 92–93)

According to Luke this is the song of Zechariah, the father of John the Baptist, at John's circumcision (Lk. 1:57–80). The first eight verses, which parallel the Magnificat, are largely phrases from the Old Testament. The last four depict John as the forerunner who will prepare the way for the true Messiah by preaching repentance. The description of the Messiah as the "dayspring" recalls Malachi 4:2. It is possible that this was a hymn originally used by the disciples of John the Baptist.

The Benedictus may be the Gospel canticle called for at Lauds in the Rule of Benedict of Nursia. In the medieval church it was the Gospel canticle used at Lauds. In the Mozarabic rite it was sung at Lauds on Sundays and festivals and daily during the first four weeks of Lent and Easter week. In the entrance rite of the Gallican eucharistic liturgy it was a song of praise. The 1549 Prayer Book appointed it for use at Daily Matins after the second lesson, taking the translation from the King's Primer of 1545. The 1552 revision set the Jubilate as an alternative because of the prejudice against Gospel canticles. In 1662 the substitution of the Jubilate was limited to those occasions when the Benedictus would be read in one of the lections.

The American revision of 1789 retained only the first four verses, printing them after the Jubilate as an alternative. The position was reversed in 1892 and the full text restored, but the use of the full text was required only on the Sundays in Advent.

Many have felt that this pre-incarnational canticle is appropriate before rather than after New Testament readings; the table of suggested canticles recommends its use at Morning Prayer on major holy days and on most Sundays as an introduction to the New Testament reading. It is also one of the three canticles suggested for use at a burial as the body is carried from the church (pp. 484 and 500). The translation in Rite Two is that of ICET.

Canticle 5 or 17: *The Song of Simeon: Nunc dimittis* (pp. 51–52 and 93)

The Song of Simeon (Lk. 2:29–32) was used in evening offices of the church as early as the fourth century. It is the canticle of the evening office in the late fourth century Apostolic Constitutions. In the West it became the canticle for the office of Compline. The Mozarabic rite used it at Lauds on the Feast of the Purification and the Roman rite placed it before Mass on that day.

In the 1549 Prayer Book it was the canticle following the second lesson at Evensong, using the translation from the Great Bible of 1539. The phrase "the glory of thy people of Israel" was replaced by "the glory of thy people Israel" in 1552. As an alternative, Psalm 67, Deus misereatur, was provided in that version.

The American revision of 1789 substituted Psalm 103:1–4, 20–22, Benedic, anima mea, for the Nunc dimittis, but the 1892 revision restored Nunc dimittis to the traditional first place among the canticles after the second lesson at Evening Prayer.

The present revision permits its use for Morning as well as for Evening Prayer and, in accordance with Western tradition, it is used in the office of Compline. It is also among the canticles suggested for use as the body is borne from the church for burial (pp. 484 and 500). The translation provided for Rite Two and for Compline is by the Rev. Dr. Charles M. Guilbert.

Canticle 6 or 20: *Glory be to God, Glory to God: Gloria in excelsis* (pp. 52 and 94–95)

The Gloria in excelsis and the Te Deum are the only canticles not from the Scriptures. The Gloria in excelsis dates to the fourth century, with many variations in the early texts. The hymn begins with the song of the angels (Lk. 2:14). In some of the early manuscripts both of Luke and of the canticle the reading is "peace to men of good will," and in other manuscripts "peace, good will to men." This introductory verse is a form of antiphon and has been so treated in some musical settings. It is followed by a hymn addressed to God the

116

Father, reminiscent of the initial portion of the Te Deum or of the preface to a eucharistic prayer. The next verse, addressed to Christ, incorporates the text of the ancient Eastern hymns Agnus Dei and Kyrie. The final verse resembles the people's response to the invitation to communion in Eastern liturgies, "there is one Holy, one Lord, Jesus Christ, to the glory of God the Father, to whom be glory for ever." In the Apostolic Constitutions, a document from late in the fourth century, the Gloria in excelsis was the canticle of the morning office. The Eastern churches continue to use it in morning office. The West also used it at the daily office: at Matins in Roman usage; at Prime on Sundays and feasts in the Mozarabic rite; at both Matins and Vespers in the Celtic Bangor antiphonary.

In the twelfth century, when it became a normal constituent of the Mass in the Roman rite, Gloria in excelsis was dropped from the daily office. The English Prayer Books, following the late medieval Roman liturgical books, printed the Gloria in excelsis only within the Eucharist. The first American revision provided this canticle as an alternative to the Gloria Patri in both daily offices, but the 1892 Book dropped it from Morning Prayer though retaining it in Evening Prayer. The 1979 Book restores it for use in the morning as well as in the evening. The translation printed in Rite Two is by ICET. In the table of suggested canticles its use is recommended on Thursday mornings except in Advent and Lent.

Canticle 7 or 21; We Praise Thee, You are God:
Te Deum laudamus (pp. 52–53 and 95–96)

The Te Deum, like the Gloria in excelsis, is not in the Scriptures. The oldest manuscript is that of the seventh-century Bangor antiphonary, but the hymn surely dates at least to the fourth century. According to medieval legend it was composed extemporaneously by Ambrose and Augustine at Augustine's baptism. Modern scholars generally attribute it to Niceta, bishop of Remesiana in Dacia (c. 392–414). In structure and content it is very like a eucharistic prayer; perhaps it was originally composed for that purpose. The rule of Caesarius (c. 470–542), bishop of Arles, and the rule of Benedict (480–550) speak of it as the canticle at Matins. In Mozarabic use it was said on Sundays and festivals at Prime. The Sarum breviary used it after the last lesson at Sunday Matins, except in Advent, Pre-Lent, and Lent, and on certain special days of the church year.

The 1549 Prayer Book appointed the Te Deum after the Old Testament lesson "daily throughout the year, except in Lent," a restric-

117

tion removed in the 1552 Prayer Book. Cranmer's translation depended upon vernacular English forms of the time and some changes in phrasing were made between 1549 and 1552. "Heaven and earth are full of the Majesty of thy glory" was substituted for "Heaven and earth are replenished with the majesty of thy glory;" "Also the Holy Ghost the comforter" replaced "The Holy Ghost also being the comforter." Cranmer retained, as if it were a part of the canticle, a set of suffrages which in medieval times had been used after either the Te Deum or the Gloria in excelsis.

The first American revision of 1789 corrected the translation of one line "Thy honorable, true, and only Son," to read "Thine adorable, true, and only Son." Also in that revision, "Thou didst humble thyself to be born of a Virgin" replaced "Thou didst not abhor the Virgin's womb." In the present edition the set of suffrages which had been attached to the end of the Te Deum since 1549 is restored to its original use, as the alternative set of suffrages for Morning Prayer.

In several particulars the translation of ICET, which has been adopted for use in Rite Two (except for the substitution of the word "shun" for "spurn"), is closer to the original than was Cranmer's version. The first line literally translates as "You as God we praise; You as Lord we acclaim." The line "The noble fellowship of prophets" is closer to the original than "The goodly fellowship of the prophets." "The white-robed army of martyrs praise you" recaptures the allusion to Revelation 7:9–17. The meaning of "Comforter" has changed radically in English usage since 1549; "advocate and guide" captures more of the sense of the original Latin. "When you became man to set us free" is truer to the original than "When thou tookest upon thee to deliver man," and "Bring us with your saints to glory everlasting" (literally "Make us be presented with a gift with your saints in bliss, with glory everlasting") is more accurate than "Make them to be numbered with thy saints, in glory everlasting." The form of Sanctus included in this canticle, "Holy, holy, holy, Lord God of Sabaoth; heaven and earth are full of the majesty of thy glory" (Is. 6:3) (or the contemporary language equivalent), is the full form of the Sanctus in earlier eucharistic prayers when the Benedictus qui venit, if included in the rite, was still a part of the invitation to communion. The Te Deum is recommended for use in the daily office on Sundays except in Advent and Lent, and it is one of the three alternative songs of praise recommended for use at the Eucharist of the Easter Vigil (page 294).

Canticle 8: The Song of Moses: Cantemus Domino (p. 85)

This is an abbreviated version of the song sung by Moses and the people of Israel after the crossing of the Red Sea (Ex. 15:1–18). It is possibly a later elaboration of the song of Miriam (Ex. 15:19–22). At a very early stage in the development of the Easter vigil this canticle was sung after the reading from Exodus 13–14. The Eastern church used it in the morning office. The Ambrosian rite of northern Italy appointed it for Sundays. In the Mozarabic rite it was used at Lauds in Easter week and on the Sundays of the Easter season, and in the Roman rite as the Old Testament canticle for Lauds on Thursdays.

The present revision of the Prayer Book is the first to include the canticle. In the table of suggested canticles (pp. 144–145) Cantemus Domino is recommended for use after the Old Testament reading on Sundays during the Easter season, on Thursday mornings throughout the year, and on Monday evenings except in Lent. The translation is by the Rev. Dr. Charles M. Guilbert.

Canticle 9: The First Song of Isaiah: Ecce, Deus (p. 86)

This canticle is from the twelfth chapter of Isaiah which is made up of two psalms celebrating return from exile (Is. 12:1b–3 and 4b–6). The Roman breviaries appointed it for use on Mondays at Lauds. In the Mozarabic rite it was used on several saints' days. The table of suggested canticles (pp. 144–145) recommends it for use on Mondays at the morning office and on Saturdays at the evening office. The translation is by the Rev. Dr. Charles M. Guilbert. This Book is the first to include the canticle.

Canticle 10: The Second Song of Isaiah:
Quaerite Dominum (pp. 86–87)

Quaerite Dominum (Is. 55:6–11) is drawn from the last chapter of that portion of the book of Isaiah known as Second Isaiah. This chapter is among the small group of lections that has been used for the Easter vigil. The table of suggested canticles (pp. 144–145) recommends its use on Friday mornings (except in Lent when it is replaced by Kyrie Pantokrator) and on Tuesday evenings. The translation is by the Rev. Dr. Guilbert. Like Canticle 9, this canticle is included in a Prayer Book for the first time.

119

Canticle 11: The Third Song of Isaiah:
Surge, illuminare (pp. 87–88)

This canticle, a cento from a portion of Isaiah commonly known as Third Isaiah, celebrates the reestablishment of Jerusalem and the rebuilding of the temple. The vision of the heavenly Jerusalem in Revelation 21 is based largely on this chapter. The Mozarabic rite used it at Lauds on Epiphany. The Canadian revision of 1922 included it in a "Special Service for Missions," and the 1959 Canadian revision printed it among additional canticles for use at the daily office.

The 1979 revision is the first American Prayer Book to include it. In the table of suggested canticles (pp. 144–145) its use is recommended at Morning Prayer on Wednesdays (except in Lent), on Sundays in the Advent season, and at Evening Prayer on Thursdays. The translation is by the Rev. Dr. Guilbert.

Canticle 12: see Canticle 1

Canticle 13: see Canticle 2

Canticle 14: A Song of Penitence: Kyrie Pantokrator (pp. 90–91)

This cento is from the Prayer of Manasseh (Manasses) which was included in some Greek versions of the Old Testament but not in the Hebrew canon. It is a classic of penitential devotion, supposedly the prayer of repentance which is spoken of in the account of the reign of Manasseh (2 Chr. 33:1–20). This canticle is used in the Lenten Great Compline of the Byzantine Rite. The Mozarabic rite also used it during Lent.

The 1979 Prayer Book is the first to include the canticle. It is recommended (pp. 144–145) for use in Lent on Sunday, Wednesday, and Friday mornings and on Monday evenings. The translation is by the Rev. Dr. Guilbert.

Canticle 15: see Canticle 3

Canticle 16: see Canticle 4

Canticle 17: see Canticle 5

Canticle 18: A Song to the Lamb: Dignus es (pp. 93–94)

Hymns sung to the One seated on the throne and to the Lamb in the vision of heaven (Rev. 4–5) compose this canticle. These may be early Christian hymns incorporated by the author of Revelation, which correspond to the acclamations at the enthronement of a king.

The Irish revision of 1926 included this canticle in an alternative form of the evening office. The Roman breviary appoints it for use on Tuesday evenings and on the feasts of martyrs.

This is the first edition of the American Prayer Book to include the text. It is recommended (pp. 144–145) for use at Morning Prayer on Tuesdays and Fridays. The translation is by the Rev. Dr. Guilbert.

Canticle 19: *The Song of the Redeemed: Magna et mirabilia* (p. 94)

This canticle, a mosaic of Old Testament phrases, is the song of the redeemed in the vision of Revelation (15:3–4). It has links with the Song of Moses, Cantemus Domino (Canticle 8), which celebrates the crossing of the Red Sea. Possibly it is an early Christian hymn incorporated by the author of Revelation. The Roman breviary of 1970 appoints it for Friday evenings and on Epiphany and Pentecost. This is its first inclusion in an American Prayer Book.

The Prayer Book recommends it for use (pp. 144–145) at Morning Prayer on Mondays and Saturdays, and on Thursdays in Advent and Lent. The translator is the Rev. Dr. Guilbert.

Canticle 20: see Canticle 6

Canticle 21: see Canticle 7

The Apostles' Creed (pp. 53–54 and 96)

The use of the baptismal creed in the office cannot be traced back earlier than the eighth century. It was one of the several elements of personal devotion which attached themselves to the end of the little offices of Prime and Compline after the Lord's Prayer. The 1549 Prayer Book directed the people to kneel at the end of the canticle following the second lesson, the Kyrie was to be said, and the minister was then to "say the creed and the Lord's Prayer in English, with a loud voice." This was in contrast to the silent repetition in the medieval offices. In the 1552 revision, immediately after the canticle, the creed was to be said by both minister and people, standing. Quicunque Vult, commonly called the Athanasian Creed (pp. 864–865), which had been said on Sundays in the medieval office, in the 1549 Book was to be used after the Benedictus at Matins on the six principal feasts. In 1552 its use was extended to thirteen days, apparently chosen to insure its use approximately once each month. The 1662 revision allowed the omission of the Apostles' Creed on those days when the Athanasian was said.

The clause "he descended into hell" was omitted from the American Proposed Book of 1786, but restored by the interstate convention of that year. The 1789 convention, however, gave permission for "any churches" (those of a state convention) to omit the clause or to substitute "He went into the Place of departed spirits." In accordance with the 1786 resolution, a creed was not printed within the eucharistic rite of the 1789 revision, but both the Apostles' and the Nicene Creeds were printed as alternatives in Morning Prayer; the controversial Athanasian Creed was omitted from the Book. The 1892 revision withdrew permission to omit the clause "he descended into hell," but allowed the alternative clause to be used.

The present revision does not permit the substitution of "He went into the Place of departed spirits." The additional directions (p. 142) specify that the creed is to be omitted when the Eucharist with its own creed is to follow the office, and that it may be omitted at one of the daily offices on weekdays. The translation which is printed in Rite Two and permitted in Rite One is the final text prepared by ICET.

The Prayers (pp. 54–60 and 97–102)

The 1549 Book followed the medieval practice of directing the people to kneel for the Kyrie, the creed, and the prayers. The minister was also to kneel, then stand again for the collects (in accordance with medieval practice). The 1552 Book directed that all stand for the creed and kneel for the prayers, except that the minister was to stand again prior to the suffrages. It has been commonly said that Episcopalians kneel to pray, but that is not the rule for posture in any edition of the Prayer Book. Various editions have assumed that standing is the normal posture for public prayer and have directed the people to kneel only for confessions, for the decalogue, for collects of the daily office, which are petitionary, and, since the 1928 American edition, for the blessing at the end of the eucharistic rite. In addition, those being married or ordained have been directed to kneel while the congregation prays for them.

The present edition directs all persons to kneel for the confession of sin, but the people are allowed to stand for the prayers of the daily office.

The Salutation

In the medieval offices and in the 1549 Prayer Book the salutation preceded the collects of the rite. In 1552 it was moved to follow the creed and precede the prayers. (For commentary on the salutation see pp. 322–323.)

The Lord's Prayer

English Prayer Books included the Lord's Prayer at two points within the daily offices. It was to be said before the opening versicle, a remnant of the private use of the Lord's Prayer as preparation for the daily office, and again among the prayers of the rite. In the 1549 Book the minister recited the Lord's Prayer and the people responded with the clause, "But deliver us from evil. Amen," as had been the practice in the Roman rite. The 1552 revision directed that everyone say the prayer; and the Kyrie which had preceded the creed in the 1549 version was moved to a position immediately before the Lord's Prayer.

The 1662 revision followed the Scottish Book of 1637, adding the doxology which begins "For thine is the kingdom" to the Lord's Prayer at its first use in the office but not in the second place, when it immediately followed the Kyrie. The American revision of 1789 omitted both the Kyrie and the second use of the Lord's Prayer. That revision also changed "which art in heaven" to "who art in heaven," "in earth" to "on earth," and "them that trespass" to "those who trespass." In the 1928 revision the Lord's Prayer could be used at this point if the confession of sin had been omitted.

The present Book has restored the Lord's Prayer to its proper place among the prayers of the office. It may be omitted when the Great Litany or the Eucharist, each of which contains the Lord's Prayer, is to follow. The contemporary language form in Rite Two is that of ICET.

The Suffrages

The first of the alternative sets of suffrages is based upon those of the 1549 Prayer Book. Several of these had been used in the little office of Prime in the Sarum breviary, in the Primer of Henry VIII, and in the forms for the Bidding of the Bedes.

Priest: O Lord, show thy mercy upon us.
Answer: And grant us thy salvation.
Priest: O Lord, save the king.
Answer: And mercifully hear us when we call upon thee.
Priest: Endue thy ministers with righteousness.
Answer: And make thy chosen people joyful.
Priest: O Lord, save thy people.
Answer: And bless thine inheritance.
Priest: Give peace in our time, O Lord.

Answer: Because there is none other that fighteth for us, but only thou, O God.
Priest: O God, make clean our hearts within us.
Answer: And take not thine [thy, from 1662] Holy Spirit from us.

The ultimate source is Pss. 85:7; 20:9; 132:9; 28:11; 122:7 (as modified in the Primer of Henry VIII); and 51:11a and 12b. The American revision of 1789 retained only the first and last sets. In the 1892 Book the full set was restored to Evening Prayer with two changes: "state" was substituted for "king" and "For it is thou, Lord, only, that makest us dwell in safety" for "Because there is none other that fighteth for us, but only thou, O God."

The 1979 Book contains a revised version of the fuller set of suffrages in both Morning and Evening Prayer. The first two are retained from the old version (Ps. 85:7 and 132:9). The third (Ps. 122:7 and 4:8) has been enlarged into a petition for peace for all nations. The fourth set, which replaces the second of the old series, is not merely a prayer that the state may be saved but that it may be kept under God's care and guided "in the way of justice and truth," a phrase from the prayer "For Peace Among the Nations" (p. 816). The fifth (Ps. 67:2) exhibits a missionary concern, and the sixth (Ps. 9:18), a social concern. In the last, Psalm 51:13b has been substituted for Psalm 51:12b as the response. The use of this set of suffrages is particularly appropriate when the collects and prayer for mission will not be followed by general intercessions.

The second set of suffrages is restored to its historic function in this Book. It had originally been used after the Gloria in excelsis in the morning office. When the Roman rite began use of the Gloria at the Eucharist, the Te Deum took its place in the office. These suffrages eventually were considered a part of the Te Deum and were so placed in the 1549 Book and in all other revisions since. The suffrages are taken from the Psalms: 28:11; 145:2; 123:4; 33:22; 31:1; 71:1. The phrase "let thy mercy be upon us" was substituted for "let thy mercy lighten upon us" in the 1789 revision. The translation in Rite Two is the work of ICET except for the substitution of "Lord, keep us from all sin today" for "Keep us today, Lord, from all sin."

The Collect of the Day (pp. 55 and 98)

The English Prayer Books required the use of the collect of the day. Earlier editions of the American Prayer Book have directed that it be omitted from Morning Prayer if a Eucharist is to follow. In addition, the earlier Books required the use of two "fixed collects,"

124

"A Collect for Peace" and "A Collect for Grace" at Morning Prayer; a different "Collect for Peace" and a "Collect for Aid Against Perils" at Evening Prayer.

This edition requires that one or more of eight collects be said. Special collects appropriate to three of the weekdays are provided for each office, as well as four other collects which make possible a weekly cycle. The collect for the day may be used in place of or in addition to one or more of these prayers.

A Collect for Sundays (pp. 56 and 98)

William Bright wrote this collect which was printed in the appendix to his work *Ancient Collects* (p. 233).[1] The 1928 Prayer Book included it, in a revised form, under the title "Sunday Morning," among the additional family prayers. In Bright's work the petition read "Vouchsafe us this day such a blessing through Thy worship, that the days which follow it may be spent in Thy favour."

A Collect for Fridays (pp. 56 and 99)

The Rev. Dr. William Reed Huntington included this prayer in his work *Materia Ritualis* (1882); it was proposed for the 1892 revision among the occasional prayers under the title "For Patience under Suffering," but was not accepted. The 1928 revision adopted it for use as the collect for Monday in Holy Week, which previously had no proper collect.

In the present revision it is retained as the collect for Monday in Holy Week (pp. 168 and 220), and reprinted for use as the station collect in the proper liturgy for Palm Sunday (p. 272), as well as being printed for optional use at Morning Prayer on Fridays. The preamble is from the exhortation contained in the office for the visitation of the sick in Prayer Books before the 1928 revision. The source of this portion was Hermann's Consultation.

A Collect for Saturdays (pp. 56 and 99)

The author of this new collect was Edward Benson, archbishop of Canterbury (1882–1896). The word "rest" replaces "Sabbath" of the original. Scriptural allusions include Gen. 2:2–3; Mt. 6:24–34; Lk. 12:22–32; Heb. 4; and Rev. 14:23.

---

[1] William Bright, *Ancient Collects and Other Prayers Selected for Devotional Use from Various Rituals, with An Appendix, On the Collects in the Prayer-Book*, Oxford and London: J. H. and Jas. Parker, 1862.

A Collect for the Renewal of Life (pp. 56 and 99)

The Rev. Dr. William Reed Huntington called this collect, which first appeared in his *Materia Ritualis*, a "cento of phrases" from the daily morning prayers of William Bright's *Ancient Collects* (pp. 5–8). The collect clearly was inspired by the canticle Benedictus Dominus Deus of the daily office. Proposed for inclusion in the 1892 Book it was not printed in the Prayer Book until the 1928 edition when it appeared under the title "In the Morning" among the additional family prayers.

A Collect for Peace (pp. 57 and 99)

In the Gelasian (no. 1476) and Gregorian (no. 1345) sacramentaries this collect is the postcommunion prayer in a Mass for peace. It is used in the same way in the Sarum missal but is also found in the Sarum breviary as a memorial at the end of Lauds. The close of the preamble, a phrase from a meditation of Saint Augustine of Hippo, might be translated more literally "Whom to know is to live, whom to serve is to reign." In all prior editions of the Prayer Book this was one of the two "fixed collects," always to be said at Morning Prayer. Scriptural allusions include Jn. 17:3; Jn. 8:31–36; and Ps. 27:1–4.

A Collect for Grace (pp. 57 and 100)

This was the second of the "fixed collects" of Morning Prayer in all earlier Prayer Books. The Gelasian (no. 1576) and the Gregorian (no. 1491) sacramentaries, and the Gallican Bobbio missal (no. 569) contain among a series of prayers for use at Matins the prayer from which this collect developed:

> We give you thanks, Lord, Holy Father, almighty everlasting God, who have brought us through the period of night to the morning hours. We beseech you that you grant that we pass through this day without sin, so that at vespers we may return thanks to you.

The collect was used in the Sarum little office of Prime. The conclusion of the petition in the English editions of the Prayer Book reads "That all our doings may be ordered by thy governance, to do always that is righteous in thy sight." The revised version of the Proposed American Book of 1786 was accepted in the Book of 1789. The collect points out that right living requires not only resistance to temptation but also active obedience to the will of God.

A Collect for Guidance (pp. 57 and 100)

In the Canadian Prayer Book of 1922 this is the first of the additional prayers for use at family prayer, under the title "For Remembrance of God's Presence." It came into that edition from the collection *A Chain of Prayer Across the Ages*,[1] where it is designated "From an Ancient Collect." From the Canadian Book it has entered Prayer Books of other Anglican provinces.

Prayer for Mission (pp. 57–58 and 100–101)

A rubric directs that one of three prayers for mission be said after the collects if the Eucharist or a form of general intercession is not to follow.

The first of the prayers is also the first of the solemn collects of Good Friday (p. 278) and the collect of the third proper "For the Ministry (Ember Days)" (pp. 206 and 256–257). It is based upon the third prayer of the ancient series of solemn collects of Good Friday in the Gelasian (no. 405) and Gregorian (no. 343) sacramentaries, and the Missale Gallicanum vetus (no. 99). The petition in its original form has been interpreted as a prayer only for those in holy orders: "Hear our supplications for all orders, that by the gift of your grace all grades may faithfully serve you." The 1549 version includes all members of the church:

> Almighty and everlasting God, by whose Spirit the whole body of the Church is governed and sanctified; receive our supplications and prayers which we offer before thee for all estates of men in thy holy congregation, that every member of the same, in his vocation and ministry, may truly and godly serve thee; through our Lord Jesus Christ.

In the 1662 revision, following the Scottish Book of 1637, the word "congregation" was changed to "Church" because of the Puritan connotation of the word "congregation." In the present revision the words "faithful people" replace "Church" in the preamble.

The second of the prayers for mission was written by George Edward Lynch Cotton, missionary bishop of Calcutta, India (1850–1866). The original version reads:

> O God, who hast made of one blood all nations of men for to dwell on all the face of the earth, and didst send thy blessed Son

---

[1] Ed. Selina Fitzherbert Fox, first ed. New York: E. P. Dutton & Co., 1913, p. 2.

to preach peace to them that are afar off and to them that are nigh: Grant that all the people of this land may feel after thee and find thee. And hasten, O heavenly Father, the fulfilment of thy promise to pour out thy Spirit upon all flesh; through Jesus Christ, our Saviour.

It embodies a number of scriptural quotations: Acts 17:26; Eph. 2:17; Is. 57:19; Jl. 2:28; and Acts 2:17. A revised version appears among the occasional prayers of the 1892 Book:

O God, who hast made of one blood all nations of men for to dwell on the face of the whole earth, and didst send thy blessed Son to preach peace to them that are far off and to them that are nigh; Grant that all men everywhere may seek after thee and find thee. Bring the nations into thy fold, and add the heathen to thine inheritance. And we pray thee shortly to accomplish the number of thine elect, and to hasten thy kingdom; through the same Jesus Christ our Lord. *Amen.*

The prayer underwent further change in 1928 and in this revision.

Charles Henry Brent, bishop of the Philippines (1901–1918) and of Western New York (1918–1929), wrote the third of the prayers for mission. It was published in his work *With God in Prayer*.[1]

Hymn or Anthem (pp. 58 and 101)

Late in the middle ages it was customary to sing an antiphon, usually in honor of the Virgin Mary, at the end of Lauds and Vespers. Anglicans in exile on the continent during the reign of Mary Tudor developed a love for the hymnody and metrical psalmody of the continental churches. Injunctions issued by Elizabeth in 1559 directed the use of plainchant for the services and stated:

For the comforting of such as delight in music, it may be permitted, that in the beginning or at the end of the Common Prayer, either at morning or evening, there may be sung a hymn or suchlike song to the praise of Almighty God, in the best sort of melody and music that may be conveniently devised; having respect that the sentence [sense] of the hymn may be understood and perceived.

---

[1] Charles Henry Brent, *With God in Prayer*, Philadelphia: George W. Jacobs & Co., 1907, pp. 40–41.

In the 1662 revision a rubric after the fixed collects noted, "In Quires and places where they sing here followeth the Anthem." This rubric was deleted from the first American revision. Printed as part of the American Prayer Book, however, were the Tate and Brady metrical versions of the Psalms and a selection of twenty-seven hymns with a preface which authorized their use "before and after Morning and Evening Prayer; and also before and after Sermons, at the discretion of the Minister." In the 1892 revision a rubric was introduced after the fixed collects of Evening Prayer: "In places where it may be convenient, here followeth the Anthem." The current rubric was substituted in this revision and included in Morning Prayer as well.

Authorized Intercessions and Thanksgivings (pp. 58 and 101)

A rubric allows the use of intercessions and thanksgivings after the prayer for mission, or after the hymn or anthem if one is sung. In earlier editions of the Prayer Book, Morning Prayer ended with the fixed collects. Intercessions were covered by the use of the Litany (required in the 1549 Prayer Book on Wednesdays and Fridays; required on Sundays, Wednesdays, and Fridays from 1552 to 1928) in Morning Prayer, and by the prayer for the church in the Eucharist. The Scottish Book of 1637 inserted after the fixed collects a rubric which required that, when the Litany was not to be said, the fixed collects should be followed by prayers which were printed at the end of the Litany: for the king and the royal family; for the clergy; the Prayer of Saint Chrysostom, and the Grace (2 Cor. 13:14). An analogous rubric was printed after the fixed collects in the 1662 Book, and these prayers were printed after the rubric. Included also among the occasional prayers in that Book was "A Collect or Prayer for all Conditions of men, to be used at such times when the Litany is not appointed to be said."

The American Book of 1789, following the lead of the Proposed Book of 1786, included among these prayers a general thanksgiving which had been printed among the occasional thanksgivings of the 1662 Book. The 1892 revision allowed the omission of the series of intercessions on any day other than Sunday or on any day when the Litany was said or "when the Holy Communion is immediately to follow." It also allowed the minister to conclude Evening Prayer "with such Prayer, or Prayers, taken out of this Book as he shall think fit." The 1928 revision permitted the minister, after the fixed collects, to end Morning Prayer "with such general intercessions, taken out of this Book, as he shall think fit, or with the Grace."

The General Thanksgiving (pp. 58–59 and 101)

Bishop Edward Reynolds of Norwich composed this prayer, inspired, some think, by a private prayer of Queen Elizabeth issued in 1596:

> I render unto thee, O merciful and heavenly Father, most humble and hearty thanks for thy manifold mercies so abundantly bestowed upon me, as well for my creation, preservation, regeneration, and all other thy benefits and great mercies exhibited in Christ Jesus.

Others have pointed out parallels between this prayer and the regulations for the construction of a eucharistic prayer in the Directory for the Publique Worship of God (1644).

Bishop Reynolds' prayer thanks God for His threefold activity as creator, preserver, and redeemer. The benefits of His redemption are described as the means of grace and the hope of glory. Scriptural allusions include Col. 1:27, Ps. 51:15, and Lk. 1:75. Some believe that this prayer—or possibly a fuller form from which it was excerpted—had been composed for use as a eucharistic prayer at some time during the interregnum when the Book of Common Prayer was banned from use. The Puritans before the 1604 revision had constantly complained about the dearth of prayers of thanksgiving in the Book. As a result, six thanksgivings for particular benefits were added. Reynolds' prayer was inserted in 1662 prior to the others under the heading "A General Thanksgiving."

The first American edition (1789) printed the form in Morning and Evening Prayer and at the conclusion of the Litany before the Prayer of Saint Chrysostom, thereby requiring its use each time a daily office was said. A rubric inserted in 1892 allowed its omission except on a Sunday when the Litany or Holy Communion was not immediately to follow. The revision of 1928 followed the lead of the Irish Book of 1877, inserting a rubric which allowed the congregation to say this prayer with the minister. The present edition directs that the prayer be said by officiant and people.

A Prayer of Saint Chrysostom (pp. 59 and 102)

This prayer is in the entrance rite of the late medieval manuscripts of the liturgies of Saint John Chrysostom and Saint Basil, but is not in the earliest manuscripts. The title was first given in the Prayer Book of 1662, following the lead of the Scottish Book of 1637. The prayer

130

itself was printed at the conclusion of Cranmer's English Litany (1544). The 1662 revision placed it there and at the end of the daily offices as well. The 1928 edition removed it from the Litany.

Cranmer was apparently misled by a Latin translation of the prayer which resulted in an unfortunate conflation of two sayings of our Lord in Matthew 18:19–20. Until the present revision the conclusion to the preamble read "When two or three be gathered together [or, are gathered together] in thy name, thou wilt grant their requests." The petition of this revision now conforms with Matthew 18:20.

In the Eastern liturgies the priest said this prayer during the singing of a diaconal litany, with a doxology at the end of both litany and prayer: "For you are a good God, and love mankind, and unto you we ascribe glory, to the Father, and to the Son, and to the Holy Spirit, now and ever, and unto ages of ages." Cranmer's version lacks this doxology, for he probably did not realize that the doxology concluding the litany in the Eastern liturgy also concluded the prayer.

Revisions from 1662 through 1928 required this prayer at the conclusion of every service of Morning and Evening Prayer, except that from 1892 on it could be omitted on weekdays or on Sundays if the Eucharist immediately followed. The word "expedient" was changed to "best" in the present revision—"expedient" has come to mean "politic" or "opportune" rather than "profitable." Cranmer provided the address "Almighty God" although the original prayer was addressed to Christ. In accordance with the principle that liturgical prayers should be addressed to the First Person of the Trinity in most instances, the phrase "through thy well beloved Son" has been inserted in the present revision.

The Dismissal (pp. 59–60 and 102)

The use of Benedicamus Domino, "Let us bless the Lord," with the response "Thanks be to God," has been a customary way to conclude services for many centuries. It was probably the common form for dismissal in the Gallican rite, corresponding to "Ite, missa est" in the Roman rite. The Roman rite began use of the Benedicamus about A.D. 1000. The form is restored for optional use in this revision.

The Pauline text commonly called "the Grace" (2 Cor. 13:14) was printed at the conclusion of the Litany and the daily offices in the revision of 1559. The 1928 edition dropped it from the Litany. This verse is used in many Eastern liturgies to introduce the Sursum corda at the Eucharist. In the Prayer Books since 1559, at the conclusion of

131

the daily offices, the Grace has served both as a final trinitarian doxology and as a prayer for the principal gifts of the Three Persons of the Trinity. Two alternative sentences, Romans 15:13 and Ephesians 3:20–21, have been added to the present Book.

An Order of Service for Noonday (pp. 103–107)

As early as the second century, writers speak of the third, sixth, and ninth hours of the day (9 A.M., 12 Noon, and 3 P.M.) as times which Christian people mark with private devotions associated with the events of the Passion. As monasticism developed, these became the hours for the "little offices," Terce, Sext, and None. The Primers of Henry VIII and Elizabeth made provision for these hours, as did John Cosin's work, *A Collection of Private Devotions*. No such offices were included in any edition of the Prayer Book, however, until the present century. Especially at conferences and conventions it has become a custom to mark the noon hour with prayers for mission which recall the Passion, and the conversion of Paul. A "Special Service for Missions," including the prayers which had become customary at noonday, was printed in the Canadian revision of 1922. The 1959 Canadian revision printed materials from that rite under the title "Prayers at Mid-day," with the sub-heading "For Missions."

The present edition of the Prayer Book provides a little office for optional use at noon. The structure can be traced at least as far back as the sixth century Benedictine Rule: each of the little offices was to begin with Psalm 70:1, "O God, make speed to save us," and the Gloria Patri. A "proper hymn" (one suited to the hour of the day or season of the church year) followed, then three selections from the Psalms (Pss. 119–128 were to be used for the little offices), a lesson from scripture, a response, the Kyrie, and concluding prayers.

The service provided in this edition of the Prayer Book is so constructed that it may be used for any or all of the traditional little offices—Terce, Sext, or None. The first lesson and the first collect have reference to the Holy Spirit, traditional for the office of Terce. The second lesson and collect relate to the crucifixion. Both the second and third collects mention the noon hour and are prayers for the church's mission. The third lesson and final collect may be used at None.

The Opening Versicle and Hymn (p. 103)

The opening versicle and response (based on Ps. 70:1) have been traditional for the beginning of daily offices at least since the sixth century. Only in Matins was this versicle preceded by "Lord, open our lips" (Ps. 51:16). The 1552 Book introduced that versicle into Evening Prayer also. In the first American revision "O God, make speed to save us" was omitted from both offices. This present revision restores it as the opening versicle for this office, for Evening Prayer, and for Compline. After the Gloria Patri a hymn may be sung.

The Selection from the Psalms (pp. 103–105)

The selections from the psalms which are printed within the rite are from those traditionally associated with the little offices. Other suitable psalms are also suggested in the rubric which precedes the first psalm of the rite.

The Lesson (pp. 105–106)

An appropriate passage of scripture follows. For convenience three short passages are printed within the rite. Meditation, silent or spoken, may reflect on the lesson.

The Prayers (pp. 106–107)

The prayers begin with the Kyrie, the traditional manner for a little office. The Lord's Prayer follows. When the doxology was first added to the Lord's Prayer, in the 1662 revision, it was not added in places where the Prayer was preceded by the Kyrie. The traditional language form of the Lord's Prayer is the 1549 version as revised in 1789. The contemporary language forms of both Kyrie and the Lord's Prayer are the texts prepared by ICET. The versicle "Lord, hear our prayer," with its response "And let our cry come to you" (Ps. 102:1a), appears before prayers in some of the medieval offices and has been used in some of the Prayer Book rites ever since 1549.

The use of one collect is required. The collect of the day may be used prior to, or in place of, one of the collects printed in the rite.

The first collect is from the 1928 revision of the American Book where it is used on the Monday of Whitsun week which previously had no collect. The author is unknown, but several of the phrases resemble those of the various collects appointed in the Sarum missal for use in the week following Pentecost. Using strong verbs we pray that the Holy Spirit may direct and rule us, comfort us, defend us, and lead us into all truth.

According to the Rev. Dr. John W. Suter, Sr., the second of the collects was composed by Bishop Arthur Cleveland Coxe (1818–1896) who was instrumental in publishing the works of the

Ante-Nicene Fathers. The prayer reminds us of the traditional association (in private devotions and in the office of Sext) between the noon hour and the Passion of our Lord. It recalls John 12:32: "I, when I am lifted up from the earth, will draw all people to myself." It has been included in recent revisions of the Prayer Book for other provinces of the Anglican Communion, beginning with the Canadian revision of 1922.

The Rev. Dr. William S. Langford, who for twelve years before his death in 1897 was General Secretary of the Board of Managers of the Domestic and Foreign Missionary Society, wrote the third prayer, according to the Rev. Dr. Suter. The scriptural reference is to the story of Paul's conversion (Acts 9:1–31 and 26:1–20). The Canadian revision of 1922 was the first edition to include this prayer. Since then it has been included in revisions for other provinces.

The fourth prayer, based on John 14:27, first appeared in the 1928 revision, printed as the first of a series of six collects, "To be used after the Collects of Morning or Evening Prayer, or Communion, at the discretion of the Minister." This revision prints it in the noonday office and also as the sixth collect for use after the Prayers of the People (p. 395). In late medieval missals, including some of the books of the Sarum rite, it is found as a private devotion of the priest in conjunction with the peace.

A rubric allows the use of free intercessions after the collect. The rite ends with the Benedicamus Domino, "Let us bless the Lord," and its response, "Thanks be to God," a traditional way to conclude a daily office. This is the first American edition of the Prayer Book to include this dismissal.

An Order of Worship for the Evening (pp. 108–114)

At the evening meal the Jews conducted a ritual blessing of light. The oldest regular evening services among Christians followed this Jewish custom at the dinner table. Evidence of such Christian ritual appears in the Apostolic Tradition of Hippolytus (Rome, c. A.D. 215). The evening service was introduced by a blessing of light (lucernarium) and included psalmody and prayers. It sometimes included an agapé meal.

Later the rite was transferred to the church building and the lamp lighting ceremony preceded a short service of psalms and prayers, and (on occasion) lessons from the Scriptures. Such a service is still the core of Vespers in the Eastern Orthodox churches. In the West it continued in the Mozarabic rite of Spain and the Ambrosian rite of northern Italy, but in much of the West it died out as the monastic hours of prayer replaced the old congregational or cathedral daily services.

A remnant of the lucernarium was retained, however, in the occasional blessing of light at evening in Christian homes. A *Book of Christian Prayers* (1578), put out under the authority of Queen Elizabeth, and a collection of private prayers, *Preces Privatae,* by the famous Anglican bishop Lancelot Andrewes, both contained thanksgivings for light, to be used in the evening.

The modern ceremony of lighting the candles in an Advent wreath may be a remnant of the ceremonies done in homes. Blessing of the new fire and the paschal candle developed from the primitive lucernarium. In recent years many places have revived the lucernarium because of its significant texts and ceremonies. This present revision is the first Prayer Book to contain this ancient rite.

Concerning the Service (p. 108)

The first paragraph points out the various ways the rite may be used. The longer form is a complete evening service for times when the gathered congregation includes a number of persons who do not say Evening Prayer daily and for whom the psalmody and lections of that rite would be unsuitable. The shorter form (see rubrics, p. 112) may serve as an introduction to Evening Prayer, which would then begin with the psalmody of the day, or to the Eucharist, which would begin with the salutation and the collect of the day. The shorter form is also appropriate for use in the home as an alternative, in the early evening, to the daily devotions for individuals and families; or it may precede a meal or other evening activity in the church or the parish house.

The second paragraph assigns portions of the rite to the various orders of ministers.

This rite is not appropriate for Monday, Tuesday, or Wednesday in Holy Week, or for Good Friday, as the third paragraph indicates. The mood of those days is penitential, and the lighting of the paschal candle will have more significance for the congregation that has not participated in a service of light so short a time before Easter. Maundy Thursday is exempted because an evening Eucharist on the eve celebrating its institution may appropriately begin with lighting of candles.

Alternatives for use in special seasons or on special days of the church year are suggested in place of the short lessons printed in the rite.

As with other rites printed only in contemporary language (see p. 14), the text may be adapted to traditional language by changing the pronouns and verbs.

The Entrance of the Ministers

The ministers may enter the dark church preceded by one or two lighted candles which would be held in a prominent place to provide light for the officiant. In the Easter season candles would not precede the officiant, since the paschal candle should be burning in its customary place and the officiant should go to that place to begin the service by its light. A musical prelude or processional is not suitable at this service (see pp. 142–143).

The Opening Acclamation (p. 109)

The normal greeting, adapted from the Mozarabic form, is like that which precedes the Exsultet and the blessing of the paschal candle at the Easter Vigil (p. 285). Throughout the Great Fifty Days, and in Lent and on other penitential occasions, the initial greeting is the same as the opening acclamation appointed for the Eucharist at such times.

The Short Lesson of Scripture (pp. 109–110)

The optional alternative lessons are provided for general use, to be read without announcement or conclusion. The section "Concerning the Service" (p. 108) suggests other lessons for certain days or seasons. The short lesson probably should be omitted if one or more lessons from scripture are to be read later in the service.

The Prayer for Light (pp. 110–111)

The rubric designates the prayer for light but permits the use of any of those printed here within the rite, or any other suitable prayer. The two prayers printed at the conclusion of the order (p. 113) would be suitable alternatives.

An eleventh century Ambrosian book appointed the first prayer for use at Vespers on common Fridays of the year.[1] Though good for general use, this prayer is particularly suitable for Pentecost, for light is used within the prayer as a sign of the Holy Spirit. The translation is by Capt. Howard E. Galley and the Rev. Dr. H. Boone Porter.

---

[1] Manuale Ambrosianum ex Codice Saec. XI, ed. M. Magistretti, Milan, 1905.

The second prayer, of Celtic origin, was adapted by the Rev. Grant M. Gallup from a prayer of Saint Columbanus.[1] In this prayer the light symbolizes charity.

The third prayer is of ancient Mozarabic origin, its source the Mozarabic breviary, Breviarium Gothicum,[2] where it was a fixed collect for use at the end of Vespers throughout the year. Capt. Howard E. Galley and the Rev. Dr. H. Boone Porter translated the prayer for this revision.

"A Collect for Aid Against Perils," the fourth prayer, has been included in every edition of the Prayer Book. It was among the prayers for Vespers in the Gelasian sacramentary (no. 1589) and in the Gallican Bobbio missal (no. 565). The Gregorian sacramentary (no. 936) places it with the prayers for the daily office; the Sarum rite appoints it for Compline.

Collects printed elsewhere in the Book are suggested for use in the season of Advent, and on Christmas, Epiphany, and other feasts of the incarnation.

Collects, based on earlier compositions by the Rev. Dr. H. Boone Porter, are provided for use at certain other times. The first is a prayer for light to be used in Lent and other times of penitence; the second a prayer for the Easter season which begins in the same way as the collect for use after the fifth lesson of the Easter Vigil. This prayer recalls the pillar of cloud by day and the pillar of fire by night which led the Hebrews out of Egypt, symbolized by the paschal candle. The third is a prayer for use on saints' festivals. Its address is related to the first of the proper prefaces for a saint (pp. 348 and 380) which is based on the conclusion of the prayer for the whole state of Christ's church in the Scottish Prayer Book of 1637. The petition contains an allusion to Hebrews 11:16.

The Lighting of Candles (p. 112)

When the service is held in a church, the altar candles are lighted after the prayer for light. Other candles in the hands of the congregation or placed about the building may then be lighted. At a service in a home, candles on the table, or on the Advent wreath in Advent season, or other candles may be lighted at this point.

The congregation should be able to focus on the action of the candle-lighting. A period of silence is suitable, or an appropriate

---

[1] John Gott, The Parish Priest of the Town, London: S.P.C.K., 1895.
[2] Patrologia Latina, ed. J. P. Migne, LXXXVI, cols. 50 and 1012.

psalm or anthem may be sung by cantor or choir. (See *The Book of Occasional Services*, pp. 8–14, for traditional anthems, including anthems for various seasons and holy days.)

O Gracious Light: Phos hilaron (p. 112)

The traditional candle-lighting hymn follows. This may be sung either in the prose version printed in the rite or in a metrical version, such as "O gladsome light," or "O brightness of the immortal Father's face," or "O gracious light, Lord Jesus Christ." Some other suitable evening or seasonal hymn may be used in its place, but Compline hymns and other hymns which speak of going to bed are not suitable in this context.

The Phos hilaron is a traditional hymn associated with the lucernarium. Basil the Great (A.D. 379) spoke of singing this ancient hymn as one of the cherished traditions of the church. Among the additional directions (p. 143) is the suggestion that if incense is used, it is especially appropriate during this hymn. The prose version for this edition was drafted by the Rev. Dr. Charles M. Guilbert.

The Continuation of the Service (pp. 112–113)

Rubrics designate how the service is to continue if it is an introduction to Evening Prayer or Eucharist, or if the shorter form is used. An order is also provided so that it may be extended to form a complete evening office.

The additional directions (p. 143) list suitable psalms for use with this service when the daily office lectionary or the proper of the day will not be used. The psalmody may be followed by silence or a collect or both. In some ancient rites it was customary for collects to follow the psalms of this office. The ancient psalter collects or various Prayer Book collects can be appropriately used.

A reading or readings from the Scriptures may come from the daily office lectionary or from the proper of the day, or a selection may be made especially for the occasion. A sermon, or homily, or a reading from Christian literature may follow the lections, or there may be a period of silence.

The order suggests the use of the traditional evening canticle, the Magnificat. Other suitable canticles include those which use the figure of light, such as Canticles 11; 4 or 16; 5 or 17: Surge, illuminare; Benedictus Dominus Deus; or Nunc dimittis. A hymn of praise may be used at this point instead of a canticle.

A litany (for example, one of the forms for the prayers of the people

138

in the Eucharist), a thanksgiving such as the General Thanksgiving (pp. 71 or 125), or other suitable devotions including the Lord's Prayer and possibly a hymn, precede the blessing or dismissal (p. 114). Both blessing and dismissal, of course, may be used.

Prayers (p. 113)

A rubric suggests options for a prayer to precede the blessing or dismissal. The collect for the day or a collect proper to the season is fitting on a feast day or a day of special significance. Several of the collects from Evening Prayer or Compline are suitable for use at the conclusion of this order. Two additional prayers are provided, either of which may be used as the prayer for light if they are not used at this point.

The first prayer was adapted by the Rev. Dr. H. Boone Porter from evening prayers in *Preces Privatae,* the private prayers of Bishop Lancelot Andrewes (1555–1626).

The second prayer is the evening collect for the lucernarium for Saturday and Sunday in the Taizé monastic community. We pray that we may discern the presence of God not only in His word and sacraments but also in the lives of those about us. This prayer recalls the question of the baptismal covenant, "Will you seek and serve Christ in all persons, loving your neighbor as yourself?"

The Blessing and Dismissal (p. 114)

The blessing printed on page 114 is the Aaronic benediction (Num. 6:24–26) cast in three-fold form as was typical of blessings in synagogue usage and in many of the ancient sacramentaries. (See also the blessing in A Thanksgiving for the Birth or Adoption of a Child, p. 445.) A deacon or lay person conducting the service is directed to substitute "us" for "you." One of the forms for dismissal from the Eucharist (pp. 339–340 and 366) or another form suited to the occasion may be used. An exchange of the Peace may also end the rite.

Daily Evening Prayer (pp. 61–73 and 115–126)

The structure of this office is the same as that of Morning Prayer. The 1549 Prayer Book titled the service "An Order for Evensong throughout the Year" using the popular name for the office of Vespers—"Evensong." The title in 1552 was changed to "An Order for Evening Prayer throughout the Year." The 1662 revision made another change, "An Order for Evening Prayer, Daily throughout the

Year," which the American Book of 1789 shortened to "An Order for Daily Evening Prayer." In the present revision, the word "order" has been dropped from the title; strictly speaking the service is not an order but a rite.

As in Morning Prayer, the service may begin with an opening sentence of scripture or may begin immediately with the versicle preceding the initial Gloria Patri. The first three sentences date from the 1892 revision; the remainder are new to this Book. An alternative beginning is the service of light (pp. 109–112) from An Order of Worship for the Evening. When that is used, Evening Prayer begins after the Phos hilaron with the psalmody of the office.

The longer bidding to the confession is an abbreviated version of that for Morning Prayer.

The Invitatory and Psalter (pp. 63 and 117)

The versicle, "O God, make speed to save us," and its response, "O Lord, make haste to help us" (Ps. 70:1), was retained from the Sarum offices in the 1549 Book for the beginning of Evensong. In 1552, for some reason, it was preceded by the opening versicle of Morning Prayer, "O Lord, open thou our lips." The first American Book retained the opening versicle in both rites, but the second versicle was dropped. The present edition restores the versicle at the beginning of Evening Prayer, as at the opening of the little offices for noon and for the close of the day.

O Gracious Light: Phos hilaron (pp. 64 and 118)

The medieval offices normally used a variable hymn near the beginning of the office, before the psalmody or immediately after it. The 1979 Book restores this for the noonday office, the Order of Worship for the Evening, and Evening Prayer. Printed in the rite is the ancient candle-lighting hymn, the Phos hilaron (see above, p. 138, for commentary). This hymn or a metrical version of it, or some other evening hymn, or a seasonal hymn, is especially fitting at this point in the rite. The Venite or Jubilate from Morning Prayer may be substituted.

The Lessons (pp. 64–65 and 118–119)

The lectionary for the daily offices assumes the use of one New Testament lesson at Evening Prayer (the Gospel in Year One and the Epistle in Year Two). If the proper Old Testament lesson has been used in the morning and an Old Testament reading is still desired as the first of two lections at Evening Prayer, the reading of the alternate year is used (p. 934).

The Canticles (pp. 119–120)

Each reading is followed by a canticle. Any of those printed in Morning Prayer (pp. 47–52 or 85–95) may be used. The Magnificat was the climactic canticle in the medieval breviaries of the Western church, on occasion accompanied by incense, which introduced the prayers of the rite at Vespers (see p. 152). The Nunc dimittis was sung at Compline. Cranmer retained the Magnificat as a response to the first lesson and the Nunc dimittis as response to the second. Though alternatives were provided in 1552, the two canticles have occupied these positions in every Prayer Book except that of 1789. The table of suggested canticles (p. 145) recommends the use of one or the other as the climactic canticle leading into prayers, and suggests the use of another canticle after the first reading when two lections are read except on Sundays and holy days.

The Prayers (pp. 67–73 and 121–126)

The first set of suffrages (A) is the same as the first set for Morning Prayer. The second set (B), new to this revision, is based on the concluding litany of the evening office in Eastern churches.

Previous editions of the Prayer Book have required the use of the collect of the day and two "fixed collects"—a "Collect for Peace" and "A Collect for Aid against Perils"—at Evening Prayer. This edition, as is true of Morning Prayer, permits one or more of eight collects to be said. The Book provides special collects for three days of the week along with four others to make possible a weekly cycle. The fourth of these is especially appropriate for Thursday evenings, since it recalls the institution of the Eucharist on that day. The collect of the day may be used in place of or in addition to one or more of these collects.

A Collect for Sundays (pp. 69 and 123)

This collect, new to this revision, is based on Revelation 21. It stresses two themes associated with the Lord's Day. Sunday is the day of the resurrection, and it is the foretaste or pledge of the eschaton. This is a revised version of one of the original prayers of William Bright printed in the appendix to his *Ancient Collects*, page 234.

A Collect for Fridays (pp. 69 and 123)

The 1892 Book adapted this prayer from *The Priest's Prayer Book*[1] as one of the three additional prayers printed at the end of the burial rite. It is retained in that position in the Burial of the Dead: Rite Two in this edition (p. 504), but is also given wider exposure through its use in the daily office. Scriptural allusions include: 1 Cor. 15:54–57; Jn. 14:6; 1 Cor. 15:17–19; 1 Thess. 4:14–15; and Rom. 6:5.

A Collect for Saturdays (pp. 69 and 123)

The present edition takes this prayer from *A Chain of Prayer Across the Ages*[2] which adapted it from the Sarum breviary. This collect is particularly appropriate for the eve of Sunday, the day of light and the foretaste of the eschaton.

A Collect for Peace (pp. 69 and 123)

In the Gelasian (no. 1472) and Gregorian (no. 1343) sacramentaries and the Sarum missal, this is the initial collect of the Mass for peace. It was also included among the prayers after the rogation litany in the Sarum processional and also used at Vespers in the Sarum breviary. Surely this was the inspiration for its position as one of the two fixed collects for Evening Prayer in all previous Prayer Books. The Latin might be more literally translated, "that the fear of our enemies having been removed, we may pass our time in rest and quietness." This revision substitutes "all enemies" for "our enemies." The preamble makes a succinct statement of the way God's grace works in our lives. It is God who kindles holy desires, transforms them into purposeful resolutions, and finally brings them to fruition in works of justice. We pray for God's peace (Jn. 14:27) in order that we may "pass our time in rest and quietness" and "that our hearts may be set to obey thy commandments." Or, in the contemporary language version, "that our minds may be fixed on the doing of your will."

A Collect for Aid Against Perils (pp. 70 and 123)

This collect is included among the prayers for Vespers in the Gelasian sacramentary (no. 1589) and the Gallican Bobbio missal (no. 565), and is also among the prayers for the daily office in the Gregorian sacramentary (no. 936), and in the Sarum office of Compline. The

---

[1] R. F. Littledale and J. Edward Vaux, seventh ed., London: Longmans, Green & Co., 1890.
[2] Fox; *Chain*, p. 210.

American revision of 1789 provided a new preamble parallel to the Collect for Grace in Morning Prayer: "O Lord, our heavenly Father, by whose almighty power we have been preserved this day; by thy great mercy defend us from all perils and dangers of this night, for the love of thy only Son, our Saviour, Jesus Christ. *Amen.*" The source of the change seems to have been *A New Liturgy* (1749). Support for the change resulted from difficulty over the play on the words "light" and "darkness" in the 1662 form and the 1786 proposal. The version of the English Book was restored in 1892. This was one of the two fixed collects of Evening Prayer in all earlier Books.

A Collect for Protection (pp. 70 and 124)

The Rev. Dr. William Reed Huntington included this prayer in his work *Materia Ritualis*. It first appeared in the 1928 Book, although it was proposed for the 1892 revision. It is a cento of phrases from William Bright's translations, *Ancient Collects* (pp. 10–11). The preamble is taken from the Mozarabic breviary[1] and the conclusion of the petition is from the Gelasian sacramentary (no. 1594).

A Collect for the Presence of Christ (pp. 70 and 124)

This collect, based upon the story of the appearance to the disciples at Emmaus (Lk. 24:13–35), is from the Roman breviary of Paul VI, where it is appointed for use at Vespers on Monday of Week 4.

Prayer for Mission (pp. 70–71 and 124–125)

The rubric directs that one of the three prayers for mission be said following the collect (or collects) if the Eucharist or a form of general intercession is not to follow.

The first prayer is from *Memorials Upon Several Occasions*, a volume published anonymously in 1933.[2]

Saint Augustine of Hippo is the source for the second prayer which is also the first of the intercessions of Compline (p. 134).

The third prayer is a revised version of one of William Bright's translations in *Ancient Collects* (p. 175). The source is the Gelasian sacramentary, in which it is the second of two prayers for those coming into a house (no. 1555).

---

[1] Migne, *Pat. Lat.* LXXXVI, col. 705.
[2] The author was the editor of the volume, Eric Milner-White.

The remaining rubrics and texts are the same as those which follow the prayers for mission in Morning Prayer.

An Order for Compline (pp. 127–135)

Compline originated in the fourth century as the night prayers of monks in their dormitories. In his *Rule,* Benedict of Nursia describes the content of the rite in the sixth century: "Let Compline be limited to the saying of three psalms, which are to be said straightforwardly without antiphons, after which let there be the hymn of that hour, a lesson, a versicle, the Kyrie, and a blessing to conclude." The psalms at Compline are fixed, "Let the same psalms be repeated every day at Compline which are Psalms 4, 91, and 134." Late in the middle ages the office of Vespers was moved earlier in the day and Compline was often said in church. It attracted various accretions: the Lord's Prayer and the Ave Maria at the beginning, antiphons for the psalms, the Nunc dimittis with an antiphon, the Lord's Prayer again, the Apostles' Creed, a confession and absolution, and prayers at the end.

From the late medieval rite the 1549 Prayer Book took the Nunc dimittis, the Lord's Prayer, the Apostles' Creed, and "A Collect for Aid Against Perils" into its service of Evening Prayer (Evensong). The Primers of Henry VIII and Elizabeth, and John Cosin's work *A Collection of Private Devotions,* provided forms for a simple office of Compline.

Over the last several decades Compline has been revived in various Anglican communities and at camps and conferences. The Irish revision of 1926, the English of 1928, the Scottish of 1929, the Canadian of 1959, and the Indian of 1963 all contain Compline rites. The present edition is the first American Prayer Book to include it.

The Blessing and the Confession of Sin (pp. 127–128)

The officiant begins the rite with a blessing, a post-Reformation Roman addition to the office, as are also the versicle and response which follow (Ps. 124:8). In the late medieval form the confession was near the end of the rite, but was moved to the beginning in the Roman rite and in the Scottish Prayer Book of 1929. This parallels the position of the confession in Morning and Evening Prayer since that was made part of the office in the 1552 revision. The first part of the optional confession is based upon modern Anglican adaptations of the Sarum form:

144

I confess to God, to Blessed Mary, to all the saints, and to you: I have sinned exceedingly through my fault, in thought, word, and deed. I pray Holy Mary and all the saints of God and you to pray for me.

The phrase "and in what we have left undone" recalls a phrase from the general confession in Rite Two versions of Morning and Evening Prayer and Holy Eucharist. The rest of the prayer depends upon the first form of confession in the Holy Eucharist: Rite One (p. 331). The absolution is a shortened form of that from the Sarum office of Compline.

Versicle and Response (p. 128)

The basic portion of the rite opens with the traditional versicle for the beginning of an office (Ps. 70:1) followed by the Gloria Patri—the model given by Benedict for beginning the various offices of the day.

The Psalms (pp. 128–131)

The three fixed psalms of Benedict's Rule (4, 91, and 134) are printed in the rite. Psalm 31:1–5, which was used in the Sarum office of Compline, is also included, and a rubric gives freedom to use other suitable psalms.

The Lesson (pp. 131–132)

A suitable passage of scripture is to be read. Four short passages are printed in place for the convenience of the reader, the first of these a fixed lesson at Compline in the Sarum breviary. The next two have been provided in other recent editions of Anglican Prayer Books. The fourth, in the Roman rite and in some of the recent Anglican provisions, has been read immediately after the blessing at the opening of the office.

The Hymn (p. 132)

In the Sarum breviary, the early English primers, and other Anglican Prayer Books, the hymn follows the lesson rather than preceding it as was the custom in the Rule of Benedict and the old Roman rite. The ancient hymn, Te lucis, is traditionally used in this office; the most familiar translation of it begins "To thee before the close of day." Another ancient hymn, Christe qui lux est et dies, was substituted for it in many medieval forms of Compline.

145

The Versicles (p. 132)

The first, "Into your hands, O Lord, I commend my spirit," and its response, "For you have redeemed me, O Lord, O God of truth" (Ps. 31:5), have been included in some of the recent Anglican versions of the office. The second versicle, "Keep us, O Lord, as the apple of your eye," and its response, "Hide us under the shadow of your wings" (Ps. 17:8), are found in the medieval Sarum and Roman forms. The prayers begin as is traditional with a little office, with the Kyrie. The Lord's Prayer ends with "deliver us from evil" as did all uses of the Prayer in earlier editions of the Prayer Book. In the revision of 1662, following the custom of the Scottish Prayer Book of 1637, a doxology was added in some places where the Prayer was not preceded by the Kyrie. The traditional language version of the Lord's Prayer is that of 1549 as revised in 1789; the contemporary form of both Kyrie and Lord's Prayer are those of ICET. The versicle, "Lord, hear our prayer," and the response, "And let our cry come to you" (Ps. 102:1a), preceded some prayers in the medieval books and has been used in some Prayer Book rites ever since 1549.

The Collects (p. 133)

The first of the four alternative collects of Compline is "A Collect for Aid Against Perils," a part of the service of Evening Prayer in every edition of the Prayer Book. It had been included among the prayers for Vespers in the Gelasian sacramentary (no. 1589) and the Gallican Bobbio missal (no. 565). It is also among the prayers for the daily office of the Gregorian sacramentary (no. 936) and in the Sarum office of Compline.

The second prayer dates to the Leonine sacramentary (no. 593) and the Gregorian (no. 941) where it is found among the prayers for the daily office. The Irish revision of 1926 included it in its alternate evening rite, the English revision of 1928 in the Compline rite, and it is in the Scottish (1929) and Canadian (1959) Compline services. The translation from William Bright's *Ancient Collects* (p. 10) reads:

> Be present, O Lord, to our prayers and protect us by day and night; that in all successive changes of times we may ever be strengthened by Thine unchangeableness; through Christ our Lord.

The third prayer, a revised version of an ancient prayer common to the Compline office of other recent Anglican Prayer Books, reads (in other versions):

146

Look down, O Lord, from thy heavenly throne, illuminate the darkness of this night with thy celestial brightness, and from the sons of light banish the deeds of darkness; through Jesus Christ our Lord. *Amen.*

The fourth prayer is the Compline collect of the Roman breviary which has also been included in the Compline office of several recent Anglican revisions.

A *Collect for Saturdays* (p. 134)

The Saturday collect of the daily office of the Taizé community is the source for this prayer, with some changes made for the present revision.

Intercessory Prayer (p. 134)

The first two of the printed intercessory prayers, from the writings of Saint Augustine of Hippo, is also printed in Evening Prayer as one of the collects for mission.

The Rev. Dr. Charles Guilbert composed the second of the intercessory prayers—for those who work while others sleep.

The rubric provides for a period of silence and for individual intercessions and thanksgivings after the prayers of office.

The Conclusion (pp. 134–135)

In the Sarum office and in recent Anglican Prayer Books, the Nunc dimittis (see p. 116) with its traditional Compline antiphon preceded the prayers, coming after the lesson and the hymn. In this revision it is suitably placed near the close of the rite. Only the Benedicamus, with which the offices have often ended, follows it and finally, the blessing of the officiant, which is found in the Roman rite and in the offices of recent Anglican Prayer Books, though not in the rite of the Sarum breviary.

Daily Devotions for Individuals and Families (pp. 136–140)

As early as the time of Queen Elizabeth a series of "Godly Prayers" for individual or family use was sometimes bound with the Prayer Book. The first American revision included forms for family prayer abbreviated from those published by Edmund Gibson (1705), later bishop of London, for use in his Lambeth parish. These owed some of their phrases to "A Form of Prayers Used by His Late Majesty King

147

William III," printed in the works of John Tillotson, Archbishop of Canterbury. Gibson's prayers were reprinted many times through the years and distributed liberally in the colonies by the Society for the Propagation of Christian Knowledge (SPCK). The work had been through thirty editions by the year 1789. Popularity of the forms faded by the time of the 1928 revision which provided shorter forms for both morning and evening. Each called for a brief passage of scripture followed by the Lord's Prayer and a collect ("A Collect for Grace" in the morning; "A Collect for Aid Against Perils" in the evening). The Grace (2 Cor. 13:14) concluded the morning prayers and the Aaronic benediction (Num. 6:24–26) the evening prayers. The present revision gives more flexible forms which follow the structure of the daily offices, corresponding to the regular services for morning, noon, early evening, and the close of the day.

The directions (p. 136) recommend possible options for use as psalms, readings, and prayers. The basic structure of each office is psalmody, a lesson from the scripture, and prayer. The morning office may be enriched by a hymn or canticle and the Apostles' Creed following the lesson and a period of silence. The rite for the early evening begins with the Phos hilaron, the ancient candle lighting hymn, rather than with psalmody. The Order of Worship for Evening may be substituted. In a service in which prayers of thanksgiving for the blessings of the day and of penitence for sins have closed the day, Nunc dimittis is a most appropriate canticle.

The prayers are from the regular offices: "A Collect for Grace" from the morning rite; prayers from An Order of Service for Noonday (p. 107) at noon; "A Collect for the Presence of Christ" for early evening; and a prayer and blessing from Compline (pp. 133 and 135) for the close of the day.

Additional Directions (pp. 141–143)

Morning and Evening Prayer (pp. 141–142)

Opening Sentences (p. 141)

Any of the opening sentences may be used at any time at the discretion of the officiant. Those of Epiphany, for example, or the last of those for the Easter season, would be suitable when a missionary theme is stressed. The last of those appointed for use at any time might appropriately be used during Lent, even though it is not printed among those for Lent.

Antiphons (p. 141)

The proper antiphons printed before the Venite may be used with either the Venite or the Jubilate. Antiphons may also be used with the psalmody of the day or with the biblical canticles (1–5 and 8–19). These may be drawn from the psalms or from the opening sentences or from other passages of scripture. (For further discussion of how antiphons may be used see p. 935 of the Prayer Book. See also *The Prayer Book Office,* compiled and edited by Howard Galley, New York: The Seabury Press, 1980.)

Gloria Patri (p. 141)

Normative uses of the Gloria Patri are these: among the opening preces; at the end of the psalmody; following the canticles with which it is printed. The directions here also permit the use of the Gloria Patri after the invitatory psalm or the canticle Pascha nostrum, and after each psalm and each section of Psalm 119. It is not to be used after any canticle in which it is not printed since these canticles have special doxologies of their own (i.e. canticles 1, 2, 6, 7, 12, 13, 14, 18, 20, and 21). The Gloria Patri may be omitted after any canticle even though it is printed there. Within the text of the rites the Gloria Patri is divided in halves for use with plainchant, a single Anglican chant, or the last half of a double chant. An alternative pointing for use with a double chant is printed here. The translation from the previous editions of the Prayer Book is also printed, with permission for its use in Rite One services of the daily office. The use of this form may be advisable when the people have this text printed with the music being sung (e.g. canticle settings in the Hymnal 1940).

Metrical Versions of Invitatory Psalms and Canticles (p. 141)

The use of metrical (poetic) versions of the invitatory psalms and canticles is explicitly permitted. For example, there is the version of Psalm 100 (Jubilate) which dates to the earliest Anglican metrical psalter, "All people that on earth do dwell," or the Song of the Redeemed, Magna et mirabilia, by Henry U. Onderdonk, an early bishop of Pennsylvania, worded "How wondrous and great thy works, God of praise."

Hymns (p. 142)

The permission to use a hymn in place of a canticle in special circumstances should not be abused. When the daily office is done with small children not adept at chanting, or on some special feast when none of the canticles makes clear reference to the doctrine or

149

event being celebrated, it would be fitting to substitute a hymn for one of the canticles.

The Creed (p. 142)

The Nicene Creed or the Apostles' Creed (within the reaffirmation of baptismal vows) is required at the Eucharist on Sundays and major holy days. On these days and on other occasions when the Creed will follow at the Eucharist, the Apostles' Creed may be omitted from an office which precedes it. On weekdays the Creed is required at only one of the daily offices.

The Lord's Prayer (p. 142)

Because the Lord's Prayer occupies a climactic place in the Great Litany and in the Eucharist, it may be omitted from the daily office when the Litany or the Eucharist is to follow immediately.

Intercessions and Thanksgivings (p. 142)

At the time of intercessions and thanksgivings in the office individual members of the congregation may add their own petitions and thanksgivings. There is also opportunity for silent prayer.

A Sermon (p. 142)

For the first time an Anglican Prayer Book gives explicit permission to preach a sermon in the context of the daily office. Rubric allots three positions, but the most logical place with the most precedent is immediately following the lessons. In the early years of the church, homilies or instructions frequently followed the readings at liturgies of the word or at daily offices. The 1662 Prayer Book designated the place for instruction and catechizing immediately after the second lesson at Evening Prayer; through much of Anglican history this seems to have been the place for a sermon preached outside the context of Ante-Communion. There is also substantial precedent in Anglicanism for placing the sermon soon after the lections, following the collects and anthem of the daily office. Though Sunday morning sermons were preached as part of the Ante-Communion until the last century, on Sundays at Evening Prayer or on other occasions they occurred after the fixed collects. The practice of preaching a sermon after the conclusion of Morning Prayer, widely separated from the lections, began only within the past few decades. Before the 1892 revision, all editions of the Prayer Book had assumed that the Sunday morning rite would consist of Morning Prayer, the Litany, and the Eucharist, with the sermon as part of the Eucharist. If there were not a representative group of communicants, however, the service might conclude with the prayer for the whole state of the church, collects, and the blessing. The 1789 revision permitted the Ante-Communion to be read through the Gospel, followed by sermon, prayers, and blessing. Toward the end of the last century the Litany and Ante-Communion were eliminated, leaving the sermon widely separated from the scripture readings. Since this revision gives permission to preach immediately after the readings, perhaps the sermon will return to its right relationship with the lessons in the daily office, just as it now is in the Eucharist.

Non-Biblical Readings (p. 142)

Biblical readings may be followed by a reading from non-biblical Christian literature. A few of the many possibilities for such use on occasion are expositions or writings from the church fathers, writings of metaphysical poets, passages from certain of the lives of the saints, or the devotional writings of preachers such as Andrewes and Donne.

An Offering (p. 142)

This is the first Anglican Prayer Book which clearly allows an offering from the general congregation at a daily office. Previously the Prayer Books had confined this action to the Eucharist. Probably the most suitable time for receiving such an offering would be during the hymn or anthem after the collects and prayer for mission, and prior to the intercessions and thanksgivings.

When There is a Communion (p. 142)

Morning or Evening Prayer may be used as the liturgy of the word at the Eucharist. In such circumstances a lesson from the Gospel is always to be read. When Morning Prayer is used in this way on weekdays, making use of the daily office lectionary, the Gospel would be read in the morning rather than in the evening in Year One. For an Evening Prayer preceding the Eucharist the Gospel would be read in the evening rather than in the morning of Year Two. On Sunday mornings, all three lections for the Eucharist would be used in the order planned over two centuries ago by Thomas Rattray, a Scottish Episcopal bishop: first lesson, canticle, second lesson, canticle, Gospel, sermon, creed, and prayers. The celebrant using the daily office as liturgy of the word may pass directly from the creed and salutation to the collect of the day; the Lord's Prayer will follow the Great Thanksgiving, and the content of the suffrages will be covered within the form of the prayers of the people conforming to the directions on page 383. The prayer for mission may be omitted since a full form of the prayers of the people is required.

Order of Worship for the Evening (pp. 142–143)

These additional directions provide various alternatives and indicate ceremonial actions which pertain to this order. The content has largely been included in the commentary on the rite.

Incense (p. 143)

This is the first edition of the Prayer Book to mention the use of incense. A similar direction is provided in describing the setting apart of the altar at the consecration of a church (p. 576). In the ancient Jewish temple an incense offering was burned by the priest every morning and evening at the altar of incense located in front of the veil shielding the holy of holies (Ex. 30:1–10; Lk. 1:8–23). Incense, thought to have purificatory powers, was used in times of sickness and to cleanse places where animals were slaughtered for sacrifice. It was a worthy expensive gift (Song of Songs 3:6; Mt. 2:11; Phil. 4:18; Rev. 18:13), thought to be pleasing to God and efficacious for the atonement of sins (Lev. 16:12–13; Num. 16:46–48; Dt. 33:10). Incense signified the ascent of prayers of the people to God (Ps. 141:2; Rev. 5:8 and 8:3–4). The smoke of incense is also seen in both the Old and New Testaments as the manifestation of God's glory (1 Kg. 8:10–11; Is. 6:6–8; Ezek. 44:4; Rev. 15:8). Zechariah's vision comes at the offering of incense (Lk. 2:8–23).

The use of incense was rejected by the early church because of the Roman custom of offering incense to a pagan deity or to the emperor, for Christians a sign of apostasy. From the fourth century, after the legalization of Christianity and the conversion of Constantine, incense was on occasion carried before the clergy in procession (as it had been carried on state occasions before civic officials) or before the dead. Eventually it was also carried before the Gospel book which symbolized the presence of Christ in His word, or at the offertory which symbolized Christ present in His sacrament. Its function was honorific, fumigatory, and festive. Later it attracted allegorical interpretations, based on various references to incense in the Scriptures. Hence it came to be used at the Phos hilaron or Psalm 141 in evening services; at the climactic canticle of Lauds, the Benedictus Dominus Deus, or of Vespers, the Magnificat, which introduced the prayers of the rite; and during the eucharistic prayer.

152

Suggested Canticles at Morning Prayer and at Evening Prayer (pp. 144–145)

This table of canticles is based upon certain historic associations of canticles and themes with particular days of the week. The Te Deum, for example, has been used in the West from very early times as the climactic canticle of Matins on Sundays and some of the major feasts except in Advent, Pre-Lent, and Lent. These associations are described in the commentaries on the individual canticles.

Psalm 95: Traditional (p. 146)

Psalm 95 in the version of the 1549 Prayer Book (except for the substitution of "hand" for "hands" in 1662) is printed here in its entirety so that this version may be used with Rite One on Ash Wednesday, Holy Saturday, and the Fridays in Lent when it is appointed for use in the morning office in place of the 1789 version of the Venite (printed in the rite itself). It may be used in place of the Venite at any time.

The Great Litany

The original meaning of "litany" in Greek was "prayer" or "supplication," but its modern connotation limits it to a particular type of prayer in which the people make fixed responses to short biddings or petitions sung or said by a lay person, deacon, or priest. Other religions, including Judaism, have used the form for hymns and psalms as well as prayers. Psalm 136, for example, must have been sung by a cantor with the congregation making the fixed response, "For his mercy endures for ever." This responsorial method of singing psalms and prayers came into use in the Eastern church within the fourth century, if not earlier. It is the method prescribed for gradual psalm and for the prayers of the people in the Apostolic Constitutions (c. A.D. 380). Within the prayers the people's response was Kyrie eleison.

The responsorial psalm or prayer was used not only in the church but in public processions, often in rivalry with similar public processions of the Arian heretics. Soon the West adopted responsorial psalmody and prayer, replacing pagan processions with processional litanies begging divine protection for the crops. About 467, when the city of Vienne was terrorized by earthquakes, Mamertus, the bishop, inaugurated processional litanies on the Monday, Tuesday, and Wednesday before Ascension Day. Other churches in Gaul soon adopted these "rogation days" which gradually spread throughout the Western church. The synod of Clovesho decreed that they should be observed in England and they were eventually adopted in Rome under Leo III (795–816). Before this, furthermore, in the papacy of Gregory the Great (590–604), April 25 had been observed as the day of the "major litany" replacing a pagan festival, the Robigalia, which had been celebrated with processions in honor of Robigo, believed to be a protector of the crops.

The litany form of prayer was in use in the church in Rome as early as the time of Pelagius I (492–496). He inaugurated the use of a litany of intercession, known as a "deprecatio," at the beginning of the Mass. Gregory the Great confined the use of the litany to certain special days, but nine repetitions of the litany response, Kyrie eleison, were retained. The use of threefold and sixfold repetitions probably came several centuries later. Litanies of the type of the Gelasian deprecatio spread throughout the West and are still used in conjunction with the Kyrie in the Ambrosian rite of Milan.

Another type of Eastern litany was introduced in Rome by a Greek-speaking Syrian pope, Sergius I (687–701). Originally intended for private rather than public use, this litany included an invocation of saints and special devotions to the cross and to Christ as the Lamb of God. It contained only one intercession with the response, "We beseech thee to hear us."

Eventually the two types of litanies were fused. The litany in general use throughout the West late in the middle ages can be divided into six parts: after an introductory Kyrie were (1) invocations to the Holy Trinity with the response "have mercy on us;" (2) invocations to the saints with the response "Pray for us;" (3) deprecations, or prayers for deliverance, with the response "Deliver us, Lord;" (4) obsecrations, or appeals for deliverance recalling events in the life of our Lord, also with the response "Deliver us, Lord;" (5) intercessions, with the response "We beseech thee to hear us;" and (6) concluding invocations addressed to Christ as the Son of God and the Lamb of God. The litany was followed by the Kyrie. If a Eucharist were to follow, the concluding Kyrie took the place of the Kyrie in the Mass. In the Sarum processional the Kyrie was followed by the Lord's Prayer, suffrages, and collects. The litany was used not only on rogation days and April 25, but also, in whole or in part, preceding the blessing of the font at the Easter Vigil and at the ordination of priests and deacons. During Lent it was said kneeling daily after the little office of Terce, and sung in procession after the office of None before the Mass on Wednesdays and Fridays. In times of emergency it was used in procession on Wednesdays and Fridays.

The Litany was the first rite published in English, in 1544, as a special supplication when Henry VIII was at war with Scotland and France. Prefixed to it was an exhortation to prayer "to be read to the people in every church afore processions." The Litany was to be used in procession on the accustomed days.

155

In constructing the Litany of 1544, Thomas Cranmer, then Archbishop of Canterbury, had for his principal sources the Sarum litanies for rogations and processions and the hour of death, Luther's litany, and the litany from the liturgy of Saint John Chrysostom. He added various details from litanies used in England and Germany. Like the Sarum litany for the dying, Cranmer's litany begins with the invocation of the Trinity rather than with the customary Kyrie and "Christ, hear us." The third of the invocations is filled out from the Nicene Creed; the fourth, addressed to the Trinity, uses an antiphon to the Athanasian Creed from the Sarum breviary. The Kyrie eleison is expanded to read "have mercy upon us miserable sinners."

The invocations are not treated as versicles and responses; each is repeated in full by the people. For the several invocations to Mary, Cranmer substituted one, "Holy Virgin Mary ["Saint Mary" in another printing], Mother of God our Savior Jesus Christ, pray for us." The invocations addressed to the angels were grouped into one, "All holy angels and archangels, and all holy orders of blessed spirits, pray for us." In place of the lengthy invocation of many saints by name he had "All holy patriarchs, and prophets, apostles, martyrs, confessors, and virgins, and all the blessed company of heaven, pray for us."

In the medieval litanies the deprecations had been introduced by a brief versicle, "Be gracious," and a response, "Spare us, Lord." Cranmer substituted for this a long petition from an antiphon based on Tobit 3:3 and Joel 2:17 which was appointed in the Sarum breviary for use with psalms said prior to the litany in Lent. The latter portion was also used with the penitential psalms before the litany for the dying. Both medieval and Lutheran litanies contained a number of short deprecations, each followed by the response "Deliver us, Lord." Cranmer grouped several of the deprecations together and followed each group with the response "Good Lord, deliver us." Sarum and Lutheran litanies were his principal sources for the various petitions. Among the deprecations was one asking to be delivered from "the tyranny of the bishop of Rome and all his detestable enormities."

The obsecrations were essentially the fuller form of Luther's litany, though the circumcision, found in the Sarum litany, but not in Luther's, is included. This section ends with petitions from Luther's litany, that we may be delivered both in times of tribulation and of wealth, in the hour of death and in the day of judgment. The intercessions were also grouped together and the response "We beseech thee to hear us" was expanded to, "We beseech thee to hear us, good Lord." Some intercessions are from the Sarum litany, but more are from Luther. Cranmer was possibly also influenced by Quiñones' litany, by the litanies of the liturgy of Chrysostom, and by litanies from other as yet unidentified sources. The first several intercessions expressed concern for the life of the church and the state. These were followed by intercessions for those with special needs, and the section concluded with supplications for material and spiritual blessings. The petition, "Son of God, we beseech thee to hear us," was followed by an unusual form of the Agnus Dei which retained only the last two petitions instead of the three common to medieval litanies and to Luther's. The suffrage, "O Christ, hear us," was followed by a six-fold Kyrie and the Lord's Prayer said by the minister, using the short Lukan form with the final phrase "But deliver us from evil. Amen" as a response.

Cranmer omitted a number of the suffrages which followed in medieval forms and imitated Luther in going immediately to the versicle "O Lord, deal not with us after our sins," its response, and a prayer which is Luther's version of a medieval collect found also in a Sarum Mass for the troubled in heart.

Next was an antiphon (Ps. 44:26), followed by the first verse of the psalm (probably a remnant of the use of the entire psalm), a variant form of the antiphon, and the Gloria Patri. The Sarum custom was to sing this before the procession.

The next portion of the Litany, a set of suffrages, drew from the Sarum supplication for use in time of war. This material can be traced to a tenth century pontifical associated with the name of Egbert, Archbishop of York (734–766). The Litany concluded with six prayers, which would eventually be used in various ways in later Prayer Books. (See pp. 130–131, 162, 220, and 557–558.)

In 1545 the Litany was ordered to be said in procession on Sundays and festival days, replacing the usual procession before the Mass. The Edwardian injunctions of August 1547 directed that the priest and choir sing or say the Litany kneeling in the midst of the church, "and none other procession or litany to be had or used but the said litany in English."

The 1549 Book contained the Litany printed as an appendix to the Eucharist. It was to be said or sung kneeling in the midst of the church on Wednesdays and Fridays before the liturgy of the word. Invocations beseeching the Virgin Mary, the angels, and the saints to intercede were deleted. Of the six prayers printed at the end of the 1544 Litany only the first and the last remained, although the first was amplified by incorporation of some material from the fifth prayer of the earlier series.

The Litany was placed after the daily office in the 1552 revision "to be used upon Sundays, Wednesdays, and Fridays, and at other times, when it shall be commanded by the Ordinary." Two occasional prayers, for rain and for fair weather, which had followed the Eucharist in the 1549 Book, and four prayers new to the 1552 edition, were printed between the two final prayers of the Litany. The four new prayers were alternatives for use "in time of dearth and famine," and prayers for use "in the time of war" and "in the time of any common plague or sickness."

In 1559, the revisers dropped the petition referring to the pope's enormities. The occasional prayers were printed after rather than within the Litany, followed by the first of the 1544 prayers which had not been included in 1549 and 1552. A prayer for the queen and a prayer for the clergy and people—which had been among the prayers at the end of the 1544 Litany—were printed between the last two prayers. The Grace (2 Cor. 13:14) followed the Prayer of Saint Chrysostom.

Occasional thanksgivings were provided in the 1604 revision to correspond to the occasional prayers of the 1559 Book: for rain, for fair weather, for plenty, for peace, and for deliverance from plague or sickness.

In 1662 the suffrages were amplified to include petition for deliverance from rebellion and from schisms, additions prompted by the recent civil war and by the divisions threatening the church. In the supplication for clergy the words "Bishops, Priests, and Deacons" replaced the words "Bishops, pastors, and ministers" which had been taken from Luther's work. This was an assertion of the threefold ordained ministry over the rival presbyterian and congregational polities. The occasional prayers were separated from the Litany and given their own heading. The prayers for the sovereign and for the clergy and people were printed at the end of the daily offices, along with the Prayer of Saint Chrysostom and the Grace, which continued to be printed at the end of the Litany as well. Previously the minister alone had said the Lord's Prayer and the Gloria Patri; this edition bade the people to say the Lord's Prayer with the minister and to use the Gloria Patri as versicle and response.

The American revision of 1789 made several substitutions in addition to the changes in petitions for civil rulers. "In all time of our prosperity" replaced "in all time of our wealth," "From all inordinate and sinful affections" was substituted for "From fornication, and all other deadly sin," and "to love and fear thee" replaced "to love and dread thee." The minister was also permitted to omit everything from the Agnus Dei to the prayer which begins "We humbly beseech thee, O Father." The General Thanksgiving from among the occasional prayers and thanksgivings of the 1662 Book was printed in the Litany just before the Prayer of Saint Chrysostom.

The 1892 revision inserted an additional supplication, "That it may please thee to send forth labourers into thy harvest."

Prayer Books since 1552 had directed that the Litany be used after the fixed collects of Morning Prayer on Sundays, Wednesdays, and Fridays; the 1928 revision permitted its use at any time after the fixed collects of Morning or Evening Prayer, or prior to the Eucharist, or separately. It was no longer prescribed for certain days. The phrase "miserable sinners" was removed from the end of each of the initial invocations which were treated as versicles and responses rather than being said by the minister and repeated by the people. These invocations were made to conform with the summary of the creed of the catechism. In the first, "Creator of heaven and earth" replaced "of heaven;" in the third, "Sanctifier of the faithful" replaced "proceeding from the Father and the Son." The words "three Persons and" were struck from the fourth. Among the deprecations the revision added a petition to be delivered from earthquake, fire, and flood. Prior to the supplication for all Christian rulers and magistrates another was inserted: "That it may please thee so to rule the heart of thy servant, The President of the United States, that he may above all things seek thy honour and glory." The phrase "That it may please thee to preserve all who travel by land or by water, all women in the perils of child–birth" became "That it may please thee to preserve all who travel by land, by water, or by air, all women in child–birth," reflecting changes of the time both in the manners of travel and the perils of childbirth. The rubric permitting abbreviation of the Litany was moved to a position after the Lord's Prayer. Two sentences beginning "O Lord, arise" which had, in previous editions, been responses of the people, were to be said by people and minister together. The General Thanksgiving, the Prayer of Saint Chrysostom, and the Grace had ended the Litany in the 1892 Book. The 1928 edition ended the Litany with the prayer beginning "We humbly beseech thee, O Father" and a rubric which allowed the minister to conclude the Litany at this point or to add prayers from the Book at his discretion.

The Great Litany[1] (pp. 148–154)

This present revision uses the title, "The Great Litany," for there are a number of other litanies in the Book. Previous editions gave no directions for the posture of the congregation. Late in the middle ages, the Litany was usually to be sung in procession, but occasionally it was to be said or sung kneeling. The royal injunction of 1547 ordered that it be said kneeling; the Elizabethan injunctions recognized the processional use of the Litany on occasion. This Book allows for it to be said or sung "kneeling, standing, or in procession." The rubric also emphasizes its appropriateness for Lent and rogation days.

Since it is often not recognized that the Litany is addressed to the Second Person of the Trinity, after the initial invocations, the address has been expanded from "Lord" to "Lord Christ."

In the initial deprecation the clause "be not angry with us" is now "by thy mercy preserve us." "Wickedness" has been substituted for "mischief" in the next deprecation and the phrase "from thy wrath" is deleted. In the next we ask to be delivered "from all want of charity" rather than "from all uncharitableness," a change made for musical reasons. The last two deprecations of the 1928 Book are divided and rearranged in a more logical order. We seek first to be delivered from spiritual evils, then from physical evils, and third from social evils. "Oppression" replaces "sedition," "conspiracy" stands unqualified by the adjective "privy," and a petition to be delivered from violence has now been added. For over three hundred years the petition to be delivered "from sudden death" has been criticized as misleading. In the medieval litany the petition asked that we be delivered from an unexpected death—one for which we were not prepared. The phrase "from dying suddenly and unprepared" replaces "from sudden death" in this revision.

The obsecrations which follow remind us that our Lord's atoning work was not limited to His death upon the cross but was manifest in all of His life on earth, from the incarnation to the sending of the Holy Spirit. A broader concept, "By . . . thy submission to the law" replaces "By . . . thy Circumcision."

The previous order of the supplications was haphazard; this revision changes to a classical order like that suggested for the prayers of

---

[1]This present revision was drafted by the Rev. Donald L. Garfield; it is heavily indebted to the detailed study of Dr. James Waring McCrady of Tennessee who is responsible for the clear ordering of the petitions and material in the supplications.

the people in the Eucharist: the universal church, its members and its mission; the nation and all in authority; the welfare of the world; the concerns of the local community; those who suffer and those in any trouble; and the departed (with commemoration of a saint where appropriate). The phrase "to draw all mankind into thy kingdom" has been added to the supplication "That it may please thee to send forth laborers into thy harvest." The petition for the president, which seemed to be based on the assumption that this office would always be held by a professing Christian, and the prayer for Christian rulers and magistrates, have been replaced by a prayer for all in authority "that they may do justice, and love mercy, and walk in the ways of truth." Petitions for peace and liberty, for the homeless and the hungry, for all persons in their vocations, for those in dangerous occupations, for those whose homes are broken or torn by strife, for the lonely and the elderly, and for the departed all are new to this revision. The more conventional forms of the Agnus Dei and the Kyrie, familiar from the Eucharist, have been substituted for the forms used in earlier litanies.

A new rubric permits the Eucharist to begin with the salutation and the collect of the day immediately after the Kyrie of the Litany; the Kyrie may be sung in threefold, sixfold or ninefold form. On other occasions the Litany concludes with the Lord's Prayer, the last versicle and response of the previous editions (Ps. 33:22), a prayer and the Grace. In 1662, when the doxology was added to the Lord's Prayer on some occasions of use, it was not added when the Kyrie immediately preceded the Prayer.

The prayer which follows had been printed among the collects provided for use after Ante-Communion in earlier editions of the Prayer Book; and also for use after the Litany or after the collects of the daily offices or of the Eucharist in the 1552 and later editions. Cranmer may have composed it, drawing from the Prayer of Saint Chrysostom and a collect from the Gregorian sacramentary (no. 1195) for the twenty-third Sunday after (the octave of) Pentecost. In the Sarum missal it was the collect for the twenty-third Sunday after Trinity as was also true in earlier editions of the Prayer Book. This prayer replaces the versicle and response and the prayer of Luther's litany (the prayer used in the Sarum rite at a Mass for the troubled in heart) used in earlier editions of the Book.

The Supplication (pp. 154–155)

Material from the conclusion of the Litany in earlier editions is restored in this Book to the use it also had in the Sarum rite—special supplication in time of war. The rubric also recommends its use in times of national anxiety or disaster. It may be used in the Litany in place of the concluding versicle and response, prayer and Grace, or it may be used at the end of Morning or Evening Prayer, or as a separate devotion. It consists of the first verse of Psalm 44, perhaps a remnant of the use of the entire psalm, with the Gloria Patri. The last verse of the psalm (44:26) is used as an antiphon before and after the first verse of the psalm, and after the Gloria Patri. This is followed by a set of suffrages which can be traced to the tenth century pontifical attributed to Egbert, Archbishop of York (734–766). The prayer following dates to 1549. At that time two of the prayers from the end of the 1544 Litany were joined. One of these, the substance of which forms the introduction to the prayer, had been placed at the end of the Sarum litany to be said on the last of the rogation days. It dates to the Gregorian sacramentary where it is a collect for the feast of Saint Cornelius and Saint Cyprian (no. 687). The other, which forms the conclusion of the prayer, was the collect of the Sarum rogation Mass and of the Mass for April 25, the occasion for a major litany in the Gregorian sacramentary (no. 472).

The Collects for the Church Year

In the Western church some of the prayers used within the eucharistic rite varied with different days and occasions. The Gallican liturgies provided a number of these variable prayers. In the early Gallican Missale Gothicum, for example, the Mass for Christmas Day included a number of variable prayers suited to the day and to the place in the rite. The first followed the initial song of praise, Benedictus Dominus Deus. Others came after the litany form of prayers of the people, after a bidding or "preface" to the liturgy of the table (the Gallican equivalent of our collect of the day), at the reading of names of those to be remembered, at the peace, before and after the Lord's Prayer, as a postcommunion prayer, and as a final prayer over the people. A variable blessing before communion was also provided.

The Leonine and Gelasian, earliest of the Roman sacramentaries, regularly include four prayers for each day or occasion: an opening prayer, a prayer probably to be said at the spreading of the cloth for the liturgy of the table, a prayer at the offering of bread and wine, and a postcommunion prayer. The Leonine sacramentary also provides a super populum—a prayer or blessing said over the people at the close of the rite. This prayer occurs frequently in the later Gelasian sacramentary. The second of the variable prayers dropped from use and is not provided in the Gregorian sacramentary; this sacramentary gives a super populum only for the weekdays of Lent. The first of the variable prayers of the Roman rite, the opening prayer, was later designated the "collect," a word which may signify the summing up of the prayers of the individuals who have been called to pray. Or it may designate the prayer said at the collecting of the people at the start of the Mass, for the collect was inserted immediately after the salutation which, at an earlier stage, had served to call the people to attention before the reading of the first lection.

Although the word "collect" generally designates the first of the variable prayers of the Mass in the Roman rite, it came to be applied to a particular form of prayer which is as rigid in structure as a sonnet or haiku. The simplest form of a collect has three parts: a preamble (address, invocation), a petition, and a conclusion (mediation). Collects of more complex structure include in the preamble a descriptive phrase or attribution which states the grounds on which we make the petition; the petition is modified by a result or consequence clause. The attribution in the preamble, the petition, and the result clause may be either simple or complex. The collect for the second Sunday of Advent (p. 159 or 211) is in the most commonly used regular form:

> Merciful God, who sent your messengers the prophets to preach repentance and prepare the way for our salvation: Give us grace to heed their warnings and forsake our sins, that we may greet with joy the coming of Jesus Christ our redeemer; who lives and reigns with you and the Holy Spirit, one God, now and for ever.

The collect for the first Sunday of Advent lacks an attribution as does that for the third Sunday of Advent which, in addition, does not begin with the address but with one of its two petitions. Despite the variations, however, which are no greater in English than in Latin, all collects display a certain succinct rhythm and symmetry.

A classic collect can be contrasted in style with the rhetorical structure traditionally used for eucharistic prayers or with the more diffuse forms of other prayers in the Eastern and Gallican rites. Compare, for example, the prayers of the Eastern tradition, such as the Prayer of Saint Chrysostom at the end of Morning and Evening Prayer, with the classic collect for Advent 2. Compare the classic collect also with prayers of Gallican and Celtic origin—the collect for Protection in Evening Prayer (p. 70 or 124) or the collect for Saturday in Easter Week (pp. 172 or 224).

The 1549 Prayer Book contained new collects for several of the Sundays and major holy days, and new collects for a number of saints' days. Many of the medieval collects which it retained were revised in order to eliminate the intercession of saints and doctrine of merit, and to stress the initiative and liberality of God's grace. The new saints' day collects do not ask for the prayers of the person, but tell something about the saint being commemorated and pray for grace to follow the example so set for us.

Revision of the collects in the Prayer Book began with the 1552 edition which substituted a new collect for Saint Andrew's Day. Other new collects were provided and a number were substantially revised in 1662. Each of the American revisions made further changes and additions.

Approximately half of the collects of this present revision are from the 1928 Book; less than thirty of the 1928 collects have been dropped. Some no longer appointed as collects of the day are actually given greater exposure: in An Order of Service for Noonday (Monday in Whitsun Week); in the Burial of the Dead (Easter Even and the Twenty-first Sunday After Trinity).

Concerning the Proper of the Church Year (p. 158)

The first paragraph lists those fixed elements in the rites which vary with the day and the occasion. The second paragraph, the direction to make use of the Sunday proper on weekdays which follow unless otherwise ordered, first appeared in the 1892 Book. The third paragraph gives directions for determining the correct proper for each of the Sundays after Pentecost. The fourth, inserted in the 1892 revision, was taken from the 1662 Book except that "may be used" was substituted for "shall be used."

The Collects for the Church Year (pp. 159–251)

First Sunday of Advent (pp. 159 and 211)

This collect was composed for the 1549 Prayer Book. The Sarum missal provided a "stir up" collect similar to that for the third Sunday of Advent.

The collect is based on verse 12 of the Epistle (Rom. 13:8–14) presently retained in the eucharistic lectionary for Year A. This expands the old Sarum Epistle (Rom. 13:11–14). The conclusion relates closely to a postcommunion prayer in the Gelasian sacramentary (no. 1145) which was included in the Gregorian under "Other Prayers for Advent" (no. 813): "that they who rejoice at the advent of your only–begotten according to the flesh, may at the second advent, when he shall come in his majesty, receive the reward of eternal life."

The striking antitheses are remarkable: cast away darkness, put on light; mortal life, life immortal; great humility, glorious majesty. The word "now" is crucial: remembering the first advent and looking toward the second, we are now, in this time, to cast off the works of darkness and put on the armor of light. From 1662 until the current revision this collect was to be repeated daily throughout the Advent season, a custom analogous to the use of memorials after the collect of the day in late medieval missals.

Second Sunday of Advent (pp. 159 and 211)

This new collect is based on that for the third Sunday of Advent in the Book of Common Worship of the Church of South India; the theme is "The Fore-runner":

> O Lord Jesus Christ, who at thy first coming didst send thy messenger to prepare thy way before thee: Grant that we, paying urgent heed to the message of repentance, may with hearts prepared await thy final coming to judge the world; who with the Father and the Holy Spirit ever livest and reignest, one God, world without end. *Amen.*

The petition is similar to that of the first of the collects for the Nativity: Christmas Day. The prayer might be compared to this collect for the third Sunday in Advent which entered the Prayer Book in 1662, generally attributed to John Cosin:

> O Lord Jesus Christ, who at thy first coming didst send thy messenger to prepare thy way before thee; Grant that the ministers and stewards of thy mysteries may likewise so prepare and make ready thy way, by turning the hearts of the disobedient to the wisdom of the just, that at thy second coming to judge the world we may be found an acceptable people in thy sight, who livest and reignest with the Father and the Holy Spirit ever, one God, world without end. *Amen.*

The essential difference between Bishop Cosin's collect and that in the present revision lies in the placing of responsibility not only upon the ministers and stewards but upon all of us to be prepared for Christ's coming again.

Third Sunday of Advent (pp. 160 and 212)

The Gelasian sacramentary is the source for this collect which is included in the first of the propers for Advent (no. 1121), and is addressed to the Son. In the Gregorian it is changed to a prayer addressed to the Father in a proper for a Sunday, included after the provisions for a winter ember vigil (no. 805). The Gallican Bobbio missal provides it as a second prayer in the first of the three Masses for Advent (no. 38). In the Sarum missal it was appointed for the fourth Sunday in Advent. Cranmer retained it in that version with slight changes, adding the phrase "among us" and, at the end of the petition, "through the satisfaction of thy Son our Lord." Revisers in 1662 added the phrase "in running the race that is set before us," and expanded "deliver us" to "help and deliver us." Cranmer's second phrase was deleted in the 1928 revision and the first of the additions of the 1662 edition has been dropped in the present revision, thus restoring the prayer to a form close to its original. The prayer echoes Psalm 80:2 and Hebrews 12:1. The one remnant of a series of four prayers which began with "excita" (stir up) used on four of the last five Sundays before Christmas in the Sarum missal, this prayer sets forth better than the others the themes of the two advents: the first in which He came in humility, and the second in which He comes in power; the first in which He came to save, and the second in which He comes to help and relieve.

The rubric following is a reminder that the Wednesday, Friday, and Saturday of this week are the traditional winter ember days, though these may now be transferred to a time related to local or diocesan occasions for ordination. (For propers for the ember days, see those for various occasions, no. 15, "For the Ministry," pp. 205–206 or 256–257 and 929.)

Fourth Sunday of Advent (pp. 160 and 212)

This collect is a revised version of William Bright's translation of a Gelasian collect (no. 1127) found in *Ancient Collects*, p. 16. It is included in the Gregorian sacramentary under "Other Prayers for Advent" (no. 809), in the Missale Gallicanum vetus as the collect in the first of three Advent Masses (no. 40). The collect, provided for use in the season when the first advent is recalled and the second anticipated, reminds us of our Lord's entry into Jerusalem (Lk. 19:44), "you did not know the time of your visitation," and prays that our consciences may be purified by His "daily visitation." It prays that, in contrast to His first advent when there was no room for Him in the inn, "he may find in us a mansion prepared for himself." This collect is especially in accord with the Annunciation theme of the lections for the day.

167

The Nativity of Our Lord: Christmas Day (pp. 160–161 and 212–213)

The first of the collects for Christmas Day is in the Advent Masses of the Gelasian sacramentary (no. 1156) and in the Gregorian sacramentary (no. 33) and the Sarum missal as a collect for the vigil Mass of Christmas. It began, "God, who makes us glad with the annual expectation of our redemption." Cranmer changed the opening and retained it for use "At the First Communion" on Christmas Day. The 1552 revision dropped it, retaining only one proper for Christmas Day; in 1892 it was recovered when the 1549 provision was restored for optional use at the first service "if in any Church the Holy Communion be twice celebrated on Christmas–day." The collect provides a good transition from Advent to the Christmas season.

The second of the collects was appointed for the vigil in the Gelasian sacramentary (no. 5) and for the midnight stational Mass at St. Mary Major's in the Gregorian (no. 36). The Sarum missal has it as the collect for the Mass at cockcrow. Its content recalls the origin of the celebration of the Nativity at the December solstice as a rival festival to the pagan ceremonies of dies natalis Solis Invicti (the Birthday of the Unconquerable Sun). This is the first Book of Common Prayer to include this collect.

The third collect was composed for the 1549 Book for use "At the Second Communion." The revisers in 1662 replaced "this day" with "as at this time." The substance is closely related to the new 1549 proper preface for Christmas Day and to the initial paragraph of the note on the second article of the Creed in *The King's Book*. Among the ancient collects the one most closely related seems to be in the Gelasian sacramentary (no. 17), the initial collect for the Mass on Christmas Day, and in the Gregorian a collect among "Other Prayers for the Birthday of the Lord" (no. 58). There are also similar collects in several of the fifteenth and sixteenth century German breviaries. In his *Commentary* Massey H. Shepherd, Jr. said of this collect:

> . . . it is of all the Prayer Book collects the most notable for its theological content, for the whole of the doctrines of the Trinity and the Incarnation are encased in it. Specifically, the Collect is woven about three themes: (1) the birth of the Only-Begotten Son of God in the substance of our human nature is linked with the idea of our rebirth in Baptism by 'pure' water . . . and the Holy Spirit; (2) the eternal Sonship of Christ is contrasted with our adoption as sons by the free grace of God; and (3) the historic birth of our Lord at a specific time and place is spiritually renewed in the hearts of his followers daily. (Cf. 2 Cor. iv. 16:

168

"Though our outward man perish, yet the inward man is renewed day by day"; note also Col. iii. 10; Eph. iii. 16.)[1]

A rubric analogous to the one which follows the collect was inserted in 1892 to make it clear that the Christmas proper (rather than that of the fourth Sunday of Advent) was to be used on any weekdays which might follow Holy Innocents' Day.

First Sunday after Christmas Day (pp. 161 and 213)

In keeping with the principle of the priority of the Lord's Day, this revision provides a rubric that, if the Sunday after Christmas Day falls on December 26, 27, or 28, the Sunday proper is to be used, and the observance of one, two, or all three of these feasts is to be postponed one day.

The collect has as its source the Sarum collect for a Mass celebrated on Christmas Day. Its ultimate source is the dawn stational Mass at St. Anastasia's found in the Gregorian sacramentary (no. 42). It entered the Prayer Book in 1928 as the collect of the second Sunday after Christmas Day. The petition in the original reads: "Grant that the light which through faith shines in the heart may shine forth in our works."[2]

The Holy Name (pp. 162 and 213)

This revised version of a prayer from *The Cambridge Bede Book* (1936) is suited to the emphasis on the holy name of Jesus. It replaces a 1549 collect which, along with the Epistle assigned to the day at that time (Romans 4:8–14), caused the renowned English scholar F. E. Brightman to comment: "[they had] altered the proportion of things, and in fact had turned the day into a commemoration of circumcision, rather than of the Circumcision of our Lord, not to edification." The 1549 collect as corrected in 1552 reads:

> Almighty God, which madest thy blessed Son to be circumcised, and obedient to the law for man; Grant us the true circumcision of the spirit, that our hearts, and all our members, being mortified from all worldly and carnal lusts, may in all things obey thy blessed will; through the same thy Son Jesus Christ our Lord.

[1] Massey H. Shepherd, Jr., *The Oxford American Prayer Book Commentary*, New York: Oxford University Press, 1950, pp. 96–97.
[2] The Prayer Book translation is a slight condensation of that by the Rev. Atwell M. Y. Baylay, *A Century of Collects*. Alcuin Club, 1913.

169

The 1549–1552 collect is closely related to an episcopal benediction for the octave of Christmas which is found in the supplement to the Gregorian sacramentary (no. 1743) and was included in various medieval liturgical books. The collect of the day in the Sarum missal commemorated the octave of Christmas:

> God, you permit us to celebrate the octave of the birth of our Savior; grant, we beseech you, that we may be defended by his perpetual divinity, as we have been renewed by his sharing of the flesh.

Second Sunday after Christmas Day (pp. 162 and 214)

The collect, included for this day in the English revision of 1928, is new to this American edition. It dates to the Leonine sacramentary (no. 1239), the earliest of the sacramentaries, as the collect of the first Christmas Mass. The Gelasian sacramentary places it among the Christmas prayers for Matins or Vespers (no. 27) and the Gregorian in "other Prayers of the Birthday of the Lord" (no. 59).

In a wonderful manner God created the dignity of human nature and restored that dignity in an even more wonderful manner, therefore we can ask to share in the divinity of His Son who shared in our humanity. The petition echoes a sentence attributed to Saint Leo the Great: "The Son of God became the Son of Man that the sons of men might become the sons of God." This collect is also used after the first lesson at the Great Vigil of Easter, the story of creation.

The Epiphany (pp. 162 and 214)

The 1549 version of this collect, retained until the present revision, substantially weakened the contrast between faith and sight (cf. 2 Cor. 5:7) of the original Gregorian text (no. 87). The translation of the petition, based on that prepared by Capt. Howard E. Galley,[1] restored the original integrity. As the wise men were led by a star, so we are led by faith to His presence. The petition of previous Books read: "Mercifully grant that we, who know thee now by faith, may after this life have the fruition of thy glorious Godhead." The word "gentibus" is clarified in the new translation by the reading "the peoples of the earth."

The revised rubric eliminates the octave of Epiphany, which had been restored in the 1928 revision, thus giving greater prominence to the primary emphasis of Epiphany, the baptism of our Lord.

---

[1] A Short Book of Common Prayer, New York: The Church Hymnal Corp. 1970.

First Sunday after the Epiphany: The Baptism of Our Lord (pp. 162 and 214)

In keeping with the restoration of Epiphany as the celebration of the baptism of our Lord and as a baptismal season, a new collect is provided for this day. It stresses the baptism of Jesus with water and the Holy Spirit as the model for our own initiation into the covenant. This prayer, drafted by the Rev. Dr. Charles M. Guilbert, is based upon two of the alternative collects in the Roman sacramentary for this day.

Second Sunday after the Epiphany (pp. 163 and 215)

New to this edition of the Prayer Book, this collect is based upon the collect for the twentieth Sunday after Pentecost in the Book of Common Worship of the Church of South India:

> Almighty God, who hast manifested thy Son Jesus Christ to be a light to mankind: Grant that we thy people, being nourished by thy word and sacraments, may be strengthened to show forth to all men the unsearchable riches of Christ, so that he may be known, adored, and obeyed, to the ends of the earth; who liveth and reigneth with thee and the Holy Spirit, one God, world without end. *Amen.*

Like many of the post-Epiphany collects, this relates to the Gospel of the day.

Third Sunday after the Epiphany (pp. 163 and 215)

The Rev. Dr. Massey H. Shepherd, Jr. drafted this collect which recalls phrases from the collect for the feast day of Saint Andrew, the story of whose calling by Christ is the Gospel of Years A and B. The Gospel for Year C is the story of our Lord's sermon at Nazareth which is also echoed in the collect. We pray that we may not only answer His call but also proclaim the Good News, and that "we and all the whole world may perceive the glory of his marvelous works."

Fourth Sunday after the Epiphany (pp. 164 and 215)

This collect is found in the Gregorian sacramentary among the daily prayers (no. 922), and in the supplement (no. 1099), as well as in previous editions of the Prayer Book, as the collect for the second Sunday after the Epiphany. The Sarum missal appoints it for the

171

second Sunday after the octave of the Epiphany. Cranmer translated the petition "grant us thy peace all the days of our life," but this revision restores the original wording.

Fifth Sunday after the Epiphany (pp. 164 and 216)

This new collect was drafted by the Rev. Dr. Massey H. Shepherd, Jr. Scriptural allusions include Gal. 4:3–5; Rom. 8:15 and 8:19–21; Jn. 10:10; and Lk. 4:16–21.

Sixth Sunday after the Epiphany (pp. 164 and 216)

In the Gelasian sacramentary this prayer is found as the first collect for the sixth of the Sundays after the Paschal octave (no. 566), the first Sunday after the octave of Pentecost. The Gregorian sacramentary appoints it (no. 1129) as the collect for the first Sunday after Pentecost (actually the first Sunday after the octave of Pentecost, later to become the second Sunday after Pentecost or the first Sunday after Trinity). In the Gallican Missale Francorum it is a collect (no. 141) used before reading the names of those to be remembered in prayer, and it is the offertory prayer at the second of the five Sunday Masses in the Gallican Bobbio missal (no. 507). Sarum use and previous Prayer Books appointed it for the first Sunday after Trinity.

Cranmer, in his translation for the 1549 Book, rendered "mortal weakness" as "the weakness of our mortal nature," and substituted "trust" for "hope" and "can do no good thing" for "can do nothing." The revisers in 1662 inserted "put their," "through," and the first "we." The collect reminds us that without the grace of God we can neither will nor do any good thing nor be pleasing to God.

Seventh Sunday after the Epiphany (pp. 164–165 and 216)

This collect was composed for the 1549 Prayer Book for use on Quinquagesima, the Sunday next before Ash Wednesday, where it was associated with the Epistle, 1 Corinthians 13. In the revised lectionary it reinforces the Gospel injunction in Years A and C: "Love your enemies."

Eighth Sunday after the Epiphany (pp. 165 and 216–217)

This original collect by William Bright is printed in the appendix to his *Ancient Collects* (pp. 234–235). The 1928 revision printed it among additional family prayers. In the preamble are biblical allusions to 1 Timothy 2:1, Philippians 3:8, and 1 Peter 5:7. In the Gospels the antithesis of faith is not doubt but fear, for faith is essentially trust in God's love and care.

Last Sunday after the Epiphany (pp. 165 and 217)

The Epiphany season may have as few as four or as many as nine Sundays depending upon the date of Easter (see the table on pp. 884–885 of the Prayer Book). The rubric makes clear that, regardless of the number of Sundays after the Epiphany, this proper is used on the Sunday before Ash Wednesday.

The English revision of 1928 first included this modern collect for the feast of the Transfiguration, the subject of the Gospel lesson in all three years for this Sunday in the eucharistic lectionary. It is particularly appropriate on this Sunday, when we recall our Lord's having set His face to go to Jerusalem, for us to pray that we "beholding by faith the light of his countenance, may be strengthened to bear our cross, and be changed into his likeness from glory to glory."

Ash Wednesday (pp. 166 and 217)

The Sarum collect for Ash Wednesday can be traced to the Gelasian sacramentary where it is the initial collect for the fall ember days (no. 1037). In the Gregorian sacramentary it is used on the Wednesday before the first Sunday in Lent (no. 154). It might be translated:

> Grant, we beseech, Lord, to your faithful people, that they may undertake the sacred solemnities of the fasts with fitting piety, and that they see them through with undisturbed devotion.

Cranmer's new collect for the 1549 Book places the emphasis on penitence rather than upon the fast. His preamble is similar to that of the form for the blessing of the ashes and to the introit appointed for that day in the Sarum missal. The petition is obviously inspired by Psalm 51 which has traditionally been used on this day. We pray for "remission and forgiveness." The word "remission" normally refers to debts, and "forgiveness" to offenses.

The rubric following the collect was inserted in the 1892 revision to insure that the proper of Ash Wednesday rather than that of the preceding Sunday would be used on the following Thursday, Friday, and Saturday. Such a rubric is also found in the Scottish Book of 1637. From 1662 until the 1928 revision the Ash Wednesday collect was to be repeated throughout Lent daily, a custom analogous to the use of memorials after the collect of the day late in the medieval period. The 1928 Book qualified this by adding "until Palm Sunday."

173

First Sunday in Lent (pp. 166 and 218)

The Sarum collect for the first Sunday has as its source the collect in the Gregorian sacramentary (no. 166):

> God, you cleanse your church with the annual observance of Lent: grant your family that what they strive to obtain from you by fasting they may follow up with good works.

Cranmer provided a new collect with reference to the Gospel lection and without the Pelagian overtones or the implication that we must strive to obtain the gifts which God is anxious to give to those who seek. His collect reads:

> O Lord, which for our sake didst fast forty days and forty nights; Give us grace to use such abstinence, that, our flesh being subdued to the spirit, we may ever obey thy godly motions in righteousness, and true holiness, to thy honor and glory, which livest and reignest, etc.

The new collect provided in the present edition is a revised version of one of the original collects in William Bright's *Ancient Collects* (appendix, pp. 237–238). It relates closely to the Gospel for all three years—the account of our Lord's temptation in the wilderness—and is particularly fitting as we enter this season of penitence in preparation for baptism or for renewal of baptismal vows.

The rubric points out that the Wednesday, Friday, and Saturday of this week are the traditional spring ember days, though these may now be transferred to a time related to local or diocesan ordinations. (See pp. 205–206 or 256–257 and 929 for the propers for ember days among those for various occasions, no. 15, "For the Ministry.")

Second Sunday in Lent (pp. 166–167 and 218)

This collect has links to one of the Good Friday solemn collects in the Missale Gallicanum vetus (no. 107), the Gelasian sacramentary (no. 413), and the Gregorian sacramentary (no. 351). In these books it follows a bidding to pray for heretics and schismatics that they may be delivered from their errors and recalled to the catholic and apostolic church. In its new context as a Sunday collect it refers to those who have abandoned the practice of Christian faith.

Third Sunday in Lent (pp. 167 and 218)

In the Gregorian sacramentary this collect is appointed for the second Sunday in Lent (no. 202). Earlier that had been a "vacant" Sunday, a Sunday which had no proper because of the vigil and ordination Mass which had been the culmination of the ember days preceding. In that sacramentary it is also printed among the "Daily Prayers" (no. 876). In the present Book it is shifted to the third Sunday in Lent from its earlier position in the Sarum missal and older Prayer Books on the second Sunday in Lent. The text reminds us that God's protection is necessary to defend us from assaults upon the soul as well as those on the body.

Fourth Sunday in Lent (pp. 167 and 219)

The Gregorian collect (no. 256) which had been appointed for this Sunday beseeches relief from deserved punishment. It is replaced by a revised version of a collect written by F. B. McNutt.[1] The new collect is more appropriate for this Sunday, for it echoes the lections and reinforces the traditional custom of this day as "mothering Sunday" or Refreshment Sunday. When Lent began, as it originally did, on the Monday after the first Sunday in Lent (rather than on Ash Wednesday), this day marked the half-way point in the season and was observed with feasting. In some places it was customary on this day to visit the mother church of the diocese and make offerings there. In others servants and apprentices often visited their parents on this Sunday, carrying with them a present which commonly took the form of a "mothering cake."

Fifth Sunday in Lent (pp. 167 and 219)

In the Gelasian sacramentary this collect is appointed for the third Sunday after the octave of Easter (no. 551), as it is also in the supplement to the Gregorian (no. 1120). Cranmer retained the original preamble which read: "Almighty God, which dost make the minds of all faithful men to be of one will." This was revised in 1662. In the Sarum missal and earlier Prayer Books this collect was appointed for the fourth Sunday after Easter; the present revision has shifted it to this Sunday in order that it may replace one of the Gregorian collects (no. 285) asking for protection and not at all suited to the time of the

---

[1] *The Prayer Manual*, London: Mowbray, 1952, no. 488.

175

church year. The changes of 1662 introduce an antithesis between the "unruly wills and affections" of sinners, and the love for God's commandments and the desire for what He has promised—gifts of God's grace.

Sunday of the Passion: Palm Sunday (pp. 168 and 219)

The collect dates to the Gelasian (no. 329) and Gregorian sacramentaries (no. 312). Cranmer inserted "of thy tender love toward man" in the preamble, and translated "grant that we merit both to have the teaching of his patience and a share in the resurrection" as "grant that we both follow the example of his patience, and be made partakers of his resurrection." The 1662 revision altered the collect slightly. (The word "patience" connotes suffering as well as endurance.) The traditional Palm Sunday Epistle (Phil. 2:5–11) inspired this collect. Massey H. Shepherd, Jr. has written:

> This Collect is the nearest thing to a statement of the doctrine of Atonement to be found in the Prayer Book, and it is significant that it associates it with Christ's Incarnation no less than his Passion. Also the stress upon the 'humility' of Christ in coming into the world for our redemption is noteworthy.[1]

Monday in Holy Week (pages 168 and 220)

This collect was written by the Rev. Dr. William Reed Huntington, printed in his work *Materia Ritualis*, 1882, and proposed for inclusion in the 1892 revision among the occasional prayers under the title "For Patience under Suffering." It was adopted in the 1928 revision for use as the collect for this day, which prior to that time had no proper collect. (The collect of Palm Sunday had been used, and from 1662 it had been followed by that of Ash Wednesday.) In this revision this collect is also printed in Daily Morning Prayer under the heading "A Collect for Friday," and as a station collect in the proper liturgy for Palm Sunday. The preamble is from the exhortation which was contained in the Visitation of the Sick until the 1928 revision. This particular portion came from the Consultation of Hermann of Cologne.

---

[1] Massey H. Shepherd, Jr., *The Oxford American Prayer Book Commentary*, New York: Oxford University Press, 1950, pp. 134–135.

Tuesday in Holy Week (pages 168 and 220)

This collect is a slightly revised version of that provided in the 1928 English Prayer Book for Holy Cross day. We are reminded of Galatians 6:14, "Far be it from me to glory except in the cross of our Lord Jesus Christ, by which the world has been crucified to me, and I to the world."

Wednesday in Holy Week (pages 169 and 220)

This collect, by an unknown author, was proposed for inclusion in the 1892 book. It made its way into the Prayer Book at the 1928 revision for use on Tuesday before Easter. In this revision it has been shifted to Wednesday where it ties in with the Epistle of the day, replacing a collect which now introduces the liturgy of the palms on Palm Sunday. It contains allusions to Is. 50:6, Is. 53, and Rom. 8:18.

Maundy Thursday (pp. 169 and 221)

The 1928 revision commission wrote this collect which includes phrases from a collect proposed for use on this day at the time of the 1892 Book. It also reflects the emphases of Cranmer's postcommunion prayer printed in The Holy Eucharist: Rite One (p. 339) and of the exhortation (p. 316). It is worthwhile to compare this collect with the communion exhortations of earlier Prayer Books.

Good Friday (pp. 169 and 221)

This collect dates to the Gregorian sacramentary (no. 327) where it is used, as also in the Sarum missal, as a blessing said over the people (super populum) at the end of the Mass on the Wednesday of Holy Week. Its use on that day explains the very explicit reference to the betrayal. In the Sarum missal it is also the postcommunion prayer for Good Friday. The Gallican Missale Gothicum provides it for Sext, the little office at noon, on Good Friday and Holy Saturday (no. 216); the Missale Gallicanum vetus places it among the office prayers for Maundy Thursday and the two days following (no. 113). The 1549 Prayer Book ordered that the collect of the preceding Sunday was to be said at the Eucharist on Good Friday, along with this collect and two others. This was also to be the collect of the day at the daily office. The other two collects were based on forms from the traditional solemn collects of Good Friday and are so used in this revision, with some changes. The first of these is also included as the first of

177

the prayers for mission in Morning Prayer and as the collect for the votive "For all Christians in their vocation."

Holy Saturday (pp. 170 and 221)

Earlier Prayer Books provided no special collect; that for Palm Sunday was used through the week. The Scottish Book of 1637 provided this collect:

> O most gracious God, look upon us in mercy, and grant that as we are baptized into the death of thy Son our Saviour Jesus Christ, so by our true and hearty repentance all our sins may be buried with him, and we not fear the grave: that as Christ was raised up from the dead by the glory of thee, O Father, so we also may walk in newness of life, but our sins never be able to rise in judgment against us; and that for the merit of Jesus Christ that died, was buried, and rose again for us. *Amen.*

A revised version appeared in the English Book of 1662 and in subsequent editions:

> Grant, O Lord, that as we are baptized into the death of thy blessed Son our Saviour Jesus Christ, so by continual mortifying our corrupt affections we may be buried with him; and that through the grave, and gate of death, we may pass to our joyful resurrection; for his merits, who died, and was buried, and rose again for us, thy Son Jesus Christ our Lord. *Amen.*

The restoration of the Easter baptismal vigil in the present edition stresses the relation between baptism and the death and resurrection of Christ in several prayers of that rite. The new collect, drafted by Bishop Otis Charles, emphasizes the Sabbath theme of expectant waiting. The substance of the old collect is retained among the prayers of the burial rite (p. 480); a collect which has certain affinities with it is provided for use in the votive "For all Baptized Christians" (pp. 201 and 252–253).

Easter Day (pp. 170–171 and 222)

The Gregorian sacramentary is the source for the first collect; it is appointed there as the second collect for the Wednesday of Holy Week (no. 324). In the Sarum rite it was included among the devotions associated with the solemn Easter procession. The 1549 Book provided it for use prior to Matins on Easter Day in a form consisting of the second and third anthems of what is now the Pascha nostrum, a versicle and response, and this prayer. This collect does not appear in the Prayer Book again until its inclusion in the 1892 revision where it is provided for a second celebration on Easter. Its content, and its original association with Holy Week, makes it a fitting transition from the time of meditation upon the passion to the celebration of the resurrection. The Sarum collect, which was amplified by Cranmer, read:

> God, who willed your Son to suffer death upon the cross for us, that you might cast out of us the power of the enemy; Grant to us your servants that we may ever live in the joy of his resurrection.

The second of the collects is from the Eucharist of the Easter Vigil in the Gelasian (no. 454) and Gregorian (no. 377) sacramentaries, the Bobbio missal (no. 258), and the Sarum missal. This is the first edition of the Prayer Book to include it. The phrase "may worship thee in sincerity and truth" is a free translation of "puram tibi exhibeant servitutem."

The preamble of the third collect is that of the "first communion" of Easter in the 1549 Book, a translation of a collect from the Sarum missal and originally drawn from the Gregorian sacramentary (no. 383). The petition which followed read: "we humbly beseech thee, that, as by thy special grace, preventing us, thou dost put in our minds good desires, so by thy continual help we may bring the same to good effect." In this revision the petition has been replaced by the conclusion of this collect found in the Missale Gallicanum vetus (nos. 186 and 223) and the Gelasian sacramentary (no. 463).

Monday in Easter Week (pp. 171 and 222–223)

This collect dates to the old Gallican books, the Missale Gallicanum vetus (no. 226), where it is an alternative collect for the Friday after Easter, and the Missale Gothicum (no. 285) and Bobbio missal (no. 285), where it is used at the exchange of the peace. A variant version is in the Gregorian sacramentary (no. 429) and in the Sarum missal for the Saturday in Easter Week. The 1928 Book appointed it for Tuesday in Easter Week. This collect has been edited in translation. The Gregorian petition read: "grant that we who have kept with reverence this Paschal feast may through it be found worthy to arrive at everlasting joys." The collect is noteworthy in that it links together the ancient Passover or Pascha, the celebration of our

179

Lord's resurrection and our new life in Him, and the anticipation of the heavenly banquet.

Tuesday in Easter Week (pp. 171 and 223)

This is a revision of a collect included in *Parish Prayers*.[1] The preamble is based on 2 Timothy 1:10; the petition emphasizes two benefits of our Lord's resurrection: His abiding presence with us and our hope of the resurrection of which His resurrection is the assurance. This is also the first collect for the burial of an adult in the Rite Two service (p. 493).

Wednesday in Easter Week (pp. 171 and 223)

This is a revised version of the collect for the Monday in Easter Week of the 1928 Book, composed by the Rev. Dr. John W. Suter, Sr. It is associated with the story of our Lord's appearance to the disciples at Emmaus after the resurrection, when He made Himself known "in the breaking of bread" (Lk.`24:35). The original form of the result clause read: "That we may behold thee in all thy works." This collect is also appointed for the third Sunday of Easter.

Thursday in Easter Week (pp. 172 and 223)

This collect, new to this Book, is also appointed for use after the seventh lesson in the Great Vigil of Easter and as the collect of the day on the second Sunday of Easter. It dates to the Gregorian sacramentary (no. 423). The translation is a revision of that by William Bright in *Ancient Collects* (pp. 56–57). In the Gregorian sacramentary and the Sarum missal it is provided for the Friday of Easter Week. It might be compared with the collect for the third Sunday after Easter in earlier Prayer Books. The 1549 version reads:

> Almighty God, which showest to all men that be in error the light of thy truth, to the intent that they may return into the way of righteousness; Grant unto all them that be admitted into the fellowship of Christ's religion, that they may eschew those things that be contrary to their profession, and follow all such things as be agreeable to the same; through our Lord Jesus Christ.

That collect was the initial collect for one of the April Masses of the Leonine sacramentary (no. 75), and of the Mass for the second

---

[1] Edited by Frank Colquhoun, London: Hodder & Stoughton, 1967, no. 302.

Sunday after the paschal octave in the Gelasian sacramentary (no. 546) and the supplement to the Gregorian (no. 1117).

Friday in Easter Week (pp. 172 and 224)

This collect, based on Jn. 3:16, Rom. 4:25, and 1 Cor. 5:7–8, echoes the Easter anthem, Pascha nostrum. It was composed for the 1549 Book to be used for the second communion of Easter Day, Tuesday in Easter Week, and the Sunday after Easter. In 1552 its use was restricted to the Tuesday in Easter Week. The revisers in 1662, at the suggestion of Bishop Matthew Wren, appointed it for the Sunday after Easter. This revision moves it to Friday. The petition "Grant us so to put away the leaven of malice and wickedness" reminds us of the Jewish practice of removing all traces of leavened bread from the house at the time of the Passover. The result clause "that we may always serve thee in pureness of living and truth" is rendered by the Latin translation of the Prayer Book (1560) "in puritate fidei et vitae" (in purity of faith and of life).

Saturday in Easter Week (pp. 172 and 224)

This new collect is a revision of a Mozarabic collect in William Bright's Ancient Collects (page 58). In the Breviarium Gothicum it is appointed for Vespers on Friday and for Matins and Vespers on Saturday and Sunday in Easter Week. The preamble calls to mind the parallelism between the death and resurrection of Christ, and the Exodus. As the Hebrews were delivered from the bondage of slavery in Egypt and brought to the Promised Land, so we are delivered by our Lord's death and resurrection from the bondage of sin and death, and brought into the Kingdom of Christ.

Second Sunday of Easter (pp. 172–173 and 224)

See Thursday in Easter Week.

Third Sunday of Easter (pp. 173 and 224–225)

See Wednesday in Easter Week.

Fourth Sunday of Easter (pp. 173 and 225)

In many of the ancient baptistries Jesus was depicted as the Good Shepherd, a theme which became associated with one of the Sundays in the Easter season. This new collect, drafted by the Rev. Dr. Massey H. Shepherd, Jr., draws out several aspects of the theme which runs through many of the lections for this day, especially John 10 and Ezekiel 34.

Fifth Sunday of Easter (pp. 173 and 225)

This is a revision of a collect formerly appointed for the feast day of Saint Philip and Saint James. It was composed for the 1549 Book and the result clause added in 1662. It has a particular allusion to the Gospel for Year A but is appropriate for readings of the other years as well. The prayer is that we may know Christ who is truth and follow Him who is the way that we may be led to Him who is the source of eternal life.

Sixth Sunday of Easter (pp. 174 and 225)

The inspiration for this collect is undoubtedly 1 Corinthians 2:9. The prayer is found in several Gallican books: the Missale Gothicum as an opening collect (no. 519); the Missale Francorum as a prayer to be read after the Old Testament lection (no. 121); and the Celtic Stowe Missal as one of the two prayers printed for use before the Epistle. In the Gelasian sacramentary it is the first in a series of propers for ordinary Sundays (no. 1178), and in the supplement to the Gregorian for use on the sixth Sunday after (the) Pentecost (octave) (no. 1144). In the Sarum missal and earlier Prayer Books this collect was used on the sixth Sunday after Trinity. In 1549 Cranmer substituted "such good things as pass all man's understanding" for "invisible good things." The Latin original had "loving you in all things and above all things;" the 1549 version retained only the phrase "in all things" and the 1662 revision substituted "above all things." The present revision moves the collect appropriately to the Easter season with the original phrase restored. In the Latin there is a distinction between the uses of the word "love" in this collect. The word in the phrases "those who love" and "that we, loving" is related to the verb *diligere*, the root meaning of which is "to choose." This has to do with an act of will. We pray that God may pour into our hearts the affect of such love (tui amoris affectum), which is rooted in an emotion (amore—love), that we may obtain the promises. The prayer recalls 1 John 4:19, "We love, because he first loved us."

For propers for the rogation days see pp. 207–208 or 258–259 and 930.

Ascension Day (pp. 174 and 226)

The first collect dates to the Leonine, earliest of the sacramentaries (no. 169). It was selected as a postcommunion prayer for Ascension in the Scottish revision of 1912. Scriptural allusions include Eph. 4:10 and Mt. 28:20.

The second collect is essentially from the Gregorian sacramentary (no. 497). Cranmer substituted "our Lord" for "our Redeemer," added "heart" to "mind," and added the phrase "and with him continually dwell." The inspiration for the collect is Colossians 3:1–2.

Ascension Day is provided with an octave in the 1928 Book. In keeping with the restoration of the integrity of the Easter season, however, the octave has now been deleted. Ascension propers are to be used on the following two days.

Seventh Sunday of Easter: The Sunday after Ascension Day (pp. 175 and 226)

An antiphon sung at Vespers on Ascension Day is the basis for this collect, composed for the 1549 Book. For the English people the antiphon had particular significance because it had been sung by the Venerable Bede as he died at the time of Vespers on Ascension Day in 735. The antiphon, which is addressed to Christ, read: "O Lord, King of glory, Lord of hosts, who today did ascend in triumph above the heavens, leave us not orphans, but send upon us the promise of the Father, even the Spirit of Truth." Cranmer translated the word "orphans" with a weaker term "comfortless," which is used here in what is now an archaic meaning, "without strength," as well as "without consolation." Compare the petition of the traditional language version with that of the contemporary.

The Day of Pentecost: Whitsunday (pp. 175–176 and 227)

The rubric spells out the provision for a baptismal vigil for Pentecost, one of the five great baptismal days recommended in this Prayer Book. The other four are Easter, the feast of the Baptism of our Lord, All Saints' Day or the Sunday following, and the time of the Bishop's visitation (see p. 312). From the second century on, Pentecost had been a time for baptizing those who had been prepared but who, for some reason, had not been baptized at Easter. The ancient sacramentaries provide propers for a Pentecost vigil, though in the late medieval period the custom of "saving" candidates for baptism was dis-

183

couraged. Although the early Prayer Books emphasized immediate baptism of newborn infants, there was a revival of Easter and Pentecost as the two principal baptismal days. This lasted into the nineteenth century. The Pentecost vigil in this Book is modeled after the Great Vigil of Easter, though much simplified. The Pentecost vigil emphasizes the concept that we receive the Holy Spirit at baptism and are incorporated into the community of the Holy Spirit.

The first collect of Pentecost, which alludes to the Pentecost event recorded in Acts 2, is new to this revision. It stresses the universality and missionary implications of the Gospel. Basic to the collect is the second of the collects of the Mass for Pentecost in the Gelasian sacramentary (no. 638):

> God, who on this festal day sanctified your universal church for every race and nation: Pour out through the whole world the gifts of your Holy Spirit, that what was begun among them at the beginning of the preaching of the Gospel with divine magnanimity may now also be poured out through the hearts of believers.

The second collect dates to the Gregorian sacramentary where it is appointed for the morning Mass at St. Peter's Basilica (no. 526). It is also the prayer for the morning Mass in the Sarum missal and the collect for Pentecost in all earlier Prayer Books. The word "comfort" is a translation of the word for "consolation." When we exercise the right judgment, which is the gift of the Spirit for which we pray, we receive the gift of joy in His holy consolation.

Pentecost is the culmination of the Great Fifty Days of the Easter Season which this revision has restored to its integrity. The use of the Pentecost collect and preface through the week, as well as the propers for Monday and Tuesday in "Whitsun Week," has therefore been suppressed.

The second rubric designates Wednesday, Friday, and Saturday of this week as the traditional summer ember days; these may now be transferred to a time suited to local or diocesan ordination practice. In earlier times the placing of ember days in this week signified the return to the regular round of fasting which had been forbidden during the Great Fifty Days. (For the propers for ember days see pp. 205–206 or 256–257 and 929, no. 15, "For the Ministry.")

The First Sunday after Pentecost: Trinity Sunday (pp. 176 and 228)

The early sacramentaries provided no proper for this Sunday because it followed the lengthy vigil and ordination Mass which was the culmination of the ember days. Later medieval books, for example the Leofric missal, included a votive Mass of the Holy Trinity which became the basis for the prayers used on the feast of the Trinity once that feast was established. Sometime late in the middle ages the ending of the collect was changed: it was no longer addressed to the Father through Jesus Christ our Lord but to the Holy Trinity. The word "grace" in the address is a Cranmerian insertion with no equivalent in the Latin. The 1549 petition was closer to the original than was that of 1662. 1549 reads: "we beseech thee, that through the steadfastness of this faith, we may evermore be defended from all adversity." In 1662 this was changed to read: "we beseech thee, that thou wouldest keep us steadfast in this faith and evermore defend us from all adversities." The present revision again addresses the prayer to the Father and changes the petition to bring it into parallel relation to the address.

The rubric restores the pre-1549 custom of treating the proper of the Holy Trinity as the proper of the feast itself rather than as a proper for use throughout the ensuing week.

Proper 1 (pp. 176–177 and 228)

Armitage Robinson translated this collect from a prayer in one of the September Masses of the Leonine sacramentary (no. 976). It was included among the occasional prayers in the 1928 English revision.

Proper 2 (pp. 177 and 228–229)

In the Sarum missal and earlier Prayer Books this collect had been associated with the twentieth Sunday after Trinity; it has undergone numerous revisions. In the Gelasian sacramentary it is the first collect in the fifteenth of sixteen Sunday Masses (no. 1234). The supplement to the Gregorian sets it as the collect (no. 1186) for the twentieth Sunday after (the) Pentecost (octave). Cranmer translated it:

> Almighty and merciful God, of thy bountiful goodness, keep us from all things that may hurt us; that we, being ready both in body and soul, may with free hearts accomplish those things that thou wouldest have done; through Jesus Christ our Lord.

He substituted "of thy bountiful goodness" for the Latin "having been propitiated," "keep us from all things that may hurt us" for "shut out all things adverse to us," "soul" for "mind," and "that thou wouldest have done" for "the things that are thine."

185

The 1662 revisers substituted "cheerfully" for "with free hearts," and the American Proposed Book used the weaker phrase "those things which thou commandest" in place of "those things that thou wouldest have done." The new version restores Cranmer's phrase "with free hearts," and uses "those things which belong to thy purpose" in place of "those things which thou commandest," bringing the petition closer to the original and enriching the meaning of the prayer.

Proper 3 (pp. 177 and 229)

In the Sarum missal and earlier Prayer Books this collect is set for the fifth Sunday after Trinity. It dates to the Leonine sacramentary where it appears among the Masses for July (no. 633). In the Gregorian supplement it was included (no. 1141) as the collect for the fifth Sunday after (the) Pentecost (octave). It reflects conditions of the period of barbarian invasions. Cranmer translated it:

> Grant, Lord, we beseech thee, that the course of this world may be so peaceably ordered by thy governance, that thy congregation may joyfully serve thee in all godly quietness; through Jesus Christ our Lord.

A more literal translation would be: "Grant us, Lord, we beseech you, both that the course of the world may be directed peaceably for us by your governance, and (that) your church (*ecclesia*) may rejoice with tranquil devotion." The revisers of 1662, reacting against the Puritan preference for and interpretation of the word "congregation" substituted the word "Church." The present revision replaces "ordered by thy governance" with "governed by thy providence" and substitutes "serve thee in confidence and serenity" for "serve thee in all godly quietness." The word "and" is deliberately restored in the middle of the prayer so that the state of the church is not made absolutely dependent on the state of the world nor the state of the world dependent on the state of the church.

Proper 4 (pp. 177 and 229)

In the Gelasian sacramentary this collect is the first prayer of the third of sixteen Sunday Masses (no. 1186); it was included in the supplement to the Gregorian sacramentary as the collect (no. 1150) of the eighth Sunday after (the) Pentecost (octave). The Sarum missal and earlier Prayer Books appointed it for the eighth Sunday after

Trinity. The first phrase "God whose providence is never-failing in ordering its own," Cranmer translated as "God, whose providence is never deceived." This phrase was revised in 1662, restoring the thought that God orders as well as foresees. A more literal translation would be "O God, whose providence is infallible in ordering (or bringing about) that which is proper to itself." The collect teaches that though hurtful things may happen to us, nothing can deny or destroy the purposes of God who is able to overrule evil and give us that which is profitable for us.

Proper 5 (pp. 178 and 229)

Earlier Prayer Books and the Sarum missal appointed this collect for the fifth Sunday after Easter, but it has been replaced there with one more appropriate to the Easter season. The Gelasian sacramentary (no. 556) and the supplement to the Gregorian (no. 1123) both contain the collect for the fourth Sunday after the Easter octave. The opening of the petition, prior to this edition, read "Grant to us thy humble servants, that by thy holy inspiration we may think those things that are good." The word "good" in this context was subject to misinterpretation; "right" restores the original Latin connotation.

Proper 6 (pp. 178 and 230)

This collect is new, but the preamble includes quotations from the collects for the fifth Sunday after the Epiphany, the second Sunday after Trinity, and the twenty-second Sunday after Trinity in earlier Prayer Books. The prayer was drafted by the Rev. Dr. Massey H. Shepherd, Jr. It portrays the church's mission to the world—a ministry of proclamation of the gospel and of social concern and action. In order that we may fulfill this mission we pray that the church might be kept in God's steadfast faith and love.

Proper 7 (pp. 178 and 230)

This Gelasian collect for the Sunday after the Ascension (no. 586) was included in the supplement to the Gregorian sacramentary (no. 1132) as the collect of the second Sunday after (the) Pentecost (octave). In the Sarum missal and earlier Prayer Books it was appointed on the second Sunday after Trinity. Cranmer's translation reads:

> Lord, make us to have a perpetual fear and love of thy holy Name: for thou never failest to help and govern them whom thou dost bring up in thy steadfast love. Grant this, etc.

187

The expanded version of 1662 reads:

O Lord, who never failest to help and govern them whom thou dost bring up in thy steadfast fear, and love; Keep us, we beseech thee, under the protection of thy good providence, and make us to have a perpetual fear, and love of thy holy name, through Jesus Christ our Lord. *Amen.*

In the present revision the language is closer to that of the original and that of Cranmer. The Latin contains in the address the qualifying word "pariter" which was lost in the English versions. It might be rendered, "Make us perpetually to have fear, and no less, love of your holy Name." Some editions of the Prayer Book have attempted to convey this thought by inserting a comma after "fear." "Name" carries the idea of God's self-revelation.

Proper 8 (pp. 178–179 and 230)

This collect, composed for the 1549 Prayer Book, was formerly associated with the feast of Saint Simon and Saint Jude. It is based upon Ephesians 2:20–22 and 4:3. The 1662 Prayer Book, following the precedent of the Scottish Book of 1637, substituted "Church" for "congregation" because of the Puritan connotation of "congregation." In the present revision "chief cornerstone" replaces "head cornerstone." Because of its reference to the apostles the collect was deliberately placed on the Sunday closest to the Feast of Saint Peter and Saint Paul.

Proper 9 (pp. 179 and 230–231)

In the earliest of the sacramentaries, the Leonine, this prayer is associated with a September Mass (no. 971). The translation is a slightly revised version of that included in *Parish Prayers*, compiled and edited by Frank Colquhoun (London: Hodder and Stoughton, 1967), no. 1555.

Proper 10 (pp. 179 and 231)

The Gregorian sacramentary appoints this collect for a Sunday after Christmas (no. 86); in the supplement it is set for the first Sunday after Epiphany (no. 1096). The Sarum missal used it for the Sunday after the octave of Epiphany. The 1549 Book dropped the observance of the octave and restored the collect to the first Sunday after the Epiphany. A more literal translation of the preamble would be "We ask you, Lord, to attend with heavenly mercy the prayers of suppliant people." The words "and know" and "grace and" are not in the Latin original. Since that Sunday is observed in the present revision as the feast of the Baptism of our Lord, the collect was transferred to this Sunday. It summarizes succinctly the two-fold meaning and purpose of prayer: to perceive God's will, and to seek the strength which is necessary for the accomplishment of it.

Proper 11 (pp. 179 and 231)

In the 1549 Book, for which it was composed, this collect is one of six printed under a rubric "Collects to be said after the Offertory when there is no Communion, every such day one." These were provided for use as a fitting close to the service on days when the liturgy of the word, or Ante-Communion, was required but there were too few communicants for the service to continue to the end of the Eucharist. In 1552 and in later revisions these collects were also allowed after the Collects of Morning or Evening Prayer or Communion, or after the Litany. Scriptural allusions include Ecclus. 1:5, Mt. 8:8, and Rom. 8:26. The present revision changed "vouchsafe to give us" to "mercifully give us."

Proper 12 (pp. 189 and 231)

The supplement to the Gregorian sacramentary appoints this collect (no. 1138) for the fourth Sunday after (the) Pentecost (octave). The initial phrase is the same as that of a collect in the Gelasian sacramentary (no. 1548) and the Gallican Bobbio missal (no. 442). The Sarum missal and earlier Prayer Books used it for the fourth Sunday after Trinity. A more literal translation would be:

> God, the protector of all who hope in you, without whom nothing is strong, nothing is holy: Multiply upon us your mercy, that ruled and guided by you, we may so pass through temporal good things that we be not turned away from things eternal.

In keeping with the Reformation emphasis on faith, Cranmer substituted "trust" for "hope." He improved the collect by omitting the qualifying adjective "good," so that the prayer applies to times of adversity as well as times of prosperity, though the adjective could be interpreted as a positive assertion that things temporal are themselves good as well as things eternal. His insertion of the "finally" (retained in the traditional version only) was not an improvement, for

189

it may be taken as postponing the receiving of things eternal until after this earthly life.

Proper 13 (pp. 180 and 232)

This collect is the first in the eleventh of the sixteen Sunday Masses in the Gelasian sacramentary (no. 1218). The Gregorian supplement appoints it (no. 1174) for the sixteenth Sunday after (the) Pentecost (octave). The Sarum missal and previous Prayer Books set it for the sixteenth Sunday after Trinity. The 1662 revision replaced "congregation" with "Church" because of the connotation of "congregation" among the Puritans. The original is *ecclesia*.

Proper 14 (pp. 180 and 232)

This is the initial collect for one of the September Masses in the Leonine sacramentary (no. 1015) and of the fourth of the Sunday Masses of the Gelasian (no. 1190). The supplement to the Gregorian (no. 1153) appoints it for the ninth Sunday after (the) Pentecost (octave). The Sarum missal and earlier Prayer Books associate it with the ninth Sunday after Trinity. The result clause, prior to 1662, reads "which cannot be (exist) without thee;" it was changed in 1662 to "who cannot do any thing that is good without thee." The translation of the present revision is closer to the original.

The prayer was improved in the 1662 revision by the substitution of "enabled" for "able," though the original possibly calls for a stronger word, "That we may be *powerful* to live according to thy will." Cranmer inserted "by thee," reinforcing the idea of the need for God's grace. This collect is a succinct statement of the doctrine of grace: it is not only true that we cannot think or do the right or live according to God's will without His grace; we cannot even exist without the grace of God. There is an allusion, more apparent in the original, to Philippians 4:8–9.

Proper 15 (pp. 180–181 and 232)

In the 1549 Book (for which it was composed) and later editions of the Prayer Book, this collect was appointed for the second Sunday after Easter; the present revision uses a collect more appropriate for that Sunday. The substitution of the word "example" for "ensample" is a return to the text prior to 1662. The collect explains the work of Christ and the response of the Christian. Christ came both as a sacrifice for sin on our behalf and as an example of the kind of life God expects of us. Our response is thanksgiving for these benefits, issuing

190

in a daily endeavor to follow in His steps. In order to make this response we pray for God's grace.

Proper 16 (pp. 181 and 232–233)

This collect was new to the 1928 Book for Tuesday in Whitsun Week. The preamble derives from a Gregorian collect (no. 542) for the Friday after Pentecost. The Gregorian petition is that the church may not be disturbed by the assault of the enemy. The petition of the Prayer Book collect is that the church, united through the gift of the Spirit, may make God's power manifest throughout the world.

Proper 17 (pp. 181 and 233)

In the Gelasian sacramentary this is the initial collect for the second of the sixteen Sunday Masses (no. 1182). The supplement to the Gregorian (no. 1147) appointed it for the seventh Sunday after (the) Pentecost (octave). The Sarum missal and earlier Prayer Books place it on the seventh Sunday after Trinity. The Latin preamble might be translated "God of virtue (power) whose is all that is best." Cranmer's paraphrase recalls James 1:17. The word "Name" connotes the self-revelation of God. Religious controversies of the period may be reflected in Cranmer's insertion of "true" before "religion."

The next to the last phrase might be better translated "nourish what is good in us," and the original last phrase "with fatherly care guard what you have nourished" was translated by Cranmer "and of thy great mercy keep us in the same." The present revision substitutes a new phrase "bring forth in us the fruit of good works." The collect is an extended metaphor of the farmer or gardener: the fruit of good works is brought forth by the grace of God who plants, nourishes, and continues to care for His own.

Proper 18 (pp. 181 and 233)

New to this edition of the Prayer Book, this collect dates to the Leonine sacramentary where it is found among the Masses for July (no. 540). The translation is from William Bright's *Ancient Collects* (p. 74). James 4:6 is the source of the biblical allusion: pride is the enemy of trust; the Christian can boast only in the mercy of God.

Proper 19 (pp. 182 and 233)

This was the opening collect of the fourteenth of sixteen Sunday Masses of the Gelasian sacramentary (no. 1230), and was appointed for the nineteenth Sunday after (the) Pentecost (octave) in the Gregorian supplement (no. 1183). Both the Sarum missal and earlier Prayer Books used it for the nineteenth Sunday after Trinity. The Latin might be more literally translated "Direct our hearts, O Lord, we beseech you, by the working of your mercy, for without you we are not able to please you." The 1549 translation is:

> O God, forasmuch as without thee, we are not able to please thee:
> Grant that the working of thy mercy may in all things direct and
> rule our hearts; Through Jesus Christ our Lord.

In 1662 it was revised to the present form which specifically mentions the Holy Spirit.

The Wednesday, Friday, and Saturday following September 14 are the traditional autumn ember days, though these may be transferred to a time immediately preceding local or diocesan ordinations. (The propers for ember days are printed on pp. 205–206 or 256–257 and 929, no. 15, "For the Ministry.")

Proper 20 (pp. 182 and 234)

This collect reflects the tumultuous times of the barbarian invasions. It is from the Leonine sacramentary as a collect for use on Ascension Day (no. 173). The translation is from William Bright's *Ancient Collects* (page 79), and is included in the Prayer Book for the first time. Colossians 3:2 provides the biblical reference.

Proper 21 (pp. 182 and 232)

The Gallican Missale Gothicum includes this as the initial prayer of the first of six Sunday Masses (no. 477); it is the first prayer of the sixth of sixteen Sunday Masses in the Gelasian sacramentary (no. 1198). The supplement to the Gregorian appoints it (no. 1159) for the eleventh Sunday after (the) Pentecost (octave), and the Sarum missal and previous Prayer Books for the eleventh Sunday after Trinity. It has undergone several revisions. The 1549 version reads:

> God, which declarest thy almighty power, most chiefly in show-
> ing mercy and pity; Give unto us abundantly thy grace that we,
> running to thy promises, may be made partakers of thy heavenly
> treasure; through Jesus Christ our Lord.

The words "mercy and pity" would be more literally translated "sparing and showing compassion." "Give unto us abundantly thy grace" might be more literally "multiply upon us your grace."

In 1662 the revised petition read: "Mercifully grant unto us such a measure of thy grace, that we running the way of thy Commandments, may obtain thy gracious promises, and be made partakers of thy heavenly treasure." That revision seemed to make the receiving of heavenly treasure a reward for obedience to the commandments rather than a free gift of grace which we pray that we might run forward eagerly to receive. In the present revision the collect is revised to make it similar to Cranmer's version. The preamble states with striking force that the supreme demonstration of God's power is shown not in creation and providence, but in His redemptive love and mercy.

Proper 22 (pp. 182–183 and 234)

In the earliest of the sacramentaries, the Leonine, this collect is found among prayers for the autumn ember days (no. 917). Greatly revised, it appears in the Gallican Missale Francorum as the concluding collect of the prayers of the people at a Sunday Mass (no. 140) and as the first prayer of the seventh of the sixteen Sunday Masses in the Gelasian sacramentary (no. 1201). The supplement to the Gregorian appoints it (no. 1162) as the collect for the twelfth Sunday after (the) Pentecost (octave). The Sarum missal and previous Prayer Books place it on the twelfth Sunday after Trinity. The 1549 ending "giving unto us that that our prayer dare not presume to ask, through Jesus Christ our Lord," was closer to the Latin versions than the fuller ending of 1662. Our sense of our own unworthiness often makes us unwilling to pray, yet through prayer we receive forgiveness for our sins as well as "other good things which we are not worthy to ask, but through the merits and mediation of Jesus Christ."

Proper 23 (pp. 183 and 234–235)

This appears in the Gregorian sacramentary among a group of prayers for morning or evening (no. 966), and in the supplement (no. 1177) as the collect for the seventeenth Sunday after (the) Pentecost (octave). It is used for the seventeenth Sunday after Trinity in the Sarum missal and earlier Prayer Books. "All" is not in the Latin. Earlier editions had "prevent" in its archaic meaning "go before" (rather than the modern meaning "hinder"). The prayer is for grace which anticipates us as well as grace which accompanies us that we may be continually dedicated to good works—"prevenient" and "cooperating" grace.

Proper 24 (pp. 183 and 235)

New to this edition of the Prayer Book, this collect is the first of the nine solèmn collects of Good Friday in the Gelasian sacramentary (no. 401), the Missale Gallicanum vetus (no. 95), the Gregorian sacramentary (no. 339), and the Sarum missal. The translation is based on that of William Bright in *Ancient Collects* (page 98).

Proper 25 (pp. 183 and 235)

The prayer is among a series for use at Vespers in the Leonine sacramentary (no. 598). The Gelasian appoints it as the initial prayer of the eighth of the sixteen Sunday Masses (no. 1209), and the Gregorian supplement has it as the collect (no. 1168) for the fourteenth Sunday after (the) Pentecost (octave). The Sarum missal and earlier Prayer Books associate it with the fourteenth Sunday after Trinity. The message is clear and forthright: only if we love what God commands can we render cheerful obedience, and for this we need the gifts of faith, hope, and charity. The Latin form has "that we may deserve to obtain what you promise," but Cranmer eliminated any idea of merit from the collect.

Proper 26 (pp. 184 and 235)

This collect is in the Leonine sacramentary among the Masses for July (no. 574). In the Gelasian it is the second of the collects for the eighth of the sixteen Sunday Masses (no. 1206). The Gregorian supplement appoints it (no. 1165) for the thirteenth Sunday after (the) Pentecost (octave); the Sarum missal and previous Prayer Books place it on the thirteenth Sunday after Trinity. The 1549 translation reads:

> Almighty and merciful God, of whose only gift it cometh that thy faithful people do unto thee true and laudable service; grant, we beseech thee, that we may so run to thy heavenly promises, that we fail not finally to attain the same; through Jesus Christ our Lord.

The word "only" used in the sense of "alone" (whose gift alone) is not found in the Latin. "True" is used in place of the "worthy" (*digne*) of the Latin. The 1662 revisers made a change in the ending which drastically altered the meaning: "that we may so faithfully serve thee in this life, that we fail not finally to attain thy heavenly promises, through the merits of Jesus Christ our Lord." The present revision provides a more faithful translation. The imagery is similar to that of Proper 21 (above).

Proper 27 (pp. 184 and 236)

This collect was composed for the 1662 revision for use on the sixth Sunday after the Epiphany which, prior to that time, had no proper of its own. Bishop John Cosin is believed to be the author. The prayer has for its scriptural base the Epistle provided for the Sunday, 1 John 3:1–9. The present revision places the collect on the third Sunday before Advent when the lections begin to focus our attention on the second advent, the time of Christ's coming again with power and glory.

Proper 28 (pp. 184 and 236)

New emphasis on the Scriptures in the Reformation period is reflected in this collect, composed for the 1549 Book. It is based on Romans 15:4, the initial verse of the Epistle for the second Sunday in Advent, the day with which this collect was associated in earlier Prayer Books. The word "learning" means "instruction," not "memorization," and the phrase "by patience and comfort of thy holy Word," in the traditional version means "by steadfastness and by the encouragement of the Scriptures" (Revised Standard Version). The word "all" in the preamble recalls the criticism of the medieval service books in the preface to the first Prayer Book (Historical Documents, pp. 866–867): course readings from scripture were so often interrupted by saints' days that the Scriptures were never read in their entirety toward the close of the middle ages. The first Prayer Book provided an orderly arrangement for reading almost the whole of the Scriptures within the course of each year in the daily office.

Proper 29 (pp. 185 and 236)

This is a somewhat free translation by Capt. Howard E. Galley of the collect of the Feast of Christ the King in the Roman Missal. Christ is portrayed as the king who frees those who are bound and unites under His gracious rule all who are divided.

Holy Days (pp. 185–194 and 237–246)

Saint Andrew (pp. 185 and 237)

The Sarum collect, asking that Andrew be a perpetual intercessor for us, was replaced in the 1549 Book by a new prayer based on the legend of his death on a cross:

> Almighty God, which hast given such grace to thy Apostle Saint Andrew, that he counted the sharp and painful death of the cross to be an high honor, and a great glory: Grant us to take and esteem all troubles and adversities which shall come unto us for thy sake, as things profitable for us toward the obtaining of everlasting life; through Jesus Christ our Lord.

In 1552 this was replaced by the only collect new to that revision; based on the story of his call. It read:

> Almighty God which didst give such grace unto thy holy Apostle Saint Andrew, that he readily obeyed the calling of thy Son, Jesus Christ, and followed him without delay: Grant unto us all, that we being called by thy holy Word, may forthwith give over ourselves obediently to follow thy holy commandments; through the same Jesus Christ our Lord.

The collect was revised for the present Prayer Book on the basis of a draft by the Rev. Dr. Charles M. Guilbert in order to include the missionary emphasis which is also stressed in the biblical account of Andrew's call.

Saint Thomas (pp. 185 and 237)

This is a newly revised version of the collect composed for the 1549 Prayer Book. The original preamble read "Almighty everliving God, which for the more confirmation of the faith didst suffer thy Apostle Thomas to be doubtful in thy Son's resurrection." The new preamble does not attribute Thomas' doubt to any action of God. The result clause replaces "that our faith in thy sight never be reproved" with "that our faith may never be found wanting." The addition, "our Lord and our God," reminds us of Thomas' confession of faith in the risen Lord (John 20:28).

Saint Stephen (pp. 186 and 237)

This is based on the Gregorian collect (no. 62) of the Sarum missal which was freely translated in the 1549 Book:

Grant us, O Lord, to learn to love our enemies, by the example of thy martyr Saint Stephen, who prayed to thee for his persecutors; which livest and reignest, etc.

The word "enemies" was changed to "persecutors" in 1662 and the collect expanded:

Grant, O Lord, that, in all our sufferings here upon earth for the testimony of thy truth, we may steadfastly look up to heaven and by faith behold the glory that shall be revealed; and, being filled with the Holy Ghost, may learn to love and bless our persecutors by the example of thy first martyr Saint Stephen, who prayed for his murderers to thee, O blessed Jesus, who standest at the right hand of God to succour all those that suffer for thee, our only mediator and advocate. *Amen.*

The present revision provides a note of thanksgiving for the example of Stephen in a collect less complicated in structure.

Saint John (pp. 186 and 238)

In the oldest of the sacramentaries, the Leonine, this was a collect said super populum (over the people as a blessing) (no. 1283). In a shortened version it appeared in the Gregorian sacramentary (no. 67). The 1549 version reads:

Merciful Lord, we beseech thee to cast thy bright beams of light upon thy Church: that it being lightened by the doctrine of the blessed Apostle and Evangelist John may attain to thy everlasting gifts; Through Jesus Christ our Lord.

In 1662 the final clause was revised to "may so walk in the light of thy truth, that it may at length attain to the light of everlasting life." The metaphor of light was played down in the first American revision, despite its importance in Johannine writings. The word "instructed" replaced "lightened" (1549) or "enlightened" (1662), and the words "the light of" were omitted in the conclusion. The 1928 version restored some of the imagery, substituting "illumined" for "instructed." In the new revision the preamble has been strengthened and the petition has been changed so that we pray that "we" rather than the "Church" may attain life everlasting.

197

The Holy Innocents (pp. 186 and 238)

The Rev. Dr. Charles M. Guilbert drafted this collect to replace one dating to 1662:

> O Almighty God, who out of the mouths of babes and sucklings hast ordained strength, and madest infants to glorify thee by their deaths; Mortify and kill all vices in us, and so strengthen us by thy grace, that by the innocency of our lives, and constancy of our faith even unto death, we may glorify thy holy Name; through Jesus Christ our Lord. *Amen.*

The 1549 collect, a translation of one which can be traced to the Gelasian (no. 42) and Gregorian (no. 75) sacramentaries, reads:

> Almighty God, whose praise this day the young innocents thy witnesses hath confessed and showed forth, not in speaking but in dying; Mortify and kill all vices in us, that in our conversation our life may express thy faith, which with our tongues we do confess; through Jesus Christ our Lord.

The Gallican Missale Gothicum contains a variant (no. 89). The present collect portrays the Holy Innocents as victims of injustice, and prays both that God would receive innocent victims and that He would frustrate the designs of evil tyrants and establish His reign of justice, love, and peace.

Confession of Saint Peter (pp. 187 and 238)

The Gospel of the day is the obvious inspiration for this new collect. It makes plain that the rock on which the church is built is not Peter himself but the faith which he confessed. The Rev. Dr. Massey H. Shepherd, Jr. drafted the collect.

Conversion of Saint Paul (pp. 187 and 238–239)

The 1549 Book provided a collect based on the one in the Sarum missal:

> God, which hast taught all the world, through the preaching of thy blessed apostle Saint Paul; Grant, we beseech thee, that we which have his wonderful conversion in remembrance, may follow and fulfill the holy doctrine that he taught; through Jesus Christ our Lord.

The last phrase in the Sarum missal had read, "may by his example advance toward thee." The present form is essentially the revision of 1662, which fittingly puts the emphasis on the "preaching" rather than on the "teaching" of Paul. The Sarum collect had emphasized the example of Paul; the Prayer Book version emphasizes the following of his doctrine.

The Presentation (pp. 187 and 239)

Cranmer's translation of this collect which dates from the Gregorian sacramentary (no. 124) reads:

> Almighty and everlasting God, we humbly beseech thy Majesty, that as thy only begotten Son was this day presented in the Temple in the substance of our flesh; so grant that we may be presented unto thee with pure and clear minds; by Jesus Christ our Lord.

The Latin had "with the substance of our flesh," and the ending was introduced by "through" rather than "by." The 1662 revisers substituted "everliving" for "everlasting" and "clean hearts" for "clear minds." They also expanded the ending to read "by the same thy Son Jesus Christ our Lord." The present revision substitutes "thee" for "thy Majesty" and omits the phrase "in the substance of our flesh," for this metaphysical terminology tends now to be confusing rather than helpful. The collect reveals the fact that in its origin this feast was a celebration of the presentation of our Lord rather than the purification of His mother. That became the principal emphasis in the late medieval period, and was retained until this revision. Even if Cranmer did not intend it, the punctuation from 1662 indicates that the use of "by" rather than "through" means not that the petition is offered through the mediation of Christ but that we may be presented to God by Christ, a teaching set forth in the Scriptures (Eph. 5:25–27; Col. 1:21–23; Jude 24–25).

Saint Matthias (pp. 188 and 239)

This collect, based upon the lesson from Acts, was composed for the 1549 Prayer Book. The present revision omits the words "the traitor" which had appeared before the name of Judas, and the word "Apostles" which had appeared after the mention of the Twelve. The petition formerly read, "Grant that thy Church, being alway preserved from false Apostles, may be ordered and guided by faithful and true pastors."

Saint Joseph (pp. 188 and 239)

The petition of this new collect is a prayer that we may imitate Saint Joseph in righteousness and in obedience to the command of the Lord, his two virtues of special note in the Gospel account. The preamble is a variant of that in the collect for this day from the South African Prayer Book:

> O God, who didst choose thy servant Joseph to be the guardian of thine only-begotten Son, and the spouse of his Virgin Mother: Grant, we beseech thee, that in the family of thy holy Church we may ever be united with the same thy Son Jesus Christ our Lord, who liveth and reigneth with thee and the Holy Ghost, ever one God, world without end. *Amen.*

The reference in the preamble to the "family of thy servant David" is taken from the Canadian Prayer Book. The Rev. Dr. Massey H. Shepherd, Jr. drafted the collect for the present Book.

The Annunciation (pp. 188 and 240)

In the Gregorian sacramentary this collect is used as a postcommunion prayer for the feast of the Annunciation (no. 143). Cranmer translated it:

> We beseech thee, Lord, pour thy grace into our hearts; that, as we have known Christ thy Son's incarnation by the message of an angel; so by his cross and passion we may be brought unto the glory of his resurrection; Through the same Christ our Lord.

Both the 1662 revision and this Book made changes for the sake of clarification, though the substance of the original remains. In an admirable way the collect links the Annunciation and the Incarnation with the themes associated with the time of the year in which the feast occurs.

Saint Mark (pp. 188–189 and 240)

The Rev. Dr. Massey H. Shepherd, Jr. drafted this collect to replace one composed for the 1549 Book and revised in 1662. The 1549 version read:

> Almighty God, which hast instructed thy Holy Church with the heavenly doctrine of thy Evangelist Saint Mark: Give us grace so

200

to be established by thy holy Gospel, that we be not, like children, carried away with every blast of vain doctrine; through Jesus Christ our Lord.

The new collect clarifies the thought, updates the language, and brings into the prayer a note of thanksgiving for the witness of Saint Mark.

Saint Philip and Saint James (pp. 189 and 240)

Earlier Prayer Books provided for this day a collect that has been given wider exposure in the present revision as the collect for the fifth Sunday of Easter. A new collect, appropriate for the commemoration of these saints, has been modeled on the second collect of the Common of a Bishop in the South African Prayer Book (1954). "Name" as it is used in this collect signifies revelation.

The Visitation (pp. 189 and 240–241)

This is a revision of one of the original collects from William Bright's *Ancient Collects* (appendix, p. 236), under the title "On the Example of the Blessed Virgin." The preamble contains an allusion to Luke 11:27–28.

Saint Barnabas (pp. 189 and 241)

Cranmer provided a new collect for this day:

> Lord Almighty, which hast endued thy holy Apostle Barnabas with singular gifts of thy Holy Ghost; let us not be destitute of thy manifold gifts, nor yet of grace to use them always to thy honour and glory; through Jesus Christ our Lord.

Cranmer's collect, slightly revised in 1662, provided the theme for the first of the collects "Of a Theologian and Teacher" in the Common of Saints in the present revision. A new collect with specific reference to events in the life of the apostle was drafted by the Rev. Dr. Massey H. Shepherd, Jr. Allusions to the Scriptures include Acts 4:32–37; 9:19–30; and 13:1–3.

The Nativity of Saint John the Baptist (pp. 190 and 241)

This collect, composed for the 1549 Prayer Book, summarizes in a remarkably succinct manner the life and teachings of John. At the

201

time of the 1662 revision "repentance" replaced the word "penance" of the earlier editions.

Saint Peter and Saint Paul (pp. 190 and 241)

The collect for this day in the Sarum missal dates to the Leonine sacramentary (no. 280):

> God, who consecrated this day by the martyrdom of your blessed apostles Peter and Paul: Grant that your church diffused throughout the whole world may always be governed by the teaching of those through whom she received the beginning of her religion.

It is in both the Gelasian (no. 921) and Gregorian sacramentaries (no. 594); a variant reading is in the Gallican Bobbio missal (no. 329). Because the commemoration of Paul on this day was not continued in the 1549 Book, a new collect was provided based on our Lord's commission to Peter after the resurrection:

> Almighty God, which by thy Son Jesus Christ hast given to thy Apostle Saint Peter many excellent gifts, and commandest him earnestly to feed thy flock; make, we beseech thee, all bishops and pastors diligently to preach thy holy Word and the people obediently to follow the same, that they may receive the crown of everlasting glory; through Jesus Christ our Lord.

A variant form of this collect was inserted in the rite for the ordination of bishops in the 1662 Book. The new collect, drafted by the Rev. Dr. Massey H. Shepherd, Jr., commemorates the martyrdom of both Peter and Paul. The petition for unity is especially poignant when we recall the many conflicts between these two apostles. The petition alludes to 1 Cor. 3:11.

Independence Day (pp. 190 and 242)

This is a revised version of a collect, first included in the Prayer Book of 1928, composed by Bishop Edward Lambe Parsons. The preamble of the 1928 version reads: "O eternal God, through whose mighty power our fathers won their liberties of old." This had to be changed since many Americans now cannot identify with the heroes of the period of the Revolution as their ancestors. Furthermore, native Americans, many of whom are Episcopalians, never could pray

202

this prayer. The new preamble emphasizes that the founders of our country won liberties for generations yet to come as well as for themselves, and that they "lit the torch of freedom for nations then unborn." The Rev. Dr. Charles M. Guilbert drafted this revision.

Saint Mary Magdalene (pp. 191 and 242)

In the 1549 Book the collect composed for this feast read:

> Merciful Father, give us grace, that we never presume to sin through the example of any creature; but if it shall chance us at any time to offend thy divine majesty; that then we may truly repent, and lament the same, after the example of Mary Magdalene, and by lively faith obtain remission of all our sins; through the only merits of thy Son our Saviour Christ.

Commemoration of Mary was dropped from the 1552 Book but restored in recent Anglican revisions. The present collect is based on that of the English revision of 1928:

> O Almighty God, whose blessed Son did call and sanctify Mary Magdalen to be a witness to his resurrection: Mercifully grant that by thy grace we may be healed of all our infirmities, and always serve thee in the power of his endless life, who with thee and the Holy Ghost liveth and reigneth, one God, world without end. *Amen.*

Saint James (pp. 191 and 242)

The Rev. Dr. Charles M. Guilbert drafted this collect to replace the one composed for the 1549 Prayer Book:

> Grant, O merciful God, that as thine holy apostle James, leaving his father and all that he had, without delay was obedient unto the calling of thy Son Jesus Christ, and followed him; So we, forsaking all worldly and carnal affections, may be evermore ready to follow thy commandments; through Jesus Christ our Lord.

The new collect is not based upon his call, for that note is stressed in the collects for other saints (for example, those for the days of Saint Andrew and Saint Matthew), but on two other incidents in his life, narrated in the Epistle and Gospel for the day (Acts 11:27—12:3 and Mt. 20:20–28).

203

The Transfiguration (pp. 191 and 243)

This is a slightly revised version of the collect the Rev. Dr. William Reed Huntington wrote for the day, based on the Lukan story of the transfiguration. It was first included in the 1892 Prayer Book.

Saint Mary the Virgin (pp. 192 and 243)

This feast is new to the American Prayer Book and the collect is a revised form of that provided in the South African Prayer Book for the day titled "The Falling Asleep of the Blessed Virgin Mary." The Sarum collect which dates back to the Gregorian sacramentary (no. 661) reads:

> We beseech you, Lord, let us be continually aided by the sacred feast of this day on which the holy mother of God, who brought forth incarnate from herself your son our Lord, underwent temporal death yet could not be held in the bonds of death.

Saint Bartholomew (pp. 192 and 243)

The collect of the 1549 Prayer Book has essentially been restored in this Book. The 1662 revisers changed the petition to read "Grant, we beseech thee, unto thy Church, to love that word which he believed, and both to preach, and receive the same." Cranmer based his collect on that in the Sarum missal:

> Almighty, everlasting God, who this day have given us venerable and holy joy in the festivity of your blessed apostle Bartholomew: Grant, we beseech you, unto your Church both to love what he believed and to preach what he taught.

This collect, suitable for any day of an apostle or evangelist, is appointed in the Leonine (no. 1273) and the Gregorian (no. 74) sacramentaries as well as the Gallican Missale Gothicum (no. 322) for the feast of Saint John the Evangelist.

Holy Cross Day (pp. 192 and 244)

The Rev. Dr. Massey H. Shepherd, Jr. drafted this new collect. Scriptural allusions include John 3:14–15, Galatians 6:14, and Matthew 16:24. The collect for this day from the English revision of 1928 is used in this revision for the Tuesday in Holy Week.

Saint Matthew (pp. 192–193 and 244)

This new collect replaces the one composed for the 1549 Book:

> Almighty God, which by thy blessed Son didst call Matthew from
> the receipt of custom to be an Apostle and Evangelist; Grant us
> grace to forsake all covetous desires, and inordinate love of
> riches, and to follow thy said Son Jesus Christ; who liveth and
> reigneth, etc.

The Rev. Dr. Massey H. Shepherd, Jr. wrote the new collect reminiscent of that for the feast of Saint Andrew. It stresses the ready obedience of Matthew to his call and gives thanks for his witness to the gospel.

Saint Michael and All Angels (pp. 193 and 244)

The Gregorian sacramentary appoints this collect (no. 726) for the commemoration in the Basilica of the Holy Angels on September 29. In the Sarum missal it is associated with the feast of Saint Michael which was celebrated on September 29. Cranmer's translation reads:

> Everlasting God, which hast ordained and constituted the ser-
> vices of all Angels and men in a wonderful order: mercifully
> grant, that they which always do thee service in heaven, may by
> thy appointment succour and defend us in earth; through Jesus
> Christ our Lord, etc.

The phrase "by thy appointment" is not in the Latin. Revisers in 1662 made minor revisions for the sake of clarity. The present version adds "and worship," and substitutes "help" for "succour." The collect emphasizes beautifully the scriptural ideas concerning the ministry of angels: their service and worship of God in heaven and their help and protection of those on earth.

Saint Luke (pp. 193 and 244–245)

This collect is a revision of that composed for the 1928 Book by the Rev. Dr. Charles Morris Addison, a member of the revision commission. It replaced a collect composed for the 1549 Book and revised in 1662. The original version read:

> Almighty God, which calledst Luke the physician, whose praise
> is in the Gospel, to be a physician of the soul; it may please thee,

by the wholesome medicines of his doctrine, to heal all the diseases of our souls; through thy Son Jesus Christ our Lord.

The old form stressed the diseases of the soul; the newer prayer speaks of the healing of the whole person, in keeping with the renewed emphasis of the church on healing.

Saint James of Jerusalem (pp. 193 and 245)

This feast day, new to this Prayer Book, has a collect drafted by the Rev. Dr. Massey H. Shepherd, Jr. The petition calls to our minds the ministry of reconciliation performed by James in his position as head of the church in Jerusalem as he labored to reconcile Jewish and Gentile Christians in one body.

Saint Simon and Saint Jude (pp. 194 and 245)

The collect previously associated with this day has been assigned to Proper 8 (see above) for wider use and exposure. The characteristic of zeal associated with Simon provides the keynote for the collect drafted by the Rev. Dr. Massey H. Shepherd, Jr.

All Saints' Day (pp. 194 and 245)

This collect was composed for the 1549 Book. The 1662 revision substituted "blessed" for "holy," and "in all virtuous and godly living" for "in all virtues, and godly living." The present revision replaces "unspeakable" with "ineffable" since "unspeakable" has so changed and negative a connotation in modern English. The collect expresses in an admirable way Saint Paul's conception of the church as the Body of Christ.

Thanksgiving Day (pp. 194 and 246)

The Prayer Book of 1789 received the collect for this day from the Proposed Book of 1786:

> O most merciful Father, who hast blessed the labors of the husbandman in the returns of the fruits of the earth; We give thee humble and hearty thanks for this thy bounty; beseeching thee to continue thy loving-kindness to us; that our land may still yield her increase, to thy glory and our comfort; through Jesus Christ our Lord. *Amen.*

The petition is based on the occasional thanksgiving "For Plenty" from the revision of 1604. The Rev. Dr. Massey H. Shepherd, Jr. drafted the new collect which replaces that of 1789, emphasizing the dimension of stewardship, both in regard to faithful conservation of resources and provision for those in need.

The Common of Saints (pp. 195–199 and 246–250)

The rubrics refer to the regulations for "Days of Optional Observance," pp. 17–18, and to the lectionary, pp. 925–927, of the Prayer Book.

Of a Martyr (pp. 195–196 and 246–247)

The first collect was prepared for use on the feast of Saint Polycarp in Prayer Book Studies XII: The Propers for the Minor Holy Days. It is based on 1 Peter 3:15 and 4:16. "Name" means revelation.

The second is a revised version of the first of the collects provided in the Canadian Prayer Book (1959) for the commemoration of a martyr. Revelation 2:10, "Be faithful unto death, and I will give you a crown of life," is the scriptural source.

The third collect is in the Missale Gothicum, a Gallican sacramentary probably from the seventh century (no. 455), for use as the collect at the exchange of the peace at the commemoration of a martyr. William Bright's translation from *Ancient Collects* (p. 69) was the first of the two collects provided in the single proper "For a Saint's Day" in the 1928 Prayer Book.

Of a Missionary (pp. 196 and 247–248)

The first collect is a slightly revised form of one from the Indian Prayer Book supplement; this prayer was new to the English Prayer Book of 1928. Scriptural references are Eph. 3:8 and Col. 2:19.

The second is a slightly adapted form of that "Of Any Saint" in the English 1928 Prayer Book. Is. 49:3, 2 Thess. 1:9–12, and 1 Pet. 2:9 are the scriptural allusions.

Of a Pastor (pp. 196–197 and 248)

The Book of Common Worship of the Church of South India provided the theme for the first collect. The petition contains an allusion to Ephesians 4:11–13.

207

The second collect is a revision of the collect "Of a Bishop or Archbishop" in the Canadian Prayer Book (1959). Scriptural allusions include 1 Corinthians 4:1.

Of a Theologian and Teacher (pp. 197 and 248–249)

The first is a modified version of that "Of a Doctor of the Church, Poet, or Scholar" in the Canadian revision of 1959, which was dependent on the collect for Saint Barnabas in earlier Prayer Books. The preamble is based on 1 Corinthians 12:4–11.

The second collect is based on that for "Doctors of the Church" from the Book of Common Worship of the Church of South India. The added preamble contains an allusion to Ephesians 4:21. The petition has John 17:3 as its source.

Of a Monastic (pp. 198 and 249)

The first collect is a revised version of that "Of a Religious" from the Indian Prayer Book supplement. Scriptural allusions include 2 Corinthians 8:9 and Ephesians 6:5. One phrase is reminiscent of the collect for the feast of Saint Matthew in previous Prayer Books.

The collect "Of an Abbot or Abbess" in the Prayer Book of the Province of South Africa (1954) is the basis for the second collect. The petition stresses the need for discipline as well as love. Among the scriptural sources is Ephesians 5:8.

Of a Saint (pp. 198–199 and 250)

This is a revised version of the second collect provided for "A Saint's Day" in the 1928 Prayer Book. The commission drafted it, using as a basis Hebrews 12:1–2.

The second collect is a revised form of one of the original collects in the Appendix to William Bright's *Ancient Collects* (p. 236). Hebrews 11:13–16 and 12:22–24 are among the scriptural allusions.

The Rev. Roddey Reid wrote the third collect, a new one reminding us that saints support us in two ways: by their witness or example certainly, but also by surrounding us with their love and their prayers. This collect is also included (p. 395) for use after the prayers of the people.

Various Occasions (pp. 199–210 and 251–261)

The rubric refers to section 5, "Days of Optional Observance," of the Calendar of the Church Year, pp. 15–18 of the Prayer Book.

1. Of the Holy Trinity (pp. 199 and 251)

The Rev. Dr. Charles Guilbert drafted this collect for the present revision. Compare it with the collect for the First Sunday after Pentecost: Trinity Sunday (pp. 176 and 228). (For commentary, see above, pp. 184–185.)

2. Of the Holy Spirit (pp. 200 and 251)

This collect, by an unknown author, was first included in the Prayer Book in 1928 as the collect of the second proper for Pentecost. The work of the Holy Spirit is set forth as both enlightenment and strengthening for God's service.

3. Of the Holy Angels (pp. 200 and 251)

This is the collect for Saint Michael and All Angels. (For commentary, see above, p. 205.)

4. Of the Incarnation (pp. 200 and 252)

This is the collect of the Second Sunday after Christmas Day. (For commentary, see above, p. 170.)

5. Of the Holy Eucharist (pp. 201 and 252)

The rubric indicates that a commemoration of the institution of the Sacrament is appropriate on Thursdays, if no principal feast or holy day is to be observed.

The collect is a revised version of the one composed by Thomas Aquinas for the new feast of Corpus Christi recently instituted. The Scottish revision of 1929 was the first Anglican Prayer Book to include it, as "An Additional Collect for Maundy Thursday." Both the Scottish version and the original are addressed to the Second Person of the Trinity. In this form the collect is found in the Prayer Book under "Prayers and Thanksgivings," for use after receiving communion (p. 834).

6. Of the Holy Cross (pp. 201 and 252)

A commemoration of the Holy Cross is suitable on Fridays if no principal feast or holy day is to be observed. Compare with the collects for Fridays of the daily office.

The collect is adapted from one in *Daily Prayer*.[1]

---

[1] Compiled by Eric Milner-White and G. W. Briggs (Penguin Books, 1959), p. 41.

7. *For All Baptized Christians* (pp. 201 and 252–253)

The rubric indicates that a votive for all baptized Christians is appropriate on Saturdays if no principal feast day or holy day is to be observed.

This is a new collect based on Colossians 4:22. It might be compared with the older collects for "Easter Even." (See Holy Saturday, above, p. 178.)

8. *For the Departed* (pp. 202 and 253)

With the exception of the word "Give" in place of "Vouchsafe" this collect is in the form which appeared in the 1928 revision as the first of two collects provided for use at a celebration of Holy Eucharist "At the Burial of the Dead." The prayer is a slightly revised form of one adapted by Bishop John Wordsworth of Salisbury from *Words to Take with Us* by W. E. Scudamore. As an intercession for the whole church in this world and in the life beyond, the collect also sets forth the idea of an intermediate state, paradise, which precedes the "unending joy" anticipated after the last judgment.

The second collect is a revised form of a prayer introduced in the Prayer Book of 1928 and printed among additional prayers for family prayer, "For an Anniversary of One Departed." In that edition the result clause read: "that *he* may win, with thee and thy servants everywhere, the eternal victory." The thought of growth in service in the life beyond was a characteristic of prayers for the departed which were accepted in the 1928 edition. The revised result clause in the present book is the work of Capt. Howard E. Galley.[1] The whole collect is an adaptation of one written by Bishop Charles Lewis Slattery and printed in 1917 in the leaflet of Grace Church, New York, where he was then rector, under the caption "For Our Warriors."

The rubrics allow the substitution of any of the collects from the burial rites for either of the above. They also permit the substitution of forms from the burial rites for the prayers of the people and for the postcommunion prayer.

9. *Of the Reign of Christ* (pp. 202–203 and 254)

This is the collect for the last Sunday after Pentecost, Proper 29. (For commentary, see above, p. 195.)

---

[1] *A Short Book of Common Prayer*, New York: Church Hymnal Corp., 1970.

10. At Baptism (pp. 203 and 254)

This new collect, drafted by the committee on Christian initiation, stresses the moral implications of baptism, making use of both the Pauline emphasis on baptism as death and resurrection and the Johannine emphasis on baptism as new birth.

11. At Confirmation (pp. 203 and 254)

This collect was also drafted by the committee on Christian initiation. Closely related to the prayer for use at baptism, it emphasizes what has happened to us at baptism and sets forth clearly the relationship of the Holy Spirit to confirmation. The Holy Spirit is received at baptism; we pray that those being confirmed may be "renewed" in the Holy Spirit.

12. On the Anniversary of the Dedication of a Church (pp. 204 and 254–255)

The Scottish Prayer Book of 1912 was the first to provide a proper for use on this occasion. The American revision of 1928 provided a collect based on that prepared by Bishop John Dowden of Edinburgh for the Scottish Book. Dowden's version was based upon an ancient Gregorian collect (no. 1262) used also on that occasion in the Bobbio missal at the exchange of the peace (no. 390). The 1928 version reads:

> O God, whom year by year we praise for the dedication of this church; Hear, we beseech thee, the prayers of thy people, and grant that whosoever shall worship before thee in this place, may obtain thy merciful aid and protection; through Jesus Christ our Lord. *Amen.*

The new collect was influenced by a form composed by J. D. Wilkinson.[1]

The rubric gives permission on this occasion to substitute the litany of thanksgiving for a church (pp. 578–579) for the prayers of the people.

13. For a Church Convention (pp. 204 and 255)

This collect makes use of phrases from prayers for similar occasions in the South African, Indian, and Canadian Prayer Books. It replaces

[1] Printed in *The Calendar and Lessons for the Church's Year*, London: S.P.C.K., 1969, p. 89.

"A Prayer to be used at the Meetings of Convention," based upon the conclusion of the Elizabethan Homily for Whitsunday, which had been adopted by General Convention in 1799 and included in the Prayer Book by action of the convention of 1835.

The prayer, with the changes of the 1892 revision, reads:

> Almighty and everlasting God, who by thy Holy Spirit didst preside in the Council of the blessed Apostles, and hast promised, through thy Son Jesus Christ, to be with thy Church to the end of the world; We beseech thee to be with the Council of thy Church *here* assembled in thy Name and Presence. Save *us* from all error, ignorance, pride, and prejudice; and of thy great mercy vouchsafe, we beseech thee, so to direct, sanctify, and govern *us* in *our* work, by the mighty power of the Holy Ghost, that the comfortable Gospel of Christ may be truly preached, truly received, and truly followed, in all places, to the breaking down the kingdom of sin, Satan, and death; till at length the whole of thy dispersed sheep, being gathered into one fold, shall become partakers of everlasting life; through the merits and death of Jesus Christ our Saviour. *Amen.*

14. *For the Unity of the Church* (pp. 204–205 and 255)

This collect is based on a prayer by Archbishop William Temple quoted in *Parish Prayers*.[1] The scriptural reference is to John 17:20–21.

15. *For the Ministry* (pp. 205–206 and 256–257)

The rubric points out that these propers may be used on the traditional ember days (p. 18) or in conjunction with ordinations at other times, or on other occasions as suitable.

The first prayer is a variant form of the collects of the rites for the ordination of deacons and presbyters of all previous Prayer Books. The Scottish Book of 1637 printed it with other intercessions to be said at Morning Prayer on days when the Litany was not appointed to be read under a rubric: "A prayer to be said in the Ember Weeks, for those which are then to be admitted into Holy Orders; and is to be read every day of the week, beginning on the Sunday before the day of Ordination." The English Book of 1662 included it among the occasional prayers as an alternative for use during the ember weeks.

---

[1] Edited by Frank Colquhoun, London: Hodder & Stoughton, 1967, no. 494.

In the American revision (1789) the rubric was changed: "To be used in the weeks preceding the stated times of Ordination." In this revision the phrase "holiness of life" has been substituted for "innocency of life." The two primary qualifications for ordination set forth in the prayer are truth of doctrine and holiness of life.

The second collect, "For the choice of fit persons for the ministry," drafted by the Rev. Dr. H. Boone Porter, took as its inspiration a prayer from Bishop John Cosin's *Collection of Private Devotions* (1627) which had been included in the 1662 Book as one of two prayers to be said daily during the ember weeks (see above). The prayer read:

> Almighty God, our heavenly Father, who hast purchased to thy-self an universal Church by the precious blood of thy dear Son; Mercifully look upon the same, and at this time so guide and govern the minds of thy servants the Bishops and Pastors of thy flock, that they may lay hands suddenly on no man, but faithfully and wisely make choice of fit persons, to serve in the sacred Ministry of thy Church. And to those who shall be ordained to any holy function, give thy grace and heavenly benediction; that both by their life and doctrine they may show forth thy glory, and set forward the salvation of all men; through Jesus Christ our Lord. *Amen.*

This second collect also replaces a prayer added at the 1928 revision for the increase of the ministry, which emphasized the inclination of the individual rather than selection by the church:

> O Almighty God, look mercifully upon the world which thou hast redeemed by the blood of thy dear Son, and incline the hearts of many to dedicate themselves to the Sacred Ministry of thy Church; through the same thy Son Jesus Christ our Lord. *Amen.*

The collect "For all Christians in their vocation" is also the first of the solemn collects of Good Friday, and the first of three prayers for mission in Morning Prayer. (For commentary on this prayer see above, p. 127.)

16. *For the Mission of the Church* (pp. 206 and 257)

The first collect is the second of the prayers for mission in Morning Prayer. (For commentary, see above, pp. 127–128.)

The second collect is a revised form of an occasional prayer, "For the Spread of the Gospel," of the Indian Prayer Book supplement.

17. *For the Nation* (pp. 207 and 258)

The new collect is a revised form of a prayer by Henry Scott Holland included in *Parish Prayers*.[1]

A rubric allows for the substitution of the collect for Independence Day when this votive is used.

18. *For Peace* (pp. 207 and 258)

This collect is based on a prayer by Francis Paget, bishop of Oxford (1902–1911); it is included in the English revision of 1928, the South African, the Indian, and the Canadian Prayer Books.

19. *For Rogation Days* (pp. 207–208 and 258–259)

The rubric indicates that these propers may be used on the traditional days or at other times, for example, local times of planting, or the beginning of the season for the fishing industry. (See *The Book of Occasional Services*, pp. 101–103, for provisions for a rogation procession and special petitions for use in the Great Litany and Form V of the prayers of the people.)

The collect "For fruitful seasons" is a revised and amplified version of the collect for the rogation days included in the 1928 revision. It seems to have been influenced by a prayer "For the Fruits of the Earth" written by Bishop John Cosin and first printed in his *Collection of Private Devotions* (1627). The revision uses phrases from a prayer by E. W. Benson.[2]

The second collect, "For commerce and industry," is modeled after the occasional prayer "For Industry" in the Canadian Prayer Book.

"For stewardship of creation" is a new version of a collect first included in the 1928 Book under the caption "For Faithfulness in the Use of this World's Goods." The original apparently was a prayer "For the Rich" in the Book of Offices proposed to the General Convention of 1889 (p. 89).

20. *For the Sick* (pp. 208 and 260)

The collect is an emended and amplified version of the prayer "For the Recovery of a Sick Person" printed among the additional prayers in the 1928 edition:

---

[1] *Parish Prayers*, ed. Frank Colquhoun, no. 1114.
[2] *Parish Prayers*, no. 348.

O merciful God, giver of life and health; Bless, we pray thee, thy
servant, [N.], and those who administer to *him* of thy healing
gifts; that *he* may be restored to health of body and of mind;
through Jesus Christ our Lord. *Amen.*

The prayer was a condensation of one written by Bishop John Dowden and included in the Scottish Prayer Book of 1912.

The rubric allows the substitution of the postcommunion prayer
from the Ministration to the Sick (p. 457) when this votive is used.

21. *For Social Justice* (pp. 209 and 260)

The original prayer "For Social Justice" was included among the
occasional prayers in the 1928 Book. Some authorities have stated
that this was composed by the Rev. James Martineau, the English
Unitarian minister and philosopher. Others claim that Bishop
Edward Lambe Parsons, a member of the revision commission, was
the composer. Bishop Parsons noted that he had shared in work on
the prayers concerning social justice and social service. The new
prayer is a slightly revised version of the 1928 form.

22. *For Social Service* (pp. 209 and 260)

This is a slightly altered version of the prayer "For Christian Service" added to the occasional prayers in the 1928 revision. Bishop
Edward Lambe Parsons is believed to have written it. The preamble
quotes Mark 10:45.

23. *For Education* (pp. 209 and 261)

A prayer "For Religious Education" was included among the occasional prayers in the 1928 revision. The preamble read: "Almighty
God, our heavenly Father, who hast committed to thy holy Church the
care and nurture of thy children," and the petition began "Enlighten
with thy wisdom those who teach and those who learn." The author
was the Rev. John W. Suter, Jr.

24. *For Vocation in Daily Work* (pp. 210 and 261)

This is a modified form of the prayer "For Every Man in his Work"
first placed among the occasional prayers in the Prayer Book of 1928.
The original was an abridged version of a prayer by Bishop Frederick
Dan Huntington which appeared in the Book of Offices and Prayers
edited by Charles Morris Addison and John W. Suter, under the cap-

tion "For the Emancipation of Workers." Scriptural allusions include Ps. 19:1, Mt. 6:24, and Lk. 22:27. For the sake of clarification, "callings" has been replaced by "occupations" and "mammon" by "self alone."

25. *For Labor Day* (pp. 210 and 261)

This new collect by the Rev. Dr. Charles M. Guilbert recognizes the right of the laborer to a proper return, but it also sets our work within the context of the common good and the "rightful aspirations of other workers." In it we pray that God might also "arouse our concern for those who are out of work."

Proper Liturgies for Special Days

Special rites and ceremonies to mark many days of the church year were included in medieval books. Many of the ceremonies associated with these days were condemned in the fifth of the homilies issued in 1547, and were prohibited by the injunctions of Edward VI.

The first Prayer Book made special provisions for very few days, providing propers for two celebrations of the Eucharist at Christmas and Easter and an introductory rite of anthems, preces, and a prayer for Matins on Easter Day. For Good Friday there were two additional collects based on the solemn collects of the Good Friday rite and appointed for use after the collects of the day in the liturgy of the word. A special penitential rite was provided for Ash Wednesday, to be used between Matins and the Eucharist. Cranmer seems to have anticipated the publication of special rites for the principal feasts, however, for at the end of the 1549 Book is a note: "Also upon Christmas Day, Easter Day, the Ascension Day, Whitsunday, and the feast of the Trinity may be used any part of Holy Scripture, hereafter to be certainly limited and appointed, in the stead of the Litany." Some of the work on these rites may have survived in the special psalms, lections, and prayers for the days Cranmer noted, and for Good Friday, which were printed in *Preces Privatae* (1564), the Latin primer of Elizabeth's time.

Special rites were cut back in the 1552 revision; the provisions for a second communion on Easter and Christmas Day were deleted. On Easter the anthems from the introductory rite for Easter were to be said in place of the Venite. The 1549 preces and collect were omitted, as was the note anticipating the publication of further rites for special days.

The American Book of 1789 reduced the Ash Wednesday rite to two prayers to be said in Morning Prayer before the General Thanksgiving, but a need for special rites for certain days developed in the nineteenth century. "A Penitential Office for Ash Wednesday" was restored in the 1892 revision, as well as a second set of propers for Christmas and Easter. The 1928 revision added the second set of propers for Pentecost.

The third edition of the Book of Offices, compiled by the Standing Liturgical Commission and commended for use by General Convention (1960), included "Benedictions for Certain Occasions in the Church Year." The preface states: "A new section has been added to this edition of the Book of Offices providing forms for certain traditional ceremonials of the Christian Year that have had a widespread revival throughout the Church in recent times." The section "Proper Liturgies for Special Days" in this revision of the Prayer Book greatly enlarges on those provisions.

Ash Wednesday (pp. 264–269)

The observance of Ash Wednesday originated in the penitential discipline of the early church when those whose notorious sins had caused scandal were excommunicated. After a period of penitence, which included sackcloth and ashes, fasting and prayer, intercession of the faithful, and dismissal from the services before communion, these persons were reinstated. The rite, at which the bishop usually presided, ordinarily consisted of prayer, the laying on of hands, and readmission to communion. Such readmissions were presumably a part of the Easter vigil.

Public penitence became associated with the Lenten season in the time of the sacramentaries. In Rome at an early stage, Lent began on the Monday after what we know as the First Sunday in Lent. Sometime in the sixth century, observance of Lent was moved back to begin on the previous Wednesday, so that the season might include forty weekdays. The penitents were placed under discipline on this Wednesday, admonished and prayed for. They received the laying on of hands and then were dismissed from the church prior to the Eucharist. The imposition of ashes and the use of the seven penitential psalms (Pss. 6, 32, 38, 51, 102, 130, and 143) were added to the rite of dismissal in the ninth century, and the day came to be known as Ash Wednesday. Services in Lent contained readings, scrutinies, and prayers for the penitents, who continued to be excluded from

218

communion. Near the end of Lent (Maundy Thursday in the Roman rite, Good Friday in the Gallican) the penitents were reconciled.

Few instances of the discipline of public penance remained beyond the eleventh century, but the old texts continued in use and Lent was given a new dimension as a time in which all received ashes and underwent penance.

In the Sarum use the seven penitential psalms were to be said with an antiphon after the little noonday office of Sext and before the Eucharist. The antiphon read: "Remember not, Lord, our offences, nor the offences of our forefathers, neither take thou vengeance of our sins." This was followed by the Kyrie, the Lord's Prayer, and suffrages. Next were seven collects, four of which can be traced to the Gelasian sacramentary (nos. 78–81), followed by an absolution and another collect. The ashes were then blessed and distributed while anthems were sung. After two more collects, one of which is in the Gregorian sacramentary (no. 843) among a group of prayers for sinners, the Mass was begun with the entrance song.

One aim of English reformers was to restore public penance as a means of discipline. As an interim measure the 1549 Prayer Book provided a rite entitled "The First Day of Lent, commonly called Ash Wednesday," which was designed to follow Matins and Litany and precede the Eucharist. The rite opened with a homily which included "the general sentences of God's cursing against impenitent sinners" (Deut. 27f.), an exhortation to repentance and an assurance that God is ready to pardon. Psalm 51 followed, then the Kyrie, Lord's Prayer, suffrages, and one of the Gelasian collects (no. 78) which had found its way into the Sarum rite. A second prayer included phrases from the sixth collect, a form for the blessing of ashes, and the Gregorian collect said after the distribution in the Sarum use. An anthem followed, composed principally of phrases from the epistle of the day (Jl. 2:12–17) and the first anthem sung at the distribution of ashes in the Sarum rite.

In 1552 the title was changed to read "A Commination Against Sinners, with Certain Prayers To Be Used Divers Times in the Year." It ordered that the anthem be said by both minister and people. The title changed again in 1662 to become "A Commination, or Denouncing of God's Anger and Judgements against Sinners, with Certain Prayers To Be Used on the First Day of Lent, and at Other Times, as the Ordinary Shall Appoint." The words "Through the merits, and mediation of thy blessed Son, Jesus Christ our Lord. Amen" were added to the anthem and a concluding blessing provided. That revision also appointed the other six penitential psalms for use at Morning and Evening Prayer on Ash Wednesday.

The American revision of 1789, in accord with the Proposed Book of 1786, omitted the service but retained the two prayers, printing them after the collect of the day for use after the Litany and before the General Thanksgiving in Morning Prayer. Except for the homily, the 1892 revision restored the rite under the title "A Penitential Office for Ash Wednesday," inserting a collect just before the blessing. This collect is in the Gregorian sacramentary among a group of prayers for sinners (no. 851), and in the supplement as the super populum (blessing over the people) at the end of the rite in a Mass for Sinners (no. 1327). It had previously been printed in the Litany of 1544, was omitted from the 1549 revision and restored in 1559. The first American revision had dropped it because, according to Bishop White, it was "too much play on words." The 1928 revisers struck the last two verses from the psalm in the rite, thus making a better climax.

The Penitential Office had fallen out of use because it seemed redundant prior to the Eucharist in which substantial penitential material of similar general nature was invariably required; yet many felt the need of a special service for Ash Wednesday. Unauthorized forms, which frequently included the use of ashes, had come into use and seemed to meet a real pastoral need. In the present revision, therefore, a special liturgy of the word is provided for Ash Wednesday, including the option of imposition of ashes as a sign of mortality and penitence.

The Liturgy of the Word (p. 264)

The special liturgy for Ash Wednesday begins with the salutation and the collect of the day. The lesson of the Sarum rite, which dates to the earliest Roman epistle lectionary, was Joel 2:12–19. Cranmer, who rarely shortened a lection, cut this back to Joel 2:12–17, thereby ending on a more somber note. The present revision uses Joel 2:1–2 as a prefix to the lection, "the day of the Lord is coming." The alternative lection, Isaiah 58:1–12, has precedent in the fact that from the time of the 1892 revision, which used the 1786 Proposed Book in this instance, Isaiah 58 had been appointed for use at Morning Prayer on Ash Wednesday. The lection from Joel is a call to fasting; that from Isaiah a description of the fast which is acceptable to the Lord. Psalm 103 is a paean of praise to God who forgives all our sins and remembers that we are but dust. The Epistle (2 Cor. 5:20b—6:10) includes that appointed in Sarum use and in earlier Prayer Books for the first

Sunday in Lent (2 Cor. 6:1–10). The Gospel, which reminds us that God is not impressed by outward signs of fasting, has been used on this day from the time of the earliest extant Roman lectionaries.

The Exhortation (pp. 264–265)

This is a slightly revised version of the form which, at the last revision of the Canadian Prayer Book, had replaced the homily of earlier English and Canadian Books. It reminds us of the various actions which became part of the development of the Lenten season: the preparation for baptism at the Easter vigil, and the penitence, fasting, and instruction which that entailed; the discipline and penitence expected of those who, through their sins, had been separated from the body of the faithful. The congregation is urged to observe Lent "by self-examination and repentance; by prayer, fasting, and self-denial; and by reading and meditating on God's holy Word."

The Imposition of Ashes (p. 265)

Late medieval forms, such as that of Sarum for the blessing of the ashes to be imposed, influence this prayer. The ashes are a sign of our mortality and of our penitence. The result clause, with its note of grace, is not paralleled in the Sarum form which reads:

> God, you desire not the death but the repentance of sinners: Look kindly upon the fragility of our human condition, and of your mercy deign to bless these ashes which we have resolved to put upon our heads as a token of humility and for the obtaining of pardon, that we, whom you have admonished are but ashes and know that for our depravity we deserve to revert to dust, consequently may be found worthy to receive pardon of all sins and the rewards promised anew to penitents.

The present revision, in restoring a form for optional use for the imposition of ashes, did not provide an explicit blessing for several reasons: the blessing of the ashes seemed to be a late medieval innovation, a distaste for blessing material objects remains strong in Anglicanism, and the use of unblessed ashes would be a more potent sign of mortality and penitence than were there some sense of holiness attached. Capt. Howard E. Galley composed the prayer for optional use over the ashes.

The sentence associated with the imposition is found in the Sarum and other medieval rites.

221

Psalm 51 (pp. 266–267)

In the 1549 Prayer Book the rite for Ash Wednesday moved directly from the homily to Psalm 51. When the first American revision dropped the Commination rite the Psalm was also dropped, but was restored in the Penitential Office for Ash Wednesday in the 1892 revision. The 1928 revisers dropped the last two verses, thus providing a better climax.

Litany of Penitence (pp. 267–269)

This litany, drafted by the Rev. Dr. Massey H. Shepherd, Jr., takes the place of suffrages, two prayers, and an anthem which were in the 1549 Book, another prayer added to the rite in 1892, and a blessing dating from 1662. All of these prayers and the anthem were generalized prayers for pardon. The new litany is the most explicit form of general confession yet to be included in a Prayer Book. It begins as an amplified version of the general confession of the daily office and the Eucharist. The ten petitions following provide a good basis for self-examination. Suffrages taken from Psalm 85:4 are a part of the conclusion.

The Absolution (p. 269)

The 1552 revision of the Prayer Book introduced a general confession and this absolution for use prior to both daily offices. The form incorporates some phrases from the confession and absolution of Forma ac ratio—a liturgy based on Calvin's work—which was drafted by John a Lasco for German refugees living in London. Other phrases possibly came from the Consultation, the liturgy Bucer prepared for Hermann, reforming archbishop of Cologne; this work served as a source for a number of rubrics and texts in the 1549 Prayer Book. The quotation from Ezekiel 33:11 in the preamble was used in the Sarum rite for the blessing of ashes. It also is found in the initial prayer of votives provided by both the Gelasian sacramentary (no. 1377) and the Gregorian supplement (no. 1007) for use in times of great mortality.

The absolution begins with a statement of God's disposition toward sinners and his commitment of both power and authority to his ministers to declare forgiveness (John 20:22–23). The priest pronounces "absolution and remission"; God "pardons and absolves." "Absolve" and "absolution" signify a setting free from sin; "remission" connotes the withholding of deserved punishment; "pardon" is based on a root meaning "to give." Forgiveness is the free gift of God; true repentance and sincere faith, also gifts of God, enable us to receive the good news of forgiveness of our sins (Mk. 1:14-15; Lk. 24:47; Acts 2:38). The absolution then becomes a prayer that God will grant us true repentance and His Holy Spirit in order that our worship on this day may please Him, that from this time on our life may be pure and holy—not only free from sin but also actively dedicated or set apart for God's purposes for us—and that we may enter into the eternal joy of the Kingdom.

The rubrics direct that the Peace be exchanged after the absolution. A deacon or lay reader may lead this liturgy in the absence of a bishop or priest, but must substitute the form found on page 42 or on page 80 for the absolution printed within this rite. Permissions and directions are given for the use of the litany of penitence on other occasions.

The Sunday of the Passion: Palm Sunday (pp. 270-273)

The pilgrim Egeria describes a special observance of Palm Sunday in Jerusalem about 381-384; an old Armenian lectionary supports this in a manuscript which claims that it was based on the services at the holy sites in Jerusalem. After the Eucharist, at which the story of our Lord's entry into Jerusalem had been read (Mt. 21:1-11), the people hastened home for a quick meal. At one o'clock they met the bishop near the top of the Mount of Olives at the Eleona (Helen or "compassion"), one of the churches which Helen, the mother of Constantine, had built to mark certain sacred sites. There they participated in a service of hymns, antiphons, and lessons "suitable to the place and day." At three o'clock they moved to the Imbomon ("On the mount") at the top of the Mount of Olives for a similar service. The Matthean account of the entry into Jerusalem was repeated at five o'clock followed by a procession down the Mount and into the city. As the people walked they waved branches of palm or olive trees, sang psalms, including Psalm 118, and all shouted the antiphon, "Blessed is he who comes in the name of the Lord!" The procession moved slowly because it included elderly people and people carrying babies, traveling down into the city to the site of the Lord's tomb where the lucernarium (Order of Worship for Evening) was held. A prayer followed at the site of the cross and the people were then dismissed.

This celebration of the entry into Jerusalem spread to other areas. The procession for Palm Sunday was picked up in Spain possibly as early as the fifth century. In the Gallican Bobbio missal are related lections and prayers (nos. 186–193) and a form for the blessing of branches (no. 558). By the twelfth century the custom of blessing the "palms" with a procession following was accepted everywhere, though the texts and ceremonies varied greatly.

The Sarum form was extraordinarily complicated. After two lessons, Exodus 15:27—16:10 and John 12:12–19, the "flowers and leaves" were exorcised. The priest then said four prayers for a blessing on the branches and on the people who would carry them. Before the last prayer the branches were sprinkled with holy water and censed. As the branches were distributed and the procession formed to move to the first station, anthems were sung, their content mainly taken from the gospel accounts of the entry into Jerusalem. Christ's presence in the procession was symbolized by the reserved Sacrament; in Rome and other places the custom was to carry a book of the Gospels. At the first station the Matthean account of the entry (21:1–9) was read. At the second station, seven boys sang the ninth century hymn "All glory, laud, and honor," with the first stanza repeated as a refrain after each stanza of the hymn. Three clerks chanted at the third station, their text John 11:49–50, "It is expedient for you that one man should die for the people, and that the whole nation should not perish." The procession stopped before the rood for the fourth station; the cross on the rood screen, which had been veiled during Lent, was uncovered for the day and the choir sang, "Hail, our King, Son of David, Redeemer of the world, whom the prophets have proclaimed the Savior of the house of Israel who is to come; for the Father sent you into the world to be a saving victim, whom all the saints have expected from the beginning of the world, and now, Hosanna to the Son of David; blessed is he that comes in the name of the Lord; Hosanna in the highest."

The Mass following the procession contained no reference to the Palm Sunday entry. Its prayers, chants, and lections related Christ's passion and marked the day as the beginning of Holy Week. The distinctive feature of this Mass was the singing of the whole of the passion narrative (Mt. 26:1—27:61). The reading was announced simply "The Passion of our Lord Jesus Christ according to Matthew." The Gloria tibi did not follow. Three singers shared the text: a tenor to represent the evangelist, a bass to take the words of Christ, and an alto for the parts of the Jews and the disciples. At the mention of our Lord's death there was a pause for silent acts of devotion. A deacon then read the continuation of the narrative (Mt. 27:51–61). The Gospel, sung in an ordinary manner, consisted of the final verses (Mt. 27:62–66).

A simple title "The Sunday next before Easter" marks the day in the 1549 Prayer Book. The collect and Epistle are retained from the Sarum Mass and the Matthean account of the passion (26:1—27:56) is appointed for the Gospel. Because of the reformers' aversion to the blessing of material things the blessing of branches and the procession were eliminated, leaving the rite with no commemoration of the triumphal entry. In some later revisions the account of the entry, or the prophecy from Zechariah 9:9ff., was appointed to be read at the daily office. Few people, over the past several decades, have attended both Morning Prayer and Eucharist, in actual practice, with the result that the contrast between the king joyously greeted by the crowd and the king reigning from a tree, condemned to death by the crowd, and the contrast between the shouts of "Hosanna" which greeted our Lord at his entry into Jerusalem and the cries of "crucify" later in the week—the particular contrasts which give the day its pathos and power—were lost to the worshiper.

The phrase "commonly called Palm Sunday" was added to the title of the day in 1928. The Book of Offices (1960) commended for use by General Convention provided "forms for certain traditional ceremonials of the Christian Year that have had widespread revival throughout the Church in recent times." Among these was a form for the blessing of palms and a procession for Palm Sunday. This revision provides a fuller and more flexible form. The full title of the Sunday, "The Sunday of the Passion: Palm Sunday," incorporates two of the traditional names for the day.

The Liturgy of the Palms (pp. 270–272)

The rubrics encourage the restoration of the outdoor procession and the use of branches of palm or of other trees or shrubs rather than fronds of palm or small crosses which can hardly be waved and certainly fail to signify a parade. In northern climates indigenous greenery, such as box, yew, or willow, was frequently used as the "palm" of Palm Sunday, and such greenery was often supplemented with flowers.

The Anthem (p. 270)

The anthem printed is the version of the shout of the multitude in the Lukan account of the entry into Jerusalem (Lk. 19:38).

225

A Collect (p. 270)

This collect was appointed in the 1928 edition of the Prayer Book as the collect of the day for the Wednesday before Easter. It is based upon one used in the Sarum missal as a super populum (prayer of blessing over the people) on the Monday of Holy Week. It was similarly used in the Gregorian sacramentary (no. 318). The Gelasian sacramentary has it as the second collect for Sexagesima (no. 74), the second of the three Sundays prior to the beginning of Lent. A more literal translation would be "Assist us, God of our salvation, and grant that we come joyfully to the recollection of the benefits by which you have restored to us our dignity." (Compare the collect for the second Sunday after Christmas, pp. 162 and 214.) In this revision the word "contemplation" was substituted for "meditation," the word used in the 1928 Book.

The Gospel of the Palms (p. 271)

The story of our Lord's entry into Jerusalem is read or sung by a deacon or some other person, from the synoptic Gospel for the Year.

The Blessing of the Palms (p. 271)

This prayer may be said by a deacon or lay person, if necessary, in the absence of a priest, thus making it possible for any congregation on this day to celebrate the liturgy of the palms. It might be compared with the alternative form in the new Roman sacramentary. It has the form of a eucharistic preface, preceded by Gratias agamus. (Cf. the thanksgiving over the water in the baptismal rite, pp. 306–307, and the form for the blessing of a font in the rite for the consecration of a church, p. 570.) Some phrases are retained from the form in the Book of Offices.

The Anthem (p. 271)

This optional anthem is the Matthean version of the shout of the crowd at our Lord's entry into Jerusalem (Mt. 21:9). If the palms have not been distributed to the people before the rite, they are to be distributed at this time.

The Procession (pp. 271–272)

As we have seen in the details of Egeria's account and in the Sarum rite, there is a long tradition behind the use of Psalm 118 and of the hymn "All glory, laud, and honor" as part of the Palm Sunday procession.

Many of the medieval rites called for one or more stations; the procession would halt at an appropriate place for a lesson, prayer, or anthem. Most had a station at the principal door before entering the church for the Mass. The station collect which is provided is the collect of the day for Monday in Holy Week. This is also printed in Daily Morning Prayer under the heading "A Collect for Fridays."

The first rubric on page 272 gives permission for the liturgy of the palms to be led by a deacon or lay reader when a bishop or priest is not available.

The second rubric permits suitable portions of the rite to be used at services other than the principal celebration. The opening anthem, the collect and the Gospel, for example, might be used as an entrance rite in situations in which the blessing and distribution and procession would be undesirable or impossible. Or the service might begin with the blessing over the branches, pronounced by the celebrant standing just inside the church or chapel and the people standing in their places facing the celebrant. "All glory, laud, and honor" might be sung or Psalm 118:19–29 said or sung as the celebrant proceeds up the aisle to the chancel. This would be appropriate especially for an early service with few people present.

At the Eucharist (pp. 272–273)

The rubric provides for the celebrant to begin the liturgy of the word with the salutation and collect of the day if the liturgy of the palms has immediately preceded.

The collect, psalm, and lections point us toward the approaching death of Christ upon the cross. The alternative Old Testament lections from Second Isaiah have been traditionally interpreted by the church in terms of the passion of our Lord. The gradual, Psalm 22 or Psalm 22:1–11, has been used as a tract since the middle ages, that is, a psalm used before the Gospel of the day. Philippians 2:5–11 as the Epistle for the day was appointed in the earliest Roman lectionary and has been the Epistle in all editions of the Prayer Book. Some commentators consider this to be a quotation from an early Christian hymn. It is certainly one of Paul's primary statements of the doctrine of Christ, stressing as it does both our Lord's humble obedience unto death and his exaltation as Lord. It might be compared with Colossians 1:11–20.

227

The Passion Gospel (pp. 272-273)

In some of the oldest lectionaries the Matthean account of the passion (Mt. 26:1—27:66) was read on Palm Sunday. The Lukan and Johannine accounts were read respectively on Wednesday and Friday, the traditional station days. Mark was omitted because it was mistakenly considered to be extracted from Matthew. At a later stage, when a liturgy developed for the Tuesday in Holy Week, the Markan account was read on that day. The 1549 Book used an abbreviated version of the traditional Matthean passion (Mt. 26:1—27:56, omitting the burial) on Sunday and appointed that of John for Good Friday. The narrative in Mark was split between Monday and Tuesday and that in Luke between Wednesday and Thursday. In the 1662 revision Matthew 26 was shifted to Morning Prayer as the second lesson and verses 55 and 56 of chapter 27 were omitted in order to give a better climax, the confession of the centurion, "Truly this was the Son of God." The present revision appoints the three synoptic accounts to be read on Palm Sunday in a three-year cycle.

The rubrics restore certain traditions, such as the manner in which the passion is announced, and the possibility of a dramatic presentation in which different persons may take specific roles with the congregation speaking as the crowd. So that the people may be more attentive to readings of such length, the congregation is permitted to sit until the verse which mentions the arrival at Golgotha.

In a liturgy of this content and weight the use of the Nicene Creed and the confession of sin seems unnecessary if not redundant; a rubric allows their omission.

Maundy Thursday (pp. 274-275)

Originally no Eucharist was celebrated within the week preceding the Paschal vigil. In some areas by the end of the fourth century, however, a celebration was held on Maundy Thursday. Egeria, who visited Jerusalem on her pilgrimage (c. 381–384), describes how the Eucharist was celebrated at 2 P.M. in the Martyrium, a large basilica built by Helen, the mother of Constantine, over the site of the discovery of the true cross. (The Armenian lectionary appoints Mt. 26:20–39, the account of the Last Supper, as the Gospel for this rite.) After the dismissal at 4 P.M. the congregation moved to the courtyard behind the church, where a cross was erected at the supposed site of the crucifixion, for a second celebration. Prayers at the tomb followed; then the people hurried home for a meal before meeting at the

Eleona. This church was built near the top of the Mount of Olives over the site of a cave believed to be the place where our Lord delivered his teachings to the disciples during that week in Jerusalem before his death. Egeria wrote: "There they sing hymns and antiphons suitable to the day and the place, interspersed with readings and prayers, until about 11 P.M. Then they read passages from the gospel which recount what the Lord said to his disciples as he sat in the very cave which is in the church." At midnight the congregation moved to the Imbomon, the church at the top of the Mount, for a similar service which lasted until cockcrow. Singing, the congregation moved down the Mount to the church built at the supposed site where our Lord prayed, and from there to the site of the arrest in Gethsemane. Appropriate prayers, hymns, and lections were used at each of the stations. At daybreak the congregation returned to the site of the crucifixion for the reading of the Johannine account of the trial before Pilate (Jn. 18:28—19:16, according to the old Armenian lectionary). Then the congregation was dismissed until the first service of Good Friday, though "those with the energy go to Sion to pray at the column at which the Lord was scourged."

The custom of an evening celebration of the Eucharist on this day spread throughout the church under the name "Cena Domini" (the Supper of the Lord). This is the emphasis of the Masses of the Gallican books, of the evening Mass of the Gelasian sacramentary (nos. 391–394), and of the basic prayers of the proper in the Gregorian (nos. 329–332). Since the time of the earliest Roman lectionaries the Epistle for this Mass has been Paul's account of the institution of the Eucharist (1 Cor. 11:20–32) and the Gospel John's account of our Lord's washing the feet of the disciples (Jn. 13:1–15). The reading of this Gospel and, in some places, the ceremonial reenactment of it as early as the seventh century has given the day the name "Maundy Thursday," the word "mandatum" coming from the antiphon based on our Lord's "commandment" in the gospel, "A new commandment I give you, that you love one another even as I have loved you" (Jn. 13:34). In many places abbots washed the feet of monks and kings washed the feet of peasants on this day. Other observances came to be a part of this day, especially in Rome where the reconciliation of penitents, presumably done at the Easter vigil in the early church and on Good Friday in Gallican territory, by the time of the sacramentaries occurred as part of the Maundy Thursday observances. In the Gallican churches altars were stripped and washed on Good Friday; this action, also, was done on Thursday in Rome. In earlier rites the oils had been blessed at the Easter vigil; the Gelasian sacramentary

229

provided a special Mass for this ceremony on Maundy Thursday (nos. 375–390) and the Gregorian incorporated it as part of the Mass of the Lord's Supper (nos. 334–336). On this day the eucharistic elements were consecrated in sufficient quantity to serve for the Good Friday communions as well. A procession to the place where the Sacrament was reserved, or a vigil there, however, does not seem to have developed until late in the medieval period.

The Sarum rite for Maundy Thursday began with the reconciliation of penitents after the little office of None at 3 P.M. The penitents waited outside the western door as the bishop approached within the church. The archdeacon made an address which drew a parallel between the baptism of catechumens and the reconciliation of penitents, the washing of water and the washing of tears. The penitents were then brought inside the church during the singing of Psalm 34 with verse eleven as antiphon, "Come, children, and listen to me; I will teach you the fear of the Lord." All then prostrated themselves for the singing of the seven penitential psalms, followed by the Kyrie, Lord's Prayer, and suffrages from the Ash Wednesday rite. Three prayers and an absolution followed. The address and the first two of the prayers are in the Mass for the public reconciliation of penitents in the Gelasian sacramentary (nos. 353–357). The Gregorian supplement also contains these first two collects in a Mass for the reconciliation of penitents on the Thursday of the Lord's Supper (nos. 1383 and 1385). The second of these "collects" in the Sarum rite was the precatory absolution from the older books. There followed in the Sarum rite an absolution in declaratory form, a type which does not date earlier than such tenth century books as the pontifical of Egbert. Then began the Mass of the Lord's Supper. The oil for the sick, the oil of exorcism, and the chrism were all blessed within the Mass, and three eucharistic hosts were consecrated: one for that day, one for the priest on Good Friday, and one to be deposited in the Easter sepulcher. Vespers followed communion. After a brief period for refreshment, the clergy returned to the church to strip the altars and wash them. They then moved to the chapter house for the washing of feet, as psalms and antiphons were sung, and to partake of a loving cup during the reading of John 13:16—14:31.

Of these rites the 1549 Prayer Book retained only the Lord's Supper, and from the propers only the Epistle, expanded to 1 Corinthians 11:17–34. The title for the day was "Thursday before Easter." To provide a Gospel the Lukan passion narrative (22–23), which previously had been appointed for the preceding Wednesday, was split between the two days. Though the early editions of the Prayer Book made no provision for it, one of the traditions which did live on in Anglicanism until well into the eighteenth century was the "royal maundy." For example, it is recorded that in 1560 Queen Elizabeth "kept her maundy" in the great hall at Westminster by washing the feet of twenty poor women.

The 1662 revision reduced the Gospel for the day from Luke 23 to Luke 23:1–49. The words "commonly called Maundy Thursday" were added to the title in 1928, the Epistle was reduced to 1 Corinthians 11:23–26, and the traditional Gospel of the day (Jn. 13:1–15), the account of our Lord's washing the feet of the disciples, was provided as an alternative Gospel. The present revision of the Prayer Book gives "Maundy Thursday" as the proper title of the day and restores the ceremony of washing of feet as an option. (See *The Book of Occasional Services*, pp. 91–94, for additional provisions for Maundy Thursday.)

The Liturgy of the Word (p. 274)

The liturgy of the word begins in the usual manner. The institution of the Passover is narrated in the Old Testament lesson. The psalm recalls the wandering in the wilderness and the provision of manna. Paul's account of the institution of the sacrament remains the Epistle, and the account of the foot-washing, the traditional Gospel of the day, is restored to prior position with the Lukan account of the institution of the Eucharist as an alternative.

The Washing of Feet (pp. 274–275)

Provision is again made for the washing of feet, an optional ceremony. Anthems are provided for use during the ceremony; some of these texts had been used as antiphons with the psalms in the medieval rite. The sources are John 13:12 and 15; 14:27a; 13:34; and 13:35.

A rubric notes that it is from this service, rather than from some other, that consecrated elements are reserved for a Good Friday communion.

Good Friday (pp. 276–282)

In the first centuries the Christian Passover was a unitive feast commemorating both the death and resurrection of Jesus Christ. Even though the Paschal Vigil was preceded by a fast extending over the Friday and Saturday, there was no sense of separate commemorations

231

of the death and the resurrection. It was a single observance of Christ's victory through death and rising to life again and of the Christian's death and rebirth through baptism.

The pilgrim Egeria gives us the first evidence of special rites to mark the day in her description of the Good Friday rites in Jerusalem about A.D. 381–384. From eight o'clock in the morning until noon, the wood and superscription of the supposed true cross were exposed on a linen-covered table at the site of the crucifixion in the courtyard behind the Martyrium, the great church built by Constantine's mother Helen. There the faithful came to venerate them as the bishop held his hands firmly on the cross while the deacons stood guard. At noon the people assembled in the courtyard for a service of psalms, lections, hymns, and prayers which lasted until three o'clock. They then moved into the church for a service and afterward to the tomb where the Johannine account of the burial was read (Jn. 19:38–42). A voluntary vigil at the tomb continued through the night.

After a time other churches acquired portions of the true cross and conducted rites similar to those performed in Jerusalem. Eventually veneration of a cross became a practice in churches which did not possess any piece of the true cross.

The Gallican books contain only some special prayers and lections for use in the daily office between the Eucharist of Maundy Thursday and the Easter Vigil. The Missale Gallicanum vetus, however, provided a simple liturgy of the word with the Roman solemn collects (nos. 92–111). The Gregorian sacramentary had only the solemn collects (nos. 338–355), but the Gelasian contained a Good Friday rite (nos. 395–418), a liturgy of the word, which began in the manner of the early church with the first lection, preceded only by a silent procession and a period of silent prayer. The solemn collects, veneration of the cross, and a general communion from the reserved Sacrament followed the readings. In the early years of the church people carried the eucharistic elements from the Sunday celebration to their homes for communion during the week. Later, even though eucharistic celebrations were forbidden on fast days, the congregation received communion from the reserved Sacrament. This custom was still practiced in the East at the time of the early Roman sacramentaries—as it continues to be on certain days—but in Rome the practice was confined to Good Friday. After the liturgy of the word, the deacons brought the reserved Sacrament, both Bread and Wine, from the sacristy and placed it upon the altar. The priest then came to the altar and, after the usual bidding, said the Lord's Prayer and the brief prayer ("Deliver us") which follows in the Roman rite, then administered the Sacrament to all present, often apparently in silence.

The Sarum rite began the liturgy of this day with a silent procession. The first words spoken were at the reading of the first lection. After two Old Testament lessons (Hos. 6:1–6 and Ex. 12:1–11), each followed by psalmody, the passion narrative in John 18:1—19:37 was read. After a pause for acts of devotion the account of the burial was read from John 19:38–42, followed by the traditional solemn collects. Two priests then held a veiled cross behind the altar and began the singing of the Reproaches, a hymn of Gallican origin composed of two parts. Only the older first half is in the Sarum missal or many of the other medieval uses. In the text Christ recounts what he has done for His people in bringing them out of Egypt and how they have repaid Him with crucifixion. The response to each of the three verses is the Eastern Trisagion, "Holy God, Holy and Mighty, Holy Immortal One, have mercy upon us." At the uncovering of the cross which followed an anthem was sung, "Behold the wood of the cross, on which hung the salvation of the world; come, let us adore." During the veneration of the cross Psalm 67 was sung with the antiphon, "We glory in your cross, O Lord, and praise and glorify your holy resurrection; for by virtue of your cross joy has come to the whole world." The sixth century Gallican hymn, "Sing, my tongue, the glorious battle," followed, with the stanza which begins "Faithful cross" as a refrain. After another anthem the cross was returned to the altar and the priest made private preparation. The reserved host from Maundy Thursday and a mixed chalice were placed on the altar and censed. After the Lord's Prayer and the prayer "Deliver us" the priest communicated himself only. The priest then washed his hands and Vespers was said ending with a postcommunion prayer which dates to the Gregorian sacramentary (no. 327). There it is used, as in the Sarum missal, for a super populum (prayer or blessing said over the people) at the end of Mass on the Wednesday of Holy Week. The cross and the one consecrated host remaining from Maundy Thursday were carried to be placed in an Easter "sepulcher" while anthems were sung.

The 1549 Prayer Book assumed the use of the daily office on "Good Friday." It provided proper Old Testament lessons for Matins and Evensong and a special collect, the old Gregorian collect used at the end of the Sarum liturgy as the postcommunion prayer on Good Friday. Psalm 22 was appointed for use as the entrance song "at the Communion." The collect of Palm Sunday and the collect of Good Friday were followed by two prayers from the solemn collects of Good Friday. Hebrews 10:1–25 was the Epistle, and John 18:1—

19:42, both the passion narrative and the Gospel for Good Friday in the Sarum rite, was appointed as the Gospel.

In the 1552 version the entrance song was dropped and the 1662 revision transferred the first chapter of the Gospel to Morning Prayer and omitted the last five verses of chapter 19. The next to the last of the Good Friday collects was revised in 1662 and the last in 1928; both have been further altered for this Book. Despite the universal tradition of having no celebration of the Eucharist on Good Friday, there has been no prohibition in any edition of the Prayer Book and the Eucharist has been celebrated frequently in Anglican churches until the present century.

This edition of the Prayer Book revives the tradition of prohibiting the celebration of the Eucharist on Good Friday and Holy Saturday. It also recovers some venerable texts and ceremonies. It provides a fuller form of the solemn collects and an opportunity for devotion before an exposed cross as well as for communion from the Maundy Thursday Eucharist.

The Liturgy of the Word (pp. 276–277)

Observing ancient custom the ministers enter in silence. After a period of silent prayer the people are bidden to pray with a form reserved for this day. Although many rites omitted the normal salutation, the Ambrosian rite provided a substitute form which has been incorporated in this present rite. Three alternatives are provided for the Old Testament lesson: one of the Suffering Servant songs of Second Isaiah; the story of Abraham's sacrifice of Isaac; and a passage from the apocryphal book of Wisdom, "Let us lie in wait for the righteous man." Psalm 22, which the 1549 Book appointed as the entrance song, and Psalms 40:1–14 and 69:1–23 are provided for gradual and tract. The use of Hebrews 10:1–25 as the Epistle dates to the 1549 Prayer Book.

The Passion Gospel (p. 277)

Many of the oldest lectionaries appoint the Johannine Gospel to be read this day, as do the Sarum missal and all editions of the Prayer Book.

The rubrics restore the simple form for announcing the passion narrative. The option provided for Palm Sunday, a dramatic presentation in which different persons are assigned different roles with the congregation taking the part of the crowd, is also permitted here. The congregation is permitted to sit until the verse which mentions the arrival at Golgotha.

The Solemn Collects (pp. 277–280)

In this form of prayer the deacon bids the people to pray, after which there is a silence followed by a prayer in which the celebrant sums up the prayers of the people. This is believed to be the form used in Rome for the prayers of the people from the third or fourth century until those prayers were dropped from normal use in the Roman liturgy. The solemn collects were preserved in the Good Friday rite, however, illustrating a liturgical principle that the more important the day the more likely the rite is to preserve ancient elements (Baumstark's Law). The solemn collects were not retained in this form in the first Prayer Book, but Cranmer did provide two prayers to be said following the collects for Palm Sunday and Good Friday in the liturgy of the word for Good Friday. Both were derived from the ancient solemn collects.

The earliest extant form of the solemn collects is in the Gelasian (nos. 400–417) and the Gregorian (nos. 338–355) sacramentaries and in the Missale Gallicanum vetus (nos. 94–111). The biddings may date to the fourth or even the third century; the collects are believed to date to the fifth century. Separate biddings and collects were provided for the church, the pope, the various clerical orders and all the people of God, the emperor, catechumens, those in trouble, heretics and schismatics, Jews, and pagans. Late medieval missals provided directions to kneel after each bidding for prayer and then stand for the collect, a practice that can be documented as early as the sixth century.

This is the first Prayer Book revision to restore the solemn collects. The initial invitation to prayer, which is new, begins with a paraphrase of John 3:16–18 and continues with a result clause in Pauline terms.

The first bidding summarizes and extends the intentions expressed by the first, third, and fifth biddings of the ancient form. The collect associated in the ancient series with the first bidding is included in this edition as Proper 24. This collect is based on the third prayer of the series. (For commentary, see p. 127 above.)

The second bidding replaces the fourth bidding of the ancient form, a call to pray that God may make all barbarous nations subject to the emperor for the sake of perpetual peace. The prayer, which is the collect for the votive "For Peace" (pp. 207 and 258), is based upon one composed by Francis Paget, bishop of Oxford (1902–1911), and included in the 1928 English revision as well as other more recent Prayer Books.

The third bidding replaces the sixth bidding of the ancient form. The new form provided for this Book incorporates some phrases from a prayer by Eugene Bersier printed in a revised version in *Prayers in Time of War*.[1]

The fourth bidding takes the place of and enlarges upon the seventh, eighth, and ninth biddings of the ancient forms. Those prayers contributed to the last of the Good Friday collects in the 1549 Book:

> Merciful God, who hast made all men, and hatest nothing that thou hast made, nor wouldest the death of a sinner, but rather that he should be converted and live; have mercy upon all Jews, Turks, Infidels, and heretics, and take from them all ignorance, hardness of heart, and contempt of thy word; and so fetch them home, blessed Lord, to thy flock, that they may be saved among the remnant of the true Israelites, and be made one fold under one shepherd, Jesus Christ our Lord; who liveth and reigneth, etc.

In the 1928 revision the petition was changed to read:

> Have mercy upon all who know thee not as thou art revealed in the Gospel of thy Son. Take from them all ignorance, hardness of heart, and contempt of thy Word; and so fetch them home, blessed Lord, to thy fold, that they may be made one flock under one shepherd, Jesus Christ our Lord.

The prayer has been cast in more positive language in this revision. The concluding portion is based on John 10:16.

The final bidding incorporates material from the conclusion of the prayers of the people in *The Eucharistic Liturgy of Taizé*.[2] The prayer is from the Gelasian sacramentary (no. 432), in which it is appointed for use after the first lection, Genesis 1, at the Easter Vigil. A prayer in the Gregorian sacramentary (no. 514) for the vigil of Pentecost uses the preamble.

---

[1] Ed. Hugh Martin, London: SCM Press, 1939, pp. 89–90.
[2] London: Faith Press, 1962, p. 43.

The rubric indicates how the service is to conclude if there are to be no devotions before the cross and no communion.

Devotions before the Cross (pp. 281–282)

Restored as an option are traditional texts associated with the bringing in or uncovering of a wooden cross as a center for devotional acts. The first anthem is a portion of Psalm 67 (verses 1–3) with an antiphon from the Sarum rite and other medieval missals. The second anthem has 2 Timothy 2:11b–12a as text with an antiphon used on this day in some late medieval rites after the devotions before the cross, at the time when the deacon was bringing the reserved Sacrament from its place of repose to the altar. The antiphon antedates this usage, however, for it initiates the memorial of the cross which was frequently found in earlier medieval primers or Books of Hours, devotional manuals designed for lay people to be used for hours of the daily office.

The third anthem was used in the same manner as the second in some late medieval missals, but was also used in the liturgy for the visitation of the sick, where it is found in the Sarum manuale as an antiphon for use with Psalm 71. The 1549 Prayer Book retained the psalm in the order for the visitation of the sick and printed this antiphon immediately after it. In the 1789 revision Psalm 130 replaced Psalm 71 but the antiphon was retained. Although other psalms were substituted in the 1928 revision, each given its proper antiphon and followed by a collect, this antiphon was retained for use before the address and examination by the minister and the "special confession" and assurance of pardon.

The first rubric on page 282 directs that a hymn be sung after the anthems. A specific recommendation is the sixth century text by Fortunatus, "Sing, my tongue, the glorious battle," which had been used in many medieval rites, including the Sarum, at the time of devotions before the cross, with the stanza which begins "Faithful cross" as a first stanza and as refrain after each of the other stanzas.

The rubrics explain how the service is to be concluded if communion is not to be administered; they state specifically that all which precedes may be led by a deacon or lay reader if no priest or bishop is present.

The Communion (p. 282)

Early sacramentaries make clear that on this day the reserved Sacrament in both kinds was brought to the altar in a simple manner.

Following the Lord's Prayer communion was administered in silence. This was an especially dramatic contrast to other days when there was an offertory procession, the eucharistic prayer, the Lord's Prayer, and the breaking of bread accompanied by a song of the people and the peace. Late in the middle ages, after private prayers had developed for use by the priest in his preparation, and when in most places only the priest received communion, those prayers of preparation were said by him prior to the Lord's Prayer. The use of one of the forms of confession of sin by the celebrant and people preceding the Lord's Prayer is analogous to the late medieval custom.

The Final Prayer (p. 282)

The earlier sources provide no postcommunion prayer for Good Friday, nor any blessing or dismissal. At a later stage a postcommunion prayer was said. The form provided in this revision is from the memorial of the cross which was frequently included in medieval primers, small books provided for the lay people with devotions for different hours of the daily office. This translation is a slightly revised version of that printed in *A Procession of Passion Prayers*.[1]

Holy Saturday (p. 283)

In the first centuries Christians fasted during the two days before the Paschal vigil in preparation for the commemoration of the death and resurrection of our Lord at the vigil. If pregnancy or illness prohibited fasting for both days, one was still to fast on the Saturday in preparation for the vigil. Aside from special rites for those to be baptized, most of the Western liturgical books provide no ceremonies for this day other than the daily office. The Ambrosian missal, which represents the use of the area around Milan, and the Gallican Bobbio missal, however, contain provisions for a special liturgy of the word for this day. The story of the flood (Gen. 6:9—8:21) was read as the Old Testament lesson, followed by a Psalmellus, "Arise, Lord" from Psalm 68. There followed the Gospel account of the burial of Christ (Mt. 27:62–66) and a collect which in the Gelasian sacramentary is used after the story of the flood within the Easter Vigil (no. 433).

The 1549 Book provided a psalm (88) as entrance psalm, an Epistle and a Gospel for use "At the Communion" on "Easter Even." The Gospel was the Matthean account of the burial (27:57–66) which had been read at the conclusion of the passion narrative on Palm Sunday

---

[1] Ed. Eric Milner-White, London: SPCK, 1956, p. xiii.

in the Sarum rite. (The 1549 Book had concluded the Palm Sunday Gospel with Mt. 27:56.) For the Epistle the Book provided 1 Peter 3:17–22, an account of our Lord's descent into hell, linking his death and resurrection with baptism. The Palm Sunday collect would have been used for this day. The Scottish Book of 1637 provides a special collect, a revised version of which was included in the 1662 revision. Though celebration of the Eucharist on Good Friday became a common practice in Anglicanism, the Saturday before Easter retained the nature of a period of preparation for the celebration of Easter.

The present Book preserves the almost uniquely Anglican provision for a liturgy of the word and restores the title "Holy Saturday." The restoration of this title should insure that this liturgy is not confused with the Easter Vigil.

The Liturgy of the Word (p. 283)

The initial rubric reinforces the tradition by explicitly stating that there is to be no celebration of the Eucharist. The liturgy begins in a stark manner with the collect. There is no salutation preceding the collect of the day, in accordance with the widespread tradition of omitting the salutation on Good Friday and Holy Saturday. Job 14:1–14, "If a man die, shall he live again," is appointed for the Old Testament lesson. Alternative psalms, Psalm 130, "O Israel, wait for the Lord," and Psalm 31:1–5, "Deliver me in your righteousness," are provided. 1 Peter 4:1–8, "The gospel was preached even to the dead," replaces 1 Peter 3:17–22 which was the Epistle for the day in the earlier Prayer Books. The Johannine account of the burial (Jn. 19:38–42), which had been the conclusion of the Passion narrative on Good Friday in the Sarum rite and early Prayer Books, but which had been severed from the account in 1662, is given as an alternative Gospel reading to the Matthean account (27:57–66).

The rubric directs that after the Gospel (and homily) the service concludes with the anthem from the burial rite (p. 484 or 492), "In the midst of life . . . ," the Lord's Prayer, and the Grace (the first of the concluding sentences of Morning or Evening Prayer). In many of the ancient liturgies some elements from the burial rite are read in commemoration of our Lord's burial.

The Great Vigil of Easter (pp. 284–295)

The Jewish Passover commemorated the slaying of the first-born, the exodus from Egypt, and the entry into the Promised Land. Jesus

Christ was the fulfillment of the old feast for the early church. In almost every language except English the same word is used for the Jewish Passover and the Christian Easter—pascha. Some authors find the feast, reinterpreted, celebrated within New Testament times and associated with baptism, with the imagery of the Passover recalled—the Exodus, the Passover, and the entrance into the Promised Land.

If the Christian Passover or Paschal Vigil does not date to New Testament times, it can certainly be documented in the second century. We have a description of the ceremony in the Apostolic Tradition of Hippolytus, a work which probably originated in Rome about A.D. 215. The candidates for baptism fast on Friday and Saturday; others fast with them on both days if they are able, or only on Saturday if ill or pregnant. Saturday night is spent in vigil, listening to readings and instructions. At cockcrow the baptismal water is blessed, a prayer of thanksgiving is said over the "oil of thanksgiving" (chrism), and an exorcism said over the "oil of exorcism." The candidates renounce Satan, his servants, and his works, then are anointed with the oil of exorcism. They are baptized, assenting to a baptismal formula which is a profession of faith, the basis for the "Apostles' Creed." When they emerge from the water they are anointed with the oil of thanksgiving in the Name of Jesus the Christ (the Anointed One). They are then led into the assembly where the bishop says a prayer with laying on of hands, completes the anointing, and signs each on the forehead. The newly baptized participate then in the prayers of the people, the exchange of the peace, and the Eucharist. On this occasion they receive water (an internal baptism), and milk and honey (the food of babies, the Promised Land) as well as the elements of bread and wine.

Later, in the time of the sacramentaries, the Vigil began with the blessing of the new fire and the chanting of the Exsultet. Then a series of four to twelve Old Testament readings followed, interspersed with psalms, canticles, and prayers. The readings typically included the stories of Creation, the Fall, the Flood, the sacrifice of Isaac, the Passover, the crossing of the Red Sea, the entry into the Promised Land, Isaiah 4 (the Song of the Vineyard), Isaiah 55 (Come to the waters), the Valley of Dry Bones, and Jonah. The water of the font was exorcised and blessed with a form filled with biblical imagery of water; in some places the people were sprinkled as a reminder of their baptism. Generally the oils had been blessed earlier in the week. The candidates were then called to make a three-fold renunciation of Satan, followed by a three-fold confession of faith. After immersion they were anointed. Gallican rites indicate that a ranking

240

clergyman washed the feet of the newly baptized. A peculiarity of Roman rites was that the anointing, common to all liturgies from the fifth century on, was followed by a second anointing done by the bishop. The newly baptized were clothed in white garments which they would continue to wear for several days, and then the Eucharist was held at which the newly baptized, regardless of age, would make their first communion. The lessons and prayers of this rite were filled with baptismal references for the Eucharist was not only a celebration of the death and resurrection of Jesus Christ but especially a celebration for the Christian of death and resurrection in Him through baptism.

As pressure grew to baptize infants within a short period after birth, the Easter Vigil no longer was the principal time for baptisms. The rites were shortened and pushed to the day before. The Sarum form began, after the little office of None at 3 P.M., with a procession to the west end of the south aisle during which Psalm 27, "The Lord is my light and my salvation," was said. The new fire was kindled, blessed, and sprinkled with holy water, incense was exorcised and blessed, and the new fire was censed. After a taper was lighted from the new fire, the procession moved to the choir singing a hymn by the fifth century writer Prudentius, "Thou leader kind." (This ceremony, which is not in the old Roman sacramentaries, is believed to be of Celtic origin, and the form differs in many particulars from that in the first printed Roman missal of 1474.) The deacon then sang the Exsultet, followed by the Sursum corda and the blessing of the candle. The text of the Exsultet dates to the old Gallican sacramentaries, the Missale Gothicum (no. 225), the Missale Gallicanum vetus (nos. 132–134), and the Bobbio missal (no. 227). After the deacon lighted the paschal candle from the new fire, candle bearers lighted the candles throughout the church.

Of the original readings, four remained, the Creation, the Exodus, Isaiah 4, and Deuteronomy 31:22–30. A collect followed the first lection, and a very brief sung response (Ex. 15:1–3; Is. 5:1–2, 7; Dt. 32:1–4) and a collect followed each of the others. Then Psalm 42:1–3 was sung followed by two collects. A lengthy litany of the saints covered the procession to the font where, since there was probably not a candidate for baptism, only the blessing of the font took place. The celebrant first said a prayer which is in the Gelasian sacramentary (no. 444), the Missale Gallicanum vetus (no. 164), and the Bobbio missal (no. 235). The blessing of the font is in the Gelasian sacramentary (nos. 445–448) but has been somewhat elaborated on—as it also is in the Gallican Bobbio missal (nos. 235–238)—by the addition of the Sursum corda and the first phrases of the eucharistic preface, a multiplication of signs of the cross, and other ceremonial actions. These included the plunging of a candle into the font. The prayer is filled with biblical allusions. If there was a baptism, oil and chrism were added to the water, another feature of Gallican origin. Another litany was sung as the procession returned to the altar where the Mass began with a troped Kyrie, during which the celebrant said his private preparation and censed the altar. The ministers, who had worn black copes until this point in the rite, removed them at the beginning of the Gloria in excelsis and all the bells were rung with a joyous clash. The collect of the day was one appointed in the Gallican Bobbio missal (no. 258), the Gelasian (no. 454) and Gregorian sacramentaries (no. 377). The Epistle, Colossians 3:1–4, was followed by Alleluias, with a verse, and a tract. Matthew 28:1–7, the account of the resurrection, was the Gospel. The Agnus Dei was not said at the fraction. A shortened form of festal Vespers preceded the postcommunion prayer and dismissal.

The 1549 Prayer Book did not retain the Easter Vigil as such. It provided Easter Day rites which incorporated the Passover and baptismal themes associated with the Vigil, and introduced other elements appropriate to the baptismal nature of the day. One of its rubrics referred to the tradition of public baptisms at Easter. Matins is preceded by two anthems (Rom. 6:9–11 and 1 Cor. 15:20–22) and a collect. The proper psalms are 2, 57, and 111. There follows a reading of Exodus 12, the Te Deum laudamus, Romans 6, baptisms, and the Benedictus Dominus Deus. The Epistles appointed for the two Communions are Colossians 3:1–7 (from the Sarum vigil) and 1 Corinthians 5:6–8. Evensong includes Psalms 113, 114, and 118, and the reading of Acts 2, the account of the Pentecost, in full. In the 1892 revision, when Morning Prayer was no longer required with the Eucharist, some of the lections stressing the connection between baptism and the resurrection of our Lord were deleted, much to the impoverishment of the rite.

This edition of the Prayer Book recovers the ancient Vigil, the keystone about which the rest of the church year is built. Other baptisms of the year reflect this primary baptismal rite. Other Eucharists of the year are, to use the analogy of Augustine of Hippo, the repeatable part of this rite. In the Great Vigil of Easter we celebrate and make present (*anamnesis*) the pivotal events of the Old and New Testament heritage, the passover of the Hebrews from the bondage of slavery in Egypt to the freedom of the Promised Land, the passover of our Lord Jesus Christ from death, and our own passover from the bondage of sin and death to the glorious liberty of new life in Christ Jesus.

Concerning the Vigil (p. 284)

Because of its content the rite should begin in the darkness, as it did in the first centuries, when it began at sunset and concluded after sunrise. Depending on local circumstances the rite may begin soon after sunset or may be scheduled so that the Eucharist is celebrated at midnight as is currently practiced in many Roman Catholic and Eastern Orthodox churches. For the most dramatic effect, it may be so scheduled that the congregation gathers before dawn and the light of the sun would stream into the church at the beginning of the Eucharist.

The second paragraph lists the four parts of the rite. Omission of any one of these components greatly impoverishes the Vigil.

It is customary for all the ordained ministers present, as well as others with liturgical functions in the church, such as readers and singers, to perform their liturgical functions within this rite which is the prototype for other services of the year. The four paragraphs following spell out this principle for the four orders of ministers: lay persons, bishops, priests, and deacons.

The next paragraph defines the limitations upon a deacon or lay person who, in the absence of a bishop or priest, functions as celebrant at this liturgy.

The last paragraph allows the use of the Service of Light prior to the liturgy on Easter Day if the Vigil has not been celebrated.

The Lighting of the Paschal Candle (pp. 285–286)

Eusebius, who died in 339, mentions the part played by lights in the Paschal Vigil. The first ceremonial use of lights on this occasion may have been simply the lucernarium, or Order of Worship for Evening, before the readings. Eventually special texts and ceremonies became part of the Easter Vigil. The lighting of the new fire may be of Celtic origin; seventh century documents speak of it in legends about Saint Patrick. By the later middle ages it seems to have become a normal component of the rite. The new fire was originally kindled with a flint.

The Prayer Book provides a model for an address by the celebrant after the kindling of the new fire; this may be adapted to particular circumstances. The model provided is an independent translation of that of the new Roman sacramentary. The prayer of blessing is a shortened version of one in the York missal, the first printed Roman missal of 1474, and other medieval books. It differs substantially from that provided by Sarum. The original of this prayer reads:

> O God, through your Son, the cornerstone, you have bestowed upon the faithful the fire of your glory: Sanctify this new fire, produced from flint for our use, and grant that by this paschal feast we may be so inflamed with heavenly desires, that with pure minds we may come to the feast of everlasting light.

The rubric designates that the paschal candle, which represents the pillar of cloud by day and the pillar of fire by night, which led the Hebrews in the Exodus, is to be lighted prior to the procession. Traditionally, it is the prerogative of the deacon to carry the candle in the procession and to sing the Exsultet. In many of the medieval rites, however, a taper was carried in the procession and used to light the paschal candle after the paragraph in the Exsultet in which the candle is offered. The hymn to be sung during this procession was often specified, in the medieval rites, as "Thou leader kind" by the fifth century writer Prudentius. Other candles were then lighted within the course of the Exsultet after the lighting of the paschal candle. The directions in this Prayer Book are based on the order of the Roman rite as revised by Pius XII in 1950. The paschal candle is lighted from the new fire and carried in procession by the deacon, or by the celebrant if no deacon is present. During the procession the deacon pauses three times and sings or says "The light of Christ" to which the people respond "Thanks be to God." If candles have been distributed to the congregation prior to the rite, they are then lighted from the paschal candle, and other candles and lamps, except for those at the altar, are also lighted. The paschal candle is then placed in its stand, and the deacon (or priest or lay person taking the place of the deacon) sings or says the Exsultet.

The rubrics suggest the use of the paschal candle in baptisms (see page 313) and that the paschal candle lead the procession into the church at burials (see page 467). Use of the candle signifies the paschal nature of these occasions.

The Exsultet (pp. 286–287)

The text dates at least to the Gallican sacramentaries, Missale Gothicum (no. 225), Missale Gallicanum vetus (nos. 132–134), and the Bobbio missal (no. 227). The Gregorian supplement also included it (nos. 1021–1022). There were other forms equally as old if not older. Two by Ennodius, bishop of Ticinum (513–521), have survived, as well as the forms of the Gelasian sacramentary (nos. 426–429) and of the Mozarabic Liber Ordinum. Passages in the writings of Jerome and Augustine of Hippo are also thought to refer to a blessing of a paschal candle.

First the deacon calls upon the whole company of heaven, then the creatures of earth, and then all the members of the church to rejoice in the victory of the mighty and eternal King. The deacon then asks those present to join in prayer for the grace to sing the praise of this great light. The prayer which follows the introductory Gratias agamus is reminiscent of a Gallican eucharistic preface. Christ is praised as the Paschal Lamb who by His blood delivered His people as the Hebrews had been delivered from Egypt. The Easter feast is likened to the Exodus: as the children of Israel were brought out of bondage in Egypt, so those who believe in Christ are delivered from sin and restored to life. By the passover of Christ from death to life "earth and heaven are joined and man is reconciled to God." The Exsultet ends with the offering of the candle as an evening sacrifice to God. Many of the older versions of the text, though not all, have included two sections not found in the Prayer Book version. After the exclamation of praise for God's loving-kindness in sending a Son to redeem a slave, some versions contain these lines: "O truly needful sin of Adam which was blotted out by the death of Christ! O happy fault which merited so great a Redeemer!" Other manuscripts have included a lengthy section in praise of wax and the bee. Some contained intercessions prior to the doxology.

The rubric states that it is customary to burn the paschal candle at all services throughout the Great Fifty Days from Easter Day through the Day of Pentecost. This custom symbolizes the importance of this period and its unitive nature.

The Liturgy of the Word (pp. 288–292)

A substantial number of readings from the Scriptures, interspersed with psalms or canticles and prayers, is basic to a vigil. The lighting of the new fire and of the pschal candle constitutes an entrance rite for this liturgy of the word which is climaxed by Christian initiation or the renewal of baptismal vows and the first Eucharist of Easter. In the early church this series of readings extended from soon after sunset until cockcrow. Later the liturgy was more highly formalized; medieval books show no fewer than four lections and as many as twelve. Though the choice of lections varied from rite to rite, all

245

lections were drawn from a group of about eighteen of the most striking passages in the Old Testament. The stories of the Creation and Exodus were invariably read, the second always followed by the singing of Exodus 15 (Canticle 8, the Song of Moses, page 85). In the Gallican rite the prayers which followed the psalms or canticles were intercessions resembling the solemn collects of Good Friday, but in other rites they often referred to the lesson which had just been read. See, for example, the Gelasian (nos. 432–441) and Gregorian (nos. 362–369) sacramentaries. The Prayer Book provides a liturgy of the word with nine lessons, each followed by psalms or canticles and prayers.

The book gives a model for an introductory address to initiate the liturgy of the word. This address depends on that of the new Roman sacramentary. It may be varied for particular circumstances.

A rubric specifies that at least two of the nine lessons be read and that the lesson from Exodus, the story of Israel's deliverance at the Red Sea, never be omitted. An appropriate psalm or canticle is listed for use after each lesson, though others may be substituted. Other suitable collects may be used in place of the optional collects provided.

The first lesson, the story of Creation (Gen. 1:1—2:2), is followed by Psalm 33:1–11, "By the word of the Lord were the heavens made," or by Psalm 36:5–10, "In your light we see light." The collect is the same as that for the second Sunday after Christmas and of the votive "Of the Incarnation." It dates to the Leonine sacramentary (no. 1239), the earliest of the sacramentaries, where it was the collect for the first Christmas Mass. It is also included among other prayers for Christmas in the Gelasian (no. 27) and the Gregorian (no. 59) sacramentaries. It reminds us that God is the restorer as well as the creator of the dignity of human nature.

The second lesson is an abbreviated version of the story of the Flood (Gen. 7:1–5, 11–18; 8:6–18; 9:8–13) of readable proportions. Psalm 46, "God is our refuge and strength," follows. The collect, based upon an earlier composition by the Rev. Dr. H. Boone Porter, recalls the traditional use of the story of the eight in the ark "saved by water" as a type of baptism; the rainbow as a sign of the covenant has been interpreted as a figure of the new covenant of our Lord Jesus Christ.

Abraham's sacrifice of Isaac is the third story (Gen. 22:1–18), followed by Psalm 33:12–22, "Let your loving-kindness, O Lord, be upon us, as we have put our trust in you," or Psalm 16, "Protect me, O God, for I take refuge in you." The collect is based on that used after this lection in the Gelasian sacramentary (no. 434). The translation is revised from that provided by John H. Uhrig and Capt. Howard E. Galley for inclusion in "Music for Holy Week."[1]

The fourth lesson, the story of the passover, Israel's deliverance at the Red Sea (Ex. 14:10—15:1), is followed as in all the early liturgical books by the Song of Moses (Canticle 8, p. 85). The prayer is based on that associated with this lesson in the Gelasian sacramentary (no. 435) and the Sarum missal. The Gregorian sacramentary had a somewhat different version of this same prayer (no. 365) in conjunction with this reading. As Israel was delivered from bondage, so through baptism may all people come to be numbered among the offspring of Abraham and enter into the inheritance of Israel. The translation is revised from that of Uhrig and Galley.[2]

The fifth lesson prophesies God's presence in a renewed Israel, Isaiah 4:2–6. In many of the medieval rites it was followed by the Song of the Vineyard from the chapter following (Isaiah 5). The response to the lesson is Psalm 122, "Pray for the peace of Jerusalem." The collect, based upon an earlier composition by the Rev. Dr. H. Boone Porter, combines themes from both the lection and the psalm.

Isaiah 55:1–11, which begins "Ho, everyone who thirsts, come to the waters," is the sixth lesson. The response is the First Song of Isaiah, Isaiah 12:2–6 (Canticle 9, page 86), "You shall draw water with rejoicing from the springs of salvation," or Psalm 42:1–7, "As the deer longs for the water-brooks, so longs my soul for you, O God." The latter psalm was frequently used in ancient rites for the procession to the font for baptism. The petition of the collect, based upon an earlier composition by Dr. Porter, is obviously based on the lection.

The seventh lesson is Ezekiel 36:24–26, "I will sprinkle clean water upon you, . . . A new heart I will give you, . . . And I will put my spirit within you." The same alternatives are provided for the response as for the sixth lesson. The collect is from the Gregorian sacramentary (no. 423) where, as in the Sarum missal, it was used on Friday of Easter Week. This translation is revised from one by William Bright in *Ancient Collects* (pages 56–57). It is also used as the collect for Thursday of Easter Week and for the Second Sunday of Easter.

The account of the valley of dry bones (Ezek. 37:1–14), "I shall put my spirit within you and you shall live, and I will place you in your own land," is the eighth lection. The response is Psalm 30, "You brought me up, O Lord, from the dead," or Psalm 143, "Revive

---

[1] Edited by Mason Martens, New York, 1972, p. 57.
[2] Martens, p. 58.

me, O Lord, for your Name's sake." The petition of the collect, based upon an earlier composition by the Rev. Dr. H. Boone Porter, alludes to the seal of baptism (see page 308 in the Prayer Book).

The ninth lesson is the vision of Zephaniah of the gathering of God's people (Zeph. 3:12–20). The response is Psalm 98, "The Lord has made known his victory," or Psalm 126, "The Lord has done great things for us, and we are glad indeed." The prayer, which is also the last of the solemn collects of the Good Friday liturgy and the collect of the ordination rites, is from the Gelasian sacramentary (no. 432), where it was used after the first lection, Genesis 1, at the Easter Vigil. The translation is based upon that of William Bright in *Ancient Collects* (pages 98–99).

The rubric permits a homily after any of the readings.

Holy Baptism or the Renewal of Baptismal Vows (pp. 292–294)

The Easter Vigil was the time of baptisms in the early church. At a later period Pentecost and Epiphany also became baptismal days, but Easter remained the principal feast. No other day of the church year so powerfully reinforces the concept of baptism as the passover from death into life as this day on which we commemorate the passover of the children of Israel from bondage to freedom and the passover of our Lord Jesus Christ from death into life.

The second rubric on page 292 designates the two places in the rite where baptism may be administered. Baptism may precede the liturgy of the word of the eucharistic rite, as in the medieval books, or may come after the whole series of readings and the homily and lead into the prayers of the people, as in the earlier church orders and the new Roman rite.

The Prayer Book provides for a renewal of baptismal vows when there are no candidates for baptism or confirmation. In such circumstances the renewal of vows may be preceded by an address which is an independent translation of that in the new Roman sacramentary. This address may also be adapted for use before the baptismal covenant of the rite of baptism or confirmation when either is celebrated on this occasion (see rubric at the bottom of page 303 and that near the top of page 416). The text of the renewal of vows introduces the covenant of the rite (pages 304–305) with a preliminary question which summarizes the renunciations and act of commitment (pages 302–303). A prayer of a super populum type, based on that in the new

248

Roman sacramentary, concludes the renewal of vows. The translation is that of Capt. Howard E. Galley.

At the Eucharist (pp. 294–295)

The first rubric directs that candles at the altar may be lighted from the paschal candle immediately after the reception of the newly baptized, if baptism has been administered immediately before this point; or they may be lighted after the prayer following the renewal of vows if that followed the service of readings. A third place for lighting of the altar candles is immediately after the last collect of the service of readings if the baptism or renewal of vows is to take place after the Gospel (and homily).

The Eucharist begins with one or another of three songs of praise. This makes a clear contrast with Lent when no song of praise is to be used in the entrance rite. Medieval Roman rites began the Eucharist with the Gloria in excelsis which was the only option for a song of praise at that point. An alternative in this Book is the Te Deum laudamus with its initial paean of praise followed by a proclamation of the passover of our Lord through death to life. The other alternative is the Pascha nostrum, the initial song of praise in the Anglican rite for Easter Day from the 1549 Prayer Book until the cessation, in recent years, of the practice of preceding the Sunday Eucharist with Morning Prayer. It is traditional for bells (which may have been silenced since Maundy Thursday) to be rung at the time of the opening song of praise. As the rubric of the Sarum rite expressed it, "All the bells shall be rung together in a clash."

The song of praise may be introduced by an opening acclamation from the Eastern Orthodox tradition: "Alleluia, Christ is risen." with its response, "The Lord is risen indeed. Alleluia." Either of the first two collects of Easter Day may be used. For the Epistle, Romans 6:3–11, "Do you not know that all of us who have been baptized into Christ Jesus were baptized into his death?," is excerpted from the full chapter which had been the New Testament lesson at Morning Prayer in Anglicanism from 1549 until the revision of 1892. In the Mozarabic rite this was the Epistle at the Easter Vigil; Cranmer had turned to this rite for other baptismal material as well. A rubric explicitly recommends the use of Alleluia on this occasion. Throughout the season of Lent this exclamation has been suppressed, following the tradition of the Western church, and it is most appropriate to

249

restore its use on this occasion. Psalm 114, "When Israel came out of Egypt," with its exodus and baptismal associations, is especially recommended for use after the Epistle and Alleluia. Matthew 28:1–10, the story of the empty tomb, is the Gospel that has been used in the Easter Vigil since the time of the earliest Roman lectionaries. It is expected that a sermon or homily will follow the Gospel if it has not followed one of the readings of the Vigil. Since the Apostles' Creed (the baptismal creed) is incorporated in the rite of baptism or the renewal of baptismal vows, the Nicene Creed is omitted.

Holy Baptism

I n all cultures the rites of initiation have been the models for other rites of the community, for initiation is the central liturgy of the community. The rites centering on other crises take as their model the initiation practices. Those associated with the sanctification of time—the cyclical rites—are typically repetitions of elements of initiatory rites. A child, at an appropriate age, passes ritually from childhood to maturity, becoming a full member of the community with the responsibilities and privileges of such membership. The initiate is instructed in the traditions and sacred history of the community and tested for readiness to act as an adult member. The rites, which are almost invariably spoken of as new birth and as death and resurrection, are designed to make an indelible impression on the initiate and to reinforce the impressions of earlier initiations on those who share the ritual. Those who have undergone the same rites are blood kin, people who can be depended on to death itself, people who bear their weight within the adult community.

The rite of initiation for one not born into Judaism involved circumcision and baptism. After a period as a "God-fearer" attending synagogue services, the individual was brought for examination and admission as a candidate or proselyte. The person was questioned— why would one wish to become a Jew? The new candidate then entered into a period of intense instruction—dogmatic, ethical, and eschatological—and was brought to repentance and renunciation of the former manner of life. After instruction in the Law and the Jewish heritage, the candidate was brought to baptism, having first been circumcised (if male). At baptism there were witnesses to vouch for the candidate. The person was baptized nude in living water, with some dialogue concerning the Law, an oath of loyalty or an act of

251

adherence, at the moment of immersion. Coming out of the water, the candidate was signed as God's sheep, slave, and soldier by the marking on the forehead with a Taw (T), the last letter of the Hebrew alphabet, symbol of the name of God (compare the mark of Cain, of Ezekiel, of Paul, of Revelation). The baptism signified that person's crossing of the Red Sea, entering into the promised land, accepting the heritage and hopes of the Jewish people as one's own heritage and hopes.

John the Baptist preached the baptism of repentance which signified a new beginning and incorporation in a new community. His baptism had eschatological implications. Jesus submitted Himself to baptism by John before entering into His ministry, and He referred to His death as baptism.

The early Christian baptismal rite took its basic form from the Jewish initiation of converts. The practice of circumcision (for males) was not maintained, because it suggested a nationalistic cult, ritual purity, exclusion of women from full membership, and the blood of the old covenant. The church proclaimed the true circumcision to be the circumcision of the heart (Jer. 4:4; Gen. 17:10ff.). The early Christians, however, retained the cultic act of baptism which spoke of repentance, cleansing, new birth, adoption, death, and resurrection. The act was reinterpreted in terms of the Christian gospel: it meant a cleansing by the blood of Jesus, new birth in Christ, death and resurrection in Christ, incorporation into His Body, the "mark" or "seal" of the Lord Jesus. To be baptized was to be adopted by God, to share in Christ's Sonship and His anointing (as kings and priests were anointed), to receive the Holy Spirit, to confess one's faith in Christ, to swear one's loyalty to Him. Later generations were to distinguish between baptism and repentance, between baptism and confession of faith. For the New Testament writers to be baptized was to repent, to confess the faith.

Along with the Jewish customs, the rites of the mystery religions of the time contributed to the development of the baptismal liturgy. In such mysteries as those of Eleusis, Orpheus, Isis, and Mithra, initiates were typically admitted as candidates, given instruction, subjected to tests (fasting, acts of humility, immersion), sealed on the forehead as a soldier of the god, given honey (the food of babies), offered the right hand of fellowship, and fed a meal of bread, and wine mixed with water.

The fullest description of the process of Christian initiation that we have from the pre-Nicene period is in the Apostolic Tradition (c. A.D. 215), which is generally considered a Roman document. Converts

who wished to be admitted as hearers—catechumens—were brought
to teachers by those who could vouch for them. Those admitted entered a three-year period of study; they attended services of readings,
instructions, and prayers, concluding with laying on of hands by the
teacher. After three years, those who had proved themselves worthy
by their sober lives, their good works, and their appropriation of the
Old Testament heritage were admitted, several weeks before Easter,
as candidates, and entered a period of instruction in the Gospel and
of daily exorcisms. Those whose reactions did not seem yet to be of
the right sort had their baptisms postponed.

The candidates bathed on Thursday and fasted on the Friday and
Saturday immediately before the baptism. On Saturday the bishop
himself performed the final exorcism in the form of an ordeal. Saturday night was spent in vigil, listening to readings and instructions. At
cockcrow prayer was said over the water. The early church fathers
compared the water of baptism to the primordial waters, the water of
the grave, the Red Sea waters, the water from the rock, the water in
which Naaman was immersed, the water of Mary's womb, the Jordan
River, the living water promised the woman at the well in Samaria,
the healing pool of Bethsaida, the water from the side of Christ, and
the waters of Paradise. Baptismal water was to be cold and to flow
through a tank or pour into it from above.

The bishop also set apart two oils, exorcising the "oil of exorcism"
and giving thanks over the "oil of thanksgiving," later to be known as
the "chrism." The candidates individually renounced "Satan, all his
servants, and all his works." This was a renunciation not just of sin
but of a former way of life. The presbyter then anointed the candidate's whole body with the oil of exorcism—comparable to the
Roman custom of anointing oneself with oil before entering the bath,
and to the athlete's oiling himself before entering the arena. The
presbyter said "Let all spirits depart far from you." A deacon then
took the candidate into the water. A presbyter or the bishop asked
"Do you believe in God, the Father almighty?" The one being baptized replied "I believe." The presbyter then, laying on hands,
pushed the candidate down into the water. Next the presbyter asked:

Do you believe in Jesus Christ, the Son of God, who was born of
the Holy Spirit from the Virgin Mary, and was crucified under
Pontius Pilate, and was dead and buried, and rose again the third
day, alive from the dead, and ascended into heaven, and sat at the
right hand of the Father, and will come to judge the living and
the dead?

The one being baptized again said "I believe" and was immersed a second time by the presbyter. The presbyter then asked "Do you believe in the Holy Spirit, and the holy church, and the resurrection of the flesh?" The one being baptized answered "I believe." (The Christian creeds were to grow from such baptismal forms.)

Having thus made a confession of faith the person was immersed for the third time. In some rites, as late as the end of the fourth century, the newly baptized person, after donning a robe, was taken immediately into the church to share the exchange of the peace and the prayers of the people for the first time. At Rome and in North Africa, however, the newly baptized was first anointed fully with the oil of thanksgiving, the chrism, an action comparable to the Roman custom of anointing oneself with perfumed oil after the bath, or to the first bathing of a new baby with oil, or to the anointing of kings and priests. At the anointing the presbyter said "I anoint you with holy oil in the name of Jesus the Anointed One." The newly baptized, possibly wearing new white robes, were led back into the congregation. In Rome and North Africa they were presented to the bishop—an action comparable to that of a midwife taking a newborn child to the father for public recognition of the child as a member of the family. The bishop recognized publicly before the congregation the fact of baptism by laying on hands and anointing the initiate—a token of the presbyter's laying on of hands in the act of immersion and of the anointing with oil after immersion. Like the giving of a diploma or certificate, this was a public acknowledgment of something which had occurred privately. The bishop then signed the newly baptized person on the forehead, possibly with a Taw (T), an act comparable to the branding of sheep, slaves, and soldiers.

The newly baptized then joined the faithful in prayer for the first time and exchanged the peace which led into preparation of the table for the Eucharist, with the newly baptized supplying the oblations.

Because of the *disciplina arcani*, the discipline of secrecy, the initiates did not learn the meaning of these rites until after their participation. The experience of initiation was so traumatic that those who experienced it felt that they had died and been raised, that they had been reborn, that the ones with whom they now had most in common were those who had undergone the same initiation. An old baptistry inscription reads: "Nothing can separate those who are reborn. They are one: one baptism, one Spirit, one faith, one God and Father."

The establishment of Christianity by Constantine brought changes in these rites. The loss of tension between the church and the world, a lack of zeal on the part of many new converts, and the scarcity of clergy were to curtail the ritual. Out of the Donatist controversy over the relationship of the character of the priest to the validity of the sacrament came a definition of what constitutes a valid baptism—water and the word. The Pelagian controversy over the nature of man and the necessity of grace brought an increased emphasis on the doctrine of original sin which resulted in increased numbers of clinical and infant baptisms. Rites and instructions were confined to a period of several weeks instead of three years. Though adult baptism was still the norm, increasingly young children were carried through the rites and instructions physically or vicariously by their parents or godparents. At the beginning of Lent a person was made a catechumen, and was expected to attend a number of services during the weeks following to hear lections chosen for their association with baptism, and lectures or instructions on the meaning of these lections. The catechumens were exorcised at these services and received laying on of hands. Generally the person was made a candidate on the Sunday before Easter; in many rites this became the day when the candidate was given the creed, *traditio symboli*, which would be returned, *redditio symboli*, at or before the baptism.

The baptism itself was associated with the Easter Vigil. This usually began with the blessing of the new fire, the Exsultet, and the blessing of the paschal candle. There followed a series of four to twelve Old Testament readings interspersed with canticles and prayers. The readings normally included the stories of the creation, the fall, the sacrifice of Isaac, the Passover, the crossing of the Red Sea, the entry into the promised land, Isaiah 55 ("Come to the waters"), the valley of dry bones, and Jonah. The water of the font was then exorcised and/or blessed with a form rich in biblical typology. The blessing of the water was sometimes followed by the blessing of oil and an anointing, although in the West these tended to be moved to days before Easter. The candidate was called upon to renounce Satan three times and to make a threefold confession of faith. In Eastern rites the renunciation was often followed by an act expressing rejection of Satan, such as spitting toward the West. An act of adherence to Christ preceded the profession of faith. The newly baptized, after immersion, were anointed (chrismated, christened) with the chrism. Peculiar to the Roman rite of central Italy and northern Africa was the custom of following this first anointing with a second anointing by the bishop. The neophytes were then clothed in white garments which they would wear for several days. In Gallican rites their feet were washed by the ranking prelate.

255

The Easter Eucharist immediately followed the post-baptismal ceremonies so that the newly baptized might make their first communion. The lections and prayers of this Eucharist were filled with baptismal references, as were those of the seven days following (the Easter octave) which they would attend still attired in their white robes. In these rites the classical pattern of Christian initiation had been retained, even though the time of preparation had been reduced from three years to a few weeks, the several-week candidacy to one week, and the Great Fifty Days to an octave. Pentecost, which signified baptism as the receiving of the Holy Spirit, and Epiphany, which signified baptism as new birth, became two secondary times for baptisms.

The emphasis on the doctrine of original sin and the increased frequency of infant baptism eventually caused compression of the process into one short rite. In the West manuscripts as early as the eleventh century provide for the baptism of infants in a single rite. Typical of the late medieval period is the Sarum rite which retained elements from various rites which had been parts of Christian initiation in the past. Signation on the forehead and the breast remained from the period of the catechumenate, as did laying on of hands, and the receiving of salt in the mouth. An exorcism and a signation with a prayer for "the light of understanding" remained from the old period of candidacy. This was followed by forms reminiscent of the old Holy Saturday morning rite, including the reading of the Matthean version of the blessing of the children and the repetition by the godparents of the Lord's Prayer, the Ave Maria, and the Apostles' Creed. All of this took place at the door of the church. The child was then blessed and carried into the church. If the water in the font was to be renewed the blessing of the font was added to the service. This order was composed of a litany of the saints, a collect, and the Gelasian blessing, rich in biblical imagery. A threefold renunciation, an anointing, a threefold interrogation concerning the Creed, and an expression of the desire to be baptized followed. The child was then immersed in water three times in the name of the Holy Trinity, anointed with chrism on the crown of the head, clothed in the chrysom (a remnant of the white garment), and given a lighted candle. "If a bishop is present he must immediately be confirmed and next communicated, if his age require it." The godparents were admonished to teach the child the Creed, the Ave Maria, the Lord's Prayer, and how to make the sign of the cross, and to see to it that the child is confirmed "as soon as the bishop comes within a distance of seven miles." From the thirteenth century only those born within eight days of the Easter or

256

Pentecost vigils were to be "saved" for baptism at the vigil. The priest was to instruct the people how to baptize in emergencies. Altogether, the fear of limbo had caused baptism to precede catechetical instruction and to lose its integral connection with the church year, with the bishop, and with the local congregation. Baptism was no longer the time of repentance, confession of faith, death and resurrection, the conferring of the Holy Spirit, manumission, the binding together of blood kin. Much of this imagery had been deleted from the rite. It was now a bath to wash away the taint of original sin. The practice of infant baptism and the new eucharistic piety worked together to separate first communion from baptism. Though remnants of the earlier practice lingered into the Reformation period, legislation in some areas as early as the thirteenth century forbade communion prior to "confirmation" and linked "confirmation" with the "years of discretion."

In addition to the post-baptismal anointing with chrism, a normal component of most baptismal rites from the fifth century, there was in the territory where the Roman rite prevailed a second post-baptismal anointing applied by the bishop, not found in other historic rites. Water and the word sufficed for a person baptized in an emergency and the varying post-baptismal ceremonies were not considered necessary. Should the person subsequently recover, one or another of the post-baptismal rituals seems to have been applied publicly. A person who had been excommunicated might at reinstatement have public administration of such ceremonies, at least in some places. And a person received into the Catholic church after having been baptized into or associated with a heretical or schismatic group might be admitted with public administration of one or more of the ceremonies. The word "confirmation" came to be used as a term defining these various situations as early as the fifth century. Eleventh century manuscripts, however, indicate that the term was also used to apply to administration of communion to the newly baptized.

As strong efforts were made to Romanize the previously Gallican territories, it was typical to insist upon use of certain Roman ceremonies or texts in addition to or in place of the former Gallican ritual. This explains many of the duplications in the late medieval rites of ordination or rites for the consecration of a church. The use of that strange second anointing in the Roman rite, ordinarily performed by a bishop, was apparently one of the tests of submission to the Roman rite in formerly Gallican territories. The second anointing had been administered in Roman practice shortly after the post-baptismal chrismation by the officiating presbyter. But in Gallican territories and missionary areas there were many fewer bishops than in the environs of Rome. In outlying areas, therefore, this second anointing was to be supplied as soon as possible after the administration of baptism. The central prayer seems to have taken fairly standard form by the time of the eleventh century Leofric missal, but in that book it is simply placed among a series of episcopal blessings of objects or persons. The form which is its basis and which closely resembles it is in the Gelasian sacramentary as the public reception by a bishop of a person who had been baptized in extremis (no. 615). Eventually this prayer with the anointing came to be known as "confirmation." Twelfth and thirteenth century pontificals contained a rite titled "confirmation of infants" which consists of this prayer, chrismation on the forehead, another prayer, and a blessing.

Medieval theologians explained this rite as a strengthening for spiritual combat which would come with adolescence. The rationale of Thomas Aquinas and other theologians has been succinctly summarized:

> We . . . do sign *him* with the sign of the cross, in token that hereafter *he* shall not be ashamed to confess the faith of Christ crucified, and manfully to fight under his banner against sin, the world, and the devil, and to continue Christ's faithful soldier and servant unto *his* life's end.

To equate this "confirmation" and this rationale with earlier practice in Rome, with Eastern chrismation, or with post-immersion ceremonies of the Gallican rites is highly questionable. As early as the thirteenth century the idea was fostered by certain local church councils that "confirmation" should be deferred until the child could be taught certain texts; a rationale was being constructed for the peculiar second anointing. In some areas the bishop or his "deputy" began to postpone such anointing until the child had learned the texts. In some areas first communion also began to be postponed until the second anointing. The integrity of the earlier initiation rite had been lost and the way was being prepared for another development which would be fostered by the Renaissance and the Reformation.

Luther tried to restore the emphasis on baptism as death and resurrection and as the anointing of kings and priests. In 1523 he published a much-abbreviated rite in which the one missing element of the medieval rite was the blessing of the water. The one new element was a "Flood Prayer," based upon the flood and the exodus as types of baptism, and the baptism of Jesus as the sanctification of water for baptizing. German church orders of the period broke further with the Roman rite, setting a span of time between admission to catechumenate and the baptism, inserting lengthy exhortations and prayers, linking the naming of the child with the application of water, insisting that the rite be performed at the Sunday Eucharist, setting new rules for the godparents, and requiring that they make promises for themselves. The Reformed (in contrast to the Lutheran) churches rejected the doctrine of infant damnation and the practice of baptism by lay persons, allowing private baptisms only in extreme circumstances. They rejected all of the ceremonies save the baptism itself and typically administered baptism by pouring, which had become the normal practice in their area before the Reformation. The Anabaptists insisted that baptism represent adult commitment and rebaptized, often by immersion, those who had been baptized in infancy.

Wycliffe spoke of the rite which was being called "confirmation" in the late middle ages as a "frivolous rite." The Bohemian Brethren substituted for a second post-baptismal anointing a rite which consisted of an examination at the end of instruction, an expression of desire to renew the baptismal covenant, prayer for the strengthening of the Holy Spirit, and a laying on of hands with an invocation "for strengthening their hope of heavenly grace." This was designed as a rite for admission to communion. Erasmus made similar recommendations, suggesting that such a rite would have greater significance if performed by bishops. Luther rejected "confirmation" as "mumbo-jumbo" which could add nothing to baptism, and instead devised catechisms which explained the significance of baptism and then gave explications of the Creed, the Ten Commandments, the Lord's Prayer, and the sacraments. He stated that children should give an account of these before being admitted to communion, but devised no rite to be associated with such graduation from catechetical instruction. He did state that he found no fault if a pastor examined the faith of the children and "confirmed" them by laying on of hands. (Compare this sign with the second anointing which was considered the "matter" of the late medieval "confirmation.")

Martin Bucer, in reaction to Anabaptist criticism, prepared a rite for use at Strassburg: an examination in the catechism, a renewal of baptismal vows, and admission to communion with laying on of hands and prayer for defense and for the strengthening gifts of the Holy Spirit. By the time he was involved in the compilation of the Consultation for Hermann, the reforming archbishop of Cologne, Bucer had come to feel that this rite should be the prerogative of a

259

bishop, or at least of an outside visitor rather than a local pastor. He had four reasons for this:

(1) it would get the bishops out into the parishes;
(2) examination in the catechism would be conducted by an outsider;
(3) dignity or impressiveness would be added to the occasion;
(4) this would be a sign of the catholicity of the church.

Calvin denounced "confirmation" as it was designated in the late medieval period, particularly the use of the chrism. Yet Calvin, with many others of the time, believed there had once existed a pure form of "confirmation" in which, after instruction, children openly professed their faith and were catechized, and then received imposition of hands as a "benediction."

The initial rubric of the 1549 Prayer Book baptismal rite indicates that baptism should be a public act. Except in emergencies, it "should not be ministered but upon Sundays and other holy days, when the most number of people may come together." When baptism is a public act, the congregation can receive the newly baptized into their fellowship and be reminded of their own baptismal vows. Much of the content of the rubric and some of the phrasing is derived from the homily "Of Baptism" which introduced the baptismal rites in the Consultation of Hermann. The service, like that of the Sarum rite, was to begin at the church door with an exhortation on the necessity and meaning of baptism, which clearly has points of contact with the initial exhortation of Hermann's rite and with the section on baptism in the *King's Book*. This was followed by Luther's "Flood Prayer," found in many of the German rites. The child is then called by name and signed with a form which derives both from Hermann and from the English reformation Rationale of Ceremonial (1543). There follows a prayer which was associated with the exorcisms in rites as old as that in the Gregorian supplement (no. 1074). The translation is not from the Latin, however, but from the German Lutheran version of the prayer. An exorcism follows, based upon those of the Sarum rite which in part evolved from the Gelasian sacramentary (nos. 296–297) but modified and amplified by German forms. The English rites had used Matthew's account of the blessing of the children (Mt. 19:13–15) in conjunction with the exorcism; the German Lutheran rites had used Mark's account at this point (Mk. 10:13–16). Later Lutheran orders, including Hermann's, detached this from the exorcism and used it as the introduction to an exhortation which was an apologia for the practice of infant baptism. Cranmer followed the new German tradition, and the exhortation printed in the Book owes something to Hermann. The Creed and the Lord's Prayer—remnants of the ancient *redditio symboli*—follow, with no laying on of hands, and then a slightly modified version of a prayer first found in the Consultation.

The entrance into the church is accompanied by a revised version of the Sarum form, but Cranmer completely disregarded the Sarum blessing of the font, except for two biblical allusions, the water and the blood from the side of Christ and the command to baptize in the Name of the Trinity, which are allusions common to many rites. The water is not "blessed" as in the Sarum rite, but "sanctified" or "prepared for the ministration of thy holy sacrament." The order is not called "The Blessing of the Font" but "these prayers." The form consists of an opening prayer for the effective operation of baptismal grace in those baptized, eight supplications, a salutation, and a summary collect. The closest parallel to these eight supplications and to certain phrases in the initial and concluding prayers is in the Easter rites of the Mozarabic Missale Mixtum. An older version dates to the Missale Gallicanum vetus (no. 168). The entrance into the church (or the prayers over the water which were required only once a month) was followed by an exhortation to the godparents influenced by one in Hermann's rite. The threefold form of renunciation which follows is not the traditional one of Satan, his works, and his pomps, but the devil, the world, and the flesh. The renunciation of the world has precedents in Lutheran forms, but the renunciation of the flesh has no known liturgical antecedents.

Cranmer replaced the threefold Sarum confession of faith, an abbreviated version of the Creed, with a slightly amplified variant reading of the Creed which was influenced by the Consultation. This is followed by two questions from the Sarum rite concerning the desire for baptism. The baptism itself is to be done as threefold immersion accompanied by a form—"I baptize thee in the name of the Father, and of the Son, and of the Holy Ghost. Amen."—which several centuries before had replaced the Creed or a longer form. The postbaptismal anointing of the Sarum rite is omitted. The 1549 Book follows the baptism immediately with the giving of the token of the white garment, accompanied by a form based on the English reformation Rationale of Ceremonial. There is then the anointing and a charge to the godparents related to one of the questions in Hermann's rite as well as to passages in the writings of Saint Basil and in the Rationale of Ceremonial. The anointing is made on the forehead as in the medieval "confirmation" rather than on the top or crown of the

Rites of Initiation

SARUM (typical late medieval rite)	1549 PRAYER BOOK	HERMANN'S CONSULTATION
At the door: Signing forehead & breast Prayer Signation (Naming?) Prayer Exorcism & Giving of salt Prayer Prayers, Adjurations, & Exorcism	*At the door:* Exhortation Prayer Signation (Naming) Prayer & Exorcism	*Saturday evening:* Exhortation Interrogations Renunciations Profession of faith Questions regarding duties of godparents & Exhortatio Exorcism Signation Two prayers (Luther)
Gospel (Matt.) Effeta	Gospel (Mk.) Exhortation	Gospel (Mk.) Exhortation & Laying on of hands
Lord's Prayer, Ave Maria & Creed Signing right hand	Lord's Prayer & Creed Prayer *Entrance into the church*	Lord's Prayer & Creed Psalms 114, 115 & 135 Prayer *After creed at Sunday* *Eucharist:*
Entrance into the church Charge to godparents Litany of Saints & Prayer Blessing of font	"These prayers" over the water Charge to godparents Renunciations	Prayer Lessons: Titus 3:4-7 Matt. 28:18-20
Renunciations Unction Profession of faith Desire for baptism Three-fold immersion Unction (crown of head) Vesting in white robe Giving of candle Gospels: Mk. 9:17-29 Jn. 1:1-14 *Confirmation by bishop or* *deputy* Preces and Form for conferring gifts of the Spirit Chrismation (forehead) Pax Prayer Psalm verses	Profession of faith Desire for baptism Three-fold immersion Vesting in white robe	Prayer Baptism (Naming) Chrismation prayer, but without an anointing Pax
	Chrismation (forehead) Exhortation to godparents *"Confirmation" by bishop* Catechism Preces and prayer for gifts of the Spirit Signation & Laying on of hands Pax Prayer	Hymn or Psalm 67 *"Confirmation" by "Visitor"* Catechism Prayer Laying on of hands with prayer
Blessing *Holy Communion* ("if age require it")	Blessing *Holy Communion*	Hymn *Holy Communion*

262

head as in the medieval rite of baptism. The phrase at the time of anointing, "the unction of his Holy Spirit," was a phrase common to medieval theologians in relation to the second post-baptismal anointing normally performed by a bishop, the anointing thought to be the "matter" of the medieval rite of "confirmation."

The 1549 Book contains a section titled "Of them that be baptized in private houses in time of necessity." Elements of that rite which are not found also in the public rite are dependent upon Hermann's Consultation, or possibly upon the Saxon church order which underlies it.

Having provided in a sense for the perpetuation of the medieval rite called "confirmation" within the baptismal rite, the 1549 Book then provided another rite titled "confirmation" which had for its precedents the forms of the Bohemian Brethren which Erasmus and Luther had approved, and which Bucer and other German and Swiss reformers had put into practice. Like their rites, this "confirmation" is not to be administered until the child can say the Creed, the Ten Commandments, and the Lord's Prayer, answer questions of the catechism, and "ratify and confess" what had been promised by the godparents. This rite, like its continental predecessors, was a prerequisite for receiving communion. It was to be administered when the child had reached the age of culpability, since a benefit of the rite is the receiving of "strength and defense" against the temptations associated with that period in a child's life. Such timing is said to be "agreeable with the usage of the church in times past," an argument which depends on a misreading of the church fathers which was common in the period. An integral portion of "confirmation" in the 1549 Book is a catechism with an introductory section on baptism followed by expositions of the Creed, the Lord's Prayer, and the Ten Commandments, principally based on English reformation formularies. The administration of the rite is limited much more severely to the bishop than were either the "confirmation" rite of the German church orders or the medieval practice of the second post-baptismal anointing. The reasons may lie in the argument spelled out by Bucer (see above, pp. 259–260), but they may also lie in the argument of the King's Book in which the function of the bishop is seen as necessary to the maintenance of civil order.

After the initial examination in the catechism, the order of the other components of the 1549 rite is deceptively close to that of the medieval rite called "confirmation." The introductory versicles are unchanged. The "Minister" then says a prayer which is a revised and amplified version of that in the Sarum rite. The ceremonial action is not an anointing "without which it [confirmation] is counted no sacrament," but, like that in the German church orders, a laying on of hands. The peace, a prayer, and a blessing follow. The prayer, made up of phrases from the "collect" of Hermann's rite, replaces the Sarum prayer. The order of some components and portions of certain texts may resemble the rite called "confirmation" in the medieval books, but the rationale is clearly that of the Consultation and other German church orders.

In the 1552 revision the whole of the baptismal rite was to be performed at the font. The signation, the exorcism, and the godparents' repetition of the Lord's Prayer and Creed were deleted. The traditional threefold form of the renunciations and the profession of faith were made single questions, and the two questions concerning baptism combined into one: "Wilt thou be baptized in this faith?" "That is my desire." The initial prayer for the sanctification of water was omitted and the phrase "prepared for the ministration of thy holy sacrament" was deleted from the final prayer. Four of the eight supplications remained. The prayers, instead of being required at least once each month, were required at each baptism. As in the Eucharist the prayer over the elements was moved to a place immediately preceding the act of taking communion, so in this rite the prayers over the water were moved to come immediately before the immersion of the child. The naming of the child was linked to the act of baptism as it had been in the German church orders. There is no longer requirement for threefold immersion, for vesting, or for unction. These actions had stirred controversy long before 1549 but that Book had retained them although the anointing was not considered an essential part of baptism; no provision had been made for it when a child privately baptized was brought to the church. At the point occupied by the anointing in the 1549 Book, the 1552 rite instructs the priest to make the sign of the cross on the child's forehead, the site of the second or "confirmation" anointing in the medieval rites, whereas the top or crown of the head was the site of the baptismal anointing in the middle ages. Associated with this signation was the text quoted above (p. 258) as the summary of medieval teaching on the meaning of the second or "confirmation" anointing. The words associated with the signation, "do sign *him* with the sign of the cross," are equivalent to those associated with the signing in the medieval "confirmation" rather than to the words "Receive the sign of the holy cross" of medieval baptism signations. The form explicates the "sealing" in baptism; the text uses analogies of the branding of sheep or a slave after the transfer of ownership or the tattooing of a

264

soldier after enlistment. This 1552 revision inserts a bidding to give thanks that this child is "regenerate," the Lord's Prayer, and a prayer of thanksgiving (which echoes the postcommunion prayer of the Eucharist) prior to the charge to the godparents.

The prayer for the sevenfold gifts of the Holy Spirit in the "confirmation" of 1549 was further revised in 1552. A new prayer, equivalent to forms in Hermann's Consultation and other German church orders, replaced the form which accompanied the laying on of hands in 1549. The changes made more explicit the rationale which the writings of the various reformers (including Cranmer), the German church orders, and the introductory rubrics to the 1549 rite had spelled out.

The 1604 edition added a section on the sacraments of Baptism and the Eucharist to the catechism and reworked the rite of private baptism. The Puritans wished to do away with private baptisms altogether; this edition did not abolish the practice but did regulate it. In emergencies people were no longer to baptize children but to "procure" a "lawful Minister."

The 1662 revision regulated the number of godparents: each child was to have two of the same sex and one of the opposite sex. An additional question was inserted after the expression of desire for baptism: "Wilt thou then obediently keep God's holy will and commandments, and walk in the same all the days of thy life?" A petition for the sanctification of the water, following the lead of the 1637 Scottish Book, was inserted in the last prayer prior to the baptism. The doctrinal upheavals of the period, the growth of the Anabaptist movement, and the establishment of the church in the new world where it faced a missionary challenge among the Indians and slaves prompted the revisers to include a rite for baptism of those able to answer for themselves, basically the public rite with appropriate substitutions for the Gospel (Jn. 3:1–8) and in the exhortation and promises.

In 1662 the text of the catechism was printed before the rite of "confirmation" rather than within it. A preface and question calling upon the candidates to ratify and confirm the vows of their baptism before God and the congregation replaced the examination in the catechism. A collect among those printed after the Eucharist, asking for direction "in the ways of thy laws and in the works of thy commandments," was inserted prior to the blessing. This collect had been used in the little office of Prime in the Sarum breviary.

The 1789 revision allowed parents to serve as sponsors for their children at baptism. It also allowed the omission of either of the first

265

two prayers. The word "sin" replaced "sins" at two places within the rite, implying that baptism remits original sin but does not suffice for remission of actual sins. A question about belief in the faith was substituted for the repetition of the Apostles' Creed, and permission was given to omit the baptismal signation and the form which accompanied it, "although the Church knows no worthy cause of scruple concerning the same." The rubric which stated that baptized children are "undoubtedly saved" was omitted. All of these changes had been frequently proposed, some as far back as the early days of Puritanism. In the rite for "confirmation" the question was revised in 1789 to take into account situations where the candidate had been baptized as an adult or situations in which the parents had served as sponsors.

The last half of the nineteenth century was racked by controversy over baptismal regeneration, with both sides often straining the meanings of Prayer Book texts. An author writing in 1911 could rejoice that, due to the hard work of the last generation of clergy, baptisms were now normally in private soon after the birth of the child. Late in the nineteenth century several authors attempted, often making use of mistaken or strained readings of the fathers and of early liturgies, to establish the laying on of hands or anointing as necessary to the *completion* of baptism.

In the 1892 revision there were only two significant changes in the initiation rites. One was the provision in the "confirmation" rite for a presentation of the candidates which was like the presentation in the ordination rites. The other was the addition, apparently as a scriptural warrant for the rite, of the option to read Acts 8:14–17. The use of this lection in this manner would be defended by few New Testament scholars today.

The 1928 Book omitted Luther's "Flood Prayer," thereby omitting all reference to the Old Testament types of baptism and to the baptism of our Lord. Questions asked of the godparents replaced the old charge at the end of the rite. The 1928 Book restored the requirement to use the sign of the cross and the form which accompanied it, thereby restoring as a requirement a signation and form which are associated with the medieval "confirmation" which had derived (see p. 264 above) from the second post-baptismal anointing of the Roman rite. For persons who come into the Episcopal Church from a communion which has no equivalent form, however, this signation has never been required. The 1928 revision allowed any baptized person to baptize "if a Minister cannot be procured." It dropped the preface to the rite for "confirmation" and added a promise to follow

266

Jesus Christ as Lord and Savior. Within the last century the typical age for "confirmation" had dropped several years so that it came to be associated with entrance into puberty rather than with entrance into adulthood.

The baptismal rite of the present edition maintains the traditional Prayer Book pattern of baptism with water, followed by a signation which represents the "confirmation" of the Roman rite. The revisions in this edition attempt to restore the centrality of initiation to the ritual pattern, the public nature of the rite and congregational involvement in it, the bishop as the normal minister, the relationship to the church year, and admission to the Eucharist as the climax. Though provision is made for the baptism of infants and children, adult baptism is restored as the model which manifests the meaning of the sacrament. The context is that of five baptismal occasions, or, when it is impossible to reserve baptisms to those occasions, the principal Sunday Eucharist. Promises are phrased in terms more easily grasped. The baptismal creed—the Apostles' Creed—is restored to the rite, and the promises also constitute a rite of renewal of baptismal vows for the entire congregation. The new thanksgiving over the water uses the principal biblical types of baptism: creation, the exodus, and the baptism, death, and resurrection of our Lord. Chrismation is permitted, and there are references to the anointing of priests and kings. The seal of the Spirit is explicitly mentioned. The rite includes the peace and, under normal circumstances, first communion.

Concerning the Service (p. 298)

The first paragraph is a clear statement of the principle that baptism constitutes full initiation into the church and that the bond established in baptism is indissoluble. Baptism is not to be repeated. This point had been stressed in the Sarum rite and in earlier Prayer Books with a requirement that the celebrant ask "Hath this child (person) been already baptized or no?"

The second paragraph establishes the principle that this sacrament should be administered as a public rite in the context of the Eucharist. One major concern of this revision is to reestablish the relationship of baptism to the church year. In the additional directions (p. 312) it is recommended that baptisms be reserved, so far as possible, for five traditional occasions which emphasize the meaning of baptism: the Easter Vigil, which signifies baptism as death and resurrection—the Pauline emphasis; the Day of Pentecost, which sig-

267

nifies baptism as the receiving of the Holy Spirit—the Lukan emphasis; the first Sunday after the Epiphany: The Baptism of our Lord, which signifies baptism as new birth, regeneration—the Johannine emphasis; All Saints' Day or the Sunday after All Saints' Day, which signifies baptism as the reception into the communion of saints; and the time of the visitation of the bishop, which signifies baptism as the reception into the holy catholic church. The baptismal significance of these days is so important that, in the absence of a priest, a deacon may be specially authorized to preside omitting only the signation (p. 312). Because of the implications for the congregation baptisms which cannot be reserved for these occasions are "appropriately administered within the Eucharist at the chief service on a Sunday or other feast." This principle was that of the 1549 Prayer Book. The reasons for administration of baptism at the principal Sunday service were there spelled out in terms partly dependent on the Consultation of Hermann, reforming archbishop of Cologne:

> that the congregation there present may testify the receiving of them that be newly baptized into the number of Christ's Church, as also because in the baptism of infants every man present may be put in remembrance of his own profession made to God in his baptism.

Only in case of emergency should a person be baptized privately.

The third and fourth paragraphs establish the relationship of this sacrament to the bishop. When present, the bishop is expected to preach the word and to preside at the baptism and Eucharist. In the absence of a bishop the priest functions as celebrant and may use chrism only if it has been consecrated by the bishop. This regulation is in accord with the tradition that dates from the end of the fourth century when a post-baptismal chrismation came into general use.

The remaining paragraphs concern sponsors. Early in the history of the church sponsors were persons well known to the congregation who could vouch for the sincerity and manner of life of those wishing to be baptized. Later, when infant baptism became the norm, sponsors were persons who accepted responsibility for the material and spiritual welfare of the child and for the raising of the child in the Christian faith. Over the centuries the number of sponsors has varied. In the early period one person was responsible for the catechumenate, one for the candidacy, and one for the baptism. The Sarum rite specified two sponsors for children. The 1549 Book does not specify the number of godparents, though it does speak of them in the plural. A rubric in the 1662 revision designates three godparents, two of the same sex as the child and one of the opposite sex. The 1789 revision, taking account of the conditions of pioneer life as well as acknowledging proposals that dated before 1662, permitted parents to act as sponsors for their children.

The present revision attempts to take into account the increased mobility of the population as well as to underline the seriousness of the responsibilities which a sponsor undertakes. Each candidate is to be sponsored by one or more persons who must be baptized Christians. Sponsors of adults or older children must "signify their endorsement of the candidates and their intention to support them by prayer and example in their Christian life." Sponsors of infants must make promises in their own names as well as taking vows on behalf of their candidates. This edition makes a more positive statement with regard to the suitability of parents serving as godparents: editions from 1789 on allowed this action; this revision states that it is "fitting" that parents be included among the godparents of their children. The content of the instruction which is to be given parents and godparents is outlined.

Holy Baptism (pp. 299–314)

On a day when baptism is administered, special versicles take the place of anything which might otherwise come between the opening acclamation and the salutation and collect of the day. The Gloria in excelsis or some other song of praise may precede the salutation (see p. 312). Ephesians 4:4–6a is the source of the special versicles. Because of the relationship of the rite to the church year, it is only on the occasion of the bishop's visitation, "or on other occasions for sufficient reason," that the collect or one or more of the lections appointed for baptism (pp. 203 or 254 and 928) may be substituted for those of the day. The rite proceeds as usual with the Old Testament lesson, gradual psalm, Epistle, (Alleluia, sequence, or tract,) and Gospel of the day. The sermon may be preached after the Gospel, or may be postponed until after the peace. The Nicene Creed is not said, since the ancient baptismal creed—the Apostles' Creed—is used within the rite. The presentation of the candidates follows immediately after the sermon, or after the Gospel if the sermon has been postponed.

Presentation and Examination of the Candidates (pp. 301–303)

Since the baptism of adults is historically and theologically normative, adults and older children are presented before infants and younger children. The candidates are presented by name. An adult candidate must express desire to receive the sacrament of baptism. When younger children and infants are presented the question is asked "Will you be responsible for seeing that the child you present is brought up in the Christian faith and life?" The concept of this question is much broader than that of the questions it replaces (which had been framed from the charge to the godparents in editions before 1928). The godparents had been asked simply if they would see to it the child learn the Creed, the Lord's Prayer, and the Ten Commandments, "and all other things which a Christian ought to know and believe to his soul's health," and see that the child when sufficiently instructed was brought to confirmation. New to this revision is the question calling for the godparents to make a commitment to prayer and witness. Some of the early German church orders called for such promises from the godparents, and the proposal that such be included in the Prayer Book goes back at least as far as Bucer's *Censura* of 1551.

The Renunciations (p. 302)

The traditional threefold form of the renunciations, replaced by a single renunciation in 1552, is restored. The content of the renunciations—renunciation of Satan and the forces of wickedness, of evil powers which corrupt and destroy, and of sinful desires—is closer to the traditional renunciation of Satan, his works, and his pomps than that of previous Prayer Books. Cranmer, partly following Lutheran precedent, had substituted a renunciation of the devil, the world, and the flesh. Though the renunciation of the world and the flesh had been explained as renunciation of "the vain pomp and glory of the world, with all covetous desires of the same, and the sinful desires of the flesh," it still was open to misinterpretation. The Manichean heresy declares that flesh and material things are in themselves bad; Christian doctrine is that "Everything created by God is good, and nothing is to be rejected if it is received with thanksgiving" (1 Tim. 4:4).

The Act of Adherence (pp. 302–303)

At least as early as the fourth century Eastern catechetical instructions of Cyril of Jerusalem and John Chrysostom of Antioch, the renunciation of Satan was followed by an act of adherence to Christ, when one master was exchanged for another. In some rites the renunciation of Satan was said facing West as a sign of rejection, of detestation, of Satan. The candidate then turned to the East, which signified light and life and the eschaton, for the act of adherence. As the renunciations are in threefold form so is the act of adherence. The three questions summarize what it means to be a Christian: to turn to Jesus and accept Him as Savior; to put one's whole trust in His grace and love; and to follow and obey Him as Lord. Some of the phrasing reflects a question which had entered the rite in 1928 for use at the baptism of adults: "Dost thou accept him [Jesus Christ], and desire to follow him as thy Saviour and Lord?" In that revision a question had also been inserted in the confirmation rite, "Do ye promise to follow Jesus Christ as your Lord and Saviour?"

Presentation of Candidates for Confirmation, Reception, or Reaffirmation of Baptismal Vows (p. 303)

The section "Concerning the Service" (p. 412) specifies the situations in which it is appropriate for persons to be presented to the bishop for reaffirmation of baptismal vows and laying on of hands. Baptism is reestablished as the gateway to communion; the House of Bishops in their Pocono Statement of 1971 stated explicitly that "Confirmation should not be regarded as a procedure of admission to the Holy Communion." Admission to communion became separated from baptism in the West late in the middle ages. Doubts about the propriety of giving Holy Communion to infants arose only after the Radbertus-Ratramus controversy of the eleventh century over the nature of the presence of Christ in the Eucharist. Evidence from the twelfth century indicates that infants in some places were given only the consecrated wine by means of the priest's dipping his finger into the wine and then placing it in their mouths. Later when the laity communicated in one kind only—the bread—infant communion died out in the West, and had generally ceased by the sixteenth century, with rare exceptions.

Since it is baptism rather than confirmation which admits to communion, confirmation can now be reestablished as a time for a mature public affirmation of faith and commitment. It is specified that in two situations a reaffirmation of baptismal vows with laying on of hands by the bishop is "expected." The first is when those baptized as infants or young children "are ready and have been duly prepared, to make a mature public affirmation of their faith and commitment to the responsibilities of their Baptism." This is based upon the Renaissance-Reformation rationale for the rite of "confirmation." The element of conscious decision against Satan and for Christ integral to

271

adult baptism is lacking in the baptism of infants. The church expects this lack to be supplied when the person can make a voluntary "mature" decision not unduly influenced by parental or peer pressure. For the same reasons that baptisms should be public, "administered within the Eucharist as the chief service," so should this affirmation of faith and commitment. This rite continues under the title "confirmation." Persons baptized as adults but not with the laying on of hands by the bishop are also "expected" to be presented to the bishop as symbol of the diocese and the worldwide church for the renewal of vows and laying on of hands. (Roman Catholic rites of "confirmation" contain no public affirmation of faith, and the "confirmation" rites of other bodies are not ordinarily presided over by a bishop.)

In this revision there are provisions for two other situations when it is suitable for persons to renew their vows and receive the laying on of hands. The rationale of the first of these is given in a position statement issued by the Standing Liturgical Commission and the Theological and Prayer Book Committees of the House of Bishops:

> When a person who has been baptized in some other fellowship of Christians wishes to become a member of the Episcopal Church, it is desirable and appropriate that this person be presented to the Bishop as representing the world-wide episcopate, and that the new relationship be blessed with the laying on of hands and a recommissioning to Christian service.

The liturgical precedents for rites receiving those baptized in other communions who wish to affiliate themselves with the Episcopal Church extend back to the late seventeenth or early eighteenth century when the existence of other denominations was first recognized and tolerated in England. Forms were devised to admit "Protestants" or "converted Papists" into the Anglican communion. Eventually the rite of "confirmation" which was intended for those brought up in Anglicanism superseded the other rites designed for this purpose. The earlier rites had been bound into some eighteenth century Prayer Books and other forms had been made public in other ways, but this is the first edition of the Prayer Book to include specific forms for reception.

The other occasion when it is suitable for persons to renew their vows and receive the laying on of hands is also explained in the document cited:

When a person whose practice of the Christian life has become perfunctory, or has completely lapsed, awakes again to the call of Christ and desires to signalize his response publicly, and to receive a strengthening gift of the Spirit for renewal.

A presentation of the candidates appears in the 1892 revision, but in both the 1892 and 1928 Books the presentation was made to the bishop by the "Minister." Though the minister or others who had been active in preparing the group for presentation can function as presenter, it would be appropriate, as for baptism, for there to be individual presenters who would "thereby signify their endorsement of the candidates and their intention to support them by prayer and example in their Christian life." The two questions correspond to the renunciations and the act of adherence of the baptismal rite.

The Question and Bidding Addressed to the Congregation (p. 303)

The role of the congregation in sustaining and supporting the persons who have come to be baptized or to renew their baptismal commitment is recognized in the question and in their pledge to "support *these persons* in *their* life in Christ." The congregation is then bidden to join with the candidates in the baptismal covenant: each rite of baptism is an act of covenant renewal for the congregation. This question and bidding do not appear in earlier Prayer Books. It might be noted that for the bidding the celebrant may use "these or similar words." On occasion, as, for example, the Easter Vigil (p. 292), it is appropriate for the celebrant to rephrase this bidding in terms suited to the day or occasion.

The Baptismal Covenant (pp. 304–305)

From New Testament times, to be baptized was to confess the faith. The creeds had their origins in the forms used during the threefold immersion in water at baptism. Later, possibly under pressure of time or possibly because Matthew 29:19 came to be looked on as a dominical formula for baptizing, a briefer statement was substituted and the threefold affirmation was said before baptism. The 1552 revision reduced the threefold affirmation to a single question. The first American Book (1789), assuming that baptism would be administered within a Sunday service in which the Creed would be said, asked the single question, "Dost thou believe all the Articles of the Christian Faith, as contained in the Apostles' Creed?"

273

The traditional affirmation of faith has been restored in this revision. The translation is by ICET.

In the 1662 revision a question was added after the renunciations and the affirmation of faith, "Wilt thou then obediently keep God's holy will and commandments, and walk in the same all the days of thy life?" This question dates from the liturgy compiled and used by Robert Sanderson, later bishop of Lincoln, during the interregnum when the use of the Book of Common Prayer had been outlawed. The five questions that replace that one question spell out what is needed to "keep God's holy will and commandments." First there is a community life that involves teaching and fellowship, Eucharist and prayers. There must be resistance to evil and a desire, having fallen into sin, to repent and return to the Lord. There must be a life of witness to the Good News by both word and example. There must be a life of service, seeking and serving Christ in all persons. And there must be commitment to work for justice and peace among all people, and respect for the dignity of every person.

Prayers for the Candidates (pp. 305–306)

The celebrant now bids the congregation to pray for the candidates. It is appropriate for the petitions to be led by one of the sponsors (p. 312). In the prayers, which were drafted for this revision, intercession is made for the candidates that they may persevere in fulfilling what they have promised, and that finally they may be brought to the fullness of God's peace and glory. The concluding collect, drafted by the Rev. Dr. Louis Weil, brings out not only the symbolism of death and resurrection in baptism but also the eschatological implications of the rite.

Thanksgiving over the Water (pp. 306–307)

Early church fathers pointed out that all water has been sanctified for the sacrament of baptism by the baptism of our Lord Jesus Christ in the Jordan River. Nevertheless, special prayers were said over the water at least as early as the time of the Apostolic Tradition of Hippolytus (c. A.D. 215). Many of these prayers used biblical typology involving water. The prayer of the Sarum rite dates to the Gelasian sacramentary (nos. 444–448), though it had been elaborated, as in the Gallican rite, with the Sursum corda and an introduction copied from the eucharistic preface, a number of ceremonial actions, and the infusion of oil and chrism. In it are allusions to the waters of creation, the flood, the heavenly city, the womb, the rivers of Paradise, the water

274

from the rock, and the wedding feast at Cana. It also speaks of the baptism of Jesus, the water which flowed from His side, and the command to go baptize all nations. The rites of the continental reformers eliminated any prayer or blessing over the water, but Luther inserted a "Flood Prayer" in his rite, naming the flood and the exodus as types of baptism and speaking of the baptism of Jesus as a sanctification of all water for the washing away of sins. Many of the German church orders adopted this prayer, and Cranmer (rejecting the Sarum form) inserted Luther's "Flood Prayer" as the first prayer of the baptismal rite in the 1549 Book. He also provided a series of prayers for use when the water is changed, which was to be at least once each month. The form consisted of an initial prayer, with a sign of the cross over the font, for the sanctification of water, eight short supplications for those to be baptized therein, and a salutation and summary collect. The closest parallel to these supplications and to certain phrases in the initial and concluding prayers is in the Easter baptismal vigil of the Mozarabic Missale Mixtum. The Missale Gallicanum vetus contains an older version of this material (no. 168).

In the 1552 revision the prayer for the sanctification of the water was dropped, four of the supplications eliminated, and the phrase "prepared for the ministration of thy holy sacrament" deleted from the final prayer. The petition "sanctify this water to the mystical washing away of sin" was, however, added to that prayer in 1662. The 1928 Book prefaced the prayer with the Sursum corda and the first sentence of the eucharistic preface. The 1789 Book had made the two prayers at the beginning of the rite alternatives; the 1928 Book omitted the "Flood Prayer," stripping the rite of all reference to classical biblical archetypes. The primary allusions are restored in the new prayer drafted by the Rev. Dr. Leonel L. Mitchell. The prayer recalls the waters of creation, the exodus, and the baptism of Jesus in the Jordan River, and portrays the font, in the classical manner, as a bath, a womb, and a tomb. Prayer is made that those baptized may be cleansed, reborn, and buried and resurrected in Jesus Christ.

Consecration of the Chrism (p. 307)

Oil is a symbol of baptism in the New Testament (2 Cor. 1:21–22; 1 Jn. 2:20; 1 Jn. 2:27; Lk. 4:18; Acts 4:27). The very title "Christ" means the anointed one. The use of oil in baptisms dates to the second century, possibly earlier. At the same time, as the Apostolic Constitutions points out (c. A.D. 380), "If there is neither oil nor chrism, the water is sufficient both for the anointing, and for the seal, and for the confession." The use of oil signified the anointing of kings and priests in the Old Testament, the "royal priesthood" (1 Pet. 2:5, 9; Rev. 1:6 and 5:10), the "seal" (Gen. 4:15; Ezek. 9:4–6; 2 Cor. 1:21–22; Eph. 1:13 and 4:30; Rev. 7:3, 9:4 and 14:1), the Anointed One. Uses of oil in daily life as a soap before bathing and perfume afterward, as unguent for athletic events, and as medicine, further enriched the symbolic use in connection with baptism. From early times two oils were used—the oil of exorcism which was used with the exorcisms preceding baptism, and the chrism or oil of thanksgiving generally applied after the baptism.

By the end of the fourth century or beginning of the fifth an anointing with chrism after the immersion had become a general custom. At about the same time local councils forbade anyone but a bishop to consecrate the oil of chrism. Chrismation in the late middle ages came to signify "confirmation." Because New Testament evidence on the use of oil was ambiguous and because many abuses had developed in association with its use, most of the German church orders and all of the Reformed churches rejected its use. The 1549 Prayer Book retained a post-baptismal anointing, but it disappeared in the revision of 1552.

This is the first Book to restore the rite of chrismation. The chrism is to be consecrated at the time of the bishop's visitation and in the sight of the people. Its use on baptismal occasions, in addition to the time of the bishop's visitation (in addition to other significations), vividly symbolizes the connection between baptism and the bishop. Chrism is composed of olive oil to which some perfumed oil, generally balsam, is added. The prayer, composed for this Book, alludes to the classical signs—Jesus the Anointed One, the "seal," and the "royal priesthood."

The Baptism (p. 307)

In the early church baptism was normally by immersion (the word "baptize" means "dip"). Baptism by pouring water over the candidate (affusion), however, was practiced at least as early as the second century when there was not sufficient water for immersion or when the physical condition of the candidate made it impossible or inadvisable. In the West, late in the middle ages, affusion came to be accepted as customary in some areas. The 1549 Book called for a triple immersion to be "discreetly and warily done," but did allow, as the Sarum rite did not, "if the child be weak, it shall suffice to pour water upon it." The 1552 Book called for one immersion in the water. In 1662 the rubrics were revised:

(If they certify that the Child may well endure it) he shall dip it in the Water discreetly and warily, . . . But if they certify that the Child is weak, it shall suffice to pour Water upon it.

Architectural evidence shows that immersion continued to be the normal method of baptism for some time after this revision. The first American Book simplified the rubric: "He shall dip it in the water discreetly, or shall pour water upon it." In the present revision the word "immerse" is used rather than the weaker word "dip." In early liturgies it was normal, when a bishop presided at a baptism, for the immersion to be done by assisting presbyters and deacons.

At the time of baptism the candidate is called by name. There is evidence for this custom as early as the Gallican Missale Gothicum (no. 260), and it had become general by the end of the medieval period. Some of the continental Reformation liturgies connected naming with baptism, as did the revision of 1552. There are various precedents. In Judaism naming was part of the rite of circumcision on the eighth day. As early as the third century, there is evidence that converts exchanged names with pagan associations for names with Christian significance at some point in the process of initiation. Since in the late medieval period it had been legislated in some areas that baptisms should be within the first eight days after the birth of the child, the baptism became the occasion on which the name was made known. The catechism printed within "confirmation" in 1549 began with the questions "What is your name?" and "Who gave you this name?" The answer to the second was "My godfathers and godmothers in my baptism." The 1552 revision connected naming with the baptismal action. Since baptisms have ceased to be the time of publication of the name, and since only rarely is a person's name changed at baptism, there seems to be little merit in perpetuating this tradition and much merit in restoring the earlier, more catholic custom of presenting the candidate by name. At a very early stage the names of the candidates accepted for baptism were called out and written in a book sometimes known as the "Book of Life" (see Rev. 21:27).

The baptismal formula is based on Matthew 28:19: "Go therefore and make disciples of all nations, baptizing them in the name of the Father, and of the Son, and of the Holy Spirit." The use of this

277

formula can be traced back to the Missale Gallicanum vetus (no. 174), the Missale Gothicum (no. 260), and the Bobbio missal (no. 248), in each of which it was amplified. The addition in Gothicum reads, "Unto the remission of sins, that thou mayest have eternal life." In some Eastern rites it has taken the form "Thou art baptized in the Name of the Father, and of the Son, and of the Holy Spirit." The word "Name" here means self-revelation. Through the first several centuries of the church's life the threefold immersion of the candidate was accompanied by the threefold affirmation of faith. The creeds developed from these formulae, which were amplified in the course of time to offset the various heresies which threatened the integrity of the church's faith. Possibly because of the pressures of time or possibly because Matthew 28:19 came to be read as a formula for use rather than as a succinct statement of the faith into which candidates were to be baptized, the use of this or similar forms displaced the creedal statements. In earlier editions of the Prayer Book the Amen had been printed in Roman type, indicating that it was to be said by the officiant alone. In this revision it is in italics, to be said by the congregation as indication of their consent and authorization, and as affirmation of their pledge to support the newly baptized in their life in Christ.

The Post-Baptismal Rites (p. 308)

In rites as late as that described in the catechetical instructions of Saint John Chrysostom (c. A.D. 390), those who were immersed came out of the water and, as soon as they were clothed, took their places among the congregation to participate for the first time in the prayers of the people and the exchange of the peace. In other areas, however, various rites developed as explications for baptism. The vesting of the newly baptized person might be accompanied by an explicatory form. The ranking prelate washed the feet of the newly baptized in Gallican rites. Some places had laying on of hands. From the late fourth or early fifth century it was almost universal to have an anointing with chrism blessed by the bishop and an accompanying form or prayer: this rite was generally performed by the officiating presbyter or by the bishop. In and around Rome the anointing was done by the baptizing presbyter and then a token of the anointing, either to complete or to symbolize the initial anointing, was done in the sight of the congregation by the bishop. The late medieval books of the West associated this with a prayer for the sevenfold gifts of the Holy Spirit (Is. 11:2). The form is in the Gelasian sacramentary (no. 615) as a

278

prayer to be said when a person baptized in extremis recovers and is presented to the bishop. A less highly developed form is in the same sacramentary (no. 451) for use with the uniquely Roman second anointing by the bishop. This, in turn, was an amplification of the form associated in that sacramentary (no. 450) with the presbyteral anointing. It is also in many other sacramentaries including the Gallican Bobbio missal (no. 249) and the Missale Gallicanum vetus (no. 175), the Celtic Stowe missal, and a tenth century Ambrosian manual. In these the form is used with the only post-baptismal anointing whether done by a priest or a bishop. The form reads:

> Almighty God, the Father of our Lord Jesus Christ, who has regenerated you by water and the Holy Spirit, and has given you remission of all your sins, himself anoints you with the chrism of salvation in Jesus Christ unto eternal life.

Cranmer made use of this preamble in the prayer associated with the one post-baptismal anointing by the priest of the 1549 Prayer Book. The petition, however, was revised to incorporate a phrase used by medieval theologians not in connection with the first of the two Roman anointings, that by the priest, but with the second anointing of the Roman rite normally performed by the bishop, "Vouchsafe to anoint thee with the unction of his Holy Spirit."

In the 1552 revision the act of anointing was replaced by a sign of the cross on the forehead, the site of the second anointing, rather than the top or crown of the head, the site of presbyteral anointing in the middle ages. The prayer was replaced by a form (see above, pp. 258, 264) which was a summary of the teachings of medieval theologians regarding the meaning of the peculiar second anointing. A revised version of the fuller form of the prayer, which underwent further revision in 1552, was retained in the rite of "confirmation." A prayer, drafted by the Rev. Dr. Charles M. Guilbert, based upon the fuller form of the ancient prayer, is in the current revision associated with the signation and optional anointing. If the bishop is celebrant, the bishop is to say this prayer. If not, it is said by the priest who functions as celebrant. Note that this prayer may be said after the form which is printed after it.

The bishop, or in the absence of a bishop, the priest who is celebrant, places a hand on the head of the newly baptized person. This act is associated in scripture and tradition with blessing, commissioning, identification, and transfer of powers. In Christian tradition it has been associated with the reconciliation of penitents, prayer for the sick, ordinations, and simple blessings as well as with baptismal rites.

279

In some areas the catechumens received laying on of hands by the catechist at the end of instruction. At the Sunday liturgy, in some locales, hands were laid on the catechumens at the time of their dismissal prior to the liturgy of the table. The act of immersing the candidates in the water of baptism was interpreted as a laying on of hands. Sometimes a bishop or presbyter laid hands on the newly baptized after their emergence from the water. Whereas the anointing had been the action or matter of the medieval rite of "confirmation," the laying on of hands was so considered by the continental reformers and was put in the 1549 Prayer Book as the action or matter of the reformed rite of "confirmation."

The celebrant marks on the forehead of the newly baptized the sign of the cross. In Judaism the newly baptized person was branded as God's sheep, slave, and soldier by being marked on the forehead with the Taw (T), the last letter of the alphabet, signifying the name of God. This was comparable to the "mark" of Cain and of Ezekiel. The Apostolic Tradition of Hippolytus, generally dated about A.D. 215, testifies to a "sealing on the forehead" which some writers see as a continuation into Christianity of the marking on the forehead in the Jewish proselyte baptism. The Taw was soon interpreted as the sign of the cross. In the early church the devotional use of the sign of the cross was a reminder of one's baptism. Until late in the middle ages the sign of the cross, as an act of personal devotion, was made on the forehead as at baptism. Some early descriptions say that it is to be preceded by a spitting and blowing upon the hand as a reminder of the water and Holy Spirit. The vestigial anointing of later rites was apparently done as a sign of the cross. In many rites signation was associated with the enrollment of a catechumen. The 1549 Prayer Book retained that form of signation, but in 1552 the one required signation was that associated with the form which had replaced the anointing of the 1549 Book.

This became a source of controversy among the Puritans and the canons of 1604 included an apologia for continued use of the sign. In 1662 a rubric was inserted:

> To take away all scruple concerning the use of the sign of the Cross in Baptism: the true explication thereof, and the just reasons for the retaining of it, may be seen in the XXXth Canon, first published in the year MDCIV.

The 1789 revision permitted the signation and the accompanying form to be omitted "If those, who present the infant, shall desire the sign of the cross to be omitted." In 1928 the permission to omit the signation and accompanying form was eliminated.

The use of the chrism, which is optional, signifies the cleansing of the bath, the anointing of kings and priests, the "seal" of baptism, and incorporation into Christ, which title means "The Anointed One." The word "christen" derived from the chrism: to be "christened" is to be "anointed." Because the chrism can be consecrated only by a bishop, its use in the absence of a bishop signifies the relationship of that office to baptism.

The form associated with the signation or chrismation reinforces the teaching that in baptism, by the operation of the Holy Spirit, we are sealed or marked as Christ's own for ever. The Taw of Jewish baptisms was interpreted as the brand of God's ownership. Early church fathers explained the baptism as the seal, brand, or tattoo which was a mark of ownership of a slave, a sheep, or a soldier. The three images were used in the form which accompanied signation in Prayer Books from 1552 until this revision. (On the seal see Gen. 4:15; Ezek. 9:4–6; 2 Cor. 1:21–22; Eph. 1:13 and 4:30, and Rev. 7:3; 9:4; and 14:1.)

Though some authors find witnesses to the exchange of the peace in such New Testament passages as 1 Cor. 16:20, 2 Cor. 13:12, Eph. 6:23–24, Phil. 4:21, 1 Thess. 5:26, 2 Thess. 3:16, 1 Tim. 6:20, 2 Tim. 4:22, Tit. 3:15, Philem. 25, Heb. 13:24, 1 Pet. 5:12 and 3 Jn. 15, the first clear reference to the action is in baptismal liturgies. Prior to baptism the catechumens had been dismissed before the peace and it is not certain whether the peace was exchanged at the normal Sunday or weekday rite in that period. The newly baptized were welcomed into the fellowship with the exchange of the peace, a tradition recovered in this Book. The peace is preceded by a form of welcome said by celebrant and people, which contains an exhortation to the newly baptized to confess the faith, proclaim the resurrection, and share in His eternal priesthood. On the occasion of a bishop's visit, if there are people to be confirmed or received, or people who wish at this time to renew their baptismal vows, the exchange of the peace is postponed until the point at which they, too, may be included.

At Confirmation, Reception, or Reaffirmation (pp. 309–310)

If there are people to be confirmed, or to be received, or people who wish to renew their baptismal vows, the bishop bids the congregation to prayer. This prayer and the forms which follow are not to be used over an adult who has just been baptized and received signation from the bishop. To make such use of them would be not only need-less duplication but would say in effect that the text of a liturgy is not to bè taken seriously; it would denigrate the rite. The prayer, drafted by the Rev. Bonnell Spencer, O.H.C., begins with a thanksgiving for what God has done for us in the death and resurrection of Jesus Christ and in the sealing of Holy Baptism. The petition is that the covenant made in baptism may be renewed, and that these persons may be recommissioned for service. This prayer might be compared to that proposed by Bishop John Henry Hobart of New York in 1826 as an alternative to the prayer of the confirmation rite in the 1789 Book:

> Almighty and everliving God, who hast vouchsafed, in baptism, to regenerate these thy Servants, by water and the Holy Ghost; thus giving them a title to all the blessings of thy covenant of grace and mercy, in thy Son Jesus Christ, and now dost graciously confirm unto them, ratifying the promises then made, all their holy privileges: grant unto them, we beseech thee, O Lord, the renewing of the Holy Ghost; strengthen them with the power of this divine Comforter; and daily increase in them thy manifold gifts of grace, the spirit of wisdom and understanding, the spirit of counsel and ghostly strength, the spirit of knowledge and true godliness, and fill them, O Lord, with the spirit of thy holy fear, now and for ever. *Amen.*

For Confirmation (p. 309)

The second of the two forms for use with the laying on of hands at "confirmation" dates to the 1552 Prayer Book. The present revision replaces "child" with "servant" which underlines the direction (p. 412) that "confirmation" be a "mature" affirmation of faith and com-mitment. This is an abbreviated form of the prayer associated with laying on of hands in various German church orders, including that of Hermann of Cologne which contributed so many elements to the Prayer Books of 1549 and 1552.

The first form, which was drafted by the Very Rev. Dr. Urban T. Holmes, embodies the content of the second and adds a petition that the person on whom hands are being laid may be empowered for God's service.

For Reception (p. 310)

The form designed for use with the laying on of hands for a person baptized within another tradition who wishes to affiliate with the Episcopal Church incorporates a recognition of membership in the church which is described in the Offices of Instruction of the 1928 Book and in the Catechism of this edition (p. 854) as "the Body of which Jesus Christ is the Head and of which all baptized persons are members." This form is comparable to those provided for the reception of "Protestants" or "Converted Papists" in the late seventeenth or early eighteenth century when the Church of England first recognized and tolerated the existence of other Christian communions. It might be compared also to forms authorized by Pope Paul VI for the reception into the Roman communion of persons who have been baptized in the Name of the Trinity.

For Reaffirmation (p. 310)

The form provided for those who had fallen away from their baptismal commitment to the Christian faith and life and wish to renew their commitment before the bishop and the congregation is based on Philippians 1:6.

The Concluding Prayer (p. 310)

This is an abbreviated version of a prayer from the 1549 Book, which in turn was abbreviated from one found in Hermann's Consultation and other German church orders. The laying on of hands signifies the fatherly hand of God. The 1549 version reads:

> Almighty everliving God, which makest us both to will and to do those things that be good and acceptable unto thy majesty: we make our humble supplications unto thee for these children, upon whom (after the example of thy holy apostles) we have laid our hands, to certify them (by this sign) of thy favor and gracious goodness toward them; let thy fatherly hand (we beseech thee) ever be over them, let thy Holy Spirit ever be with them, and so lead them in the knowledge and obedience of thy word, that in the end they may obtain the life everlasting, through our Lord Jesus Christ, who with thee and the Holy Ghost liveth and reigneth, one God, world without end. Amen.

The Peace (p. 310)

For commentary on the Peace in conjunction with this rite see page 281 above.

At the Eucharist (p. 310)

The normal expectation, as outlined in the section "Concerning the Service" (p. 298), is that baptism will be administered within the context of the Eucharist. The service continues with the prayers of the people or with the offertory. The use of Eucharistic Prayer D in Rite Two provides an opportunity to incorporate intercessions without the need to make use of a full form of the prayers of the people. The bishop, if present, should function as the principal celebrant. This provides an opportunity to model the roles of the various orders, lay persons, bishops, priests, and deacons.

The proper preface of baptism (pp. 348 or 381) may be used in place of the proper preface of the day except on principal feasts (those listed on p. 15).

Alternative Ending (p. 311)

For urgent and unusual circumstances in which it is impossible to complete the rite with the Eucharist, an alternative ending is provided. The newly baptized join in saying the Lord's Prayer. In the early church the occasion of baptism was the first time in which the newly baptized were exposed to this prayer. At a later stage in the development of the rite the Lord's Prayer was taught during the catechumenate, but was not prayed until after the baptism when the newly baptized could join the congregation in addressing "Our Father." The Lord's Prayer was added to the Prayer Book rite in 1552.

This is followed by a prayer which states the effects of baptism: adoption by God, incorporation into the church, and inheritance with the saints. The prayer is based on one first appearing in the 1552 revision:

> We yield thee hearty thanks, most merciful Father, that it hath pleased thee to regenerate this infant with thy Holy Spirit, to receive him for thy own child by adoption, and to incorporate him into thy holy congregation. And humbly we beseech thee to grant that he, being dead unto sin, and living unto righteousness, and being buried with Christ in his death, may crucify the old man, and utterly abolish the whole body of sin; that as he is made partaker of the death of thy Son, so he may be partaker of his resurrection; so that finally, with the residue of thy holy congregation, he may be inheritor of thine everlasting kingdom; through Christ our Lord. Amen.

The prayer underwent changes in the revisions of 1662 and 1928. The concluding super populum prayer, or blessing (based on Eph. 3:14–19), was added to the rite in 1928. It would be appropriate to use

284

this form as the blessing after the Eucharist on some baptismal occasions.

Additional Directions (pp. 312–314)

The Baptismal Days (p. 312)

The first four paragraphs deal with the five occasions for which baptisms should be reserved. The baptismal importance of these days is such that, in the absence of a bishop or priest, a deacon may be authorized to preside under certain limitations spelled out here. Legislation which extends back to the council of Toledo in 398 forbids deacons to chrismate, and these directions state that when a deacon presides the analogous portion of the rite is to be omitted. That portion may be administered by a bishop or priest at a subsequent occasion of public baptism. This is analogous to situations in the middle ages when the rite of chrismation was applied to persons who had been baptized in extremis and had recovered. The rite of private baptism in the 1549 Book called for public administration of certain portions of the rite in such circumstances, but not for the chrismation. The Brandenburg church order which contributed to the 1549 Book at various points was one of the few German orders which retained chrismation. In the Brandenburg directions for the public reception of a person baptized privately it is spelled out that the chrismation is not to be administered lest it be interpreted as necessary to a valid initiation. In 1552 the chrismation was replaced by a signation and a formula which summarized the late medieval teaching about "confirmation." The rites of subsequent Prayer Books for the public reception of a person baptized privately did not supply the signation until the 1928 revision, which lists it among the parts of the service to be used in such circumstances.

The nature of the four great baptismal days may be emphasized on occasions where there are no baptisms by the use of the form for the renewal of baptismal vows, which includes the baptismal creed (p. 292), in place of the Nicene Creed at the Eucharist.

The Liturgy of the Word (p. 312)

The next two paragraphs allow for the use of the Gloria in excelsis (or the song of praise used in its stead) within the entrance rite on baptismal occasions, though it is not required or printed within the rite. They also allow, in limited circumstances, for elements of the proper for baptism to be substituted for the proper of the day.

The next paragraph points out that it is appropriate for sponsors to read the lessons and to lead the petitions on pages 305–306.

Since the use of the baptismal creed is integral to the rite, it is explicitly stated that the Nicene Creed is not to be used at this Eucharist.

The Baptism (pp. 312–313)

The next two paragraphs are particularly pertinent to situations in which the service is not as clearly visible or audible at a font which, because of local circumstances, must be used, as from some other place in the church. In such a situation the first portion of the rite should take place where it is most visible and audible, and the movement to the font precede the thanksgiving over the water. This movement may take place during or before the baptismal litany (pp. 305–306). It may be accompanied by a suitable psalm, hymn, or anthem. (Psalm 42 was used immediately before the litany which preceded the blessing of the font in the Sarum rite.) Even in situations where the font is more fortunately located, the procession to the font is still an available option and may be a desirable one.

The thanksgiving over the water, with its rich biblical imagery, is a high point in the rite, analogous to the Great Thanksgiving at the Eucharist. As the table is prepared and the bread and wine placed upon it just prior to the eucharistic prayer, calling the attention of the congregation to the elements and preparing them to enter into the thanksgiving, so, where practicable, the font should be filled with water in the sight and hearing of the congregation just prior to the thanksgiving over the water. The celebrant and the sponsors should arrange themselves in such a way that the congregation can see the action at the time of the thanksgiving and of the administration of the baptism. An implication which can be drawn from these directions is that when chrism is to be consecrated, the bishop should stand in a place where the congregation will have a clear view, and that a sufficient quantity of the olive oil and the perfumed oil should be poured out before the people so they can see and smell the chrism which on subsequent occasions will symbolize the connection of the bishop with the baptism. On those occasions, prior to the chrismation, the chrism might be poured from its container into a bowl, in the sight of the people, in sufficient quantity to release its perfume and remind them of the occasion of its consecration.

The next paragraph directs that a candle, which may be lighted from the paschal candle, may be given to each of the newly baptized or to a godparent. The giving of a burning candle to the newly baptized can be traced to the eleventh century. The form which accompanied the action in the Sarum rite stressed the eschatological implications of baptism. It was based on Matthew 25:1–13:

> N., receive a lamp burning and without fault; guard your baptism; keep the commandments, so that when the Lord comes to the wedding feast you may meet him together with the saints in the heavenly hall, that you may have eternal life and live for ever and ever. Amen.

It is appropriate outside the period of the Great Fifty Days for the paschal candle to be placed near the font as a reminder of the paschal implications of baptism.

If it is easier for the congregation to see and hear what happens at the front of the church than what is done at the font, or possibly in other situations as well, it is best for the prayer and signation to take place at the front of the church. A suitable psalm, hymn, or anthem may be sung during this procession. There is precedent in some liturgies for the use at this point of Psalm 23 which is filled with relevant imagery: water, the shadow of death, a table prepared, a full cup, an anointing with oil.

As far back as the Apostolic Tradition of Hippolytus in the third century the candidates brought bread and wine to offer at the rite in which they would be baptized and receive their first communion. The direction emphasizes the appropriateness of having the oblations for this first Eucharist presented by the newly baptized or their godparents.

Conditional Baptism (p. 313)

Out of the Donatist controversies of the early fifth century there arose a definition of what constitutes a valid baptism: the use of water and the word. Baptisms in which water and the Trinitarian formula were used, even in the most unusual circumstances (including jest), were not to be repeated, so important was the concept of the seal of baptism. For circumstances in which persons are uncertain whether they were baptized or whether the proper form and matter (water and the Name of the Trinity) were used, a rite of conditional baptism emerged. The provisions of this Book in essence are those of the Sarum use, which have been continued in every edition of the Prayer Book.

Emergency Baptism (pp. 313–314)

Three new elements have been inserted in the provisions for emergency baptism which are essentially those of the 1928 revision: the use of the Lord's Prayer, an optional additional prayer (for which the editorial committee has drafted a model), and a direction to inform the priest of the appropriate parish so that the baptism may be recorded. The 1549 Book included a lengthy provision "Of them that be baptized in private houses in time of necessity." The major change in the rite before 1928 was in 1604 when, as a concession to the Puritans, the rite was rewritten so that "the minister of the parish, or any other lawful minister that can be procured" were the only ones allowed to baptize. This was contrary to tradition, which extended at least as far back as the second century, that in case of imminent death a lay person could baptize. This limitation was removed in the 1928 revision. A person baptized in an emergency, and who recovers, should have that baptism recognized at a public celebration of the sacrament in which that person would take part in everything except the administration of the water.

The Holy Eucharist

The common sacrifice and the common meal, shared by the community at certain intervals, are a part of every culture, even the most primitive. Such sharing reinforces the cohesion of family, clan, group, and community. Those who eat together share ideas, values, actions, beliefs, and loyalties as well as traditions and sacred history. Sacrifices and meals center on three elements: meat, bread, and alcohol. Meat is essential to the sacrifice. We identify with the animals killed and offered in thanks and propitiation. To eat meat is to gain the qualities of that which is the source of the meat: in primitive societies gazelle is eaten to improve speed, elephant to improve memory, the ox to give strength, the lion to acquire courage. Admirable qualities of one's human enemies can be gained by cannibalism. Blood binds together and blood is the element of life and fertility.

Bread is basic to existence; some form of grain food has been a part of human diet in every culture. Further, there is a link between blood and grain since blood sacrifice, whether of actual or of symbolic blood (wine), was considered necessary for the promise of a good harvest. Bread symbolizes human labor as we work "to put bread on the table;" and bread represents the life of the community, for various members of the community contribute their time and labor to grow, harvest, grind, and cook in order to provide bread for the people. It is also a symbol of fellowship—a "companion" is one with whom one shares bread.

Alcohol is associated with vitality, joy, fellowship, celebration, numbing of pain, liberating of inhibitions, overcoming of fatigue, opening of communication, swearing of loyalty, and the libation of the sacrifice.

The significance of these three elements in Judaism is indicated by the association of the three great pilgrimage feasts with them: Passover with the new flock, the slaying and sharing of the paschal lamb; Pentecost at the end of the seven weeks of harvest following the offering of barley; and Tabernacles (Booths) celebrating the new wine. The worship of the temple centered on the offering of animal sacrifices; the worship of the home centered on bread and wine, with the Sabbath meal as climax of the Jewish week. Other sacred meals, such as the annual Passover Meal, followed the pattern of the Sabbath meal, as did the *chaburah* meals shared by groups which had special intentions or vows in common. Following the liturgy of the word at the synagogue, participants came home, performed ritual ablutions, and then shared conversation over wine before coming to the table to eat. Assembling at the table, participants thanked God over the bread: "Blessed be God, King of the universe, who brings forth bread from the earth." The bread was then broken and distributed, providing the means for eating from common dishes. To break bread was to share one loaf, to eat together—unleavened bread at the Passover, leavened bread at other times.

After the meal the diners shared a cup of wine which was first blessed by the *pater familias* who called upon the group to stand: "Lift up your hearts," and asked their permission to give thanks in their name: "Let us give thanks to the Lord our God." God was then blessed as creator, sustainer, and redeemer, in relation to the particular day or occasion, and prayer was offered for the community of Israel, usually in petitions with an eschatological overtone. The wine was blessed by blessing God: to "bless" in Hebrew is the equivalent of to "thank," to name the Name of God, to associate with the revelation of God. The forms of blessing (*berakoth*) varied with the different days of the Jewish year. To participate in this blessing and sharing of the cup was to express one's *credo*, to be bound together with those with whom the cup was shared, to symbolize one's heritage and hopes (*anamnesis* and *prolepsis*), and to reaffirm one's commitment to God and to the community.

Jesus shared many sacred meals with His disciples. John 6 describes the feeding of the multitude, using some of the liturgical terms associated with such meals. Jesus and the disciples gathered immediately prior to His betrayal and arrest. The Synoptic Gospels state that this was the Passover Meal; the Johannine account states that it was not. The procedure on that occasion was evidently that which any good Jew would have followed in presiding over such a meal. The new elements were the words of administration associated with the bread and wine: "This is my Body," and "This is my Blood." Jesus added one more dimension to an old rite.

The resurrection appearances generally occur in the context of sacred meals. The early disciples continued to gather as a family for such occasions; as they broke bread and shared the cup, they remembered Jesus who was present with them. Probably they continued the Jewish ritual, using forms of prayer appropriate to the day or the occasion, but the time of the meal soon shifted from the Sabbath to the first day of the week, the Lord's Day, which symbolized the creation, light, the resurrection, the new covenant, the outpouring of the Spirit, the coming kingdom, the eschaton. The day and the rite reinforced each other. Were the early gatherings for the breaking of bread a continuation of the resurrection meals or commemorations of the Last Supper? At a relatively early stage they certainly came to bear the weight of both interpretations; whether the Last Supper was a Passover Meal or not, it soon developed Passover connotations for the early Christians.

Before the end of the New Testament period, the rituals involving the bread and the cup were separated from the meal because of practical difficulties of accommodating greater numbers in a home, because of abuses sometimes connected with the meal, and because of the need for a brief ritual in times of severe persecution. The rituals before the meal (the taking of bread, blessing God over it, breaking the bread, and sharing it) and the rituals following it (taking the cup, blessing God over it, and sharing the wine) were compressed into a rite which consisted of taking the bread and wine together and blessing God over them, then breaking and distributing the bread and sharing the cup. The meal, separated from these significant actions, in some places developed into an agapé.

The early church organized its life around the Sunday Eucharist. Those who could not attend the weekday liturgies of the word came on Sundays. The liturgy began with the salutation "The Lord be with you," of the celebrant, followed immediately by readings from the Old Testament, psalmody, and readings from the New Testament. A lector (reader) read the lessons from a reading stand; the celebrant followed with a sermon preached from a chair set in a prominent place; and the catechumens were dismissed, apparently in some places with a blessing. A deacon then led the intercessory prayers "of the faithful," and the liturgy concluded with the kiss of peace. On Sundays the rite continued with the *Anaphora*, or liturgy of the faithful, the liturgy of the table. A white cloth was spread on a small table which often was not put in place until this point in the service. The faithful brought their offerings of bread and wine to the table, or deacons moved among them to receive the offerings. A sufficient quantity for all present to share was selected and placed on the table; the remainder was placed at one side for the use of the clergy and for distribution to the poor.

The celebrant and assisting presbyters gathered about the table and laid their hands on the bread and wine. This was an ancient sign of separation, offering, identification, transfer, or consecration. As the clergy and people stood with hands raised, the celebrant said the Great Thanksgiving, the text of which was not fixed. We have several prayers or fragments of prayers which date to the pre-Constantinian period, including prayers of thanksgiving, prayers for communicants, prayers which name the Name of God over the elements, and prayers which entreat the descent of the Spirit. Some resemble Jewish blessings; others seem to have incorporated elements from prayers associated with the mystery religions.

At the close of the eucharistic prayer the bread was broken and the celebrant, the assisting presbyters, and the deacons received the bread and wine. Some of the ministers then stood at the sides of the table and administered to the people, who came forward and moved from one side to the other to receive. In some places, however, the ministers moved among the people to administer to them. After all present had received, the deacons left to take the bread (and the wine) to members of the congregation who had not been present. In some localities the communicants took bread (and wine) home to receive privately during the week, as both a reminder and a foretaste of the Sunday Eucharist.

The establishment of Christianity brought great numbers of new members into the church; as buildings grew larger, the services became more formalized. In place of a simple salutation to call the people together for the readings, entrance rites developed to prepare the congregation for the liturgy of the word. Many of these rites included a procession of clergy and readers with the Gospel book carried in procession. Hymns and psalms were sung at this time to unite the people as one congregation. Lectionaries developed to systematize the readings. The reading or readings from the Old Testament were separated from those in the New Testament by a responsorial psalm (which some of the early church fathers called "a lesson from the psalms"). The reading of the Gospel came to be the deacon's prerogative, and was sometimes preceded by a canticle or psalm and greeted with the singing of Alleluias or other acclamations. After the sermon or homily, the catechumens were dismissed. In some places the prayers of the people took the form of a litany led by the deacon and concluded with a prayer said by the celebrant. At an early stage, in the Eastern and Gallican rites, the gifts of bread and wine, which had been brought to the sacristy before the rite, were transferred to the altar during the exchange of the peace. In the Roman rite the people continued to present their gifts just prior to the eucharistic prayer; the exchange of the peace took place while the bread was broken for the communions of the people. A formal procession and hymnody accompanied the movement of the elements in the later Eastern and Gallican rites, and the transfer attracted ceremonials similar to those which accompanied the procession with the Gospel book preceding the liturgy of the word. Once the transfer of gifts was formalized into what became known as the "Great Entrance," the peace, which had previously accompanied the transfer, was moved to a position after the transfer.

"Sacramentaries" developed, containing the texts of eucharistic prayers. In the Eastern churches the prayers varied with the day or occasion. The Gallican rites, within a fixed framework of Sursum corda, Sanctus and Benedictus qui venit, institution narrative, and people's Amen, inserted three variable portions to be sung by the celebrant. The Roman rite had one fixed eucharistic prayer within which a proper preface was inserted on each occasion at an early stage, but later the number of prefaces used was drastically reduced. In Eastern and Gallican rites the bread was broken and placed in the chalice. The sacrament was then administered by means of a spoon. In the Roman rite, at the breaking of the bread, sometimes a portion of the bread from a Eucharist celebrated by the bishop, or from a prior Eucharist, was put in the chalice to symbolize unity in space or time. The patens and extra chalices needed for administration to the people were then brought to the altar. The broken bread was placed on the patens and the chalices were filled or had wine added to them from the one chalice which stood on the altar throughout the eucharistic prayer. These actions symbolized the sharing of one loaf and one cup. To prepare the people for worthy reception, communion devotions were added to the rites; the Lord's Prayer was part of such devotions, though in the Roman rite it was moved by Gregory the Great to form the conclusion or extended Amen of the eucharistic prayer. Communion devotions in the Eastern rites usually included the Benedictus qui venit and Sancta sanctis, "Holy (set apart) things for holy (set apart) people." In Gallican rites the devotions included a blessing of the people, varying with the day or occasion. In the various rites, popular hymnody and psalmody became a part of the communion of the people.

As both the entrance of the clergy in procession with the Gospel book and the transfer of the elements became increasingly formalized, so did the close of the rite. One or two prayers were said, followed by a formal dismissal. Communicants no longer carried home the consecrated bread (and wine) for reverent consumption later in the week; the elements were reserved in the sacristy for communions of the sick.

In the ninth century eucharistic piety underwent great change. Language was a major factor in the West, since Latin was less and less likely to be a language familiar to most of the people. Another contributing factor was the gradual displacement of local rites by the Byzantine or Constantinopolitan rites in the Eastern localities and by the Roman rite in the West. These developments set the stage for the eucharistic controversies of the ninth and eleventh centuries, which resulted in a fearful (rather than joyful) approach to the Sacrament as well as a rapid decline in frequent communion by the people.

In the East the celebrant began to sing some portions of the rite at the same time that other portions were being sung by the deacon or choir. A screen of icons, an "iconostasis," separated the people from the sanctuary.

In the West the portion of the eucharistic prayer that followed the Sanctus was said inaudibly while the choir completed an elaborate Sanctus. Screens or veils were erected in some churches to separate the people from the altar. More and more the rite came to be something done *for* the people rather than an offering by the whole congregation of God. Masses for special intentions flourished, and liturgical books were rearranged so that the low Mass, a late development, could be said even at times when only a priest and server were present.

The multiplication of Masses required additional altars, ending the patristic principle of one altar about which the people of God gathered each Lord's Day. Thanks to the number of weekday Masses, the close relationship between the Eucharist and Sunday and other major feasts was lost; people's weekday worship became no longer a participation in daily offices, but presence at Mass as observers. The daily offices no longer prepared for nor stemmed from the Sunday Eucharist; they were individual obligations of monastics and clergy. To economize on space, as the altars multiplied they were often placed against the church walls where they functioned not only as tables for the Eucharist but also as ambos or lecterns for the liturgy of the word. Psalms were reduced to one or two verses. Since the people seldom made offerings, the paten and chalice were sometimes prepared by a server before the Mass. Kissing of a "pax board" substituted for the exchange of the peace.

Fear and awe at the mystery associated with the Mass fostered concern about even the tiniest fragments of the Host; in the West wafers frequently replaced real bread so that no crumb might be dropped and overlooked. As a further protective measure, the priest placed the consecrated wafer in the communicant's mouth. A chalice-like ciborium, which had no symbolic relation to bread, substituted for the plate-like paten on which the bread could be seen. Communion was no longer given in both kinds. Both bread and wine were withheld from infants. The concluding ablutions were formalized.

Private prayers of confession and preparation for the priest worked their way into the rite; the communions of the people were administered outside the rite after confession. Ceremonies and appurtenances acquired allegorical meanings, and the rite itself was explained in allegorical terms. One explanation, for example, based on the life of Christ, likened the entrance song to the prophets, the Kyrie to Zechariah, the Gloria in excelsis to the song of the angels, the collect to the visit of Christ to the temple at the age of twelve, the epistle to the preaching of John the Baptist—and so on. Other systems were based upon Old Testament typology, the forty works of Christ's life, the thirty-three years, the thirty-nine lashes. . . .

During the thirteenth century, in the West, some people began to kneel at various points within the Eucharist; the bread was elevated after the words of institution. In the fourteenth and fifteenth centuries the people were directed to kneel when the Sacrament was carried to the sick. Processions of the Sacrament developed and the place of reservation changed from the sacristy to an aumbry, dove, or tower within the church itself. Occasionally it was exposed in a monstrance. In some places on the continent the faithful genuflected to the Sacrament.

Like the bread, the cup came to be elevated at the words of institution. Altars looked increasingly like tombs, equipped with retables and crosses, sometimes with crucifixes (especially in Germany), so that they might provide a more impressive background for the elevations which became the focus of eucharistic piety. Since seeing had become far more important than participating and receiving, the element of dramatic setting and spectacle was emphasized. Pews having come into use, some people initiated lawsuits for seats that provided the best view of the elevations. By the end of the fifteenth century, many of the laity had almost ceased to receive communion, and legislation was necessary to get the people to communicate once a year. An extant sixteenth-century document explains to the laity that some of the prayers in the Mass are in the plural because, in the first days of the church, others besides the priest received communion.

Preaching became less and less a part of the services. Friars attempted to revive it and legislation in some areas required a sermon from one to four times each year. The sermon, when given, was set within the "prone," sometimes after the Gospel but often outside the body of the Mass. The Prone typically included biddings or intercessions, a general confession and absolution, and was likely to contain the Ave Maria (Lk. 2:42, often without the later addition), the Lord's Prayer, and the Creed—the three things that a child was required to know in the late medieval period prior to "confirmation."

Luther did not provide a new eucharistic rite but attempted to purify the medieval Roman rite by eliminating elements which he believed to be later accretions. In his Latin rite of 1523 he omitted all of the private prayers which had come into use late in the medieval period and which varied from place to place. He removed the late medieval sequences and allowed a vernacular hymn in their place. He also dropped the variable offertory verses and collects as well as the variable postcommunion prayers, elements which had been used since the fourth or fifth century. Luther's most radical deletion was that portion of the eucharistic prayer which was said inaudibly by the priest during the late middle ages. He preferred the use of the whole of the psalms which had come to be entered only "by title." He allowed vernacular hymns after the Sanctus and Agnus Dei, both of which were sometimes troped in complicated fashion in the medieval rites. A sermon was to be part of every Eucharist, and there was to be a weekly communion during which the communicants would come to the chancel for the liturgy of the table. Two years later Luther instituted a somewhat more radically revised form in German for those who did not understand Latin.

Various German church orders instituted "in course" reading to replace the old Epistles and Gospels, restored the prayers of the people, and, in some cases, preceded the entrance song with a general confession, "comfortable words," and an absolution. The decalogue was sometimes added to the rite and a "peace of God" blessing included at the end of the Eucharist.

Zwingli's reformed rite for Zurich (1523) was quite conservative. The lections and sermon were in the vernacular, the commemoration of saints' days was eliminated, the lectionary simplified, and a substitute provided for that portion of the eucharistic prayer which had been said silently in the late medieval period. This substitute consisted of four paragraphs: a thanksgiving, a sort of epiclesis upon the communicants, an anamnesis, and a prayer for worthy reception. Zwingli retained ceremonies, vestments, music, and even the Ave Maria. He, like Luther, proposed weekly communions of the faithful. His revision did not satisfy the iconoclastic radicals, however, and in 1525 he proposed a rite without music, in which he attempted to omit everything he deemed non-scriptural. His model seems to have been the late medieval Prone: it consisted of intercessions, the Lord's Prayer, the Ave Maria, readings and a sermon, notices of deaths and a prayer of thanksgiving for the departed, a general confession and an absolution. At Easter, Pentecost, the Zurich patronal festival in the Fall, and Christmas, this was followed by a preparatory prayer, a fixed Epistle (1 Cor. 11:20–29), the Gloria in excelsis, a fixed Gospel (Jn. 6:47–63), the Apostles' Creed, an exhortation, the Lord's Prayer, a prayer that the communicant might give thanks faithfully and might live as becomes a member of His Body, the institution narrative, administration to the people in their seats (from wooden trays and cups), Psalm 113:1–9, a postcommunion prayer, and a dismissal.

Calvin found in Geneva a rite similar to that of Zurich. During his exile in Strassburg, however, he instituted with his congregation a rite which more closely resembled that of the German congregation. One unique feature of his rite was a metrical version of the decalogue in which each verse ended with the Kyrie. When he was recalled to Geneva, Calvin instituted a simplified version of the Strassburg rite. Following the Reformed tradition, his rite directed that the people take communion as they sat or stood at tables.

The reformed Roman liturgy of the sixteenth century standardized the private prayers of the priest, reduced the number of proper prefaces and sequences, and eliminated tropes altogether. Later, the Sacrament was reserved in a tabernacle on the altar, the practice of genuflection to the Sacrament became customary, and the extraliturgical Benediction of the Blessed Sacrament and the Forty Hours devotion became popular. Churches were built or remodeled to resemble theaters so that the elevations and the exposition of the Sacrament would be dramatized; reredoses and lengthy altars placed against the wall heightened the effect.

In England the first major reform of the Eucharist was the issuing of the Order of the Communion in 1548. This Order encouraged the receiving of communion within the Eucharist, and replaced the various orders for communion after confession which had come into use in the late middle ages. The English Order, inserted in the Latin Mass immediately after the priest's communion, consisted of a lengthy exhortation followed by an invitation to those who intended to communicate to come into the chancel. One of the people, or one of the ministers on behalf of the people, was to say a general confession, followed by the priest's absolution and "comfortable words," and a prayer for worthy reception. The Sacrament was then administered in both kinds. A blessing concluded the Order. The Consultation of Hermann, the reforming archbishop of Cologne, strongly influenced this Order.

"The Supper of the Lord and the Holy Communion, commonly called the Mass" of the 1549 Prayer Book, preceded by Morning Prayer and the Litany, began with the use of a whole psalm or a section of Psalm 119, replacing the remnants of the old entrance psalms. While the psalm was being sung, the priest said the Lord's Prayer and a collect retained from the elaborate priest's preparation in the Sarum rite. A ninefold Kyrie followed the psalm, then the Gloria in excelsis. The Sarum rite forbade the Gloria during Advent, Pre-Lent, and Lent, but there was no such prohibition in the 1549 Book. Next came the salutation, the collect of the day, and the prayer for the king, a new addition to the rite replacing the memorial collects which had followed the collect of the day in the medieval rites. After the "minister" read the Epistle, the Gospel was to be read by the "priest, or one appointed to read the gospel," "immediately after the epistle ended." The intervening remnants of the gradual psalm, the Alleluia, or tract, and the sequence had been eliminated. The service basically retained the Epistles and Gospels of the Sarum rite, which varied slightly from those of Roman use, although some were lengthened. The Creed followed, then a sermon or homily, and an exhortation to worthy communion. In 1547 some homilies had been published for use at the Eucharist; if no sermon was preached, one of these was to be read. If a sermon was preached, "or for other great cause," the celebrant could omit the Litany, the Gloria in excelsis, the Creed, and the exhortation to communion. Twenty sentences of scripture were provided, to be sung while the people placed their offerings in "the poor men's box." Those who had indicated their desire beforehand to receive communion were to remain in the chancel after making their offerings, men on one side, women on the other. The priest was to put on the altar sufficient bread and a chalice

The Eucharist

SARUM (typical late medieval rite)	1549 PRAYER BOOK	HERMANN'S CONSULTATION
Priest's preparation	Communicants hand in names	*Saturday evening preparation*
	Morning Prayer & Litany	Psalm(s)
		Antiphon or Scriptural hymn
Priest's private preparation	*Priest's private preparation* (during the	Magnificat & collect
Veni Creator	Introit)	Psalm
Collect for Purity	Lord's Prayer	Account of Institution or John 6
Vesting		Sermon
Kyrie, Lord's Prayer	Collect for Purity	Prayer for the faithful
& Ave Maria (short		Private confession & absolution
form)		*Sunday and Holy Day Rite*
Confiteor & Pax	Introit	General Confession
The Rite	*Sunday and Holy Day Rite*	Comfortable Words
Introit: Psalm verses	Introit: Psalm	Absolution
Kyrie	Kyrie	Introit
Gloria in excelsis	Gloria in excelsis	Kyrie
Collect of the day &	Collect of the Day	Gloria in excelsis
"Memorial" Collects	Prayer for the King	Collect of the Day
Epistle	Epistle	
Gradual, Sequence,		Epistle
Alleluia		Alleluia, Gradual, or
Gospel	Gospel	Sequence
Creed (on major days)	Creed	Gospel
	Sermon	
		Sermon
		Prayer "for all states of men"
		Creed & alms-giving
	Exhortation	Exhortation
Offering of elements	Offering of alms,	
with prayers	bread & wine	
Sursum corda, Preface,	Sursum corda, Preface,	Sursum corda, Preface,
Sanctus, Benedictus qui	Sanctus, Benedictus qui	Sanctus, Benedictus qui
Prayers of offering and	Prayer "for the whole state	
petition	of Christ's Church"	
An epiclesis-type petition	An epiclesis	
Institution Narrative	Institution Narrative	Institution Narrative
Anamnesis, oblation,	Anamnesis, self-oblation	
and intercessions	& prayer for church	
Protocol & Lord's Prayer	Protocol & Lord's Prayer	Lord's Prayer
Embolism		
Fraction		
Pax/Pontifical blessing	Pax	Pax
	"Christ our Paschal Lamb . . ."	
	Invitation	
	General Confession	
Agnus Dei	Absolution	
Commixture	Comfortable Words	
Priest's devotions	Prayer of Humble Access	
Priest's Communion	Communions: Agnus Dei	Communions: Agnus Dei
Postcommon sentence	Postcommunion sentence	& hymns
Postcommon collect(s)	Postcommunion prayer	Postcommunion prayer
	Blessing	Blessing
Dismissal		Ablutions
Priest's devotions		
(People are communicated outside Mass after private confession & absolution)		

or cup of wine mixed with water. All of the private devotions of the priest and the offertory prayer of the medieval rite were omitted.

The eucharistic prayer began with the salutation and Sursum corda. It was followed by the Lord's Prayer and a text associated with the peace, or in the late middle ages with the kissing of the pax board. There are, however, no directions with regard to any ceremonial action to accompany this text.

A rubric at the end of the service directs that the bread (wafer) is to be "something more larger and thicker than it was, so that it may be aptly divided in divers pieces," but when the fraction is to take place is not specified. Presumably it would have been at the time of the fraction in the historic rites. None of the private prayers of the priest at the time of the fraction and of the peace was retained. The late medieval text which followed, "Behold the Lamb of God, behold who takes away the sins of the world," which was associated with a showing of the consecrated bread to the people, was replaced by a new text: "Christ our paschal Lamb is offered up for us once for all, when he bare our sins on his body upon the cross, for he is the very lamb of God that taketh away the sins of the world; wherefore let us keep a joyful and holy feast with the Lord." Next was the invitation, the general confession (preceded by the only direction to kneel within the rite), the absolution in a revised form, the "comfortable words," and the prayer for worthy reception from the Order of 1548. After this prayer, which later came to be known as the "prayer of humble access," came the communion of the priest and other ministers and the administration to the people. The words of administration, retained from the 1548 Order, were typical of the Lutheran rites. During the administration, the Agnus Dei, historically associated with the breaking of the bread, was sung. Twenty-two scriptural verses were provided in place of the variable verses of the medieval rite (these were remnants of the psalm sung during the time of administration in an earlier period). One from among these twenty-two was to be sung after the communion of the people. One fixed postcommunion prayer replaced the variable prayers of earlier rites and the service ended with a fixed blessing, following the Lutheran custom.

The rubrics presume that Morning Prayer shall be read daily; that it shall be followed on Wednesdays and Fridays by the Litany and the eucharistic rite through the offering, ending with one or two collects and the blessing; and that the Eucharist shall be celebrated in every church every Sunday and holy day for which a proper is provided. The Eucharist may not be celebrated, however, if there is no one disposed to communicate with the priest. A rotation is to be planned among the people of the parish in order to provide bread and wine; each Sunday those who offer as well as others who wish to communicate are to receive communion with the priest. Every confirmed person is "to communicate once in the year at least." The Book explains that to protect against persons' carrying away the consecrated bread for superstitious use, as had been done on occasion in the late middle ages, the priest is to continue to place the bread in people's mouths rather than following the ancient practice of placing it in their hands.

The 1549 rite was not well received. Some conservatives complained that it was like a "Christmas game;" conservative priests celebrated it without regard for its rubrics or rationale, "counterfeiting Masses." On the other hand, the revision was too conservative for many. In some places communion was administered to people seated in their pews. In 1550, "for the sake of godly quietness," altars were ordered to be replaced with "honest tables." For a time Archbishop Cranmer was almost the only person to defend the rite against detractors of one persuasion or another.

The 1552 Book made no provision for the entrance psalms which had covered the priest's preparation in the 1549 Book. The Lord's Prayer and the Collect for Purity were to be said aloud as the opening ritual of "The Order for the Administration of the Lord's Supper, or Holy Communion." There followed, in place of the ninefold Kyrie, recital of the Ten Commandments with the response "Lord, have mercy upon us, and incline our hearts to keep this law." This use of the decalogue had precedents in various medieval troped Kyries and in the reformed rites of Bucer, Calvin, and Pullain. The collect for the day and the prayer for the king, without salutation, were followed by the Epistle and Gospel, both now read by the "priest." The Nicene Creed and a sermon or homily came next in order, with no provision to omit the Creed under any circumstances. After the sermon was the declaration of holy days or fasting days for the following week. The scriptural sentences for the offertory were said by the priest, rather than being sung by "clerks." Wardens gathered the offerings of the people for the "poor men's box." Nothing is said about placing wine and bread on the altar; this the priest or the clerk presumably did prior to the rite. The prayer for the whole state of Christ's Church, a revised version of the intercessions included within the 1549 eucharistic prayer, followed the offertory, and then came the exhortations. At least one of these exhortations was always to be said, the one reminding the congregation of the seriousness of communion; on occasion the exhortation urging the people to worthy preparation was to

301

be repeated; and, as it was needed, the exhortation reminding those who were reluctant to receive communion of their special need for it.

At the invitation to "draw near," those who before or immediately after Morning Prayer had signified their intention to receive communion were to come into the chancel. They were directed to kneel while one of them or one of the ministers said the general confession "in the name of all." They remained kneeling for absolution, but presumably stood, if we can judge by directions in later devotional manuals, for the "comfortable words." This section, which had been a communion devotion in the 1548 Order and 1549 Book, was now placed before the eucharistic prayer. The prayer itself was drastically revised. The salutation no longer preceded the Sursum corda; the preface and Sanctus of 1549 were retained, but Benedictus qui venit was reduced to one line, "Glory be to thee, O Lord, most high." This was followed by "the prayer of humble access," a communion devotion in 1548 and 1549, and by a revised version of what had been the first paragraph of the post-Sanctus in the 1549 Book. The phrase of the 1549 Book, "one oblation once offered," became "one oblation of himself once offered." A petition for worthy reception replaced the 1549 epiclesis. Communion was administered, immediately after the institution narrative, to people kneeling to receive, and the bread was placed in their hands. Different sentences of administration, capable of a Zwinglian interpretation, replaced the Lutheran sentences of 1549. The peace, the "Christ our paschal Lamb," the Agnus Dei and the scriptural postcommunion sentences were all eliminated. The administration was to be followed immediately by the Lord's Prayer and one of two postcommunion prayers. The first of these was an abbreviated version of the final paragraph of the eucharistic prayer in the 1549 Book. The second was a slightly revised version of the post-communion prayer in that Book. As a result of this rearrangement the act of receiving communion occurred in the midst of the revised 1549 eucharistic prayer at precisely the place occupied by the elevations in the medieval rite—a deliberate attempt to substitute a eucharistic piety based on receiving the Sacrament for one based upon adoration of the consecrated elements. Gloria in excelsis followed the post-communion prayer, which some think to be an attempt to imitate the psalm of praise sung after the communion of the people in the rites of the Reformed churches. The people were than dismissed with a blessing.

Use of the "Ante-Communion" was no longer required on Wednesdays and Fridays, but was mandatory on holy days as well as on Sundays when there was not "a good number to communicate with the priest." In contrast to the larger and thicker wafers (capable of being broken into several pieces) required by the 1549 Book, "it shall suffice that the bread be such as is usual to be eaten at the table with other meats, but the best and purest wheat bread that conveniently may be gotten." Instead of the people providing the bread and wine, these elements were provided "at the charges of the parish." The priest is to have what remains "to his own use." The Book required at least three communions each year, rather than the one of 1549, and one of these had to be at Easter. Added at the last minute, and printed in black rather than in red like the other rubrics, was a rubric asserting that the new direction in this Book for the people to kneel to receive the Sacrament signified thanksgiving and helped to avoid profanation and disorder but was in no wise intended to imply adoration of the "sacramental bread or wine" or "any real and essential presence there being of Christ's natural flesh and blood"—the somewhat controversial "black rubric." Though kneeling to receive had spread through some parts of the West in the late medieval period, standing was still the normal posture in many places. The issue had been forced by clergy in England who had begun to administer to people seated in their pews, by the popular writings of Bishop John Hooper who had returned from exile in Zurich in 1549, and by a sermon of John Knox before the Council in September 1552.

The two important changes in the eucharistic rite in the 1559 revision were the deletion of the "black rubric" and the amplification of the sentences at administration of communion, prefacing those of the 1552 Book with those of the 1549 Book. No changes were made in 1604.

In 1563 the Apostolic Constitutions was printed, providing the earliest liturgical texts then available. Some Anglicans accorded this, and the Eastern liturgies, great authority. Others developed increased respect for certain features of the 1549 Book which had been changed or eliminated in the 1552 revision. When the rite was revised for the Scottish Book of 1637, the Gloria tibi was restored from 1549 at the announcement of the Gospel, and a response was added at the end. The offerings of the people were to be received in a basin by the deacon, if one was present, or by the churchwardens. Several oblationary sentences were substituted for some of the sentences of the earlier rites. Money offerings were placed on the holy table by the presbyter, after which he was to "offer up and place" the bread and wine upon the table. A revised version of both the petition for the communicants and the commemoration of saints from the 1549 prayer for the church was restored at the conclusion of the prayer,

303

but it included no petition for the departed. The "prayer of consecration," as it was now designated in the rubric, followed immediately after the Sanctus. The opening portion of the prayer, with a few additions, was that of the 1604 Book, but an epiclesis which combined the 1549 epiclesis with the petition for worthy reception from 1552 was inserted prior to the 1552 institution narrative. The manual acts of the 1549 Book were restored, and the prayer proceeded, immediately after the institution narrative, to a revised form of the continuation of the prayer from 1549. The Lord's Prayer, as in the 1549 Book, followed immediately, said by all present; the Matthean doxology, in common use in Scotland, was added at the conclusion. Then followed the "collect of humble access to the Holy Communion." The sentences for the ministration of communion from 1549 were spoken and the people responded Amen. Should additional elements be needed, a rubric provided that the institution narrative be said over them. Another rubric required that the "presbyter," the word consistently used for "priest" in this Book, cover the remaining elements until the end of the service, after which he, with assistance of some of the communicants, was reverently to consume all that remained. A postcommunion prayer, the Gloria in excelsis, and the blessing concluded the service.

Despite many proposals from Laudians on the one hand and Puritans on the other, the revision of 1662 was quite conservative. The place for announcements was shifted, making an awkward break after the Creed and before the sermon. The money offerings, and the bread and wine were to be placed on the holy table at the time of the offering. A thanksgiving for the departed and a petition that we might "follow their good examples," added to the prayer for the church, had not been a part of the 1549 or 1637 Books but was from the bidding prayer of 1604. Because people had ceased to remain in church to watch the celebration of communion in the chancel, the phrase "before this congregation" was deleted from the bidding to confession. The word "absolution" was inserted in the rubic prior to the form. An Amen was added to the Sanctus. The 1552 prayer, with two slight verbal additions from the Scottish Book, was printed under a rubric which included the title "Prayer of Consecration." Manual acts in the institution narrative included a direction to break the bread at the words "he brake it," and the institution narrative concluded with Amen. Additional elements could be consecrated by saying, over either the bread or the wine, the relevant words of the institution narrative. There were directions as in the Scottish Book for covering the elements remaining and consuming them later. The

1552 black rubric was restored in a revised form which denied, not "any real and essential presence," but "any Corporal Presence of Christ's natural Flesh and Blood."

From the end of the seventeenth century there were many revisions or proposals for revision of the Eucharist. Edward Stephens, William Whiston, John Henley, and others published and put into use with small groups liturgies based on the Apostolic Constitutions and other older models. In 1718 some of the English Non-jurors published and began to use a liturgy influenced by Eastern rites. Beginning in 1722 Scottish Non-juring Episcopalians republished the rite of 1637 in "Wee Bookies" which went through several revisions. Also, early in the eighteenth century, various Latitudinarian revisions or proposals began to appear in print. In 1784, John Wesley published a revision for use by American Methodists.

The revision of the American Proposed Book of 1786 was essentially conservative. The initial Lord's Prayer was dropped, as was the Nicene Creed, but it was expected that the Apostles' Creed would have been said in Morning Prayer immediately preceding the Eucharist. Some phrases were removed from the exhortations, and the Gloria in excelsis was abbreviated. The prayer for the church, which duplicated the Litany, was no longer required in Ante-Communion. The black rubric was deleted. Charles Wheatly, whose commentary was the most widely used throughout the eighteenth and nineteenth centuries, had said that this rubric denied a doctrine so ridiculous that it was "needless to offer any confutation of it."

Except for the restoration, for permissive use, of the initial Lord's Prayer and the full text of the Gloria in excelsis, the changes of the Proposed Book were incorporated in the 1789 revision. In the eighteenth century the Summary of the Law had frequently been used in Non-juror and Latitudinarian groups in place of the decalogue, or (among Scottish Non-juring Episcopalians) in addition to it, and its use was permitted after the decalogue. Scottish Non-juring clergy and possibly others as well had substituted another prayer, "the decalogue collect," for the prayer for the king. It was printed in place of that prayer in the 1789 revision. The Gloria tibi was restored; it had not been in English Books since 1552, but had been in the Scottish liturgies and in some Latitudinarian proposals. A rubric provided that either the Apostles' or the Nicene creed was to be read if a creed had not been said in Morning Prayer immediately before, a provision made for occasions when the rite would be used for the communion of the sick, since any Eucharist would otherwise be preceded by Morning Prayer. The 1789 revision gave permission to omit the proper preface for Trinity Sunday and provided an alternative form which set forth the doctrine in less metaphysical terms. The people were instructed to say the Sanctus with the priest, beginning with the words "Therefore with angels and archangels," legalizing an already common practice. In place of the 1662 eucharistic prayer was a form which combined elements from the 1764 Scottish prayer and elements from earlier Scottish revisions. A hymn was to be sung after the prayer and a hymn might be used in place of the Gloria in excelsis. Additional elements could be consecrated by repeating a substantial portion of the eucharistic prayer, as in the proposed liturgy of 1689, the liturgies of Whiston and Wesley, and the 1764 Scottish revision. This contrasted with the mere repetition of pertinent words from the institution narrative which the 1662 Book permitted. The rubric requiring the people to communicate three times a year was dropped, since by this time the custom of more frequent communions had become firmly established.

The revision of 1892 required the decalogue only once on each Sunday. The Kyrie followed the Summary of the Law, for use "if the Decalogue hath been omitted." The Nicene Creed was to be said on five major feasts. Some additional offertory sentences were added, largely from the Scottish tradition, and the exhortation was required only once each month. The communion hymn was no longer obligatory. Because noncommunicating rites had been instituted in some places, it was made explicit that "sufficient opportunity shall be given to those present to communicate."

The 1928 revision required the decalogue once a month and the exhortation three times a year. It provided several enrichments: permission to use a hymn or anthem after the Epistle and the Laus tibi after the Gospel; three additional proper prefaces—one for Epiphany; one for Purification, Annunciation, and Transfiguration; and one for All Saints. The principal changes, which stirred tremendous controversy since they were seen by some to encourage Romish errors of purgatory and eucharistic adoration, were the inclusion of a petition for the departed and some changes in the order which brought it more into accord with the Scottish Book of 1637: the Lord's Prayer followed the eucharistic prayer and the prayer of humble access came after that, as a communion devotion.

Following the restoration, in 1789, of a more adequate eucharistic prayer, the significant changes have been in eucharistic ceremonial and piety rather than in the text. Certain practices were imported or revived after the mid-nineteenth century, and justifications for change tended to be allegorical, aesthetic, or antiquarian. The changes often promoted an individualistic, pietistic approach to worship, to make seeing and hearing more difficult for the congregation, and to curtail actual congregational participation. Variants included the shift in the position of the celebrant at the Eucharist so that his back was to the people; the substitution of round wafers for broken bread, often administered from a cup-like ciborium rather than the more significatory paten; the substitution of sips of "sacramental" wine for substantial drinks of the more symbolic red wine (often homemade). In many places the ceremonial appropriate to the Western Roman type of eucharistic prayer was imposed on a prayer which followed an Eastern outline. The rubrics of the 1892 Book allowed Morning Prayer to be said on Sundays without requiring the Ante-Communion to follow; the former requirement had the merit of reminding the people that Sunday Eucharist was the climax of the liturgical week. Rubrics also allowed a celebration of the Eucharist on Sunday without a preceding service of Morning Prayer, which left the Eucharist with a very sparse liturgy of the word. The service patterns which developed, sometimes with a multiplication of small weekday communions as extensions of or preparations for a principal Sunday service of Morning Prayer or a noncommunicating "high Mass," did much to break down the last vestiges of understanding of the liturgical week and of the integral relationship between Sunday and the Eucharist.

The influence of the liturgical movement, the advance in historico-critical study of the liturgy, and the renewed emphasis upon biblical theology, patristics, and ecumenism stirred the awareness of many people. The Eucharist of the 1928 Book was subjected to much criticism because of its lack of psalmody, its paucity of lectionary material (particularly the Old Testament), its inflexibility, the lack of opportunity for congregational participation, the invariable length, the separation of the essential actions, and the failure to provide for a real breaking of the bread. The eucharistic prayer failed to offer thanks for the creation and incarnation, which is needed to place the sacramental action in the proper theological context. The absence of an epiclesis upon the people and the lack of any eschatological reference were other serious defects. In comparison to Morning Prayer, many persons felt the supposedly festal eucharistic service to be excessively penitential. A revision was needed to recapture the family aspect of the feast, its basic eucharistic nature, its kerygmatic function, and its eschatological implications. The sharing and worshiping community needed a rite that would remind them of the creation, death, and resurrection, and provide a foretaste of the heavenly banquet.

The 1979 Prayer Book provides many more options in the entrance rite and a full liturgy of the word with Old Testament lection, psalm, New Testament lection, Gospel, and sermon. Flexibility and congregational participation are provided in the prayers of the people. The historic exchange of the peace is restored. The preparation of the table is in the logical place in the action, immediately before the eucharistic prayer. Additional eucharistic prayers restore important elements missing from the prayers of the earlier Books. Elements which are now known to be late additions and of secondary importance to the rite are made optional, at least on occasion. A breaking of bread for the communion of the people is restored, together with an optional fraction anthem. The historic Sancta sanctis bids the people to approach for communion. The sentences of administration are brief enough to be said in full to each communicant. The rite may be concluded almost immediately after its climactic point, the Holy Communion. Various options, including the dismissal, are provided. In addition to the full texts in Rite One and Rite Two there is also An Order for Celebrating the Holy Eucharist which lists those elements essential for a Eucharist but allows the rite to adapt to particular occasions and settings. Altogether, this revision provides more flexibility and a greater richness than any previous Anglican Prayer Book ever offered for the eucharistic celebration.

The Holy Eucharist:
The Liturgy for the Proclamation of the Word of God
and Celebration of the Holy Communion (pp. 315–409)

The early church used various terms to refer to the principal service of Sundays, the days of the Easter season, and other holy days. Many of the terms focused on one aspect or other of the rite: Eucharist, Lord's Supper, the Offering, Communion, the Sacrament, the Holy Mysteries. In the Eastern churches the comprehensive term "liturgy" was used. "Mass," in early sacramentaries the word used for the proper of the day, became a common title for the rite in the West. "Lord's Supper" came eventually to be limited in use to Maundy Thursday after that day became one on which the sacrament was celebrated; it was retained in medieval missals for the rite of that day. The 1549 Prayer Book titles the rite "The Supper of the Lord and the Holy Communion, commonly called the Mass." In 1552 this was changed to "The Order for the Administration of the Lord's Supper, or Holy Communion." A rubric in the rite for the institution of ministers, accepted by the General Convention of 1804, made use of the patristic title "Eucharist," a use which has spread increasingly not only in Episcopal churches but in other communions. The Constitution on the Sacred Liturgy of Vatican II and other contemporary Roman Catholic documents and writings now use this title. The catechism of this Prayer Book (p. 859) gives six names for the rite: Holy Eucharist, Lord's Supper, Holy Communion, Divine Liturgy, Mass, and Great Offering. The subtitle describes the content and emphasis of the rite—it is a liturgy of both Word and Sacrament.

The Exhortation (p. 316)

The Order of the Communion of 1548 contained an exhortation to worthy preparation for receiving the Sacrament. It was to be read on the Sunday or holy day prior to the ministration of communion. The order for ministration itself began with an exhortation to approach worthily, and a warning to unrepentant sinners and anyone not in charity with the world not to come to the holy table lest "the Devil enter into him as he did into Judas, to fulfill in him all iniquity, and to bring him to destruction, both of body and soul." The two exhortations and the warning seem to depend on the chapter "Of the Lord's Supper" and the two alternative exhortations (one from the Cassel church order and the other from that of Brandenburg-Nürnberg) in the Consultation of Hermann. Both exhortations remained in the 1549 Book, which amplified the exhortation to preparation and incorporated the warning into the text of the exhortation for worthy reception of the Sacrament. The latter was to be read after the sermon on Sundays, if in the sermon people were not exhorted "to the worthy receiving of the holy sacrament." The other was printed for use "if upon the Sunday or holy day the people be negligent to come to the communion."

In 1552, revised forms of these exhortations were printed between the prayer for the church and the bidding to draw near for confession and communion. The exhortation to worthy reception was to be read at every celebration; the exhortation to preparation was also to be read prior to communion at times left to the discretion of the curate. A strong exhortation, the work of Peter Martyr, a continental reformer who had come to Oxford as Regius Professor of Divinity, was provided after the prayer for the church to be read if the people be "negligent to come to the Holy Communion." The 1662 and 1789 revisions made some changes in these exhortations; the 1892 revision allowed the exhortation which had previously been required at every celebration to be omitted except on one Sunday of each month. The 1928 revision reduced this requirement to the first Sunday in Advent, the first Sunday in Lent, and Trinity Sunday.

The three exhortations of prior Books are conflated in the present revision, on the basis of a draft by Capt. Howard E. Galley, and there is no longer any requirement that the exhortation be used on any specific occasion. It may be read, in whole or in part, during the liturgy or at other times. Two phrases, "the sacrifice of his death" and "the banquet of that most heavenly food," are from the exhortation of Peter Martyr. Much of the remainder comes from the other two exhortations. The initial line is from the collect for Maundy Thursday; the conclusion of the first paragraph, which speaks of other benefits of the sacrament, is new to this Book. The second paragraph, echoing the eucharistic prayers of this revision, restores and emphasizes the conception of the Eucharist as encompassing not only the death and passion of Christ but thanksgiving to God for His creation, His continual providence, the incarnation, His making us His children and exalting us to everlasting life. The phrase "not recognizing the Lord's Body" (1 Cor. 11:29), in the next paragraph, restores a phrase omitted in the 1789 revision. The next to the last paragraph has been revised to conform more closely to the Prayer Books which preceded the first American Book. The final paragraph, new to this revision, contains allusions to the oblation or self-oblation of prayers I, II, A, B, and C (pp. 333, 340, 361, 367, and 369).

The Decalogue (pp. 317–318 and 350)

The decalogue, Exodus 20:1–17, is printed in traditional language (pp. 317–318) and in contemporary language (p. 350) for use in the penitential order of either Rite or in the Rite One Eucharist.

In the 1552 Book the decalogue replaced the ninefold Kyrie of the 1549 Prayer Book. The revisers may have wished to include in every Sunday rite the three things which were to be known by every child before confirmation—the Lord's Prayer, the Creed, and the Ten Commandments. From Elizabethan times it was required that the three texts be displayed prominently before the people in every church, a custom which has fallen into disuse only in recent decades. The medieval troped Kyries were the precedent for the use of the decalogue in the Eucharist; Luther provided a metrical version with Kyrie eleison as a response which was translated into English by

310

Miles Coverdale and published in 1539. Various continental Reformed rites contained the decalogue. In Calvin's Strassburg rite was a metrical version to be sung with every verse ending with the Kyrie. This in turn was incorporated in the Liturgia Sacra of Valérand Pullain prepared for Protestant refugees who settled in England.

The 1892 revision allowed omission of the decalogue, "provided it be said once on each Sunday," and the 1928 revision altered the requirement to "at least one Sunday in each month." In that revision, also, some of the parts of longer commandments appeared in smaller type and permission was given to omit such parts at any time. The abbreviated version is included in this Book for use in Rite One, or with the Penitential Order for Rite One, at the discretion of the celebrant. A contemporary translation, based upon that of the English Series Three (1973), is provided for optional use with the Penitential Order of Rite Two. The present revision puts the decalogue into its proper theological context: the first commandment is preceded, as in the Bible and in the Catechism (since 1552), by the inclusion of Exodus 20:1, which reminds us that the God who makes these demands of us is the God who has delivered us from bondage.

A Penitential Order (pp. 319–321 and 351–353)

A penitential order is provided for optional use in Lent or at other times when it is desired to emphasize the penitential element in the Eucharist or when a special service of preparation for the Eucharist seems appropriate. Precedents for the use of a penitential order at this point include the mutual confession of priest and server in the late medieval rites, the custom of continental Protestant liturgies, and of the Prayer Book daily offices after 1552.

A hymn, psalm, or anthem may be sung before the opening acclamation. As in the eucharistic rite, three opening acclamations are provided.

If this order is used as a separate service, the exhortation (p. 316) or a sermon may follow the acclamation. When the order is used as an entrance rite for the Eucharist, the celebrant moves from the opening acclamation to the decalogue or scriptural sentences, or to the bidding to confession.

The celebrant may then read the decalogue (pp. 317–318 or 350) while the people kneel and make the appropriate responses.

One of three sentences of scripture may be read. The first is the Summary of the Law, added to the Prayer Book of 1789 for permissive use after the decalogue. The 1892 Book also allowed its use as an

311

alternative to the decalogue except at one service on each Sunday; the 1928 Book permitted it as an alternative except on one Sunday of each month. In the present Book the Summary is retained in Rite One (p. 324) for optional use. In Rite Two, at the discretion of the celebrant, any of these three sentences may be said prior to the bidding to confession (p. 359).

The bidding, general confession, and absolution are the same as those in the eucharistic rites. In addition the Rite One form contains the general confession from Rite One Morning Prayer. The restriction placed on the deacon or lay person with regard to the use of the absolution is the same as that rubricated for Morning and Evening Prayer.

When the order is used as an entrance rite for the Eucharist, the service continues with the song of praise, or the Kyrie, or the Trisagion. If used as a separate service, it concludes with suitable prayers, and the Grace or a blessing.

Concerning the Celebration (pp. 322 and 354)

The Various Liturgical Ministries

The initial directions designate particular liturgical functions for each of the four orders: lay persons, bishops, priests, and deacons.

The bishop has a clear prerogative to be the principal celebrant and to preach. The role of the bishop as chief liturgical officer, as preacher and defender of the faith and as symbol of the catholicity of the church is symbolized by the exercise of these functions within the liturgy at visitations and on diocesan occasions. The roles of the bishop are hardly expressed symbolically if the liturgical role on such occasions is limited to pronouncing the absolution and blessing, neither of which are elements basic to the structure of the rite. For the first several centuries of the church's life, a presbyter exercised the functions of principal celebrant and preacher only by delegation of the bishop. The representative nature of the priesthood can best be conveyed if it is expressed liturgically—when the bishop is in a congregation or at a diocesan function—by the bishop's exercise of the prerogatives of the order.

The second paragraph is designed to encourage celebrations in which the functions of various orders, the nature of the church, and the symbol of the Eucharist as a sacrament of unity are expressed liturgically within the rite. The priests, the bishop's local representatives, assist as concelebrants. The deacons act out their roles as servants of the church and heralds of the gospel. Lay persons exercise

312

special gifts and present the eucharistic elements in the name of the congregation and as representatives of the people.

Concelebration

The third paragraph encourages a revival of the practice of concelebration. Many of the earliest liturgical documents describe this practice: assisting presbyters were likely to place their hands upon the gifts when they moved to the table (prepared by the deacon), to hold up their hands with the chief celebrant, and to share in the breaking of the bread and in the ministration of communion. Visiting bishops or presbyters were invited to concelebrate with the local bishop and presbyters as a sign of the unity of the church. The practice of saying the eucharistic prayer in unison with the chief celebrant, however, cannot be documented before the seventh century.

The practice of concelebration has continued in the East, but died out in the West, except for certain remnants, after the rise of a eucharistic piety which placed more value upon the multiplication of Masses than upon the Eucharist as a symbol of unity and an icon of the church and its ministry. In Anglican churches there was a recovery of the practice, until recent decades, expressed ritually in that the participating clergy vested alike, stood about the altar, alternated in reading parts of the rite, possibly helped with the breaking of the bread, and shared in the distribution of communion. The eucharistic prayer itself was often shared: a priest at one end of the altar read from the Sursum corda through the Sanctus; a priest at the other end read the "Prayer of Consecration." The principle of concelebration was undermined in Anglicanism in recent years, however; when two or more priests were present one was likely to read all the texts and perform all the functions pertinent to the priesthood while the others read texts and performed functions historically associated not with the priesthood but with the diaconate (reading the Gospel and taking part in the preparation of the table). This paragraph in the 1979 Book lists traditional ways in which concelebration has been enacted ceremonially. The concelebrating priests, probably vested in the same manner as the chief celebrant, stand at the altar with the celebrant. They join in the consecrating of the gifts through assuming the same posture, extending hands over or toward the bread and the cup along with the celebrant. Though the rubrics do not require or suggest that they read anything aloud, they might possibly read portions of the eucharistic prayer such as the Post-Sanctus or the supplications, or might read along with the celebrant throughout the prayer or from the beginning of the institution narrative through the epiclesis.

313

At the fraction the principal celebrant breaks the loaf into enough portions so that there is one for each of the concelebrating priests, who then share in the breaking of the bread and the distribution of communion.

The Deacon

The fourth paragraph lists the traditional duties of the deacon. Since the fourth century, in most rites, the deacon has read the Gospel. Traditionally, at least from the fourth century, the deacon has bidden the prayers of the people. These prayers are not restricted to the deacon in the present Book, since active lay participation is encouraged, but it is certainly fitting that the deacon lead the prayers of the people. On Good Friday a deacon says the biddings of the solemn collects. At least as early as the second century the deacon prepared the table, placed bread and wine upon it, and administered the Sacrament or assisted in administration. A deacon also bids the people to confession (pp. 330 and 360) and says the dismissal (pp. 339–340 and 366). Some of the duties of the deacon, which had been partially usurped by priests in the late middle ages, are recovered in the present Book. In the absence of a deacon it is appropriate that these duties be performed by an assisting priest rather than by the principal celebrant, if another priest is present.

Lay Ministers

The fourth paragraph makes clear that lay persons should normally read the lessons preceding the Gospel. Representatives of the congregation (pp. 333 and 361) bring the people's offerings of bread and wine, of money and other gifts, to the deacon or celebrant. The recovery of the gradual psalm, traditionally sung by the cantor with the congregation responding, provides an opportunity for a person with musical gifts to make a special contribution to the rite. More opportunities are provided than in any previous Book for special contributions by a choir or instrumentalists. The congregation has more opportunity to participate vocally, and the standing posture which is encouraged by the rubrics symbolizes active participation. The rites thus restore the dignity of liturgical roles to the laity who should be recognized as integral to the liturgy rather than as passive spectators.

Morning or Evening Prayer as the Liturgy of the Word

The directions on page 142 explain the procedure when Morning or Evening Prayer is used as the liturgy of the word at a Eucharist.

The Holy Eucharist:
Rites One and Two (pp. 323-343 and 355-376)

The Entrance Rite (pp. 323-325 and 355-357)

Until the fourth or fifth century the Eucharist began with the first of the readings, probably preceded by the salutation of the celebrant. With the vast increase in numbers and the larger buildings which resulted from Constantine's legalization of Christianity, there was need for a more ritually formal opening to the rite which would settle the congregation and prepare them to be attentive to the readings. The clergy, rather than visiting with the people in the congregation prior to the rite, began to enter in formal procession bearing the book of the Gospels which symbolized the liturgy of the word, and often preceded by candles and incense, like civil officials on state occasions. No later than the early fifth century this processional entrance began to include psalmody; the selection was generally appropriate to the day or occasion, or as an approach to worship. Litanies and popular hymns or canticles were interspersed between the entrance psalm and the salutation before readings. Kyrie eleison was a customary response within such litanies, and they were concluded with a prayer led by the celebrant. Ordinarily, the hymns and canticles were brought into the rite from the daily office, and were often followed by a prayer which had some relation to the particular text which had been sung. Many of the Eastern liturgies also included a blessing of God within the entrance rite. The later missals in the West contain psalms, prayers, and a mutual confession and absolution exchanged between priest and server during or prior to the entrance psalm. In the Lutheran rites this became a general confession and absolution for the whole congregation.

There has been a general tendency for entrance rites to become increasingly cumbersome, to take on a significance of their own rather than to prepare the people to hear the Word. Almost every major liturgical reform has sought to excise various accretions in the entrance rite so that it may better serve its function.

In the 1549 Book the entrance rite consisted of a psalm—during which the priest said private devotions—the Kyrie, the Gloria in excelsis (except when a sermon was to be preached), the salutation, the collect of the day, and a prayer for the king. The 1552 revision eliminated the psalm and required that the private prayers be said aloud. The decalogue replaced the Kyrie and was followed immediately by

315

the prayers. Various revisions thereafter allowed options within the rite: permission to sing a psalm or hymn prior to the rite; permission to omit the initial Lord's Prayer; the addition of the Summary of the Law and, later, permission to substitute it for the decalogue on occasion; the addition of the Kyrie when the decalogue was not said; substitution of another prayer in place of the prayer for the king; the restoration of the salutation, and (on occasion) the directions to use other collects after the collect of the day.

The 1979 Book provides special entrance rites for certain days and occasions: Ash Wednesday, Palm Sunday, Good Friday, Holy Saturday, the Easter vigil, the Pentecost vigil, baptism, confirmation, marriage, burial of the dead, ordinations, the celebration of a new ministry, and the consecration of a church. For other occasions there are often five available options or choices: from Christmas Day through the feast of the Epiphany, on Sundays from Easter Day through the Day of Pentecost, on all the days of Easter Week, and on Ascension Day (p. 406), the use includes the Gloria in excelsis or some other song of praise. This is also permitted at other times except in Advent or Lent. The normal use for Advent and Lent, which is permitted on many other occasions, includes the Kyrie or the Trisagion. The Penitential Order (pp. 319–321 and 351–353) provides an appropriate entrance in Lent and on certain other occasions. In addition, the Great Litany may be used as an entrance rite (see p. 406); it is especially appropriate in Lent and on rogation days. The Order of Worship for the Evening (pp. 108–114) may also be used as an entrance rite (see p. 112).

The Hymn, Psalm, or Anthem (pp. 323 and 355)

The custom of accompanying the entrance procession of the clergy with a psalm was introduced in Rome by Pope Celestine (422–432). The choir sang the text and the congregation responded with an antiphon, generally a verse of scripture, repeated after each psalm verse or group of verses. Ordinarily, this introit psalm was one of approach to worship or one particularly suited to the day or occasion. If it was long, as much was used as might be needed for the entrance, and the celebrant signaled the choir when to stop. In the West, beginning in the fifth century, the Gloria Patri was added to give climax to the psalm, or portion of psalm, and to call everyone to attention for the salutation and first reading. Late in the middle ages, in the low Mass, the introit was typically reduced to the antiphon, the initial verse of the psalm, the Gloria Patri, and a repetition of the antiphon. On Epiphany, for example, the introit consisted of the antiphon "Behold the Lord, the ruler, comes; and dominion, power, and empire are in his hand," the first verse of Psalm 72, the Gloria Patri, and a repetition of the antiphon. Obviously, Psalm 72 had been used at this point principally for verses ten through fifteen, but now it was simply entered by title. This was satisfactory, perhaps, for the clergy bound to the weekly saying of the psalms, and for whom the first verse was suggestive of the whole, but not for a congregation much less familiar with them.

Luther preferred the use of a whole psalm rather than just the initial verse; the 1549 Book substituted short psalms or sections of Psalm 119. Certain ones seem to have been chosen for their appropriateness to a particular day: Psalm 98 for Christmas, Psalm 96 for Epiphany, Psalm 6 on Ash Wednesday, for example. The first half of the church year was filled in with shorter psalms used in course, and the first twenty-one Sundays after Trinity with sections of Psalm 119. During the singing of the psalm the priest said the Lord's Prayer and the collect for purity, and repeated the text of the entrance psalm.

The 1552 Book did not retain these psalms; under Elizabeth permission was given to precede the rite with a metrical psalm or hymn. In later Anglican history it is at this point that elaborate settings of the Sanctus were often sung. The Prayer Book of 1789 included, in its preface to the metrical psalter and the hymnal, the permission to sing a psalm or hymn. By the time the 1892 Book came into use, psalms and hymns were in a separate volume. A rubric which permitted the use of a hymn at this point was printed just before the lectionary. The present Book omits that general rubric; the word "hymn" in the rubric now printed in the rite refers to one of the hymns authorized by General Convention (see p. 14). "Psalm" presumably denotes the traditional method of responsorial psalmody in which the congregation participates through use of the antiphon. "Anthem" indicates music sung by the choir. Late in the nineteenth century a practice without precedent was accepted in many Anglican churches—the choir entered with the clergy in procession during the entrance song. It should be noted that on certain days or occasions which have their own proper entrance rites, or when the Order of Worship for the Evening is used as the entrance rite, a hymn, psalm, or anthem is not to be used at the entrance of the clergy. If the Great Litany is sung as the entrance rite, it should not be preceded by a hymn, psalm, or anthem.

The Opening Acclamation (pp. 323 and 355)

In the manner of the Eastern liturgies and of recent Western revisions, including the Roman rite, the service begins after the entrance of the ministers with an acclamation or greeting. Three are provided, of which only one is to be used on any given occasion. The use of an acclamation is required in Rite Two and optional in Rite One.

The first acclamation is for normal use. Its wording is reminiscent of the beginning of Jewish prayers and of the opening greeting in Eastern rites, "Blessed be God." As Christians baptized in the Name of the Trinity, we bless God as Father, Son, and Holy Spirit. The people's response, "And blessed be his kingdom, now and for ever. Amen." picks up the Eastern opening greeting, "Blessed is the kingdom of the Father, and of the Son, and of the Holy Spirit, now, and ever, and unto ages of ages. Amen." This acclamation is replaced during the Great Fifty Days from Easter through Pentecost with the traditional Christian Easter greeting (Lk. 24:34), in keeping with the greater emphasis the 1979 Book has placed upon the distinctiveness of the Easter season. This greeting may also be used at the daily offices throughout the Great Fifty Days. In Lent and on other penitential occasions an acclamation based on Psalm 103:1–3 and Psalm 136:1–26 replaces the normal acclamation. This form sets penitence in its proper perspective: the God we worship is the God who forgives, whose mercy endures for ever. Because of God's self-revelation as a forgiving God, we can approach Him when burdened with our sins.

The Collect for Purity (pp. 323 and 355)

This collect, reminiscent of Psalm 51, is in the eleventh century Leofric missal and the Sarum missal as the collect of the day in a Mass invoking the graces of the Holy Spirit. It is also found in the Sarum missal as a collect to be said by the priest after the Veni Creator Spiritus as a part of his private preparation as he vests for Mass. This and the Lord's Prayer were the only portions of the private preparation retained in the 1549 Book, to be said by the priest during the singing of the entrance psalm. The 1552 revision made them part of the public rite. In 1789 permission was given to omit the Lord's Prayer. The use of the collect for purity continues to be required in Rite One, but it may be omitted in Rite Two. Its omission is appropriate in festal seasons when it interrupts the movement upward from the entrance song to the opening acclamation to the song of praise.

The Ten Commandments (p. 324)

(For commentary see the discussion on pp. 310–311)

The Summary of the Law (p. 324)

The American revision of 1789 was the first Prayer Book to include the Summary of the Law (Mt. 22:37–40) as part of the Eucharist. It had appeared in the Non-juror liturgy of 1718, where it was substituted for the decalogue. Apparently this custom was not limited to Non-juring circles; a proposal of 1734, the Book of Common Prayer Revis'd, Corrected, and Enlarged, states that the Ten Commandments "are now never used as part of the Communion Service." Bishop John Dowden's reconstruction of the Scottish use for Ante-Communion includes the Summary as an alternative. Various proposals in the last half of the eighteenth century, as well as the 1789 Book, included it for optional use after the decalogue. The 1892 revision allowed omission of the decalogue except at one service each Sunday, and the 1928 Book required its use on only one Sunday of each month. These editions required the use of the Summary whenever the decalogue was omitted. The present Book leaves the use of the Summary of the Law in Rite One to the discretion of the celebrant. The Summary is also included among the optional sentences of scripture in the Penitential Order of both rites (pp. 319 and 351). The version in Rite Two restores the text of the Jewish *shema* (Deut. 6:4–5). The Summary may also be said in Rite Two prior to the general confession (p. 359).

The Kyrie (pp. 324 and 356)

In secular usage the text of the Kyrie eleison was an acclamation used at the approach of an emperor. Though the text can be said to have a penitential meaning, it is comparable to the Aramaic Hosanna, "Save us now," or the British "God save the queen." The use of the Kyrie as a response to the petitions of a litany can be traced to the fourth century in the East. Such litanies spread to the West in the fifth century, keeping the responses in Greek, as was true of other Eastern rites in various languages. Pope Gelasius I (492–496) inaugurated the use of such a litany at the opening of the Mass. Under Gregory the Great (590–604) such use was limited to certain days, but nine repetitions of the litany response, Kyrie eleison, were retained in the Mass. Litanies of this type, or the Kyrie eleison alone, were increasingly

319

used in the West; in many instances, when the ninefold Kyrie was used, three of the responses were changed to Christe eleison. The use of a threefold Kyrie in the daily office before the Lord's Prayer is attested to as early as the sixth century.

Late in the middle ages, with the elaboration of plainchant, the Kyrie of the Mass was often troped; that is, it was paraphrased or the text was filled out in a way that provided a syllable for every note of music. The continental reformers and the reformed Roman rite suppressed the tropes in the mid-sixteenth century. The 1549 Book retained the ninefold Kyrie without tropes; the 1552 revision substituted the decalogue with responses similar to the wording of the Kyrie. In 1892 the Kyrie was restored to the Prayer Book in the threefold version, to be said as a response to the Summary of the Law "if the Decalogue hath been omitted."

The present Book prints both the traditional Greek text and an English version of the Kyrie in the two eucharistic rites. It may be sung in threefold, sixfold, or ninefold form (p. 406). It, or the Trisagion, must be used on days when the Gloria in excelsis, or some other song of praise, is not said or sung; it may also be used in place of the song of praise on any day except for Christmas Day through the Feast of the Epiphany, the days of Easter Week, Ascension Day, and the Sundays from Easter through the Day of Pentecost. The translation in Rite Two is by ICET. This briefer form conveys more of the spirit of the original than does Cranmer's translation, though that is retained in Rite One.

The Trisagion (pp. 324 and 356)

The Trisagion is an ancient hymn of the Eastern churches which is sung after the Little Entrance, the entrance of the clergy with the Scriptures (originally the entrance for the opening of the rite). It soon came to be used in the same manner in the Gallican liturgies of the West, and made its way into the Roman rite with the Gallican reproaches for Good Friday which used this hymn as a response. The Sarum rite also used it within the antiphon for the Nunc dimittis at Compline from the third Sunday in Lent until the fifth. This anthem was popular in Germany; Luther made a metrical translation which was suggested for use at a burial in Hermann's Consultation. Probably this use suggested to Cranmer the inclusion of a paraphrase in the burial office. That version has been retained in every edition (see pp. 484 and 492). In Rite Two the traditional shape of the anthem is restored (p. 492). The present Book also appoints the burial anthem containing the Trisagion for use on Holy Saturday (p. 283). This is the first Book to include the Trisagion as an alternative for the Kyrie at the place in the rite with which it is associated in the Eastern and Gallican liturgies. It may be sung or said once or three times, and it may be sung antiphonally (p. 406).

Song of Praise (pp. 324–325 and 356)

In the liturgies of Saint Basil and Saint John Chrysostom the entrance is separated from the Trisagion by variable hymns. From the time of the earliest Gallican books, a hymn or canticle of praise, typically the Benedictus Dominus Deus, followed the entrance. Apparently this occurred after the Trisagion in some places, in others the canticle and the Trisagion were probably used alternatively on various days. In Western rites the hymn sung at this point in the Eucharist seems to have been one in daily or frequent use in the daily office, therefore well known to the people. As a result, the congregation had an opportunity to participate at the beginning of the rite in a familiar and popular song of praise. The Gloria in excelsis, used in the morning office since the fourth century, was one of the options and apparently one of the most popular daily office canticles.

The Roman rite, in contrast to the Gallican, included such a song of praise only on certain festive days at Masses celebrated by the Pope, a custom introduced by Pope Symmachus (498–514). The Gloria in excelsis was the song used on such occasions. As late as the eleventh century people were questioning why a priest could not use this song, at least on Christmas. In the eleventh or twelfth century the Gloria in excelsis became customary on Sundays and certain other feast days, except those in Advent, Pre-Lent, and Lent. This canticle replaced other options in the Ambrosian, Mozarabic, and Celtic rites; in the Ambrosian rite it preceded the Kyrie rather than following it (as in the Roman rite). The earlier settings were designed for the congregation, being put in a form for syllabic recitation. Late in the middle ages, as musical settings became increasingly elaborate, the text was also elaborated or troped. The Reformed church liturgies omitted the tropes. The Roman church banned them when the rite was reformed under Pius V (1566–1572). The 1549 Book printed the Gloria in excelsis after the ninefold Kyrie, with no restrictions on its use. The revisers in 1552 moved it to a position between the postcommunion prayer and the blessing, a position similar to that occupied by a psalm in the rites of the Reformed churches. It was required at every Eucharist.

The first American revision gave the option to substitute a "proper hymn," presumably one appropriate to the day or to this point within the Eucharist. At the same time, the Gloria in excelsis was restored to the daily offices as an option in place of the Gloria Patri after the psalms. The 1892 revision dropped it from Morning Prayer but retained it in Evening Prayer. The 1979 Book restores it as an option for either office.

Following the lead of other recent Anglican revisions, the present Book restores the Gloria in excelsis to a place in the entrance rite. It is not to be used during Advent or Lent. This hymn, or some other song of praise, is mandated for use daily from Christmas Day through the Feast of the Epiphany, on all Sundays from Easter Day through the Day of Pentecost, on all the days of Easter Week, and on Ascension Day (p. 406). The traditional Gallican use and the options listed for use at the Easter Vigil (p. 294) indicate the intention of the rubric to be that the alternative song of praise be a canticle from the daily office. For a saint's day, as an example, the Te Deum is more appropriate than the Gloria in excelsis, unless a daily office including the Te Deum has immediately preceded. The Pascha nostrum or Dignus es would certainly be suitable during the Easter season; the Benedictus Dominus Deus, the Surge, illuminare, or the Magna et mirabilia for Epiphany; the Magnificat for Marian feasts.

The Kyrie or Trisagion (see commentary, pp. 319–321)

The Salutation (pp. 325 and 357)

The salutation which precedes the collect of the day is a remnant of the salutation or bid to attention at the beginning of the liturgy, just before the first reading, in the years before the development of the entrance rite. As the entrance rite evolved, various elements were inserted between the initial salutation and the first reading. Older liturgies used the greeting "Peace be with you" or "The Lord be with you" and a response, "And also with you." The latter bidding and response is based on the greeting of Boaz and the response of his reapers (Ruth 2:4). Eventually, in the Roman rite, this greeting was inserted to call the people back to attention for the Gospel, for the offertory chant, for the eucharistic prayer, for the postcommunion prayers, and for the dismissal. The 1549 Book retained three uses: before the collect of the day, before the Sursum corda of the eucharistic prayer, and before the postcommunion prayer. All uses of this dialogue were deleted in the 1552 revision, and were not restored to the Prayer Book preceding the collect of the day until 1928. The present Book restores the use prior to the eucharistic prayer. These two uses of the ancient greeting initiate the two major portions of the Eucharist—the liturgy of the word and the liturgy of the table.

The Collect (pp. 325 and 357)

For the origin and structure of the collect see the essay which precedes the commentary on individual collects (pp. 163–165).

As early as the fifth century, perhaps before, a prayer came to be included within the entrance rite in some places. That of the Egyptian sacramentary of Serapion is a prayer related to the lessons which follow. It prays for grace that the people be helped by the reading and interpretation of the Scriptures. Corresponding prayers within the Eastern and Gallican rites were related to the hymnody of the entrance rite. The liturgies of Saint Basil and Saint John Chrysostom, for example, contain a "prayer of the Trisagion." In the Gallican Bobbio missal there are prayers for use after the Trisagion, after the Gloria in excelsis, and after the Benedictus. These prayers use ideas or phrases from the canticle which has just preceded; those for principal days link the canticle with the occasion. The collect of the Roman rite, though it occupied a similar place, came into use after the time of Celestine (422–432), and in if not before Leo's time (440–461), prior to any insertion of a canticle in the rite. In the fifth and sixth centuries a diaconal litany, of which the Kyrie is a remnant, introduced the Roman Eucharist. Some believe the collect to have originated in the celebrant's prayer at the close of that litany. Others suggest that the insertion of a collect between the initial greeting and the first reading antedates the use of the litany and is related neither to the song of praise nor to the litany, but forms a conclusion to the entrance of the clergy.

On special occasions the collect of the Roman rite was related to the lections or to the theme of the day. On other occasions, however, it was of a more general nature or consisted of a petition related to special needs of the time. The fact that the collect was inserted in the rite at the time of the barbarian invasions and the decline of the Roman empire surely explains why so many of the collects from earlier sacramentaries are petitions for peace and protection. Attempts to link many of the collects with the lections for the day are a waste of time and artificial. The earlier sacramentaries simply provided a number of formularies for use on ordinary Sundays. A comparison of the printed Sarum missals with the first printed Roman missal reveals that, for the period after Pentecost, though the series of collects and of lections was basically the same, the collects were frequently not related to the same lections and not said on the same Sunday. Essentially the collect of the day is the conclusion to the entrance rite. On special days and throughout certain seasons it expresses the emphasis of the day or season and sometimes does echo the lections to be read. On other occasions it expresses the more general concerns or special needs of the time. In the late medieval period other collects were said frequently as commemorations or "memorials" after the collect of the day. Cranmer returned to the early practice of using only one collect of the day, with the single exception of Good Friday. From the time of the 1662 revision the collects of certain special days were to be said after the collect of the day throughout the season or the octave. In this revision the older principle of having only one collect is restored. Only at a burial or ordination may a second collect be said.

The Lessons (pp. 325–326 and 357–358)

The early Christians met from the first for services which consisted principally of the reading and exposition of the Scriptures. For this they had the precedent of the services in the Jewish synagogue. Readings in the synagogue were either chosen at the reader's discretion or were a part of "in course" readings (*lectio continua*) or were from a fixed lectionary. The early Christians soon added readings from Christian writings to those from the Old Testament; the books of the New Testament were in fact largely selected from Christian writings which had come into general use in the church's worship. Gradually lectionaries developed which provided systematic patterns for the readings. Many scholars believe that some of the older lectionaries in the Eastern churches had their beginnings in a synagogue lectionary.

As the church year took shape lessons which were particularly appropriate for principal days and feasts became fixed. The remainder of the year was filled by readings in course. Surviving fragments of older lectionaries show that many readings were appointed, often of substantial length. As the entrance rite developed and the congregation became increasingly unfamiliar with the language used in the liturgies, the lections were drastically cut both in number and length. The Gallican rites fixed three lessons: the first, normally, came from the Old Testament, with readings from Acts substituted during the fifty days of the Easter season; the second was usually from the Epis-

324

tles, replaced by readings from Revelation during the Easter season; the third was from one of the four Gospels. Some of these lections were as much as two or three chapters in length.

The Roman rite eventually settled on a two-lesson lectionary: the first lesson was normally from one of the Epistles, but occasionally (and daily on Lenten weekdays) from the Old Testament; the second was always taken from one of the Gospels. The Catholic Epistles were read during the Easter season, the Pauline Epistles throughout the remainder of the year. In the pre-Vatican II Roman lectionary we see remnants of a system by which, over the course of approximately twenty of the Sundays after Pentecost, the Epistles of Paul were read in the order in which they appear in the New Testament. The drastic cutbacks that were made in the medieval period severely limited such readings. For example, of the sixteen chapters of Romans that, at an earlier time, would have been read on three Sundays, or at least within a three-week period, there remained three lections averaging six verses in length. The Roman lectionary was the basis of the Sarum missal, although by the time of the Reformation there were some divergencies between the then current Roman lectionary and that of the Sarum use. In some cases, the newer Roman lectionary substituted a different lesson; in others the Sarum had done so. On most of the Sundays after Pentecost the use of the lections generally varied by one Sunday.

Cranmer retained the Sarum lectionary, for the most part, though he made some substitutions, lengthened some lessons and abbreviated a few. The octave of Epiphany was eliminated, which put the lections for the Sundays after the Epiphany one week off from the Roman rite. Similar changes have been made over the course of successive revisions, including the insertion in the 1928 revision of a new Gospel for the second Sunday after the Epiphany, shifting the old Gospels for the second and third Sundays to the following Sundays and dropping the old Gospel for the fourth Sunday after the Epiphany, thereby separating Epistles and Gospels which had previously been linked. Cranmer had restored a substantial number and length of lessons and psalmody to the Sunday service, however, through his radical emendation of the daily office lectionary. Until the 1892 revision of the Prayer Book, Morning Prayer had been required before the Eucharist. According to the system of the first two Prayer Books, the congregation would have heard almost all of the Old Testament read on Sundays within the course of every seven years, and the New Testament (except for Revelation) within every period of two years and four months. The whole of the Psalter would

325

have been read on Sundays almost twice every year. Proper Old Testament lessons for the Sundays were provided during the reign of Elizabeth and proper New Testament lessons in the first American revision. The Sunday service still contained a substantial portion of the Scriptures until the 1892 revision allowed the celebration of the Eucharist without requiring that Morning Prayer precede. This left a meager diet of scripture for celebrations of the Eucharist.

The new eucharistic lectionary adopted for this Book provides for the reading of a substantial amount of the Old Testament and almost all of the New Testament over a three-year period. The lectionary is a revision of that adopted by the Roman Catholic Church after the Second Vatican Council. It has been refined on the basis of trial use in the Episcopal Church, and on the basis of revisions in other Christian churches which have adopted the Roman lectionary. The foundation of the lectionary is the reading from the Gospels: the Gospel according to John is read in Lent and Easter season and on certain other occasions; in a three-year cycle, each of the Synoptic Gospels is read in course throughout the remainder of the church year, except for certain special days or seasons.

The first reading at a Eucharist is from the Old Testament, except in the Easter season when, in accordance with an old tradition, the first choice is a reading from Acts. Many of the Old Testament readings were chosen for their substantial relationship to the Gospel of the day. The psalm appointed for the gradual is often linked to the Old Testament lesson preceding it. The second reading is normally from the Pauline Epistles in course, with the Catholic Epistles or Revelation in Easter season.

Until the present revision, the eucharistic rite itself provided only two lections, although up to the 1892 revision Morning Prayer with psalms and two lessons immediately preceded. In this revision a full liturgy of the word, including Old Testament, psalmody, New Testament, and Gospel is provided, though one of the two lessons which precede the Gospel may be omitted and the use of the psalm is not obligatory. At weekday services when most of the congregation has probably been exposed to the full set of lections on Sunday, the omission of one lection and the omission of the psalm or the substitution of another appropriate psalm is quite defensible.

The Announcement of a Lesson (pp. 325 and 357)

The custom of announcing the lesson dates to the twelfth century. Earlier Prayer Books required that the reader announce the chapter and verse as well as the name of the book. The citation of the chapter was new to the 1549 Book and that of the verse new to the 1662. This is now optional, for it is likely to be meaningful only in situations where people follow the lessons in their Bibles, possibly in another language or translation, or in situations where the level of biblical scholarship is such that the citation puts the reading into context for members of the congregation. In such situations, the new order which gives the book first, then the chapter, then the verse, should prove helpful.

The Response (pp. 325 and 357)

"Here endeth the epistle" was new to the 1662 Book, following the Scottish Book of 1637. The alternative is a translation of the response in the Roman sacramentary of Paul VI. The response "Deo gratias" ("Thanks be to God") was used in the medieval period as an acknowledgment of having heard what was said. It was used not only after readings but also after the dismissal and even, in some cases, after announcements made at the services. It is new to this revision of the Prayer Book.

Silence (pp. 326 and 357)

In this revision the rubric "silence may follow" has been inserted at many points in the various services. Earlier Prayer Books ordered a period of silence in one place only, before the Veni Creator Spiritus in the rite for ordination of priests. In this edition provision for silence is made when a period of recollection or reflection is appropriate. The rubric here is intended to encourage silent reflection on the readings.

The Gradual (pp. 326 and 357)

The use of a psalm after the readings from the Old Testament can be documented as early as the mid-fourth century. It is mentioned by Saint Athanasius (c. 293–373) and prescribed by the Apostolic Constitutions (c. 380). This represents the oldest regular use of psalmody in the liturgy. Whereas in some liturgies those psalms which came into the rite at a later time to cover the actions at the four processions (the entrance, the Gospel procession, the presentation of the oblations, and the communion of the people) could be omitted, the gradual psalm could not. The name "gradual" probably derives from "gradus" (step) indicating that it was traditionally, like the lessons and Gospel, sung from the ambo (pulpit) or its "gradus." This psalm was normally sung responsorially: the cantor, or later the choir on occasion, sang the text, first singing the antiphon which would be repeated by the people after each psalm verse or group of verses. This antiphon was a verse from the psalm which best summed up its message or related it to the reading which had preceded. When the Old Testament lesson was dropped from certain rites, the gradual was sometimes moved: in the Roman rite it followed the Epistle; in some other rites it retained its place prior to the Epistle.

The Gloria Patri was added to psalms at various places in the rite to provide a climax or a cut-off point for the processional psalm at the entrance of the clergy, for the psalm at the presentation of the oblations, and for the psalm at the communion of the people. It was never used with the gradual psalm, however, for the appointed portion was never cut. This psalm had its own reason for its use in the liturgy; its integrity was never to be compromised by additions or by using it to cover actions. When the time came that few of the people understood the Latin of the Roman rite, and after the elaboration of music for the gradual, however, the psalm was reduced to the antiphon and one verse, usually the first.

Luther retained the use of the gradual, although he expressed a preference for reciting the whole of a psalm. Other reformers deleted the gradual, as did the 1549 Prayer Book, although it did restore the use of a whole psalm at the entrance. The rationale was that Morning Prayer, with its substantial psalmody, would precede the Eucharist, obviating the need for a special gradual psalm.

The rubric of the present Book allows use of a "Psalm, hymn, or anthem" after each reading. On some occasions a hymn which is a metrical version of an appointed psalm, or an anthem setting of the text, would be an appropriate substitute for the responsorial or direct singing or reading of the gradual. (See p. 582 of the Prayer Book for traditional methods of psalmody.)

The Psalms, Hymns, or Anthems (pp. 326 and 357)

Either or both of the first two lessons may be followed by a psalm, hymn, or anthem. The use of a psalm, the "gradual," after the first reading is dealt with earlier in this section. At an early stage other psalmody or hymnody entered the rite in anticipation of the reading of the Gospel. The use of any of the traditional materials at this point was discontinued in the 1549 Book, which followed the Epistle with a rubric that the Gospel was to follow "Immediately after the epistle ended." The 1928 Book restored permission to sing between the

328

Epistle and Gospel "a Hymn or an Anthem." The present Book broadens this permission.

The Alleluia (pp. 326 and 357)

At least as early as the *Martyrdom of Matthew* (third century) Alleluias were sung in anticipation of the reading of the Gospel. Apparently this at first involved those psalms which contained Alleluia, or those which expressed joy and to which Alleluia could suitably be added. These Alleluia psalms were sung responsorially like the gradual, by a cantor, with the people responding Alleluia after each verse. Eventually, as with the gradual, the text sung by the cantor was reduced to one verse. Later other scriptural verses were used in addition to verses from psalms. Some of these were taken from the Epistle which had just been read and others from the Gospel which was to follow immediately after, but some had no relationship whatever with the lections of the day. Texts not taken from the Scriptures also came into use with the Alleluia. In the rites of both Eastern and Western churches the use of Alleluia was normal before the reading of the Gospel, but in the Roman rite the Alleluia was replaced in penitential seasons by a tract and eventually was supplemented or replaced, on many occasions, by a sequence.

The Tract (pp. 326 and 357)

In Eastern and Gallican rites the Alleluia continued to be used during Lent, but in the Roman rite it was replaced in Pre-Lent and Lent with a tract, a psalm or portion of a psalm sung straight through without a responsorial verse. This emphasized the penitential nature of the season; the return to the use of the Alleluia at Easter heightened the festal celebration of the day. The tract was sung to a simpler melody than the gradual or sequence. This possibly represented the music for the psalms of an earlier period. Eventually the tract came to be sung antiphonally by a choir.

The Sequence (pp. 326 and 357)

During the last half of the ninth century, when the music of the Alleluia verses had become more elaborate, Notker, a monk of Saint Gall (d. 912), set to work to elaborate the texts as well so that there would be only one syllable for each note in order to make chanting easier for the singers. These amplified texts were called "sequences." The anthem used in the burial rite (pp. 484 and 492), "In

329

the midst of life," is based on a text by Notker. About A.D. 1000, a new type of sequence developed which made use of rhyme. Rome gave the sequences a frigid reception, but the northern countries in the late middle ages seem to have welcomed them. The northern missals contained a sequence for almost every day on which the Alleluia was used. Vernacular hymnody in Germany developed from these sequences; vernacular verses written in imitation of the Latin of the sequence were sung by the congregation after each strophe of the Latin. The old German hymn Christ ist erstanden, which can be traced to the twelfth century, was used in this manner with the Easter sequence, Victimae paschali; Komm, Heiliger Geist, Herre Gott, was used in this way with the sequence for Pentecost, Veni Sancte Spiritus. Adam of Saint Victor (d. 1192) was the most famous writer of sequences. The Reformed churches retained very few of the medieval sequences and in the revision of the Roman missal under Pius V only four sequences were kept: Victimae paschali for Easter; Veni Sancte Spiritus for Pentecost; Lauda Sion for Corpus Christi; and Dies Irae (which has been suppressed in the reform stemming from Vatican II) for requiems.

The Gospel (pp. 326 and 357–358)

The reading from the Gospels, the climactic reading, has attracted special ceremonies at least as far back as the late fourth century. Standing for the Gospel reading can be traced to the Apostolic Constitutions, a document which also indicates that the deacon was to read the Gospel. From that time on (late fourth century) the Gospel reading was normally assigned to the deacon. In some areas or on some occasions, however, the celebrant or bishop read the Gospel. Even earlier is the greeting of the Gospel reading with Alleluias.

The movement of the deacon (or other reader) to the ambo (pulpit) for the reading was emphasized in importance, at least as early as the seventh century, by a formal procession with two lights which were carried by acolytes before the Gospel book. The acolytes remained below while the deacon ascended the pulpit for the reading. In Gallican rites seven lights were used in this procession. In many rites the Gospel book had been carried into the church by the deacon at the entrance of the clergy. Sometimes it was placed upon the ambo immediately after the entrance procession; in a number of places, however, the richly decorated book used in the procession was put on the altar until the time for the procession to the ambo. The reading of the Gospel and the book itself symbolized the presence of Christ in

330

the liturgy of the word just as the eucharistic prayer and the eucharistic elements symbolized His presence in the liturgy of the table. In some places in both the East and the West the announcement of the Gospel was greeted with Benedictus qui venit, "Blessed is he that cometh in the name of the Lord. Hosanna in the highest." The most common acclamation in Eastern and Gallican territory was that which eventually made its way into the Roman rite—"Glory to you, Lord." In the ninth century there is evidence that people made a sign of the cross on their foreheads at the announcement.

Incense was carried before the book in the entrance procession at an early period and eventually, also, in the Gospel procession. From the eleventh century the practice of censing the book before the reading gradually spread. The conclusion of the Gospel in the Gallican liturgies was greeted with the exclamation "Praise to you, Christ." In some rites Alleluias or other acclamations were used.

The 1549 Book retained the Gloria tibi response at the announcement of the Gospel ("Glory be to thee, O Lord"). No special ceremonies are noted. The injunctions of 1547 had directed that all readings were to be done from the pulpit, a return to the practice followed before the changes accompanying the development of low Mass. The Book directed that "the priest, or he that is appointed" should read the Epistle, and "a priest or deacon" the Gospel. In the 1552 revision the priest is to read both Epistle and Gospel. The 1637 Scottish Book directed that the "presbyter" read both the Epistle and Gospel and that the people were to stand for the Gospel. The Gloria tibi was restored at the announcement and a response at the conclusion. The 1662 revision made no change, except that the people were to stand. The Gloria tibi was included in the first American revision and the rubric indicated that "the Minister" was to read the Epistle and Gospel. This opened the door for the recovery of the deacons' traditional role as readers of the Gospel at regular services, not just at their ordinations, and allowed the use of lay persons as readers of the Epistle. In the 1928 revision the Laus tibi was provided for optional use after the Gospel.

The rubric of the present Book directs the people to stand for the Gospel, which is to be read by "the Deacon or a Priest." The response after the Gospel is no longer optional. A hymn or anthem is permitted immediately before the Gospel, which allows once again for recovery of the traditional Alleluias.

A model of the announcement is provided for the reader (pp. 479 and 495), "The Holy Gospel of our Lord Jesus Christ according to John." This represents a return to catholic tradition in the simplicity of the announcement. The citation of chapter and verse is no longer required. The additional directions (p. 406) point out that it is desirable that the Gospel be read from the same lectern as the other readings, "or from the pulpit, or from the midst of the congregation." Until the development of the low Mass, readings were from the ambo, a custom which continued at high Mass. Injunctions which preceded the 1549 Prayer Book ordered that the readings at all rites be from the pulpit. Only in recent years have the lectern and pulpit become two separate pieces of furniture in Anglican churches or has the reading been done from the altar in imitation of the low Mass custom. This present revision may encourage a return to the pulpit as the symbol of the word both read and preached, of the presence of Christ in His word, as the altar is a symbol of Christ present in His sacrament. The additional directions also allow the reading of the Gospel in other languages which are the native tongue of a portion of the congregation. Various rites have provided for this option, especially on the two primary feasts, Easter and Pentecost.

The Sermon (pp. 326 and 358)

A sermon or homily has been required at the Eucharist from the time of the 1549 Prayer Book. The exposition of the lections just read was a regular part of the Eucharist in the early centuries. Later in various areas, first of all in Rome apparently, preaching became less regular. So infrequent was a sermon in the late middle ages that friars came to consider preaching a part of their calling, and various local councils legislated that in every church sermons should be preached with a certain frequency, sometimes no more than one to four times each year. The infrequent sermons were often preached within the context of the Prone rather than of the Mass.

Luther required a sermon at every Mass. In the Reformed churches sermons were preached not only every Sunday but in many places also during the week. In 1547, before the appearance of the first Prayer Book, a book of homilies was issued in England providing a homily to be read each Sunday. The first Prayer Book required a sermon or the reading of a homily at each Sunday or holy day Eucharist. The exception for the weekdays was not included in the 1552 revision.

It is to be noted that the permission in many of the previous Prayer Books to allow announcements, hymns, or prayers to be inserted between the Gospel and the sermon has been totally deleted in this present revision.

The Nicene Creed (pp. 326–328 and 358–359)

During the first centuries of the church's existence it was clearly understood, in keeping with the tradition of Jewish mealtime prayers, that the creed of the Eucharist was the eucharistic prayer. People heard the faith proclaimed over the bread and wine, and gave their assent in acclamations and Amen. The first use of the Nicene Creed in the Eucharist seems to have been among the Monophysite heretics late in the fifth century or early in the sixth; they used it as a retort to the formula of Chalcedon (p. 864). This Creed originated in the East as a baptismal profession of faith with a structure modeled on Matthew 28:19 and an emphasis on oneness that reflects Ephesians 4:4. The council of Nicaea in 325 amplified the Creed in an effort to combat the Arian heresy. It was further amplified at the council of Constantinople (381) to combat Apollinarianism, and was adopted at the council of Chalcedon (451) as the profession of the council of Constantinople. Over several centuries its use extended to most of the other Eastern rites where it was used after the transfer of the bread and wine to the altar, before or after the peace, as a monotoned prelude to the sung thanksgiving.

In the West, the third council of Toledo in Spain (589) first introduced the Creed to remind the Arian converts continually of the true faith. This council also inserted the *filioque* (and the Son) clause which was not in the original Creed propagated by the ecumenical council. Slowly, over the course of the next few centuries, use of the Creed spread northward. The Celts first adopted it, then the Anglo-Saxons. Charlemagne, possibly influenced by Alcuin, inserted it in the liturgy of his chapel. By the tenth century it had reached Germany where, following the pattern of the Celtic rite, it was inserted in the Eucharist after the readings and homily and prior to the prayers of the people. Rome did not accept the Creed as part of the Eucharist until the eleventh century and even then confined it to Sundays and certain feasts.

After the people had largely ceased participating in the Mass vocally and after a number of private prayers by the priest were normally included in the liturgical books, the custom of the priest's saying the Creed in the first person singular began to spread. As late as the sixteenth century, however, some of the printed books retained the plural form of the council document. The inclusion of the *filioque* was a slow process as liturgical manuscripts were copied. This clause has never been accepted in the East, and the Roman Catholic Church is presently in communion with some uniate groups which have never accepted the clause.

Some continental reformers, rejecting the Creed because it contained nonscriptural phrases, substituted the Apostles' Creed. The 1549 Prayer Book retained the Nicene Creed in the Eucharist, allowing it to be omitted if a sermon was preached. In that edition it was moved from after the sermon to a place after the Gospel. The 1552 revision made it a fixed part of the rite. At the time when the American Proposed Book was being prepared there was considerable opposition to its being included in the Eucharist, largely because of the "unscriptural phrases" it was said to contain. The English bishops wrote that they hoped the Nicene Creed would be given "a place in your book" though the use of it might be "left discretional." This letter, far from being the cause of its restoration (as has been asserted by some authors), says itself that it was written after the bishops had "prepared a bill for conveying to us the powers necessary" for ordaining bishops for the American church. The Nicene Creed was restored at an interstate convention in 1786 as an alternative to the Apostles' Creed for use in Morning Prayer, which was always to be said prior to the Eucharist. The 1789 convention adopted this resolution. When the Eucharist was used without being preceded by Morning Prayer (*i.e.* at the communion of the sick), either the Apostles' Creed or the Nicene Creed was to be said. In 1892 the rubric was revised; the Nicene Creed was to be used at the five feasts with proper prefaces. The present revision provides eucharistic prayers which proclaim the faith in its fullness, and the Creed is required only on Sundays and at major feasts (for these feasts see pp. 15–17). The Creed in this revision is also in its earlier position after the sermon so that the sermon may be preached immediately after the readings.

The ICET translation, which left the inclusion of the *filioque* clause optional, has been adopted for this Book. The plural form is restored, true to the document of the council and fitting for use in the Eucharist as a proclamation of the faith of the Church. For Rite One the translation of prior Prayer Books is provided as an alternative, with the restoration of the word "holy" which was for some unaccountable reason omitted from the 1549 Book and subsequent revisions.

The Prayers of the People (pp. 328 and 359)

We know that the prayers of the people followed the readings and sermon, at least as early as the second century. By the end of the fourth century in the East these prayers had become a litany with biddings by the deacon to which the people responded Kyrie eleison. In Rome the prayers also consisted of biddings which, in the fifth century or earlier, were followed by a period of silence and a collect said by the celebrant. The solemn prayers of Good Friday (pp. 277–280) follow that tradition. In the fourth century intercessions also became a part of the eucharistic prayer; Eastern litanies made their way to the West to become the form used for the prayer of the people in the Gallican rites. The Roman rite of the late fifth century prefaced the Eucharist with a litany of which the Kyrie is a remnant. This litany seems to have replaced the earlier solemn collects except on Good Friday, though they remained in use at certain other places on some days. Some Eastern rites also inserted a litany into the entrance rite, possibly one cause of the reduction or disappearance of the prayers of the people in some liturgies. Intercessions within the eucharistic prayer in the Roman rite may have been a factor in the displacement of the introductory litany on most occasions in the time of Gregory the Great (590–604).

As it became increasingly the custom to say the major part of the eucharistic prayer inaudibly, the audible portion of the Roman rite was left without intercessions. This may have contributed to the multiplication of votive Masses for special needs.

Most of the continental reformers restored substantial intercessory prayers to the rites, often inserting these between the sermon and the eucharistic prayer as had been done in the early centuries and continued to be done in the Eastern liturgies.

The Prayer Book of 1549 contained a revised version of the 1544 litany (for discussion see the section on the Litany in this book) to be said before the Ante-Communion on Wednesdays and Fridays. That Book also included—following the Sanctus—a "prayer for the whole state of Christ's Church." This was the point, in the Roman canon, at which intercessions for the living were included. There is some reason to believe that Cranmer originally intended to have this prayer read prior to the eucharistic prayer, as in Justin Martyr's second-century account of the Eucharist, but conservative sentiments prevailed. In the 1552 revision, which required the Litany on every Sunday as well as on Wednesdays and Fridays, the prayer for the church was moved to a place before the eucharistic prayer. The original version of that prayer for "the whole state" has been revised in the Books of 1552, 1662, 1789, 1928, and in this present Book. It is printed in Rite One.

The 1979 Book restores the prayers of the people to the historic position after the sermon and Creed and prior to the peace and the offertory of the Eucharist. Rather than provide one fixed text, the Book gives directions to which, except on special days and occasions, the prayers of the people must conform. These directions (p. 383) require prayers for the church and the world to cover specific categories, but allow adaptations or insertions suitable to the occasion. In addition to the prayer for the whole state of Christ's Church and the world in Rite One (pp. 328–330), six forms are provided (pp. 383–395) which may be done in traditional or contemporary language suited to the context of the rite. Adaptations or insertions suited to the occasion may be made in any of these, and there is freedom to devise other forms. A series of collects or occasional prayers may be used (pp. 809–841), or a prayer from some other source, or a prayer composed for the occasion, so long as the directions on page 383 are followed.

Forms I, IV, and V are particularly appropriate for the principal service on Sundays and major feasts because of the range and fullness of these forms and the fixed congregational responses. In forms I, V, and VI there are penitential sections. Forms II, III, and VI, with varying responses and the opportunity for individuals to add their own petitions, are especially suitable for small groups and for groups which come together frequently. Petitions which have a bar beside them in the left margin may be omitted as desired. The celebrant may introduce the prayers with a bidding related to the occasion, the season, or the proper of the day. (For commentary on these forms, see below, pp. 405–407.)

A concluding collect, said by the celebrant, ends each of the six forms of the prayers of the people, following the custom of ancient litanies. The rubric (p. 394) suggests the use of a collect appropriate to the season or occasion, but much freedom is allowed in the choice of collect. Editions of the Prayer Book from 1662 through 1928 directed that certain collects be repeated after the collect of the day throughout the season (Advent and Lent) or for several days after the feast (Christmas, Epiphany, Palm Sunday, Easter, Ascension, Pentecost, and All Saints) to emphasize the season or feast. An analogous use of a seasonal collect is appropriate at the conclusion of the prayers of the people.

This is also the place to use a collect which expresses some special need in the life of the local congregation when more emphasis is necessary than the form of the prayers may provide. A collect for the mission of the church, such as one of those in the daily offices, is also fitting. Eight collects are provided for general use (pp. 394–395). The first five are petitions for God to accept the prayers of His people.

336

These provide among them a theology of prayer. The sixth is especially appropriate when used immediately before the peace, the seventh for the season of Advent, and the eighth for saints' days. (For commentary on these collects, see below, pp. 407–408.)

The Prayer for the Whole State of Christ's Church and the World (pp. 328–330)

The bidding of this prayer has changed with various revisions of the Book. In 1549 it read "Let us pray for the whole state of Christ's Church," which is similar to the rubric preceding the prayer of the people in Hermann's Consultation. The 1552 revision eliminated the commemoration of the departed and changed the bidding to read "Let us pray for the whole state of Christ's Church militant here in earth." This is close in wording to a bidding in a 1531 Primer. In the first American revision the words "here in earth" were dropped. The 1928 Book inserted a petition for the departed and restored the 1549 bidding. The present Book broadens the prayer to include persons and concerns that are not explicitly Christian; the bidding is expanded to "Let us pray for the whole state of Christ's Church and the world."

The 1928 revision attempted to provide for personalizing of the intercessions by inserting a rubric "Here the Priest may ask the secret intercessions of the Congregation for any who have desired the prayers of the Church." The present Book gives an opportunity, at appropriate places within the prayer, to insert the names of those whom the congregation should remember in prayer before God. There is also opportunity, before the final paragraph, to insert additional petitions and thanksgivings.

In the present Book the people may make an appropriate response after each paragraph of the prayer. One which seems in keeping with this prayer is the familiar response, "We beseech thee to hear us, good Lord."

The order of the petitions in 1549 was church, the king and his council, "Bishops, Pastors, and Curates," God's people, the congregation assembled, and the departed. The order is that of the prayers of the people in Hermann's Consultation which was copied from the liturgy of Cassel. Though various portions of the original prayer were revised or omitted, the order of the elements remained constant until this revision. The petitions for the clergy and people are now placed ahead of those for the nation and those in authority, in conformity with the classical order of prayers of the people (p. 383).

The beginning of the prayer is similar to that of the prayers of the people in various German church orders. The original Cranmerian version of the first paragraph had "which by thy holy Apostle hast taught us to make prayers and supplications, and to give thanks for all men." In this revision "who in thy holy Word" is substituted. The quotation is from 1 Timothy 2:1; since many scholars no longer consider this a Pauline epistle, the preamble is changed to eliminate a stumblingblock. The middle portion resembles the section immediately following the Sanctus in the medieval Roman canon. In the 1552 revision a phrase was inserted in the next line "to accept our alms." The words "and oblations" were added to the phrase in 1662. The phrase was to be omitted when no alms (offerings for the poor) or oblations (other money offerings) were presented. In 1928 the brackets were removed from all but the words "alms and," to clarify or reinterpret the meaning of the two key words: "oblations" was interpreted as a reference to the offerings of bread and wine; "alms" as a reference to any offering of money. This revision returns the prayer to the traditional place for the prayers of the people, prior to the offerings, and deletes the phrases inserted in 1552 and 1662.

The second paragraph upholds both word and sacrament following traditional Anglican principle, emphasizing neither at the expense of the other. The 1549 form used the Lutheran trilogy for the various pastoral ministries, "Bishops, Pastors, and Curates [clergy in charge of a cure]." The 1662 revision omitted "Pastors" because of the Puritan connotations of the word. In 1789 the phrase was changed to "Bishops and other ministers."

The third and fourth paragraphs resemble the prayers of Hermann's Consultation. The third reflects the Renaissance-Reformation emphasis upon the Scriptures, which were then newly available in both the original languages and vernacular translations, and upon the preaching of the word. The wording is possibly influenced by Luke 1:74.

The fourth paragraph originally read:

> Specially we beseech thee to save and defend thy servant Edward our king, that under him we may be godly and quietly governed. And grant unto his whole council, and to all that be put in authority under him, that they may truly and indifferently minister justice, to the punishment of wickedness and vice, and to the maintenance of God's true religion and virtue.

In the 1552 revision the petition was broadened to include "all Christian kings, princes, and governors." In the first American revision the paragraph was changed:

> We beseech thee also, so to direct and dispose the hearts of all Christian rulers, that they may truly and impartially administer justice, to the punishment of wickedness and vice, and to the maintenance of thy true religion and virtue.

This paragraph has been severely criticized for many years because of the limitation of the petition to Christian rulers, because justice should be administered but tempered with mercy, because wickedness and vice often need to be corrected rather than punished, and because it is not the duty of a nation based upon the principle of freedom of religion to maintain the Christian religion as a matter of secular obligation. The paragraph in this revision intercedes for all who bear authority "that they may be led to wise decisions and right actions for the welfare and peace of the world."

The next paragraph, which expresses ecological concern, is new to this revision. It is composed of portions of two collects new to the Prayer Book in 1928: the first two lines are from a prayer "For Joy in God's Creation" by the Rev. John W. Suter, Jr.; the remainder of the petition is from the prayer "For Faithfulness in the Use of this World's Goods." Both of these prayers have been retained among the prayers and thanksgivings (pp. 814 and 827). The first, in a revised form, is also provided as the collect for the Wednesday of Easter Week and the third Sunday of Easter; the second, as the collect of the third of the propers for the rogation days.

The sixth paragraph, except for the updating of the language in the 1662 and 1789 revisions, retains the Cranmerian form. There is a much longer parallel section in the prayers of the people found in the Consultation and other German church orders.

In the 1549 Book the preceding paragraph was followed by a petition, for which there are parallels in both German church orders and medieval eucharistic prayers, for the assembled congregation: "And especially we commend unto thy merciful goodness this congregation which is here assembled in thy name to celebrate the commemoration of the most glorious death of thy Son." This was dropped in 1552.

The 1549 version of this prayer concluded with a commemoration of saints and a petition for the departed:

> And here we do give unto thee most high praise and hearty thanks, for the wonderful grace and virtue declared in all thy saints from the beginning of the world; and chiefly in the glorious and most blessed Virgin Mary, mother of thy Son Jesus Christ our Lord and God, and in the holy patriarchs, prophets, apostles, and martyrs, whose examples, O Lord, and steadfastness in thy faith, and keeping thy holy commandments, grant us to follow. We commend unto thy mercy, O Lord, all other thy servants, which are departed hence from us with the sign of faith and now do rest in the sleep of peace; grant unto them, we beseech thee, thy mercy and everlasting peace, and that at the day of the general resurrection we, and all they which be of the mystical body of thy Son, may altogether be set on his right hand, and hear that his most joyful voice: Come unto me, O ye that be blessed of my Father, and possess the kingdom which is prepared for you from the beginning of the world. Grant this, O Father, for Jesus Christ's sake, our only mediator and advocate.

Sources for this section include the medieval Roman eucharistic prayer, the Liturgy of Saint Basil, and Matthew 25:34. Very few Lutheran reformed prayers contained any commemoration of the departed. The medieval abuses associated with the doctrine of purgatory and the invocation of saints had caused many people to reject prayers for the departed. Pressure from such persons caused the deletion of all but the last sentence of this section in the 1552 Book. A revised version of this section was restored to the prayer in the Scottish Book of 1637.

The revisers in 1662 inserted a commemoration of the departed (but with no petition for them) which was developed from the bidding prayer of the Elizabethan injunctions of 1559. This was ordered to be "used before sermons" in a slightly revised form by Canon 55 of 1604:

> And we also bless thy holy Name for all thy servants departed this life in thy faith and fear; beseeching thee to give us grace so to follow their good examples, that with them we may be partakers of thy heavenly kingdom.

The American Book of 1892 adopted a prayer which is a Scottish revision of the final section of the 1549 prayer, placing it among the additional prayers printed after the burial office. This prayer is retained in this Book (p. 487).

In 1928, amid great controversy, a petition for the departed was restored to the prayer for the church, "beseeching thee to grant them continual growth in thy love and service." The idea of growth in the life beyond, which is hardly typical of traditional prayers for the departed, was characteristic of those which made their way into the 1928 Book.

The present revision has finally responded to the frequently reiterated point that many who have departed this life in the faith and fear of the Lord have nevertheless not set examples which we should pray to follow. The final petition is changed to read: "so to follow the good examples of . . . all thy saints."

The rubric following the prayer directs that when the liturgy of the word is used at times when a priest is not available, or when communion is not to follow, the service should be concluded at this point according to the directions on page 406 of the Prayer Book.

Confession of Sin (pp. 330–332 and 359–360)

A confession of sin on the part of the whole congregation was new to the liturgies of the Reformation period. In the early church Christians acknowledged their sinfulness by giving thanks to God, in the eucharistic prayer, for having redeemed them. Once the litany form was introduced, the prayers of the people normally contained the Kyrie eleison as a response; the Lord's Prayer which eventually became a regular part of the rite contained the petition "forgive us as we forgive." No absolution was included, for one of the benefits of communion was understood to be the forgiveness of sins. Late in the middle ages, however, there were several developments which prepared the way for a general confession to be included in the reformed rites.

Toward the end of the middle ages it became customary for the priest and assistant to exchange a mutual confession and absolution prior to the Mass. There is also some evidence at this time of a vernacular confession followed by an absolution just before the act of receiving communion. In 1548 the Order of the Communion was published consisting of an exhortation, invitation, confession, absolution, scriptural assurances of forgiveness, and a prayer which later came to be known as the "prayer of humble access." This Order, replacing the medieval forms, was inserted in the Mass after the communion of the priest. The exhortation and invitation were ad-

341

dressed to the congregation; those who were to receive communion were invited to the chancel where they would kneel and participate in this devotion before receiving the Sacrament. The 1549 Book retained a revised form of this confession of sin, following the eucharistic prayer and prior to the communion of priest and people. The 1552 revision placed the confession before the Sursum corda. The present Book, in keeping with revisions in many of the other provinces of Anglicanism, moves it to a place among the prayers, prior to the preparation of the table for the eucharistic rite. In this position the confession of sin does not break into the basic actions of the eucharistic liturgy but serves as a preparation for that rite.

The rubric designates that a confession of sin is to be said here if it has not been said earlier. A penitential order is supplied for both rites (pp. 319–321 and 351–353), which provides a solemn introduction to the service appropriate to Lent or to other penitential occasions. Forms I, V, and VI of the prayers of the people contain penitential supplications or a general confession. The Great Litany may be used as the entrance rite of either service and the decalogue with its responses may be part of the entrance actions of Rite One. Both the Great Litany and the decalogue with its responses have the tone and nature of confession of sin. Confession is the obverse of thanksgiving; to give thanks for redemption is to acknowledge one's sinfulness. On the great festal days of the church year, when it may be more appropriate not to make use of explicit acts of confession, this is allowed by rubric, "On occasion, the Confession may be omitted."

In Rite Two the confession may be preceded by one of the sentences from the Penitential Order (pp. 351–353). The first of these is the Summary of the Law, which in Rite One may be used as part of the entrance liturgy. The second and third are calls to confession in words of scripture. The sentence may be read by the deacon.

It is appropriate for the deacon to bid the people to confession and to initiate the reading of the confession. In the absence of a deacon the celebrant gives the bidding and leads the confession.

The Bidding to Confession (pp. 330 and 360)

The first of the two biddings to confession in Rite One dates to the Order of the Communion (1548). It sets forth the three conditions of true repentance: earnest repentance for sins of the past, love for one's neighbor, and the intention to lead a new life. In the 1548 form "draw near" literally meant that those who intended to receive were to move from the nave to the chancel near the altar. This custom persisted in many churches until well into the nineteenth century and, in a few, into the twentieth. Until the late Victorian period the chancel, or the area about the altar, was thought of as the room for the sacrament, and the nave, or the area around the pulpit, as the room for the daily office and the liturgy of the word. This architectural distinction makes clear the phrase which was in the earlier versions (which assumed that only a small number of those present would communicate, and that everyone else would remain in the nave), "and to his holy Church here gathered together in his Name" [1548 and 1549], or "before this congregation here gathered together in his holy name" [1552 until the revision of 1662]. The concluding line, "meekly kneeling upon your knees," of earlier Prayer Books was changed to "devoutly kneeling" in the American revision of 1789.

The second bidding in Rite One entered the Book in 1892 as an alternative to the exhortation to confession in Evening Prayer. In the 1928 version it was printed in Morning Prayer as well.

The bidding in Rite Two is new.

It is appropriate that a period of silent reflection precede the general confession; the new rubric gives express permission for such a silence.

The General Confession (pp. 331 and 360)

The first of the forms for general confession in Rite One dates to the Order of the Communion of 1548, and is, in essence, a condensation of a much longer form in Hermann's Consultation. Until the 1662 revision this confession was to be said by one of the communicants or by one of the ministers "in the name of all those that are minded to receive the Holy Communion." Since 1662 it has been said by all present.

The general confession in Rite Two, which is also printed in Rite One as an alternative form, is based on a form proposed by a British ecumenical organization, the Joint Liturgical Group.[1] That version read:

> Most merciful God, we confess that we have sinned against thee in thought, word, and deed. We have not loved thee with our whole heart. We have not loved our neighbors as ourselves. We pray thee of thy mercy to forgive what we have been, to help us to amend what we are, and to direct what we shall be; that we may delight in thy will and walk in thy ways, through Jesus Christ our Lord. Amen.

---

[1] The Daily Office, London: S.P.C.K., 1968, p. 77.

343

The phrases peculiar to the revision included in this edition of the Prayer Book derive from the forms for general confession in prior Prayer Books for the daily office and the Eucharist (retained in this Book on pp. 41–42 or 62–63 and 331). This new form is also printed in Morning and Evening Prayer: Rite Two. In this form we confess not only our sins of commission but also those of omission and our lack of love for God and neighbor. Not only do we ask that we may walk in God's ways, but also that we may delight in His will.

The Absolution (pp. 332 and 360)

The absolution in Rite One dates to the Prayer Book of 1549. The second part is originally the absolution said by priest and server in the Sarum rite carried over into the Order of 1548. The first half, which states the conditions of forgiveness—hearty repentance and true faith—was new to the 1549 Book. It replaced the first half of the 1548 absolution which was dependent on the Consultation of Hermann:

> Our blessed Lord, who hath left power to his church to absolve penitent sinners from their sins, and to restore to the grace of the heavenly Father such as truly believe in Christ.

The absolution of Rite Two is derived from the older portion of Rite One.

The Sentences of Scripture (p. 332)

In Rite One four optional sentences from scripture follow the absolution. All previous editions of the Prayer Book required that all four be said at every celebration. The first two sentences were introduced with the words "Hear what comfortable words our Saviour Christ saith unto all who truly turn to him." The third was preceded by "Hear also what Saint Paul saith," and the fourth by "Hear also what Saint John saith." The word "comfort" has changed drastically in its connotations, the second of the sentences is a word of the Johannine author rather than of Christ, and serious doubts have been raised about the Pauline authorship of 1 Timothy. Because of these difficulties, the traditional introductions are replaced in the 1979 Book by a simple bidding, "Hear the Word of God to all who truly turn to him." The conclusion, "and not for ours only, but for the sins of the whole world," was added to the fourth sentence in this Book, and the words "perfect offering" substituted for "propitiation."

All four of the sentences were in the Order of the Communion (1548). The last three, along with two additional sentences (Jn. 3:35–36a and Acts 10:43), were read in the Consultation of Hermann immediately after the confession and prior to the absolution, introduced by the words "Hear the Gospel." The use of "comfortable words" in the reformed German church rites can be traced at least as far back as the first reformed service in Strassburg, conducted by Diobald Schwarz on February 16, 1524. The first of the sentences, the one not found in the Consultation, is in some of the other German church orders.

The Peace (pp. 332 and 360)

Some authors find evidence of the exchange of the kiss of peace in various New Testament passages:

1 Corinthians 16:20	2 Timothy 4:22
2 Corinthians 13:12	Titus 3:15
Ephesians 6:23–24	Philemon 25
Philippians 4:21	Hebrews 13:24
1 Thessalonians 5:26	1 Peter 5:12
2 Thessalonians 3:16	3 John 15
1 Timothy 6:21	

The first unambiguous references to the peace, however, are in the baptismal liturgies. The peace could not be exchanged with the uninitiated, but the newly baptized were welcomed with the kiss of peace. In early liturgies the peace formed the conclusion of the liturgy of the word, after the dismissal of the catechumens and the prayers of the faithful. In early Eastern liturgies it extended through the time that the offerings were being transferred from the sacristy to the table. Later, in both the Eastern and Gallican liturgies this transfer of gifts assumed ceremonial significance, and the peace followed it as an introduction to the liturgy of the table. The Roman rite, in the fifth century, transferred the peace to the time of the breaking of the bread, as an immediate preparation for communion.

In various cultures the exchange of the peace has taken the form of a kiss on the cheek, an embrace, a clasping of hands with or without the kissing of the hand, or a bow. In the late medieval period the kiss came to be exchanged in a hierarchical movement, beginning with the celebrant who first received the kiss of the Lord by kissing the altar, the paten, the consecrated bread, or a paxboard (a wooden plaque bearing the image of a saint or of the crucifixion). If it was a paxboard, that was then passed around among the communicants, at least on occasion. Eventually the exchange of the peace was confined normally to the celebrant and the deacon, and then only on certain occasions.

The reformed liturgies did not include the exchange of the peace, although the accompanying text was retained in some of the German church orders and in the 1549 Prayer Book. It was revived in modern times in the Book of Common Worship of the Church of South India, and has spread to most of the revisions of the second half of the twentieth century. An exchange of the peace among the people has also been revived in Roman Catholic rites. This present revision restores the peace. The salutation is required, after which "the Ministers and People may greet one another." The medieval hierarchical method of exchange is expressly not recommended for this exchange. No special form of words is prescribed for the ministers and people to speak to one another. In the present rite the peace is printed at the point at which it was exchanged in the early church, though an additional direction (p. 407) permits its use at the place customary in the medieval Roman rite, after the breaking of the bread.

Offertory Sentences (pp. 333 and 361)

The 1549 Book provided sentences of scripture to be sung while the people placed their offerings in "the poor men's box." Otherwise one of these sentences was to be said by the minister immediately before the offering. The 1552 Book directs the minister to say one or more of the sentences, and the offering is to be gathered by the churchwardens. Rubrics in the 1662 Book make clear that the minister is to continue reading the sentences while the offering is gathered by deacons, churchwardens, or others. The 1928 revision provides that one or more sentences be said to "begin the offertory," but the celebrant is no longer obligated to read during the gathering of the offerings. Previous editions of the Prayer Book provided a series of scriptural sentences, and the offertory sentence (or sentences) was to be chosen from among them. The present revision permits the minister to use one of the offertory sentences printed in the Book (pp. 343–344 or 376–377) or some other sentence of scripture appropriate to the day or occasion. The use of a sentence is not required, however. Instrumental or vocal music may often make a more effective beginning for the offertory than the repetition of a familiar sentence, its value blurred by overuse. In a service with no music it is often smoother and more edifying for the minister simply to begin the preparation of the table in the course of the exchange of the peace than to attempt to say an offertory sentence while the peace is still being exchanged.

The Preparation of the Table and the Presentation of the Offerings (pp. 333 and 361)

One of the additional directions (p. 407) states "It is the function of a deacon to make ready the Table for the celebration." The association of the deacon with the preparation of the table can be documented in the second century. In some places the table was not brought into the room or moved into the center of the congregation until the catechumens had been dismissed and the prayers of the people were concluded. A white cloth was placed on the table and the offerings of bread and wine brought to the deacons (or the deacons circulated among the people to gather them). Sufficient bread and wine for the sacrament was set out and the remainder put aside for the clergy and for the poor. Water was added to the cup to dilute the wine. These acts of preparation directed the attention of the congregation from the ambo or pulpit at which the lessons had been read (and the sermon sometimes preached)—the piece of furniture symbolizing Christ's presence in His word—to the table (altar)—symbol of His presence in His sacrament. In the Eastern and Gallican liturgies the offerings were brought to a sacristy or "treasury" by the people on their arrival at the church. During the exchange of the peace, the deacon prepared the table and brought the gifts from the sacristy to place upon it, assisted by others if necessary. In the later middle ages a rite developed for the preparation of the gifts, the *prothesis*, and the transfer itself acquired ritual significance. Hymnody and prayers became part of this transfer which came to be called the "Great Entrance." Some remnants of the offertory procession with the gifts persisted in the West, even after the decline in the people's communions and the shift from bread to wafers. One of these was the presentation of alms for the poor at "the poor men's box."

In many places, late in the middle ages, the actual preparation of the eucharistic elements and the placing of them on the altar was separated from the time of the procession. Sometimes the elements were placed on the altar before the Mass or before the Gospel. The 1549 Prayer Book, like various German church orders, directed the people to come into the chancel and place their alms in "the poor men's box." The minister was then to select sufficient round, un-

347

leavened breads, "larger and thicker than it was, so that it may be aptly divided in divers pieces," and to pour sufficient wine into a cup, adding "a little pure and clean water," and then place those upon the altar.

The 1552 revision directs the churchwardens to gather the alms and place them in the poor men's box. (For generations the people came forward to the place where the wardens stood to present their offerings.) Nothing is said about when to place the bread and wine on the altar. Apparently many priests or clerks performed this action prior to the rite. Like the Scottish Book of 1637, the 1662 revision restored the gathering of the offerings of the people as a function of the deacon. Money offerings were to be received by the deacons, churchwardens, or others, in a decent basin and brought to the priest, "who shall humbly present and place it upon the holy Table." The priest was then to place sufficient bread and wine on the table for the communions. The 1892 revision permitted the singing of a hymn or anthem at the presentation; at that time a sentence apparently designed for use at the presentation was added to the end of the offertory sentences, "All things come of thee, O Lord, and of thine own have we given thee." The 1928 revision played down the presentation which had been previously featured in various ways; the rubric was recast: "when the Alms and Oblations are being received and presented, there may be sung a Hymn, or an Offertory Anthem." This was apparently an attempt to use music at the offertory in the traditional manner as an accompaniment to the whole action of gathering the gifts and placing them upon the altar in preparation for the eucharistic prayer. No presentation sentence is given in the present revision, since the oblation is spoken of in the eucharistic prayer which immediately follows. Making use of such a sentence in a proleptic fashion diminishes the force of the oblation in the prayer itself.

The present revision returns the deacon's functions of preparing the table and placing the bread and wine upon it (see p. 407). Others may assist. The recovery of the almost universal pre-Reformation custom of diluting the wine with a little water is rubricated: "It is customary to add a little water to the wine." "Representatives of the congregation" replaces "Deacons, Churchwardens, or other fit persons appointed for that purpose" in designating what persons shall bring the offerings to the minister.

The Hymn, Psalm, or Anthem (pp. 333 and 361)

Soon after Constantine legalized Christianity, when congregations had grown and moved into larger buildings, it became customary for

348

a hymn or psalm to be sung at the presentation of the gifts of bread and wine, or when they were brought from the sacristy, where they had been presented, to the table for the eucharistic prayer. The most frequently used offertory hymn in the Eastern liturgies, familiar in English translation as "Let all mortal flesh keep silence," rapidly spread to the West and was used in Gallican rites. In the Roman rite, at the offertory procession, a psalm was sung by a cantor or by a choir or antiphonal choirs, with the congregation participating in an antiphon, in a form similar to that of the entrance procession and the procession at the time of communion. When the people had made their offerings, the cantor sang the Gloria Patri, which provided the climax for the psalm. As the communions of the people declined in the medieval period, this psalm was reduced to the antiphon and one or two verses of the psalm. The 1549 Prayer Book eliminated such use of psalm segments, providing instead twenty scriptural sentences, most of them dealing with alms for the poor. The clerks were to sing as many of these as was necessary during the presentation of alms by the people; if there were no clerks to sing, the priest was to initiate the offering by reading one of the sentences. From 1662 until the 1928 American revision a rubric directed that the minister read the offertory sentences during the entire time the offering was being received. The 1892 revision permitted the singing of a hymn or anthem as the money offerings were presented. Revisers of the 1928 Book permitted the singing of a hymn or anthem "when the Alms and Oblations are being received and presented." The present Book extends the permission to include a "hymn, psalm, or anthem."

The Thanksgiving over the Bread and Wine (pp. 333–336, 340–343, 361–363, and 367–375)

The Jewish blessings over the bread and wine, the two items with particular religious significance, were blessings of God, expressions of thanksgiving, naming the Name of God. "Blessed be God, King of the universe, who brings forth bread from the earth" was the thanks over the bread. In the primary blessing over the cup, God was blessed as creator, sustainer, and redeemer, in the context of the particular celebration. The acts of God were recalled and prayer was offered for Israel, usually with petitions having eschatological significance. The prayers ended with another expression of praise. The blessing was an expression and reaffirmation of the creed of the community, and declared the heritage and hopes of the Jewish people.

Early Jewish Christians probably continued to use familiar Jewish

349

prayers at their sacred meals. The oldest of the common, fixed elements of the prayer come from Jewish liturgical tradition: the bidding to stand, "Lift up your hearts," with its response, followed by the celebrant's request for permission to pray in their name, "Let us give thanks to the Lord our God," and their assent "It is right to do so," is typical of the dialogue which introduced the Jewish *berakoth* (form of blessing). The acclamation "Amen" (so be it) at the end was also retained from Jewish tradition.

For the first several centuries the texts of eucharistic prayers were not fixed. We have prayers, or fragments of prayers, from the second and third centuries; the different forms show different emphases. God is blessed or thanked, the communicants are prayed for, the name of God is spoken over the elements, or the Spirit is invoked. Some of these prayers resemble Jewish blessings; others are more like the prayers associated with mystery religions. A prayer from the second century Acts of John 109 is still used in the Ethiopian Anaphora of Saint John the Evangelist; another from the third century Acts of Thomas 49–50 is incorporated in a eucharistic prayer found in an Irish palimpsest[1] dated to the seventh century. The prayer of Addai and Mari in an amplified form is still used in the East. The prayer which was to have greatest influence on later eucharistic prayers is associated with the ordination of bishops in the Apostolic Tradition of Hippolytus (c. 215 at Rome). The opening dialogue is followed by a giving of thanks for creation, incarnation, and redemption. This leads into a recital of the institution narrative and an anamnesis (a recalling of the death and resurrection of Christ) followed by the offering of the bread and the cup. The Holy Spirit is then invoked (epiclesis) and prayer offered that the communicants may be gathered into one and may be filled with the Spirit. The prayer ends with an expression of praise addressed to God, through Christ, with the Holy Spirit. This text is a reconstruction. The inclusion of the institution narrative is unique in a prayer dated earlier than the middle of the fourth century, and there are problems in deciphering the text of the epiclesis.

Both the social changes and the theological developments of the fourth century encouraged greater formalism, more theological clarity within the rites, and a fixity of texts. Christianity had become the accepted religion with increasingly large congregations and church buildings. The eucharistic prayers in the East developed along a

---

[1] A manuscript in which the original text has been covered and a second written over it.

Trinitarian pattern similar to that of the creeds. Like the creed in baptism, the eucharistic prayer in the rite was an affirmation of faith. God the Father was blessed for creation and redemption, the redemptive work of Christ was recalled, and the benefits of the Spirit were invoked. The prayer ended with a Trinitarian doxology. The congregation participated in the prayer through the responses in the opening dialogue, shared in singing the Sanctus, which became a normal part of the prayer in the fourth century, and joined in the Benedictus qui venit which was eventually added. In many prayers, after the institution narrative, the congregation shared in a memorial acclamation as well as in other acclamations, and they joined in the final Amen. The blessing of God contained a thanksgiving for creation, for not having forsaken humanity after its fall, for the incarnation, and for the death and resurrection of Jesus Christ. The thanksgiving for creation and incarnation provided a theological context for the command "do this for the *anamnesis* of me." The anamnesis recalled the death, resurrection, and ascension of our Lord, ending with an eschatological reference. The Spirit was invoked upon the elements and the communicants. Prayer was offered for the unity of the church and other benefits of communion, and intercessions were included within the prayer as early as the fourth century, as evidenced in the catechetical lectures of Cyril of Jerusalem. The Eastern rites had several fixed eucharistic prayers which varied to suit the day or occasion.

The Gallican ideal seems to have been a different prayer for each Sunday and holy day of the church year. Sursum corda or the initial dialogue led into a variable preface introducing the Sanctus and Benedictus qui venit. There followed a variable section (post Sanctus) which led into a fixed institution narrative, a brief anamnesis which included an eschatalogical reference, and another variable section ending with the people's Amen. The three variable sections stressed the reason for the commemoration of the particular day, largely by praise and thanksgiving. Explicit notes of oblation, epiclesis, and prayer for the communicants were not always present in the prayers for a particular day, though all of these did appear in the course of several celebrations. In many prayers, God was blessed for creation, incarnation, and redemption; in all prayers the redemptive work of Christ was recalled with an eschatological reference; in many the Spirit was invoked.

The Roman rite developed a fixed eucharistic prayer within which a proper preface was inserted for each occasion. On some special occasions there were also insertions after the Sanctus or near the end of the prayer. The oldest text we have is that quoted in *De Sacramentis* IV, which is generally attributed to Ambrose (339–397). The prayer is introduced by Sursum corda and a preface, which are not quoted. There is no hint of the use of a Sanctus in this writing nor any evidence to suggest that it had reached the West by Ambrose's time, though it did soon after. The portion quoted begins with a short petition that "this oblation, which is the figure of the body and blood of our Lord Jesus Christ," might be made "for us right, spiritual, and worthy." This leads into the institution narrative which is followed by an eschatological reference, an anamnesis, an oblation of "this holy bread and cup of eternal life," and a petition that this oblation might be accepted on God's "altar on high." The epiclesis of this prayer is not so explicit as those of the Eastern prayers, but the institution narrative, the eschatological reference, the anamnesis and oblation—by this time considered normal constituents of a eucharistic prayer in the East—are all present. The portion which precedes the central core probably included a partly variable expression of praise and thanksgiving; the core may have been followed by intercessions. A doxology is used later in the lecture which some have thought was the conclusion of the eucharistic prayer.

Eventually the proper prefaces were drastically curtailed in number and variety. The oldest sacramentary, the Leonine, contains a proper preface for every complete Mass; various Gelasian manuscripts contain between fifty and two hundred; the Gregorian contains about a dozen. This left the Roman prayer quite impoverished in elements of praise, thanksgiving, and the recital of salvation history compared to other rites. Petitions for the acceptance of offerings, for the church and clergy, for those who had offered the gifts, and for all present, were said in communion with the saints whose merits and prayers were invoked. These insertions are reminiscent of, or found among, the variable prayers during the presentation of gifts in other rites. The petition preceding the institution narrative, which is quoted above, was changed into a petition that this oblation "may become for us the body and blood of your dearly beloved Son, our Lord God, Jesus Christ," which is like the epiclesis of some Eastern rites, though lacking the explicit mention of the Spirit. The eschatological reference was struck from the end of the institution narrative. The anamnesis and oblation were expanded. At first occasionally, later regularly, there was an intercession for the departed, followed by a prayer that "we, your sinful servants" might be admitted into the company of the saints. Preceding the final doxology was another which some believe to represent a blessing for other gifts which, in the early days, were presented at the altar along with the bread and wine. Eventually the Benedictus qui venit, originally associated in some rites with the invitation to communion, was attached to the Sanctus on most occasions, as had also come to be true in the Eastern and Gallican rites.

At a period when few of the people other than educated professionals, and some of the nobility, understood the Latin of the Mass, the priest continued with the remainder of the eucharistic prayer as the choir completed the Sanctus. The elaborate music robbed the people of any opportunity to participate in the Sanctus. The portion of the prayer following the Sanctus came to be thought of as the eucharistic prayer; its title "the canon" was shifted by those who copied the manuscripts from its earlier place preceding the Sursum corda to immediately after the Sanctus (and Benedictus qui venit). In the West attention centered more and more on the institution narrative, the "moment of consecration" as people came to think of it. The prayer became the "action" of the priest alone and the people ceased to think of it as the great thanksgiving for the mighty acts of God, the recalling of the redemptive work of Christ, and the invoking of the benefits of the Spirit, with definite parts assigned to them. A late medieval document defined the part of the people as to "see God made and eaten." Changes in texts and ceremonials, decline of communions, and the changes in eucharistic piety late in the middle ages all were accompanied by a shift of emphasis from participating and receiving to the seeing and adoring of the consecrated elements.

Luther, sweeping away all that he considered later accretions to the Mass, eliminated the portion of the prayer that had been said inaudibly in the medieval Mass; as an heir of late medieval piety, however, he inserted the institution narrative in that place occasionally occupied by the proper preface. Later German church orders rewrote the preface to include a recital of salvation history, possibly on the basis of some exposure to the most widely used of the Eastern liturgies, those of Saint Basil and of Saint John Chrysostom, which had recently become available in print. Zwingli's eucharistic prayer of 1523, the Scottish prayer of John Knox based upon Calvinistic sources, and many other prayers from the Reformed tradition recover a fuller recital of salvation history, with explicit mention of the creation and incarnation. Some also recover a more explicit epiclesis on the elements or on the people.

The 1549 eucharistic prayer begins, as did the Sarum prayer and many in the German church orders, with the salutation, the Sursum corda, the Roman common preface, and the Sanctus. Many of the

German church orders (perhaps following Luther's action) inserted the institution narrative or a fixed preface at the place in which a proper preface was frequently inserted in the medieval rites. Cranmer retained the principle of using a proper preface, but provided prefaces only for the five principal feasts: Christmas, Easter, Ascension, Pentecost, and Trinity Sunday. In the late medieval use the Sanctus was ordinarily followed by Benedictus qui venit; Cranmer retained both but translated the second Hosanna in the highest as "Glory to thee, O Lord in the highest." In contrast to the inaudible repetition of the remainder of the prayer, practiced during the past several centuries, the priest was to "say or sing, plainly and distinctly." At this point the priest or deacon bade the people to pray for "the whole state of Christ's Church." There are reasons to believe that Cranmer had composed the form with the traditional place for the prayers of the people in mind, as in the writings of the church fathers and in some of the German church orders familiar to him. Evidently a conservative element had prevailed, however, and this prayer followed immediately after the Sanctus as had the intercessions for the living in the Roman form. The intercessions for the departed which had come at the end of the Roman prayer were joined to those for the living.

After the intercessions is a new beginning which would have more logically followed the Benedictus qui venit:

O God, heavenly father, which of thy tender mercy didst give thine only son Jesu Christ to suffer death upon the cross for our redemption, who made there (by his one oblation once offered) a full, perfect, and sufficient sacrifice, oblation, and satisfaction, for the sins of the whole world, and did institute and in his holy Gospel command us, to celebrate a perpetual memory of that his precious death, until his coming again: Hear us (O merciful Father) we beseech thee; and with thy holy spirit and word, vouchsafe to bless [✝] and sanctify [✝] these thy gifts, and creatures of bread and wine, that they may be unto us the body and blood of thy most dearly beloved son Jesus Christ. Who in the same night that he was betrayed: took bread [*Here the priest must take the bread into his hands*], and when he had blessed, and given thanks, he brake it, and gave it to his disciples, saying, Take, eat, this is my body which is given for you; do this in remembrance of me.

Likewise after supper he took the cup [*Here the priest shall take the Cup into his hands*], and when he had given thanks, he gave it to them, saying, Drink ye all of this, for this is my blood of the new Testament, which is shed for you and for many, for re-

354

mission of sins; do this as oft as you shall drink it, in remembrance of me. [*These words before rehearsed are to be said, turning still to the Altar, without any elevation, or showing the Sacrament to the people.*]

Wherefore, O Lord and heavenly Father, according to the institution of thy dearly beloved son, our saviour Jesu Christ, we thy humble servants do celebrate, and make here before thy divine majesty, with these thy holy gifts, the memorial which thy son hath willed us to make, having in remembrance his blessed passion, mighty resurrection, and glorious ascension, rendering unto thee most hearty thanks for the innumerable benefits procured unto us by the same, entirely desiring thy fatherly goodness, mercifully to accept this our sacrifice of praise and thanksgiving; most humbly beseeching thee to grant that by the merits and death of thy son Jesus Christ, and through faith in his blood, we and all thy whole church, may obtain remission of our sins, and all other benefits of his passion. And here we offer and present unto thee (O Lord) our self, our souls, and bodies, to be a reasonable, holy, and lively sacrifice unto thee; humbly beseeching thee, that whosoever shall be partakers of this holy Communion, may worthily receive the most precious body and blood of thy son Jesus Christ and be fulfilled with thy grace and heavenly benediction and made one body with thy son Jesus Christ, that he may dwell in them, and they in him. And although we be unworthy (through our manifold sins) to offer unto thee any sacrifice, yet we beseech thee to accept this our bounden duty and service, and command these our prayers and supplications, by the ministry of thy holy angels, to be brought up into thy holy tabernacle before the sight of thy divine majesty; not weighing our merits, but pardoning our offences, through Christ our Lord, by whom, and with whom, in the unity of the Holy Ghost, all honor and glory be unto thee, O Father Almighty, world without end. Amen.

This section begins with a recalling of the one sacrifice on the cross and the command "to celebrate a perpetual memory of that his precious death." The theological definition of this section has no precedent in eucharistic prayers, but depends on the *King's Book* and the *Antididagma,* the Cologne chapter's answer to Hermann's Consultation. It is followed by an epiclesis of an Eastern form:

Hear us, O merciful Father, we beseech thee; and with thy holy spirit and word, vouchsafe to bless [✝] and [✝] sanctify these thy gifts and creatures of bread and wine, that they may be unto us the body and blood of thy most dearly beloved Son Jesus Christ.

355

The last clause is a literal translation of that which preceded the institution narrative in the Roman rite. The calling upon the Holy Spirit, the use of the verbs "bless and sanctify" and the description of the elements as "gifts" are all in the Eastern liturgy of Saint Basil. There is some precedent in Eastern liturgies for an invocation of the incarnate Word, but by "word" Cranmer probably meant the recitation of the institution narrative. It is not capitalized in the 1549 Book but that tells us nothing since neither was "holy spirit." Cranmer's reading of the church fathers and of Eastern liturgies had probably caused him to feel the need for a fuller form of epiclesis with specific mention of the Holy Spirit rather than the clipped form of the Roman rite. "Word" indicates a continuation of the Western emphasis on the institution narrative.

A number of nonscriptural phrases had gradually been inserted in the Roman institution narrative. Some of the German church orders and the catechism of Justus Jonas which Cranmer had translated into English substituted a narrative which conflated the four biblical accounts (1 Cor. 11:23–26; Mt. 26:26–28; Mk. 14:22–24; and Lk. 22:19–20). The Mozarabic rite had done the same thing. Cranmer either used one of the existing forms or made the same sort of conflation. Rubrics in the margin directed that "the priest must take the bread into his hands" for the words over the bread, and "shall take the cup into his hands" for the words over the cup. In the middle ages, the growing custom of elevation at the institution narrative had concentrated attention on showing the people the Sacrament. The 1549 Book followed the institution narrative with the rubric: "These words before rehearsed are to be said, turning still to the Altar, without any elevation or showing the Sacrament to the people."

The lengthy final paragraph of the prayer includes portions from the Roman canon, the Liturgy of Saint Basil, Hermann's Consultation, the *Antididagma*, and a quotation from Romans 12:1. The anamnesis was amplified in a manner that took in phrases from the Consultation. The offering of the "perfect, holy, and spotless victim" and the prayer for the acceptance of the offering of the priest of the Roman prayer were not retained. The anamnesis was followed by a prayer that God might accept "our sacrifice of praise and thanksgiving" and our offering of "our self, our souls, and bodies." These petitions are dependent on the Consultation and the *Antididagma* and Romans 12:1. The petition that those who partake may be "fulfilled with thy grace and heavenly benediction" which follows is from the Roman form. The next petition, "that he may dwell in them, and they in him," is from the Consultation and also has affinities with the

Liturgy of Saint Basil. Cranmer then returned to the Roman prayer, "and command these our prayers and supplications, by the ministry of thy holy angels, to be brought up into thy holy tabernacle before the sight of thy divine majesty," substituting "prayers and supplications" for the word "offerings." The final phrase, "not weighing our merits, but pardoning our offenses," and the doxology, omitting the phrase "in whom," also came from the Roman prayer. Despite his use of Eastern and Mozarabic liturgies in this Book, Cranmer did not include, as some other reformers did, the proclamation of salvation history with explicit references to the creation and the incarnation, an eschatological reference, or an epiclesis upon the people. In keeping with the Lutheran tradition he systematically excised all references to an oblation of the elements.

The 1552 revisers dealt harshly with this prayer, omitting the salutation before the Sursum corda, abbreviating the Benedictus qui venit to one phrase "Glory be to thee, O Lord most high," substituting the word "continue" for "celebrate" in the section after the Sanctus. They substituted a prayer for worthy reception in place of the 1549 epiclesis:

> Hear us, O merciful Father, we beseech thee, and grant that we, receiving these thy creatures of bread and wine, according to thy Son our Savior Jesus Christ's holy institution, in remembrance of his death and passion, may be partakers of his most blessed body and blood.

The duplication which Cranmer had allowed to slip into the institution narrative, "blessed and," was removed, and the instructions for the priest to take the bread and cup into his hands deleted. Perhaps the rubric concerning elevations had been ignored by some priests; perhaps the eucharistic piety of the people had continued to center on the recital of the institution narrative and adoration of the elements rather than on the receiving of communion. Whatever the reason, in 1552 the ministration of the elements was moved to precisely this point in the rite. Following the ministration to the people, the prayer continued, beginning with the petition to "accept this our sacrifice of praise and thanksgiving." All that remained of the anamnesis was the phrase which had been incorporated into the petition preceding the institution narrative, "in remembrance of his death and passion." There was no recalling of any other mighty acts of redemption.

Reservation for the sick was eliminated by the 1552 revision, reflected by the change of "whosoever shall be partakers" to "all we which be partakers." The petition that the communicants may be "made one body with thy Son Jesus Christ, that he may dwell in them, and they in him" was deleted. The second half of this petition, however, was a duplication of a phrase in the prayer that later came to be called "the prayer of humble access." That phrase was given more prominence in the 1552 revision by being shifted to the very end of that prayer. The revision also deleted the petition that their prayers would be brought up by the angels "into thy holy tabernacle before the sight of thy divine majesty." Further, the postcommunion prayer was made an alternative to this conclusion of the eucharistic prayer.

No changes were made in the prayer either in 1559 or 1604. In the meantime, however, some Anglicans had come to have high regard for Eastern liturgies, especially for the Apostolic Constitutions, available in print for the first time in 1563, and for the 1549 eucharistic prayer. The Scottish revision of 1637 reworked the prayer, including an epiclesis in it, as had prior Scottish liturgies; the 1637 prayer overall is based on 1549. It retained the Sursum corda, preface and Sanctus from 1552, following them immediately with the "prayer of consecration," a term used here for the first time in a Book of Common Prayer. Unfortunately it was placed after the Sanctus, as had been the title "the Canon" in late medieval books, rather than before the Sursum corda. The portion which followed the Sanctus is the 1552 revision of the 1549 form with one addition in the phrase "memory of that his precious death *and sacrifice*." The petition for worthy reception, included in English Books from 1552, is modified by an epiclesis like that of the 1549 Book:

> Hear us, O merciful Father, we most humbly beseech thee, and of thy almighty goodness vouchsafe so to bless and sanctify with thy word and Holy Spirit these thy gifts and creatures of bread and wine, that they may be unto us the body and blood of thy most dearly beloved Son; so that we, receiving them according to thy Son our Saviour Jesus Christ's holy institution, in remembrance of his death and passion, may be partakers of his most precious body and blood.

The institution narrative is the 1552 revision, but with the manual acts restored from 1549. It is to be followed immediately by the paragraph which had come at this point in 1549 except for the removal of the petition that the prayers may be brought by the angels to the tabernacle on high. The administration of the Sacrament is separated from the prayer by the Lord's Prayer and the "Collect of humble access to the Holy Communion."

Prior to the 1662 revision both Laudians and Puritans wanted the restoration of an epiclesis and the breaking of bread. In the 1662 revision the only changes in the prayer, however, were these: the addition of two words, "most humbly," from the Scottish Book, in the petition; the use of the title "prayer of consecration" in the rubric; manual acts which included a direction to break the bread at the words "he brake it;" and the addition of an Amen after the narrative. Changes in rubrics and addition of the Amen were significant, although the textual changes themselves were minimal.

Beginning in 1722, Scottish Non-juring Episcopalians published a series of "Wee Bookies," editions of the rite of 1637 with some modifications. The rite of the English Non-jurors and the reconstruction of the ancient Liturgy of St. James by Thomas Rattray, a Scottish bishop, were the most important influences on these revisions. In 1735 the eucharistic prayer was modified by the insertion of a phrase "which we now offer thee" as an oblation; in 1755 the epiclesis was shifted from its place prior to the institution narrative to a position after the anamnesis. In 1764 the changed reading of the initial line, "All glory be to thee, Almighty God," linked the prayer to the Sanctus. The epiclesis was drastically shortened; the words "that they may become the body and blood" replaced "that they may be unto us the body and blood," and the remainder of the petition omitted. In America some Scottish clergy used one or another of the Wee Bookies, at least for the eucharistic prayer, after they no longer felt bound to the 1662 Book. When the Proposed Book of 1786 came off the press, even before any copies were bound, the sheets were sent to the Maryland state convention which had two powerful Scots members, both named William Smith. The convention proposed to insert into the eucharistic prayer an excerpt from the epiclesis of the Scottish prayer of 1637 and of the Wee Bookies before the 1764 revision. The proposal, sent to Pennsylvania, was adopted there and then sent on to Boston, where Samuel Parker, most prominent of the area clergy, expressed his desire that the whole of the Scottish eucharistic prayer be adopted.

What was Samuel Seabury's role in the whole procedure? Recently available manuscripts indicate that his activities should be reevaluated. A year and a half before the convention of 1786, Seabury had signed a concordat with the Scottish bishops who ordained him, agreeing to make an attempt to introduce the Scottish eucharistic rite into the American Book; he had not yet mentioned this in any of his proposals for eucharistic revision put forth to the Connecticut committee on revision nor in any extant letters to other Americans. After the state conventions of Maryland and Pennsylvania, and Samuel Parker of Boston, had committed themselves to revision of the eucharistic prayer along Scottish lines, Seabury presented a revised version of the Scottish liturgy to the Connecticut convocation. According to a contemporary account, the convocation "with *a noble spirit rejected*" the rite. Nothing daunted, Seabury copied his revision of the Scottish prayer, altering it slightly in the process, into a notebook which he took to the convention of 1789.

Prior to that convention the younger William Smith, who had been one of those using the Scottish prayer before 1786, wrote to a number of the delegates urging them, as a safeguard against the Romish error of transubstantiation, to adopt a eucharistic prayer based upon ancient models, a prime example being the Scottish prayer. The convention of 1789 adopted a prayer which included some of Seabury's proposals, based upon the Scottish prayer of 1764, for insertion in a eucharistic rite which was still essentially the English rite of 1662. At the epiclesis, however, it relied on the earlier Wee Bookies, as had the Maryland and Pennsylvania conventions. Omitted from the fuller form of the epiclesis were the words "that they may be unto us the body and blood of thy most dearly beloved Son." The prayer adopted at that convention, except for minor updating in 1892, is retained in this Book as Eucharistic Prayer I of Rite One. Seven other prayers, however, restore a number of traditional elements still lacking in this prayer, including fuller or more precise forms of the anamnesis and the epiclesis.

The Great Thanksgiving (pp. 333–336, 340–343, 361–363, and 367–375)

In ancient liturgies the eucharistic prayer, from the Sursum corda through the people's Amen, was considered a unit and given a single title in the manuscripts. The early title Eucharistia (thanksgiving) was soon replaced by others: in the East the word "anaphora" was common; in the West various Latin words designated "the prayer"—*oratio, prex, praedicatio,* and *praefatio* (from which we get the word "preface"). Another designation was "the action." The word "canon" for this prayer seems to come from a phrase in the ancient sacramentaries, "Incipit canon actionis." Later the word stood alone in this place. After the portion of the prayer following the Sanctus came to be said inaudibly, the word "canon" appeared in liturgical books after the Sanctus rather than before the Sursum corda. The word *praefatio*, which had designated a public prayer in pre-Christian times, and which appeared before the introductory portion of the eucharistic prayer, came to signify that portion only rather than the whole of the prayer. The first Prayer Books gave no title to the eucharistic prayer (though a rubric in the 1549 form for the Communion of the Sick referred to it as "the Canon"), but the Scottish Book of 1637 included a title "Prayer of Consecration" in the rubric which, unfortunately, came after the Sanctus rather than before the Sursum corda. The 1662 revision picked this up and American Books perpetuated it. The present revision has dropped both the division and the title, restoring the most ancient title for the prayer, "The Great Thanksgiving" (Eucharistia megale). The individual prayers are termed "Eucharistic Prayer." The title, as in the ancient liturgies, is now at the beginning of the prayer, which once again is a unit from the Sursum corda through the people's Amen.

Elements Common to the Eucharistic Prayers of Rite One and Rite Two

The Opening Dialogue

As early as the Apostolic Tradition of Hippolytus the opening dialogue of the eucharistic prayer was introduced by a salutation which called the people together for the liturgy of the word, based on Ruth 2:4, or by the Grace (2 Cor. 13:14). The practice spread and appears in all later medieval missals. The 1549 Book retained the salutation, but the 1552 revision dropped it. Although it was restored at the blessing of the font in the baptismal rite in 1928, this is the first revision to restore the salutation before the Sursum corda in the Eucharist. The dialogue following echoes Jewish forms of blessing. "Lift up your hearts" was a command to stand, the normal posture for prayers of thanksgiving, a posture which fosters and signifies the participation of the congregation in the action, the appropriate posture for public prayer shared by those who had been raised in baptism. "Let us give thanks" was the celebrant's request for permission to offer thanks in the name of those present. The response was their consent. The Sursum corda and the people's Amen at the close of the eucharistic prayer are elements which seem common to all prayers, as far back as the time when many eucharistic prayers were extemporaneous. The translation of the opening dialogue in Rite Two is by ICET.

Praise and Thanksgiving (pp. 333–334, 340–341, 361–363, 367–368, 369–371, and 372–374)

The principal Jewish blessings, those said over the cup, continued into an expression of praise to God for His mighty acts of creation, the sustenance of His people, and redemption. As the eucharistic prayer developed fixed forms, a major portion of the prayer in the Eastern liturgies was devoted to a recital of salvation history, always including the acts of creation and incarnation to provide the theological basis for celebration of the sacrament. Ordinarily praise was also offered to God for not having forsaken His creatures after they had fallen into sin, and for the death of our Lord upon the cross. In contrast to the Eastern prayers with the proclamation of the major acts of salvation history, the Western prayers contained variable portions which often centered upon the particular commemoration of the day. When the Roman rite curtailed the use of proper prefaces, there were few occasions on which there was specific reference to salvation history until the institution narrative. In this respect the eucharistic prayers of the early Prayer Books improved on the Roman rite. The death on the cross was proclaimed; after the 1789 revision it was prefaced by an acclamation of praise. Both prayers in Rite One and Prayers A and B of Rite Two continue the Roman tradition of a common preface into which proper prefaces are inserted. In place of the eight prefaces with limited use provided by the 1928 Book, the present revision gives prefaces for every Sunday, for major seasons of the church year, for saints' days, and for certain other occasions. (For commentary on the prefaces, see below, pp. 397–404.) The basic note of praise and thanksgiving has been given more prominence.

Though the 1928 Prayer is retained in the body of Rite One, an alternate prayer is provided which, following the Sanctus, restores the elements basic to sacramental theology—thanksgiving for creation and incarnation. All four prayers of Rite Two embody these elements. Prayer A recalls the fall and the human condition. Prayer B gives thanks for God's goodness in the calling of Israel and in the message of the prophets, emphasizing also the incarnational theme of the Eucharist. Prayer C recalls the fall and offers thanks to God for his repeated calls to return to Him and for His revelation of the law through prophets and sages. Prayer D incorporates all of these notes. Prayers C and D, rather than providing for insertion of a proper preface, follow the Eastern model of the fixed recital of salvation history. At least as far back as the fourth century the Sanctus was the climax of this expression of praise and proclamation, or has been inserted in it.

362

The Sanctus (pp. 334, 341, 361, 367, 371, and 373)

In the praise of God the congregation shares the song of the angels and the whole company of heaven. The Sanctus is the song of the seraphim in Isaiah's account of his vision of the Lord "in the year that King Uzziah died" (Is. 6:1–3; *cf.* Rev. 4:8). The Jewish synagogue liturgy used the Sanctus, and it became an acclamation of the people at least as early as the fourth century. Historically this is a song of the people (rather than of the choir) as is made clear by the older musical settings, which are continuations of the music of the preface. In the Mozarabic rite some highly complicated settings of the preface led into much simpler settings of the Sanctus. Only with the separation of the preface and Sanctus from the "canon" in the middle ages was the function of the Sanctus as a people's acclamation obscured or lost. The 1549 Book directed it to be sung by the clerks with the priest. In the 1552 Book the Sanctus was still set apart as a separate paragraph and it was thought of as a song of the people. The 1789 Book directed the people to join with the priest at the words "Therefore with Angels and Archangels," a common practice in that period, but the 1892 revision restored the original custom. The simplicity of the musical settings composed for this text, which included that introduction, indicates the understanding in Anglicanism that the Sanctus is for the people to share, not for elaborate settings that only a skilled choir might sing. When elaborate settings were used it was often between the Litany and the Eucharist. The practice of accompanying the Sanctus with bells dates from the fifteenth century. The translation in Rite Two is by ICET.

Benedictus qui venit (pp. 334, 341, 361, 367, 371, and 373)

The Apostolic Constitutions (c. 380) is the first liturgical work to contain this text associated with our Lord's entry into Jerusalem (Mt. 21:9). In that rite it is part of the invitation to communion. Its use as an expansion of the Sanctus seems to have originated in Gaul, spread to Rome, and then to most of the Eastern liturgies. The Coptic rite is an exception. Late in the middle ages the Sanctus was sometimes sung while the celebrant said inaudibly the portion of the prayer before the institution narrative; the Benedictus qui venit followed.

Luther retained this chant in his Latin Mass and Cranmer included it in the 1549 Book, translating the second "Hosanna in the highest" as "Glory to thee, O Lord in the highest." In the 1552 revision only the revised version of that line remained, "Glory be to thee, O Lord, most high." The present revision provides the remainder of the Benedictus qui venit as an option in Rite One and includes it in all the eucharistic prayers of Rite Two, using the ICET translation. Traditionally the Benedictus qui venit, like the Sanctus, is an acclamation of the people. Because of its optional character in Rite One, it is printed in a form which allows it to be used as versicle and response.

Except in Prayer C of Rite Two the Benedictus qui venit is followed by a rubric which permits the people to stand or kneel for the remainder of the eucharistic prayer. Standing was the universal posture for this prayer until late in the middle ages and continues to be the posture in the Eastern churches. The council of Nicea forbade kneeling for prayer on Sundays or during the Great Fifty Days of Easter, days when the Eucharist would be celebrated. Late in the middle ages, when the focus of the congregation had changed from participation in the Great Thanksgiving and receiving of communion to being present for adoration at the "moment of consecration," we find evidence that some people had begun to kneel for the elevations which had been introduced into the rite at the institution narrative.

The 1549 Book assumed standing to be the posture for this prayer; Prayer Books have traditionally embodied the principle that people stand for prayer unless expressly bidden to kneel, as at the prayers of confession and petition. Some older Anglican manuals direct the people, if they are kneeling, to stand when addressed by the priest, and specifically to assume a standing posture after the absolution when the priest says "Hear what comfortable words." Clearly this meant that they stood for the eucharistic prayer which followed immediately. Standing for this prayer symbolizes our new life in Christ and the congregation's participation in the prayer offered in their name.

The institution narrative is preceded by a direction to hold [or lay a hand upon] the bread and [upon] the cup, and any other vessel containing wine to be consecrated as the pertinent words are said. The 1549 Book included such rubrics which were deleted in 1552 but restored in 1662 with an additional direction to break the bread at the words "he brake it." The fraction has been restored to its traditional place in the present Book, after the prayer, and the direction for breaking the bread in the course of the institution narrative is deleted. The rubric speaks of "the cup" and of "any other vessel containing wine to be consecrated." This accords with the additional direction (p. 407): only one cup should be on the altar at the Great Thanksgiving as a sign of our sharing the cup; additional wine should be consecrated in a flagon, cruet, or bottle from which the wine may be poured into additional chalices after the breaking of the bread. In keeping with the spirit of this rubric the bread also should be on one paten or plate, symbolizing the sharing of one loaf. Any additional patens or plates needed for ministration of the Sacrament should be brought to the altar at the breaking of the bread.

The Institution Narrative (pp. 334–335, 342, 362–363, 368, 371, and 374)

With the possible exception of the prayer in the Apostolic Tradition of Hippolytus, eucharistic prayers surviving from the pre-Nicene period do not contain the institution narrative. After the last part of the fourth century, however, this became a regular component of the eucharistic prayer. In most of the Eastern liturgies and most of the Gallican, it linked the thanksgiving for and the proclamation of the mighty acts of God with an anamnesis of the Lord's redemptive work. In Egyptian and Roman rites the intercessions and epiclesis upon the elements came between the expression of thanksgiving and the institution narrative. Late in the middle ages attention in the Western church centered more and more on this portion of the prayer, the recitation of which came to be considered "the moment of consecration," rather than the warrant for doing what is done in the whole sacramental action.

The earliest texts, those of Hippolytus and Serapion, are simple accounts from the Scriptures. Later texts embellish the accounts of the institution to varying extents, but the Mozarabic text conflated the New Testament accounts without non-scriptural additions, a course also taken by the continental reformers in many cases. For the 1549 Book Cranmer either used one of the conflations already existing or made one of his own. The 1552 revision dropped "blessed" since it was synonymous with the other part of the phrase "given thanks." This 1552 version is the text maintained in the present Rite One except for the initial phrase ("who in the same night that he was betrayed") which was changed in 1789 to read "for in the night in which he was betrayed." In Prayer II, "to thee" is added after "given thanks," and "broke" replaces "brake," "Drink this, all of you" replaces "Drink ye all of this," and "New Covenant" is substituted for "New Testament." The institution narratives in Rite Two are also conflations of the scriptural sources.

The Memorial Acclamation (pp. 363, 368, 371, and 375)

In many Eastern liturgies the people were more active participants than in the Western liturgies in which their participation was limited to the opening dialogue, the Sanctus, and the final Amen. The Book of Common Worship of the Church of South India included in its eucharistic prayers the two acclamations most frequently used in the Eastern liturgies; the use of one or more acclamations has been introduced into many recent Western liturgical revisions, including the modern Roman rite. An acclamation of the people is most frequently found after the institution narrative and after the anamnesis and oblation. In Eastern rites the praise of the Father reached its climax in the institution narrative which often ended with a quotation of 1 Corinthians 11:26, frequently in an amplified form which included a memorial of the resurrection like the non-Roman eucharistic prayers of the West. This often introduced an acclamation of the people which stemmed from the content of the conclusion of the narrative and anticipated the anamnesis which followed. The memorial acclamation of Prayer B of Rite Two is the one most frequently found at this place in Eastern liturgies, "We remember his death, we proclaim his resurrection, we await his coming in glory." In Prayer A the acclamation, clearly based on the same text, becomes also a proclamation.[1] The people's first response after the institution narrative in Prayer C, "We celebrate his death and resurrection, as we await the day of his coming," is also based on this text.

In Prayer A, as in most of the Eastern forms, the memorial acclamation anticipates the anamnesis said by the priest immediately after. In Prayer B, as in some Ethiopian liturgies, the acclamation itself is the anamnesis of the prayer; this is also true, to an extent, in Prayer C. The acclamation in Prayer D, "We praise you, we bless you, we give thanks to you, and we pray to you, Lord our God," is found in almost all rites which contain the memorial acclamation and in some which do not, where it follows the anamnesis and oblation and precedes the invocation. This acclamation comes at the climax when we turn from thanksgiving for the mighty acts of God and the anamnesis of the work of Christ, which has culminated in the offering of the bread and the cup, to prayer for the benefits of the Holy Spirit.

The Anamnesis (pp. 335, 342, 363, 368, 371, and 374)

The concept of anamnesis is basic to Jewish-Christian tradition. Anamnesis is the antithesis of amnesia. A person with amnesia has lost identity and purpose. To know who you are, to whom you belong, and where you are headed, you must remember. A Jew was one who through anamnesis had crossed the Red Sea and entered the prom-

---

[1] This is one of two translations of the traditional form by the Roman Catholic International Consultation on English in the Liturgy (ICEL).

ised land. The heritage and hopes of the Jewish people were the individual's heritage and hopes. An anamnesis of the mighty acts of God was basic to Jewish blessings which reminded God of what He had done in the past, in this way also asking Him to continue to act as He had acted in the past.

A Christian is one for whom, through anamnesis, the death and resurrection of Jesus Christ is a present reality, and one who has already entered the kingdom though it is not yet realized in its fullness. Anamnesis was an important part of many early eucharistic prayers and had become a normal component by the end of the fourth century. The offering of praise to the Father flowed into a remembrance of the redemptive work of the Son. Two basic components of the anamnesis were the death and resurrection, but the ascension and second coming were usually included as well. When the second coming was not included in the anamnesis, the institution narrative often ended with an eschatological reference.

The medieval Roman canon lacked both eschatological reference and anamnesis of the second coming, as did the 1549 Prayer Book which contained anamnesis of death, resurrection, and ascension, but not of the second coming. The only remnant of anamnesis in the 1552 revision was the phrase "in remembrance of his death and passion" which was moved into the petition for worthy reception before the institution narrative. When the 1789 Prayer Book accepted a eucharistic prayer based on the text of the Scottish prayer, the 1549 anamnesis was restored. In the present Book in the anamnesis itself or in the memorial acclamation, a congregational acclamation closely related to the anamnesis, the recalling of the second coming has been recovered in all of the prayers except Prayer I of Rite One, the prayer from the 1928 Book.

The Oblation (pp. 335, 342, 363, 369, 371, and 374)

In the Apostolic Tradition the anamnesis immediately precedes an offering or oblation: "remembering his death and resurrection, we offer you the bread and the cup." Church fathers of the time, Irenaeus for example, spoke of the Eucharist as an offering or sacrifice. Early manuscripts of fixed eucharistic prayers included an oblation, though not on every occasion in the Gallican liturgies. In Eastern rites the oblation usually came at the end of the offering of praise to the Father and the anamnesis of the redeeming work of the Son. The oblation of the prayer in the Liturgy of Saint Basil (Prayer D in Rite Two) is typical: "We offer you, from the gifts you have given us, this bread and this cup." The offering in some Eastern and Galli-

367

can prayers and in the prayer of the Roman rite, in use throughout almost all of the West at the end of the medieval period, was an offering of a "sacrifice" or a "victim." It is easy, therefore, to see how, after the institution narrative had come to be considered the consecratory formula in the West, the Mass was envisioned in popular piety as a repetition of Calvary and a propitiatory sacrifice. Petitions for the acceptance of the sacrificial oblation appeared in the prayer both before and after that at the climax of the anamnesis, and the note of oblation was stressed in the variable offertory prayers.

All of the reformers rejected the popular concept of the Mass as a repetition of Calvary; by way of contrast, the Roman council of Trent clearly defined the "sacrifice of the Mass." In reaction to the popular concept, Luther deleted from the rite all offertory prayers and everything that followed the Sanctus-Benedictus qui venit of the eucharistic prayer. The 1549 Book omits the oblation, and the word "sacrifice" is always qualified. We ask God "mercifully to accept this our sacrifice of praise and thanksgiving." We present ourselves as a "reasonable, holy, and lively sacrifice." "And although we be unworthy . . . to offer unto thee any sacrifice, yet we beseech thee to accept this our bounden duty and service, . . . our prayers and supplications."

The 1552 revision moved the act of receiving communion to a place immediately after the institution narrative in an effort to make it the climax of the rite, replacing a piety based on adoration of the elevated Sacrament with a piety based on the receiving of the Sacrament. An additional motive for that change was to separate all references to sacrifice from references to the eucharistic elements. This section of the prayer was made an alternative to the postcommunion prayer and came to be popularly designated as the "self-oblation."

The Scottish Book of 1637 and the early "Wee Bookies" did not restore the historic oblation to the anamnesis, but they did restore an anamnesis and print the self-oblation of the prayer immediately after it, prior to the ministration of the Sacrament. Some English Non-jurors considered the lack of an oblation a serious deficiency; their liturgy of 1718 contained the oblation from the Apostolic Constitutions, "we Offer to Thee, our King and our God, according to his holy Institution, this Bread and this Cup." The influence of the English Non-jurors may have caused the phrase "which we now offer unto thee" to be inserted in the Wee Bookie of 1735. The American Book of 1789 retained the phrase in the revised form of the Scottish prayer which it adopted. These words were printed in capital letters in several early printings of the American Prayer Book.

Each of the prayers of Rites One and Two contains an oblation. The oblation of Prayer II in Rite One is the same as that of Prayer I, from the 1928 Book. In the prayers of Rite Two, the oblation is placed in the traditional relationship to the anamnesis, as the climax of the offering of praise to the Father and recalling the redeeming work of the Son (rather than in the inverted order of the prayers in Rite One). Prayer C of Rite Two also contains a phrase reminiscent of the offering of the gifts prior to the epicletic phrase in the traditional Roman eucharistic prayer.

The Epiclesis or Invocation (pp. 335, 342, 363, 369, 371, and 375)

One of the eucharistic prayers in the third century Acts of Thomas (49–50) calls upon the Spirit under various images, seeking its presence. The eucharistic prayer in the Apostolic Tradition (c. 215) contains an epiclesis of problematical reconstruction. It is generally represented to contain an invocation of the Spirit upon the oblations and a petition that the communicants may be filled with the Spirit. From the late fourth century, prayers in the Eastern liturgies usually contained an invocation of the Spirit upon the people and the gifts. The epiclesis in the oldest manuscript of the Liturgy of Saint Basil is a petition that "through the benevolence of your goodness your Holy Spirit may descend upon us and upon these gifts placed here and sanctify them to be the holy of holies." In most of the Eastern prayers the epiclesis upon the gifts was a prayer that they might be "made" or "shown to be" the Body and Blood of Christ. In many liturgies, following the anamnesis and oblation, the transition to the epiclesis was marked by an acclamation of the people, "We praise you, we bless you, we give thanks to you, and we pray to you, Lord our God" (see p. 375).

As the institution narrative came to be thought of as the "moment of consecration" in the West, some Eastern groups began to think of the epiclesis upon the elements in that sense. Coptic prayers contained a preliminary epiclesis just before the institution narrative. A notable variation was the eucharistic prayer of Serapion in which there was an epiclesis of the Word rather than of the Spirit. The variable portion of the Gallican prayer included a number of supplications for the descent of the Spirit upon the gifts. The Roman rite had no explicit epiclesis; in the place occupied by the preliminary epiclesis of the Coptic rite, before the institution narrative, was a prayer that God might bless this oblation "that it may be unto us the body and blood of your dearly beloved Son Jesus Christ." Cranmer retained that clause immediately before the institution narrative in

369

1549 but prefaced it with an invocation derived from the Liturgy of Saint Basil, "Hear us, O merciful Father, we beseech thee; and with thy holy spirit and word, vouchsafe to bless and sanctify these thy gifts and creatures of bread and wine." "Word" surely meant the institution narrative. He had combined in this epiclesis both the Eastern and Western emphases.

In 1552 a prayer for worthy reception replaced the epiclesis:

> Hear us, O merciful Father, we beseech thee, and grant that we, receiving these thy creatures of bread and wine, according to thy Son our saviour Jesus Christ's holy institution, in remembrance of his death and passion, may be partakers of his most blessed body and blood.

Some of the continental and Scottish reformers restored the epiclesis in their rites.

Anglicans who became aware of the Eastern liturgies and of the Apostolic Constitutions felt a growing need for an epiclesis in the Prayer Book. The Scottish Book of 1637 modified the petition for worthy reception in a manner that suggested the epiclesis of 1549:

> Hear us, O merciful Father, we most humbly beseech thee, and of thy almighty goodness vouchsafe to bless and sanctify with thy word and Holy Spirit these thy gifts and creatures of bread and wine, that they may be unto us the body and blood of thy most dearly beloved Son; so that we, receiving them according to thy Son our Saviour Jesus Christ's holy institution, in remembrance of his death and passion, may be partakers of his most precious body and blood.

The Westminster Directory which had guided public worship during the interregnum when the Prayer Book was forbidden, the Savoy liturgy proposed by the Puritans as an alternative to the Prayer Book (at the time of Charles' restoration), and the proposed revision of the eucharistic prayer by Sancroft all contained an epiclesis. But the 1662 revisers would not include it. Scottish Non-juring Episcopalians, beginning in 1722, republished the eucharistic rite of the 1637 Book. The 1764 revision of the Wee Bookies drastically abbreviated the epiclesis, and replaced "that they may be unto us the body and blood" with "that they may become the body and blood."

The American Book of 1789 inserted an abbreviated form from the Wee Bookies which preceded the 1764 printing, a form which omitted "that they may be unto us the body and blood of thy most dearly

370

beloved Son." "Word" was capitalized in the first Standard Book (1793), thereby appearing to refer to the incarnate Word rather than to our Lord's promise in the institution as the lower case "word" had done. Only Serapion's prayer includes an epiclesis of the incarnate Word, and it had not been discovered in 1793. The form adopted in 1789, with the capitalization of 1793, is the one included in Prayer I of Rite One in this Book. In Prayer II the result clause is changed from that which is capable of a receptionist interpretation to conform with that of the 1549 Book and the Scottish Wee Bookies which preceded 1764. In the prayers in Rite Two there are variations upon this: "to be for your people" (A); "that they may be the Sacrament of" (B); "to be" (C); and "showing them to be" (D). Prayers A, B, and D have also recovered the epiclesis on the people. The Eastern position for the epiclesis, adopted in the Scottish Wee Bookie of 1755, is maintained in all of the prayers except C, where it occupies the position of the preliminary epiclesis in the Coptic prayers and in those of the Roman Church.

The Supplications (pp. 335–336, 342–343, 363, 369, 372, and 375)

Supplications for various benefits of the Spirit have stemmed from the epiclesis since very early times. In the Apostolic Tradition of Hippolytus, in close conjunction with the epiclesis, is a petition that those who communicate may be gathered into one and that their faith may be confirmed. Prayer for the unity of the church has been a regular part of the supplications. In the description of the eucharistic rite of the fourth century, the catechetical lectures attributed to Cyril of Jerusalem note that there follows after the epiclesis a prayer for the church, then "for all who need help," and "then we make mention also of those who have fallen asleep." Prayer made at this point was said to be especially effective for any who were the subject of supplication. The Coptic rite placed intercessions in the preface; the Roman rite inserted prayers for the living soon after the Sanctus, and intercessions for the dead, with prayer to be admitted to the company of saints, before the concluding doxology. The continental reformers excised all intercessions from the eucharistic prayer, reacting to the abuses linked to the custom of indulgences and Masses for the dead late in the middle ages.

The 1549 Prayer Book put the intercessions in a place analogous to that of intercessions for the living in the Roman rite, but 1552 moved them to a place before the eucharistic prayer. The 1549 Book followed the anamnesis with supplications for the acceptance of "our sacrifice of praise and thanksgiving," our offering of ourselves, and

371

our offering of "our bounden duty and service," as well as with petitions for forgiveness and worthy reception, for grace, and that we may be made one body with Christ. The 1552 revision separated these supplications from the initial portion of the eucharistic prayer by the ministration of communion. The Scottish Book of 1637, the Wee Bookies and the first American Book restored these supplications to the eucharistic prayer, prior to the ministration of the Sacrament. The supplications in Rite One (Prayer I) are a slightly revised form of the 1637 Scottish text. Those of Prayer II are an abbreviated form of the material. Prayer A of Rite Two includes supplications for worthy reception that we may serve God in "unity, constancy, and peace," and that we may be admitted with all the saints "into the joy of your eternal kingdom." Prayer B includes supplications that we may be united with Christ "in his sacrifice," that all things may be put in subjection "under your Christ," and that we may enter with all the saints "the everlasting heritage of your sons and daughters." In Prayer C we seek that our eyes may be opened to see God's hand at work in the world about us and that we may come to the Sacrament with right intentions, be made one body, and worthily serve the world in Christ's name. We pray for the unity, faith, and peace of the church in Prayer D, and that we may find "our inheritance with all the saints." In this prayer we also have the option of offering intercessions within the eucharistic prayer. These are not to substitute for the prayers of the people, but this prayer does provide opportunity for intercessions within the rite when the prayers of the people have been displaced or may be omitted (Ash Wednesday, Thanksgiving Day, the feast of the dedication of a church, baptism, confirmation, marriage, and burial).

The Doxology (pp. 336, 343, 363, 369, 372, and 375)
In the Apostolic Tradition of Hippolytus the eucharistic prayer concludes with a doxology, "through your Child Jesus Christ, through whom be glory and honor to you, with the Holy Spirit in the holy church, now and unto the ages of ages." As the text of the prayers became fixed, the Trinitarian doxology, which differed slightly from rite to rite, was the invariable conclusion of most eucharistic prayers. That of the Roman rite, "by whom and with whom and in whom, in the unity of the Holy Ghost, all honour and glory be unto thee, O Father almighty, world without end," was brought over by Cranmer into the 1549 Book, except that he omitted the phrase "in whom." The Cranmerian doxology has been retained in every revision; in the present Book the missing phrase is restored

in Prayer II and in Prayers A, B, and D of Rite Two. A different doxology is provided for Prayer C.

Apparently in some churches early in Christian history the bread and the cup were elevated at the close of the eucharistic prayer, the bread by the celebrant and the cup by the deacon. This may have symbolized the offering to God, or it may have been a non-verbal signal for the people to affirm their assent by "Amen."

The People's Amen (pp. 336, 343, 363, 369, 372, and 375)

The mid-second century description of the eucharistic rite in Justin Martyr's *Apology* stresses the Amen of the people: "Bread and wine and water are brought up, and the president offers prayers and thanksgivings to the best of his ability, and the people assent, saying the Amen." Even late in the middle ages, when most of the prayer was said silently, the priest raised his voice at the last words of the prayer so that the people might know when to respond Amen. The present Book prints the Amen in small capital letters, unlike any other "Amen" in the Book, to give emphasis to this assent and affirmation by the people.

Eucharistic Prayer I (Rite One: pp. 333–336)

For the background, history, and sources of this prayer, see the discussion above, in the material on the eucharistic prayer (pp. 353–360).

The adoption of this prayer, from the Scottish rite, for the first American Book represented a great enrichment in comparison to the prayer in the 1662 Book. As the prayer in the 1662 Book had not, this prayer included a clear verbal link from the Sanctus to the rest of the prayer, a fuller anamnesis in the traditional position after the institution narrative, an oblation, an epiclesis, supplications, and a doxology before the communion of the people.

Eucharistic Prayer II (Rite One: pp. 340–343)

This is a revised version of Prayer I, based on a draft by the Very Rev. Dr. Robert H. Greenfield. References in the thanksgiving to the creation and incarnation, and a reference to the second coming (in the anamnesis) have enriched this prayer, providing a theological basis for the understanding of the sacrament. The word "Covenant" replaces "Testament" in the institution narrative. The result clause "that they may be unto us the Body and Blood of thy dearly beloved Son Jesus Christ," part of both the 1549 Book and of the Scottish liturgies before 1764, has replaced the 1552 petition for worthy reception. The supplications are abbreviated with no loss of any essential concept. The petition for unity now includes the whole church, not just those communicating on this occasion. The "sacrifice of praise and thanksgiving" and the sacrifice of "our selves" have been linked with the word "whereby." "In whom," the phrase from the traditional doxology, has been restored. Some of these changes were proposed as early as *Prayer Book Studies IV* (1953), and many were included in *The Liturgy of the Lord's Supper* (1967). The prayer has been abbreviated but greatly enriched.

Eucharistic Prayer A (Rite Two: pp. 361–363)

This prayer, a shorter, modern adaptation of the prayers of previous American Books and of Prayer I of Rite One, was drafted by the Rev. Dr. H. Boone Porter. It opens with the traditional Sursum corda and a contemporary version of the common preface which was revised for the 1549 Book from the Roman common preface. The modern English version of the preface is the work of Capt. Howard E. Galley.

Throughout the principal seasons of the year, on special days, and on all Sundays, a proper preface is inserted in accord with the Gallican and pre-Gregorian tradition, when a proper preface was provided for almost every Mass. The preface leads into the Sanctus, followed by thanksgiving for the creation and incarnation, and a statement of the human condition ("fallen into sin"). In this it resembles the 1967 prayer in *The Liturgy of the Lord's Supper*.

"He stretched out his arms upon the cross" dates from the time of Hippolytus and has been included in various liturgies. To the early church fathers this concept was symbolic of the redemption of all peoples. The phrase "a perfect sacrifice for the whole world" succinctly states the emphasis of the post-Sanctus of earlier Books upon "the one oblation of himself once offered, a full, perfect, and sufficient sacrifice, oblation, and satisfaction for the sins of the whole world." The institution narrative, like that of earlier Books, conflates the New Testament accounts. The phrase "the mystery of faith" (the expression is drawn from 1 Tim. 3:9) has been used in eucharistic prayers at least since the seventh century. The memorial acclamation, which elucidates the phrase, is a translation by ICEL of the most frequently used of the Eastern memorial acclamations; another translation is given in Prayer B. "Sacrifice of praise and thanksgiving" has been in Anglican Prayer Books since 1549. The anamnesis moves in traditional style into the oblation of the gifts, and the epiclesis is based on that of 1549 and on Scottish liturgies before 1764. The concluding phrase, "the holy food and drink of new and unending life in him," the conclusion of the memorial acclamation, "Christ will come again," and the final petition, "at the last day bring us with all your saints into the joy of your eternal kingdom" add eschatological dimensions lacking in earlier Books. An epiclesis upon the people has been restored. The petition that "we may serve you in unity, constancy, and peace" gathers into a concise statement some of the lengthier petitions of self-oblation in earlier Books. "And in him" is restored to the doxology.

Eucharistic Prayer B (Rite Two: pp. 367–369)

Like Prayer A this begins with the traditional Sursum corda and common preface. In keeping with the Gallican and early Roman tradition the proper prefaces emphasize many aspects of salvation history. Following the Sanctus is a thanksgiving for God's goodness and love shown in creation, the calling of Israel, and the incarnation of our Lord. This section conflates two eucharistic prayers from Services for Trial Use (1970), one based on the eucharistic prayer of Hippolytus, the other drafted by the Rev. Frank T. Griswold III. The institution narrative is the same as that in Prayers A and D. The memorial acclamation is a literal translation of the Eastern memorial acclamation and, as in some Ethiopian eucharistic prayers, it constitutes an anamnesis. In presenting "this bread and this wine" we offer "our sacrifice of praise and thanksgiving," a phrase used in the self-oblation of Anglican liturgies since 1549. The epiclesis upon the gifts is explicit, that upon the people more subtle. We pray to be united to Christ in his sacrifice. The ending is eschatological, beseeching God to "put all things in subjection under your Christ" and to bring us with all the saints to the eternal heritage of God's sons and daughters. The name of a saint may be inserted if there is a commemoration.

Biblical allusions include 2 Thessalonians 2:13–14; Ephesians 1:9–11 and 21–23; Hebrews 11:16; Colossians 1:15–20; and Hebrews 5:9. The conclusion to the paragraph preceding the doxology was drafted by the Rev. Dr. H. Boone Porter. The traditional doxology with the inclusion of "in him" ends the prayer. Reference to the prophets, emphasis on the incarnation, and the eschatological emphasis at the conclusion make this prayer particularly suitable for use during Advent, Christmas, Epiphany, and on saints' days. The beginning and ending are the same as those of Prayer A; the same music may be used for both.

Eucharistic Prayer C (Rite Two: pp. 369–372)

This prayer is distinctive in many ways. Like some Eastern prayers it contains much congregational response. Also an Eastern characteristic is the fact that there is no provision for a proper preface, but the fixed preface recites a salvation history which covers many of the aspects treated in the various proper prefaces of Prayers A and B. There is special emphasis on the creation, more than in any of the other prayers, and reference to the fall with a penitential petition. The prayer reminds us of the Old Testament drama of God's continuing effort to draw His people back to Himself. The recital of salvation history reaches its climax in the proclamation of the incarnation and atonement. The people's variable responses are largely in words from the Scriptures.

The introduction to the Sanctus lists various categories of the company of heaven. In contrast to the other prayers in Rites One and Two, this prayer follows the Roman tradition of placing an oblation of the elements before the institution narrative. Like Coptic prayers, the traditional Roman prayer, the English Prayer Book forms, and the Scottish liturgies before 1755, Prayer C has its epiclesis immediately before the institution narrative. The oblation reminds us of our baptism and the epiclesis is more direct than that in the other prayers: "Sanctify them by your Holy Spirit to be the Body and Blood of Jesus Christ our Lord." The institution narrative uses words of scripture, but is a variant reading. As in Prayer B, the oblation of the gifts is in typical Anglican terminology: "a sacrifice of thanksgiving." The anamnesis and oblation are followed by another translation of the most frequently used of the memorial acclamations. "Celebrate" is from the 1549 Book.

The address which begins the supplications is from Genesis 26:7, Exodus 3:15–16, 1 Chronicles 12:17 and 29:18, Acts 3:13, 5:30, and 7:32, and 1 Peter 1:3. The first petition resembles the petition of the first of the occasional prayers (p. 814: "For Joy in God's Creation") and the collect for Wednesday in Easter Week and the third Sunday of Easter. The prayer petitions further for right dispositions as we approach the Lord's table, and concludes with a supplication for unity that we may worthily serve the world in Christ's name. The response recalls the story of our Lord's appearance at Emmaus (Lk. 24:30–35). The petition to accept these prayers and praises echoes that of the 1549 Book. Reference to Christ as our high priest reminds us of Hebrews 4:14 as well as the phrase about the church in the doxology of the Apostolic Tradition. The prayer was drafted by Capt. Howard E. Galley.

Eucharistic Prayer D (Rite Two: pp. 372–375)

The fourth prayer in Rite Two is adapted from the Liturgy of Saint Basil, generally dated to the time of Basil the Great (d. 379). It continues to be used on certain Sundays and feasts of special solemnity in the Greek and Slavic churches. An adaptation is also used among Coptic Christians, and an abbreviated and revised form of this lengthy prayer is one of the four eucharistic prayers of the Roman sacramentary of Paul VI. In its main substance the prayer, therefore, is authorized among more Christians than any other eucharistic prayer.

In 1974 a group of American Catholic, Anglican, and Protestant scholars gathered to draft a prayer which the major American denominations might approve. The committee studied the prayer of Saint Basil especially because of its widespread use, broad scope, ancient roots, and appeal for both Eastern and Western Christianity. Both the form in the Roman sacramentary and the earlier versions that inspired it were influential in developing an American form in a version which has also been authorized for use by the Inter-Lutheran Commission on Worship and by the Committee on Word and Table of the United Methodist Church. It is one of the prayers set forth by the committee on worship of the Consultation on Church Union (COCU).

The text of the prayer up to the institution narrative is a translation of the Latin original of the Roman sacramentary. The institution narrative is that of Prayers A and B. The anamnesis, oblation, and epiclesis are basically those of the earliest known manuscript of the prayer, with the addition of the phrase, "the bread of life and the cup of salvation, the Body and Blood of your Son Jesus Christ," from later manuscripts. The petition for the communicants is based on the Roman sacramentary Latin version; the petition for the church is from the earliest manuscript, and the bracketed intercessions are based on those of the Roman sacramentary. The final petition, that we may find our inheritance with the saints, contains phrases from the early manuscripts and from the old Roman prayer. The concluding expression of praise and the doxology are from the Latin version of the Roman sacramentary.

In this prayer we have a text of historic and ecumenical significance encompassing most of the themes found in the other eucharistic

377

prayers. In keeping with the Eastern tradition, there is no provision for use of a proper preface since the themes of various prefaces are stated in the fixed text of this prayer. Like Prayer B it allows the insertion of a saint's name if there is a commemoration. And like Eastern and Roman eucharistic prayers since the fourth century it provides for intercessions.

The Lord's Prayer (pp. 336 and 363–364)

About A.D. 400 the Lord's Prayer was included in the Eucharist as a devotion preparatory to receiving the Sacrament after the breaking of the bread. There seem to be some indications that the Lord's Prayer had been used long before this as a preparatory devotion by the people in their houses on weekdays before they consumed the eucharistic elements they had brought home from the Sunday celebration. Early church fathers identify the "daily bread" of the petition with the bread of the Eucharist. Probably the Lord's Prayer had entered the Roman liturgy as a communion devotion, but Gregory the Great (590–604) placed it immediately after the Amen of the eucharistic prayer, so that some commentators interpreted it as a conclusion to the prayer or as an extended Amen. In various liturgies a form which expressed confident or bold obedience in saying this prayer introduced the Lord's Prayer, as in the Roman form, "Taught by our Lord's command and following his divine instruction we make bold to say." The Gallican rites contain different forms for various days but the basic tone is similar to that of the Eastern and Roman forms. In many rites the Prayer was said by all, but the Roman rite directed the priest alone to say everything up to the petition for deliverance from evil which was said by the people as a response, a method the 1549 Book retained, along with the introduction "As our Savior Christ hath commanded and taught us, we are bold to say." Cranmer's version of the Prayer read:

> Our Father, which art in heaven, hallowed be thy Name. Thy Kingdom come. Thy will be done in earth, as it is in heaven. Give us this day our daily bread. And forgive us our trespasses as we forgive them that trespass against us. And lead us not into temptation. *The answer:* But deliver us from evil. Amen.

The 1552 Book directed the priest to say the Prayer with the people repeating each petition after him, immediately after the ministration of communion. The 1662 revision, following the method of the Scottish Book of 1637, added the Matthean doxology. Until 1928, how-

378

ever, the placement and manner of saying the Prayer was unchanged; at that time it was placed in the position it had in the Roman rite, the 1549 Book and the Scottish liturgies. The 1789 American revision updated the language.

The introduction in the 1928 revision is dependent on the Roman and 1549 forms, "And now, as our Saviour Christ hath taught us, we are bold to say," a form retained in the present Rite One. In Rite Two this form is used to introduce the Prayer done in traditional language; a simpler form "As our Savior Christ has taught us, we now pray," introduces the Prayer in the contemporary language of the ICET translation.

The Breaking of the Bread (pp. 337 and 364)

The practical purpose of the breaking of the bread is to divide it for the people's communions. Symbolically, the loaf is shared and Christ's body is broken. Even in the middle ages, when the people rarely received communion and a wafer replaced the loaf, the priest broke the wafer to provide communion for himself, and to provide a portion to reserve for the communion of the sick. In some areas a portion of bread broken at a communion celebrated by a bishop was sent to outlying parishes to add to the chalice as a sign of unity of the church under the bishop. In other places a piece of the bread was reserved to be placed in the chalice at a later Eucharist, a sign of unity in time. After these practices disappeared, a portion of the wafer consecrated at that Mass was placed in the cup and given an allegorical interpretation. Eventually the use of small round wafers with no symbolism of brokenness or sharing became the custom for communions of the people.

The first Prayer Book did not retain the commixture, nor did it end the use of wafers "for avoiding of all matters and occasion of dissension," but the wafers were to be larger and thicker and "every one shall be divided (1548: broken) in two pieces, at the least, or more." The 1552 Book substituted a rubric, "it shall suffice that the bread be such as is usual to be eaten at the table with other meats, but the best and purest wheat bread that conveniently may be gotten." The 1662 Book rubricated that the bread be broken at the words "he brake it" in the institution narrative, a direction maintained by the American revision of 1789, but with the action of breaking much further separated from the action of communion. Late in the nineteenth century wafers again began to replace bread and the fraction was simply an act dramatizing the institution narrative. The present Book restores the fraction as a primary action of the Eucharist, immediately before the communions of the people.

After the celebrant has made the initial fraction, it is suitable to bring additional patens to the altar and that any other priests present assist in the breaking of the bread for communion. Assisting in this manner has been one of the traditional functions of a concelebrating priest. An additional direction (p. 407), which restores the ancient tradition, points out that "it is appropriate that there be only one chalice on the Altar" during the eucharistic prayer. If more wine is needed it should be contained in a flagon, and any additional chalices should be brought to the altar to be filled after the breaking of the bread. The presence of one loaf and one cup on the altar during the eucharistic prayer signifies the central and unifying aspect of the rite.

Fraction Anthem (pp. 337 and 364)

During and after the initial breaking of the bread silence is kept. One or more anthems, however, may be sung as the bread is broken for distribution and additional chalices filled, and prior to the optional prayer of humble access or the Sancta sanctis ("The gifts of God for the people of God")—the invitation to communion. In some Eastern rites the fraction was accompanied by psalmody, in Gallican rites by a variable fraction anthem, and in the Roman rite from the late seventh century by the Agnus Dei. The optional anthem printed in both rites of the 1979 Book is "Christ our Passover," which may be said or sung by the celebrant, said as a versicle and response, or sung by the people, by a cantor, or by a choir. The principle which requires the omission of Alleluia at the daily office in Lent also applies to this anthem. The Alleluias are to be used during the Great Fifty Days, may be used at other times, but are not to be used during Lent. This anthem is derived from one included in the 1549 Book but omitted in the 1552 revision:

> Christ our Paschal Lamb is offered up for us, once for all, when he bare our sins on his body upon the cross, for he is the very Lamb of God that taketh away the sins of the world; wherefore let us keep a joyful and holy feast with the Lord.

This replaced a sentence sometimes used as the consecrated bread was shown to the people: "Behold the Lamb of God who takes away the sins of the world" (John 1:19), which was accepted into the Missal of Pius V. Another option is the Agnus Dei which is printed in Rite One. The Book includes both contemporary ICET translations, one

380

among the additional directions (p. 407) and the other within the Litany at the Time of Death (p. 463). (See *The Book of Occasional Services*, pp. 15–19, for additional Anthems at the Breaking of the Bread.)

The Agnus Dei originated in the East; the early one-line version, based on John 1:19, is an abbreviated form of the line in the Gloria in excelsis, which dates to the fourth century. Besides its use in the Gloria in excelsis at the morning office in the East, and soon afterward in the West, the line also appeared near the conclusion of a litany used in private devotions in the East and introduced to Rome by Sergius I (687–701). Its use soon spread through the West. In close connection with the fraction, some Eastern liturgies included prayers to the Lamb of God; often the word "Lamb" signified the eucharistic bread. Sergius introduced the line "Lamb of God that takest away the sins of the world, have mercy on us" at the fraction in the Roman rite. For several centuries the one line was repeated, as a song of the people, as long as was necessary to cover the breaking of bread for the communions. Once the people had ceased to receive frequent communion the repetitions were reduced to three. Later, when the anthem became part of the exchange of the peace, the conclusion changed, at the third repetition, to "grant us your peace."

Late in the middle ages the peace was rarely exchanged and then usually only between celebrant and deacon. The Agnus Dei, in elaborate sung form, extended through the communion of the priest and came to be considered a communion hymn rather than a fraction anthem. The 1549 Book retained it to be sung during the communions, but the 1552 revision deleted it and amplified the Gloria in excelsis to include the three repetitions of the basic line. The extra line was deleted in 1928, restoring the Gloria in excelsis to its traditional Roman form. A proposal to include the Agnus Dei in the 1928 Book was not approved, although it was printed in the service music of unofficial editions of the hymnals of 1892 and 1916. It was accepted in the official Hymnal (1940) to be used as an optional hymn after the prayer of humble access. The present Book restores it to its traditional use as an optional fraction anthem. Other suitable anthems may be sung or said in place of Christ our Passover or the Agnus Dei.

The Prayer of Humble Access (p. 337)

The Gallican liturgies contained a blessing of the people, the Eastern liturgies a prayer of inclination, after the fraction and prior to the communion. After the decline of the communions of the people, private prayers by the priest for worthy reception came into common use. Such prayers were not an official part of the liturgy, and varied from book to book.

The 1548 Order of the Communion was designed for use in the Mass after the communion of the priest and as a replacement for orders for the private ministration of communion from the reserved Sacrament in the late medieval period. It included (after the exhortation, a bidding to confession, general confession, absolution, and "comfortable words") a prayer for worthy reception. The form was not apparently a translation of any existing prayer, but incorporated phrases or concepts from the Liturgy of Saint Basil, Mark 7:28, a Gregorian collect (nos. 851 and 1327) which had been printed at the end of the 1544 litany, John 6:56, and the writings of Thomas Aquinas (*Summa Theologica*, Part 3, Question 74, Article 1). The 1549 Book kept this form for use immediately before communion. Since the institution narrative in 1552 was placed immediately before the ministration of the Sacrament to emphasize the receiving of communion as the center of the rite, this prayer was placed after the Sanctus. The conclusion of the 1549 form had read, "Grant us therefore, gracious Lord, so to eat the flesh of thy dear Son Jesus Christ, and to drink his blood in these holy Mysteries, that we may continually dwell in him and he in us, that our sinful bodies may be made clean by his body and our souls washed through his most precious blood." In the 1552 revision, in keeping with the changed position of the prayer, the phrase "in these holy Mysteries" was omitted, and "and that we may evermore (1549: continually) dwell in him and he in us" was moved to the end where it provided a better climax. In the Scottish Book of 1637 this prayer was returned to a position immediately before communion, designated in the preceding rubric as the "collect of humble access to the Holy Communion." The 1552 position, however, was retained in 1662, 1789, and 1892; the 1928 revision restored the prayer to the place it held in 1549 and 1637. In the present Book it appears in Rite One as an optional communion devotion after the fraction, and a revised rubric allows the people to say it with the priest. A portion of the conclusion, which seemed to imply dualism of body and soul, attributing benefits for the body to one element (bread/body) and for the soul to the other (wine/blood), is a medieval concept found in Aquinas' work. It is omitted in the present Book, as it also is in English Series 3.

The Sancta sanctis: "The Gifts of God for the People of God": (pp. 338 and 364–365)

Eastern liturgies of the fourth century contain the Sancta sanctis— "the holy for the holy" or "holy things for holy people"—associated with the showing of the Sacrament to the people. The people's typical response was "One is holy, one is Lord, Jesus Christ, to the glory of God the Father." In the Apostolic Constitutions this is followed by "Glory to God in the highest, peace on earth, goodwill among men" and the Benedictus qui venit. The Sancta sanctis is to be used in Rite Two and may be used in Rite One. The additional optional sentence, which derives from the form used at the ministration of the eucharistic bread in the 1552 Book and subsequent editions, is in the first of the alternative words of ministration in Rite One, but is included only in this form in Rite Two.

The Ministration of Communion (pp. 338 and 365)

The present Book does not prescribe either the posture of the communicants at the ministration nor the place where communion is to be ministered. In addition, it is the first edition of the Prayer Book to legalize the use of intinction, within certain restrictions (pp. 407–408).

The traditional posture for Christians receiving communion is standing, a tradition the Eastern churches have always maintained. The church fathers interpreted such posture as a sign of our approach to God as His children rather than as slaves, as a symbol of our being raised by Jesus Christ, as reminiscent of the command to eat the Passover in haste so that one may be ready to go about the Lord's business. Only late in the middle ages did the custom of kneeling to receive begin to spread in the West. Among the Reformed churches in Zurich and elsewhere on the continent, sitting was the accepted posture; in the German church orders standing is the position still presumed.

The 1548 Order of the Communion directs the people to kneel, a direction omitted in 1549; possibly kneeling was assumed or perhaps the omission of any direction implied standing as the posture. Some of the refugees to the continent during the reign of Henry VIII returned under Edward VI and instituted the practice of sitting for the ministration. In reaction to this the 1552 Book directed that the Sacrament be received kneeling, justifying such action "for a signification of the humble and grateful acknowledgment of the benefits of Christ given unto the worthy receiver, and to avoid the profanation and disorder which about the Holy Communion might else ensue." The present revision deletes the direction to kneel in order that the traditional posture, and the eucharistic concepts which it signifies, may be recovered.

In the early centuries those administering the elements apparently moved among the people, a practice which continued for a long period in some areas. In other places, however, the people began to move toward the altar to receive the Sacrament from deacons or priests, or to go to tables at various locations throughout the church nave. As early as the time of Augustine of Hippo (early fifth century) in Africa and in several other places, a chest-high rail was built around the altar to keep the people from pressing too closely upon the ministers thus impeding their movement in the course of the service. The people then came to such rails to receive.

The earliest use of rails in Anglicanism dates to the early seventeenth century, but these were "altar rails" rather than "communion rails" and were latticed to prevent dogs from desecrating the holy table, as episcopal injunctions explain. In the nineteenth century people still took the invitation "draw near" to mean to come up into the chancel, or close to the chancel, which was looked upon as a room for the sacrament just as the nave was a room for the liturgy of the word. Until early in the eighteenth century, at least, the clergy had still moved about among the people to minister the elements. Gradually the custom of using the rail as a "communion rail" spread among the churches, but the usage was never rubricated in the Prayer Book.

People in the early church received communion in both kinds, taking the bread into their hands, or possibly taking it from the paten. The late fourth century catechetical lectures attributed to Cyril of Jerusalem instruct on the receiving of the bread: "When you approach, do not come with your hands stretched or your fingers separated, but make your left hand a throne for the right which is to receive a king." Changes in eucharistic piety in the middle ages and the risk of the Sacrament being carried from the church for some superstitious use led to intinction in the East and in some parts of the West. The method generally used involved placing the bread in the chalice of wine. Communions were then administered with a spoon. In Roman territory, from the ninth through the fifteenth centuries, the desire to protect the Sacrament led to changes in administration: wafers replaced bread and portions were put into the communicant's mouth rather than being placed in the hand. The bread was withheld from children. Small individual wafers then replaced larger broken wafers. Eventually the chalice was no longer given to the laity. One effect of these gradual changes was that, by the sixteenth century, small children were denied communion except in a very few places; the adult laity rarely received except at the one time mandated during the year—Easter season.

The 1548 Order of the Communion restored communion in both kinds. The 1549 Book, while acknowledging that early custom was to place the bread into communicants' hands, directed that the priest place the bread in the mouths of the people so that it might not be carried away to be used for superstitious or wicked (i.e. Black Mass) purposes. In 1552 the rubric directed that it be delivered into the hands of the people, a stipulation continued in every edition through that of 1928.

The rubrics of the present Book specify that the clergy receive in both kinds. The additional directions (p. 407) state that this is to be done *while the people are coming forward to receive,* a ceremonial direction intended to emphasize the fact that clergy and laity alike receive at one table. Every communicant is to be given opportunity to receive in both kinds separately but the elements may be received in both kinds simultaneously "in a manner approved by the bishop." The additional directions point out that it is customary for the celebrant to minister the bread. Deacons often ministered the communion in early churches, even when several bishops and priests were present. Previous editions of the Book limited the action of the deacon to ministration of the cup; the additional directions of this Book state, "When several deacons or priests are present, some may administer the Bread and others the Wine." The directions also legitimize the canonical legislation of General Convention (1967), "In the absence of sufficient deacons and priests, lay persons licensed by the bishop according to the canon may administer the Chalice."

The Words of Administration (pp. 338 and 365)

In the New Testament accounts of the institution of the sacrament the words "This is my body" and "This is my blood" are not consecratory formulae, as they were interpreted in the middle ages in the West, but sentences of administration. The words "The Body of Christ" and "The Blood of Christ" were sentences of administration from very early times. They constituted a profession of faith to which the recipient answered Amen as an assent. Apocryphal books of the second and third centuries give accounts of the Eucharist with sev-

385

eral forms for administration, typical of which are "Let this eucharist be for you for remission of transgressions and sins, and for the everlasting resurrection," and "Let this eucharist be for you for grace and mercy and not for judgment and vengeance." In the baptismal liturgy of the Apostolic Tradition the bread is distributed with the words: "The bread of heaven in Christ Jesus," with the communicant responding Amen. Then the communicant is to drink three times from the chalice. The words of administration constitute a threefold creedal form, "In God the Father Almighty," "And in the Lord Jesus Christ," and "And in the Holy Spirit and the holy Church." The communicant responds Amen after each. In the Apostolic Constitutions the words of administration are "The Body of Christ" and "The blood of Christ, the cup of life." The people respond Amen.

The basic form used in the West in the middle ages was "The body (blood) of our Lord Jesus Christ keep you in eternal life." Some variants inserted "for the remission of sins." "Your soul" was often substituted for "you."

In the Order of the Communion of 1548 the texts were "The body of our Lord Jesus Christ, which was given for thee, preserve thy body unto everlasting life" and "The blood of our Lord Jesus Christ, which was shed for thee, preserve thy soul unto everlasting life." The phrases "which was given for thee" (Mt. 26:28 and Mk. 14:24) and "which was shed for thee" (1 Cor. 11:24) are inserted in the medieval form in various German church orders, including that of Hermann of Cologne. The idea that the body of Christ benefits the body while the blood benefits the soul was a distinction found in some late medieval writings, including the *Summa Theologica* of Thomas Aquinas, and was already enshrined in the prayer of humble access prior to communion. The 1549 Book maintained the distinction in the prayer, but the phrase in both sentences of administration is "preserve thy body and soul." The 1552 revision replaced these sentences with Zwinglian forms: "Take and eat this in remembrance that Christ died for thee, and feed on him in thy heart by faith with thanksgiving;" and "Drink this in remembrance that Christ's blood was shed for thee, and be thankful." The 1559 Book joined the two forms; the Scottish Book of 1637 retained the 1549 form and added Amen as the response of each communicant. The 1662 Book and every American revision has kept the 1559 texts, and the present edition provides this form as one of three alternatives for Rite One. The second (first of the two alternatives in Rite Two) is the basic Western text of the eighth century. The other alternative consists of the basic text for the administration which was used in the very early church, with phrases in apposition typical of those added at an early period. In each of the forms both the anamnetic and the eschatologic aspects of the feast are spoken. It is the intention that these shorter forms be said individually for each communicant, and that the communicant be given opportunity to say "Amen" as an act of faith before receiving.

Communion Hymns, Psalms, or Anthems (pp. 338 and 365)

Psalmody was used during communion at least as early as the fourth century, treated like other processional psalms, at the entrance and at the offertory, which became part of the rite soon after. Originally the cantor sang the psalm; later a choir or antiphonal choirs did the singing; the congregation participated in an antiphon. When all had communicated, a signal was given and the cantor or choir sang the Gloria Patri as a climax to the psalm. Apparently the people once more sang the antiphon as a conclusion. Psalm 34, with verse 8 as the antiphon, and 145, with verse 16, seem to have been the most popular of the communion psalms. The East favored Alleluia psalms, especially Psalms 148 and 150, with Alleluia as the response. Often the antiphon might not be from the psalm but from another verse of scripture with eucharistic connotations. In Rome, and in some Eastern churches, the psalms varied with the occasion and special psalms were used at the great feasts. On other days psalms were used in course, or the entrance psalm was repeated. (By way of contrast, on Good Friday communion was administered in silence.) In the Celtic rite a hymn best known in the translation "Draw nigh and take the body of the Lord" was used in place of a psalm at times. As the people's communions disappeared late in the middle ages, the psalm was dropped, leaving only the antiphon. The celebrant received communion while the Agnus Dei was being sung, and the remaining antiphon from the communion psalm came to be thought of as a postcommunion song. Some German church orders directed that a hymn be sung in this place, after the communion of the people and prior to the postcommunion prayer. In the Reformed churches the communion of the people was often followed by the singing of one or more of the Hallel psalms.

The 1549 Book printed the Agnus Dei to be sung at communion time by the clerks, and followed it with twenty-two "sentences of holy Scripture, to be said or sung every day one, after the Holy Communion, called the post Communion." All are from the New Testament, arranged according to their appearance in the Bible. They are not communion sentences but exhortations to lead a moral life, to

387

love and to serve, or they are warnings to prepare for the second coming. Though they are the equivalent of the remnants of earlier communion psalms in the medieval missals, only one of these sentences appears in the Sarum rite. Both Agnus Dei and the sentences dropped from the 1552 Book. The Non-juror liturgy of 1718 directed that Psalm 33 be sung or said at the communion of the people "or the great Hallel, usually sung at the close of the passover supper, and which was supposed the hymn sung by Christ at the institution of the sacrament, consisting of Psalms 113, 114, 115, 116, 117, 118." The 1734 liturgy of Thomas Deacon, the Non-juror, directed the singing of one or more of these psalms in order: 34, 45, 133, and 145. Thomas Rattray, the Scottish Non-juring bishop, in his proposed liturgy suggested the optional use of Psalms 24 and 145. Though the Prayer Book made no provision for such use, most of the Anglican metrical psalters contained a hymn or hymns for use at the time of the people's communion. The first American revision required a hymn prior to the priest's communion, a requirement made permissive in 1892 and 1928. The present edition permits the singing of "hymns, psalms, or anthems" during the ministration of communion, and an additional direction (p. 409) allows the use of a hymn before the postcommunion prayer. This might serve to cover the ablutions or the removal of the Sacrament to the place where the ablutions will be completed.

The Consecration of Additional Bread and Wine (pp. 338 and 365)

Supplementary consecration of additional bread and wine is a uniquely Anglican practice. Even when congregations had grown so large that all could not partake from one chalice, the concept of one cup was signified by permitting only one chalice to be on the altar. At the presentation of the gifts, one cup was filled and additional wine poured into a large vessel not placed on the altar. After the fraction, a small portion of the chalice contents was poured into the large vessel from which cups would be filled for communion; if there was not enough wine for the communion of the people more was taken from the sacristy to fill the chalice. For a time both bread and wine were reserved for Good Friday communions, but eventually only the bread was reserved and, at the Good Friday rite, after the Lord's Prayer, a portion of this was broken off and put into the chalice of wine for communion in both kinds. Communion for the sick had parallel development. Not until the eucharistic controversies of the ninth century did the theological explanation appear that the wine was consecrated by contact, and a natural development was that additional

388

bread was consecrated by sprinkling consecrated wine upon it. The more dynamic views of the Eucharist of earlier centuries required no explanation of the consecration. In the thirteenth century the scholastic theologians developed a theology of consecration by formula: in the West the necessary form was recital of the words of institution; parallel to this in the East was a development which identified the necessary form as the epiclesis of the Holy Spirit. Once a "moment of consecration" had been set, there was a shift from the earlier dynamic view of the Eucharist to passivity and adoration rather than participation and reception. The theology of consecration by formula brought with it scruples for the theologians to deal with—spillage, forgetfulness, the poisoned chalice, the twisted tongue, the empty chalice. Such defects were rectified by saying the institution narrative or the narrative and the rest of the prayer. In the medieval church this was not a means of consecrating additional bread and wine, however, but a remedy for defects in the consecration. The theory of consecration by contact was rejected, and legislation of the Roman Catholic Church still forbids the consecrating of elements outside a whole Mass. If insufficient quantities of bread and wine are consecrated at a Mass, then some simply cannot receive, which preserves the integrity of the rite at the expense of communion of some of the people.

If there was a theology of consecration in Lutheran rites it was a theology of consecration by use of the institution narrative. Calvin and the Reformed churches were influenced on this point by the newly available Eastern liturgies and writings. Theology of consecration, if there was such, in the Reformed rites was by prayer, sometimes with explicit mention of the Holy Spirit.

In the 1549 Book the theology of consecration seems to be by both epiclesis and institution narrative, "with thy holy spirit and word." In 1552 the explicit epiclesis of the Holy Spirit was replaced by a petition for worthy reception and a theology of consecration apparently by prayer and the institution narrative. The Order of the Communion of 1548 had included a rubric specifying that if the "wine hallowed and consecrate" were not sufficient the priest was to refill the chalice and say over it the relevant portion of the institution narrative. This was the remedy for defects in consecration in the late middle ages, but the 1548 Order was using it in a totally new way without precedent in liturgical history. Nothing is said in 1549 or 1552, nor in 1559 and 1604, about what to do when additional Sacrament is needed. In 1573, Robert Johnson was brought to trial for adding more wine to the chalice without saying over it the relevant portion of the institution narrative, but this seems to be an isolated case which drew little notice. The canons of 1604, however, required that the relevant portion of the narrative be said over any additional bread or wine, a provision included in the Scottish Book of 1637 and the English Book of 1662. By the end of the century, however, some Anglicans seem to have become uncomfortable with this solution or with the theology which it implied but were, at the same time, ignorant of the practice of the early and medieval church. The proposed Book of 1689 required that the insitution narrative be preceded by a brief petition. Charles Wheatley, in his commentary on the Prayer Book (1710), argued against the 1662 form as being insufficient; Whiston's liturgy of 1712 required the use of the whole of the post-Sanctus portion of the eucharistic prayer. Wesley adopted this practice in his revision of the Prayer Book for American Methodists. The Scottish revision of 1764 changed the rubric to require the whole of the prayer from "All glory be to thee" through the epiclesis, and this practice was adopted in the first American Book. The present revision provides a brief form (p. 408) which contains both an epiclesis and the recital of the relevant sentence of institution. The fuller form of the Scottish 1764 rite and of prior American Books continues to be recognized as an alternative.

The Conclusion of the Rite (pp. 339–340 and 365–366)

Until the fourth century the rite ended with the communion of the people. Some scholars believe that there was a formal dismissal by the deacon (corresponding to the formal dismissal at other public assemblies in that period) but there is no documentary evidence. If so, it would be the counterpart of the opening salutation of the celebrant which in places preceded the readings which were the beginning of the liturgy of the word. With growth in numbers and the move to larger buildings a more formal conclusion to the rite was needed. The dismissal can be documented in some places as early as the fourth century. Soon it was preceded by either or both of two types of prayers: a prayer which gave thanks for the sacrament and prayed that it might have good effect upon the lives of the communicants; and a prayer for the people, who were being sent forth into the world. This was variously known as a laying on of hands, an inclination (that is, a prayer for which people bowed), or a super populum, a prayer over the people. It was possibly accompanied by a laying on of hands or a stretching out of a hand or hands over the assembly. This prayer, and the ceremonial which accompanied it, was analogous to the dismissal of the catechumens and penitents after the liturgy of the word.

For this prayer the deacon often bade the people to bow their heads. After it or after the dismissal, the clergy exited, and the deacons took the Sacrament from the celebration to those who could not be present. In contrast to their ceremonious entrance, the exit of the clergy was almost abrupt. The people apparently fell in behind them and left the church, visiting on their way with their neighbors. Those who had rendered thanks for all that God had done for them and who had feasted with Him and on Him must quickly be about His business.

Just as the entrance rite tended to mushroom, however, so did the rather abrupt exit rite. Eventually litanies and additional prayers were added. The Roman and Gallican rites were for a long time resistant to such elaboration, but in the late medieval period ablutions worked their way into the public service, accompanied by private prayers of the celebrant. Other private prayers and thanksgivings added to the rite in the medieval period became a part of the public rite by the time of the Reformation.

In some places, in the middle ages, the bishop had said a blessing over the people as he walked through the church at the close of the Eucharist. By the time of the Reformation, the bishop in many places said the blessing over the congregation before leaving the altar, an action imitated by priests in France and Germany.

So that the exit rite might better serve its function of sending the people on their way with dispatch to go about the Lord's business, acting out what they had celebrated, nearly every major liturgical reform has attempted to cut away the accretions. German and French reformers cut back the conclusion of the service to a prayer and a blessing, though among Calvinistic reformers a hymn, imitating the hymn sung by our Lord and His disciples before departing from the upper room, might be included. The 1549 Book concluded the rite with a sentence of scripture, a fixed prayer, and a blessing. The 1552 revision expanded this part of the service to include the Lord's Prayer and the Gloria in excelsis. In various congregations other elements accrued: for example, an eighteenth century author complained about the length of the rite after the communion, saying that by the time he left the church all his good resolutions made at his communion had dissipated. The 1892 revision permitted the singing of a hymn after the blessing, probably a common custom by that time despite the rubric directing the priest to "let them depart with this Blessing." Within the last few decades the rubrics of the Prayer Book have been violated by the ablutions which, rather than being done by the priest and other communicants after the blessing and departure of the people, have been done publicly before the congregation. Just as entrance rites tended to become increasingly cumbersome, and to take on a significance of their own rather than serving as a means of preparing the people to hear the word, so exit rites have taken on extrinsic significance, working against rather than for the sending forth of the people to witness and to serve. This revision has made several changes in an effort to restore the conclusion to its due proportion and to emphasize its function in the service.

The Postcommunion Prayer (pp. 339 and 365–366)

The use of a formal conclusion after the communions of the people was another development of the fourth century following upon the increase in numbers and the move to larger buildings once Christianity was legalized. The sacramentary of Serapion (c. A.D. 350), thought to have originated in Egypt, contains a fixed thanksgiving for communion. The Apostolic Constitutions (c. 380), a Syrian document, follows communion with a prayer of dedication. Augustine of Hippo (d. 430) mentions a prayer after communion. Probably the use of a variable postcommunion prayer began in the Roman rite in the last half of the fifth century; such variable prayers were also used in Gallican territory. A few of these Roman and Gallican prayers are related to particular celebrations or to some special need, but most incorporate thanksgiving for communion or a petition which refers to the efficacy of communion. Luther and the German church orders abandoned the variable prayer, although retaining some prayers from the medieval rite to be used as alternatives.

The 1549 Book provides one fixed postcommunion prayer which is equal in length to several of the Sarum postcommunion prayers joined together. In one prayer it brings together many of the themes scattered through the variable prayers. Massey H. Shepherd, Jr., has written of this text:

> [It is] one of the most remarkable summaries of doctrine to be found in all the formularies of the Prayer Book. In particular it gathers up all the varied meanings of the Holy Communion: thanksgiving, mystery, grace, incorporation into Christ, fellowship in the Church, anticipation of the Kingdom of God. Its definitions of the Eucharist and of the Church have become classic, being firmly based on the terms of the New Testament (cf. 1 Cor. x. 3–4, xii. 27; Tit. iii. 7). Moreover, the prayer serves as a felicitious translation of the worshiping congregation from the mysteries

392

of the sanctuary to the 'good works' of Christian service in the world's life (cf. Eph. ii. 10), and it relates the sacrament of the altar to the tasks of everyday living.[1]

The prayer is thought by some to be related to the second answer of the catechism in the 1549 Book which states that in baptism a person is made "a member of Christ, the child of God, and an inheritor of the kingdom of heaven." The Eucharist is portrayed as an assurance of what happened in baptism.

The 1552 revision substituted "thou dost vouchsafe to feed us, who have duly received these holy mysteries" for "thou hast vouchsafed to feed us in these holy mysteries," "dost assure us thereby" for "hast assured us, duly receiving the same," and "now" for "therefore." That revision also shifted an abbreviated version of the final paragraph from the eucharistic prayer in the 1549 Book—the self-oblation—to the postcommunion position and printed it just before this prayer. Either was to be used. The 1637 Scottish edition restored a fuller form of the self-oblation to the eucharistic prayer, leaving again the one fixed postcommunion of 1549, but the 1662 Book retained both prayers as alternatives after communion.

The 1789 American Book restored the self-oblation to the eucharistic prayer. This present edition retains a revised version of the postcommunion prayer in Rite One. The 1549 phrase "thou dost feed us, in these holy mysteries" has been restored. The phrase "by the merits of his most precious death and passion" has been deleted, for it centers too much on one aspect of the redemptive work of Christ to the neglect of others. A shorter version of this prayer in contemporary language is provided in Rite Two as the second of two alternative postcommunion prayers. The other was drafted by the Rev. Dr. Leo Malania.

An additional direction (p. 409) permits the singing of a hymn after the postcommunion prayer. In various Eastern rites, as opposed to the rites of the West, a hymn was sometimes included after the postcommunion prayer. Calvin's rite included a metrical psalm of praise after the postcommunion prayer. The 1552 revision of the Prayer Book moved the Gloria in excelsis from the entrance rite to a position between the postcommunion prayer and the blessing. Some commentators have thought that this position was in imitation of the

---

[1] Massey H. Shepherd, Jr., *The Oxford American Prayer Book Commentary*, New York: Oxford University Press, 1950, pp. 83–84.

psalm of Calvin's rite. The first American revision allowed a hymn to be substituted for this canticle. The 1892 Prayer Book included permission to sing a hymn after the blessing as well, but this has been withdrawn in the present revision. The blessing or dismissal is a sending out of the people, and the use of any text after the blessing or dismissal denigrates the text of those forms.

The Blessing (pp. 339 and 366)

There is no evidence of a blessing at the end of the Eucharist, or of any equivalent, before the fourth century. The Egyptian sacramentary of Serapion contains after the postcommunion prayer a prayer to be said by the celebrant with or as a laying on of hands. Many Eastern liturgies have at this point a prayer with inclination or laying on of hands; for the faithful this is the equivalent of a prayer with laying on of hands which was said for the catechumens (or other special groups) at their dismissal prior to the liturgy of the table. If a few individuals were present the prayers may have been accompanied by individual laying on of hands; for a larger group, laying on of hands was symbolized by extending a hand or hands over the congregation during the prayer. A super populum after the postcommunion was a regular feature of every Mass in the oldest Roman sacramentary, the Leonine. For this prayer, the deacon bade the people to bow their heads and the content differed from other prayers. The celebrant was not included in it; it was a prayer by him for a blessing upon or benefits for the people. Gallican rites have no equivalent. The Gregorian sacramentary restricted the super populum to the weekdays of Lent, a restriction the Roman missals retained until the revision of Paul VI. It had become no longer a prayer of blessing for the congregation but a prayer or blessing on public penitents. When the public penitential discipline died out and Lent took on the character of a penitential season for the whole church, this prayer was continued as appropriate to the Lenten season.

This Lenten super populum was not kept in the 1549 Book, though some of the medieval prayers were used as collects of the day. The collect for Good Friday (pp. 169 and 221), for example, was the super populum for Wednesday in Holy Week. Earlier editions of the Prayer Book replaced the Gloria in excelsis at ordinations with collects in the form of a super populum, prayers for a blessing upon a special person or group of persons within a congregation.

Although the Gallican sacramentaries do not contain a super populum, they do have a blessing (reserved to the bishop) prior to communion, which is generally proper to the day or season and is thought by some to be a blessing upon the people prior to communion; others think it a blessing on the people who will be leaving the church before communion. This episcopal blessing was retained in some territories when the Roman rite replaced the Gallican. Since it happened to come at approximately the place occupied by the peace in the Roman rite, it served as an introduction to the peace. By the eleventh century it had assumed a standard form in the sacramentaries and benedictionals: it began with three sentences related to the day or occasion, to each of which the congregation responded Amen; a Trinitarian blessing followed, ending with the peace, to which the congregation answered "And with you." The Aaronic blessing (Num. 6:24–26) was one used for general occasions. Ordo Romanus Primus (8th century) describes another type of blessing, given by the bishop as he left the church. This was a private blessing for which no forms are provided in the liturgical books. Late in the middle ages in some places the bishop gave this blessing from the altar before his departure; it came to be imitated by priests in France and Germany, and the blessing at the end of the rite came to be a common feature of German church orders, although hardly any of the medieval missals included a text for a blessing at the close of the Eucharist. Many of the Reformed churches also closed the rite with a blessing.

The Order of the Communion of 1548 has the people depart with this blessing: "The peace of God which passeth all understanding, keep your hearts and minds in the knowledge and love of God, and of his Son Jesus Christ our Lord." The people are to respond Amen. The 1549 Prayer Book provides one of the blessings from Hermann's Consultation as an addition to the 1548 blessing: "And the blessing of God Almighty, the Father, the Son, and the Holy Ghost, be amongst you and remain with you alway."

The present revision includes a slightly revised form of the conclusion of the 1549 blessing as an alternative. This is also the blessing said by the new priest at ordination with "among" substituted for "upon" and "always" for "for ever." A blessing is permitted in Rite Two but no formal text is given. The celebrant at that Rite is free to seek out or compose a blessing proper to the day or season, adapt a traditional Anglican blessing to contemporary language, or use any of the Prayer Book blessings in contemporary language. At the ordination of a bishop the new bishop blesses the congregation (p. 523) with an impressive form introduced by versicles and responses in the manner of medieval pontifical blessings. This is also suitable for use by the bishop at visitations and on other occasions. The newly or-

395

dained priest blesses the congregation with a form suited to general use (p. 535). The Aaronic blessing is printed at the conclusion of the Order of Worship for the Evening (p. 114) in the threefold form typical of the medieval period, and a threefold form is also provided at the conclusion of the Thanksgiving for the Birth or Adoption of a Child (p. 445). Another blessing is that printed at the conclusion of the burial rite (p. 503). (See *The Book of Occasional Services*, pp. 20–27, for Seasonal Blessings and Lenten Prayers over the People.)

The Dismissal (pp. 339–340 and 366)

The first unambiguous evidence of a formal dismissal of the assembly is from the fourth century. The Apostolic Constitutions and other early Eastern liturgies have a simple announcement by the deacon, "Depart in peace." A typical response to this form of dismissal was "In the name of Christ." It corresponded to the dismissals at other public assemblies, as did the "Ite missa est" of the Roman rite, which many believe would have been used from earliest Christian times in Rome but which cannot be documented before the eighth century. The corresponding form in Gallican territory was "Benedicamus," "Let us bless the Lord." As the Roman rite supplanted the Gallican rite in the West, a number of features of the old Gallican rite made their way into the Roman rite. One of these was the Benedicamus. The Roman "Ite missa est," "Go, you are dismissed," or "Go, the assembly is concluded," came to be considered of a festive nature, and it was replaced in times of penitence and on other more solemn occasions by "Let us bless the Lord." Alleluias were added to the dismissal at Easter. The response, "Deo gratias," "Thanks be to God," was used in the medieval period as an acknowledgment of having heard what was said, not only after the dismissal, but also after certain readings, and even in some cases after announcements made in the services. In the late medieval period, with the elaboration of the melodies of the dismissal, the text was often troped.

The use of the dismissal was retained in some of the continental Reformed rites, but not in the Book of Common Prayer. This is the first edition to restore it. The use of the dismissal is permitted in Rite One and required in Rite Two. The first three forms correspond to the troped dismissals of the late medieval period. The fourth is the old Gallican dismissal. On Palm Sunday the procession of the liturgy of the palms begins with a form which corresponds to the early Eastern dismissals, "Let us go forth in peace" with the response "In the name of Christ. Amen."

Offertory Sentences (pp. 343–344 and 376–377)

The 1549 Book provided twenty sentences of scripture to be sung while the people were placing their offerings in "the poor men's box." A number speak particularly of giving to the poor or giving for the support of the ministry. The 1892 revision added five sentences from the Scottish Book, and the 1928 edition added three, two of which had missionary emphasis, and deleted twelve, leaving a total of sixteen. Sentences appealing to unworthy motives for giving and those appealing for support of the clergy were among those removed. The rubric of the present Book permits the celebrant to use any sentence of scripture or none at all. If one is used, a sentence from the psalm might be appropriate, or one from one of the lessons for the day, or a sentence with seasonal associations. Of the eight sentences printed for general use, Hebrews 13:15–16 dates back to the 1549 Book (though in earlier Books only verse 16 was used) and 1 Chronicles 29:11 to the 1892 revision. The others are new. Prayer Book Studies IV (1953) proposed the first four and the 1967 Liturgy of the Lord's Supper suggested the other two. Printed after the sentences is a bidding retained from the 1967 proposal which summarizes the meaning and purpose of the action. No sentences are provided for use at the presentation, for within the eucharistic rite the presentation is spoken through the eucharistic prayer which follows the offering immediately.

Proper Prefaces (pp. 344–349 and 377–382)

One difference between Eastern and Western liturgies was the Western use of proper prefaces. The various Eastern rites contained a number of eucharistic prayers which varied with the day or occasion, but each recalls the mighty acts of God in creation, redemption, and the outpouring of the Spirit. Each prayer is a confession of faith and a proclamation of the gospel. One of the oldest and most widely used of Eastern prayers is seen in abbreviated form in Eucharistic Prayer D. Characteristically, it does not contain a proper preface. But in the West, after the development of the church year, eucharistic prayers tended to center on a particular aspect of the Christian Mystery being celebrated on the occasion. The Gallican liturgies, except for three fixed elements (the Sursum corda, the Sanctus, and the institution narrative), varied the eucharistic prayer from Sunday to Sunday. In the Roman rite a substantial portion of the prayer was fixed, but the Leonine sacramentary provided a proper preface for each Mass and other insertions within the prayer for various occasions. The Gelasian sacramentary provided more than fifty proper prefaces, but the Gregorian sacramentary, later, reduced the number to about a dozen and the Sarum missal contained ten.

Under the influence of the German church orders, the 1549 Book provided five proper prefaces—Christmas, Easter, Ascension, Pentecost, and Trinity—eliminating the Sarum prefaces for Epiphany, Ash Wednesday, apostles and evangelists, feasts of the Holy Cross, and feasts of the Virgin Mary. Further, the prefaces of the Sarum rite might be used on many occasions; those of the 1549 Book were limited to the five feast days. The 1552 Book allowed use of the Christmas, Easter, and Ascension prefaces through the octaves, and permitted the Pentecost preface to be used until Trinity Sunday. The American revision of 1789 provided an alternative preface for Trinity Sunday and changed the rubric so that neither of the prefaces was required. No further changes were made until 1928 when the use of a proper preface on Trinity Sunday became obligatory, the Pentecost preface was shortened, and, following the lead of other Anglican revisions, three new prefaces were added: for Epiphany and its octave; for Purification, Annunciation, and Transfiguration; for All Saints and its octave.

The present revision increases the number of proper prefaces to twenty-two. The only days without proper prefaces are weekdays after Pentecost which are not saints' days. Even on these occasions a proper preface is said if one of the propers for various occasions is used.

Preface of the Lord's Day (pp. 344–345 and 377–378)

In keeping with the renewed emphasis upon Sunday in this revision, three proper prefaces of the Lord's Day are provided. One or the other of these three is to be used on any Sunday for which a special proper preface is not appointed. The three alternative prefaces of the Lord's Day, written for this revision by the Rev. Dr. H. Boone Porter, stress Sunday as the day of creation, of the resurrection, and of the outpouring of the Holy Spirit. These forms also stress the eschatological and baptismal implications of the day.

Prefaces for Seasons (pp. 345–357 and 378–380)

The 1549 Prayer Book provided only five proper prefaces, Christmas, Easter, Ascension, Pentecost, and Trinity, each to be used only on the feast day itself. The 1552 revision accepted the principle of the use of octaves. The prefaces for the first three of these days were to be used throughout the octave, and that for Pentecost was to be used until Trinity Sunday. The preface for that day was to be used "upon the feast of Trinity only." In this revision the use of the prefaces has been extended throughout the season, on Sundays and weekdays as well, except for holy days and various occasions celebrated within the season. Additional seasonal prefaces are also provided.

The preface for the season of Advent was composed for the trial Liturgy of the Lord's Supper, 1967. Some of the phrasing was suggested by the Advent preface of the Book of Common Worship of the Church of South India.

The preface of the Incarnation is appointed to be used not only during the twelve days of Christmas but also on the feast day of Saint Mary the Virgin (August 15). It is a revised version of the Christmas preface of earlier Prayer Books. The 1549 version read:

> Because thou didst give Jesus Christ, thine only Son, to be born as this day for us, who by the operation of the Holy Ghost was made very Man, of the substance of the Virgin Mary his mother, and that without spot of sin, to make us clean from all sin.

This preface, composed for the 1549 Book, is similar to a passage in the *King's Book* of 1543. The Sarum preface dates to the Gregorian sacramentary (nos. 38 and 51) and its supplement (no. 1537). It is appointed in the sacramentary for Christmas Masses, and in the supplement for the feast of the Purification of the Virgin Mary. That preface, which was replaced in the 1549 Book, reads:

> Because by the mystery of the Word made flesh the light of your brightness has shone upon the eyes of our mind, so that while we know God visibly, we may be drawn by him to love things invisible.

The preface of Epiphany entered the Prayer Book in the 1928 revision. The first phrase is based upon the Gregorian preface for Christmas and the feast of the Purification (cited above) and the remainder on 2 Corinthians 4:6. In the 1928 Book this was the preface for the feasts of the Purification (Presentation), Annunciation, and Transfiguration. In the present Book its use is retained for those days, but it also replaces a preface for Epiphany which had entered the American Book in 1928 from the Scottish Book of 1912:

399

Through Jesus Christ our Lord; who, in substance of our mortal flesh, manifested forth his glory; that he might bring us out of darkness into his own glorious light.

Anglican Prayer Books prior to the Scottish revision of 1912 had no proper preface for Epiphany. The Sarum preface, which dates to the Gelasian sacramentary (no. 59) and the Gregorian (no. 89) and its supplement (no. 1526), read:

> Because when your only-begotten appeared in the substance of our flesh, he restored us into the new light of his immortality.

This is the first American Prayer Book to include proper prefaces for Lent. The first of the alternative prefaces is basically that of The Liturgy of the Lord's Supper (1967). The use of this preface is particularly appropriate on the first Sunday of Lent, when the Gospel in all three years is the story of our Lord's temptations. The form is a revised version of that of the Book of Common Worship of the Church of South India which was indebted to the Scottish revision of 1929. Biblical allusions include Hebrews 4:15 and 2 Corinthians 5:15.

The second of the alternative proper prefaces for Lent, which is particularly appropriate for use on Ash Wednesday and most Sundays in Lent, is a paraphrase by Capt. Howard E. Galley of the Church Army of the first preface for Lent in the Roman sacramentary of Paul VI. This preface expresses very powerfully the meaning and purpose of Lent and the disciplines which it entails. The translation of the Roman Catholic ICEL reads:

> Each year you give us this joyful season when we prepare to celebrate the paschal mystery with mind and heart renewed. You give us a spirit of loving reverence for you, our Father, and of willing service to our neighbor. As we recall the great events that gave us new life in Christ, you bring the image of your Son to perfection within us.

The proper preface for Holy Week includes allusions to John 12:32 and Hebrews 5:8-9. It is based upon that of the Scottish revision of 1929, which reads:

> Because thou didst give thine only Son, our Saviour Jesus Christ, to redeem mankind from the power of darkness; who, having finished the work thou gavest him to do, was lifted up upon the cross that he might draw all men unto himself, and, being made

perfect through suffering, might become the author of eternal salvation to all of them that obey him.

The proper preface for Easter is the one provided in the 1549 Book. Scriptural allusions include John 1:29 and 2 Timothy 1:10. It is a loose paraphrase of the Easter preface in the Sarum missal which dates to the Gelasian (no. 458) and the Gregorian (nos. 379, 385, 394, and 417) sacramentaries. It is also found in the Gallican Bobbio missal (no. 261), and in what is probably an earlier version in Missale Gallicanum vetus (nos. 182 and 233) and Missale Gothicum (no. 286). The Sarum version might be more literally translated:

And to extol you indeed at all times, but more gloriously on this day especially, when Christ our Passover was sacrificed, for he is truly the lamb that took away the sins of the world, who by dying destroyed our death, and by rising again restored life.

Except for two changes, the proper preface for the Ascension is that of the 1549 Book. In this present revision "there we might also be" was substituted for "thither we might also ascend." The 1549 version, "appeared to all his disciples," was changed in 1552 to "appeared to all his Apostles." This revision substitutes "appeared to his disciples." The Sarum version upon which this is based read:

Through Jesus Christ our Lord, who after his resurrection manifestly appeared to all his disciples, and as they watched him was lifted into heaven, that he might grant us to be partakers of his divinity.

It is the proper preface for the Ascension of the Gregorian sacramentary (no. 499).

Much of the content of the proper preface for Pentecost is taken from Cranmer's new composition for the 1549 Book. That preface read:

Through Jesus Christ our Lord, according to whose most true promise, the Holy Ghost came down this day from heaven, with a sudden great sound, as it had been a mighty wind, in the likeness of fiery tongues, lighting upon the Apostles, to teach them, and to lead them to all truth, giving them both the gift of diverse languages, and also boldness with fervent zeal, constantly to preach the Gospel unto all nations, whereby we are brought out of darkness and error into the clear light and true knowledge of thee, and of thy Son Jesus Christ.

The Sarum version, which was that of the Gelasian sacramentary (no. 627), the Gallican Missale Gothicum (no. 357), and the Gregorian sacramentary (nos. 522 and 528), reads:

> Through Christ our Lord, who ascending above all heavens and sitting at your right hand, poured out the promised Holy Spirit this day on the sons of adoption. Wherefore the whole world rejoices with exceeding joy and the heavenly hosts and angelic powers sing together a hymn to your glory, saying without ceasing, Holy . . .

This revised version of the Prayer Book preface—inspired by English Series 3—states more concisely the thoughts of the longer version, and gives thanks also for two other graces of the Holy Spirit, "uniting peoples of many tongues in the confession of one faith," and giving the church the power to serve God as a "royal priesthood."

Prefaces for Other Occasions (pp. 347–349 and 380–382)

This preface for Trinity Sunday is a new translation by the Rev. Dr. Charles M. Guilbert, Custodian of the Standard Book of Common Prayer, and member of the editorial committee for this revision, of a preface thought to be of Mozarabic origin. Its style and content are more typical of Gallican than of Roman prefaces. It is found in the Gelasian sacramentary (no. 680) and the Gregorian (no. 1621) for the Sunday in the octave of Pentecost. It is also found in the Celtic Stowe missal and in a Mozarabic sacramentary. In the Sarum missal it was appointed for use on every Sunday from Trinity Sunday until Advent and at nuptial Eucharists. It was one of the five proper prefaces retained in the 1549 Book, in an abbreviated version for use on Trinity Sunday only. Cranmer's version reads:

> Which art one God, one Lord, not one only person, but three persons in one substance: For that which we believe of the glory of the Father, the same we believe of the Son, and of the Holy Ghost, without any difference or inequality: whom the angels, etc.

The original proceeded:

> that in the confession of a true and everlasting Godhead, both distinction in persons, and unity in essence, and equality in majesty might be adored; whom angels and archangels praise,

402

the cherubim also and seraphim, who cease not to cry with one
voice, saying, Holy . . .

The 1789 revision provided an alternative proper preface, and permission was given to use either or neither. The alternative, composed
by Bishop William White, read:

> For the precious death and merits of thy Son Jesus Christ our
> Lord, and for the sending to us of the Holy Ghost the Comforter;
> who are one with thee in thy eternal Godhead.

In the 1928 revision the use of a proper preface on Trinity Sunday
was again required. The older of the two forms was revised to read:

> Who, with thine only-begotten Son, and the Holy Ghost, art one
> God, one Lord, in Trinity of Persons and in Unity of Substance.
> For that which we believe of thy glory, O Father, the same we
> believe of the Son, and of the Holy Ghost, without any difference
> of inequality.

The new translation of this Book is better adapted for use as a proper
preface, more in keeping with the other proper prefaces than the
older versions which were more like doctrinal formularies than
eucharistic prayers. In fact, it sets forth more clearly than the old the
unity, equality, and co-eternity of the Triune God. The Trinity Sunday preface in this Book is also appointed for Independence Day, the
feast of Saint Michael and All Angels, and Thanksgiving Day. It is
also the preface for the votives "Of the Holy Trinity," "Of the Holy
Angels," and "For the Nation," and an alternative at "For the Unity of
the Church" and with the common "Of a theologian and teacher."

The preface for All Saints, based on Hebrews 12:12, came into the
American Prayer Book in the 1928 revision from the Scottish Book of
1912.

Three alternative proper prefaces are provided in this revision for
use on the feast day of a saint. The first of these is drawn from a prayer
included in the American Prayer Book in the 1928 revision as one of
the additional prayers printed after the burial office. This prayer, the
first of the additional prayers (p. 487) in this edition, is essentially the
final paragraph of the prayer for the church from the eucharistic rite
of the 1637 Scottish Prayer Book. The first phrase can be traced back,
through the Scottish Book, to the first Prayer Book of 1549, where it is
in the conclusion of the 1549 prayer for the church, deleted in 1552.

The second of the alternative proper prefaces for a saint is a revised version of the first half of the proper preface for saints of the Book of Common Worship of the Church of South India.

The third preface for the feast day of a saint dates at least to the first printed Roman missal of 1474 where, surprisingly, it is the preface of the eucharistic introduction to the blessing of the palms on Palm Sunday.

The proper preface for apostles and ordinations is from the trial Liturgy of the Lord's Supper (1967). It is a revised form of that proposed in Prayer Book Studies IV (1953), which had been based upon the preface for ordinations in the Scottish revisions of 1912 and 1929. Biblical sources include John 10:11–18, 21:15–19, Hebrews 13:20, and Matthew 28:18–20. This preface is appointed for use with the first of the votives "For the Ministry" as well as on the feast days of apostles and at ordinations.

The proper preface for the dedication of a church was written by Capt. Howard E. Galley. Biblical allusions include Hebrews 4:14, 1 Peter 2:5, Ephesians 2:20–22, and Hebrews 13:15. This preface is provided for use on the anniversary of the dedication of a church as well as at the time of its consecration.

The proper preface for use at a baptism, written by the committee on baptism, gives stress to three of the effects of that sacrament: in baptism we are adopted by God, become citizens of the kingdom, and receive the Holy Spirit. This preface may be used with the proper for the last Sunday after Pentecost (Proper 29), as well as with the votives "For All Baptized Christians," "At Baptism," "At Confirmation," "For the Unity of the Church," and the third of the propers "For the Ministry."

The proper preface for use at a marriage was written by Capt. Howard E. Galley. Biblical allusions include Hebrews 12:22, Revelation 21:2, 2 Corinthians 5:17 and Ephesians 5:25–27.

The oldest extant version of the proper preface for the commemoration of the dead is that of the Mozarabic Missale Mixtum in which it is the proper preface in a Mass for a deceased priest.[1] In the Roman Church it was adopted in a revised form in 1919 for use at a requiem. A translation of this preface was proposed in Prayer Book Studies IV (1953); the present translation uses both the version adopted in 1953 and the revised form of the prayer from the Sacramentary of Paul VI. The preface in the 1979 Book is appointed for burials and for votives "For the Departed."

---

[1] J. P. Migne, ed., *Patrologia Latina*, LXXXV, col. 1019.

Prayers of the People (pp. 383–395)

Form I (pp. 383–385)

This prayer is based upon litanies from the Eastern liturgies of Saint Basil and Saint John Chrysostom. The initial line is the call to prayer after the Gospel. The first and second petitions are the opening petitions of the prayers of the faithful and of the initial Great Litany. The petitions for the clergy, the community, fruitful seasons, those who travel, and those with various needs parallel and show some verbal dependence upon the analogous petitions in the Great Litany of those rites. The petition for the departed is based upon those of the "Litany of fervent supplication" after the Gospel. The petition for deliverance is paralleled in the litany which follows the preparation of the table. The remaining petitions are based upon supplications found both in that litany and in the litany at the conclusion of the eucharistic prayer. The fifth of the concluding collects (p. 395) is based upon the prayer associated with the "litany of fervent supplication," the first of the litanies following the readings in these two ancient Eastern liturgies. A petition may be inserted to cover concerns not explicitly mentioned and certain petitions may be omitted, such as the petition for forgiveness when a confession of sin is said within the eucharistic rite. As a whole this prayer incorporates current concerns, but it is also closely related in structure and spirit to the ancient litanies which are its primary sources.

Form II (pp. 385–387)

The Rev. Alfred Shands drafted this series of biddings, new to the 1979 Book. In a concise manner the prayer covers subjects for which intercessions are offered and provides opportunities for the people to offer individual petitions silently or aloud.

Form III (pp. 387–388)

In the classical collects, the petition is followed by a statement of the reason for the petition. The leader, in this prayer, states the petition and the people respond by stating the reason for the petition. The prayer is a revised form of the third alternative intercession in the experimental liturgy of the Anglican Church of the Province of New Zealand (1966). In that form the first response was extended to include the phrase "so that the world may believe." The fifth response in the New Zealand version read "That we may be blessed in all our

405

works." The final bidding in the present American Book replaces a versicle "Lord, hear our prayer," and response "And let our cry come to you." The present revised form allows the people to add their own petitions.

Form IV (pp. 388–389)

The history of this form is interesting. Services for Trial Use (1970) included a form of intercession adapted from the English Series Two experimental liturgy of 1967. The English form was revised for Series Three (1973) and further revised for the South African liturgy of 1975. The structure of this prayer follows the English forms with the response the same in all. With slight variations, the first two supplications are common to all the revisions, the third and fourth petitions are based on petitions peculiar to the South African liturgy, and the two final supplications on petitions peculiar to English Series Three.

Form V (pp. 389–391)

This should be compared with Form I. It is based upon a skillful modern Western adaptation of the Eastern litany form.[1] As in the Western collect form, each petition is followed by a statement of the reason for which the petition is made. A petition may be inserted for special needs or concerns; at appropriate places, names may be inserted in the supplications. Several petitions are marked as optional, and it is appropriate to omit the petition for forgiveness when a fuller form of confession will be used in the service.

Form VI (pp. 392–393)

The responsive portion of this prayer is based on a litany authorized by Special General Convention II (1969) for use with the 1967 trial liturgy, The Liturgy of the Lord's Supper. The petitions of that litany, which were drafted by the Rev. Dr. Carroll E. Simcox, were rearranged in this responsive form, and the concluding portion was added for Services for Trial Use (1970). The scriptural verses which follow the periods of silence are from 2 Samuel 24:14, 1 Chronicles 21:13, Psalm 34:3, Isaiah 25:1, Titus 3:4, Psalms 52:8 and 55:26. The general confession is a conflation of phrases from two sources: the general confession printed in Rite One which dates to

---

[1] *Santa Misa, Acción de Gracias de la Comunidad Cristiana*, New York: Pro Musica Press, 1965, pp. 16–19.

the Order of the Communion of 1548, and a petition for forgiveness from the 1967 Liturgy of the Lord's Supper.

The Collect at the Prayers (pp. 394–395)

The first collect is dependent upon two from earlier editions of the Prayer Book. It dates to the Gregorian sacramentary (no. 1195) in which it is the collect for the twenty-third Sunday after [the octave of] Pentecost. In the Sarum missal and prior editions of the Prayer Book it was appointed as the collect of the day for the twenty-third Sunday after Trinity. The petition was included also in another form in the 1549 Book, within a longer prayer printed among the collects provided for use after Ante-Communion. The longer form is retained in this Book to be used at the conclusion of the Great Litany (p. 153), and among the occasional prayers under the title "For the answering of prayer" (p. 834). Cranmer's translation of the original version read:

> God, our refuge and strength, which art the author of all godliness; be ready to hear the devout prayers of thy church, and grant that those things which we ask faithfully we may obtain effectually; through Jesus Christ our Lord.

The second collect is a contemporary adaptation of another Cranmerian collect which was printed among those provided for use after Ante-Communion in the 1549 Book. In the 1552 Prayer Book and subsequent Books use of these prayers was also allowed after the collects of either of the daily offices or the Eucharist, or after the Litany. In the present edition it is the collect of Proper 11. The contemporary adaptation was made for An Order of Worship prepared and recommended for experimental use by the commission on worship and the executive committee of the Consultation on Church Union (1968). In that rite it was the one optional collect printed for use at the end of the prayers of the people.

The third collect was written by Capt. Howard E. Galley. It reminds us of an important aspect of prayer, seeking to discern the will of God. Right praying leads to right action.

The fourth is another contemporary adaptation of the Cranmerian collect which in the 1979 Book is appointed as the collect of Proper 11.

The fifth collect is the prayer of the celebrant associated with the litany form of the prayers of the people in the Eastern Orthodox liturgies of Saint Basil and Saint John Chrysostom. It dates to the

407

earliest manuscript, the Barberini Euchologion of the late eighth century.

The 1928 Book first included the sixth collect, based on John 16:27, as the first of six collects which might be used after the collects of the daily office or the Eucharist. In the present Book it is included also among the prayers of the office for noonday (p. 107). The original form of the prayer is in late medieval missals, including some of the books of the Sarum rite, as a private devotion by the priest at the time of the peace. Its use is especially appropriate when the peace follows immediately after the prayers.

The seventh collect is a revised form of a collect printed after the prayers of the people in the Indian Liturgy (1960) and in the liturgy for Africa (1964). It is particularly appropriate for the season of Advent.

The Rev. Roddey Reid wrote the last collect.[1] It is also the third of the collects provided in the common "Of a Saint" (pp. 199 and 250). This prayer, which is particularly suited for use on saints' days and at All Saints', reminds us that the saints support us in two ways—not only by their witness or example but also by surrounding us with their love and their prayers.

Communion Under Special Circumstances (pp. 396–399)

This form is intended not only for use with the sick (p. 457), but also with those who because of work schedules or physical or other types of limitations cannot be present at a public celebration. Every edition of the Prayer Book had included special provisions for the communion of the sick, but it was not until the 1892 revision that provision was made for the communion of "aged and bed-ridden persons or such as are not able to attend the public Ministration in the Church." The present revision gives a more flexible form for the administration of communion to those who for any reason cannot be present at the public celebration for extended periods of time.

At a Eucharist celebrated with such persons, the proper of the day, or one of those appointed for various occasions, may be used. When limited time makes it necessary, the priest may begin with the offertory. It is desirable, however, that at least a passage from the Gospel be read as a liturgy of the word. One of the four Gospel passages printed at the beginning of this rite might be used.

---

[1] The Rev. Roddey Reid served on the editorial committee for the 1979 Book of Common Prayer.

The rubric which states that it is desirable to have periodic celebrations with a person who cannot be present at the public service for an extended period is followed immediately by a rubric which permits communion from the reserved Sacrament "At other times, or when desired."

In the mid-second century the deacons left the celebration of the Eucharist with the Sacrament to take it to those who, because of sickness or imprisonment or for any other reason, could not be present at the public rite. In some areas communicants took a portion of the Sacrament home with them in order that they might begin each day by receiving communion from the Sunday Eucharist. This was an anamnesis of the last eucharistic assembly which spoke of Sunday as the first day of the week and all which that represented, and a foretaste of the next eucharistic assembly which represented Sunday as the "eighth day" and all which that signified. This custom apparently died out in the fourth century, but the deacons or the priests continued to carry the Sacrament to those unable to be present. And in the East and in Gallican territory the communions on fast days were administered from the reserved Sacrament. In Roman territory this practice was followed on Good Friday. With the decline in communions of the people which accompanied the shifts in eucharistic piety in the medieval period, the communion of the sick from the reserved Sacrament began to be thought of as a "last rite," but continued to be a communion from a public rite. In the late middle ages, when private confession was required before communion, the devout communicant often received immediately after confession from the reserved Sacrament rather than within a public celebration.

During and after the thirteenth century in the West, piety centered more upon seeing the Sacrament than upon receiving it. The place of reservation, which in earlier times was the sacristy (which is still true in some places in the East), was changed to the church itself. In reaction to the late medieval developments, most of the reformers did away with the ancient practice of reservation for those unable to be present at the public rite. Many forbade any private celebration of the Eucharist.

The 1549 Prayer Book allowed reservation for the communion of the sick on the day of a public celebration. The 1552 Book eliminated reservation entirely, and this is the first American revision to permit the practice, though it was restored earlier in revisions for some other provinces of Anglicanism. It is restricted (pp. 408–409) to the reservation of that which is needed for the communion of those who cannot be present at a public celebration, for administration by a deacon to a congregation when a priest is not available, and to the reservation on Maundy Thursday for the Good Friday communion (pp. 275 and 282).

The fourth rubric states that it is desirable that those who will receive in special circumstances have fellow parishioners, relatives, and friends present, when possible, to communicate with them. The 1549 Prayer Book, like the Brandenburg church order, to symbolize the corporate nature of the Sacrament, directed that a sick person, receiving privately, "shall always desire some, either of his own house, or else of his neighbor's, to receive the Holy Communion with him." The 1552 Book revised this: a "good number" were expected to communicate with the sick person, but in times of contagious diseases and "upon special request of the diseased" the minister alone could communicate with the sick person. The 1662 Book required that there be "three, or two at the least" to communicate with the sick person, and the 1789 revision changed this to "which shall be two at the least." The 1928 revision dropped this requirement, but the sick person was still to signify to the minister "how many there are to communicate with him." In this present revision it is explicitly stated that it is desirable that others communicate with the person receiving in special circumstances.

Printed for the convenience of the priest or deacon and the people are texts needed for administration from the reserved Sacrament. The service begins directly, as in the first centuries, with a reading from the Scriptures. Four passages appropriate in general circumstances are printed. (At the great feasts it is, of course, desirable to read a passage appropriate to the day.) The celebrant may comment on the reading. Suitable prayers may be offered, with a concluding collect. That printed is the collect of Maundy Thursday. A confession of sin may follow. The confession and absolution printed in the service are those of Rite Two. The peace may then be exchanged. The rite then turns from the liturgy of the word to the liturgy of the sacrament. The Lord's Prayer is followed by the Sancta sanctis, and the ministration of communion. A sentence of administration common to Rite One and Rite Two is printed, but another of the forms may be used. One of the usual postcommunion prayers may be said, but an alternative, the work of the Rev. Dr. Massey H. Shepherd, Jr., is provided. The service concludes with a blessing or dismissal. The form printed is the fourth of the forms in Rite One and Rite Two. The postcommunion prayer and the dismissal which are printed in the rite would always be appropriate; there are times when other forms which speak of being sent out into the world would not be suitable.

An Order for Celebrating
the Holy Eucharist (pp. 400–405)

This order, which lists the elements considered essential for a eucharistic celebration, follows the traditional form which has been adopted in Rite One and Rite Two. It provides freedom for situations in which those rites, principally designed for the Sunday gathering of the congregation, are too formal, too verbose, or too demanding. The order provides flexibility for use when the congregation is principally composed of children or other particular age groups, or of special ethnic or cultural groups. It allows for appropriate adaptations when members of the congregation have limited sight, hearing, or other physical abilities, or have minimal reading ability or attention span. It is also appropriate for use with groups which have gathered for prayer, study, sharing, or committee work. It provides flexibility for situations in which time is at a premium. The order also provides the freedom, within certain limitations, to use some of the great historic liturgies of the church, to celebrate according to different traditions, to use texts from previous editions of the Book of Common Prayer or the Prayer Books of other provinces of Anglicanism (so long as the peace is included and the preparation of the table is reunited with the eucharistic prayer rather than preceding the prayer for the world and for the church). When there is sufficient reason to modify Rite One or Rite Two, the basic texts of those rites can be used with subtractions, variations, or additions allowed by this order.

The form allows freedom for experimentation or adaptation when texts particularly appropriate to the day or occasion are available. For example, devotional treasures from the writings of some of the saints or other worthies may be included in their commemoration on a black letter day. During the twelve days of Christmas a service of lessons and carols might serve suitably as the entrance rite and the proclamation and response to the word of God, though not as the principal service on a Sunday.

The initial rubric emphasizes that this order is not intended to provide license for a casually improvised service. It demands more careful attention and preparation than Rite One or Rite Two in which the choices are more limited and the structure largely detailed.

What is provided here is not a rite but an order of those elements which this church considers essential to a eucharistic celebration: the people and priest gather in the Lord's Name, proclaim and respond to the word of God, pray for the world and the church, exchange the

411

peace, prepare the table, make eucharist, break the bread, and share the gifts of God. The order of the elements is exactly the same as that of Rite One and Rite Two.

The People and Priest

The order of this listing is significant. The church is the *laos*, the people of God. For the Eucharist there must be a gathering of the people of God. Anglicanism has never allowed a priest to say a Mass without a representation of the people. The inclusion of a specific mention of the priest makes clear, however, that the presence and participation of a priest is required for the celebration. The subsequent rubrics indicate that the priest need not in this celebration occupy as prominent a role as in Rite One or Rite Two, but it is required that a priest say the eucharistic prayer in the name of the gathering.

Gather in the Lord's Name

This corresponds to the entrance rite of Rite One or Rite Two. In some circumstances, as in the first centuries of the church's life, this could be a simple bidding to attention or a salutation. On the other hand, this rite is often appropriate at the close of an evening spent in prayer, study, committee work, listening to music, singing, or some other activity. The evening's activity would then function as the entrance rite for the celebration.

Proclaim and Respond to the Word of God

The only restriction with regard to the reading or readings is that a passage from one of the four Gospels must be included. The pattern of Old Testament, Psalm, New Testament, and Gospel need not be adhered to, nor is the order of the readings prescribed. At times, one brief reading as the basis for reflection may be the appropriate choice. At other times a much longer reading than is appropriate within the setting of the normative rites may be desirable, as for example, the whole of the Sermon on the Mount (Mt. 5–7), or the whole of one of the Epistles. Or a great number of readings in which one theme is traced throughout the Scriptures may be desirable. The listing of appropriate responses to the readings is intended to be all inclusive, "readings, song, talk, dance, instrumental music, other art forms, silence." It should be noted that the more inclusive word "song" is used, in contrast to "hymn, psalm, or anthem" of the rubrics of Rite One and Rite Two.

Pray for the World and the Church

One of the forms of the prayers of the people (pp. 328–330 or 383–395), or prayers in conformity with the directions on page 383, may be used, but while various categories must be mentioned in the prayers of the people of Rite One or Rite Two, this order requires only that both the world and the church be remembered in prayer. Various published forms which do not necessarily fulfill the requirements for use in Rite One or Rite Two, or forms composed for the occasion, or free prayer may be used.

Exchange the Peace

In Rite One and Rite Two the exchange of the peace is printed in the traditional place, as the conclusion of the liturgy of the word and introduction to the liturgy of the table. The only exception normally allowed is that it may be done at the place to which it was shifted in the Roman rite, in connection with the breaking of the bread. At baptism or at confirmation, reception, or reaffirmation, it comes prior to the prayers as a sign of welcome. In this order, however, which assumes a congregation of a more intimate nature, possibly one which has spent the evening or several days in each other's company, more freedom is allowed. It may be appropriate to exchange the peace at the beginning or at the conclusion of the celebration, or possibly in connection with a particular reading or as a response to a reading.

Prepare the Table

At this point the bread and wine should be placed upon the table by some of the people, and, if the wine is not in a cup or glass suitable for drinking, some should be poured into the cup over which the blessing will be said. If there are other offerings, they should also be placed upon the table at this time.

Make Eucharist

The priest is to say the eucharistic prayer in the name of the gathering. Any of the eucharistic prayers of Rite One or Rite Two may be used. Two additional forms are provided (pp. 402–405), in which only a basic core is prescribed. As long as thanks and praise are offered for the work of God the Father in creation and in His revelation of Himself and for the salvation of the world through Jesus Christ our Lord, this prayer may be filled out by the use of relevant material from various traditional or published prayers, or a text may be composed for the occasion. The form may provide for a number of responses by the people; two are required: participation in the opening dialogue and the concluding Amen.

Break the Bread

As in Rite One and Rite Two the breaking of the bread is to follow the conclusion of the eucharistic prayer and precede the communion of the people.

Share the Gifts of God

The phraseology is reminiscent of the traditional Sancta sanctis, "The Gifts of God for the People of God," the invitation to communion of Rite One and Rite Two. Whereas in those rites it is prescribed that a deacon or priest (or a person licensed by the bishop) minister the Sacrament making use of prescribed texts, that is not required in this order. The Sacrament may be ministered by some of those present, the communicants may themselves receive from the sacramental elements on the table, or the elements may be passed from one to another, so long as they are "shared in a reverent manner." The rubric directs that any of the elements which have been designated for the Sacrament be consumed prior to sharing in any other food.

The agapé or love feast of the early church had its analogue in the *chabûrah* or brotherhood meal which was held by certain groups among the Jews on significant occasions. In the earliest decades of the church's life, the Eucharist was celebrated in the context of such a meal. Because abuses crept in (see 1 Cor. 11:17–34), because of the increase in numbers so that the group could not be accommodated in most private houses, and because of the need for haste in times of persecution, the meal was separated from the eucharistic celebration. The agapé itself continued for generations; the distribution of blessed bread or other food at the end of the eucharistic rite in many Eastern churches, and on certain occasions in the West during the medieval period, may be a remnant of this agapé meal. The "love feast" of the Moravians, adopted by the Methodists, was a conscious attempt to revive the agapé of the early church.

The descriptions which we have of the agapé meals of the early church indicate that they began with the sharing of blessed bread.

414

This blessing of the bread was not restricted to a priest, and the form avoided terms which might lead to confusion between this bread and the bread of the Eucharist. The agapé typically included the serving of wine, but this was not considered essential to the occasion. (A wine blessing, when used, frequently preceded the bread blessing.) The agapé was, at least on occasion, prefaced by the lucernarium or blessing of light (see the Order of Worship for the Evening, pp. 108–114), and was customarily followed by the singing of psalms and hymns and by prayers appropriate to the time of day. The final rubric of the order directs that an agapé or common meal should not be intermingled with or should not immediately precede the eucharistic celebration. If it is to be a part of the celebration it should not begin until after the eucharistic elements have been consumed.

At the Great Thanksgiving (pp. 402–405)

Any of the eucharistic prayers of Rite One or Rite Two may be used in An Order for Celebrating the Holy Eucharist. In addition, two forms are provided which permit the use of portions of other eucharistic prayers or the preparation of prayers particularly suited to the group or occasion. These forms are not authorized for use in Rite One or Rite Two.

Form 1 (pp. 402–403)

The salutation and Sursum corda are to be followed by the giving of thanks to God for creation and for His revelation of Himself to His people. The particular occasion may be recalled, and the proper preface of the day may be incorporated as it is printed, or adapted to make it better suited to the context. In keeping with the precedent of prayers of the first centuries, the inclusion of the Sanctus is not obligatory. If it interferes with the progression to the section in which God is praised "for the salvation of the world through Jesus Christ our Lord" it should be omitted. The fixed text, like Eucharistic Prayer C of Rite Two, follows the order of the traditional Roman eucharistic prayer: an offering of the gifts and the epiclesis precede the institution narrative. This is followed by an anamnesis, prayer for the benefits of communion, and the final doxology. The oblation and epiclesis are an abbreviated version of those of Eucharistic Prayer C. The oblation is that of Prayer III in the Roman sacramentary of Paul VI. The institution narrative is identical with that of Prayer C. The anamnesis, which is reminiscent of the common memorial acclamation, is an abbreviated version of that of Roman Prayer IV. The peti-

415

tion resembles the conclusion of Prayer C. Its final phrase is from Roman Prayer IV. The doxology is identical with that of Prayers A and B.

Form 2 (pp. 404–405)

Like Form 1 above, this prayer is to be filled out by those preparing the particular service. They choose or prepare not only the text of the section in which God is blessed for His work in creation and for His revelation of Himself, and for the salvation of the world through the redemptive work of Christ, but also the concluding section in which prayer is offered for "the benefits of Christ's work, and the renewal of the Holy Spirit." This form maintains the Eastern, Scottish, American order of institution narrative, anamnesis and oblation, and epiclesis. The Sursum corda is not introduced with the usual salutation, but, as in many of the Eastern liturgies, with the Grace (2 Cor. 13:14). As in Form 1, following the precedent of many of the earliest eucharistic prayers, the Sanctus is not required, and it should be omitted if it interferes with the flow of the thanksgivings. The institution narrative is identical with that of Eucharistic Prayer A of Rite Two, and, except for the introduction, the same as that of Prayers B and D. The anamnesis is an amplified version of the memorial acclamation in Eucharistic Prayer B. The oblation incorporates phrases from that of Eucharistic Prayer A. The epiclesis upon the gifts incorporates phrases from both Prayers A and B. The petition for the benefits of communion is based upon the Australian experimental liturgy of 1973. The doxology is that of Eucharistic Prayer A.

Additional Directions (pp. 406–409)

The Covering of the Holy Table

The first sentence states, "The holy table is spread with a clean white cloth during the celebration." One third century account (Acts of Thomas) has the deacon bring the table into the midst of the congregation at the beginning of the liturgy of the table and place upon it a white cloth. At least as late as the eighth century, when the attention turned from the pulpit to the table after the liturgy of the word, deacons spread a white cloth upon the table. With the development of low Mass, in which the altar began to function as both table and pulpit, the altar was prepared before the rite, and was covered with a white cloth. Eventually, in order to protect the cloth, a smaller piece of cloth which could be laundered more easily was put over the center of it, much like putting a place mat under a child's plate to protect a treasured cloth on the dinner table. The use of this "corporal" has never been required by the Prayer Book. It came back into use in Anglicanism in the late nineteenth and early twentieth century. The word "linen" in the description of the required cloth in prior editions of the Prayer Book was used in the sense in which people speak of tablecloths made of various materials as "linens." This rubric is a clarification of the corresponding rubric of prior editions. The cloth may be put on the table before the service, or at the time of the offertory.

The Entrance Rite

The second paragraph gives directions for occasions on which the Great Litany is sung or said in the entrance rite. This is equivalent to the entrance rite in Rome from the late fifth century until the end of the sixth.

The third paragraph gives specific permission to make use of the Gloria Patri at the conclusion of an entrance psalm. This was traditional after the processional psalms used at the entrance, at the offertory, and at the communion. The Gloria Patri was never used, however, after the gradual or the tract; these psalms were not in the service to cover a procession but for the sake of the psalm texts themselves. The importance attached to them is signified by the fact that they were not omitted even when there were no processions. The Gloria Patri provides a climax for processional psalms, but its addition to graduals or tracts, which have their own integrity and reason for being in the rite, is certainly not traditional and is thought by many to denigrate these elements of the rite. The use of the translation of the Gloria Patri in prior editions of the Prayer Book is allowed in Rite One. This is probably wise when this translation is printed with the music used by the congregation.

The fourth paragraph gives, for the first time, explicit permission to sing or say the Kyrie in either threefold, sixfold, or ninefold form. The ninefold form is that which was traditionally used through the time of the 1549 Prayer Book. It is the form which was continued in one sense in the decalogue which replaced the Kyrie in the revision of 1552. It was restored to the Prayer Book in a threefold form in the 1892 revision. The sixfold form is increasingly favored in rites of various churches and by composers, for it provides that a cantor or choir may sing each of the three lines and the congregation repeat what they have just heard as a response. Freedom is also explicitly granted to sing the Trisagion three times or antiphonally.

417

The fifth paragraph lists those occasions on which the use of the Gloria in excelsis or some other song of praise is required in the entrance rite, and the occasions on which the Kyrie or Trisagion must be used in place of the song of praise.

The Liturgy of the Word

The sixth paragraph encourages the recovery of the tradition of reading (and preaching) the word from a prominent pulpit or ambo which symbolizes the importance of the word, the integrity of the liturgy of the word, and the presence of Christ in His word. Even before the publication of the first Prayer Book, injunctions ordered that in every church there should be a pulpit for the reading and preaching of the word. This was a recovery of the tradition of the early church and of the medieval high Mass which had been abandoned at low Mass. The Roman sacramentary of Paul VI states:

> The dignity of the word of God requires the church to have a suitable place for announcing his message so that the attention of the people may be easily directed to that place during the liturgy of the word.
> Ordinarily the lectern or ambo should be a fixed pulpit and not a simple movable stand. Depending on the structure of the church, it should be so placed that the ministers may be easily seen and heard by the faithful.
> The readings, responsorial psalm, and *Exsultet* are proclaimed from the lectern. It may be used for the homily and general intercessions (prayer of the faithful).

The Prayer Book rubric also states plainly, "It is desirable that the Lessons and Gospel be read from a book or books of appropriate size and dignity."

The seventh paragraph permits the reading of the Gospel in other languages if a portion of the congregation is composed of people whose native tongue is not English. The reader of the Gospel in another language need not be a deacon or priest. In some rites the Gospel is read in several languages, especially at the two primary feasts, Easter and Pentecost.

When There is No Communion or When No Priest is Present

The next two paragraphs give directions for the use of the liturgy of the word in situations where there is to be no communion, or where there is no priest present.

418

The Peace

The next paragraph clarifies the fact that there is to be a verbal exchange at the peace, whether or not the people greet each other, and that the people in their greetings are not bound to any particular form of words. It also allows the exchange of the peace in connection with the breaking of the bread, the place which it has occupied in the Roman rite since the fifth century.

Announcements

The Prayer Books before 1662 directed that announcements follow the sermon. The 1662 revision unfortunately placed them between the readings and the sermon, a permission deliberately withdrawn in this revision. Announcements are allowed in four places within the rite, each of which has its own rationale. Things that people need to know before the Creed may be announced before the service. Announcements which it would be helpful for people to know prior to the prayers of the people (so that they might become subjects of prayer) may be made after the Creed. Any announcements which involve welcomes or other greetings may appropriately be made at the time of the peace. Reminders of activities immediately after the service might most appropriately be made just prior to the blessing (Rite One) or [blessing and] dismissal (Rite Two).

The Preparation of the Table

The twelfth paragraph defines the role of the deacon in the preparation of the table, and emphasizes the tradition of mixing water with the wine. The "ministers" who may assist the deacon should, in keeping with tradition, be lay ministers.

So highly valued was the symbolism of one cup upon the altar that after the growth of the church additional wine needed for the administration of the Sacrament was poured into another vessel which was not placed upon the altar. After the breaking of the bread a few drops from the chalice which had been upon the altar during the eucharistic prayer were added to the wine in that vessel. In keeping with Anglican tradition, from 1662 on, the flagon with additional wine is to be placed upon the altar, but no other cup or cup-like vessel, whether it contains wine or bread, should be upon the altar to soften the symbolism of the one cup. In a few rites the act of pouring the wine from the flagon into other cups, after the breaking of the bread, has been considered symbolically significant.

419

The Fraction Anthem

One of the two translations of the Agnus Dei by ICET is printed here for use on occasion as the anthem at the breaking of the bread. (For the history and use of this anthem, see above, pp. 380–381.)

The Ministration of Communion

The last full paragraph on page 407 makes explicit a direction that the celebrant is not to receive communion until "the people are coming forward." The symbolism which is being safeguarded is that celebrant and congregation alike partake of one table. There should be no "high table" for the clergy apart from the sharing of the people.

The last direction on page 407 safeguards the right of every communicant to receive the consecrated bread and wine separately, but also permits the practice of intinction within certain restrictions.

In documents as early as the second century, the deacon is described as the minister of communion. Not long afterward, the celebrant and assisting presbyters also took part in the ministration. Anglican Prayer Books prior to the current revision limited the deacon to the ministration of the cup. This direction restores to the deacon the right to administer the bread as well as the cup, and recognizes the decision of the General Convention of 1967 to allow lay persons specially licensed to administer the chalice.

Supplementary Consecration

Making use of a form of words over additional bread or wine needed to complete the communions of the people is a uniquely Anglican tradition. (For the history of this, see above, pp. 388–390.) A brief text which includes both epiclesis and words of institution is provided in this edition of the Prayer Book; a fuller form equivalent to that required from the time of the 1789 revision is permitted as an alternative.

Ministration of Communion by a Deacon

Historically deacons have been ministers of communion to those unable to be present for the Eucharist. The council of Arles (A.D. 314) forbade the deacon to function as celebrant when a priest was not available, but deacons have administered to congregations from the reserved Sacrament using the historic liturgy of the presanctified gifts, the liturgy anciently appointed for the ministration of communion on days when a celebration of the Eucharist was considered inappropriate. This is the first Prayer Book to authorize a restoration of this tradition. The rite which is outlined here can be used only with the authorization of the bishop.

Reservation and Ablutions

The paragraph which begins at the bottom of page 408 gives directions for ablutions, in particular the disposition of consecrated elements which remain after the communion. Reservation of the Sacrament for the communion of those who for good reasons cannot be present at the public celebration, for administration by a deacon, and on Maundy Thursday for the Good Friday communion (see pp. 275 and 282) is explicitly allowed. Other elements which remain are to be reverently consumed, after the communion of the people or after the dismissal. The additional directions for the ordination rites are more explicit: "it is appropriate for the deacons to remove the vessels from the Altar, consume the remaining Elements, and cleanse the vessels in some convenient place." The intention is that the ablutions not be a focus of attention.

Hymns after Communion

The last of the additional directions allows a hymn before the postcommunion prayer. The 1549 Book had provided sentences of scripture, one of which was to be sung at that time, but the 1552 revision omitted these. This is the first Prayer Book to restore permission to have a sung text at this point. In some situations it would help to make the ablutions less obtrusive. A hymn is also allowed after the postcommunion prayer, in a position analogous to the Gloria in excelsis in Prayer Books since the 1552 revision. It is to be noted that the permission to have a hymn after the blessing, which was in the revisions of 1892 and 1928, has been withdrawn. The blessing and dismissal is itself a sending out.

Disciplinary Rubrics

The first three paragraphs of the disciplinary rubrics are basically a version in modern language of two rubrics from the 1549 Prayer Book. Until the 1928 revision they were printed among the rubrics which followed the title of the service and prior to the text of the eucharistic rite, but in that Book they were moved to the end of the service. The first of the 1549 rubrics, the basis for the first two paragraphs, directed the minister to warn anyone who was such "an open and notorious evil liver" that the congregation was scandalized, and any who had wronged their neighbors, not to come to communion. In the 1662 revision the qualification of having scandalized the congregation was extended to both categories of persons. In this revision that qualification is attached to having done wrong to neighbors, and removed from the other. The third paragraph, which was based upon the royal injunctions (26) of 1547, directs the minister to give warning to those between whom there is hatred. The requirement that the bishop be notified within fourteen days was added in the 1662 revision. Canon law protects the laity from arbitrary acts of excommunication, and specifies that communion may not be refused penitent persons at the point of death.

Pastoral Offices

This section of the Prayer Book contains rites which mark significant turning points (crises) in the lives of individuals within the community. In the late middle ages rites of this type were contained in a book known in various places as the "manuale," "rituale," or "agenda." The Prayer Book included them because they were part of community concern and were normally to be conducted in public with a congregation to participate. Revised forms of all the rites from previous Books are in the present Book; several rites not in any earlier edition have been included to meet the needs of the contemporary community.

Confirmation (pp. 412-419)

For times when there is no one to be baptized at the bishop's parochial visit, but there are persons who wish to make public affirmation or reaffirmation, or to be received from other communions, material from the baptismal rite is repeated under this heading in order to make the service easier to follow. Among the propers for various occasions the Book also provides a collect and lections (pp. 203 or 254, and 929), for use subject to the rules of precedence governing principal feasts, Sundays, and holy days (see pp. 17–18). On this occasion the bishop may consecrate chrism for use at subsequent baptisms, using the prayer on page 307. (See *The Book of Occasional Services*, pp. 209–210, for a bidding and additional directions about consecrating chrism.)

For commentary on this rite, see the section on Holy Baptism.

A Form of Commitment to
Christian Service (pp. 420-421)

I n the New Testament we have accounts of a special service for those who ventured from the Christian community into a new ministry or into missionary enterprises (Mt. 10:1—11:1; Acts 13:1-3; Gal. 2:9). The Acts of Peter, a late second century book of the New Testament Apocrypha, contains the account of a rite in which persons were commissioned for a new ministry with prayer and laying on of hands, culminating in the Eucharist. Such rites have not been limited to clergy or those employed professionally by the church. The chief liturgical model for one who undertakes a special responsibility involving commitment to the service of Christ in the world has been the rite for coronation of a ruler. Throughout the history of the church, rites have been devised locally for persons who enter into various civic offices or who undertake some special responsibility. This is the first edition of the Prayer Book to include a model for such a rite.

As the first rubric makes clear, the rite is not intended to be a commissioning for lay ministries within the church (rites for this purpose are in *The Book of Occasional Services*, pp. 160–176). It marks personal commitment to the service of Christ "in the world." The commitment may be a general one or may carry special responsibility for some undertaking; it may be a commitment to exercise a lay ministry through one's profession or vocation. The shift to another vocation, or the taking on of some new or additional responsibility, may represent a commitment to service of Christ in the world to be marked by this rite.

The rite opens with an act of commitment which must be worked out for the individual situation between the celebrant and the person

425

making the commitment. It may be a statement of intention, or a series of questions and answers. Some form of reaffirmation of the baptismal vows is always included.

This action follows the prayers [and confession of sin] and precedes the peace within the eucharistic rite. It begins with the act of commitment.

The blessing, the commendation and the pledge of support, and the final prayer are provided as models. They may be adapted for the particular circumstance, or other forms may be used as seems appropriate to the celebrant and to the individual making the commitment.

This form was prepared by the Rev. Bonnell Spencer of the Order of the Holy Cross.

The Celebration and Blessing
of a Marriage

I n most societies, when persons approach marriage, a series of rites separates them from their peers (the unmarried men and women of the community), prepares them for marriage, and integrates them into the life, responsibilities, and customs of married couples in the community.

Among the Jews the rites of marriage involved a ceremony of betrothal, some time prior to the wedding, in which the father of the bride gave his consent to the union. The wedding itself was preceded by a procession of the bridegroom and friends to the bride's home. She was richly dressed, wearing a veil, which she would not remove until her entry into the bridal chamber. The ceremony included vows and a written contract ("covenant"), and a blessing over a cup of wine. During the ceremony the bride and groom stood under a canopy in the presence of at least ten witnesses (the "minyan," a minimum number necessary for a synagogue service). Following the ceremony the wedding company went in procession to the bridegroom's home while the witnesses sang love songs (see Psalm 45 and the Song of Songs); there was dancing and a feast that lasted from seven to fourteen days.

There is no hint concerning a Christian marriage rite in the New Testament, although it does provide teachings concerning the duties of husbands and wives, parents and children, and married couples within the community. Probably the rites of Judaism were followed with little modification since they were a part of ancient and familiar custom.

Among the pagan Romans wedding rites began with a betrothal at

427

the home of the bride, where a contract was signed before witnesses. The man gave a betrothal present, kissed the bride, and placed a ring on the fourth finger of her left hand as a symbol of possession. The hands of the two were joined. A banquet generally followed. Some time later, on the day of the wedding, the bride was arrayed in her wedding garments, which included a cincture (a symbol of virginity), a yellow dress, flame-colored veil, and floral crown. The bride and groom made a solemn declaration before witnesses after which the *pronuba* (representing Juno, goddess of marriage, domesticity, and childbearing) joined their hands. The couple offered a sacrifice at the family altar to propitiate the *lares*, and the *auspex nuptiarum* (priest of the marriage rites who would guarantee the auspiciousness of the rite) recited a prayer which the couple repeated as they processed around the altar. At some point a veil or pall was held over the couple. A banquet followed, lasting until nightfall when the bride was led to her new home, accompanied by virgins and young unmarried men singing wedding songs, and was carried over the threshold by her husband. They lit the hearthfire together and she was sprinkled with water, a symbol of fertility among other things. The *pronuba* prepared the marriage bed as the couple went through the rites of loosening the marriage cincture and praying to the gods of marriage. On the following day the bride received her new relatives and sacrificed to the gods of her new home.

Incidental references to marriage in the writings of the church fathers indicate that the rites were not radically different among early Christians, except for evidence of the consent and possibly the attendance of the bishop who participated in some marriages. Christian prayers and blessings were, of course, substituted for pagan ones, and a Eucharist replaced the pagan sacrifices.

When the liturgical books developed, lections, psalms, and prayers were provided for the Eucharist, with a special blessing before the communion of the newly married couple. Forms for blessing the newlyweds in bed were also provided. Some books contained propers for use at a daily office, and propers for a Eucharist after thirty days and at one year. Late in the middle ages marriage rites came completely under purview of the church and were considerably abbreviated. Banns were posted to advise the community of the coming marriage. The equivalent of the old civil marriage was held in the church porch immediately before the wedding, and the giving of blessed bread and wine often substituted for communion.

Many theologians, from the time of Clement of Alexandria and Augustine, had looked upon marriage as a concession to human weakness; Luther considered it a vocation appropriate for Christian living. He greatly abbreviated the marriage rite, retained the publication of banns, and followed the custom of asking questions of betrothal in the church porch. These were followed by the verse "Those whom God hath joined together" and a proclamation of the marriage. These two elements were not in the English rites but did have medieval German precedents. The couple were then led to the altar for the reading of Genesis 2:18, 21–24, and an exhortation which consisted mainly of scriptural quotations followed by a prayer.

The rites of later German church orders were generally more elaborate; that of Hermann of Cologne required an examination of the couple and their parents as well as the publication of banns on three holy days before the wedding. The rite itself was performed within the Sunday service and began with an exhortation which included several scriptural quotations. There followed a silent prayer by the congregation, the betrothal questions, exchange of rings, proclamation of marriage, the singing of Psalms 127 and 128, and prayer. The German rites deleted the blessing of the ring. In the Reformed churches marriages were also conducted within the Sunday service, with banns published beforehand. Reformed tradition rejected the blessing or the giving of rings within the rite.

The 1549 Prayer Book drew its marriage rite from the Sarum and York traditions, the Consultation of Hermann and some other German church orders,[1] and the exposition of marriage from the *King's Book*. The rite was to be preceded by the publication of banns on three Sundays or holy days. The marriage took place in the church on Sunday after Morning Prayer and the Litany and before the Eucharist. An Exhortation lists three reasons for the institution of marriage: (1) the procreation of children; (2) "a remedy against sin, and to avoid fornication"; and (3) "mutual society, help, and comfort." The couple is charged to declare any known impediment. The charge is followed by the betrothal, the giving of the bride, the vows, and the giving of the ring (not blessed). "Other tokens of spousage, as gold or silver," are also to be given. A prayer for grace to keep the vows and live according to God's law, a proclamation of the marriage, and a blessing follow. The priest and couple move to the altar during the saying or singing of Psalm 128 or 67, and the couple kneel for the Kyrie, the Lord's Prayer, preces, prayers for the gift of children and for graces necessary to marriage, and for the priestly blessing. A hom-

---

[1] Probably that of Brandenburg.

ily is provided for use if the sermon does not expound on the duties of husbands and wives according to the Scriptures. The couple is required to receive communion.

The 1552 revision made minor changes in prayers, omitted the requirement of other gifts along with the ring, and changed the form connected with the ring accordingly.

The 1662 revision no longer requires the couple to receive communion at their marriage but they are urged to do so either at that time or at the first opportunity thereafter. This was a concession to the Puritans who objected to having weddings on Sundays or at the Eucharist because of the festivities traditionally associated with weddings.

The American revision of 1789 deleted from the opening exhortation the "causes for which Matrimony was ordained," and eliminated the words "with my body I thee worship" from the form used with the giving of the ring. The procession to the holy table and all that followed were omitted, leaving an abridged rite which represented the old civil espousal, cut short before the sacramental reinforcement of the civil action.

The 1892 Book restored references to marriage as instituted by God, as signifying the union between Christ and His church, and as "adorned and beautified" by the miracle at Cana.

The 1928 revision eliminated the phrase "with all my worldly goods I thee endow," the use of Old Testament models for marriage, and the promise of the woman to "obey." It provided an optional form for blessing the ring, a prayer for children, and another prayer for the couple. Eucharistic propers were given.

The present revision again sets marriage within the context of the liturgy of word and sacrament. In place of one set of propers, a choice of psalms and scriptural readings from the Old and New Testaments is listed within the rite. The "giving away of the bride" is optional as is a new form for the presentation of both bride and groom. The congregation is asked to uphold this couple in their marriage.

A form is provided for the blessing of a civil marriage (pp. 433–434), based on the one first included in the 1949 Book of Offices.[1] An order for marriage (pp. 435–436), analogous to the orders for the Eucharist and for burial (pp. 400–401 and 506), lists elements which are to be included in any alternative or newly composed rite.

---

[1] Compiled by the Liturgical Commission, commended for use by General Convention; second edition, New York: The Church Pension Fund, 1949.

Concerning the Service (p. 422)

The Church's Requirements for a Christian Marriage

The first paragraph defines Christian marriage: "a solemn and public covenant between a man and a woman in the presence of God." It then states the canonical requirements for a marriage in the Episcopal Church: at least one of the parties must be a baptized Christian; there must be at least two witnesses; and the marriage must conform to the laws of the state and the canons of the church.

The Various Liturgical Ministers

A bishop or priest normally presides, for only a bishop or priest can pronounce the nuptial blessing and celebrate the Eucharist. A bishop, when present, should pronounce the blessing and preside at the Eucharist. A deacon or assisting priest may deliver the charge (p. 424), ask for the declaration of consent (p. 424), read the Gospel, and perform the usual assisting functions at the Eucharist. If no bishop or priest is available, and if it is permitted by civil law, a deacon may perform a marriage, but must omit the nuptial blessing which follows the prayers. As at a Eucharist, it is desirable for the Old Testament lesson and the Epistle to be read by lay persons.

The Use of Names

In the opening exhortation, at the symbol *N.N.* (p. 424), the full names of the man and woman to be married are declared. At other places in the rite, where the symbol *N.* occurs, only the Christian names are used (pp. 424, 427, and 428).

The Celebration and Blessing of a Marriage (pp. 425–434)

The title, which is new to this revision, replaces the earlier Prayer Book title, "The Form of Solemnization of Matrimony."

The first rubric designates that a marriage is to be celebrated in the church or some other appropriate place. Marriages in the medieval period were performed on the porch of the church and the couple entered afterward for the blessing of the marriage and the Eucharist. The 1549 Prayer Book prescribed that the marriage be "in the body of the church." The first American Book (1789), perhaps because of pioneer conditions, added permission for the marriage to be performed "in some proper house." English Prayer Books assumed that the marriage would be celebrated within the context of a Sunday service, after Morning Prayer and Litany and prior to the Eucharist.

431

The 1892 revision allowed the use of a hymn before any service in the Book. The 1979 Book allows the use of a hymn, psalm, anthem, or instrumental music during the entrance of the wedding party.

The direction that the woman stand to the right and the man to the left, as they face the celebrant, has been part of the service since 1662. It is from the Sarum rite which explains "the reason being that she was formed out of a rib in the left side of Adam."

The Exhortation (pp. 423–424)

This exhortation goes back to the 1549 Prayer Book where the form included quotations from the exhortation of the Sarum rite, from the Cologne *Encheiridion*, from Luther's marriage rite (picked up by many of the German church orders), and from the *King's Book*. The 1549 form reads:

> Dearly beloved friends, we are gathered together here in the sight of God, and in the face of his congregation, to join together this man and this woman in holy matrimony, which is an honorable estate instituted of God in paradise, in the time of man's innocency, signifying unto us the mystical union that is betwixt Christ and his Church: which holy estate Christ adorned and beautified with his presence and first miracle that he wrought in Cana of Galilee, and is commended of Saint Paul to be honorable among all men; and therefore is not to be enterprised, nor taken in hand unadvisedly, lightly, or wantonly, to satisfy men's carnal lusts and appetites, like brute beasts that have no understanding: but reverently, discreetly, advisedly, soberly, and in the fear of God, duly considering the causes for which matrimony was ordained. One cause was the procreation of children, to be brought up in the fear and nurture of the Lord, and praise of God. Secondly, it was ordained for a remedy against sin, and to avoid fornication, that such persons as be married might live chastely in matrimony, and keep themselves undefiled members of Christ's body. Thirdly, for the mutual society, help, and comfort that the one ought to have of the other, both in prosperity and adversity. Into the which holy estate these two persons present come now to be joined. Therefore, if any man can show any just cause why they may not lawfully be joined so together, let him now speak, or else hereafter for ever hold his peace.

In the first American Book the section on the causes for which marriage was ordained was deleted from the exhortation. In 1949, however, a canon (Title I, Canon 17, Section 3) was passed which re-

432

quired a couple to sign a declaration of intention which included a modified form of this section in which the causes are rephrased and listed in a different order. (The assertion that procreation was the first cause for which marriage was instituted was objected to as far back as Bucer's *Censura* of 1551, in which he maintained, on the basis of Genesis 2:18, that the primary cause was mutual society, help, and comfort.) The 1949 declaration reads:

> We believe it [marriage] is for the purpose of mutual fellowship, encouragement, and understanding, for the procreation (if it may be) of children, and their physical and spiritual nurture, for the safeguarding and benefit of society.

The present Book updates the language of the exhortation and restores to it some of the content of the declaration of intention.

The Charge (p. 424)

The charge is an abbreviated form of that in earlier Prayer Books, which was dependent upon the charge in the York marriage rite. The 1549 form reads:

> I require and charge you, as you will answer at the dreadful day of judgment, when the secrets of all hearts shall be disclosed, that if either of you do know any impediment, why ye may not be lawfully joined together in matrimony, that ye confess it. For be ye well assured, that so many as be coupled together otherwise than God's Word doth allow are not joined of God, neither is their matrimony lawful.

The last sentence has been dropped in the present revision because it refers to English civil law, not to canon law or church tradition.

The Declaration of Consent (p. 424)

The declarations of consent are a contemporary form of the man's pledge to the woman in the 1549 Prayer Book. It was formed by combining those of the Sarum rite and Luther's marriage rite. The 1549 form reads:

> N., Wilt thou have this woman to thy wedded wife, to live together after God's ordinance in the holy estate of matrimony? Wilt thou love her, comfort her, honor and keep her, in sickness and in health; and forsaking all other keep thee only to her, so long as you both shall live?

433

Until the 1928 revision the second question asked of the wife had read, "Wilt thou obey him, and serve him, love, honor and keep him, in sickness and in health?" In the present Prayer Book, in contrast to previous editions, the question is asked first of the woman and then of the man. These promises are equivalent to a final ratification of the engagement. Originally they were made at some time prior to the marriage. They publicly acknowledge that the choice is a matter of free consent rather than of constraint.

The Pledge of Support (p. 425)

A new part of this revision is the congregational pledge to "uphold these two persons in their marriage." The role of family, friends, and the community, which is often crucial in sustaining or breaking a marriage, is openly recognized by this question.

The Presentation or Giving in Marriage (pp. 425 and 437)

The Sarum rite included a giving of the bride in marriage by the father or a friend, but no text was associated with this action. In the York rite, however, was a question "Who gives me this wife?" The 1549 form reads "Who giveth this woman to be married to this man?" The form is a survival from a period when women were thought of as property. This revision makes the form optional. The forms provided (p. 437) also allow the substitution of "presents" for "gives" and provide for the presentation of the man to the woman as well as the woman to the man.

A Hymn, Psalm, or Anthem (p. 425)

Vocal music may be used to separate the opening section from the ministry of the word which follows. One possibility is the Gloria in excelsis or some other song of praise. This is an appropriate time for members of the wedding party to move to seats in the nave or chancel for the ministry of the word.

The Ministry of the Word (pp. 425–426)

The collect, drafted by the Rev. Dr. Charles M. Guilbert, preserves the main themes of the first prayer of the marriage rite in the 1549 Prayer Book, which was based upon the Sarum form for the blessing of the ring. The 1549 version reads:

O Eternal God, creator and preserver of all mankind, giver of all spiritual grace, the author of everlasting life: send thy blessing upon these thy servants, this man and this woman, whom we bless in thy Name, that as Isaac and Rebecca (after bracelets and jewels of gold given of one to the other for tokens of their matrimony) lived faithfully together, so these persons may surely perform and keep the vow and covenant betwixt them made, whereof this ring given, and received, is a token and pledge, and may ever remain in perfect love and peace together, and live according to thy laws; through Jesus Christ our Lord. Amen.

The 1552 revision deleted the phrase in parentheses; the 1928 revision the reference to Isaac and Rebecca.

Earlier editions of the Prayer Book had assumed that marriages would take place within the principal Sunday liturgy. When that custom fell into disuse it left a marriage rite devoid of the reading and exposition of scripture. The 1928 Book provided a Collect, Epistle, and Gospel for use at a nuptial Eucharist. This revision provides a full liturgy of the word with Old Testament lesson, psalmody, Epistle, Gospel, and homily. Prayer Books before 1789 had included a homily, partially based on that in the Consultation of Hermann, which was to be read if the sermon did not declare "the office of man and wife . . . according to holy scripture." The Apostles' Creed may be said at the conclusion of the readings (and homily) (see p. 437). The baptismal creed rather than the Nicene is especially suitable at such a time of commitment; furthermore it is more likely to be familiar to non-Episcopalians at the wedding than is the Nicene.

The Marriage (pp. 427–428)

The sacramental sign of marriage is the joining of hands, a custom practiced by the Jews (Tobit 7:13), by the Greeks, and by the Romans. The form is a contemporary version of that in earlier Prayer Books which was based on the Sarum form. In the 1549 Book the words for the man are: "I, N., take thee, N., to my wedded wife, to have and to hold from this day forward, for better, for worse, for richer, for poorer, in sickness, and in health, to love and to cherish, till death us depart, according to God's holy ordinance; and thereto I plight thee my troth." The woman's vow, until 1928, included a promise to "obey." Whereas the man was called upon to "plight" his troth, the woman was required to "give" hers. In the Sarum form the

435

woman promised to be gentle and obedient in the bed and at the table.

The Blessing of the Ring or Rings (p. 427)

Because of the reformers' distaste for the blessing of material objects, the 1549 Book omitted any blessing of the ring. An optional form, based on that in the Sarum rite, was provided in 1928: "Bless, O Lord, this Ring, that he who gives it and she who wears it may abide in thy peace, and continue in thy favour, unto their life's end; through Jesus Christ our Lord. Amen." In this revision a new form has been provided which explains the significance of the wedding ring.

The Giving of the Ring or Rings (p. 427)

It was an ancient Roman custom for the man to give a ring to the woman as a sign of betrothal; by the ninth century this action was duplicated in the giving of a ring at the time of marriage. The growing custom of the woman's also giving a ring to the man is recognized in the rubric in the 1979 Book. The 1549 form associated with the giving of the ring, based on the Sarum form, reads: "With this ring I thee wed; this gold and silver I thee give; with my body I thee worship; and with all my worldly goods I thee endow, in the Name of the Father, and of the Son, and of the Holy Ghost. Amen." In the 1552 revision the phrase "this gold and silver I thee give" was dropped. The 1789 revision eliminated "with my body I thee worship," and the 1928 Book omitted "and with all my worldly goods I thee endow." The fuller form in the present Book carries an echo of the original form. The alternative ending, "in the Name of God," may be used when the Trinitarian formula might become an imposition upon a non-Episcopalian who does not subscribe to the doctrine of the Trinity. A new provision (p. 437) allows the substitution of some other suitable symbol, such as the mangalasutra in Indian cultures, for the wedding ring.

The Declaration of Marriage (p. 428)

A declaration of the marriage with a joining of hands was part of the German rites late in the middle ages which Luther included in his rites and the German church orders also retained. From these it came into the 1549 Prayer Book. The present revision modernizes the wording, and the scriptural sentence (Mt. 19:6) has been moved to follow rather than precede the declaration. The 1549 form reads:

> Forasmuch as N. and N. have consented together in holy wedlock, and have witnessed the same here before God and this company, and thereto have given and pledged their troth either to other, and have declared the same by giving and receiving gold and silver, and by joining of hands, I pronounce that they be man and wife together, in the Name of the Father, of the Son, and of the Holy Ghost. Amen.

In the 1979 Book the Amen is said by the congregation.

The Prayers (pp. 428–430)

The Lord's Prayer is printed for use immediately after the declaration of marriage if communion is not to follow.

As at other Eucharists the prayers are to be read by a deacon or by some other person appointed rather than by the celebrant.

The prayers, drafted by the Very Rev. Robert H. Greenfield, begin with a preamble based on that of the first prayer at a marriage in earlier Prayer Books, originally from the Sarum rite. The next two paragraphs have as their source a prayer for parents by Bishop Angus Dun (p. 444). The supplication that the couple may acknowledge their faults and seek forgiveness is new. The next paragraph is based on a prayer in Services for Trial Use (1970, p. 316) which was drafted by Virginia Harbour (Mrs. Richard L.). The optional petition for children is based upon a prayer which entered the American Book in 1928 from the Scottish revision of 1912. The remainder of the prayer is based on the intercession in Services for Trial Use (pp. 319–320), also drafted by Ms. Harbour.

The Blessing of the Marriage (pp. 430–431)

The first prayer, drafted by the Rev. Dr. H. Boone Porter, sets Christian marriage within the context of the incarnation and the cross. The imagery is from the marriage rite: the ring is a seal; the festal clothing normally associated with a wedding, the mantle; and the crowns, still associated with a wedding in the Eastern churches (of which we have a remnant in the wedding veil), the crown. The reference to the heavenly banquet anticipates the conclusion of the service in the Eucharist.

437

The second prayer is a slightly revised form of one which was first used in the 1928 Book. It was based in part on a prayer in the English Books which the 1789 American Book had omitted. In the 1549 version the prayer, derived from the sacramental blessing in the Sarum rite, read:

O God, which by thy mighty power hast made all things of naught, which also after other things set in order didst appoint that out of man, created after thine own image and similitude, woman should take her beginning, and knitting them together, didst teach that it should never be lawful to put asunder those whom thou by matrimony hadst made one: O God, which hast consecrated the state of matrimony to such an excellent mystery that in it is signified and represented the spiritual marriage and unity betwixt Christ and his church: look mercifully upon these thy servants, that both this man may love his wife according to thy word, as Christ did love his spouse the church, who gave himself for it, loving and cherishing it even as his own flesh; and also that this woman may be loving and amiable to her husband as Rachel, wise as Rebecca, faithful and obedient as Sara, and in all quietness, sobriety, and peace be a follower of holy and godly matrons. O Lord, bless them both, and grant them to inherit thy everlasting kingdom, through Jesus Christ our Lord. Amen.

It is worth noting that in this revision, in the preamble, the phrase "the covenant of marriage" has been substituted for "the state of matrimony." The word "state" connoted an idea of "natural law" in medieval theology, but has in modern use a secular connotation and no theological implications.

The Blessing (p. 433)

This form dates to the 1552 Prayer Book. The 1549 form, derived from Sarum, began "God the Father bless you. ✝ God the Son keep you. God the Holy Ghost lighten your understanding," and ended "that you may have remission of your sins in this life, and in the world to come life everlasting." In the English Books this concluded the portion of the rite conducted in the nave of the church and preceded the movement into the chancel for additional prayers and a blessing and the Eucharist.

The Peace (p. 431)

The peace may be exchanged between the newly married couple and throughout the congregation. The custom of kissing the bride is a

438

survival of the medieval kiss of peace. It is appropriate for the couple to kiss at this time.

If Eucharist is not to follow, the wedding party leaves the church.

At the Eucharist (p. 432)

The Eucharist continues with the offertory, at which the newly married couple may present the offerings of bread and wine and receive the Sacrament before other members of the congregation (see p. 438). A proper preface is provided for use at a marriage (pp. 349 and 381). A proper postcommunion prayer, drafted by the Rev. Dr. Massey H. Shepherd, Jr., is also provided.

The Blessing of a Civil Marriage (pp. 433–434)

The Book of Offices[1] contained a form for "The Blessing of Married Persons," which was designed for the blessing of civil marriages. It was adapted from the marriage rite of the 1928 Prayer Book. This is the first Prayer Book to include such a rite among the pastoral offices.

The rubric prescribes that the service begin as at a celebration of the Eucharist, since the initial portion of the marriage rite is not appropriate for blessing a marriage which has already taken place. The collect and lessons of the marriage rite are to be used, however.

The address of the celebrant is based on that in the Book of Offices. The promises are those of the declaration of consent (p. 424) and the question asked of the congregation closely approximates that asked in the regular form (p. 425). The blessing of the ring(s) is also the usual form (p. 427), followed by the sentence which comes after the declaration of marriage (p. 428). From this point the rite proceeds in a regular manner beginning with the prayers (p. 428).

An Order for Marriage (pp. 435–436)

This order, new to this edition of the Prayer Book, allows use of the rite of another edition of the Book of Common Prayer, a rite from some other source, or a rite composed for the occasion, so long as certain conditions are met. It is analogous to the orders for Eucharist and for Burial (pp. 400–401 and 506). The elements listed are those considered essential by this Church for a Christian rite of marriage: a brief statement of the Church's teaching concerning marriage; an

---

[1] Compiled by the Liturgical Commission and commended for use by the General Convention; second edition, New York: Church Pension Fund, 1949.

assurance of the intention of the couple to enter into marriage, and of their free consent; an exchange of vows using either the form of this edition or of the 1928 Prayer Book; a declaration of the marriage; intercessions; the blessing of the marriage; the peace. The use of one or more readings from Holy Scripture is normative, as is the celebration of the Eucharist.

Additional Directions (pp. 437–438)

Following the Sarum custom, the English Prayer Books required that the banns of marriage be published three Sundays or holy days before the marriage was to take place. The marriage license originated as an ecclesiastical dispensation from the publication of the banns. The form to be used became part of the Prayer Book in 1662. Prior American Books preceded the form with a rubric, "The Laws respecting Matrimony, whether by publishing the Banns in Churches, or by Licence, being different in the several States; every Minister is left to the direction of those Laws, in every thing that regards the civil contract between the parties." The language of the form is updated in the 1979 Book.

Commentary on other additional directions has been included at suitable points within the commentary on the rite itself.

(See *The Book of Occasional Services*, pp. 144–146, for a rite for the Anniversary of a Marriage.)

A Thanksgiving for the Birth
or Adoption of a Child

In most societies an expectant mother, at some point, is formally relieved of certain family and community responsibilities. After the birth of the child (whether the child lives or dies), she joins again the full life of the community, resuming her normal responsibilities within the family or (if it is a first child and it lives) assuming a different place within the life of the community from that which she formerly held.

After childbirth a Jewish woman was considered ritually unclean (relieved from certain responsibilities) for forty days after the birth of a male or eighty days after the birth of a female. Leviticus 12 prescribes both the number of days and the burnt offering and sin offering which were to be made at the conclusion of the period of uncleanness.

The early days of Christianity provide no evidence for a continued practice of ritual purification or any significance attached to ceremonies associated with the birth of a child into a family, though such rites may have continued with appropriate modifications and reinterpretations. The Canons of Hippolytus (fourth century) assign to a place among the catechumens women who have not undergone a rite of purification after childbirth. The seventeenth Constitution of Leo (c. 460) forbids women to receive communion for forty days after the birth of a child, but acknowledges that in a case of necessity she may receive without sin. In a letter to Pope Gregory, contained in Bede's *Ecclesiastical History*, Augustine of Canterbury asks how long a woman should stay away from church after childbirth. Gregory replies that the time is a "mystery" rather than a strict legal require-

441

ment and that if the woman "enters the church the very hour that she is delivered, to return thanks, she is not guilty of any sin."

In some Eastern and early Western rites, prayers are said for the mother and child at the entrance to the church. The child is then "churched" (carried into the church), and the rite concludes with the Nunc dimittis. This structure relates to the account in Luke 2:22–38 of the purification of Mary and the presentation of Christ. In later Western rites the emphasis was shifted to purification of the mother rather than presentation of the child; the rubric makes no mention of the child at the service. The purification rite in the Sarum manuale was fairly typical of medieval Western rites: Psalms 121 and 128, the Kyrie and Lord's Prayer, preces, and a prayer were all to be said at the entrance to the church. Many rites directed the woman to kneel and hold a candle for this portion of the rite. The priest then sprinkled her with holy water and led her into the church, saying the words also said when an unbaptized child was carried in: "Enter into the temple of God that you may have eternal life and live for ever and ever. Amen." Other psalms, such as 24, 51, 86, or 122, were often used and sometimes the Magnificat or Nunc dimittis. Occasionally Luke's account of the presentation was read.

The continental Reformed rites did not usually provide for the "churching of women." The 1549 Book did include a rite, not printed in conjunction with baptism or marriage as in the medieval books, but near the end of the Prayer Book. This has led some scholars to believe that the rite was a last minute addition, made in response to some conservative pressures. The service was to take place in the nave near the entrance to the choir. A model for an introductory exhortation emphasized thanksgiving for preservation through the dangers of childbirth. Psalm 121 followed, then the Kyrie and Lord's Prayer, and the preces from the Sarum rite. The concluding prayer included a reference to the vocation of women, not in the Sarum form. The woman was then to return the white garment which had been given at the baptism of the child, to present "accustomed offerings," and to receive communion, "if there be a communion." The rite was to be done within the principal Sunday service. The candle, alternative psalm, sprinkling with holy water, and the leading into church of the Sarum rite were all deleted.

The 1552 revision changed the title from "The Order of the Purification of Women" to "The Thanksgiving of Women after Childbirth, commonly called the Churching of Women." Since the giving of vesture at baptism was no longer done, mention of the return was deleted.

442

The 1662 Book replaced Psalm 121 with Psalm 116:1–13a and 16b. Psalm 127 was given as an alternative. The specific mention of the vocation of women was deleted from the prayer.

In 1789, the American Book removed the alternative psalm and excised verses 3 and 6–10 from Psalm 116. The prayer was revised along lines suggested by the 1749 book *A New Liturgy*. A rubric at the end of the rite specified that the offering of the woman "shall be applied by the Minister and the Church-Wardens to the relief of distressed Women in Childbed." The prayer was also printed among the occasional prayers for use instead of the whole office, at the minister's discretion.

The 1928 Book added an optional prayer for the child, thereby continuing a tendency to make this office less concerned with the reincorporation of the woman into the life of the community, and more concerned with giving thanks for the birth of the child.

The second edition of the Book of Offices (1949) included "The Order for the Adoption of Children."[1]

In the present revision one rite serves as a thanksgiving either for a child born into a family or for a child received by adoption. The rite contains material both from the Prayer Book thanksgiving after childbirth and from the order for adoption in the Book of Offices. Additional acts of thanksgiving and prayers are included, and both parents, as well as other members of the family, may take active part in the rite. It would normally be celebrated on a Sunday just prior to the Peace in the Eucharist.

A Thanksgiving for the Birth or Adoption of a Child (pp. 439–445)

The changes in the title for this rite in various editions of the Prayer Book indicate the changes in the rite itself as well as in the church's use and interpretation of the rite. The 1549 Book translated the Sarum title literally as "The Order of the Purification of Women." The 1552 Book changed this to read "The Thanksgiving of Women after Childbirth, commonly called the Churching of Women." The present Book titles it "A Thanksgiving for the Birth or Adoption of a Child." Any idea of ritual impurity associated with childbirth is eliminated, and the emphasis is upon thanks for the gift of a child by birth or by adoption into the family and the larger community.

The rite is to be celebrated at a public service; in the Eucharist it

---

[1] Compiled by the Liturgical Commission, commended for use by the General Convention; second edition, New York: The Church Pension Fund, 1949.

443

may follow the prayers of the people and precede the Peace; at Morning or Evening Prayer it may take place after the prayers. Traditional Anglican practice had inserted the rite in the Sunday service before the Eucharist and after Morning Prayer and the Litany. It was considered fitting that the woman receive communion after churching.

The second rubric provides an abbreviated form of the service, especially if it is used at a hospital or in a home. It also suggests two readings, either of which may precede the rite: Luke 2:41–51 (the Child Jesus' visit to the Temple) or Luke 18:15–17 ("Let the children come to me").

The third rubric explicitly permits parents who so desire to give thanks in their own words during the prayers.

For the rite, the parents and other members of the family come before the altar. Medieval rites were conducted in the porch of the church and the woman was led into the church only after her purification. The 1549 Book set the rite in the nave of the church near the entrance to the chancel; the 1552 Book moved it to a place near the holy table, and the 1662 revision advised "some convenient place, as hath been accustomed, or as the Ordinary shall direct." A pew near the pulpit and reading desk was designated in many churches as "the churching pew." The present rubric represents a return to the 1552 custom.

For the Birth of a Child (p. 440)

The new initial bidding calls upon the congregation to join the family in giving thanks for the gift of a child. This contrasts with the 1549 Book: "Forasmuch as it hath pleased Almighty God of his goodness to give you safe deliverance, and your child baptism, and hath preserved you in the great danger of childbirth: ye shall therefore give hearty thanks unto God and pray." As the rite was used in circumstances when the child had died, the 1552 Book omitted the phrase "and your child baptism."

For an Adoption (pp. 440–441)

The questions asked of the parents and the child, and the forms which follow, are based upon those of "The Order for the Adoption of Children" of the Book of Offices (1949), pages 9–11.

444

Act of Thanksgiving (pp. 441–443)

Three alternative forms are provided for the thanksgiving. Several of the medieval Western rites used the Magnificat, but this is the first Prayer Book to include it in this rite. Psalm 116:1–13a and 16b was included in the rite in 1662, from Robert Sanderson's liturgy composed for use during the interregnum when the Prayer Book was forbidden. In the first American revision verses 3 and 6–10 were deleted; the present revision deletes verses 4 and 13a as well. Psalm 23 appeared in several medieval rites, but this is the first Prayer Book to include it.

The Prayer (p. 443)

The one prayer required in the rite is an amplified version of the prayer "For the Care of Children" (p. 829) which in another form was added to the 1928 Prayer Book. It was drafted by the Rev. Dr. John W. Suter, Jr., and based on a much longer prayer by the late Rev. William Austin Smith of Springfield, Massachusetts. The scriptural allusion is to Philippians 4:8.

Prayers (pp. 444–445)

Additional prayers may be said. Four are provided and the parents may also express their thanks in their own words (p. 439)

For a Safe Delivery (p. 444)

This prayer has evolved from one in the Sarum rite which in the 1549 version reads:

> O Almighty God, which hast delivered this woman, thy servant, from the great pain and peril of childbirth: Grant, we beseech thee, most merciful Father, that she through thy help may both faithfully live, and walk in her vocation according to thy will in this life present, and also may be partaker of everlasting glory in the life to come; through Jesus Christ our Lord. Amen.

There was no equivalent to the clause concerning vocation in the Sarum form. The 1662 Book omitted this clause. The first American Book revised the prayer following the book *A New Liturgy* (1749) and also printed the prayer among the occasional prayers and

445

thanksgivings. The rite was preceded by a rubric that permitted the prayer to be used in place of the whole rite.

For the Parents (p. 444)

Angus Dun, bishop of Washington (1944–1962), composed this prayer which is new to the present edition of the Prayer Book. It was printed in the *Book of Prayers for Church and Home*.[1] Much of the content of the prayer has been included in the prayers of the marriage rite (p. 429).

For a Child Not Yet Baptized (p. 444)

New to this revision, this prayer is abbreviated from the prayer for the child in "An Office of Public Thanksgiving for Women after their Delivery from Childbirth" of *A Collection of Offices* compiled by Jeremy Taylor during the interregnum. The full form reads:

> O Eternal God, who hast promised to be a Father to a thousand generations of them that love and fear Thee; be pleased to bless this child who is newly come into a sad and most sinful world. O God, preserve his life, and give him the grace and sacrament of baptismal regeneration: do Thou receive him, and enable him to receive Thee, that he may have power to become the child of God; keep him from the spirits that walk at noon, and from the evil spirits of the night, from all charms and enchantments, from sudden death and violent accidents: give unto him a gracious heart and an excellent understanding, a ready and unloosed tongue, a healthful and a useful body, and a wise soul, that he may serve Thee, and advance Thy glory in this world, and may increase the number of Thy saints and servants in the kingdom of our Lord Jesus. *Amen.*

For a Child Already Baptized (pp. 444–445)

This prayer, new to the 1979 Book, was drafted by Virginia Harbour. It is based upon the "Dedication of Soul and Body to God's Service, with a Resolution to be growing daily in Goodness" of the forms of prayer to be used in families included in earlier editions of the American Prayer Book, which was an abbreviated version of a prayer in Bishop Edmund Gibson's *Family Devotions*.

---

[1] Ed. Howard Paine and Bard Thompson, Philadelphia: Christian Education Press, 1963, no. 203.

The Blessing (p. 445)

This optional blessing is based on that of "The Order for the Adoption of Children" in the Book of Offices (1949), page 12.

The Final Rubric (p. 445)

The final rubric dates to the 1549 Book. In that edition, in the visitation of the sick, was a rubric:

> And if he have not afore disposed his goods, let him then make his will. (But men must be often admonished that they set an order for their temporal goods and lands, when they be in health.) And also to declare his debts, what he oweth, and what is owing to him: for discharging of his conscience, and quietness of his executors.

The 1662 revision changed the wording as did the 1928 Book, when it was moved from the body of the rite to the end. The 1928 rubric reads:

> The Minister is ordered, from time to time, to advise the People, whilst they are in health, to make Wills arranging for the disposal of their temporal goods, and, when of ability, to leave Bequests for religious and charitable uses.

In this revision the duty of making prudent provision for one's family is explicitly stated.

The Reconciliation of a Penitent

I n any society certain offenses which seriously endanger or disrupt the community or bring scandal upon it result in separation from the community for the offender. After appropriate penalties, self-examination, testing, and reeducation, the person may be reincorporated into the community. So far as we can trace historically, all cultures have had various expiatory penalties for those who violate the communal codes and, where it was felt reasonable, have conducted rituals which might restore the penitent sinners to good favor in the group.

Within Judaism certain offenses or conditions brought excommunication or a condition of ritual uncleanness. Rites and ceremonies analogous to those associated with mourning and with baptism preceded or accompanied repentance, restoration, or cleansing. Such rites often included the penitential psalms, prayers of confession, the donning of sackcloth and ashes, fasting and weeping, rending of garments, kneeling and prostration, and ritual washings. Possibly the laying on of hands, signifying blessing, identification, and transfer in the Old Testament, accompanied the restoration of the penitent within the community.

The New Testament contains evidence of discipline and excommunication for those who brought scandal upon the church, whose members were subject to its discipline. Excommunication may have been a formal act following a solemn assembly of the congregation (e.g. see 1 Cor. 5; 1 Tim. 1:20; Tit. 3:11–12). Reconciliation or restoration also was a formal act, probably with laying on of hands (see 2 Cor. 2:5–11 and 1 Tim. 5:19–22).

The fullest descriptions we have of rites of excommunication and reinstatement in the early church are those of Tertullian (*De*

448

poenitentia 9) and of the *Didascalia* 5–7. The liturgy of penance was divided into three stages: (1) the excommunication or imposition of penance; (2) the acts of penitence, which included sackcloth and ashes, fasting and prayer, intercession of the faithful, and dismissal from the public services, with prayer and laying on of hands, before the communion; and (3) the absolution or reinstatement, over which the bishop normally presided and which usually consisted of prayer, laying on of hands, and readmission to the Eucharist. Such readmissions presumably were done at the time of the Easter vigil, though a dying penitent was not denied communion.

At a later period public penitence was related to the Lenten season. At the beginning of Lent, or on the Wednesday prior to Lent, the penitents were placed under discipline. They were admonished and prayed for and received laying on of hands before being ejected from the church prior to the Eucharist. In the ninth century the imposition of ashes and the saying of the seven penitential psalms (6, 32, 38, 51, 102, 130, and 143) were added to the rite of expulsion, and the day came to be known as Ash Wednesday. Lenten services contained readings, scrutinies, and prayers for the penitents who had been excluded from communion. Near the end of Lent (Maundy Thursday in the Roman rite, Good Friday in the Gallican) came the time for reconciliation. The penitents were admonished and given warning; they prostrated themselves as the congregation cried out for pardon for them. Prayers were read over them, and hands were laid upon them. Finally they were raised and admitted to communion. The books contained special forms for the reconciliation of dying penitents.

The practice of private penance developed within the Celtic church. Books called "penitentials" which prescribed penances for various offenses appeared during the sixth through the ninth centuries. The authority of these depended on the prestige of their authors or editors. Public penance was assigned for sins which brought scandal to the church; private penance was expected for matters of conscience which might be known to the offender and to God alone. We have no forms for rites of private penance before the sixteenth century; at an early stage those from the rites of public penance may have been used, being adapted by the confessors who were sometimes lay monks.

Few remnants of the discipline of public penance lasted into the eleventh century, but the old texts were retained and Lent given a new function as a time in which all persons received ashes and submitted to penitence.

Late in the middle ages the Western rites of private penance

449

underwent several changes. The order of the three stages (confession, acts of penitence, and reconciliation) was changed: first one confessed, then was reconciled, then acts of penitence were performed. The outward sign of laying on of hands was dropped. Declaratory absolutions displaced or supplemented the older precatory forms. Priests alone could be confessors, and a penitent was ordinarily required to confess to the parish priest. Confession became a requirement prior to communion and at least once each year. Also in the late middle ages general confessions and absolutions became common in connection with the daily offices and as a preparation of the priest and server before Mass.

The Lutheran and Reformed churches attempted to restore the ancient public penitence through church discipline and the "fencing of the table," and general confessions, as well as absolutions, became part of their rites.

For a time Luther considered private confession a sacrament and he, as well as many of the German church orders, provided forms with declaratory absolutions, but rejected the principle of acts of penance (satisfaction). Private confession could not be imposed on anyone, though many of the German orders considered it a normal action in preparation for communion; confession to a lay person was allowed. Calvin denied the sacramental nature of private confession, but did admit absolution as a ceremony to confirm faith in the forgiveness of sins. The council of Trent reinforced the teaching of the Scholastics about the need for private penitence, providing a standardized form in the Rituale Romanum.

In the rite for Ash Wednesday the 1549 Prayer Book included the expression of hope that the public penitential discipline of the early church would be restored. It was indeed restored to a limited extent, with public penances continuing to be imposed on occasion even as late as the first part of the nineteenth century.

A general confession and absolution was provided in the Order of the Communion (1548) and retained with slight revision in the 1549 Prayer Book. The 1552 revision preceded the daily offices with a general confession and absolution.

One of the exhortations in the 1548 Order contained an apologia for non-compulsory private confession for any whose consciences were not quieted by "their humble confession to God, and the general confession to the church." The 1549 Book retained this:

And if there be any of you whose conscience is troubled and
grieved in anything, lacking comfort or counsel, let him come to

450

me, or to some other discreet and learned priest taught in the law of God, and confess and open his sin and grief secretly, that he may receive such ghostly counsel, advice, and comfort that his conscience may be relieved, and that of us, as of the ministers of God and of the church, he may receive comfort and absolution, to the satisfaction of his mind and avoiding of all scruple and doubtfulness: requiring such as shall be satisfied with a general confession not to be offended with them that do use to their further satisfying the auricular and secret confession to the priest; nor those also which think needful or convenient, for the quietness of their own consciences, particularly to open their sins to the priest, to be offended with them that are satisfied with their humble confession to God, and the general confession to the church: but in all things to follow and keep the rule of charity, and every man to be satisfied with his own conscience, not judging other men's minds or consciences [1548: acts] whereas he hath no warrant of God's Word to [1548: for] the same.

Within the rite for the visitation of the sick, a rubric specified that the sick person was to make a special confession, "if he feel his conscience troubled with any weighty matter." A declaratory form of absolution, partly based on a form in the Sarum rite for the visitation of the sick and partly upon the absolution in Hermann's Consultation, was provided for use after the special confession. The rubric states, "and the same form of absolution shall be used in all private confessions."

The 1552 revision altered the exhortation to read:

And because it is requisite that no man should come to the Holy Communion but with a full trust in God's mercy, and with a quiet conscience, therefore if there be any of you which by the means aforesaid cannot quiet his own conscience, but requireth further comfort or counsel; then let him come to me, or some other discreet and learned minister of God's word and open his grief that he may receive such ghostly counsel, advice, and comfort as his conscience may be relieved and that by the ministry of God's Word he may receive comfort and the benefit of absolution, to the quieting of his conscience, and avoiding of all scruple and doubtfulness.

The rubric directing the sick person to make a special confession if troubled in conscience was retained, but the sentence which immediately preceded the 1549 form of absolution was revised to read "After which confession the priest shall absolve him after this sort."

451

Mention of the use of this absolution in other private confessions was deleted.

The 1662 revision qualified the rubric preceding the absolution in the rite for the visitation of the sick, "After which Confession, the Priest shall absolve him (if he humbly and heartily desire it) after this sort."

Since the Prayer Book provided no form for use in private confession, other than the absolution, clergy compiled their own rites. Joseph Glanville, in 1679, described his procedure which he had learned from "godly and eminent divines." He began with the Lord's Prayer, preces, the Gloria Patri, and Psalm 139. Then he sat in a chair and questioned the penitent who knelt beside him. Finally he pronounced the absolution, read some sentences from the Scriptures and Psalm 32, said some prayers, and gave a blessing.

In the first American Book the conclusion of the exhortation in the eucharistic rite read "let him come to me, or to some other minister of God's word, and open his grief; that he may receive such godly counsel and advice, as may tend to the quieting of his conscience, and the removing of all scruple and doubtfulness." The rubric concerning a special confession and the absolution were removed from the rite for the visitation of the sick. In the rite for the visitation of prisoners, taken into the 1789 edition from the Prayer Book of the Church of Ireland, however, the "minister" was instructed to move the prisoner to make a confession, and "After his confession, the minister shall declare to him the pardoning mercy of God, in the form which is used in the Communion-service."

The 1928 Prayer Book dropped the form for the visitation of prisoners, but included a rubric modeled on that of the English Book in the rite for visitation of the sick, "Then shall the sick person be moved to make a special confession of his sins, if he feel his conscience troubled with any matter; after which confession, on evidence of his repentance, the Minister shall assure him of God's mercy and forgiveness."

Recent revisions in other provinces of Anglicanism have contained a form for private confession, normally modeled on that of the Roman rite. The absolution has customarily been the one included in English Books since 1549.

The present Book gives two forms. Form One is like the forms in other recent revisions in the various Anglican provinces. Form Two is a much fuller rite, containing material similar to the Byzantine form for confession and other material similar to the recently revised

Roman Catholic form. Possibly it is better suited than Form One for the penitent who has come to confession when such an action marks a radical turning point in that person's life.

Concerning the Rite (p. 446)

This page was drafted by the Rev. Donald L. Garfield.

The Ministry of Reconciliation

The first paragraph and the first sentence of the second are analogous to the section on confession in the exhortations of the English Prayer Books. Private confession is available for all who desire it, but it is not compulsory. The Anglican attitude has been summarized: "All can; some should; none must."

The Availability of Confession

The second paragraph points out that private confession is not restricted to times of sickness. This is a misapprehension which was probably fostered by the fact that the rubrics concerning private confession and the form of absolution in earlier editions of the Prayer Book had been printed within the rite for the visitation of the sick. "Confessions may be heard anytime and anywhere." It is not necessary that a confession be made in a church building or that it be reserved to a particular time. However, for the convenience of priest and people, stated times for confession, particularly at the beginning of Lent and Advent and before the principal feasts, are observed in many congregations.

The Forms Provided in This Revision of the Prayer Book

Two forms for the reconciliation of a penitent are provided in this present edition of the Prayer Book. The first is briefer and more direct. The second is a much fuller form which is particularly appropriate when a person has turned or returned to the Christian faith, or at other possible "crisis" points in a person's life. In keeping with Western tradition since the thirteenth century, only a bishop or priest may pronounce absolution at a private confession. Another Christian may hear a confession, but must make clear that a priestly absolution will not be pronounced. A declaration of forgiveness is provided for use by a deacon or lay person.

The Place for a Confession

Though confessions may be heard in any setting, the directions point out that a confession in a church building should be in a place which allows privacy. Illustrations from the medieval period show the penitent kneeling before the priest in the nave or chancel of the church with the priest either standing or seated facing the penitent, in a position where the absolution could be accompanied by its sacramental sign of the laying on of hands. In the Baroque period special booths to ensure privacy were erected in many Roman Catholic churches. Recent regulations of the Roman Catholic Church suggest that there should be a room available for private confessions which would include facilities for the priest and the penitent to sit facing each other, or for the penitent to kneel for the confession. The directions of this Prayer Book also point out that if it is preferred, the confessor and the penitent may sit face to face for a spiritual conference leading to an absolution or declaration of forgiveness.

Counsel, Signs of Penitence, and Acts of Thanksgiving

The rubrics of the forms for reconciliation permit the priest to offer counsel, direction, and comfort. While these forms are not intended as either a substitute or an opportunity for extended counseling, it may be that an occasional confession would lead to or conclude a period of counselling. In this context such counsel or comfort as is offered should be direct and to the point of the matters which are troubling the conscience of the one making the confession. On occasion, acts of reparation or reconciliation or other appropriate signs of penitence may be advised. In other circumstances, the penitent may be assigned a psalm, prayer, or hymn to be said as a sign of penitence or act of thanksgiving.

The Secrecy of the Confession

The content of a confession is not normally a matter of subsequent discussion. If the penitent wishes to reopen the subject with the confessor, this may be done, but even that option is not open to the confessor. The secrecy of a confession is morally absolute for the confessor. This right and responsibility has been upheld in the courts of some states.

The Reconciliation of a Penitent (pp. 447–452)

Form One (pp. 447–448)

The Blessing (p. 447)

The form with which the penitent begins the confession, "Bless me, for I have sinned," can be traced to the sixteenth century for-

454

malization of the rite of private penance. It is analogous to the enrollment of the penitent in earlier rites of public penance. The blessing
with which the priest responds is comparable to the binding of the
sinner in preparation for loosing him in the rites of public penance.

The Confession (p. 447)

At an early stage in the development of the rite of private penance,
there was probably no particular form of words used. Eventually texts
were drawn from the rites of public penance. After the *confiteor* came
to be said before the Mass or after the daily office, this formula, which
varied from place to place, was used in private confessions. The first
half of this form is similar to a common form of the *confiteor* of the late
medieval period. A form similar to this first half (though lacking the
phrase, "in things done and left undone," which is based upon the
general confessions of the daily office and the Eucharist) is included
in the English revision of 1928, the Scottish of 1929, and the Canadian of 1959. The second half cannot be traced back as far as the first.
It probably developed for use at private confessions. A similar text,
though lacking the last phrase, has been included in the South African revision of 1954 and the Indian of 1960.

The Absolution (pp. 447–448)

The first of the two forms of absolution dates back to the 1549
Prayer Book. The opening comes from Hermann's Consultation, the
second half from a Sarum form for the visitation of the sick. In the
1549 and subsequent editions of the English Prayer Book, it is
printed in the rite for the visitation of the sick. The 1549 Book precedes
it with a rubric which directs the sick person to make a special confession if troubled in conscience, "After which confession, the priest
shall absolve him after this form: and the same form of absolution
shall be used in all private confessions." In the 1552 revision the latter
portion of the rubric was changed to read, "After which confession
the Priest shall absolve him after this sort." In the 1662 revision the
sentence was expanded, "After which Confession, the Priest shall
absolve him (if he humbly and heartily desire it) after this sort." This
form of absolution has not been included in previous American editions of the Prayer Book. In the one service of the 1789 and 1892
revisions which included a special confession of sins, "A Form of
Prayer for the Visitation of Prisoners," the absolution was to be "in
the form which is used in the Communion-service." The 1928 revision, though it restored the rubric concerning a special confession in

455

the rite for the visitation of the sick, provided no form of absolution. Instead the "Minister" was to "assure him of God's mercy and forgiveness."

The alternative is a form approved by the Roman Consilium after the Second Vatican Council. The translation was drafted by the Rev. Dr. Massey H. Shepherd, Jr. It is analogous to earlier forms of absolution, whereas the second half of the first form is the type of absolution which became common in the thirteenth century and was regarded by Thomas Aquinas as the essential sacramental form.

In the early church, absolutions were accompanied by a laying on of hands, which was the sacramental action, the outward and visible sign of absolution.

The Dismissal (p. 448)

After the absolution the priest says to the penitent the words of Nathan to David (2 Sam. 12:13), "The Lord has put away all your sins." The priest then says "Go in peace," the words of Jethro to Moses (Ex. 4:18), of the priest of Micah to the Danites (Jg. 18:6), and of Jesus to the woman who was a sinner (Lk. 7:50), and asks of the penitent, "and pray for me, a sinner." These scriptural verses also provide one of the alternative forms of dismissal in the Roman rite for the reconciliation of a penitent.

Declaration of Forgiveness to be used by a Deacon or Lay Person (p. 448)

This declaration is based upon the alternative form of absolution given above.

Form Two (pp. 449–452)

The beginning of this rite, Psalm 51:1–3 and the Trisagion, is reminiscent of the Byzantine form of confession, which begins with the Trisagion, the Kyrie, the Lord's Prayer, and Psalm 51. The form for the special confession of sins in the visitation of the sick of the Prayer Book of the Church of Ireland consists of Psalm 51:1–3, 8, 10, and 13. One of the alternative forms for confession of the new Roman Catholic rite for the reconciliation of individual penitents uses Psalm 51:2–3.

456

The Blessing (p. 449)

The blessing is a revised version of that in Form One (above), which is dependent upon the first of the alternatives in the new Roman Catholic rite for the reconciliation of individual penitents.

The Sentences of Scripture (pp. 449–450)

An optional reading from scripture has been inserted at this point in the new Roman rite. The sentences which are printed here for the convenience of the priest are the "comfortable words" which have followed the absolution in the Eucharist of earlier editions of the Prayer Book and in Rite One of this edition.

The Bidding and the Confession (p. 450)

This bidding and confession were prepared for this edition by the Rev. Dr. Thomas J. Talley. The confession is set in the theological context of creation and redemption. In the early church and in the current Byzantine rite confession is spoken of as a "second baptism;" in this form we are reminded of our baptism in which we were clothed with righteousness and established among the children of the kingdom. Scriptural allusions include Genesis 1:27 and 2:7, Luke 15, and Colossians 1:12.

The Examination (pp. 450–451)

The two questions are reminiscent of the affirmations in the baptismal rite (pp. 302–305). The Byzantine form has a repetition of the creed at this point in the rite.

The form which follows is dependent upon the absolution in the Rite Two daily office and the Rite Two Eucharist; it was derived from the Sarum *confiteor,* and is typical of the older forms of absolution in liturgical books which antedate the appearance of the declaratory form which first became common in the thirteenth century.

The Laying on of Hands and the Absolution (p. 451)

The rubric explicitly mentions the laying on of hands or the extending of a hand over the penitent (the traditional sacramental sign of absolution) during the saying of one of the two forms which follow.

457

The texts are the same as those in Form One but are printed in reverse order.

The Dismissal (p. 451)

Scriptural allusions include Luke 15 (the stories of the lost sheep, the lost coin, and the lost son), in addition to the verses included in the dismissal for Form One.

Declaration of Forgiveness to be used by a Deacon or Lay Person (p. 452)

This is the same as the text provided in Form One.

Ministration to the Sick

I t was Jewish practice to offer prayer for the sick and to anoint them with oil, a common medicine of the time. The law of purity concerning lepers (Lev. 13–14) may provide us with something of a prototype for rites of ministration to the sick which included cleansing and exorcism, anointing, and the offering of a sacrifice.

James 5:13–16 seems to indicate a continued use of a rite for the sick with confession of sins, prayer, and anointing by the "presbyters of the church."

In the Apostolic Tradition of Hippolytus (c. 215) are two notes concerning ministry to the sick: the bishop is to be informed of the sickness so that he may visit; a form is provided for giving thanks when oil is offered at the Eucharist. This form provides a prayer for health for those who "use" or "partake of" the oil which was offered with the bread and wine, blessed at the eucharistic thanksgiving, and then returned to the giver for use. Similar forms from that period also contain blessings over water or bread as well as oil. The substance was probably self-administered. Many accounts also come from the pre-Nicene period which tell of clergy or laity with healing gifts who visit the sick, pray over the person, and then anoint. In addition, the deacons often carried the Sacrament from the Eucharist to sick persons.

Both Eastern and Gallican rites contain forms for visitation and anointing of the sick, dating to the early middle ages. The Mozarabic form consists of a sprinkling with holy water, an anointing, psalmody, a prayer for healing, and a blessing. The longer and more elaborate Celtic rite began with a bidding, prayers for healing and lections. In one version a short form of the creed, and in another version a blessing of water and "blessing of the man," preceded the anointing with "the

459

oil of gladness." The Lord's Prayer followed the anointing. A short blessing, which may have been associated with the peace, precedes the communion. The rite ended with postcommunion prayers, anthems, and a blessing. It may be a reasonable assumption that sprinkling with holy water and anointing were later additions to the original rites for visitation and communion of the sick.

In the late middle ages the rites for visitation underwent great changes. In the ninth century there was an effort to revive the use of unction, not for healing but for remission of sins. Later, when communions became infrequent and confession obligatory before communion, prayers for healing disappeared from the rites and penitential actions multiplied. The rite came to be used principally for the dying, although the late Sarum books distinguished between visitation of the sick and extreme unction. The visitation rite included the seven penitential psalms with antiphons (said during the procession to the person's house), the peace, the adoration of a crucifix, asperges, nine collects, an exhortation to faith and love, the confession, and seven absolutions, one being the old form for reconciliation of public penitents. Extreme unction, on the other hand, involved Psalm 71 with the antiphon "O Savior of the world," the anointing of seven parts of the body while eight psalms were read, a prayer, communion from the reserved Sacrament, and additional psalmody, prayers, and blessings. At the point of death the Nicene Creed, the seven penitential psalms, and a litany of the saints were to be said.

Most of the continental Reformed rites eliminated the anointing with oil. Lutheran forms typically provided for exhortations, absolution, psalms, lections, and a celebration of the Eucharist. That of Electoral Brandenburg provided communion from the reserved Sacrament on days of a public Eucharist. Reformed rites ordinarily left the order at the visitation to the discretion of the minister: some favored communion of the sick from the public rite, some a celebration for the sick, and some were so opposed to private communions that they objected to either method.

In the 1549 Prayer Book the visitation office begins with the salutation "Peace be in this house and to all that dwell in it," abbreviated from the Sarum rite. Psalm 143, one of the seven penitential psalms, followed, with an antiphon "Remember not, Lord, our iniquities," also based on Sarum. Then came the Kyries, Lord's Prayer, and preces from the Sarum rite and revised forms of the ninth and third of the Sarum collects. The suggested form for an exhortation contains material from the homily "Against the Fear of Death," Hermann's Consultation, and an exhortation from the Sarum office: the essential theme

460

is that sickness is God's chastisement to correct sinful humanity. The baptismal form of the Apostles' Creed replaces the fourteen articles of the Sarum profession of faith; and the Sarum exhortation to faith, hope, and charity gives way to rubrics which direct the priest to treat these topics as seems fit. In accord with the Sarum order, the person is to "make a special confession, if he feel his conscience troubled with any weighty matter." The form of absolution, derived from Sarum and the Consultation, is to be "used in all private confessions." The Sarum form for reconciliation of dying penitents follows, a form which is in the Gelasian sacramentary (no. 364) and the supplement to the Gregorian (no. 1396). The rite concludes with Psalm 71 with its antiphon "O Savior of the world," a blessing with no known liturgical antecedents, and optional anointing, "If the sick person desire to be anointed." If anointing is requested, it is to be "upon the forehead or breast only," with a single sign of the cross, using a form partly derived from Sarum. Psalm 13 (one of the eight psalms for anointing in the Sarum rite) ends the anointing. The Book provides for communion of the sick from the reserved Sacrament on the day of a public Eucharist, or for a celebration in the sick person's home on other days. If the visitation and communion take place at the same time, certain elements of the visitation rite may be omitted.

The 1552 revision omitted the initial psalm and revised the second of two collects after the preces. There was no anointing nor was there permission to administer from the reserved Sacrament nor to abbreviate the rite when celebrating in the home of the sick person.

The rubric on confession was strengthened in 1662: the sick person is to "be moved" to make a special confession. This revision added the Aaronic blessing (Num. 6:24–26) and four prayers composed by Robert Sanderson at the end of the rite, but removed references to healing and recovery. In the prayer before the exhortation, a petition "sanctify, we beseech thee, this thy fatherly correction to him, that the sense of his weakness, may add strength to his faith, and seriousness to his repentance" replaced "Visit him, O Lord, as thou didst Peter's wife's mother, and the captain's servant." The last five verses of Psalm 71, which included a promise of thanksgiving for expected recovery, were also deleted.

The American Book of 1789 eliminated all references to the special confession. *The Rule and Exercises of Holy Dying*, Bishop Jeremy Taylor's popular devotional book, was available to the revisers and, using chapter V, section 7, they substituted Psalm 130 for Psalm 71, and added three additional prayers, two of which were based on prayers in Taylor's manual.

461

The revisers of the 1928 Book reworked the visitation office, eliminating the exhortation and examination, and generally using other substitutions to make less of the older thesis that sickness was God's chastisement for sin. The rite was restructured to consist of an introductory portion made up of the initial greeting, an abbreviated form of the antiphon, the Kyrie, the Lord's Prayer, preces, and the first collect of the old office. There was permission to say one of the penitential psalms after the antiphon. A section of antiphons, psalms, and collects followed, for use at discretion. Five psalms with proper antiphons and collects were provided, and additional psalms listed. After the anthem "O Savior of the world," the sick person was to be exhorted and examined and moved to make a special confession if troubled in conscience. The rite ended with the Gelasian prayer for a dying penitent, the blessing from the 1549 Book, and the Aaronic blessing which was added in 1662. Four of the seven additional prayers from the 1789 Book were retained and three new prayers replaced the three which were deleted. The 1928 revision also added a litany for the dying and provisions for unction.

The present Book provides a liturgy of the word, with New Testament lessons as well as psalms, the laying on of hands with or without anointing, and a private communion of the sick or communion from the reserved Sacrament. There is also provision for laying on of hands or anointing at a public celebration of the Eucharist. Prayers for use by a sick person are also included.

Ministration to the Sick (pp. 453–457)

The first rubric, designating that the minister of the congregation is to be notified of an illness, dates to the 1662 Book.

The rite is divided into three parts, of which one or more may be used. If more than one is used, the parts should be in the order given: first the ministry of the word; then the laying on of hands; then, as the climax of the rite, the communion of the sick. If only the first part is used, the Lord's Prayer should be included among the prayers.

Part I may be led by a deacon or lay person under any circumstances; anointing of the sick, in cases of necessity, may also be done by a deacon or lay person using oil blessed by the bishop or a priest (see p. 456); and a deacon may administer communion from the reserved Sacrament (see p. 396).

The laying on of hands or anointing may be used at a public service, as the fourth rubric indicates, preferably just before the exchange of the peace. (See *The Book of Occasional Services*, pp. 147–154 for a Public Service of Healing.)

The Greeting (p. 453)

The greeting which opens the rite was taken into the 1549 Book from the Sarum rite for visitation of the sick.

Part I. Ministry of the Word (pp. 453–455)

The order of the elements for the ministry of the word is the same as that at a Eucharist: readings and commentary on the readings, prayers, and confession of sin. Four sets of lections are listed, though the celebrant is not bound to use any of these. Psalm 91 and a portion of Psalm 103 are among those recommended in the 1928 Book. The Epistle and Gospel recommended for use if communion is to follow were added in 1928 as an alternative proper for the communion for the sick. Prayers for the sick are given (pp. 458–460) and other suitable prayers may also be said. The priest may suggest that the sick person make a special confession, if troubled in conscience; one of the forms for reconciliation of a penitent may be used (pp. 446–452). The general confession and absolution from the Holy Eucharist: Rite Two are printed for optional use if a special confession is not made. In keeping with the rubric on page 14, the form in traditional language from Rite One may be substituted (pp. 330–332).

Part II. Laying on of Hands and Anointing (pp. 455–457)

The Blessing of Oil for the Anointing of the Sick (p. 455)

The Apostolic Tradition of Hippolytus contains the oldest form for blessing of oil for the sick: "Sanctify this oil, O God, with which you anointed kings, priests, and prophets, you that would grant health to those who use it and partake of it, so that it may bestow comfort on all who taste it and health on all who use it." The oil was offered with the bread and wine at the Eucharist, blessed at the prayer, and returned to the offerer for use. The Roman rite eventually reserved the blessing of oil for the sick to the bishop, who blessed it on Maundy Thursday within the service at which chrism was consecrated. The 1549 Prayer Book retained the use of oil for the sick "If the sick person desire to be anointed" but provided no form for the setting apart of the oil; the 1552 revision eliminated the use of oil; it was not restored in the American Prayer Book until 1928, but even that Book

463

made no provision for blessing the oil. The intention of the revision is that the local priest bless the oil for the sick in the presence of the people. The form, an abbreviated version of that proposed in Prayer Book Studies III: The Order for the Ministration to the Sick (1951), is based on an old Roman form.

The Anthem (p. 455)

This anthem was used as the antiphon for Psalm 71 in the Sarum rite for extreme unction. The 1549 Prayer Book retained it as an anthem to be said after Psalm 71, though this was to be said as a regular part of the office of visitation, whether or not anointing followed. When the American 1789 Book replaced Psalm 71 with Psalm 130, this anthem was retained for use after it. The 1928 revision used it after the collect following the final psalm of the visitation rite. This present Book revives its connection with the anointing (or laying on of hands). The anthem is also printed in the Good Friday liturgy (p. 282) in the traditional language, for use among the devotions before the cross.

The Laying on of Hands (p. 456)

Although the 1549 Book provided for anointing of the sick, the 1552 Book omitted this action and it was not restored until the American revision of 1928 which provided laying on of hands as an alternative for anointing. The 1979 Book permits anointing as a supplementary rite to the laying on of hands. In the 1928 Book the words accompanying the laying on of hands are:

> I lay my hand upon thee In the Name of the Father, and of the Son, and of the Holy Ghost; beseeching the mercy of our Lord Jesus Christ, that all thy pain and sickness of body being put to flight, the blessing of health may be restored unto thee. Amen.

That form is replaced in this revision by two alternative new forms.

The Anointing (p. 456)

The Sarum rite of extreme unction included the application of oil with the sign of the cross to seven different parts of the body. The 1549 Prayer Book prescribed anointing "upon the forehead or breast only, making the sign of the cross." Omitted in 1552, the anointing was restored in the 1928 revision as an option without any specification about either blessing the oil or anointing with the sign of the

464

cross. The present edition specifies the use of "holy oil" with the sign of the cross on the person's forehead. (If the forehead is bandaged, or if anointing it would cause pain, the anointing should be done on some other part of the body, such as the breast or the back of a hand.)

The form for the anointing is an abbreviated version of that in the 1928 Book where the form continued with words unsuited for use with the dying, "beseeching the mercy of our Lord Jesus Christ, that all thy pain and sickness of body being put to flight, the blessing of health may be restored unto thee. Amen." An optional addition has been substituted for this conclusion. The present form is essentially abridged from the 1549 statement, portions of which were derived from the Sarum use:

> As with this visible oil thy body outwardly is anointed: so our heavenly Father, almighty God, grant of his infinite goodness, that thy soul inwardly may be anointed with the Holy Ghost, who is the Spirit of all strength, comfort, relief, and gladness. And vouchsafe for his great mercy, if it be his blessed will, to restore unto thee thy bodily health, and strength to serve him, and send thee release of all thy pains, troubles, and diseases, both in body and mind. And howsoever his goodness, by his divine and unsearchable providence, shall dispose of thee: we, his unworthy ministers and servants, humbly beseech the eternal majesty, to do with thee according to the multitude of his innumerable mercies, and to pardon thee all thy sins and offences, committed by all thy bodily senses, passions, and carnal affections: who also vouchsafe mercifully to grant unto thee ghostly strength, by his Holy Spirit, to withstand and overcome all temptations and assaults of thine adversary, that in no wise he prevail against thee, but that thou mayest have perfect victory and triumph against the devil, sin, and death, through Christ our Lord: Who by his death hath overcome the prince of death, and with the Father and the Holy Ghost evermore liveth and reigneth, God, world without end. Amen.

In the early church, deacons and lay persons as well as priests anointed the sick. Rubrical directions in the 1928 Book used the word "Minister" rather than "priest." The present Book uses the word "Priest" in the rubric which precedes the anointing but the rubric provides that in cases of necessity a deacon or lay person may anoint, making use of oil blessed by the bishop or a priest.

As in other rites (pp. 407 and 428), if communion is not to follow, the Lord's Prayer is to be said prior to the dismissal.

The Blessing (pp. 456–457)

This is an abbreviated version of the blessing which concludes the visitation of the sick in the 1549 Prayer Book, which seems to have no liturgical precedents. Scriptural bases for the blessing are Psalm 61:3, Philippians 2:10–11, and Acts 4:12. The fuller ending in prior editions of the Prayer Book reads "that there is no other Name under heaven given to man, in whom and through whom thou mayest receive health and salvation, but only the Name of our Lord Jesus Christ."

Part III. Holy Communion (p. 457)

Every edition of the Prayer Book has included provisions for the communion of the sick. The 1549 Book, following the Brandenburg church order, provided for communion in both kinds from the reserved Sacrament on a day when the Eucharist was celebrated in the church, and for an abbreviated celebration on other days. The 1552 revision eliminated the provision for communion from the reserved Sacrament, and the permission to abbreviate the rite. Though it was not required that it be preceded by Morning Prayer and Litany, as at a public celebration, the whole of the eucharistic rite was to be read in the sick person's house. The 1662 revision allowed the priest to begin the celebration with the collect, and after the Gospel to go directly to the bidding to confession. In the 1892 revision further concessions were allowed. In "times of contagious sickness or disease, or when extreme weakness renders it expedient," the rite could be reduced, as in the Irish Book of 1877, to the general confession and absolution, the Sursum corda through the Sanctus, the "Prayer of Consecration" through the epiclesis, the communion, the Lord's Prayer, and the blessing. The 1928 revision required that the prayer of humble access be included in the minimal form, but provided shorter alternative forms for the general confession and absolution. This present revision provides more flexibility. The Eucharist, which may be preceded by a brief liturgy of the word (and laying on of hands), begins with the [peace and] offertory. An alternative postcommunion prayer, drafted by the Rev. Dr. Massey H. Shepherd, Jr., and a dismissal (the fourth of the forms printed in Rite One and Rite Two) are provided for use when forms which stress being sent into the world might be inappropriate.

A rubric explicitly permits administration from the reserved Sacrament, using the form for Communion under Special Circumstances, pages 398–399. (On the history of reservation, see above, pages 409–

410.) Until the continental Reformation, communion of the sick was normally from the reserved Sacrament. The 1549 Prayer Book allowed reservation for the communion of the sick on the day of a public celebration, and allowed a celebration for the sick on other days, from which the reserved Sacrament could be carried to other sick persons. The 1552 revision eliminated reservation. This is the first American revision to restore the practice, though it was restored earlier in some revisions for other provinces of Anglicanism. It is particularly appropriate to bring the reserved Sacrament directly from a public service in which prayers have been said for the sick, thereby including them in the fellowship.

This is the first edition of the Prayer Book to allow for communion in one kind only. It is probable that in the early church, on occasion, the Sacrament carried to the absent or the Sacrament reserved was in one kind. Theologically the whole Christ was believed to be present in either the bread or the wine. Late in the middle ages, as a new eucharistic piety developed, the cup was withheld from the laity to protect the Sacrament from possible spilling or dribbling. The continental reformers restored the cup, a return to the practice of the early church and an assertion of the priesthood of the laity. The 1548 Order of the Communion restored the cup in England. The new rubric is not intended as a denial of the cup (or the bread) to the laity but as an encouragement to administer communion to the sick in circumstances when it might be difficult or impossible for the sick person to receive one or the other of the eucharistic elements.

The final rubric (the bottom of p. 457) is a simplified form of a rubric which dates to 1549, the equivalent of the Sarum rubric:

> If the probability of vomiting or other irreverence is feared, the priest shall say to the sick, "Brother, in this case true faith and good will suffices, only believe and you have eaten."

This can be compared to the commentary of Augustine on John 6:27–29. The rubric in the 1549 Book reads:

> But if any man either by reason of extremity or sickness, or for lack of warning given in due time to the curate, or by any other just impediment, do not receive the sacrament of Christ's body and blood: then the curate shall instruct him, that if he do truly repent him of his sins, and steadfastly believe that Jesus Christ hath suffered death upon the cross for him, and shed his blood for his redemption, earnestly remembering the benefits he hath thereby, and giving him hearty thanks therefor, he doth eat and

467

drink spiritually the body and blood of our Savior Christ, profitably to his soul's health, although he do not receive the sacrament with his mouth.

The 1552 revision adds to the impediments "or for lack of company to receive with him," a phrase removed in the 1928 Book. The doctrine stated in this rubric is equivalent to the doctrine of baptism by desire in cases where baptism is desired but not available.

Prayers for the Sick (pp. 458–460)

The first prayer "For a Sick Person" was printed among the occasional prayers in the 1928 revision. A longer version, created by joining portions of three prayers from the 1662 office for the visitation of the sick, was among four occasional prayers introduced in the 1789 American Book. These four prayers are found in the same order in a manuscript of liturgical forms which Bishop Samuel Seabury of Connecticut compiled from diverse sources such as the writings of Bishop Thomas Wilson of Sodor and Man, the Scottish liturgy, and the revised Prayer Book of King's Chapel, Boston, which he carried with him to the General Convention of September 1789. Another prayer from that notebook, retained in this revision, is "For a Person in Trouble or Bereavement" (p. 831). Until 1928, this prayer for the sick ended "Or else give *him* grace so to take thy visitation, that, after this painful life ended, *he* may dwell with thee in life everlasting." The preamble, from 2 Corinthians 4:16, had been the preamble of a prayer added in the 1662 revision. The remainder of the prayer is basically a conflation of the first two prayers of the visitation office in the 1662 Book. The portions used date back to the 1549 Book and to the Sarum rite.

The second prayer entered the Book in 1928. The Rev. Howard Baldwin St. George, a professor at Nashotah House (1902–1932), and secretary of the subcommittee responsible for this section of the 1928 revision, is believed to be the one chiefly responsible for this collect.

The third prayer was added to the 1928 Book from William Bright's *Ancient Collects* (pp. 109–110). It originates in the Gelasian sacramentary (no. 1537) and the supplement to the Gregorian (no. 1390) where it is among the prayers for the sick. In the Bobbio missal it is the collect of a Mass (no. 380). Although it was in the Sarum rite for visitation of the sick, the 1549 Book did not include it.

The fourth prayer, "For a Sick Child," was new to the 1928 revision.

468

The Rev. Dr. John W. Suter, who wrote several of the prayers added to the Book at that time, was responsible for some of its phrasing.

The alternative prayer for a sick child, new to this revision, is an amended form of a prayer in the Irish Prayer Book of 1926.

The prayer "Before an Operation" is a revised version of one which was new to the 1928 Book among the additional prayers in family prayer. The conclusion uses Psalm 56:3 as scriptural source.

The alternative prayer, new to this edition, is revised from a prayer by the Rev. Dr. Robert N. Rodenmayer, published in a collection edited by him.[1]

The prayer "For Strength and Confidence" was adapted by the Rev. Dr. Charles M. Guilbert from one added to the American Prayer Book of 1928. The original prayer, abbreviated in 1928, was by the bishop of Edinburgh, John Dowden (1886–1910), and had been included in the Scottish Book of 1912. The 1928 version reads:

> O merciful God, giver of life and health; Bless, we pray thee, thy servant, N., and those who administer to him of thy healing gifts; that he may be restored to health of body and of mind; through Jesus Christ our Lord. Amen.

The prayer "For the Sanctification of Illness" (p. 460) is from the 1928 Book and basically a conflation: the initial petition dates from 1928, the result clause from 1662, and the remainder from a collect in the 1549 Book. The 1662 version reads:

> Hear us, Almighty and most merciful God and Savior; extend thy accustomed goodness to this thy servant who is grieved with sickness. Sanctify, we beseech thee, this thy fatherly correction to him; that the sense of his weakness may add strength to his faith, and seriousness to his repentance: That, if it shall be thy good pleasure to restore him to his former health, he may lead the residue of his life in thy fear, and to thy glory; or else, give him grace so to take thy visitation, that, after this painful life ended, he may dwell with thee in life everlasting; through Jesus Christ our Lord. Amen.

The 1549 version reads:

> Hear us, almighty and most merciful God and Savior: Extend thy accustomed goodness to this thy servant, which is grieved with

---

[1] *The Pastor's Prayerbook*, New York: Oxford University Press, 1960, no. 252.

sickness; visit him, O Lord, as thou didst visit Peter's wife's mother, and the captain's servant. And as thou preservest Tobit and Sara by the angel from danger, so restore unto this sick person his former health, if it be thy will, or else give him grace so to take thy correction, that after this painful life ended, he may dwell with thee in life everlasting. Amen.

This was based upon the third of the Sarum collects for the visitation of the sick.

The prayer "For Health of Body and Soul" is new to this revision. It was drafted by the Rev. Dr. Charles M. Guilbert on the basis of a prayer from *The Pastor's Prayerbook*.[1] It is the initial portion of the final blessing in the Sarum rite of extreme unction.

The prayer "For Doctors and Nurses" is new to this Book. It is an abbreviated version of one written by the Rev. Dr. John W. Suter.[2]

The "Thanksgiving for a Beginning of Recovery" is a revised form of a prayer in the Prayer Book of the Church of Ireland, and replaces a prayer from the 1789 revision:

Great and mighty God, who bringest down to the grave, and bringest up again, we bless thy wonderful goodness, for having turned our heaviness into joy, and mourning into gladness, by restoring this our *brother* to some degree of *his* former health. Blessed be thy name, that thou didst not forsake *him* in *his* sickness, but didst visit *him* with comforts from above, didst support *him* in patience and submission to thy will, and, at last, didst send *him* seasonable relief. Perfect, we beseech thee, this thy mercy towards *him*, and prosper the means, which shall be made use of for *his* cure; That being restored to health of body, vigour of mind, and cheerfulness of spirit, *he* may be able to go to thine house, to offer thee an oblation with great gladness, and to bless thy holy name, for all thy goodness towards *him*, through Jesus Christ our Saviour: To whom, with thee and the Holy Spirit, be all honor and glory, world without end. *Amen.*

This prayer originated in the House of Bishops which was, at the 1789 Convention, composed of William White and Samuel Seabury.

---

[1] *Pastor's Prayerbook*, no. 274.
[2] John W. Suter, *Prayers of the Spirit*, New York: Harper & Bros., 1943, p. 29.

Prayers for use by a Sick Person (p. 461)

This is the first edition of the Prayer Book to include a selection of prayers specifically intended for use by the sick person. All are new to this Book.

"For Trust in God," the first prayer, is from Suter's *Prayers of the Spirit* (p. 27). The second is a revised form of a prayer in the *Army and Navy Service Book*. The third is revised from a prayer in the 1926 Irish Prayer Book. The Rev. Dr. Theodore Parker Ferris composed the fourth.[1]

---

[1] Printed in *Prayers for a New World,* compiled and edited by John W. Suter, New York: Charles Scribner's Sons, 1964, p. 200.

Ministration at the Time of Death

By the time of the council of Nicaea (A.D. 325) the practice of giving communion to the dying as a means of *viaticum* (sustenance for a journey) seems to have been regarded as an ancient custom (for commentary see below, pp. 477–478). Prayers for the commendation of the departed are extant from the fourth century.

In the middle ages the visitation of the sick came to be thought of not as a rite for healing but for the remission of sins, and its use was largely reserved to those thought to be in extremis. The litany for the dying and prayers of commendation were, therefore, added to that rite.

Although the 1549 Prayer Book did not include the litany and prayers for the dying from the medieval rite, the revision of the visitation office still contained many elements better suited to a "last rite" than to a rite for healing. The commendatory prayer for a sick person "at the point of departure" was added in the 1662 Book. In the 1928 revision the visitation office was altered to make it more suitable as a rite of healing; a litany and additional commendatory prayers were added for use when appropriate. The present Book has substituted a new prayer for the 1662 commendation, has revised the concluding collect of the litany, and added an additional commendatory prayer. Prayers for use at a vigil and a rite for the reception of the body at the church have also been added.

Ministration at the Time of Death (pp. 462–467)

The rubric specifies that the minister of the congregation should be notified when a person is near death, "in order that the ministrations of the Church may be provided."

472

A Prayer for a Person near Death (p. 462)

This prayer, thought to have been drafted by John W. Ashton, replaces two prayers from the 1662 revision which may have been composed by Robert Sanderson: "A Prayer for a sick person when there appeareth small hope of recovery," and "A commendatory Prayer for a sick person at the point of departure." The first of these reads:

O Father of mercies, and God of all Comfort, our only help in time of need; we fly unto thee for succour in behalf of this thy servant, here lying under thy hand in great weakness of body. Look graciously upon him, O Lord; and the more the outward man decayeth, strengthen him, we beseech thee, so much the more continually with thy grace and Holy Spirit, in the inner man. Give him unfeigned repentance for all the errors of his life past, and steadfast faith in thy Son Jesus; that his sins may be done away by thy mercy, and his pardon sealed in heaven, before he go hence, and be no more seen. We know, O Lord, that there is no word impossible with thee; and that if thou wilt, thou canst, even yet, raise him up, and grant him a longer continuance among us. Yet, forasmuch as in all appearance the time of his dissolution draweth near; so fit and prepare him, we beseech thee, against the hour of death; that after his departure hence in peace, and in thy favor, his soul may be received into thine everlasting kingdom, through the merits, and mediation of Jesus Christ, thine only Son, our Lord and Saviour. Amen.

The prayer had been abbreviated somewhat for the 1928 Book. The other prayer reads:

O Almighty God, with whom do live the spirits of just men made perfect, after they are delivered from their earthly prisons: We humbly commend the soul of this thy servant, our dear brother, into thy hands, as into the hands of a faithful Creator, and most merciful Saviour; most humbly beseeching thee that it may be precious in thy sight. Wash it we pray thee, in the blood of that immaculate Lamb, that was slain to take away the sins of the world: that whatsoever defilements it may have contracted in the midst of this miserable and naughty world, through the lusts of the flesh, or the wiles of Satan, being purged, and done away, it may be presented pure and without spot before thee. And teach us who survive, in this, and other like daily spectacles of mortality, to see how frail, and uncertain our own condition is; and so to number our days that we may seriously apply our hearts to that

473

holy and heavenly wisdom, whilst we live here, which may in the
end bring us to life everlasting through the merits of Jesus Christ,
thine only Son our Lord. Amen.

The final petition was omitted in 1892 and the phrase "in the midst of
this miserable and naughty world" dropped in the 1928 revision. A
briefer form of the prayer is retained among additional prayers
printed in the burial rite (p. 488).

Litany at the Time of Death (pp. 462–465)

The rubric notes that it is desirable for others to join with the
minister in the litany.

This litany, added to the Prayer Book in 1928, is based upon the
"Litany for the Dying" in William Bright's *Ancient Collects* (pp.
118–120) which was drawn from the medieval litanies of Sarum,
Fleury, Jumièges, and Rouen. The present Book abbreviates the responses to the invocations from the longer "Have mercy upon the
soul of thy servant" in both Bright's book and the 1928 edition, in
order to remove the dualistic concept of soul apart from body which
the older form implied. One of the two translations of the Agnus Dei
done by ICET is substituted for the form in the 1928 Book. As in
other rites in contemporary language, both contemporary and traditional forms of the Lord's Prayer are provided. The structure of this
litany is like that of the Great Litany (pp. 148–153): invocations,
deprecation, obsecrations, supplications, Agnus Dei, Kyrie, Lord's
Prayer, and final collect. The final collect is a revised form of that in
the 1928 Prayer Book, a condensed form of a prayer in Bishop
Charles Gore's *A Prayer Book Revised* (1913). Gore's version was
based upon a translation of "A prayer for a soul going to judgment,"
in the Eastern Orthodox rite for the dying, from William Bright's
Ancient Collects (pp. 117–118).

A Commendation at the Time of Death (p. 464)

The 1928 revision was the first Prayer Book to include this commendation which is dependent on a shortened version of the Sarum
form which William Bright had printed in *Ancient Collects* (p. 120).
That form reads:

> Depart, O Christian soul, out of this world, in the Name of God
> the Father Almighty, Who created thee; in the Name of Jesus
> Christ His Son, Who suffered for thee; in the Name of the Holy

Ghost, Who has been poured into thee; may thy place be this day in peace, and thy habitation in the Heavenly Jerusalem.

The revisions were influenced by the summary of the creed in the catechism of previous Prayer Books and by our Lord's words to the penitent thief on the cross (Lk. 23:43).

A Commendatory Prayer (p. 465)

This prayer is a slightly abbreviated version of one first included in the 1928 Book. It had been proposed for inclusion in the 1883 *Book Annexed*. The present Book also uses it at the commendation within the burial rite (pp. 483 and 499). The source is a prayer by John Cosin in *A Collection of Private Devotions* (1627).

The final form, included in the American Prayer Book for the first time, both here and in the burial rite (pp. 486 and 502), was used in the Sarum rite at the commendation of the soul and as the dismissal after the service at the grave.

Prayers for a Vigil (pp. 465–466)

The vigil, a normal part of the medieval burial liturgy, was not taken into the continental Reformed rites for burial nor into the 1549 Prayer Book, although provision for it was included in English primers. A vigil is here restored as a suitable option. The form suggests appropriate texts for use in areas where a vigil is expected or desired. It is especially useful as an additional rite which can provide opportunity for friends unable to attend the regular rites to come together for prayer with the family. Like the vigils of the church year it prepares the participants for the climactic liturgy of the word and table at the burial itself.

Psalms, lessons, and collects, such as those for the burial service, may be used, as well as psalms, collects, and lections that will not be part of the burial rite. The vigil may, indeed, be an opportunity to introduce texts which will be used at the burial or to give time for reflection upon them. The rubric also suggests that the litany at the time of death (pp. 462–464) is appropriate. The additional litany of commendation, dependent on the form used at Gethsemani Abbey, uses a response based on the last words of our Lord from the cross (Lk. 23:46) taken from Psalm 31:5. Other scriptural allusions are Matthew 22:11–12, Matthew 25:34, and Hebrews 4.

475

Reception of the Body (pp. 466–467)

This form, new to the 1979 Prayer Book, may be used whenever the body is brought to the church, and is especially suitable if the body is at the church sometime prior to the public rite. The form is composed of two prayers, one for the deceased and one for the bereaved, each of which is preceded by a bidding which may be followed by a period of silence.

The first prayer is the final collect of the litany at the time of death (p. 464). The bidding to the second prayer is based upon the last of the additional prayers in the burial rite (pp. 489 and 505). The prayer itself is an abbreviated form of "For a Person under Affliction" in the 1789 Book, one of those from Bishop Samuel Seabury's notebook of "Occasional Prayers and Offices." It incorporated phrases from the Litany, the office for the visitation of the sick, and the prayer "for all conditions of men" in the 1662 Book. In earlier Books the prayer read:

> O merciful God, and heavenly Father, who hast taught us in thy holy Word that thou dost not willingly afflict or grieve the children of men; Look with pity, we beseech thee, upon the sorrows of thy *servant*, for whom our prayers are desired. In thy wisdom thou hast seen fit to visit *him* with trouble, and to bring distress upon *him*. Remember *him*, O Lord, in mercy; sanctify thy fatherly correction to *him*; endue *his* soul with patience under *his* affliction, and with resignation to thy blessed will; comfort *him* with a sense of thy goodness; lift up thy countenance upon *him*, and give *him* peace; through Jesus Christ our Lord. Amen.

This prayer was somewhat shortened in the 1928 Book. (Compare No. 55 among the Prayers and Thanksgivings, p. 831.)

Rubrics suggest suitable additions to this rite for use if the burial office is not to follow immediately, specify that the burial rite begins with the opening anthems if it is to follow immediately, and suggest that the body be led into the church by a member of the congregation bearing the lighted paschal candle which signifies Easter and baptism.

476

The Burial of the Dead

The earliest accounts we have tell of rites and ceremonies which filled the time between death and burial. The rites were designed to insure that the dead were, in fact, dead (and not perhaps in a coma or trance) and that they stayed dead, and to carry the members of the community through their dealings with grief, realign the family structure, and redistribute the property and community responsibilities of the deceased so that the family and community could move on in the daily round.

Jewish rites and ceremonials included preparation of the body. Mourners tore their garments, dressed in sackcloth, and cut their hair. Neighbors brought bread and "the cup of consolation." Prayer and sacrifices were offered for the dead, with lamentations and funeral hymns, and the placing of bread and wine offerings on the tombs.

The kerygma of the resurrection and exaltation of Jesus Christ and the assurance of resurrection in Him is central to New Testament teaching. Except for reinterpretation in terms of the Christian gospel, the rites of burial in the New Testament period were probably not very different from those of the Jews, although customs derived from pagan practice exerted an increasing influence as the number of Gentile Christians multiplied.

Pagan burial customs included the *viaticum*, the last meal for the dead, or the coin for Charon, the ferryman who would carry the dead across the Styx only if he were paid; the final kiss; the arranging, washing, anointing, and clothing of the body; the procession to the grave with torches, lamentations, dirges, and mourners dressed in black; the (cremation and) burial of the remains; the ceremony of farewell, *vale*, and the funeral oration; and commemorations at certain intervals. A wake was customary in some areas before the burial;

477

in others following it, where burial was on the day of death and the wake was held at the grave.

The early Christians substituted communion for the *viaticum* and rejected the use of torches in procession because of their association with the emperor cult. Psalms, hymns, and Alleluias replaced the lamentations and dirges, and the church fathers inveighed against the wearing of black by the mourners. Cremation was considered unsuitable since the body was to be resurrected; psalms, hymns, and prayers substituted for the *vale*. In some places the ceremonies at the grave concluded with a Eucharist, and the Eucharist was offered in commemoration at certain intervals.

Descriptions of Christian burial rites from the fourth century indicate that certain psalms, lessons, and prayers were customary. Early sacramentaries provided prayers for use at the time of death and before the body was carried from the house. The procession was accompanied by the singing of such psalms as 23, 32, 114, 115, and 116, chosen for their baptismal and exodus themes. There were prayers and lections for Matins and Vespers and for the Eucharist, and prayers for the interment and for anniversary celebrations on the seventh and thirtieth days or similar intervals. Christian burials in this early period seem to have been dignified, triumphant, and filled with hope. Prayers were for forgiveness and rest and a place among the patriarchs, prophets, and all who pleased God from the beginning of the world.

Late in the middle ages the pattern of the burial rites remained much the same in the West: commendation, Vespers (Placebo, from the antiphon on the first psalm), Matins (Dirige or Dirge), the Eucharist, committal, and anniversary commemorations. But there were many changes in the texts and the ceremonies. Black replaced white as the color; mournful corteges accompanied by penitential psalms replaced the festal processions with Alleluias, psalms of praise, and the waving of branches. In place of hopeful commendatory prayers there were absolutions of the body and such prayers as one in the Sarum rite: "Deliver him from the hand of hell, from the deep pit, from the lion's mouth," and such hymns as Dies irae, "Day of wrath, O day of mourning," with emphasis on ashes, torment, and everlasting damnation. This hymn was not officially a part of the Roman rite until 1570, but had been used much earlier in some locations. Other evidence of the changes in piety is the addition of the daily office of the dead, the regular inclusion in the Roman eucharistic prayer of a commemoration of the dead (formerly used only on occasion), votive Masses for the dead, and the institution of

478

All Souls' Day (November 2). The growing fear of purgatory caused drastic changes in the liturgy. No longer reminiscent of the baptism and Easter liturgies, the burial rite came to have the same restrictions upon the use of Alleluia and other responses of praise and joy as the last three days of Holy Week. It acquired the character of a meditation on mortality with a heavily penitential, at times even horrifying, tone.

The continental reformers all violently opposed the doctrine of purgatory and Masses for the dead. However, they were too much imbued with the late medieval tradition to return to the baptismal and paschal imagery of the early church rites. In the Consultation of Hermann the burial rite was fairly typical of German church orders: during the procession to the grave the text "In the midst of life we are in death," Psalm 130, or hymns were to be sung; at the grave a lection from 1 Corinthians 15, Philippians 3:20ff., or Romans 6:8–11 was to be read. A short office was provided for use in the church, consisting of a lesson, an exhortation, the Lord's Prayer, and two collects. Generally the German church orders included no formal committal of the body. In the Reformed tradition the burial itself was often "without any ceremony," although it was frequently followed in the church by a service of readings, psalms, sermon, and prayers.

The 1549 Prayer Book provided a burial rite which had four parts: the procession to the church or to the grave; the burial; an office; and the Eucharist. Three anthems were provided for use during the procession from the churchyard gate to the church or grave. They were to be said by the priest or sung by the priest and clerks. The first two of these, John 11:25–26 and Job 19:25–27, had been used in the Sarum office. The third, 1 Timothy 6:7 and Job 1:21, had no medieval precedent. The service at the grave, which might precede or follow the office and Eucharist in the church, began with two anthems to be said by the priest or sung by priest and clerks. The first was Job 14:1–2 and the second the medieval antiphon "In the midst of life" used in the Sarum rite with the Nunc dimittis during the third and fourth weeks of Lent, and incorporated into burial rites in many of the German church orders. The priest then cast earth upon the body and said a form of committal which combined the Sarum form and Philippians 3:21. An anthem, Revelation 14:13, followed; this had been used as antiphon to the Magnificat in the Sarum office of the dead. The service concluded with two prayers: a commendation of the departed and a thanksgiving for the deceased, both of which included petition for the departed.

The first prayer contained allusions to John 5:22 and Matthew

479

25:34, and the second to Romans 7:24, Psalm 31:6, and Hebrews 9:39–40 and 12:23. The first prayer began like one in the Sarum rite and the second like one in the Cologne Consultation.

The office to be said in the church before or after the burial consisted of three psalms, a lesson, a threefold Kyrie, the Lord's Prayer, preces, and a prayer. The psalms, 116, 139, and 146, had been used in the Sarum rite; use of Psalm 116 can be traced back to the time of Saint John Chrysostom. The lesson, 1 Corinthians 15:20–58, was an expanded version of the lesson in some German church orders and the preces were selected from the Sarum rite. The concluding prayer, "O Lord, with whom do live the spirits of them that be dead," included several phrases from prayers in the Sarum rite, two of which are in the Gelasian sacramentary (nos. 1607 and 1627) and the supplement to the Gregorian (nos. 1398 and 1410). The first is also in the Bobbio missal (no. 535); the final petition was based, like that of the prayer for the church in the 1549 Eucharist, on the collect of the Sarum Mass of the Five Wounds of Our Lord Jesus Christ.

The proper for the Eucharist included Psalm 42, traditionally associated with the burial office, for use as an introit. The collect, the address of which includes the quotation of John 11:25–26 and 1 Thessalonians 4:13, seems to have derived in part from a Dirige of the primer of 1539 attributed to Bishop John Hilsey. The Epistle, 1 Thessalonians 4:13–18, is in the Sarum requiem and a number of Lutheran burial rites. The Gospel, John 6:37–40, was appointed in the Sarum missal for Tuesday Masses for the dead.

The 1552 revision drastically abbreviated the burial rite. No texts were provided for use in the church, although the rubric concerning the procession directed that the anthems be sung going "either unto the church or towards the grave." Accounts of burials for this period, including that of Edward VI, indicate that at least on some occasions the body was carried into the church for the daily office and Eucharist before burial.

The service at the grave began with the 1549 anthems, followed by the committal in which the initial sentence was changed from "I commend thy soul to God the Father Almighty and thy body to the ground," to "Forasmuch as it hath pleased Almighty God of his great mercy to take unto himself the soul of our dear brother here departed: we therefore commit his body to the ground." This is from the second funeral sermon in Hermann's Consultation. Rather than the priest, as a symbolic gesture, casting earth upon the body at the committal, "the earth shall be cast upon the body by some standing by" as the priest says the committal. As in many of the German church orders the anthem from Revelation precedes the reading of 1 Corinthians 15:20–58. The Kyrie and Lord's Prayer are said at the grave, but there are no preces, and the service ends with two prayers. The first of these begins like the prayer of the 1549 burial office, then appends the first portion of the prayer of thanksgiving of the 1549 committal rite, and concludes with a new form that is the nearest the 1552 Book comes to a petition for the departed:

> beseeching thee, that it may please thee of thy gracious goodness, shortly to accomplish the number of thine elect, and to haste thy kingdom, that we with this our brother, and all other departed in the true faith of thy holy name, may have our perfect consummation and bliss, both in body, and soul, in thy eternal and everlasting glory.

The final prayer combines the first part of the collect of the 1549 eucharistic rite and the conclusion of the first of the prayers at the grave from that rite. It is worth noting that the 1549 prayer asked that "both this our brother and we, may be found acceptable in thy sight;" the 1552 petition omitted the phrase "both this our brother and."

Although there was no revision of the 1552 rite until the 1662 Prayer Book, the Elizabethan Primer of 1559 contained a Dirige which had traditional psalms and lessons from the 1549 Prayer Book and older rites. In the petitions for the departed there is an attempt to emphasize the communion of saints rather than the escape from punishment.

The 1560 Latin edition of the Book (for use by individuals and communities which understood that language) contained a commemoration of benefactors and a Collect, Epistle (1 Thess. 4:13–14) and alternative Gospels (Jn. 6:37–40 or 5:25–29) for a burial Eucharist.

In the 1662 Book a rubric prefaced the rite, directing that "the Office ensuing is not to be used for any that die unbaptized, or excommunicate, or have laid violent hands upon themselves." The phrase "the souls of the faithful" replaced "the souls of them that be elected" in the first prayer, and the Grace (2 Cor. 13:14) was added at the conclusion of the service at the grave. Robert Sanderson and Jeremy Taylor, in their rites for use during the interregnum, had both provided Psalms 39 and 90 for the church service, and the 1662 Book included these in addition to moving the use of 1 Corinthians 15:20–58 to the church portion of the rite. These psalms and the lesson, if we can judge by Taylor's liturgy and by practices which continued into the nineteenth century, were intended as propers for use within a daily office.

The American Book of 1789 added a qualifying phrase to the first rubric indicating that the office was not to be used for "any unbaptized Adults." A cento from the two psalms (Pss. 39:5–9 and 12–15 and 90:1–10 and 12) replaced the use of whole psalms. The committal was revised partly on the basis of the 1662 forms for use at sea. The Kyrie was deleted, and the controversial first prayer made optional and revised in a manner which owes something to the prayer for the church in the Scottish Eucharist, the result of a proposal from the Pennsylvania state convention of May 1786.

The 1892 revision allowed the omission of the selection of verses from one psalm or the other. By this time the psalms and lesson were no longer set within a daily office; a final rubric allowed the use of a hymn or anthem, the creed, "and such fitting Prayers as are elsewhere provided in this Book" to be added after the lesson. The Kyrie was restored and three additional prayers added after the Grace. Two were based on prayers from *The Priest's Prayer Book*.[1] The third was the conclusion of the prayer for the church in the Scottish Prayer Book of 1637 and the "Wee Bookies." An additional rubric permitted the whole of the rite to be said "under shelter of the Church."

A rubric, printed at the end of the 1928 rite, replaced the initial rubric of the 1662, 1789, and 1892 Books. It read: "It is to be noted that this Office is appropriate to be used only for the faithful departed in Christ, provided that in any other case the Minister may, at his discretion, use such part of this Office, or such devotions taken from other parts of this Book, as may be fitting." The Book provided additional selections from the psalms: 27:1, 4–11, 15–16; 46:1–5, 10–11; 121; and 130. The lesson was abbreviated to 1 Corinthians 15:20–28, 35–58, and two alternative lessons were added: Romans 8:14–19, 28, 31–32, and 34–39; and John 14:1–6. There were also included a new optional prayer for the departed and a blessing; alternative anthems for use at the grave; and two additional prayers, one from the Sarum requiem for a priest and the other from the Scottish Book of 1912. A separate office for the burial of a child was added to this edition as well as a proper for a requiem Eucharist. Several of the new prayers which came into the Book in 1928, as well as the revised ending of the prayer for the church in the eucharistic rite, included petitions for the departed.

---

[1] R. F. Littledale and J. Edward Vaux, seventh edition, London: Longmans, Green & Co., 1890.

The present Book includes burial rites in both traditional and contemporary language, modeled on the Sunday liturgy of word and sacrament. Many alternatives have been added, many laudable texts and ceremonies restored. "An Order of Burial" is also provided which may be filled out by the celebrant in a manner especially suited to a particular situation. In addition there is a form for the consecration of a grave if the burial is in a place not previously set apart for Christian burial.

Concerning the Service (pp. 468 and 490)

This introductory page states the expectations of the church with regard to arrangements for burial. The death of a member should be reported to the minister of the congregation as soon as possible. The bereaved should not commit themselves to any burial arrangements before consultation with the minister and such arrangements should be made in consultation.

The second paragraph emphasizes that "Baptized Christians are properly buried from the church," a modification of the earlier Prayer Book position which assumed that all burials would be either from the church or at the grave. Because of the nature of the burial rite and the Christian community it is explicitly stated that "The service should be held at a time when the congregation has opportunity to be present."

The third paragraph reinforces the tradition that the coffin is to be closed before the service and to remain closed thereafter. It also notes that it is appropriate to place a pall or similar covering, rather than flowers, on the coffin. This is intended to restore the use of a pall, customary in Anglicanism until the middle of the nineteenth century.

The first sentence of the fourth paragraph restates a rubric introduced in the Prayer Book of 1892: "Inasmuch as it may sometimes be expedient to say under shelter of the Church the whole or a part of the service appointed to be said at the Grave, the same is hereby allowed for weighty cause." Precedent for the committal service to precede the service in the church goes back to the 1549 Prayer Book which provided an office to be said in the church "either before or after the burial of the corpse." Though not explicitly stated in later Books, this permission seems to have been assumed: while special provisions for the service in the church have been included since 1662, the opening anthems were to be said as the body was carried "either into the Church, or towards the Grave." Permission is given for the committal to precede cremation; this is the first American Prayer Book to recognize the practice of cremation.

483

The next three paragraphs designate particular liturgical ministries for the various orders. Though it is expected that a priest will preside at the burial of the dead, it is appropriate for the bishop, when present, to preside at the Eucharist and to pronounce the commendation. The rubrics indicate the traditional duties of a deacon—reading the Gospel, leading the prayers of the people, and saying the dismissal. As in other rites, "It is desirable that the Lesson from the Old Testament, and the Epistle, be read by lay persons." At least as far back as the reign of Elizabeth I, deacons and lay persons were authorized to preside at burials when a priest could not be obtained.

Until the 1928 revision, the American Prayer Book made no special provision for the burial of a child. A service was proposed for the 1892 revision but was rejected. The Scottish Book of 1912 included a special rite, and revisions for other provinces of Anglicanism followed this lead. The American rite of 1928 consisted of three opening anthems (Jn. 11:25, Lk. 18:16, and Is. 40:11), two psalms (23 and 121), a lesson (Mt. 18:1–5 and 10), prayers, a special form of committal which incorporated the Aaronic benediction from Numbers 6:24–26, an anthem (Rev. 7:15–17) and concluding prayers. The present revision incorporates much of the special material of that rite into the regular rite. The use of the passages from Lamentations, 1 John, and John 6 are especially recommended at the burial of a child.

The next to the last paragraph on this page points out that it is customary for the celebrant to meet the body and go before it into the church or towards the grave. This is the first edition to provide a form (pp. 466–467) for use at the reception of the body, which is especially fitting if the body is brought to the church at some time prior to the rite. The rubric on page 467 suggests that a member of the congregation lead the procession into the church, bearing the lighted paschal candle which symbolizes Easter and baptism (see pp. 285–287 and 313).

Since the body may be received at the church at some time prior to the burial rite, the final paragraph permits the opening anthems of the rite to be sung during the entrance of the ministers or after the celebrant is standing in the accustomed place.

The Burial of the Dead (pp. 469–489 and 491–505)

The Opening Anthem (pp. 469 and 491–492)

Rite One begins with the saying or singing of one or more of four anthems. The first two (Jn. 11:25–26 and Job 19:25–27) were used in the 1549 Book as the first two of three anthems to be said or sung in the procession from the churchyard gate ("style") to the church or towards the grave. The first had been used as an antiphon at Lauds and at the grave in the Sarum rite. The second was a response after the first lesson at Matins. Cranmer also provided a third anthem (1 Tim. 6:7 and Job 1:21), without precedent in the medieval rites, which has been replaced in the present Book by Romans 14:7–8 and Revelation 14:13. The anthem from Revelation had been used in both the Sarum rite and earlier Prayer Books after the committal at the grave. The 1550 *Book of Common Prayer Noted* by John Merbecke provided for the first half of the first and last of the three anthems of the 1549 Book to be sung as antiphons before and after the second half, which was treated as a verse. The second was to be sung straight through. These anthems may be said or sung by the minister, a cantor, a choir, or the whole congregation. In Rite Two these anthems may be used in place of the opening anthem at the committal (p. 501).

In Rite Two additional options are allowed. A hymn, psalm, or other suitable anthem may be sung instead of the opening anthems. An additional alternative anthem is printed which dates to the 1549 Prayer Book where it was to be used at the beginning of the service at the grave. It is based on an old form consisting of a series of verses each followed by a response reminiscent of the Trisagion (pp. 324 and 356). Notker, a monk of Saint Gall in Switzerland (d. 912), is said to have composed it while he was watching the construction of a bridge over a chasm and realized the peril that threatened its builders. In the Sarum rite it was a daily antiphon to the Nunc dimittis during the third and fourth weeks of Lent. The anthem was popular in Germany, and Luther's metrical translation of it was used in the burial rites in German church orders. The last line of Cranmer's version, "Suffer us not at our last hour for any pains of death to fall from thee," was inspired by Luther's metrical paraphrase or by Coverdale's English translation of it. The anthem is printed in Rite One for use at the grave; the use at the grave is permitted in Rite Two. The form printed in Rite Two (p. 492) restores the responsorial character of the original.

In Rite Two a rubric (p. 492) explicitly permits the celebrant to follow the opening anthem with an address "acknowledging briefly the purpose of their gathering, and bidding their prayers for the deceased and the bereaved."

The Collect (pp. 470 and 493–494)

At the Burial of an Adult (pp. 470 and 493)

The collect in Rite One, the second of three alternatives in Rite Two, was added to the Prayer Book in 1928 as the alternative collect for use at a burial Eucharist, and as the first of three prayers for alternative use after the committal of the body. Originally it was the collect in the requiem Mass for a priest in the Sarum missal and in the Gelasian sacramentary (no. 1634).

The first of the three alternative collects in Rite Two is new to this Book. It is also the collect for Tuesday in Easter Week. The third collect of Rite Two, drafted by Virginia Harbour, is also new to this book. Its inspiration is a prayer from "Your Word is Near".[1]

At the Burial of a Child (pp. 470 and 494)

This is a slightly revised version of a prayer first printed in the American Book in 1928. Its source was a prayer by John Dowden, bishop of Edinburgh (1886–1910), new to the Scottish Book of 1912:

> O Lord Jesus Christ, who didst take little children into thine arms and bless them; Open thou our eyes, we beseech thee, that we may perceive that thou hast now taken this child into the arms of thy love, and hast bestowed upon *him* the blessings of thy gracious favour; who livest and reignest with the Father and the Holy Spirit, one God, world without end. *Amen.*

An Additional Prayer (p. 494)

This prayer, drafted by Virginia Harbour, is new to this Book. The inspiration was a prayer from "Your Word is Near"[2] which had been in Services for Trial Use. It also uses a phrase from a prayer (on page 505) originally in the Prayer Book of the Church of Ireland.

The Liturgy of the Word (pp. 470–480 and 494–496)

This edition of the Prayer Book provides a full liturgy of the word with an Old Testament lesson, a canticle or psalm; a New Testament lesson, followed by a canticle, hymn, or psalm; a Gospel, homily, and the Apostles' Creed. No previous edition of the Prayer Book had included an Old Testament lesson in the burial office. The use of the

---

[1] Huub Oosterhuis, New York: Newman Press. Included in Services for Trial Use, 1970.
[2] Oosterhuis.

reading from Wisdom at a burial can be traced back to the Apostolic Constitutions (c. 380).

The 1549 rite included Psalms 116, 139, and 142, with Psalm 42 as the entrance psalm for the Eucharist. All had been used in the Sarum rites; and the use of Psalm 116 at burials can be found as early as the time of John Chrysostom (d. 407). The 1662 revision appointed Psalms 39 and 90, which came from the liturgies compiled by Robert Sanderson and Jeremy Taylor for use during the interregnum when the Prayer Book was banned. The American 1789 Book, following the Proposed Book of 1786, substituted a cento (Psalm 39:5–9, 12–15 and Psalm 90:1–10 and 12) in place of the whole of the two psalms. The 1928 revision added Psalms 27:1, 4–11, 15–16; 46:1–5, 10–11; 121; and 130. All of these have been retained in the 1979 Book, some in fuller forms. Psalms 42:1–7; 116; 139:1–11 (all used in the 1549 rite); Psalm 23 (used in the 1928 rite for the burial of a child) and Psalm 106:1–5 are also in the present Book. Chrysostom refers to the use of Psalm 23 at burials. For Rite One the psalms are printed within the rite in the translation used in previous Prayer Books; Psalm 23 is also printed in the King James Version, the first time this very familiar translation has been included in a Prayer Book.

The 1549 Book, following the precedent of the German church orders, appointed 1 Corinthians 15:20–58 to be read at the office, and 1 Thessalonians 4:13–18 and John 6:37–40 for the Eucharist. No propers for the Eucharist were included in the 1552 revision. The 1928 Book omitted verses 29–34 from the reading in 1 Corinthians, and provided two alternative lessons, Romans 8:14–19, 28, 31–32, and 34–39 and John 14:1–6; it also restored the 1549 Epistle and Gospel for the Eucharist. It added a separate rite for the burial of a child with Revelation 7:15–17 for use at the grave. The present Book does not keep the reading from 1 Thessalonians, and modifies the selections from 1 Corinthians 15, Romans 8, and Revelation 7. The readings from 2 Corinthians, 1 John, and Revelation 21 are new to the 1979 Book.

In the Sarum missal John 6:37–40 was the Gospel used at Tuesday Masses for the dead. The 1549 Prayer Book appointed this as the Gospel for the Eucharist at a burial, and the 1928 edition restored it as the Gospel when the Prayer Book once again included propers for the Eucharist which had been dropped from 1552 on. John 14:1–6 was provided as an alternative scripture reading in the 1928 burial office. The present edition retains both of these and three other readings from John as choices for the Gospel. If there is a celebration of the Eucharist, a Gospel, as is true in all other Prayer Book services with

487

communion, must conclude the readings (see pp. 470 and 494). The announcement of the Gospel (pp. 479 and 495) is the model for use at other services.

The rubric specifically permits the use of a homily in the burial rite.

As long as a daily office was used with burials, the Apostles' Creed was said. The revisions of 1892 and 1928 explicitly permitted its use. In a burial rite the Apostles' Creed is more suitable than the Nicene because of its Easter and baptismal connotations, and because non-Episcopalians in a funeral congregation are much more likely to be familiar with it.

A rubric gives directions for continuing the service if there is not to be a communion.

The Prayers of the People: Rite One (pp. 480–481)

This form was drafted by the Very Rev. Dr. Robert H. Greenfield from familiar prayers in the 1928 Book and other editions of the Book of Common Prayer.

The address of the first paragraph is that of the collect for All Saints' Day (pp. 194 and 245); the petition is from the first of the prayers in the votive "For the Departed" (pp. 202 and 253).

The second paragraph is based partly upon the collect of Easter Even of Prayer Books from 1662 through 1928:

> Grant, O Lord, that as we are baptized into the death of thy blessed Son, our Saviour Jesus Christ, so by continual mortifying our corrupt affections we may be buried with him; and that through the grave, and gate of death, we may pass to our joyful resurrection; for his merits, who died, and was buried, and rose again for us, the same thy Son Jesus Christ our Lord. *Amen.*

The 1662 collect was a revision of the Collect for Easter Even in the Scottish Book of 1637:

> O most gracious God, look upon us in mercy, and grant that as we are baptized into the death of thy Son our Saviour Jesus Christ, so by our true and hearty repentance all our sins may be buried with him, and we not fear the grave: that as Christ was raised up from the dead by the glory of thee, O Father, so we also may walk in newness of life, but our sins never be able to rise in judgment against us; and that for the merit of Jesus Christ that died, was buried, and rose again for us. Amen.

488

The words "may die to sin and rise to newness of life" come from a series of supplications taken by Cranmer from the blessing of the font in the Mozarabic Missale Mixtum, or from one of the older Gallican versions of that prayer, used in the setting apart of water for baptism in previous editions of the Prayer Book.

The petition of the third paragraph, based on 2 Corinthians 5:7, is from a prayer in the 1892 and 1928 Books, taken from *The Priest's Prayer Book*.[1] The result clause, which incorporates a phrase from the Benedictus Dominus Deus, is from a prayer by Jeremy Taylor first included in the Prayer Book in 1789 (for commentary see below, p. 497).

The next petition was the collect for the twenty-first Sunday after Trinity in the Sarum missal and earlier Prayer Books. It can be traced to the Gelasian sacramentary (no. 1238) where it is the collect for the last of sixteen Masses for the Sundays after Pentecost. In the Gregorian sacramentary it was appointed for Vespers on the Sunday after Easter (no. 438) and as a prayer for use at any time (no. 886); the Gregorian supplement included it for use as the collect for the twenty-first Sunday after [the octave of] Pentecost (no. 1189).

The next paragraph is based on a prayer in the 1928 Book for use at the burial of a child. It is the last of the additional prayers for burial in both Rite One and Rite Two (pp. 489 and 505). The phrase "a sure confidence in thy fatherly care" echoes phrasing in several prayers (see pp. 310, 419, 815, and 830).

The fourth paragraph on page 481, which may be omitted, has as its source a collect in the 1926 Irish Prayer Book printed among the additional prayers of Rite Two (p. 505). The phrase "in the comfort of a reasonable and holy hope" is from a prayer by Jeremy Taylor added to the Prayer Book in 1789. It is retained among the additional prayers of both Rite One and Rite Two (pp. 489 and 504).

The optional fifth paragraph is based on a prayer in the 1954 revision of the South African Book:

> O heavenly Father, who in thy Son Jesus Christ, hast given us a true faith, and a sure hope: Help us, we pray thee, to live as those who believe in the Communion of Saints, the forgiveness of sins, and the resurrection to life everlasting, and strengthen this faith and hope in us all the days of our life, through the love of thy Son, Jesus Christ our Saviour. *Amen.*

---

[1] Littledale and Vaux, p. 250. Originally a prayer from the Roman ritual.

The three petitions of the next paragraph are all from prayers included in the burial rite or from the occasional prayers (pp. 470, 488, 483, and 831).

The next paragraph is taken from a prayer included among the additional prayers (p. 488).

The first line of the concluding paragraph resembles the form for the committal of the body (p. 485). The phrase "to have our consummation and bliss in thy eternal and everlasting glory" is from one of the additional prayers (p. 488). The conclusion is based upon James 1:12 and the second of the collects for use at the votive "For the Departed" (pp. 202 and 253).

The Prayers of the People: Rite Two (pp. 497–498)

In Rite Two the form provided for use at a vigil (pp. 465–466) or the form of Rite One (pp. 480–481) may be substituted for that printed within the rite, which is from the new Roman Catholic burial rite. Scriptural allusions include John 11:1–44 and Luke 23:39–43.

The Concluding Collect: Rite Two (p. 498)

Rite Two provides two alternative concluding collects for the prayers of the people. The first, new to this edition, reminds us of the baptismal nature of the burial liturgy, which is signified by the use of the lighted paschal candle to lead the procession into the church (p. 467). The alternative collect begins as a prayer from the Scottish revision of 1929, included among the additional prayers at the bottom of page 504. The remainder consists of texts of two forms which are provided as concluding preces at the committal in this edition of the Book.

At the Eucharist (pp. 482 and 498)

The Eucharist continues after the prayers of the people with the peace and the offertory. A proper preface is provided (pp. 349 and 382). A postcommunion prayer, drafted by the Rev. Dr. Massey H. Shepherd, Jr., speaks of the Eucharist as a foretaste of the heavenly banquet. It replaces the usual postcommunion prayer. If the body is not present in the church, the rite ends with the [blessing and] dismissal. If the body is present the rite in the church ends with the commendation, unless the committal is to follow immediately in the church.

490

The Commendation (pp. 482–484 and 499–500)

The commendation was added in this revision to meet a need which has become acute since many of those in the church do not or cannot go to the graveside for the committal of the body. The celebrant and other persons stand in the appropriate places near the body.

An anthem or hymn may be sung. The Kontakion and Ikos from the Eastern Byzantine rite, attributed to Thesphanes (obit c. 842), are printed here. The Kontakion is repeated as an antiphon.

The commendation is a slightly abbreviated form of "A Commendatory Prayer when the Soul is Departed" in the litany for the dying, new to the Prayer Book in 1928. Its origin is the book *A Collection of Private Devotions* (1627) by John Cosin who later played an important part in the revision of 1662.

The commendation may be followed by a blessing or a dismissal or both.

A hymn, anthem, or canticle may be sung or said as the body is borne from the church. The first four of the five anthems printed in the rite were prepared as a unit by the Rev. Dr. Thomas J. Talley. The first is a text from the Byzantine rite which initiates the celebration of the Easter Eucharist, and which is sung as the body is carried to the grave at a burial during the Easter season. The two anthems that follow are based on the Benedictus Dominus Deus. This unit concludes with an anthem, composed by Dr. Talley, which is based on Matthew 25:34. The fifth anthem, probably of Gallican origin, is in manuscripts at least as early as the tenth century. In medieval rites it was used at the procession to the church or the procession to the grave. Benedictus Dominus Deus, the first of the three recommended canticles, was frequently used in medieval burial rites, while the Nunc dimittis is in many Lutheran orders. In the 1549 Book the Pascha nostrum was to be said before Morning Prayer on Easter. Since 1552 it has replaced the invitatory psalm at Morning Prayer on that day.

The Committal (pp. 484–487 and 501–503)

The Anthem (pp. 484–485 and 501)

The committal begins with an anthem. Printed here in Rite One, and permitted in Rite Two, is the anthem "In the midst of life," which may be used at the beginning of Rite Two (p. 501). (For commentary on this anthem, see above, p. 485.) The second anthem of Rite One, the anthem printed at this point within Rite Two, was first included in the 1928 Book. It is a cento of scriptural verses: John 6:37, Romans 8:11, and Psalm 16:9 and 11. In Rite Two the anthems which begin on page 491 may also be used at this time.

The Committal (pp. 485 and 501)

The 1549 Book preceded the committal with a rubric: "Then the priest casting earth upon the corpse shall say." In 1552 the rubric indicates that the filling of the grave was to be done at this point, and that it was something in which members of the community were to participate: "Then while the earth shall be cast upon the body by some standing by, the priest shall say." Except for the change from "priest" to "minister" this rubric remained in American Books until this edition. The sense of the rubric has not been changed, though the wording is somewhat clarified: "Then, while earth is cast upon the coffin, the Celebrant says these words."

The 1549 committal of the body, a revision of the Sarum committal, reads:

> I commend thy soul to God the Father almighty, and thy body to the ground, earth to earth, ashes to ashes, dust to dust, in sure and certain hope of resurrection to eternal life, through our Lord Jesus Christ, who shall change our vile body, that it may be like to his glorious body, according to the mighty working whereby he is able to subdue all things to himself.

In 1552 the form was changed to read:

> Forasmuch as it hath pleased almighty God of his great mercy to take unto himself the soul of our dear brother here departed, we therefore commit his body to the ground, earth to earth, ashes to ashes, dust to dust, in sure and certain hope of resurrection to eternal life, through our Lord Jesus Christ, who shall change our vile body, that it may be like to his glorious body, according to the mighty working whereby he is able to subdue all things to himself.

The first portion was taken from the beginning of the second funeral sermon in Hermann's Consultation. In the first American revision this was again revised (partly on the basis of the committal for use at sea which had been included in the 1662 Book):

Forasmuch as it hath pleased Almighty God, in his wise providence, to take out of this world the soul of our deceased *brother*, we therefore commit *his* body to the ground; earth to earth, ashes to ashes, dust to dust: looking for the general resurrection in the last day, and the life of the world to come, through our Lord Jesus Christ; at whose second coming, in glorious majesty, to judge the world, the earth and the sea shall give up their dead, and the corruptible bodies of those, who sleep in him, shall be changed, and made like unto his own glorious body; according to the mighty working, whereby he is able to subdue all things unto himself.

In the 1928 revision the first half was revised:

Unto Almighty God we commend the soul of our *brother* departed, and we commit *his* body to the ground; earth to earth, ashes to ashes, dust to dust; in sure and certain hope of the Resurrection unto eternal life, through our Lord Jesus Christ; at whose coming in glorious majesty to judge the world, . . .

The committal has been revised again in this edition. The first half essentially goes back to the 1552 Book. The second half is the Aaronic blessing (Numbers 6:24–26) which was used as the conclusion of the committal in the 1928 form for the burial of a child. This is the first edition in which the congregation participates by saying Amen at the end of the committal.

The alternatives for the committal "to the ground" allow for a burial at sea, a provision made in the revision of 1662 in the forms of prayer to be used at sea which were added in that Book. In this revision provisions are made, for the first time, for cremation ("*or* the elements") or for burial in a crypt or mausoleum ("*or* its resting place").

The Lord's Prayer (pp. 485–486 and 501–502)

From the time of the 1552 revision the service at the grave has included the Lord's Prayer. Since 1662 it has followed the committal. Prior editions have appointed the shorter Lukan form, and, except in the edition of 1789, this has been preceded by a threefold Kyrie. Because of the greater familiarity of the Matthean form, it has been substituted in this revision.

493

The Prayers (pp. 486 and 502)

Another prayer or prayers, from among the additional prayers printed after the rite (pages 487–489 or 503–505), may follow the Lord's Prayer. The prayer printed in Rite One is a slightly abbreviated version of a prayer of unknown authorship from the Scottish revision of 1912 which entered the American Book in 1928. It alludes to Revelation 14:13, which is one of the burial anthems (pages 469 and 492), Philippians 1:6, and Colossians 1:12. As in several other of the prayers for the departed which entered the Prayer Book in 1928, the life of the world to come is viewed as a life of continued growth and service.

The Concluding Preces (pp. 486 and 502)

Some revisions of the Prayer Book in this century for other provinces have restored one or both of these forms, but this is the first American edition which includes them.

The first form, which is based on 2 Esdras 2:34–35, can be traced back to the supplement to the Gregorian sacramentary (no. 1406) where it is used with the psalms of the burial rite. By the sixteenth century, in the rites of the Sarum manuale, this text recurs with great frequency from the time of the prayers with the dying until after the committal of the body. It is used as the antiphon of the gradual and as either the antiphon or the verse for each of the processional songs of the Mass (the introit, the offertory, and the communion). The term "Requiem" as the designation for a Eucharist for the departed is derived from the first word of the Latin text of this antiphon.

The brief prayer which follows was used in the Sarum rite at the commendation of the soul and as the dismissal after the committal of the body.

The Dismissal or Blessing (pp. 486–487 and 502–503)

In the 1662 revision of the Prayer Book, at the suggestion of Bishop Matthew Wren, the Grace (2 Corinthians 13:14) was added to the committal as a conclusion after the prayers, just as it had been added to the Litany and to the daily offices in the revision of 1559. The 1928 revision substituted Hebrews 13:20–21. This present edition provides an alternative form in Rite Two (printed first) which consists of the opening acclamation used in the Eucharist and the daily offices throughout the Easter season and the first of the forms for the dismissal after the Eucharist.

The Consecration of a Grave (pp. 487 and 503)

Several of the twentieth-century revisions of the Prayer Book for other provinces have a prayer for use at the consecration of a grave. This is the first American edition to include such a provision. It is intended for use "If the grave is in a place that has not previously been set apart for Christian burial." The prayer may be used at some time apart from the burial, before the committal in the rite, or among the prayers after the committal. This form dates back to the second edition of The Book of Offices: Services for Certain Occasions not provided for in the Book of Common Prayer.[1]

Additional Prayers: Rite One (pp. 487–489)

The first of the additional prayers (p. 487), which entered the Book in the 1892 revision, is the final paragraph in the Scottish revision of the conclusion to the prayer for the whole state of Christ's church in the 1549 Book (for the text of the 1549 version see above, p. 340). Sources include the medieval Roman eucharistic prayer, the Liturgy of Saint Basil, the collect of the Sarum Mass of the Five Wounds, and Matthew 25:34.

The second prayer (p. 488) was first included in the 1549 Book; it incorporates some lines from various prayers in the medieval burial offices. It underwent revision in 1552 and 1662 and was further revised on its first appearance in the American Book of 1789. The version printed here is that of 1789. The 1549 version reads:

> O Lord, with whom do live the spirits of them that be dead, and in whom the souls of them that be elected, after they be delivered from the burden of the flesh, be in joy and felicity: Grant unto this thy servant, that the sins which he committed in this world be not imputed unto him, but that he, escaping the gates of hell and pains of eternal darkness, may ever dwell in the region of light, with Abraham, Isaac, and Jacob, in the place where is no weeping, sorrow, nor heaviness; and when that dreadful day of the general resurrection shall come, make him to rise also with the just and righteous, and receive this body again to glory, then made pure and incorruptible; set him on the right hand of thy Son Jesus Christ, among the holy and elect, that then he may hear with them these most sweet and comfortable words: Come to me ye blessed of my Father, possess the kingdom which hath been

---

[1] Compiled by the Liturgical Commission, New York: Church Pension Fund, 1949.

495

prepared for you from the beginning of the world. Grant this, we beseech thee, O merciful Father, through Jesus Christ our mediator and redeemer. Amen.

The 1552 revision, which possibly owes some words to Bucer's criticism of the prayers for the departed of the Prayer Book of 1549, reads:

Almighty God, with whom do live the spirits of them that depart hence in the Lord, and in whom the souls of them that be elected, after they be delivered from the burden of the flesh, be in joy and felicity; We give thee hearty thanks for that it hath pleased thee to deliver this N. our brother out of the miseries of this sinful world, beseeching thee, that it may please thee of thy gracious goodness shortly to accomplish the number of thine elect, and to haste thy kingdom, that we with this our brother, and all other departed in the true faith of thy holy Name, may have our perfect consummation and bliss, both in body and soul, in thy eternal and everlasting glory. Amen.

The changes of 1662 were small but significant: "the souls of the faithful" was substituted for "the souls of them that be elected," and "that we with all those that are departed in the true faith" for "that we with our brother, and all other departed in the true faith." This prayer was omitted from the Proposed Book of 1786, but the Pennsylvania state convention of 1786 resolved that it be reinstated in a revised form. The prayer appears here in the version of the 1789 Book. It should be noted that the substitution which came out of the Pennsylvania convention was taken from the commemoration of the faithful of the Scottish eucharistic liturgies. The revisions of this prayer vividly indicate different emphases in regard to prayer for and commemoration of the dead in various editions of the Prayer Book.

The third prayer (p. 488) is a revised version of "A Commendatory Prayer for a Sick Person at the point of Departure" of the 1928 Prayer Book. The phrase "in the midst of this earthly life" has been substituted for "through the lusts of the flesh or the wiles of Satan." The address of that prayer has been omitted, "O Almighty God, with whom do live the spirits of just men made perfect, after they are delivered from their earthly prisons." "We humbly commend the soul of this thy servant" now reads "we commend thy servant N." Biblical allusions include 1 Peter 4:19, Revelation 7:14, John 1:29, and Ephesians 5:27. The prayer goes back to the 1662 revision. The author is unknown, though it is thought by some to have been Robert

Sanderson. Until the prayer was abbreviated in the 1892 revision it ended with this petition:

And teach us who survive, in this, and other like daily spectacles of mortality, to see how frail and uncertain our own condition is; and so to number our days, that we may seriously apply our hearts to that holy and heavenly wisdom, whilst we live here, which may in the end bring us to life everlasting.

The author of the fourth of the additional prayers (p. 488) is unknown. It came into the Prayer Book in the 1928 revision, when prayers for the departed were restored. The life beyond death is viewed as one of growth and of increase in the knowledge and love of God, as is true of other prayers which entered the Prayer Book in that revision: the petition in the prayer for the church, the prayer following this prayer, and the prayer for the departed in the additional prayers of family prayer, which in this present edition is the second of the collects for the votive for the departed (pp. 202 and 253).

The fifth prayer, also of unknown authorship, was included in the 1928 revision as an occasional prayer for use on Memorial Days. It is based on a similar prayer in *Hymns and Prayers for Use of the Army and Navy* (1917), used in World War One. The petition for mercy and light is characteristic of traditional prayers for the departed. The result clause, which speaks of growth in the life of the world to come, is based on Philippians 1:6 (see the commentary on the preceding prayer).

The American revision of 1789 was the first Book to use the sixth prayer as part of the order for the visitation of the sick as "A prayer, which may be said by the minister, in behalf of all present at the visitation." The 1928 Book deleted the words "through this vale of misery" from the phrase "let thy Holy Spirit lead us through this vale of misery." The revisers in 1789 obviously had a copy of the devotional manual *The Rule and Exercises of Holy Dying* by Bishop Jeremy Taylor (1613–1667), for not only this prayer but another prayer which followed it owed much to the prayers in that book.

The seventh prayer (mid-page 489), new to this revision, was included in the Scottish Book of 1929 as one of a series of "Collects which may be said after the Collect of the Day, or before the Blessing." *Doctrine in the Church of England*[1] says of this prayer:

---

[1] A report of the Commission on Christian doctrine appointed by the Archbishop of Canterbury, first published in 1938.

It is impossible to declare that departed saints cannot hear our prayers, and we therefore must not condemn as impossible direct address to them as a private practice, provided this be to ask for their prayers whether for ourselves or for others; anything other than this seems to us both perilous and illegitimate. But also it is impossible to have well-grounded assurance that the saints hear us, so that direct address to them may well be thought inappropriate in the official worship of the Church. On the other hand, such formal expression within the liturgy of our fellowship with them in prayer as is contained, for example, in the Collect—"O God, the King of Saints"—appended to the Scottish Liturgy represents a true balance of thought and is a legitimate enrichment of worship.

The phrase "known to us and unknown" was added in this revision, and "we also may be partakers of the inheritance of the saints in light" is substituted for "we may attain unto everlasting life."

The next to the last prayer (p. 489), in a contemporary language version, is the final prayer of the Good Friday rite (p. 282). Its source is the memorial of the cross frequently found in medieval primers, small books of devotions designed for lay persons to use at different hours of the daily office.[1]

The last prayer (p. 489) has been attributed to Bishop Charles Lewis Slattery of Massachusetts. The 1928 Prayer Book included it as the final prayer at the grave in the brief rite for the burial of a child unique to that revision. It contains an allusion to Matthew 5:4, the second of the Beatitudes.

Additional Prayers: Rite Two (pp. 503–505)

This first prayer is the same as the second of the additional prayers of Rite One.

The second prayer is the same as the sixth prayer of the additional prayers of Rite One.

The third prayer is the same as the seventh prayer among the additional prayers of Rite One.

The fourth prayer is the same as the collect for Fridays at Daily Evening Prayer.

The fifth prayer is from the Scottish revision of 1929. Compare this prayer with the alternative collect for use after the prayers of the people of Rite Two, page 498.

---

[1] This translation is a revised version of that printed in A Procession of Passion Prayers, compiled by Eric Milner-White, London: SPCK, 1956, p. xiii.

The sixth prayer (at the top of page 505) is a revised form of the collect provided in the 1549 Prayer Book for use at a requiem Eucharist before or after the service at the grave. The prayer, like many prayers of the period, is a cento of scriptural quotations: 1 Thessalonians 4:13–18 and John 6:37–40 (the Epistle and Gospel appointed in that Book), and from John 11:25–26 and Matthew 25:34. The 1549 form read:

> O merciful God, the Father of our Lord Jesus Christ, who is the resurrection and the life, in whom whosoever believeth shall live though he die, and whosoever liveth, and believeth in him, shall not die eternally, who also hath taught us, by his holy Apostle Paul, not to be sorry as men without hope for them that sleep in him: We meekly beseech thee, O Father, to raise us from the death of sin, unto the life of righteousness, that when we shall depart this life we may sleep in him, as our hope is this our brother doth, and at the general resurrection in the last day, both we and this our brother departed, receiving again our bodies, and rising again in thy most gracious favor, may with all thine elect saints obtain eternal joy. Grant this, O Lord God, by the means of our advocate Jesus Christ, which with thee and the Holy Ghost, liveth and reigneth one God for ever. Amen.

In the 1552 revision an altered form of this prayer was the final prayer to be said at the grave. The word "rest" was substituted for "sleep" in the phrase "that we may sleep in him." The conclusion was changed to read:

> and that at the general resurrection in the last day, we may be found acceptable in thy sight, and receive that blessing which thy well-beloved Son shall then pronounce to all that love and fear thee, saying, Come, ye blessed children of my father, receive the kingdom prepared for you from the beginning of the world. Grant this, we beseech thee, O merciful Father, through Jesus Christ our Mediator and Redeemer. Amen.

This new ending had been the conclusion of a prayer said at the grave in the 1549 Book. In the first American revision the two prayers at the grave were preceded by a rubric which required the use of either or both, and the phrase "as our hope is this our brother doth" was omitted in an attempt to eliminate the last vestiges of prayer for the dead from the Book. In the 1928 revision this prayer was placed among the additional prayers after the rite.

The seventh prayer (p. 505), new to this edition, is from the Irish

Prayer Book of 1926. The phrase "in the joyful expectation of eternal life with those they love" replaces "in the sure expectation of a joyful reunion in the heavenly places." Scriptural allusions include Colossians 1:11 and 1 Thessalonians 4:13.

The last prayer is the same as the last of the additional prayers of Rite One.

An Order for Burial (p. 506)

This order, new to the 1979 Prayer Book, allows the use of the rite of another edition of the Book of Common Prayer or a rite from another source "When, for pastoral considerations, neither of the burial rites in this Book is deemed appropriate." It also permits the composition of a rite to suit particular circumstances, including situations in which the deceased was not a baptized Christian or had rejected the Christian faith. (See *The Book of Occasional Services*, pp. 156–159, for appropriate texts.) The 1928 edition had included a statement that the Prayer Book rite was appropriate "only for the faithful departed in Christ, provided that in any other case the Minister may, at his discretion, use such part of this Office, or such devotions taken from other parts of this Book, as may be fitting."

This order, which provides a structure for such circumstances, is analogous to the orders for the Eucharist and for marriage (pp. 400–401 and 435–436). It includes those elements which are considered essential: one or more passages of scripture; prayer, including the Lord's Prayer; a commendation of the deceased to God; a committal of the body to its resting place; and other optional elements which would be considered a normal part of a burial rite (reception of the body; opening anthems, psalms, or hymns; an initial prayer for the bereaved; a homily; the Apostles' Creed; and communion). These elements are listed in order, except for the last.

Note (p. 507)

This note explains the theology which underlies the burial rites of this edition of the Prayer Book.

Episcopal Services

This section of the Prayer Book contains rites which require the presence of a bishop as the chief celebrant, although that function may be delegated in the Celebration of a New Ministry. Late in the middle ages the rites of ordination, consecration of a church, and certain blessings and other rites normally reserved to the bishop, were collected in a book named the "pontifical." Although the 1549 Book included rites from the other principal liturgical books—the breviary, the missal, the processional, and the manuale—it did not contain those from the pontifical.

In 1550 revised ordination rites were published: "The Form and Manner of Making and Consecrating of Archbishops, Bishops, Priests, and Deacons." Some extant copies indicate that this was to be bound with the Prayer Book, and a revision was included in the 1552 Book, although it had its own title page. In the seventeenth century this collection came to be called the "ordinal," the term which preceded the collection of ordination rites in the 1928 Book. ("Ordinal" in the middle ages designated a book of directions for the conduct of services.) The 1662 revision listed the contents of the ordinal on the title page: "The Book of Common Prayer and Administration of the Sacraments and Other Rites and Ceremonies of the Church According to the Use of the Church of England Together with the Psalter or Psalms of David, Pointed as They Are To Be Sung Or Said in Churches; and the Form or Manner of Making, Ordaining, and Consecrating of Bishops, Priests, and Deacons." Forms for the consecration of a church and for the institution of a minister were added to the American ordinal in 1799 and 1804 respectively. Revised forms of these rites, and of the three ordination rites, are included in this section of the 1979 Book of Common Prayer.

501

People sometimes ask why these rites, so seldom used, are included in pew copies of the Book. The reason is that in the Episcopal Church the Prayer Book is the standard of doctrine and discipline as well as worship. These rites are the principal source for establishing what the Church teaches about the functions, responsibilities, and ethos of the ordained ministries, and about the church building and its use.

The Ordination of a Bishop, of a Priest, of a Deacon

I t is difficult to separate the offices and functions of ministers in the New Testament. In some locales bishops (overseers or pastors and teachers) and deacons (servants) must have had at least a semi-professional status. The term "presbyter" (elder) recalls the concept of elders or leading men of the community who, within Judaic institutions, constituted a collegiate ruling body. In the New Testament certain customs—popular election, recognition by authority, prayer and fasting, and laying on of hands—were linked to the setting apart of persons for various ministries. The bishop emerged early as the chief pastor and liturgical officer, and president of the body of elders (presbyters) whose responsibility was to sustain and govern the congregation and to represent the bishop in his absence. Deacons assisted the bishop as ecclesiastical servants: they administered the charities of the church, helped with administrative and pastoral duties, and distributed the Sacrament within the service and afterwards to those unable to be present. In its role of servanthood, the order of deacons symbolized Christ who came not to be served but to serve.

Christians proclaimed Jesus as the great high priest and His body the church as His royal priesthood. The bishop, as pastor and liturgical leader, came to be spoken of as "high priest" within the body of the church. The responsibilities placed upon bishops greatly increased after Constantine legalized Christianity, and many of their duties had to be delegated to presbyters of local congregations. In early Christian writings and in both Greek and Latin Bibles one word—"sacerdos" in Latin, "hiereus" in Greek—signifies Christ, our great high priest, the bishop, and the priesthood of all baptized people. "Presbyter" designates an order of ordained ministers associated with the bishop in governing the life of the congregation. Once the presbyter began to assume certain liturgical functions previously belonging to the bishop, the presbyter came to be considered a priest. In English and other modern European languages the word "priest," which carries sacerdotal connotations, has encompassed the meaning of the more ancient term "presbyter," and largely displaced it.

The earliest extant text of ordination rites is that in the Apostolic Tradition of Hippolytus (c. 215) which is thought to be representative of early rites in Rome. A bishop, elected by a local congregation, was ordained on a Sunday by a group of bishops who laid hands on his head. One of the bishops said a prayer depicting the ministry of a bishop and the new bishop was greeted with the kiss of peace and then presided at the Eucharist. Presbyters and deacons were also elected by the people. The bishop alone laid hands on the new deacon since the deacon was directly responsible to him in diaconal works. Other members of the presbytery joined the bishop in laying hands on a new presbyter, for he was being admitted to a corporate body presided over by the bishop. In each case, the prayer of the bishop described the ministry of the order, and the newly ordained person joined others of that order in performing appropriate services at the Eucharist which followed. The deacon prepared the table and administered communion; the presbyter stood with the bishop and other presbyters during the eucharistic prayer, and joined with them in breaking the bread.

Western rites gradually became lengthier and more complicated. There were additional prayers; when the Roman and Gallican rites were combined, ordinations retained the texts and ceremonies of both, so that a person was, in effect, ordained twice—in a Gallican manner and in a Roman. In the late middle ages several more elements were added: prayers and blessings and imperative formulae (including an additional laying on of hands with the formula "Receive the Holy Spirit, whose sins you remit they are remitted, and whose sins you retain they are retained," at the ordination of presbyters), the hymn Veni Creator Spiritus, a delivery of instruments of office (a Gospel book for deacons, chalice and paten for presbyters, and a staff, ring, and mitre for bishops), and anointings. The precedent for many of these additional ceremonies, especially the anointings, can be found in the early baptismal rites; ordination was in effect replacing baptism as initiation into the church. There was great

504

debate over precisely what constituted the essential form and matter of the sacrament of ordination. Some persisted in the view that it was prayer and the laying on of hands; many other theologians taught that it was the delivery of instruments of office, and still others felt that the anointing was the principal element. Since the title "priest," formerly belonging to bishops, had become commonly associated with presbyters, the sense of the episcopate as a distinct order was largely lost; when three orders were spoken of the reference was often to priests, deacons, and subdeacons.

From an early period, certain persons, not actually ordained, had certain functions in the liturgical life of the congregation. Hippolytus lists widows, readers, virgins, and subdeacons. "Minor orders" developed in the medieval Western church as a series of steps ascending to the "major orders" of subdeacon, deacon, and priest. From the ninth century on a person was required to be ordained deacon before he might be ordained priest, an act which diminished the importance of the diaconate.

Martin Luther and other continental reformers, strongly influenced by their study of the Scriptures and of the early church fathers, concluded that the essentials of the ordination rite were prayer and the laying on of hands. Martin Bucer of Strassburg in his treatise *De ordinatione legitima* had the greatest influence on the formation of ordination rites in the Church of England; his controversies with the Anabaptists had developed a strong feeling for church order. Bucer considered ordination to be the laying on of hands before a solemn gathering of the church in the context of the word and prayer. A sermon preceding the rite declared what was offered to the people through the ordained ministry, how they were to esteem the ministry, and what the duties of a minister were. After the common prayers which followed the sermon, the congregation sang Veni Sancte Spiritus; Psalms 40, 132, and 135 followed, and a reading from one of four alternative Epistles (Acts 20:17–35; 1 Tim. 3; Eph. 4:1–16; or Tit. 1:5–9) the first two of which dated to Luther's rite. Then Psalm 67 and one of four alternative Gospels was read (Mt. 28:18–20; Jn. 10:1–16; Jn. 20:19–23; or Jn. 21:15–17). The candidates were presented and opportunity given the congregation to object to the ordination if anyone had good reason to do so. An address to the candidates concluded in an examination of nine questions, and a prayer that they might keep the promises made. The congregation was asked to pray silently for the ordinands. After a period of silence, the principal minister said a lengthy prayer depicting the work of the ministry as that of a pastor, teacher, and preacher, and invoking the descent

505

The Ordination of Deacons and Priests

SARUM (typical late medieval rite)	1550 ORDINAL *Deacons*	1550 ORDINAL *Priests*	BUCER'S DE ORDINATIONE LEGITIMA
			Veni Sancte Spiritus
Introit of the Day		Introit: Psalm 40, 132, or 135	Introit: Psalms 40, 132, and 135
		Kyrie	
		Gloria in excelsis	
Collect of the Day		Collect of the Day	
Presentation of ordinands and ordination to minor orders			
Epistle of the Day		Epistle: Acts 20: 17-35 *or* I Tim. 3	Epistle: Acts 20:17-35
			or I Tim. 3
			or Eph. 4:1-16
			or Titus 1:5-9
			Psalm 67
Tract of the Day			
Litany			
Laying of hands on deacons with "Receive the Holy Spirit"		Gospel: Matt. 28:18-20 *or* John 10-16	Gospel: Matt. 28:18-20
Silent Prayer		Veni Creator Spiritus	*or* John 10:1-16
Prayer			*or* John 20:19-23
Giving of stole, Gospels, and dalmatic		Final inquiry of the people	*or* John 21:15-17
Gospel of the Day		Litany and collect	Final inquiry of the people
	Final inquiry of the people		
	Litany and collect		
	Eucharist through Collect of the Day	"Oath of the King's Supremacy"	
	Epistle: I Tim. 3 *or* Acts 6:2-7	Allocution	Allocution
	"Oath of the King's Supremacy"	Examination with concluding prayer	Examination with concluding prayer
	Examination		

Laying of hands on priests in
silence
Silent Prayer
Prayers

Laying on of hands with "Accept
thou authority"
Giving of New Testament
Gospel of the Day

Disposition of stole
Giving of chasuble
Veni Creator Spiritus
Blessing and anointing of hands
Giving of paten and chalice

Offertory through Communion
Laying of hands on priest with
"Receive the Holy Spirit"
Vesting in chasuble
Postcommunion prayer

Dismissal

Creed
Offertory through Communion

Postcommunion prayer
Prayer
Blessing

Silent Prayer
Prayer
Laying on of hands with
"Receive the Holy Ghost"
Giving of Bible

and of chalice
and bread
Creed
Offertory through Communion

Postcommunion prayer
Prayer
Blessing

Silent Prayer
Prayer
Laying on of hands with prayer

Creed
Offertory through Communion

Prayer
Blessing
Dismissal

of the Holy Spirit upon the one being ordained. The principal minister and the presbyters joined in the laying on of hands accompanied by a blessing. The Eucharist then continued, beginning with the Nicene Creed. Bucer provided only one ordination rite (for presbyters) in his treatise, but appended a paragraph in which he stated that when anyone was ordained bishop "everything is done and carried out more solemnly and at greater length," and that some distinction should be made between the ordination of "presbyters of the second order" and those of the "third order" "whom we call deacons, or helpers."

The 1549 Prayer Book did not contain ordination rites, but "The Form and Manner of Making and Consecrating of Archbishops, Bishops, Priests, and Deacons" was published in 1550. The model and principal source of the rite for the ordination of priests was Bucer's form, modified by some rearrangement and by the inclusion of other materials, principally from the Sarum pontifical. One or another of the three psalms prior to the Epistle in Bucer's rite (Ps. 40, 132, or 135) was to be used as the introit. Either Acts 20:17–35 or 1 Timothy 3 was read as the Epistle, and either Matthew 28:18–20, John 10:1–16, or John 20:19–23 as the Gospel. As in Bucer's rite, the ordination came after the Gospel (in the medieval pontifical, ordination to major orders had followed the Epistle). The hymn Veni Creator Spiritus was sung after the Gospel. The candidates were then presented, and the congregation had opportunity to raise objections to the ordination if there was sufficient reason. The Great Litany was then said, with a special petition and a concluding collect. Then followed the administration of "The Oath of the King's Supremacy." A slightly condensed version of the address of Bucer's rite concluded in an examination making use of eight of Bucer's nine questions, followed by his prayer for grace to keep the promises. The congregation prayed in silence for the ordinands. After a period of silence the bishop read a slightly shortened version of the prayer which came at this point in Bucer's rite, omitting the petition for the descent of the Holy Spirit upon the candidates. The priests joined the bishop in the laying on of hands, which in Bucer's rite was accompanied by prayer. In Cranmer's rite the prayer was replaced by an imperative form, based partly upon that which (in the thirteenth century) came into the rite for the ordination of priests in connection with the new additional imposition of hands. Then followed the delivery of the Bible and a chalice and bread, accompanied by an authorization to preach, and to administer the sacraments. The Eucharist then continued with

The Ordination of Bishops

SARUM (typical late medieval rite)	1550 ORDINAL	BUCER'S DE ORDINATIONE LEGITIMA
		Veni Sancte Spiritus
Introit of the Day	Introit: Psalm 140, 132, or 135	Introit: Psalms 140, 132, and 135
Kyrie	Kyrie	
Gloria in excelsis	Gloria in excelsis	
Collect of the Day	Collect of the Day	
Epistle of the Day	Epistle: I Tim. 3:1-7	Epistle: Acts 20:17-35 or I Tim. 3 or Eph. 4:1-16 or Titus 1:5-9
Gradual of the Day		Psalm 67
Alleluia of the Day		
Vesting		
Litany		
Imposition of the Gospels and of hands with Veni Creator Spiritus and prayer		
Prayer		
Anointings of head and hands		
Blessing and giving of staff, ring, mitre, and Gospels		
Gospel of the Day	Gospel: John 21:15-17 or John 10:1-16	Gospel: Matt 28:18-20 or John 10:1-16 or John 20:19-23 or John 21:15-17
Creed	Creed	Final inquiry of the people
	Reading of king's mandate "Oath of the King's Supremacy"	
	Oath of obedience to the archbishop	
	Litany and collect	
		Allocution
	Examination with concluding prayer	Examination with concluding prayer
	Veni Creator Spiritus	
	Prayer	Prayer
	Laying on of hands with "Take the Holy Ghost"	Laying on of hands with prayer
	Imposition of Bible	
	Giving of staff	
		Creed
Offertory through postcommunion prayer	Offertory through postcommunion prayer	Offertory through Communion
	Prayer	Prayer
	Blessing	Blessing
Dismissal		Dismissal

509

the Nicene Creed. A super populum, which stressed the ministry of the word, preceded the blessing.

In keeping with Bucer's suggestion, the rite for the consecration of an archbishop or bishop was made somewhat lengthier and more solemn. One of the three psalms was the introit, 1 Timothy 3:1-7 served as the Epistle and John 21:15-17 or John 10:1-16 as the Gospel. The Nicene Creed, the presentation of the candidate, the reading of the king's mandate for the consecration, the administration of "The Oath of the King's Supremacy" and "The Oath of Due Obedience to the Archbishop" followed the Gospel. An exhortation which spoke of the twelve apostles, Paul, and Barnabas (evidence that the church viewed the episcopate as based upon the apostolate chosen by our Lord) bade the people to prayer. The Litany was said, with a special supplication and concluding collect (a slightly revised form of that used in the rite for the ordination of priests). An examination followed, based partly upon Bucer's form and partly upon that of the late medieval pontificals, ending with a variant of Bucer's concluding prayer. The lengthy prayer which followed incorporated a substantial amount of Bucer's form which was said at this point in the ordination of priests, but concluded with petitions from the rite of the pontificals. The bishops' laying on of hands was accompanied by a form composed of an initial phrase from a new additional laying on of hands in late medieval pontificals and the quotation of 2 Timothy 1:6-7. A Bible was then placed upon the neck of the bishop as a reminder to "Give heed unto reading, exhortation, and doctrine," and a staff was given signifying the bishop's function as chief shepherd. The Eucharist continued with the exhortation or the offertory. A special super populum, based largely upon 2 Timothy 4, preceded the blessing.

Also in keeping with Bucer's suggestion, the rite for the ordination of deacons was made less imposing than that for the ordination of priests. The candidates were presented prior to the beginning of the Eucharist. The congregation could object if there was reasonable cause. The Litany followed with the special suffrage which was inserted at the ordination of priests, and a variant of the special concluding collect. This was followed by the eucharistic rite of the day up to the Epistle. Two alternative readings, 1 Timothy 3:8-16 and Acts 6:2-7, were provided. "The Oath of the King's Supremacy" was then administered to the candidates, followed immediately by an examination consisting of seven questions. Four of the questions were from Bucer's rite, and one was based upon a medieval admonition to deacons. Then the bishop alone laid hands on the candidates saying words which authorized the person "to execute the office of a deacon in the church of God." A New Testament was delivered to each man, not a book of the Gospels (as had been customary in the late medieval rites), with an authorization to read the Gospel, "and to preach the same, if thou be thereunto ordinarily [that is, by the ordinary or authority of the diocese] commanded." The Eucharist continued with the reading by a new deacon of the Gospel for the day. A super populum, incorporating some phrases from one of the prayers of the medieval pontifical, preceded the blessing.

These three rites were printed with a preface which asserted that the three orders of bishops, priests, and deacons existed from apostolic times, that admission to these orders was by "public prayer, with imposition of hands;" that these orders were to be continued in the Church of England; and that no one not presently a bishop, priest, or deacon should function as bishop, priest, or deacon in the Church of England without ordination according to these forms.

The 1552 revision eliminated the appointed introits, the directions concerning the vesture of the candidates, and the delivery of the chalice and bread and of the staff.

The revision of 1662 provided a proper collect, based upon that for Saint Peter's Day, for the rite for the ordination of a bishop. Acts 20:17–35 was an alternative Epistle, and John 20:19–23 and Matthew 28:18–20 replaced John 10:1–16 as alternative Gospels. A phrase specifying the order being conferred was inserted in the form which accompanied the laying on of hands. In the rite for the ordination of priests the presentation and the Litany preceded the Eucharist as in the earlier rites for the ordination of deacons. The collect which had concluded the Litany was appointed as the collect of the Eucharist. Because the passages appointed for use as the Epistle had been interpreted by people of presbyterian persuasion as equating the order of bishop with that of presbyter, these alternatives were moved to the rite for the ordination of a bishop and here replaced by Ephesians 4:7–13. For the same reason, the revision moved two of the alternative Gospels to the rite for the ordination of a bishop, and appointed Matthew 9:36–38 as the Gospel, retaining John 10:1–16 as an alternative. John Cosin's metrical translation of Veni Creator Spiritus was provided as an alternative to Cranmer's version, and moved to the same position as in the rite for the ordination of a bishop. A phrase designating the order being conferred was inserted into the form which accompanied the laying on of hands. In the rite for the ordination of deacons, as in that for priests, the prayer which had concluded the Litany in prior editions of the ordinal was appointed as the collect of the Eucharist. The Epistle was abbreviated to 1 Timothy 3:18–23, and a proper Gospel (Luke 12:35–38) appointed at this revision.

In the first American revision of the ordinal (1792), in the bidding to prayer at the ordination of bishops, the example of the election of Matthias was substituted for the sending forth of Paul and Barnabas. The reading of testimonials of election was substituted for the reading of the king's mandate; and a promise of conformity to the doctrine, discipline, and worship of the Protestant Episcopal Church replaced the oath of obedience to the archbishop. The public oath to the King's Majesty was, of course, eliminated from all three rites. The most significant change in the ordination rites, however, was the provision of an alternative form for use at the laying on of hands in the ordination rite for priests similar to that used in the rite for the ordination of deacons.

The 1928 revision deleted the rubrical requirement that Morning Prayer immediately precede the rite, but provided proper lessons for the daily office prior to each of the three rites. An altered form of Edward Caswell's translation of the Veni Creator Spiritus replaced Cranmer's. A brief Litany for Ordinations was provided for use as an alternative to the Great Litany.

The ordination rites of this present revision restore the association of prayer with the laying on of hands. The prayer of consecration at the ordination of a bishop is based (as in the new Roman Catholic rite) upon the prayer of Hippolytus. The order in which the rites appear in the book has been reversed so that the ordination of the bishop comes first, as in some ancient sacramentaries, emphasizing the centrality of this ministry. Fuller liturgies of the word are provided for each rite.

The rites of ordination are intended to be used in local churches for individual candidates. In each rite representatives of the laity, and of each of the other three orders of ministers, are given opportunities to function in manners appropriate to their orders, and the newly ordained person participates in the climactic Eucharist. The diaconate is not depicted as an inferior ministry in the new rite, but restored to its ancient dignity. The ordained ministry is depicted as a ministry within rather than over the church. The addresses, examinations, and prayers of consecration depict more fully and more clearly the order being conferred.

Preface to the Ordination Rites (p. 510)

The ordinal of 1550 was printed with a preface which read:

It is evident unto all men, diligently reading Holy Scripture, and ancient authors, that from the apostles' time there hath been these orders of ministers in Christ's church: bishops, priests, and deacons, which offices were evermore had in such reverent estimation that no man by his own private authority might presume to execute any of them except he were first called, tried, examined, and known to have such qualities as were requisite for the same. And also by public prayer, with imposition of hands, approved and admitted thereunto. And therefore to the intent these orders should be continued and reverently used and esteemed in this Church of England, it is requisite that no man (not being at this present bishop, priest, nor deacon) shall execute any of them, except he be called, tried, examined, and admitted according to the form hereafter following.

And none shall be admitted a deacon except he be twenty-one years of age at the least. And every man which is to be admitted a priest shall be full twenty-four years old. And every man which is to be consecrated a bishop shall be fully thirty years of age.

And the bishop knowing, either by himself or by sufficient testimony, any person to be a man of virtuous conversation and without crime, and after examination and trial finding him learned in the Latin tongue and sufficiently instructed in Holy Scripture, may upon a Sunday or holy day, in the face of the church, admit him a deacon in such manner and form as hereafter followeth.

In the revision of 1662 the phrase "not being at this present bishop, priest, nor deacon" was deleted from the preface. The deletion of this phrase, and the addition of the phrase "or hath had formerly Episcopal Consecration, or Ordination" at the end of the first paragraph, was interpreted by some writers of the period as designed to make episcopal ordination essential for ministry in the Church of England and to put an end to the practice of accepting into its ministry men non-episcopally ordained in Scotland or on the continent. The minimum age for ordination to the diaconate was raised to twenty-three, "unless he have a Faculty." Ordinations, except "on urgent occasion," were to be limited to the times appointed in the canon, the Sundays after the ember days.

The first American revision of the ordinal retained the opening paragraph in its 1662 form. The following was substituted for the second paragraph: "And none shall be admitted a Deacon, Priest, or Bishop, except he be of the age which the Canon in that case provided may require." In the third paragraph, "finding him sufficiently instructed in the Holy Scripture, and otherwise learned as the Canons require" was substituted for "finding him learned in the Latin tongue and sufficiently instructed in Holy Scripture." The times for ordinations were those appointed in the canons, the Sundays following the ember days, "or else, on urgent occasion, upon some other day," rather than "or else, on urgent occasion, upon some other Sunday or Holy-day." This was a further departure from the custom and the ancient canon laws of the Western church.

In the 1979 revision the first paragraph from the preface of prior ordinals has been expanded, on the basis of a draft by the Rev. Dr. H. Boone Porter, for the sake of clarification and for definition of the historic functions of each order. The content of the second and third paragraphs is not retained since church canons regulate these matters.

Concerning the Ordination of a Bishop (p. 511)
Concerning the Service (pp. 524 and 536)

At the Ordination of a Bishop (p. 511)

The first paragraph of the directions concerning the ordination of a bishop emphasizes the importance of conforming to the ancient tradition that a bishop be ordained on a Sunday or other feast of our Lord, or on the feast of an apostle or evangelist.

The second paragraph directs that the Presiding Bishop (or a deputy) preside and serve as chief consecrator, and that at least two other bishops serve as co-consecrators. The canons of the church require, in accordance with ancient tradition, that at least three bishops participate in the consecration of a new bishop. So that the ministry of the church may be liturgically modeled on this occasion, representatives of each of the other orders, the presbyterate, the diaconate, and the laity, are assigned appropriate duties in the service.

In order that the people may see and hear, the chief consecrator is to preside from a chair placed close to the people. As many of the other bishops present as is convenient are to sit to the right and left of the chief consecrator.

Since the order has its own integrity, the bishop-elect is to be vested in a rochet or alb, "without stole, tippet, or other vesture distinctive of ecclesiastical or academic rank or order."

The next paragraph explains the use of the symbols *N.* and *N.N.* within the text of the rite.

The paragraph which follows states explicitly that it is appropriate for the bread and wine to be presented by the family or friends of the new bishop.

The final paragraph gives permission for the family of the new bishop to receive communion before other members of the congregation, and states explicitly that opportunity is to be given to the people to communicate on this occasion.

At the Ordination of a Priest (p. 524) *or of a Deacon* (p. 536)

When either order is to be conferred, at least two presbyters must be present.

In order that the people may see and hear, the bishop is to preside from a chair placed close to the people and facing them.

Because each order has its own integrity the ordinand is to be vested simply in a surplice or alb. The candidate for ordination to the priesthood is not to wear a stole, nor is a candidate for either order to wear "tippet, or other vesture of ecclesiastical or academic rank or order [office]."

The next paragraph explains the use of the symbols *N.* and *N.N.* within the text of the rites.

The paragraph which follows states explicitly that it is appropriate for the bread and wine to be presented by the family or friends of the newly ordained person.

The next paragraph in both sets of directions makes explicit the fact that the newly ordained person is to function at the Eucharist in a manner appropriate to that order, the priest as concelebrant with the bishop and other priests, the deacon in the distribution of communion. (See also pp. 534–535, 546–547, and 554–555 in the Prayer Book, for additional duties of the new priest or deacon.)

The final paragraph permits the family of the newly ordained person to receive communion before the other members of the congregation, and states explicitly that opportunity is to be given to the people to communicate on this occasion.

The Ordination of a Bishop, of a Priest,
of a Deacon (pp. 512-523, 525-535, 537-547)

In contrast to prior Anglican ordination rites the titles and the texts of these rites are in the singular for the ordination of individual candidates. They are designed to encourage the ordination of a candidate in a local church, where that person is known or will minister. The ancient title "ordination" is used for all three rites to emphasize the dignity and integrity of each of the three orders. The 1550 ordinal used the word "consecrating" in the title of the rite for the setting apart of a bishop, and the word "ordering" in the titles of the rites for the ordination of priests and of deacons. In 1662 "consecrating" was expanded to "ordaining or consecrating" in the rite for the ordination of a bishop, and "making" was substituted for "ordering" in the rite for the ordination of deacons.

A Hymn, Psalm, or Anthem (pp. 512, 525, 537)

As in the Eucharist and the celebration of a new ministry, the service may begin with the singing of a hymn, psalm, or anthem.

The Opening Acclamation (pp. 512, 525, 537)

The opening acclamation proper to the season of the church year is used.

The Collect for Purity (pp. 512, 525, 537)

For commentary on the collect for purity, see above, p. 318.

The Presentation (pp. 513-515, 526-528, 538-540)

In the rites of the English Prayer Books the archdeacon (or his deputy) presented the candidate for ordination as deacon or priest. The first American revision substituted the word "Priest." A candidate for ordination as bishop was presented by two bishops. In the 1979 Book the candidate for ordination as a deacon or priest is presented by a priest and a lay person, "and additional presenters if desired." A bishop-elect is presented by "Representatives of the diocese, both Priests and Lay Persons" who testify that this person was duly chosen. Testimonials are read which give evidence of a canonical election and of the consents to this ordination by a majority of the standing committees of the dioceses and by a majority of the bishops of the church. The presenters of a candidate for ordination as a deacon or priest certify that the requirements of the canons have been fulfilled, and that they believe the candidate's manner of life to be fit for the exercise of the ministry. The canonical requirements include endorsement of the candidate by representative clergy and laity—usually the rector and vestry of the candidate's parish and the standing committee of the diocese for which the candidate is to be ordained—and evidence of a suitable general and theological education. The sentences of presentation have been revised on the basis of a draft by Margaret Sloan.

The Oath (pp. 513, 526–527, 538–539)

The ordination rites of 1550 included "The Oath of the King's Supremacy:"

> I from henceforth shall utterly renounce, refuse, relinquish, and forsake the Bishop of Rome, and his authority, power, and jurisdiction. And I shall never consent nor agree that the Bishop of Rome shall practice, exercise, or have any manner of authority, jurisdiction, or power within this realm, or any other the king's dominions, but shall resist the same at all times, to the uttermost of my power. And I from henceforth will accept, repute, and take the King's Majesty to be the only supreme head in earth of the Church of England. And to my cunning, wit, and uttermost of my power, without guile, fraud, or other undue mean, I will observe, keep, maintain, and defend the whole effects and contents of all and singular acts and statutes made and to be made within this realm in derogation, extirpation, and extinguishment of the Bishop of Rome and his authority, and all other acts and statutes made or to be made in confirmation and corroboration of the king's power of the supreme head in earth of the Church of England; and this I will do against all manner of persons, of what estate, dignity or degree, or condition they be, and in no wise do nor attempt, nor to my power suffer to be done or attempted, directly or indirectly, any thing or things, privily or apertly, to the let, hindrance, damage, or derogation thereof, or any part thereof, by any manner of means, or for any manner of pretence. And in case any other be made or hath been made by me to any person or persons in maintenance, defence, or favor of the Bishop of Rome, or his authority, jurisdiction, or power, I repute the same, as vain and adnichilate: so help me God, all Saints and the holy Evangelist.

In the 1552 revision the last line was changed to read, "so help me God through Jesus Christ." In 1559 this oath was revised and sub-

517

stantially abbreviated. In addition, the English rites required that a bishop-elect swear due obedience to the archbishop. Canon 36 of the English canons of 1604 required that candidates for ordination subscribe to the Articles of Religion, the Prayer Book, and the ordinal as containing doctrine "agreeable to the Word of God." In place of these oaths and subscriptions, Article VIII of the constitution of the American church prescribed a declaration of conformity:

> I do believe the Holy Scriptures of the Old and New Testaments to be the word of God, and to contain all things necessary to salvation; and I do solemnly engage to conform to the doctrines and worship of the Protestant Episcopal Church in these United States.

(The last line was changed in 1901 to read, "and I do solemnly engage to conform to the Doctrine, Discipline, and Worship of the Protestant Episcopal Church in the United States of America." In 1979 it was changed to read ". . . of The Episcopal Church.") This document was signed by candidates prior to the rite, but an abbreviated form based upon this declaration was included within the rite for the ordination of a bishop. The present Book requires that the declaration be read and signed publicly in all three rites. In the rites for the ordination to the diaconate or to the priesthood the declaration is prefaced by a pledge of obedience to the bishop and to other ministers who may have authority over the candidate. That pledge of obedience was included in the examination in prior editions of the rites.

The Charge (pp. 514, 527, 539)

Though the congregation has been assured that all legal and canonical requirements have been fulfilled, opportunity is given for anyone who knows of any impediment to the ordination to declare it. This feature is a remnant from the early church when candidates were chosen by the congregation, generally from within their ranks. Though the opportunity for objection had not survived in Anglican rites for the ordination of a bishop, the 1979 Book includes it in that rite as well. This Book also restores a positive affirmation of the candidate, found in the ancient and Eastern rites.

The Pledge of Support (pp. 514, 527, 539)

A new feature of all three rites is a pledge to uphold this person in the ministry to which he or she is being ordained.

The Prayers (pp. 514–515, 527, 539)

The bidding to prayer in the rite for the ordination of a bishop dates to the ordinal of 1550, though the language was updated in 1662 and 1792 and again in this present revision. The American revision of 1792 substituted the election of Matthias for the sending forth of Paul and Barnabas used in the English Books. Scriptural allusions to Luke 6:12 and Acts 1:24–25 make clear that the church views the episcopate as patterned upon the apostolate chosen by our Lord. Prior editions of the Prayer Book gave no form of words for the bishop's bidding to prayer in the other ordination rites. This revision provides a model.

The Litany for Ordinations (pp. 548–551), or some other approved litany, follows the bidding. (For commentary on ordination litanies see below, pp. 530–532.)

The Concluding Collect (pp. 515, 528, 540)

On certain occasions the collect of the day would make a suitable collect for an ordination, in place of, or in addition to, the collect printed within the rites. (For commentary on that collect, see above, p. 248.) This ancient collect, not included in prior editions of the Prayer Book, replaces a prayer, apparently composed for the 1550 ordinal, to be used at the conclusion of the litany (with appropriate variations for each order):

> Almighty God, giver of all good things, which by thy Holy Spirit hast appointed divers orders of ministers in thy Church: mercifully behold this thy servant, now called to the work and ministry of a bishop, and replenish him so with the truth of thy doctrine, and innocency of life, that both by word and deed he may faithfully serve thee in this office, to the glory of thy name, and profit of thy congregation: Through the merits of our Savior Jesus Christ, who liveth and reigneth with thee and the Holy Ghost, world without end. Amen.

In the 1662 revision an amended form of this prayer was appointed for use in place of the collect of the day at the ordination of priests and of deacons. A revised version was retained for use at the conclusion of the litany at the ordination of a bishop, and a new prayer based upon the collect for Saint Peter's Day was provided as the collect. The 1979 Book retains a revised version of the prayer quoted above (which was common to the prior ordination rites) as the first of the prayers in the votive "For the Ministry" (pp. 205 and 256).

519

The Ministry of the Word (pp. 515–516, 528–530, 540–542)

The medieval pontificals had provided no proper lections for ordination, but used those for the day. For discussion of the lections appointed in earlier rites, see above, pp. 508–512.

From the revision of 1662 until that of 1928 the rubrics specifically required that the ordination rites be preceded by Morning Prayer. Though that requirement was not stated explicitly in the rubrics of the 1928 Book, proper lessons were provided: Isaiah 61 and 2 Timothy 2 at the ordination of a bishop; Ezekiel 3:1–11 and 2 Corinthians 5:11—6:10 at the ordination of priests, and Isaiah 6:1–8 and Mark 10:32–45 at the ordination of deacons. In the 1943 revision of the lectionary proper psalms were also appointed: Psalms 23 and 100 at the ordination of a bishop; Psalm 132 at the ordination of priests; and Psalms 36:5–12 and 63 at the ordination of deacons.

Though Morning Prayer is not required in this present revision as a part of the public rite, a full liturgy of the word, with three readings, Old Testament lesson, Epistle, and Gospel, is obligatory. In the rite for the ordination of a bishop, the use of Isaiah 61 dates from 1928, Psalm 100 from 1943, 1 Timothy from 1550, and John 20 from 1662. In the rite for the ordination of a priest, the use of the lesson from Ephesians dates from 1662, and Psalm 132 from 1943. The Gospel from John 10 is an abbreviated form of one which goes back to the ordinal of 1550. The Gospel from Matthew 9 dates from the revision of 1662. In the rite for the ordination of a deacon the Epistles from 1 Timothy and Acts date to the ordinal of 1550; the Gospel from Luke 12, to the revision of 1662. The 1979 Book provides more choices, not only to allow greater variety but also to gather together, for teaching purposes, readings that pertain significantly to each of the orders. The substitution of readings from the proper of the day is allowed on a Sunday or major feast, at the discretion of the bishop.

The Old Testament lesson and the Epistle are invariably to be read by lay persons, and the Gospel by a deacon, if one is present, in order that within an ordination rite each of the four orders may be seen functioning liturgically as models of the ministry.

The Sermon (pp. 516, 529, and 541)

Prior editions of the ordination rites had contained directions concerning the sermon, based upon those of Bucer's *De ordinatione legitima*. The rubric of the 1549 Prayer Book reads, "there shall be an exhortation declaring the duty and office of such as come to be admitted Ministers, how necessary such orders are in the church of Christ,

520

and also how the people ought to esteem them in their vocation." These directions are not in the present revision of the rites. Sermons should be based upon the lections.

The Nicene Creed (pp. 519–520, 529–530, 541–542)

The liturgies of the word for the ordination of a priest and of a deacon reach their climax in the affirmation of the Nicene Creed. In the rite for the ordination of a bishop a hymn is sung at this point, and the bishop's role as guardian of the church's faith is symbolized when the bishop-elect, after the examination, leads the congregation in the creed (see below).

The Examination (pp. 517–520, 531–532, 543–544)

The Address (pp. 517, 531, 543)

Earlier Anglican rites for ordination to the priesthood contained an address to the candidates which set forth the duties of the order. The present Book also provides such an address in the rites for the ordination of a bishop and of a deacon. The address in the rite for the ordination of priests in prior Anglican ordinals is essentially a translation of that in Bucer's treatise *De ordinatione legitima*. This address, which viewed the laity as a passive and helpless body, has been substantially abbreviated. The old form emphasized the teaching, preaching, and pastoral roles. The revised form incorporates emphasis upon the liturgical and sacramental roles of the priest, and the role of the priest in the councils of the church. The address on the work of a deacon portrays the deacon as one called to serve, to proclaim Christ and the Gospel to the world by both life and teaching, and to bring to the church the needs, concerns, and hopes of the world. The work of a bishop is portrayed as that of one called to proclaim and interpret the gospel, to guard the faith, unity, and discipline of the church, to celebrate and provide for the administration of the sacraments, to ordain, to be a chief pastor and wholesome example, and to share with fellow bishops the leadership of the church.

The Examination (pp. 517–518, 531–532, 543–544)

The medieval rites contained no examination for the ordination of priests or deacons. The rite for the ordination of priests in the 1550 ordinal included as an examination eight of the nine questions from the rite in Bucer's treatise *De ordinatione legitima*. Four of these questions, along with three additional ones, one of which was based upon a medieval admonition to deacons, formed an examination for candidates for the diaconate. The medieval rite for the ordination of a bishop had contained a scrutiny, some of which (supplemented from Bucer's treatise) was used for the examination of a bishop. In the 1979 Book the questions of prior ordinals are retained, but stated in a more concise form; questions which refer to other aspects of the particular orders have been added.

The examination of a bishop, following a tradition of the Eastern churches, is concluded with the bishop's acting out liturgically the role of guardian of the faith by leading the congregation in the Nicene Creed.

The examination of a priest and of a deacon concludes with a brief prayer for grace to perform what has been promised. That in the ordination of a priest, which contains an allusion to Philippians 1:6, is a more concise version of the prayer following the examination in Bucer's treatise. In varied forms, this prayer had followed the examination for both priests and bishops in prior Anglican ordinals.

The Consecration of the Bishop, of the Priest, of the Deacon (pp. 520–521, 533–534, 544–545)

The ordinand kneels before the bishop. At the ordination of a bishop other bishops present stand to the right and left of the Presiding Bishop. At the ordination of a priest other priests stand to the right and left of the bishop. These directions are intended to prevent their blocking the view of the congregation at the time of the laying on of hands.

The Hymn (pp. 520, 533, 544)

In the late medieval period it became customary to sing the metrical hymn Veni Creator Spiritus in the rites for the ordination of a bishop and for the ordination of priests. The point at which this hymn was sung varied in different pontificals. In the Sarum use for the ordination of priests it was sung after the laying on of hands and the vesting, but prior to the delivery of the chalice and paten, and the blessing and unction of the hands of the ordinand. It was sung at an analogous point in the rite for the ordination of a bishop. In Bucer's De ordinatione legitima a similar hymn, Veni Sancte Spiritus, was to be sung after the sermon, prior to the examination and laying on of hands. The ordinal of 1550 placed the Veni Creator Spiritus (in Cranmer's translation) after the Gospel, and before the examination and the laying on of hands at the ordination of priests.[1] At the ordination of a bishop, however, it came between the examination and the laying on of hands. The 1662 revision moved it to the same place in the rite for the ordination of priests which it occupied in the rite for the ordination of a bishop. In 1662 a translation by John Cosin was provided as an alternative to Cranmer's. The 1928 Book substituted an altered version of Edward Caswell's translation for that of Cranmer. The present Book, following the precedent of other recent Anglican revisions, appoints this hymn (or an alternative) to be used prior to the prayer of consecration and the laying on of hands in all three rites.

Another ancient hymn invoking the Holy Spirit, Veni Sancte Spiritus, is permitted as an alternative. This hymn had been a part of the ordination rites of Luther and Bucer, and possibly was in some of the medieval rites known to them. Any authorized translation of either of these hymns may be used. The hymn may be sung by the congregation, or a choir, or a cantor, and may be sung in full, antiphonally, or responsively (see p. 552).

Veni Creator Spiritus has generally been attributed to Rabanus Maurus (c. 776–856), abbot at Fulda and archbishop of Mainz. In the late medieval period it was the office hymn at Terce on Pentecost, and in the Sarum missal it was said regularly as a part of the priest's preparation before Mass.

Veni Sancte Spiritus, known as "The Golden Sequence," appears in manuscripts from about 1200. It has been ascribed to various writers, but most commonly to Stephen Langton (d. 1228), Archbishop of Canterbury. In the late medieval period it was used as the sequence on Pentecost, and was one of the four medieval sequences which survived the Tridentine reform of the Roman missal.

A Period of Silent Prayer (pp. 520, 533, 544)

The earliest extant description of ordination rites, that of Hippolytus (c. 215), stresses a period of silence prior to the prayer of consecration. During this silence hands were laid on the ordinand and all prayed for the descent of the Spirit. Medieval pontificals continued this tradition of a period of silence with a laying on of hands in the rites for the ordination of deacons and of priests. Bucer, in his treatise De ordinatione legitima, provided for silence between the examination and the prayer of consecration. Such a period has

---

[1] Cranmer's translation included a verse which had been omitted from many of the English pontificals.

been provided in Anglican rites for the ordination of priests; this present revision restores the period of silent prayer at the ordination of a bishop and of a deacon as well.

The Prayer of Consecration (pp. 520–521, 533–534, 545)

In the Apostolic Tradition of Hippolytus the period of silence with laying on of hands was followed, in each of the ordination rites, by a prayer during which the bishop laid hands on the ordinand. The prayer in the rite for the ordination of a bishop depicts the bishop as Christian patriarch, as pastor, and as high priest within the priestly community. The prayer for the consecration of presbyters depicts the order as successors to the Jewish elders, whose duty it is to "sustain and govern" the people. The prayer for the consecration of deacons depicts the deacon as one who serves and who informs the church.

The prayers in the sacramentaries depict the presbyters as successors of the sons of Aaron and of the seventy sent out by our Lord, as ministers of the Eucharist, and as colleagues of the bishop. The deacons are depicted as successors of the Levites and of the seven set apart in the Acts of the Apostles to serve tables.

The late medieval pontificals combined the Roman and Gallican rites. Both the Roman and the Gallican forms of the prayer of consecration were said, and various subsidiary ceremonies and texts were inserted in connection with the vesting of the newly ordained, the delivery of instruments, and the anointing of the hands or head. The laying on of hands was separated from the prayer of consecration. In the thirteenth century imperative formulae were added to the rites with a second laying on of hands. There was much debate over what constituted the essential matter of the sacrament.

In his treatise *De ordinatione legitima* Bucer argued that the essential aspect of ordination is the laying on of hands in the context of the word and prayer in a solemn gathering of the church. He provided a lengthy prayer for use after the silent prayer of the congregation and prior to the laying on of hands, which was accompanied by a blessing.

Cranmer, in the preface to the ordination rites, stated that the essential matter of ordination is "public prayer, with imposition of hands." Since in one of the rites (that for the ordination of deacons) the only prayer preceding the imposition of hands is the Litany (with a special petition and concluding collect), it seems that for Cranmer the essential "public prayer" was the Litany. The laying on of hands was not accompanied by prayer, as in the early church and in Bucer's rite, but (like the additional laying on of hands in rites from the

524

thirteenth century) by an imperative formula. The first phrases in the forms associated with the laying on of hands in the ordination of a bishop and in the ordination of priests had their precedent in late medieval pontificals. At the ordination of a bishop the form for laying on of hands was completed by the addition of 2 Timothy 1:6–7. The conclusions of the form for the ordination of priests, and the form for the ordination of deacons, seem to have been original. They were modeled on forms which accompanied the giving of instruments in the late medieval rites. In the 1550 text the forms accompanying the laying on of hands in the ordination of a bishop and in the ordination of priests and of deacons read respectively:

> Take the Holy Ghost, and remember that thou stir up the grace of God which is in thee by imposition of hands; for God hath not given us the spirit of fear, but of power, and love, and of soberness.
> Receive the Holy Ghost; whose sins thou dost forgive, they are forgiven; and whose sins thou dost retain, they are retained. And be thou a faithful dispenser of the word of God and of his holy sacraments. In the Name of the Father, and of the Son, and of the Holy Ghost. Amen.
> Take thou authority to execute the office of a deacon in the church of God committed unto thee. In the Name of the Father, the Son, and the Holy Ghost. Amen.

In the 1662 revision a phrase inserted in the first two of these specified the order to which the person was being ordained. This was to guard against presbyterian interpretations of the rites and to answer criticisms by Roman Catholics. The first American revision of the ordinal (1792) provided an alternative form for the ordination of priests modeled on that for the ordination of deacons.

The 1550 and subsequent ordinals did, however, preface the laying on of hands with prayer in the rite for the ordination of priests and in that for the ordination of a bishop. That of the rite for the ordination of priests is an abbreviated version of the prayer prior to the laying on of hands in Bucer's treatise, but Bucer's petition for the descent of the Spirit is omitted. In the 1550 ordinal the prayer read:

> Almighty God and heavenly Father, which of thy infinite love & goodness towards us hast given to us thy only and most dear beloved son Jesus Christ to be our redeemer and author of everlasting life: who after he had made perfect our redemption by his death and was ascended into heaven sent abroad into the world

his Apostles, Prophets, Evangelists, Doctors and Pastors, by whose labor and ministry he gathered together a great flock in all the parts of the world to set forth the eternal praise of thy holy Name; for these so great benefits of thy eternal goodness, and for that thou hast vouchsafed to call these thy servants here present to the same office and ministry of the salvation of mankind, we render unto thee most hearty thanks, we worship and praise thee, and we humbly beseech thee by the same thy Son to grant unto all us which either here or elsewhere call upon thy Name, that we may show ourselves thankful to thee for these and all other thy benefits, and that we may daily increase and go forwards in the knowledge and faith of thee, and thy Son, and the Holy Spirit, so that as well by these thy ministers as by them to whom they shall be appointed ministers thy holy Name may be always glorified and thy blessed kingdom enlarged; through the same thy Son our Lord Jesus Christ, which liveth and reigneth with thee in the unity of the same Holy Spirit, world without end. Amen.

Bucer's prayer provided the preface for the prayer before the laying on of hands in the rite for the ordination of a bishop. It concluded with phrases from one of the prayers used at the ordination of a bishop in the medieval pontificals:

. . . . ascended into heaven poured down his gifts abundantly upon men, making some Apostles, some Prophets, some Evangelists, some Pastors and Doctors, to the edifying and making perfect of his congregation: Grant, we beseech thee, to this thy servant, such grace that he may be evermore ready to spread abroad thy Gospel and glad tidings of reconcilement to God, and to use the authority given unto him not to destroy but to save, not to hurt but to help, so that he as a faithful and a wise servant, giving to thy family meat in due season, may at the last day be received into joy; through Jesu Christ our Lord, who with thee and the Holy Ghost, liveth and reigneth, one God, world without end. Amen.

The super populum of the rite for the ordination of deacons made use of some phrases from the ancient Roman prayer for the consecration of deacons.

The present Prayer Book, like the new Roman rite, uses the prayer of Hippolytus for the ordination of a bishop in conjunction with the laying on of hands. The prayer at the ordination of a priest incorporates material from Bucer's prayer (used in prior Anglican ordinals),

526

Ephesians 4:11–12, and the new South Indian and English proposed rites. It presents a fuller view of the priesthood than does the prayer of prior rites: a priest is to proclaim the gospel and administer the sacraments, act as pastor and teacher, and share in the councils of the church. The prayer for the rite of the ordination of a deacon is similar to that of the South Indian and English proposed rites. It incorporates allusions to Philippians 2:5–11 and Luke 22:27 and phrases from the super populum of prior Anglican rites which had been derived from the ancient Roman prayer, thus restoring these phrases to their original use.

In each instance a rubric stresses the participation of the people in the Amen. During the prayer, in accordance with ancient tradition, the bishops present lay hands on a bishop, the presbyters present join the bishop in laying hands on a priest, and the bishop alone lays hands on a deacon.

The Vesting of the Newly Ordained (pp. 521, 534, 545)

In the early church the clothing of the newly baptized in white garments was a significant ceremony in the rites of initiation. The medieval clergy, when they functioned liturgically, wore clothing that had passed out of fashion. Eventually allegorical explanations developed and additional vestments and insignia came into use. Late in the middle ages the robing of a newly ordained person in vestments associated with the particular order became a significant part of the ordination rites. The deacon was given a stole, and in some rites a dalmatic. At the ordination of a priest the stole was placed over both shoulders, and he was given a chasuble. A bishop was given a staff, a ring, and a mitre.

The 1550 ordinal requires that those to be ordained deacon or priest wear a plain alb, and that a person to be ordained bishop wear a surplice and cope. There is no provision for the vesting of the newly ordained within the rites, however, even though the rubrics of the 1549 Prayer Book Eucharist required that a deacon wear a tunicle and the priest a chasuble or cope. The medieval delivery of the stole, (dalmatic,) chasuble, and mitre at ordinations were omitted from the rubrics. The 1552 revision of the Prayer Book prescribed the surplice as the only vestment of a deacon or priest, and the rochet as the only vestment of a bishop or archbishop. The rubrics of the 1552 ordinal deleted every mention of vestments.

The Act of Uniformity which promulgated the use of the Prayer Book revision of 1559 provided that such ornaments of the church, and of the ministers thereof shall be retained, and be in use, as was in this Church of England by the authority of Parliament in the second year of the reign of King Edward the sixth, until other order shall be therein taken, by authority of the Queen's Majesty, with the advice of her commissioners appointed and authorized under the great seal of England, for causes ecclesiastical or of the metropolitan of this realm.

This "ornaments rubric" has been a matter of debate throughout the subsequent generations: did this refer to the provisions of the 1549 Book or to the use of the period immediately prior to the promulgation of that Book? Archbishop Matthew Parker's "Advertisements" of 1566 required surplices in parish churches and that the celebrant and reader of the Epistle and Gospel wear copes in cathedral and collegiate churches.

The 1662 revision of the ordinal, in the rubrics, simply stated that a candidate for ordination as a deacon or priest was to be "decently habited" for the rite. There is no mention of vesting within the rites. A candidate for ordination as bishop was to be vested in a rochet. After the examination, prior to the Veni Creator Spiritus, the bishop-elect was to "put on the rest of the Episcopal habit," that is, the black satin chimere and scarf which were customary at that time. These rubrics remained unchanged until this present revision.

In recent generations the use of some or all of the vestments mentioned in the rubrics of the 1549 Prayer Book (the alb, the tunicle, the chasuble, and the cope) has been recovered in many places. The stole and the mitre, neither of which is mentioned in the rubrics of the 1549 Book, have also been recovered.

The present revision designates, in the directions concerning the service (pp. 511, 524, and 536), that a bishop-elect is to wear a rochet or alb and that a candidate for ordination as a priest or as a deacon is to wear a surplice or alb, "without stole, tippet, or other vesture distinctive of ecclesiastical or academic rank or order." A new bishop is to be "clothed with the vesture of the episcopate" (p. 553). A new priest is to be vested with a "stole . . . about the neck, or other insignia of the office of priest" (p. 553). A new deacon is to be vested with a "stole . . . over the left shoulder, or other insignia of the office of deacon" (p. 554). While a bishop is being vested, instrumental music may be played (p. 553). If vestments (or other symbols of office) are to be dedicated before being given, it is not to be done within the ordination rite but "at some convenient time prior to the service" (see p. 552), lest the dedication and vesting (and/or delivery of instruments) assume undue proportions within the rite, the essence of which is prayer and the laying on of hands.

The Delivery of the Bible (pp. 521, 534, 545)

In the early church ordination to minor orders was often accompanied by the delivery of instruments appropriate to the order. A reader, for example, was given a book, or a doorkeeper the keys. In the late medieval period the delivery of instruments also became part of the rites for ordination to major orders. A deacon received a book of the Gospels, a priest a paten and chalice, a bishop a staff, a ring, and a mitre. In time, the delivery of instruments assumed such importance that it was thought by many to constitute the matter of the sacrament.

The 1550 ordinal substituted the delivery of the New Testament for the delivery of the book of the Gospels at the ordination of a deacon as a sign of his authority to read the Gospel. A chalice and bread, and a Bible were given to a newly ordained priest as signs of authority to preach and administer the sacraments. Continuing a medieval custom, a Bible was placed upon the neck of a bishop, that he should "give heed unto reading, exhortation, and doctrine," and a staff was given to him to symbolize his function as a shepherd who nourishes, rescues, and disciplines the flock and seeks the lost. The giving of the ring and the mitre was discontinued. In 1552 the giving of the chalice and bread and of the pastoral staff was discontinued. A Bible was given to the bishop, not laid upon his neck. The texts associated with the delivery of instruments, however, remained the same.

The 1979 Book directs that a Bible be given to all three orders. The texts are revised to incorporate more aspects of the work of the various orders. In the rites for the ordination of a bishop and of a priest other symbols of office may be given after the delivery of the Bible (see the rubric on p. 531 and the additional direction on p. 553). As is true of vestments, symbols of office may not be dedicated within the ordination rite (see above and p. 552 in the Prayer Book).

The Presentation of a Bishop or
Greeting of a Priest (pp. 522, 534)

After the delivery of the Bible (and other symbols of office) the Presiding Bishop presents the new bishop to the people, who offer their acclamation and applause.

The bishop greets a new priest at this point, signifying the acceptance of the new priest into a collegial ministry.

The Peace (pp. 522, 534, 546)

A new bishop or priest initiates the exchange of the peace. Each of the rites gives opportunity for the newly ordained person to be greeted by the clergy, and to greet family members and others, as convenient.

The Seating of a Bishop (p. 522)

If the ordination of a bishop takes place within the cathedral, or if the episcopal chair has been brought to the place of the rite, a new bishop of a diocese may be escorted to the chair at this point.

At the Celebration of the Eucharist (pp. 522–523, 535, 546–547)

In the early church a newly ordained person served within the Eucharist in a manner appropriate to his order. Western churches obscured this tradition in the medieval period, except for the fact that at the ordination Eucharist a newly ordained deacon read the Gospel. The 1979 revision has restored the older tradition. A new bishop presides as chief celebrant at the Eucharist and gives a pontifical blessing. A new priest concelebrates with the bishop and other presbyters, and joins in the breaking of the bread (on concelebration, see above, pp. 313–314). A new priest also blesses the people. A new deacon prepares the table, dismisses the people, and may also assist in the administration of communion, remove the vessels from the altar and consume the remaining elements, cleanse the vessels, and carry communion from the service to those unable to be present (see pp. 554–555).

An additional direction allows the singing of a hymn of praise after the blessing and dismissal at the ordination of a bishop (see p. 553). It is traditional to sing the Te Deum laudamus to a familiar setting.

A special postcommunion prayer, drafted by the Rev. Dr. H. Boone Porter, is provided for use in all three rites.

The Litany for Ordinations (pp. 548–551)

In medieval ordination rites, prior to the laying on of hands and the ordination prayers, there was a litany with special suffrages. The ordinal of 1550 appointed a litany in each of the three ordination rites, not derived from the medieval litanies, however, but the Litany of the 1549 Prayer Book, with an additional special suffrage. The suffrage for use at the ordination of deacons or priests read:

> That it may please thee, to bless these men, and send thy grace upon them, that they may duly execute the office now to be committed unto them, to the edifying of thy Church, and to thy honor, praise, and glory.

That in the rite for the ordination of a bishop read:

> That it may please thee to bless this our brother elected, and to send thy grace upon him, that he may duly execute the office whereunto he is called, to the edifying of thy Church, and to the honor, praise, and glory of thy name.

A proper collect was also provided at the conclusion of the Litany (see above, p. 519). In one of the rites (that of ordination to the diaconate) no other prayer is included before the laying on of hands. In the ordination rites of prior Prayer Books, therefore, the Litany seems to serve the function of the "public prayer" of the church which Cranmer believed should precede the laying on of hands as one of the actions essential for ordination.

The revision of 1662 changed the petition for use at the ordination of deacons or priests:

> That it may please thee to bless these thy servants, now to be admitted to the order of Deacons [or Priests] and to pour thy grace upon them, that they may duly execute their office to the edifying of thy Church, and the glory of thy holy Name.

The 1928 revision provided a much shorter "Litany and Suffrages for Ordinations" as an alternative. This Litany, largely the work of Bishop Charles Lewis Slattery, followed the general structure of the Great Litany. After an initial petition based upon the first suffrage of many Eastern litanies, it depended largely upon various prayers for the church and the ministry of earlier Books.

The Litany for Ordinations in the 1979 Book is based upon Form V of the prayers of the people. Trinitarian invocations, similar to those of the Great Litany (p. 148), have been prefixed, and several suffrages are added. The second suffrage is drawn from the first of the prayers for mission in Morning Prayer (pp. 57 and 100). The third was inspired by a suffrage in the 1928 Litany for Ordinations. The first two petitions for the ordinand depend upon the special suffrage which dates to the ordinal of 1550. One of the suffrages in the 1928 Litany for Ordinations is the source of the third petition for the ordinand. The petition for the family, household, or (monastic) community of the ordinand is new to the present Book. Like the Great Litany, this Litany ends with Kyrie eleison, which may be sung by the congregation or choir in threefold, sixfold, or ninefold form, and a collect.

A collect is printed within the ordination rites for use at the conclusion of this Litany on those occasions. At other times, for example on ember days (see the rubric on p. 548), when this Litany is used as the prayers of the people, another suitable collect may be substituted.

Additional Directions (pp. 552–555)

The first paragraph specifies that the ordination rites may be concluded with either Rite One or Rite Two of the Holy Eucharist.

A number of directions deal with the problems involved in a situation when it is necessary for two or more persons to be ordained to an order within the same service. Note that no provision is made for ordination to more than one order within the same service (as had been allowed in previous editions of the ordinal), for each of the rites is designed to give liturgical expression to a particular order.

A prayer for the dedication of vestments, or other symbols of office, is provided for use at some time preceding the ordination rites. This form appears in the new Roman Catholic ordination rites, which also restrict its use to a time prior to the ordination rites themselves.

Commentary on other directions is incorporated within the commentary on the rites.

Celebration of a New Ministry

Ordination is the basic rite for the conferring of pastoral responsibilities. In the early church a bishop, priest, or deacon was usually ordained for a particular position; no further ceremonies of installation were required. This has continued to be the normal pattern in Eastern churches. A new situation, however, arose in Western Europe in the medieval period: large numbers of priests were ordained to serve in minor capacities with the hope that they would at some time be given a benefice.

In England, after generations of conflict between feudal landowners anxious to secure priests for the manor parishes who would be loyal to their feudal lords, and bishops equally anxious to see the parishes held by priests who would be loyal to the diocesan, a procedure for institution and induction evolved. The person or corporate body who had control of the benefice would select the priest. The appointee then swore fealty to the bishop before witnesses. The bishop then gave him a letter of institution, and a mandate for the archdeacon, or some other church official, to induct him into possession of the premises and perquisites of the parish. This procedure continued through the Reformation. John Johnson, in *The Clergyman's Vade Mecum,* described the ceremonies of institution and induction of the early eighteenth century. They included subscription to the Articles of Religion, certain oaths, a proclamation by the inductor while the new priest had his hand on the key of the church, entering the church, ringing the bell, and reading the Articles, the declarations, and the Prayer Book service of the day.

The American church gave liturgical and spiritual significance to the essentially legal ceremonies of institution and induction. The Connecticut convocation of 1799 adopted an "Office of Induction"

533

prepared by William Smith, then rector at Norwalk. This form, with minor changes, was adopted by the New York state convention of 1802. With further changes, the New York form was adopted by the General Convention in 1804. In 1808 and 1844 further emendations were made, and other changes in the Prayer Book revisions of 1892 and 1928.

The rite of earlier American Prayer Books, "An Office of Institution of Ministers into Parishes or Churches," began with Morning Prayer, for which proper psalms and lessons were appointed. The 1928 revision made this optional. The bishop or appointed deputy stated the purpose of the rite and gave opportunity for any parishioner to show cause why this person should not be instituted. The inductor read the letter of institution; and the senior warden presented the keys of the church to the new rector, who received them as "the pledges of my Institution, and of your parochial recognition," promising to be "a faithful Shepherd over you." After a collect and the Lord's Prayer, the new incumbent was received "within the rails of the Altar" and given a Bible, a Prayer Book, and copies of the national and diocesan canons. These books were to serve as his rule in teaching, in leading worship, and in exercising discipline. After a psalm, the inductor read three prayers, based upon Prayer Book collects, and a "Benediction." The new incumbent then knelt for a prayer of self-dedication, apparently an original composition for the rite, after which he stood for a prayer for the church, made up principally of phrases from various Prayer Book forms.

The sermon and Eucharist followed (the latter was made optional in the 1928 Book). Even though the bishop was present, the new incumbent was to say the blessing, after which "the Wardens, Vestry, and others, shall salute and welcome him, bidding him God-speed."

English diocesan forms since the late nineteenth century, and the Canadian Prayer Books of 1922 and 1959, have incorporated some features from the American rite. They have also added other ceremonies symbolic of various aspects of the ministry. In a manner reminiscent of classical Anglican rites for the consecration of a church, the new incumbent is led to different parts of the church for appropriate readings, exhortations, and prayers.

The American rite, since the revision of 1844, had provided only for the induction of the rector of a parish, even though the purpose of the rite was devotional and edifying rather than legal. The form in the 1979 Book may be used, with adaptations where necessary, not only for rectors of parishes but also for assistants, vicars of missions, deans and canons of cathedrals, chaplains of institutions, or non-stipendiary clergy. And it may be used for deacons and lay persons with pastoral responsibilities as well as for priests. The rubrics allow for great flexibility and for adaptation to local conditions. At the beginning of the rite the minister declares commitment and the congregation promises support. After the lessons and sermon, the bishop, clergy of the diocese, a warden, and representatives of the congregation present signs and symbols associated with the ministry: a Bible, water for baptizing, a stole, a book of prayers, olive oil, the keys of the building, the constitution and canons of the church, and bread and wine. The congregation then greets the new minister, who initiates the peace and, if a priest, concelebrates with the bishop at the concluding Eucharist. This rite was drafted by the diocesan liturgical commission of Utah with its bishop, the Rt. Rev. E. Otis Charles.

Letter of Institution of a Minister (p. 557)

This form, drafted by Bishop Otis Charles, replaces the form of prior American Prayer Books. The 1928 version of that form reads:

To our well-beloved in Christ, A. B., Presbyter, Greeting.

We do by these Presents give and grant unto you, in whose Learning, Diligence, sound Doctrine, and Prudence, we do fully confide, our Licence and Authority to perform the Office of a Priest, in the Parish (*or* Church) of *E.* And also hereby do institute you into said Parish, (*or* Church,) possessed of full power to perform every Act of sacerdotal Function among the People of the same; you continuing in communion with us, and complying with the rubrics and canons of the Church, and with such lawful directions as you shall at any time receive from us.

And as a canonically instituted Priest into the Office of Rector of ___ Parish, (*or* Church,) you are faithfully to feed that portion of the flock of Christ which is now intrusted to you; not as a man-pleaser, but as continually bearing in mind that you are accountable to us here, and to the Chief Bishop and Sovereign Judge of all, hereafter.

And as the Lord hath ordained that they who serve at the altar should live of the things belonging to the altar; so we authorize you to claim and enjoy all the accustomed temporalities appertaining to your cure, until some urgent reason or reasons occasion a wish in you, or in the congregation committed to your charge, to bring about a separation, and dissolution of all sacerdotal relation, between you and them; of all which you will give us due notice; and in case of any difference between you and your congregation as to a separation and dissolution of all sacerdotal connection

535

between you and them, we, your Bishop, with the advice of our Presbyters, are to be the ultimate arbiter and judge.

In witness whereof, we have hereunto affixed our episcopal seal and signature, at _____, this _____ day of _____, A.D. _____, and in the _____ year of our consecration.

Concerning the Service (p. 558)

The first of these directions points out that though the service as printed is for use at the institution of the rector of a parish, it may, unlike the rite of prior American Books from the time of the 1844 revision, be used at the inauguration of other ministries as well. In such circumstances appropriate alterations may be made.

The other directions designate particular liturgical ministries appropriate to each of the four orders, lay persons, bishops, priests, and deacons. They are designed to encourage a celebration which gives liturgical expression to the new ministry which is being celebrated and to its position within the life of the diocese and the local community. The bishop is normally the chief minister, and, when present, the chief celebrant of the Eucharist. If a deputy takes the place of the bishop, in line with the provisions of prior American Prayer Books, a priest being inducted is chief celebrant. Other clergy of the diocese function as concelebrants "as an expression of the collegiality of the ministry in which they share." Deacons function "according to their order" (reading [the litany and] the Gospel, preparing the table, administering the Sacrament, performing the ablutions, and dismissing the people). Lay persons present the new minister to the bishop, read the lessons which precede the Gospel, present some of the signs of ministry to the new minister, and assist in other appropriate ways. A direction explicitly states that it is appropriate to invite ministers of other churches to participate as well. Their presence and participation symbolizes a shared ministry within the community.

The final directions designate the appropriate liturgical roles of a deacon or lay person whose new ministry is being celebrated.

Celebration of a New Ministry (pp. 559–565)

A Hymn, Psalm, or Anthem (p. 559)

As at the Eucharist or at a marriage or ordination, the service may begin with the singing of a hymn, psalm, or anthem.

The Institution (pp. 559–560)

This portion of the rite gives liturgical expression to the bishop's action of institution. Rather than being presented to the bishop by a patron, as in medieval times, the new minister is presented by the parish wardens. The letter of institution is read by the bishop, or the bishop states the purpose of the new ministry. Following the precedent of American rites, the new minister publicly makes a commitment to the new trust and responsibility. Earlier American rites permitted the congregation to object to the institution, if anyone could show just cause. This revision substitutes a pledge to support and uphold this ministry.

The Litany (p. 560)

Prior American rites included a series of prayers for the church and ministry drawn largely from other Prayer Book material. The 1979 Book uses, instead, the Litany for Ordinations (pp. 548–551) or some other appropriate litany. The collect of the day, a collect of the season, or some other suitable prayer may be used in place of the collect printed in the rite.

At the Liturgy of the Word (p. 560)

Provision is made for a full liturgy of the word with Old Testament lesson, psalmody, Epistle, Gospel, and sermon. Previous American Books provided proper psalms and lessons for a daily office at the institution of a minister. Psalms 132 and 133 are from among those appointed in earlier editions. Readings from the proper of the day, or other appropriate lessons such as those from the service for the ordination of a deacon, or from the lectionary for various occasions, may be substituted. After the Gospel a sermon may be preached by the bishop, or by the new minister or some other person. An address about the work of the congregation and the new minister may substitute for a sermon. Representatives of the congregation or community, the bishop, or other persons may respond to the sermon or address.

A Hymn (p. 560)

Prior to the induction the congregation sings a hymn.

The Induction (pp. 561–563)

Historically, the induction enabled the new minister to take possession of the parish and be recognized as the incumbent. In the American rites the senior warden presented him with the keys of the church, and the institutor gave him a Bible, a Book of Common Prayer, and a copy of the national and diocesan canons. English diocesan rites of the late nineteenth century, and the rites of the 1922 and 1959 Canadian Books, directed that the new minister be led to various parts of the church for appropriate readings, exhortations, and prayers. These actions, reminiscent of various Anglican forms for the consecration of a church, dramatized the new pastoral relationship.

The 1979 Book provides for presentation of instruments symbolic of the various aspects of ministry. Those for which directions and forms are given are appropriate at the induction of a rector into a parish. If a person is being inducted into another ministry, those which are not appropriate should be omitted and fitting substitutions may be made. The bishop concludes the presentations with a sentence reminding the congregation of the relationship of the bishop to the new minister and to the congregation.

A Prayer (pp. 562–563)

The new minister, if a priest, then kneels and says a prayer, apparently an original composition by William Smith for the 1799 Connecticut form. This prayer of self-dedication, beginning with an allusion to Matthew 8:8, centers on the primary duties of the priest as a minister of the word and sacraments, as a teacher, and as a person of prayer.

The Presentation (p. 563)

The bishop presents the new minister (and, when appropriate, the family) to the congregation. The congregation may respond with applause or some other expression of approval. The bishop greets the new minister. Previous American rites had directed that "the Wardens, Vestry, and others, shall salute and welcome him, bidding him God-speed."

The Peace (p. 563)

The first act of the new minister is to initiate the exchange of the peace.

At the Eucharist (pp. 563–564)

The Eucharist continues with the offertory. The rubric specifies that the bishop, if present, should be the principal celebrant. In the absence of a bishop, and in keeping with prior American rites, the new minister, if a priest, is chief celebrant. Other priests should serve as concelebrants, and deacons present should fulfill the roles traditionally assigned to that order. Any authorized form of the Great Thanksgiving may be used. On major feasts (those listed on pp. 15–17 of the Prayer Book) the proper preface of the day should be used; on other occasions that for apostles and ordinations is especially appropriate. The postcommunion prayer of the ordination rites is printed for use at the induction of a priest or deacon. If the new minister is a lay person, however, the usual postcommunion prayer is said. Previous American rites had specified that a newly inducted priest say the blessing on this occasion. The 1979 Book permits the newly inducted priest to say the blessing at the request of the bishop.

Additional Directions (pp. 564–565)

The additional directions point out that the rite should be conducted at the entrance to the chancel or at some other place where it can be clearly heard and seen, and that the symbols should be large enough to be seen by all. Commentary on the other directions is included within the text of the commentary on the rite.

The Dedication and Consecration
of a Church

There is no evidence of the dedication or consecration of a church prior to the peace of Constantine. A building came to be thought of as a church because it was the place where the body of the church met for the word and sacraments. Even for a period of time after the establishment of Christianity, when new buildings were built for church purposes or old buildings were converted to church use, the dedication or consecration of the building seems to have consisted of the first celebration of the Eucharist within the building. This was, however, considered a momentous occasion, and often many ecclesiastical and civic dignitaries attended.

At a later stage special and impressive rites developed in both East and West. The essential element for the dedication or consecration of a church continued to be the celebration of the Eucharist. In the Roman rite relics were deposited in the altar and, if the building had served as a pagan temple, there was apparently a preliminary sprinkling or lustration. The Gallican rites, resembling the Eastern rites, were far more elaborate. The bishop and clergy entered during the singing of a litany. The bishop consecrated a mixture of wine and water, asperged the church, and (after another litany) asperged the altar. He then anointed the altar with chrism at the center and at each of the four corners, after which he circuited the church, anointing it. He then blessed the altar linens and vessels. The altar was vested and the Eucharist celebrated. The Roman rite has been called analogous to burial, the Gallican and Eastern rites to baptism.

In later times the first act of the bishop on entering the church was to trace the alphabet in Latin and Greek on the floor of the church (possibly of Celtic origin and perhaps a remnant of the ceremony at the laying of the foundations which signified the claiming of territory). The Roman deposition of relics was also incorporated into the rite. As early as the fourth century, in some places, the dedication was commemorated annually. Late in the medieval period the Gallican and Roman rites were fused and elaborated.

English Prayer Books themselves contained no form for the consecration of churches, but a substantial number of separate forms used in the seventeenth century have survived. Early within that century some consensus was reached on the general contents and order of the rite for the consecration of a church. The most influential of the early forms was that of Lancelot Andrewes, bishop of Winchester: after an address to the bishop by the donor, the bishop and priests said responsively Psalms 24 and 122, as the bishop, the founder, and the priests entered the building. Just inside, so that the congregation gathered outside could hear, the bishop knelt, in imitation of Solomon at the dedication of the temple, for a lengthy prayer of dedication introduced with the prayer of David (1 Chr. 29:10b–18) and concluded with invocations addressed respectively to the Father, the Son, the Holy Spirit, and the Trinity. The bishop then moved about the building saying appropriate prayers at the font, the pulpit, the reading desk, the holy Table, the place at which marriages would be performed, and the pavement beneath which bodies would be buried. After further prayers for those who would worship in the building, the people entered and Morning Prayer was begun. Proper psalms (Pss. 84, 122, and 132) and lessons (Gen. 28:10–22 and Jn. 2:13–25) were appointed. A lengthy prayer followed the fixed collects, and another was provided for use after the Litany. There was an additional collect provided for the Eucharist and a proper Epistle (1 Cor. 3:16–23) and Gospel (Jn. 10:22–42). The prayer of Solomon at the dedication of the temple (1 Kg. 8:27ff.) and the Act of Consecration were read prior to the offertory. At the end of the Eucharist, just before the blessing, a prayer was said for the donor. The churchyard was blessed in the afternoon at the time of Evening Prayer. The seventeenth-century forms required that the building be put to use on that occasion for the daily offices, the Litany, and the Eucharist. They also contained rubrics specifying the points at which baptisms, confirmations, marriages, the churching of women, ordinations, and burials should take place. The ideal was to put the building to full use on the occasion of its consecration.

Efforts to secure a uniform use resulted in the approval (in 1712) by both houses of Convocation of a simplified form of Andrewes' rite, but it did not receive royal assent. This form retained the prayers related to the furnishings of the church but omitted the perambulation. A simplified version of that form was approved by the bishops in 1715, but its progress was interrupted in the lower house. Bishop Thomas Wilson of Sodor and Man revised the 1715 form for his own use. Samuel Seabury, the first bishop of Connecticut, used Wilson's form.

Since there had been no bishops in colonial times to consecrate any of the churches in this country, the first American bishops recognized the need for an official form. For its addition to the Prayer Book, they had the precedent of various eighteenth-century printings of the Irish Prayer Book which had included a rite containing material by Jeremy Taylor. At the 1799 convention Samuel Provoost, the first bishop of New York, proposed a form which was accepted. He had used this revision of the 1712 Convocation form as early as May 24, 1789, when he consecrated St. Ann's Church in Brooklyn, probably the first consecration of a church according to this form in this country. There were few changes in the 1892 or 1928 revisions of the Prayer Book except for the omission in 1892 of the requirement that a Eucharist be celebrated, a serious departure from ancient and universal custom.

The 1928 revision provided propers for both the daily office and the Eucharist for the feast of the dedication of a church.

In earlier centuries a church had generally been erected by a donor who gave it at the time of consecration. In America, in the nineteenth century, churches were often financed by the selling of pews to people of the parish area. Eventually loans were secured by mortgaging the property. To protect property from alienation a canon enacted in 1868 required that the building and ground on which it was erected be fully paid for and free of all encumbrance at the time of consecration. As a result, the traditional connection between the first use of the new building and the consecration of it was severed. The consecration came to mark the liquidation of debts rather than the first use of the building. Services of "dedication" were developed to meet the need for special solemnities to mark the first use of the church. This arrangement received official recognition in the Book of Offices, compiled by the Liturgical Commission and commended for use by the General Convention of 1940. The rite in the second edition (1949) recovered some of the traditional material which had been omitted in the Prayer Book form for the consecration of a church: a marking of the threshold with the sign of the cross; a perambulation of the building with blessing of the font and other items of furniture, vessels, and ornaments; a blessing of the altar at the conclusion. Fol-

542

lowing the blessings, the altar was to be vested and the Eucharist celebrated. This rite made the later consecration of the church largely redundant.

The revised rite in this present Book restores the traditional connection of the first use of the building and its consecration. It includes expressive visible actions such as the classic Anglican perambulation of the building. There is greater lay participation. The Anglican ideal of putting the building to full use for the sacraments and pastoral offices is encouraged by the rubrics of the rite. In contrast to the emphasis upon the separation of the building from uses other than worship in many earlier Anglican forms, the present rite, in keeping with the general tradition through the centuries, recognizes that the building may also be used for educational, humanitarian, or social purposes, or for other suitable activities. The service may be adapted for special circumstances; relevant portions may be used for the blessing of alterations, additions, or new furnishings, or for the dedication of a private or institutional chapel or oratory.[1] A Litany of Thanksgiving for a Church is also provided for use on the anniversary of the dedication of a church or on other suitable occasions (pp. 578–579).

Concerning the Service (p. 566)

The first of these directions makes clear that the service is designed for the dedication and consecration of a church and its furnishings. Portions of the rite may be used for the dedication of furnishings or parts of a building, or for the dedication of a chapel or oratory within another building. For special circumstances the service may be adapted according to directions given on page 576.

The second and third paragraphs state principles upon which the rite is based: it is designed for a time when the building is ready for regular use as a place of worship. The consecration of the building does not preclude its function for educational, social, or other suitable activities.

The fourth and fifth paragraphs deal with the participants in the rite. The consecration of a church is traditionally the prerogative of the bishop. The rector or minister in charge, as well as the warden or other representative of the congregation, has a part in the prayer of consecration. Neighboring ministers should be invited to participate and may be assigned appropriate parts in the rite. Lay persons pour water into the font, read the lessons which precede the Gospel, vest the altar, place the vessels on it, light the candles, and participate in

---

[1] The original draft upon which this rite is based was prepared by Margaret Sloan.

543

other ways. If possible, the architect, builders, musicians, artists, bene-factors, and friends who have contributed to the building or to the service of dedication should participate in the rite.

A special order for thanksgiving and recommitment to mission and ministry is provided when a building has been used for a period of time without having been consecrated (see pp. 577–579).

The Dedication and Consecration of a Church (pp. 567–579)

The Gathering of the Clergy and People (p. 567)

The clergy and people gather with the bishop in a place apart in order that they may enter the church in procession, dramatically sig-nifying the church's action in taking occupancy of the new building.

The Exhortation (p. 567)

A model provided for the opening address of the bishop states the purpose of the assembly. This replaces the opening exhortation of earlier American rites:

> Dearly beloved in the Lord; forasmuch as devout and holy men, as well under the Law as under the Gospel, moved either by the express command of God, or by the secret inspiration of the bless-ed Spirit, and acting agreeably to their own reason and sense of the natural decency of things, have erected houses for the public worship of God, and separated them from all unhallowed, worldly, and common uses, in order to fill men's minds with greater reverence for his glorious Majesty, and affect their hearts with more devotion and humility in his service; which pious works have been approved of and graciously accepted by our heavenly Father; Let us not doubt that he will also favourably approve our godly purpose of setting apart this place in solemn manner, for the several Offices of religious worship, and let us faithfully and devoutly beg his blessing on this our undertaking.

A Prayer (p. 567)

In this prayer we are reminded of three purposes of sacred build-ings: the worship of God, "the building up of the living, and the remembrance of the dead."

544

The Procession (pp. 567–568)

The congregation should circle the building, if possible, before going to the principal door (p. 575), while singing hymns or psalms in procession. Sacred vessels, ornaments, and decorations, the deed for the property and blueprint of the building, the keys, and tools used in construction may be carried in the procession. Opening the door of the church to receive the bishop has always been a normal feature of Anglican forms for the consecration of a church. The second edition of the Book of Offices (1949) included in the rite for the opening of a church a ceremony marking the threshold with the sign of the cross, an action incorporated in this rite. All three editions of the Book of Offices appoint Psalm 122 for entrance into the church. The second and third editions provide an antiphon:

> This is none other than the house of God,*
> And this is the gate of heaven.

Another psalm may be substituted; hymns and anthems may also be sung as the procession moves into the church.

The Prayer for the Consecration of the Church (pp. 568–569)

This prayer begins with Psalm 124:8 as a versicle and response. Its Trinitarian structure resembles the conclusion of the prayer of consecration in Bishop Lancelot Andrewes' form and many of the other seventeenth-century forms. Prayer Book Studies 28 noted:

> Since the building of a church today is not normally the work of a single donor or "founder," but represents the collective endeavor of the local laity, of their clergy, and of the diocese, it was felt appropriate for their representatives to have parts in the prayer.

The conclusion of the prayer is a quotation from the prayer of David after he had provided for the building of the temple (1 Chr. 29:11). It incorporates material from the prayer of consecration in earlier American rites, dating from the Convocation form of 1712:

> O Eternal God, mighty in power, and of majesty incomprehensible, whom the heaven of heavens cannot contain, much less the walls of temples made with hands; and who yet hast been gra-

545

ciously pleased to promise thy especial presence, wherever two or three of thy faithful servants shall assemble in thy Name, to offer up their praises and supplications unto thee; Vouchsafe, O Lord, to be present with us, who are here gathered together with all humility and readiness of heart, to consecrate this place to the honour of thy great Name; separating it henceforth from all unhallowed, ordinary, and common uses; and dedicating it to thy service, for reading thy holy Word, for celebrating thy holy Sacraments, for offering to thy glorious Majesty the sacrifices of prayer and thanksgiving, for blessing thy people in thy Name, and for all other holy offices: accept, O Lord, this service at our hands, and bless it with such success as may tend most to thy glory, and the furtherance of our happiness both temporal and spiritual; through Jesus Christ our blessed Lord and Saviour. *Amen.*

The Dedication of the Font (pp. 569–570)

In prior American rites following the Convocation form of 1712, a series of supplications followed the prayer of consecration. The first two were for those who would be baptized or would renew baptismal vows in that place. The present rite, like some of the earlier Anglican forms, indicates that the bishop move to the font, possibly during the singing of selected verses of a psalm or stanzas of a hymn (see p. 576). A prayer for those who will be baptized at the font is followed by a versicle and response (Eph. 4:4–6) and a sentence of dedication. A baptism may take place immediately, making use of an abbreviated form of the baptismal rite—an early Anglican custom. If there is no candidate for baptism, water may still be poured into the font by children or other lay persons (see p. 575), and the thanksgiving over the water be said. The bishop may also consecrate oil of chrism for subsequent use (see p. 575).

The Dedication of the Lectern and (or) Pulpit (pp. 570–571)

Earlier American rites, following the Convocation form of 1712, provided a prayer for those who heard the word read and preached in this place. The present rite, like some prior Anglican forms, directs that the bishop move to the lectern (and then to the pulpit), possibly during the singing of selected verses of a psalm or hymn (see p. 576). A prayer is followed by a versicle and response (Ps. 19:14 or Ps. 119:105) and a sentence of dedication. A donor, lay reader, or other lay person brings forward a Bible and puts it in place (see p. 576). If, in accordance with ancient tradition, earlier Anglican custom, and current Roman Catholic legislation, one item of furniture serves for both the reading and preaching of the word, symbolizing the presence of Christ in his word as the altar symbolizes the presence of Christ in his sacrament, only one prayer, one versicle and response, and one sentence of dedication are used (see p. 576).

At the Liturgy of the Word (pp. 571–572)

A full liturgy of the word with three lessons is required. Previous to the 1928 revision the rite for the consecration of a church concluded with Morning Prayer and the Eucharist. Psalm 84 and lessons from 1 Kings and from Revelation were among those appointed in prior editions of the Prayer Book. Psalm 48 and the readings from 2 Samuel, 1 Corinthians, and Matthew 21 were in earlier Anglican rites for the consecration of a church; the lections from 1 Peter and Matthew 21 are the Epistle and Gospel appointed as propers for the feast of the dedication of a church in the 1928 revision.

The Dedication of an Instrument of Music (p. 572)

American rites, before the 1979 Book, did not provide for the dedication of a musical instrument within the ceremony of dedication of a church. The present ceremony directs that the bishop move to an appropriate place, possibly during the singing of selected verses of a psalm or hymn (p. 576). The prayer is followed by a versicle and response (Ps. 150:3–4) and a sentence of dedication. The instrument dedicated should be silent until this point (see p. 575), but the dedication is followed by instrumental music, or a hymn, or anthem.

The Sermon or Address (p. 572)

The additional directions suggest that it is suitable for a warden or other lay person to outline the plans of the congregation for witness to the gospel, and that the bishop may respond, indicating the place of the congregation within the life of the diocese (see p. 576).

Other Pastoral Offices (p. 572)

In accordance with early Anglican custom it is suitable for other pastoral offices to be celebrated at this point in the rite. The additional suggestions specifically indicate Thanksgiving for the Birth or Adoption of a Child, Commitment to Christian Service, or Blessing of Oil for the Sick (see p. 576). On occasion, marriages or other rites have been performed within this context. In at least one historic instance the rite included the blessing of the churchyard and the burial of the dead.

The Nicene Creed (p. 572)

The Apostles' Creed may have been said if a baptism or other pastoral office was celebrated. If not, the Nicene Creed is said or sung at this point in the rite.

The Prayers of the People (p. 572)

Though any of the usual forms may be used, the additional directions suggest that a form be composed especially for this occasion, "having due regard for the distinctive nature of the community, and with commemoration of benefactors, donors, artists, artisans, and others" (p. 576). The bishop's concluding collect contains a supplication for all those who will pray in this place, a common feature of earlier Anglican forms.

Thanksgiving for the Adornment and Furnishings of the Building (p. 573)

This is a general prayer of dedication for ornaments or furnishings which cannot be mentioned individually.

The Dedication of the Altar (pp. 573–574)

American rites, following the Convocation form of 1712, contained a supplication for those who would receive Holy Communion in this place. The 1979 Book restores the dedication of the altar as a climactic point in the rite, as it was in the Irish order (though not in most of the other seventeenth-century forms). The altar is a sign of the heavenly altar and the high priesthood of Christ, and the table of the eucharistic feast. The benefits of Holy Communion are enumerated: sustenance and refreshment, forgiveness of sins, unity with one another, and strength for service. This form, which is dependent upon the Irish form from the seventeenth century, was drafted by the Rev. Dr. H. Boone Porter.

A rubric indicates that it is appropriate for bells to be rung and music played after the dedication of the altar. The additional directions note that the altar may be censed. The altar is vested, vessels are placed upon it, and candles lighted. Donors of furnishings, or other lay persons, may cover and decorate the altar—an appropriate action for members of the Altar Guild (p. 576).

The Peace (p. 574)

The bishop initates the exchange of the peace.

At the Eucharist (p. 574)

The Eucharist continues with the offertory. The bishop, as chief celebrant, should be joined by the priests of the parish and other clergy in concelebration. The proper preface of the season or one suited to the name of the church may be used instead of that for the dedication of a church (see p. 576). After the postcommunion prayer (and hymn) the bishop blesses the people and they are dismissed by a deacon or priest.

Additional Directions (pp. 575–579)

The first paragraph notes that the complete form is to be used at the opening of a church or chapel, and that it is not required that the premises be debt-free or that they be owned by the congregation. Commentary on the paragraphs which immediately follow has been incorporated within the commentary on the text of the rite.

For the Dedication of Churches and Chapels
in Special Cases (pp. 576–577)

These directions explicitly permit adaptation of the rite for special cases when a building will serve other purposes, be shared with other Christian bodies, or function as a private chapel or oratory.

For the Dedication of Furnishings, or
Parts of a Church or Chapel (p. 577)

These directions point out that, in accordance with tradition, the blessing of a new font or of an altar is reserved for the bishop, but that other portions of this rite may be used by a bishop or priest for the blessing of alterations, additions, or new furnishings. Directions explain the adaptation and use of portions of the rite in such circumstances. (See *The Book of Occasional Services*, pp. 177–194, for forms for the dedication of church furnishings and ornaments.)

For a Church or Chapel Long in Use (pp. 577–579)

During the colonial period it was impossible to obtain episcopal consecration for new churches, although at least on some occasions special services and festivities were held when a church was first opened for use. It is safe to assume that many of these churches,

549

hallowed by long use, were never consecrated by a bishop at a later time. The situation was further complicated in 1868 when the canons forbade the consecration of a church until it was debt-free. For these and other reasons, many churches have never been consecrated; it is hardly fitting to speak of consecrating such churches, as if they were not already holy places, having been consecrated by use itself. The present Book provides an order which includes thanksgiving for a church, commemoration of benefactors, and a reaffirmation of commitment, to be used on momentous occasions within the life of a congregation—the paying off of a debt, recognition as a parish, or a major anniversary.

A Litany of Thanksgiving for a Church (pp. 578–579)

This litany, based upon a draft by the Rev. Donald L. Garfield, incorporates phrases from the prayer of consecration in prior editions of the rite (see above, pp. 545–546). It recalls Solomon's prayer at the dedication of the temple (1 Kg. 8:27), our Lord's promise to be present with those gathered in his name (Mt. 18:19–20), and Psalm 46:11. The conclusion is a quotation from the prayer of David after he had provided for the building of the temple (1 Chr. 29:11), which also forms the conclusion of the prayer of consecration in the rite of the consecration of a church (Prayer Book, p. 569).

The Psalter (pp. 581-808)

The psalter of the Great Bible of 1539, Coverdale's revision of his translation made in 1535, became the psalter of the 1549 Prayer Book. The translation was not based on the Hebrew original but upon the old Latin psalter which had been translated from the Greek Septuagint.[1] The psalter of the Great Bible was, in other words, a translation from a Latin translation of a Greek translation of a Hebrew original.

The Scottish Prayer Book of 1637 used the psalms, as well as the Epistles, Gospels and other scriptural passages, from the King James Version (1611). This translation had been made directly from the Hebrew, unlike Coverdale's, and has generally been considered more accurate. The English revision of 1662 used the Epistles and Gospels from the King James Version in place of those in the Great Bible, but conservative sentiment retained the Coverdale psalter. Over the course of years hundreds of changes have been made in the Prayer Book psalter to correct, to clarify, or to provide substitutions for obsolete words (1790, 1793, 1822, 1845, 1871, and 1892). The 1928 revision made over one hundred changes after comparison with the Hebrew texts.

The psalter in the 1979 Prayer Book is the result of a much more thorough and systematic re-examination of the Hebrew text in the light of recent scholarship. Obsolete and archaic words have been removed and inaccurate renderings emended, but the rhythmic expression which characterized Coverdale's work has been carefully preserved. So that the psalms may be congruent with the services in

---

[1] The Septuagint is a Greek translation from the Hebrew, dating from the second century B.C.

551

traditional language, the vocabulary has been largely restricted to that available to Coverdale. To retain the original Hebrew form and to facilitate singing or recitation, the psalms have been printed in lines of poetry. This revision of the psalter has been judged so successful for liturgical use, both for reading and for singing, that it has been adopted by the Lutherans in their recent liturgical revision.

The 1549 Prayer Book directed that the entire psalter be read each month in the course of the daily offices. The daily office lectionary of the 1979 Prayer Book provides for distribution of the psalter over a seven-week period. For the convenience of those who wish to recite the psalter on a monthly basis, however, the Book has retained the traditional Anglican divisions of the psalter into consecutive portions for morning and evening during a thirty-day period.

The psalter in the Great Bible followed the Hebrew divisions of the psalms rather than those of the old Latin version. The Latin incipit was therefore provided as well as the number of the psalm according to the Hebrew divisions. This information is still sometimes important to those engaged in research on the psalms or to those seeking traditional musical settings.

For commentary on the distribution and use of the psalms in the daily offices and the Eucharist, see above, pp. 106–107, 132–133, 138, 144–145, 316–317, 327–329, 348–349, and 387–388.

Concerning the Psalter (pp. 582–584)

The first page of this section lists and explains the four traditional methods of reading or singing the psalms. *Direct recitation* is the reading or singing of the psalm or section of a psalm in unison, an appropriate method when the selection is relatively brief. *Antiphonal recitation* is the method traditionally used in the public recitation of the daily office. Two groups of readers or singers alternate verse by verse in the reading or singing, concluding with the Gloria Patri (or antiphon) in unison. *Responsorial recitation* is the traditional method for the invitatory psalm of the daily office, for the gradual psalm of the Eucharist, and for processional psalms in the Eucharist (at the entrance, at the offertory, and at the communion). The verses of the psalm are sung by a solo voice, or by a choir, and the choir and congregation sing a refrain after each verse or group of verses. *Responsive recitation,* in which the minister and congregation alternate verse by verse, has been used frequently in Anglican worship when the psalms are read rather than sung. If the selection is lengthy, this method is certainly less tiring than direct recitation, though not so satisfactory as antiphonal reading.

The two paragraphs at the top of page 583 explain the parallelism of Hebrew poetry.

The next paragraph deals with the asterisk. The 1662 revision divided the psalms into half verses to facilitate unison reading or chanting. The listing of the psalter on the title page of that revision was followed by the words "Pointed as They Are To Be Sung Or Said in Churches." In reading, the asterisk is observed by a distinct pause; in plainchant or Anglican chant the asterisk marks the conclusion of the first half of the chant.

The next four paragraphs explain the distinctions between the three terms used in the psalms to refer to God—Elohim, Adonai, and YHWH—and the way in which the psalter distinguishes the use of these terms.

The final paragraph notes that, though prior editions of the Prayer Book psalter had translated the Hebrew shout of praise "Hallelujah" as "Praise (ye) the Lord," the Hebrew form is retained in this Book.

Prayers and Thanksgivings

The 1549 Prayer Book included only two special prayers, for rain (see No. 43, below) and for fair weather. These were printed after the eucharistic rite, following six alternative collects for use after the offertory when the Eucharist was not to be celebrated (see Nos. 57, 60, 65, and 68, below; see also pp. 189 and 407 in this commentary). In the 1552 revision these two prayers were printed at the end of the Litany, allowing more frequent use, and additional prayers were added: two alternatives for use in time of dearth and famine, a prayer for time of war, and a prayer for time of a common plague or sickness. The 1559 revision printed the occasional prayers after, rather than within, the Litany, and added a general collect. Two new prayers were also placed near the end of the Litany, one for the queen and one for the clergy and people (see No. 9, below). The 1604 Book provided occasional thanksgivings corresponding to the occasional prayers of the 1559 revision: for rain, for fair weather, for plenty, for peace, and two alternative thanksgivings for deliverance from plague or sickness.

The revisers in 1662 added a prayer for parliament, two alternative prayers to be said daily during ember weeks (see pp. 212–213, above), and a "Collect or Prayer for all Conditions of men" (see No. 2, below) to be used after Morning Prayer on days other than Sundays, Wednesdays, and Fridays, those days when the Litany was to be said. The 1662 Book also included a general thanksgiving (see above, p. 130) and a thanksgiving "that it hath pleased thee to appease the seditious tumults which have been lately raised up amongst us."

In the first American revision of 1789 the prayer for parliament was revised to become a prayer for congress; the prayer for fair weather from *A New Liturgy* (1749) replaced that of the 1549 and later editions; the first of the 1552 prayers for use in the time of dearth and famine was revised, and the second was dropped. A prayer created partially from phrases in the visitation office replaced the prayer for a time of sickness, and new prayers were added for a sick person (see above, p. 468), for a sick child, for a person or persons going to sea (similar to a prayer in the King's Chapel liturgy), and for a person under affliction (see No. 55, below). Bishop Samuel Seabury had included these new prayers in a manuscript of liturgical forms he had compiled earlier and apparently brought with him to the convention. These may have been the four occasional prayers which the Massachusetts convention of 1785 asked Edward Bass and Nathaniel Fisher to prepare. A prayer for prisoners sentenced to die, revised from a form in *A New Liturgy*, was also added. The General Convention of 1799 approved a prayer for conventions, to be printed in the minutes; the convention of 1835 ordered that it be added to the Prayer Book. In 1789 the alternative thanksgiving for deliverance from plague was omitted. Thanksgivings were added for recovery from sickness (see Thanksgiving No. 9, below) and for safe return from sea. The thanksgiving for women after childbirth (see above, pp. 445–446) was also printed among the occasional thanksgivings and could be used as an alternative to the whole of the office. The prayer for all conditions of men and the general thanksgiving were printed in the daily offices rather than among the occasional prayers.

Before the 1892 revision a great many additional prayers were proposed for inclusion, but few were added: For the Unity of God's People (No. 14, below), For Missions (above, pp. 127–128), and alternative prayers for the rogation days (Nos. 29 and 42, below). One thanksgiving, for a child's recovery from sickness (Thanksgiving No. 11, below), was also added.

The 1928 revision included several prayers that had been proposed prior to 1892.[1] A number of others were added, either among the occasional prayers or in a new section of additional prayers printed after the forms for family prayer.[2]

The present Prayer Book has grouped together the occasional prayers and occasional thanksgivings. A table of contents is provided for this section, and cross references given for other suitable prayers

---

[1] Nos. 18, 35, 45, 58, and 64, below. Also see above, pp. 125, 126, 143, 176, 177, and 475.

[2] Nos. 1, 5, 7, 15, 19, 20, 31, 38, 46, 51, 52, 54, 63, and 70 (1 and 2). Also see above, pp. 125, 172–173, 210 (two prayers), 215–216 (four prayers), 469, and 497.

located elsewhere in the Book (pp. 810–813). Thirty-eight new prayers, two new graces, and nine new thanksgivings have been added.

Prayers and Thanksgivings (pp. 814–841)

Prayers for the World (pp. 814–816)

1. For Joy in God's Creation (p. 814)

This prayer by the Rev. Dr. John W. Suter, Jr., first appeared in *A Book of Collects,* edited by him and his father in 1919, and was added to the Prayer Book in 1928. It is closely parallel to the prayer by his father which is the collect for the Wednesday in Easter Week and the Third Sunday of Easter (pp. 171, 173, 223, and 224–225 in the Prayer Book). The conclusion is based on Colossians 1:16. In this revision a portion of the petition has been incorporated in the Prayer for the whole state of Christ's Church and the world (p. 329).

2. For All Sorts and Conditions of Men (pp. 814–815)

Some scholars have attributed this prayer to the Rev. Dr. Peter Gunning, master of St. John's College, Cambridge, and bishop of Chichester (1670–1674) and of Ely (1675–1684). Others believe it to be the work of Robert Sanderson or Edward Reynolds. It was included in the 1662 revision, among the occasional prayers, for use in Morning Prayer on those days when the Litany was not appointed to be read. The American Book of 1789 printed it in both Morning and Evening Prayer, for use daily in Evening Prayer and for use in Morning Prayer except on Wednesdays, Fridays, and Sundays, when the Litany was to be read. The optional phrase was omitted in 1789 but restored in 1892. The petition for those "who profess and call themselves Christians" is generally assumed to have been directed at the Puritans. Some scholars argue that this prayer was composed during the interregnum—when the Book of Common Prayer was outlawed—for use in place of the prayer for the church of the eucharistic rite. Since the word "Finally" appears so early in the course of the prayer, it has been believed that the prayer originally contained petitions for the king and clergy which were removed when the prayer was accepted by the revisers, since prayers for both the king and clergy were to be said immediately before this form. The prayer includes phrases from Psalm 67:2, John 16:13, Psalm 25:9, and Ephesians 4:3.

556

3. *For the Human Family* (p. 815)

This prayer, new to the 1979 Book, was drafted by the Rev. Dr. Charles P. Price, chair of the drafting committee for prayers and thanksgivings.

4. *For Peace* (p. 815)

This prayer, from *Occasional Prayers Reconsidered* (S.P.C.K., 1930), is new to this revision.

5. *For Peace Among the Nations* (p. 816)

Bishop Edward Lambe Parsons composed this prayer, first included in the Prayer Book in 1928. Its scriptural sources are James 3:18 and Revelation 11:15.

6. *For our Enemies* (p. 816)

This is a revised form of a prayer from an anonymous correspondent, printed in *The Living Church* (September 8, 1968).

Prayers for the Church (pp. 816–819)

7. *For the Church* (p. 816)

This prayer, added to the Prayer Book in 1928, was written by Archbishop William Laud. It was first published in *A Summarie of Devotions* (1677), adapted from his manuscripts. The original version reads:

> Gracious Father, I humbly beseech Thee for Thy holy Catholic Church, fill it with all truth, in all truth with all peace. Where it is corrupt, purge it; where it is in error, direct it; where it is superstitious, rectify it; where anything is amiss, reform it; where it is right, strengthen and confirm it; where it is in want, furnish it; where it is divided and rent asunder, make up the breaches of it; O Thou Holy One of Israel. Amen.

8. *For the Mission of the Church* (pp. 816–817)

Caroline Rose (Mrs. Lawrence) drafted this prayer which is new to this revision.

9. *For Clergy and People* (p. 817)

This prayer dates to the Gelasian sacramentary where it is the collect for a Mass in a monastery (no. 1429) and the postcommunion for a Mass for a household (no. 1552). In the supplement to the

Gregorian it is the collect for a Mass for abbots and congregations (no. 1308); in the Sarum missal it is the collect in a Mass for clergy and people. It was among the collects printed after the Litany in 1544, and entered the Prayer Book in 1559. The revision of 1662 printed it in Morning and Evening Prayer after the fixed collects, to be used daily except when the Litany was said after Morning Prayer. The American Book of 1789 substituted "from whom cometh every good and perfect gift" (Jas. 1:17) for "who alone workest great marvels," and "Bishops, and other Clergy, and upon the Congregations committed to their charge" for "Bishops and Curates, and all Congregations committed to their charge." In the 1892 revision permission was given to omit this prayer at Evening Prayer; the 1928 Book extended that permission to Morning Prayer as well.

10. For the Diocese (p. 817)

This new prayer was written by the Standing Liturgical Commission. Some phrases were suggested by prayers for the diocese in *The Prayer Manual*.[1]

11. For the Parish (p. 817)

The prayer "For the Congregation and District of a Charge" in the Scottish revision of 1929 is the basis for this prayer. The longer form of that Book reads:

> Almighty and Everlasting God, who dost govern all things in heaven and earth: mercifully hear our prayers, and grant unto us in this Congregation and District all things that are needful for our spiritual welfare; strengthen and confirm the faithful; visit and relieve the sick; bless and protect the children; turn and soften the wicked; arouse the careless; recover the fallen; restore the penitent; remove all hindrances to the advancement of thy truth; and bring all to be of one heart and mind within the fold of thy holy Church, to the honour and glory of thy holy Name; through Jesus Christ our Lord. *Amen.*

The prayer is new to the 1979 revision.

12. For a Church Convention or Meeting (p. 818)

This prayer, composed by the Standing Liturgical Commission for the 1979 Book, replaces a prayer composed by the bishops and

---

[1] Edited by F. B. Macnutt, London: A. R. Mowbray, 1951, nos. 564–569.

adopted by the deputies at the General Convention of 1799, "to be used at the meeting of the Convention, and to be printed with the Journal of the present Convention." The Convention of 1835 ordered that the prayer, based upon the conclusion of the Elizabethan homily for Whitsunday, be printed at the end of the occasional prayers. It read:

> Almighty and everlasting God, who by thy Holy Spirit didst preside in the Council of the Blessed Apostles, and hast promised, through thy Son Jesus Christ, to be with thy Church to the end of the world: We beseech thee to be present with the Council of thy Church *here* assembled in thy Name and Presence. Save *us* from all error, ignorance, pride, and prejudice; and of thy great mercy vouchsafe, we beseech thee, so to direct, sanctify, and govern *us* in *our* present work, by the mighty power of the Holy Ghost, that the comfortable Gospel of Christ may be truly preached, truly received, and truly followed, in all places, to the breaking down the kingdom of sin, Satan, and death; till at length the whole of thy dispersed sheep, being gathered into one fold, shall become partakers of everlasting life; through the merits and death of Jesus Christ our Saviour. *Amen.*

13. For the Election of a Bishop or other Minister (p. 818)

This prayer, new to the 1979 Book, is based upon one in the English revision of 1928. "Who will care for your people and equip us for our ministries" replaces "who shall feed thy flock according to thy will, and make ready a people acceptable unto thee."

14. For the Unity of the Church (p. 818)

The American Prayer Book, in the revision of 1892, first included this prayer which had been printed in a book issued for the armed ' forces during the Civil War. It had been in the English Book since 1714, at the accession of George I, in the Accession Service used on the anniversary of the coronation of a sovereign. The prayer was abbreviated from a longer form issued in the preceding decades. The earliest of the forms which includes this prayer is the one issued in 1689 for the accession of William and Mary. In it are allusions to Ephesians 4:3–6, Acts 4:32, and Romans 15:6.

15. For those about to be Baptized or to renew their Baptismal Covenant (p. 819)

A revised version of a prayer by Henry Somerset Walpole, bishop of Edinburgh (1920–1929), this form entered the Scottish Prayer

Book in 1912 and the American Book in 1928. The 1928 version, published under the title "For those about to be Confirmed," read:

> O God, who through the teaching of thy Son Jesus Christ didst prepare the disciples for the coming of the Comforter; Make ready, we beseech thee, the hearts and minds of thy servants who at this time are seeking to be strengthened by the gift of the Holy Spirit through the laying on of hands, that, drawing near with penitent and faithful hearts, they may evermore be filled with the power of his divine indwelling; through the same Jesus Christ our Lord. *Amen*

16. For Monastic Orders and Vocations (p. 819)

The Rev. Bonnell Spencer, O.H.C., composed this prayer which is new to the 1979 Book. The address alludes to 2 Corinthians 8:9.

17. For Church Musicians and Artists (p. 819)

This is the prayer of the Royal School of Church Music, revised to include in the petition mention of other artists as well as musicians. It is new to this revision.

Prayers for National Life (pp. 820–823)

18. For our Country (p. 820)

Though this prayer has sometimes been attributed to George Washington, it was written in 1882 by the Rev. George Lyman Locke during a visit at the home of William Reed Huntington, the most active member of the commission for Prayer Book revision which issued the Book of 1892. Included in the 1883 proposals in the service for Thanksgiving Day, this prayer did not enter the Prayer Book until 1928, when it was accepted in the emended form printed here.

19. For the President of the United States and all in Civil Authority (p. 820)

This was added to the Prayer Book in 1928 as an alternative to the prayer for the President in Morning Prayer (a revised form of that for the sovereign in the English Books). It has been attributed to Mr. George Zabriskie of the revision commission's Committee on Morning Prayer. It contains allusions to Psalm 8:1 and Isaiah 11:2.

20. For Congress or a State Legislature (p. 821)

Mr. George Zabriskie is considered to have been largely responsible for the final form of this prayer which was added in the 1928

560

Book. In the present revision "that they may enact such laws as shall please thee" replaces "that it may ordain for our governance only such things as please thee."

21. For Courts of Justice (p. 821)
This prayer was first included in the 1928 Book. Mr. George Zabriskie was responsible for the final form of the collect, which was the work of the revision commission. Its allusions are to Psalm 9:4, Isaiah 11:1–5, and the Te Deum laudamus.

22. For Sound Government (pp. 821–822)
Caroline Rose (Mrs. Lawrence) composed this new prayer.

23. For Local Government (p. 822)
This prayer, new to this Book, is a revised form of a prayer in the Canadian Prayer Book of 1959.

24. For an Election (p. 822)
The Forward Movement publication, *Prayers New and Old* (edited by Clement W. Welsh), contributed this new prayer.

25. For those in the Armed Forces of our Country (p. 823)
This new prayer is a slightly revised form of one which had been included in the *Armed Forces Prayer Book* (pp. 54–55) and in *A Prayer Book for the Armed Forces* (pp. 102–103). Its source was the Forward Movement publication, *Prayers for All Occasions* (edited by Francis J. Moore).

26. For those who suffer for the sake of Conscience (p. 823)
The Rev. Dr. Charles P. Price drafted this prayer, new to the present Book.

Prayers for the Social Order (pp. 823–827)

27. For Social Justice (p. 823)
This prayer, by an unknown author, is new to the 1979 Book.

28. In Times of Conflict (p. 824)
The source of this prayer is *The Grey Book* (Oxford University Press, 1923), a collection of proposals for the revision of the English Prayer Book. It is new to this revision.

29. For Agriculture (p. 824)

The original form of this collect was composed by the English revisers of 1689 for the Sunday before the rogation days. The collect used phrases from the prayers of the 1662 Book for time of dearth and famine, for rain, and for fair weather, and from the thanksgiving for fair weather, as well as 2 Thessalonians 3:12. The present prayer is an updated version of the original which read:

> Almighty God, who hast blessed the earth that it should be fruitful and bring forth everything that is necessary for the life of man, and hast commanded us to work with quietness and eat our own bread; bless us in all our labors and grant us such seasonable weather that we may gather in the fruits of the earth and ever rejoice in thy goodness to the praise of thy holy name, through Jesus Christ our Lord. Amen.

It was first added to the American Book in 1892 under the title "For Fruitful Seasons." In the 1892 and 1928 Books it was preceded by a rubric which commanded the use of this prayer or of an alternative (No. 42, below, p. 828 in the Prayer Book) at the daily office on Rogation Sunday and the rogation days.

30. For the Unemployed (p. 824)

This is a revision of the prayer of the Industrial Christian Fellowship.[1] The original version read:

> O Lord and heavenly Father, we commend to Thy care and protection the men and women of this land who are suffering distress and anxiety through lack of work. Strengthen and support them, we beseech Thee; and so prosper the counsels of those who govern and direct our industries, that Thy people may be set free from want and fear to work in peace and security, for the relief of their necessities and the well-being of this realm; through Jesus Christ our Lord. *Amen.*

31. For Schools and Colleges (p. 824)

The 1928 Book added the prayer of which this is the revision:

> Almighty God, we beseech thee, with thy gracious favour to behold our universities, colleges, and schools, that knowledge may

---

[1] Published in *The Prayer Manual*, ed. F. B. Macnutt, London: A. R. Mowbray, 1951, no. 117.

be increased among us, and all good learning flourish and abound. Bless all who teach and all who learn; and grant that in humility of heart they may ever look unto thee, who art the fountain of all wisdom; through Jesus Christ our Lord. *Amen.*

The prayer had been included in the English proposals of 1920; it was a revision of a prayer by an unknown author, from the Scottish Book of 1912.

32. For the Good Use of Leisure (p. 825)

This new prayer was drafted by the Rev. James G. Birney of the drafting committee on prayers and thanksgivings.

33. For Cities (p. 825)

The Rev. J. Robert Zimmerman of the drafting committee on prayers and thanksgivings drafted this new prayer.

34. For Towns and Rural Areas (p. 825)

This new prayer was drafted by the Rev. Dr. H. Boone Porter.

35. For the Poor and the Neglected (p. 826)

A prayer "For all Poor, Homeless, and Neglected Folk," first published among the proposals for the revision of 1892 in *The Book Annexed,* was added to the 1928 Book. Frederick Dan Huntington or William Reed Huntington is thought to be the author. President Franklin D. Roosevelt made it famous as "the Forgotten Man's Prayer." The 1928 version read:

O God, Almighty and merciful, who healest those that are broken in heart, and turnest the sadness of the sorrowful to joy; Let thy fatherly goodness be upon all that thou hast made. Remember in pity such as are this day destitute, homeless, or forgotten of their fellow-men. Bless the congregation of thy poor. Uplift those who are cast down. Mightily befriend innocent sufferers, and sanctify to them the endurance of their wrongs. Cheer with hope all discouraged and unhappy people, and by thy heavenly grace preserve from falling those whose penury tempteth them to sin; though they be troubled on every side, suffer them not to be distressed; though they be perplexed, save them from despair. Grant this, O Lord, for the love of him, who for our sakes became poor, thy Son, our Saviour Jesus Christ. *Amen.*

The prayer in the 1979 Book is an updated version.

36. For the Oppressed (p. 826)

Caroline Rose (Mrs. Lawrence) drafted this new prayer.

37. For Prisons and Correctional Institutions (p. 826)

The Rev. Dr. Charles P. Price drafted this prayer which replaces a prayer for prisoners adopted in the American Prayer Book of 1789 from the 1749 proposal *A New Liturgy.* The 1928 version read:

> O God, who sparest when we deserve punishment, and in thy wrath rememberest mercy; We humbly beseech thee, of thy goodness, to comfort and succour all prisoners [especially those who are condemned to die]. Give them a right understanding of themselves, and of thy promises; that trusting wholly in thy mercy, they may not place their confidence anywhere but in thee. Relieve the distressed, protect the innocent, awaken the guilty; and forasmuch as thou alone bringest light out of darkness, and good out of evil, grant to these thy servants, that by the power of thy Holy Spirit they may be set free from the chains of sin, and may be brought to newness of life; through Jesus Christ our Lord. *Amen.*

38. For the Right Use of God's Gifts (p. 827)

This collect, new to the 1928 Prayer Book, is a revised version of a prayer "For the Rich" from a Book of Offices proposed for publication to the General Convention of 1889. In the present Book the petition is incorporated in the prayer for the church in The Holy Eucharist: Rite One (p. 329).

39. For those who Influence Public Opinion (p. 827)

The 1979 Book added this prayer, in a slightly revised form, from *The Pastor's Prayer Book,*[2] which gives as its source E. Milner-White's *The Boys' Prayer Book.*

Prayers for the Natural Order (pp. 827–828)

40. For Knowledge of God's Creation (p. 827)

The Rev. J. Robert Zimmerman, of the drafting committee for prayers and thanksgivings, drafted this new prayer.

---

[1] *The Pastor's Prayer Book,* ed. Robert N. Rodenmayer, New York: Oxford University Press, 1960, no. 424.

41. For the Conservation of Natural Resources (p. 827)

This new collect was drafted by the Rev. Dr. Charles W. F. Smith.

42. For the Harvest of Lands and Waters (p. 828)

This prayer is a revised version of the second of two prayers new to the 1892 Book; one of the prayers was to be used in the daily office on Rogation Sunday and the rogation days. This prayer was taken from a collection authorized by Cortlandt Whitehead, bishop of Pittsburgh (1882–1922), for use in the diocese. Allusions in it are to Psalms 145:17 and 104:31.

43. For Rain (p. 828)

This is a slightly revised version of a prayer in the 1549 Prayer Book, printed along with a prayer for fair weather after the text of the eucharistic rite. These were the only occasional prayers in that Book. The 1552 revision printed these prayers, and other occasional prayers, after the Litany. The scriptural allusion is to Matthew 6:33.

44. For the Future of the Human Race (p. 828)

The Standing Liturgical Commission drafted this new prayer.

Prayers for Family and Personal Life (pp. 828–833)

45. For Families (pp. 828–829)

Frederick Dan Huntington, bishop of Central New York (1869–1904), wrote this prayer. Although included in *The Book Annexed* (1883), it was not added to the 1892 revision. The 1928 Book placed it among the additional prayers of family prayer. It includes a number of biblical allusions: Psalm 68:6, Hebrews 12:15, Galatians 5:26, 2 Peter 1:5–6, Genesis 2:24, and Malachi 4:6.

46. For the Care of Children (p. 829)

The Rev. Dr. John W. Suter, Jr., wrote the original form of this prayer which first entered the Prayer Book in 1928. It was based upon a much longer prayer written by the Rev. William Austin Smith. The petition of the 1928 version read "Give us light and strength so to train them, that they may love whatsoever things are pure and lovely and of good report." The biblical allusion is to Philippians 4:8.

47. For Young Persons (p. 829)

This is a new collect drafted by Sister Ann Brooke Bushong of the Church Army.

48. *For Those Who Live Alone* (p. 829)

This is a new collect drafted by the Rev. Dr. Paul E. Langpaap.

49. *For the Aged* (p. 830)

Charles W. F. Smith and Ivy Watkins Smith composed this new prayer.

50. *For a Birthday* (p. 830)

This new prayer was written by the Rev. Dr. Charles P. Price.

51. *For a Birthday* (p. 830)

This is an abbreviated version of the Groton School Graduates' Prayer, written by William Amory Gardner, one of the three original members of the faculty. New to the 1928 Book, it includes allusions to Philippians 4:7 and the Great Litany.

52. *For the Absent* (p. 830)

This prayer, based upon Psalm 139:6–9, can be traced back to *An Order of Family Prayer* (1845) which was compiled by Jonathan M. Wainwright, provisional bishop of New York (1852–54). It entered the Prayer Book in 1928.

53. *For Travelers* (p. 831)

New to the 1979 Book, this is a slightly revised form of a prayer in the Canadian Prayer Book of 1959.

54. *For those we Love* (p. 831)

This is an emended version of a prayer published by Charles Lewis Slattery, a member of the revision commission, in his *Prayers for Private and Family Use* (1922). It had been printed in *The Churchman,* January 19, 1918, as a revised form of a prayer which can be traced to *Family Prayers and Bible Readings* (1876), published in London. The 1928 American Book included it among the additional prayers of family prayer. The original text read:

> O Thou who hast ordered this wondrous world, who knowest all things in earth and heaven, so fill our hearts with trust in thee, that by night and by day, at all times and in all seasons, we may, without fear, commit those who are dear to us to thy never-failing love for this life and the life to come.

55. *For a Person in Trouble or Bereavement* (p. 831)

This is one of the occasional prayers introduced in the revision of 1789. Four, each of which was emended somewhat, are found in the same order in a manuscript of liturgical forms which Bishop Samuel Seabury had compiled from such diverse sources as the writings of Bishop Thomas Wilson of Sodor and Man, the Scottish liturgy, and the revised Prayer Book of King's Chapel in Boston. These may have been the four occasional prayers the Massachusetts convention of 1785 asked Edward Bass and Nathaniel Fisher to prepare. (Another of these prayers is retained in the 1979 Book as the first of the prayers for the sick on page 458.) The longer version of the 1789 and 1892 Books read:

> O merciful God, and heavenly Father, who hast taught us, in thy holy Word, that thou dost not willingly afflict or grieve the children of men, look with pity, we beseech thee, upon the sorrows of thy *servant*, for whom our prayers are desired. In thy wisdom, thou hast seen fit to visit *him* with trouble and to bring distress upon *him*. Remember *him*, O Lord, in mercy; sanctify thy fatherly correction to *him; endue his* soul with patience under *his* affliction, and with resignation to thy blessed will; comfort *him* with a sense of thy goodness; lift up thy countenance upon *him,* and give *him* peace, through Jesus Christ our Lord. *Amen.*

The address is based upon Lamentations 3:33, and the conclusion upon the Aaronic benediction in Numbers 6:24–26. (Compare the final prayer at the Reception of the Body, p. 467.)

56. *For the Victims of Addiction* (p. 831)

This new prayer was drafted by the Rev. Dr. Charles W. F. Smith.

57. *For Guidance* (p. 832)

This collect dates to the Gregorian sacramentary (no. 198) where it is one of the prayers to be said (after a lesson) in the liturgy of the word during the vigil at the climax of the Lenten ember days, as it also is in the Sarum missal. The 1549 Prayer Book retained it as one of six collects for alternative use after the offertory on occasions when there was no celebration of the Eucharist. In the 1552 revision the use of these collects was permitted after the collects of the daily offices or the Eucharist, or after the Litany, at the discretion of the minister. The 1662 Book required this collect prior to the blessing in all three ordination rites. The American Prayer Book of 1789 substituted the initial word "Direct" for "Prevent."

58. For Guidance (p. 832)

The 1928 Prayer Book added this collect, one of the original prayers printed in the appendix of William Bright's *Ancient Collects* (p. 234). Scriptural allusions include Psalm 25:8, Isaiah 11:2, Psalm 36:9, and Jeremiah 31:9.

59. For Quiet Confidence (p. 832)

The Rev. Dr. John W. Suter, Jr., composed this prayer which was published in *A Book of Collects* (1919) and added to the 1928 Prayer Book. It incorporates phrases from Isaiah 30:15 and Psalm 46:11.

60. For Protection (p. 832)

The Gelasian sacramentary is the original source for this collect (no. 1313), which is also in the supplement to the Gregorian (no. 1317), the Bobbio missal (no. 400), and the Sarum missal. In all four texts it was a collect in a votive Mass for travelers. The 1549 Book retained it as one of six collects, one of which was to be used after the offertory when there was to be no Holy Communion. The 1552 revision permitted the use of these collects after the collects of the daily offices or the Eucharist, or after the Litany, at the discretion of the minister.

61. A Prayer of Self-Dedication (pp. 832–833)

William Temple, Archbishop of Canterbury (1942–1944), wrote this prayer which is new to the 1979 Book.[1]

62. A Prayer attributed to St. Francis (p. 833)

This prayer, by an unknown author, cannot be traced back earlier than the present century.

Other Prayers (pp. 833–835)

63. In the Evening (p. 833)

In or before 1876, the Rev. George W. Douglas found (or composed) this prayer from a passage in Sermon XX of a volume of sermons by John Henry Newman, *Sermons on Subjects of the Day*.[2] It was added to the Prayer Book in the 1928 revision.

---

[1] *The Prayer Manual*, no. 255.
[2] See *The Living Church*, June 8, 1935.

568

64. Before Worship (p. 833)

This prayer, added to the Prayer Book in 1928, is one of the original collects included in the appendix of William Bright's *Ancient Collects* (p. 233). The address joins Zechariah 12:10 and John 4:23. Revisers in 1928 omitted the opening clause which was based on James 1:17, "from whom every good prayer cometh."

65. For the Answering of Prayer (p. 834)

This prayer is also printed for use at the conclusion of the Great Litany (p. 153). For commentary, see above, p. 161.

66. Before Receiving Communion (p. 834)

The Book of Common Worship of the Church of South India included this prayer which comes from the old Mozarabic liturgy. The 1979 revision is the first American Prayer Book to contain it.

67. After Receiving Communion (p. 834)

A revised version of this collect is printed in the 1979 Book as the collect for the votive "Of the Holy Eucharist" (pp. 210 and 252). For commentary, see above, p. 209.

68. After Worship (p. 834)

A collect which reflects the Renaissance-Reformation emphasis upon the Scriptures, this prayer was composed for the 1549 Book, one of the six collects provided for use after the offertory when there was to be no communion. The 1552 Book allowed the use of these collects after the collects of the daily office or Eucharist, or after the Litany, at the minister's discretion.

69. On Sunday (p. 835)

The Rev. Dr. Charles P. Price drafted this new prayer.

70. Grace at Meals (p. 835)

Jewish prayers at meals were always blessings of God rather than petitions for a blessing upon the food or the recipients. The third of these four forms is adapted from the Jewish *Authorized Daily Prayer Book*. The source of the other forms, which have been in common use for many years, is unknown. The first two entered the Prayer Book in 1928; the other two are new to the 1979 Book.[1]

---

[1] Prayers before meals had been included in the Gelasian sacramentary (nos. 1595–1602) and other medieval liturgical books.

General Thanksgivings (pp. 836–837)

1. A General Thanksgiving (p. 836)
This is a new prayer drafted by the Rev. Dr. Charles P. Price.

2. A Litany of Thanksgiving (pp. 836–837)
This new litany, drafted by the Rev. Dr. Massey H. Shepherd, Jr., may be used in place of the prayers of the people on Thanksgiving Day (see pp. 194 and 246 in the Prayer Book).

Thanksgivings for the Church (p. 838)

3. For the Mission of the Church (p. 838)
Caroline Rose (Mrs. Lawrence) of the drafting committee on prayers and thanksgivings wrote this prayer.

4. For the Saints and Faithful Departed (p. 838)
The source of this prayer was the 1968 liturgy of the Consultation on Church Union. It is a revised version of the commemoration of saints in the Eucharist of the Taizé community.

Thanksgivings for National Life (pp. 838–839)

5. For the Nation (pp. 838–839)
Caroline Rose drafted this litany, new to the 1979 Book.

6. For Heroic Service (p. 839)
A new prayer in the 1979 Prayer Book, this was composed by Caroline Rose.

Thanksgiving for the Social Order (p. 840)

7. For the Diversity of Races and Cultures (p. 840)
Caroline Rose drafted this new prayer.

Thanksgivings for the Natural Order (p. 840)

8. For the Beauty of the Earth (p. 840)
A new prayer in the 1979 Book, this was written by Caroline Rose.

9. For the Harvest (p. 840)

This is a slightly revised form of a prayer dating to the Proposed Book of 1786 which included it for use after the General Thanksgiving at Morning Prayer on Thanksgiving Day. In the 1928 revision it was placed among the occasional thanksgivings under the title "A Thanksgiving to Almighty God for the Fruits of the Earth and all the other Blessings of his merciful Providence." It is based upon Psalm 145 with specific quotations from Proverbs 3:20 and Genesis 8:22. The final petition is adapted from the last prayer in Forms of Prayer to be Used at Sea of the 1662 English Book.

Thanksgivings for Family and Personal Life (p. 841)

10. For the Gift of a Child (p. 841)

Caroline Rose, of the committee on prayers and thanksgivings, drafted this new prayer.

11. For the Restoration of Health (p. 841)

The thanksgiving "For a Child's Recovery from Sickness" entered the Prayer Book in 1892. It was a variant of the thanksgiving in the rite for the Thanksgiving of Women after Child-birth in the 1789 Book (see above, pp. 445–446). This present prayer is a moderately revised form.

An Outline of the Faith

The outline of the Christian faith in this Prayer Book is a revised and expanded version of the catechism or offices of instruction in previous Books. In the early church a person who hoped to be baptized was received as a catechumen and entered into a period, often three years in duration, of intensive instruction or catechesis (see above, pp. 252–256). In the early medieval period, after infant baptism had become the norm, some of the traditions of the old catechumenate were continued in ceremonies during which the Gospels, the creed, and the Lord's Prayer were given to the child in the weeks immediately preceding the Easter baptisms. Late in the middle ages, when baptism was compressed into one rite, a remnant of the old catechetical instruction survived in the exhortation to the godparents to see to it that the child learned the creed and the Lord's Prayer. Synods and councils of the period issued prescriptions for catechizing the faithful, and books were produced which contained explanations of the creed, the Lord's Prayer, and (sometimes) the Ave Maria, and other forms such as lists of the mortal sins, the godly virtues, and the works of mercy.

The word "catechism" apparently dates from the sixteenth century when the Renaissance-Reformation emphasis on religious instruction inspired both Protestants and Catholics to print many popular manuals. Luther's Short Catechism of 1529 was based upon the creed, the Lord's Prayer, and the Ten Commandments. Sixteenth-century English primers generally included these texts, sometimes with brief expositions. Those in "Marshall's Primer" (1534) owed much to Luther. The Royal Injunctions of 1536, 1538, and 1547 established these three articles as the basis for religious instruction. The *Bishops' Book* and the *King's Book* are each divided roughly into four parts, providing expositions of the creed, the Lord's Prayer, the Ten Commandments, and the sacraments. The same is true of "Cranmer's Catechism," essentially a translation of the German reformer Justus Jonas' Latin form of a German catechism, of uncertain authorship, supposedly used in Nürnberg. The catechism from Hermann's Consultation, following other German church orders, is introduced by questions and answers concerning the effects of baptism, and concludes with questions about the sacraments.

In the 1549 Book the catechism begins with questions and answers dealing with the effects of baptism. These are followed by the Apostles' Creed with a brief explanation of the doctrine of the Trinity, an abridged form of the Ten Commandments with a discussion of one's duty toward God and toward one's neighbor, and the Lord's Prayer with exposition of its meaning. Principal sources for this form were English Reformation formularies, the *Bishops' Book*, the *King's Book*, "An Exhortation to Prayer" published with the litany of 1544, the homilies of 1547, and "Cranmer's Catechism." The 1549 catechism is more succinct than most of the formularies and catechisms of the time and does not include a section on the sacraments. It is printed under the title "Confirmation, wherein is contained a catechism for children." The bishop or his appointee is, at the time of confirmation, to question the children in the catechism. A rubric requires that, as preparation for this, the priest once every six weeks, "openly in the church," for one-half hour before Evening Prayer "instruct and examine" in some part of the catechism those who have not been confirmed.

The principal change in the catechism of the 1552 Book was the printing of a fuller form of the Ten Commandments, with a scriptural preface: "I am the Lord thy God which have brought thee out of the land of Egypt, out of the house of bondage." The rubric was also changed to require that instruction be given on all Sundays and holy days to those who had not learned the catechism.

In response to requests of the Puritans, the revisers of the 1604 Book added a section on the sacraments. This is generally thought to have been the work of John Overall, Dean of St. Paul's, London, based on a catechism prepared by his predecessor, Alexander Nowell.

No substantial change was made in the catechism in 1662, but it was removed from the confirmation rite and given its own heading. The rubric directed that catechizing was to follow the second lesson at Evening Prayer.

The principal change in the first American Book (1789) was the substitution of the words "spiritually taken" for "verily and indeed taken" in the answer to the question concerning the "inward part, or thing signified" in the Lord's Supper.

No further changes were made in American Books until the 1928 revision which virtually duplicated the catechism in two offices of instruction. These provided additional questions and answers on the ministry, the church, and the duties and privileges of membership. These questions and answers were based principally upon a supplement to the catechism, adopted by the lower house of the Convocation of Canterbury in 1887, but never authorized.

Ever since the appearance of the 1549 Prayer Book, there have been frequent requests for expansion of the catechism. The 1979 Book contains a catechism that is substantially revised and enlarged. The principal sources of this revision, which was drafted by the Very Rev. Dr. Robert H. Greenfield, are the catechism and offices of instruction of the 1928 Book, "The Revised Catechism Authorized by the General Synod of the Church of England," first authorized in 1962, and "A Catechism" published in 1973 which had been prepared by a drafting committee of the Standing Liturgical Commission consisting of Bishop Stanley H. Atkins, chairman, the Rev. Donald L. Garfield, and Messrs. Dupuy Bateman, Jr., and Harrison Tillman.

Concerning the Catechism (p. 844)

These paragraphs explain the use of the catechism. It provides an outline for instruction, a point of departure for the teacher. It also provides a brief summary of the Church's teaching for an inquiring stranger.

In the revision of 1928 much of the content of the catechism, and some supplementary material, had been arranged as two offices of instruction. They included prayers and rubrics permitting or requiring hymns, so that they could be used as simple services. The final paragraph of these directions explains that sections of this catechism, with appropriate prayers and hymns, may be used in that manner.

These directions are basically those of the 1973 catechism. The phrase "for ease of reference" replaces "but it is not necessarily to be learned by heart and recited."

An Outline of the Faith Commonly Called
the Catechism (pp. 845–862)

Human Nature (p. 845)

This section, which deals with the nature of humankind and introduces themes of sin and of revelation, is new to the 1979 Prayer Book.

God the Father (p. 846)

Earlier Prayer Books contained a simple statement in the catechism: "I learn to believe in God the Father, who hath made me, and all the world." This section is an expansion of the statement.

The Old Covenant (pp. 846–847)

This theological introduction to the Ten Commandments is new to this revision.

The Ten Commandments (pp. 847–848)

The section on the Ten Commandments dates to the Prayer Book of 1549. In the 1979 revision, which is dependent upon the 1973 catechism, this discussion is rephrased in contemporary language, and concepts have been broadened and deepened to include social concerns and to emphasize spiritual virtues. Some of the new phrases come from the English revision of 1962, others are from the 1973 catechism. In earlier Prayer Books the explication of the first four commandments read:

> My duty towards God is To believe in him, to fear him, And to love him with all my heart, with all my mind, with all my soul, and with all my strength: To worship him, to give him thanks: To put my whole trust in him, to call upon him: To honour his holy Name and his Word: And to serve him truly all the days of my life.

The explication of the last six read:

> My duty towards my Neighbour is To love him as myself, and to do to all men as I would they should do unto me: To love, honour, and succour my father and mother: To honour and obey the civil authority: To submit myself to all my governors, teachers, spiritual pastors and masters: To order myself lowly and reverently to all my betters: To hurt nobody by word or deed: To be true and just in all my dealings: To bear no malice nor hatred in my heart: To keep my hands from picking and stealing, and my tongue from evil speaking, lying, and slandering: To keep my body in temperance, soberness, and chastity: Not to covet nor desire other men's goods: But to learn and labour truly to get mine own living, And to do my duty in that state of life unto which it shall please God to call me.

Sin and Redemption (pp. 848–849)

This section is new to the 1979 Prayer Book.

God the Son (pp. 849–850)

The catechism of earlier Prayer Books had dealt with this theme in one sentence: "I learn to believe . . . in God the Son, who hath redeemed me, and all mankind." The catechism of 1973 expanded this:

> I learn that God the Son, through whom all things were made, has redeemed me and all mankind by becoming man and dying for our sins. He was raised victorious over death, and has been exalted to the throne of God. There he reigns, our brother, our advocate, and our Lord. He will come again in glory to judge both the living and the dead.

The New Covenant (pp. 850–851)

The offices of instruction in the 1928 Prayer Book incorporated the Summary of the Law in answer to a question "What does our Lord Jesus Christ teach us about these Commandments?" In the catechism of 1973 the answer to this question was expanded to include the "New Commandment" (John 13:34). Both texts had also been inserted in the English revised catechism of 1962. The present Book sets the Summary of the Law and the New Commandment within the context of the New Covenant established by Jesus Christ.

The Creeds (pp. 851–852)

The earlier catechisms contained a recitation of "the Articles of thy Belief"—in the 1928 Book retitled "the Articles of the Christian Faith" in the offices of instruction—followed by a question and answer:

> *Question.* What dost thou chiefly learn in these Articles of thy Belief?
> *Answer.* First, I learn to believe in God the Father, who hath made me, and all the world.
> Secondly, in God the Son, who hath redeemed me, and all mankind.
> Thirdly, in God the Holy Ghost, who sanctifieth me, and all the people of God.

In the 1928 offices of instruction this summary statement was followed by a sentence concerning the Trinity, "And this Holy Trinity, One God, I praise and magnify," which introduced the Gloria Patri.

The English revision of 1962 added this conclusion, and mentioned the Nicene Creed along with the Apostles' Creed as a source of "a summary of the Christian Faith." That revision also amplified the summary of the creeds; these features, in turn, were part of the 1973 catechism, with some revision of the statements of summary. The 1979 Book defines the creeds as "statements of our basic beliefs about God." The three creeds of the Western church are then set in historic context, and the summary statements concerning the articles of belief are greatly expanded within the catechism (see pp. 846, 849–850, and 852–853 in the Prayer Book).

The Holy Spirit (pp. 852–853)

The catechism in earlier Prayer Books summarized the work of the Holy Spirit: "I learn to believe . . . in God the Holy Ghost, who sanctifieth me, and all the people of God." The 1928 text of the offices of instruction substituted "Holy Spirit" for "Holy Ghost" in this summary. The English revision of 1962 expanded the statement:

> The Church teaches that God the Holy Spirit inspires all that is good in mankind; that he came in his fullness at Pentecost to be the giver of life in the Church, and that he enables me to grow in likeness to Jesus Christ.

In the 1973 catechism the equivalent statement read:

> I learn that God the Holy Spirit is the Life-giver, who has spoken through the prophets. He came at Pentecost to be the giver of power in the Church, and he sanctifies me and all the people of God.

The 1979 Prayer Book adds questions and answers concerning the recognition of the presence of the Holy Spirit in our lives and the recognition of truths taught by the Holy Spirit.

The Holy Scriptures (pp. 853–854)

No statements concerning the Holy Scriptures were in the catechisms of prior Books. The Canadian revision of 1959, the English revised catechism of 1962, and the catechism of 1973 all include brief sections on the Bible. A few phrases in the present Book are adapted from the 1973 catechism. This section might be compared with Article VI (pp. 868–869) and with the solemn oath of the ordination rites (pp. 513, 526, and 538).

The Church (pp. 854–855)

In 1887 the lower house of the Convocation of Canterbury adopted a supplement to the catechism containing questions and answers on the church, the sacraments, and the ministry. The upper house did not adopt this, but the 1928 American Prayer Book and other recent Anglican revisions, including the Canadian revision of 1959 and the North Indian revision of 1963, used the material. The 1928 Book placed it in the second office of instruction. This present Book defines the church as "the community of the New Covenant" (see also pp. 850–851 of the Prayer Book on the New Covenant). The first sentence of the answer to the question "How is the Church described in the Bible?" is the answer to the question "What is the Church?" of the second office of instruction in the 1928 Book. It is structured upon Paul's conception of the church as the body of Christ (Col. 2:19; Eph. 1:22–23, 4:15) and of baptized persons as the different members of the body (Rom. 12:4–5; 1 Cor. 6:15, 12:12ff.; Eph. 4:25, 30). To this are added other scriptural analogies: "the People of God" (1 Pet. 2:9); "the New Israel" (cf. Gal. 6:16 and Rom. 9:6); "a holy nation" (1 Pet. 2:9); "a royal priesthood" (1 Pet. 2:5 and 9); and "the pillar and ground of truth" (1 Tim. 3:15). The explication of the church as described in the creeds is based upon that of the 1928 office. Revised answers about the church incorporate a number of phrases from the 1973 catechism. The three final questions and answers on the mission of the church, added in this present Book, are an expansion of a question and the initial sentence of its answer in the 1973 form.

The Ministry (pp. 855–856)

A section on the ministry based, like that of the section on the church, on the 1887 supplement, was introduced in the second office of instruction in the 1928 Book. The 1979 Book substantially amplifies this section, setting forth more fully the biblical and patristic concepts of the ministry for the various orders—lay persons, bishops, priests, and deacons. (The laity are designated as an order in patristic writings, including the First Epistle of Clement which is generally dated A.D. 96.) The question and answer on the ministry of the laity is new to this Book. The answers to questions on the ministry of bishops, priests, and deacons are greatly amplified, to define these ministries as they are proclaimed in the rites of ordination. The final question and answer on the duty of all Christians is from the second office of instruction in the 1928 Prayer Book.

Prayer and Worship (pp. 856–857)

Earlier editions of the catechism contained an exhortation to prayer, a repetition of the Lord's Prayer, and an exposition of it. The English revision of 1962 included a question on the meaning of worship and a question "What is Prayer?" to which the answer was "the lifting up of heart and mind to God," with a listing of the principal kinds of prayer. Questions and answers under the title "Prayer" were also in the catechism of 1973, which again contained the question "What is prayer?" and listed the kinds of prayer. Answers to the first and fourth questions in this section of the 1979 Book are based on those of the 1973 catechism. The initial portion of the answer to "What is adoration?" is derived from the English revised catechism (1962); the answer to the final question "What is corporate worship?" is also related to the question and answer on worship in the 1962 revision. The other questions and answers are new to the 1979 Book.

The Sacraments (pp. 857–858)

The 1604 Prayer Book added a section defining the nature of the sacraments and explained the meaning of the two great sacraments, Baptism and Eucharist. The definition of a sacrament in the present Book is based on that of previous editions: "an outward and visible sign of an inward and spiritual grace given unto us; ordained by Christ himself, as a means whereby we receive the same, and a pledge to assure us thereof."

Augustine defined a sacrament as "a sign of a sacred thing," and medieval theologians stressed the fact that a sacrament not only signified but also conveyed what it signified. The definition of the word "grace" and the listing of the ways in which God's grace works in our lives were added in the present Book. The final question and answer, which derive from the 1973 catechism, replace those of prior editions which read:

> Question. How many Sacraments hath Christ ordained in his Church?
> Answer. Two only, as generally necessary to salvation; that is to say, Baptism, and the Supper of the Lord.

Holy Baptism (pp. 858–859)

The substance of the first question and answer dates to the Prayer Book of 1549, where it is the answer to the second question of the catechism. The other questions and answers are based upon the section concerning the sacraments, added in the revision of 1604, though the answers to the last four questions have been enriched on the basis of biblical teaching and in conformity with the revised baptismal rite (pp. 297–314 of the Prayer Book). The questions and answers of previous Books read:

> *Question.* What is the inward and spiritual grace?
> *Answer.* A death unto sin, and a new birth unto righteousness: for being by nature born in sin, and the children of wrath, we are hereby made the children of grace.
> *Question.* What is required of persons to be baptized?
> *Answer.* Repentance, whereby they forsake sin; and Faith, whereby they steadfastly believe the promises of God made to them in that Sacrament.
> *Question.* Why then are Infants baptized, when by reason of their tender age they cannot perform them?
> *Answer.* Because they promise them both by their Sureties; which promise, when they come of age, themselves are bound to perform.

In the 1604 Prayer Book, the answer to the last question read:

> Yes, they do perform them by their Sureties, who promise and vow them both in their names, which when they come to age themselves are bound to perform.

That answer was revised in 1662. The new answer to the first of these questions is based upon that in the 1973 form.

The Holy Eucharist (pp. 859–860)

Questions and answers concerning the Eucharist were included in the additions to the catechism in the 1604 Book:

> *Question.* Why was the Sacrament of the Lord's Supper ordained?
> *Answer.* For the continual remembrance of the sacrifice of the death of Christ, and of the benefits which we receive thereby.
> *Question.* What is the outward part or sign of the Lord's Supper?
> *Answer.* Bread and Wine, which the Lord hath commanded to be received.
> *Question.* What is the inward part, or thing signified?

Answer. The Body and Blood of Christ, which are verily and
indeed taken and received by the faithful in the Lord's Supper.

Question. What are the benefits whereof we are partakers
thereby?

Answer. The strengthening and refreshing of our souls by the
Body and Blood of Christ, as our bodies are by the Bread and
Wine.

Question. What is required of them who come to the Lord's Supper?

Answer. To examine themselves, whether they repent them truly
of their former sins, steadfastly purposing to lead a new life;
have a lively faith in God's mercy through Christ, with a
thankful remembrance of his death; and be in charity with all
men.

The revision of 1789 substituted the word "spiritually" for "verily
and indeed."

In the present Book the emendations of answers to these questions
incorporate a number of phrases from the catechism of 1973 which
was, in turn, dependent on the English revision of 1962. The question
and answer on the eucharistic sacrifice and several phrases in other
answers are new to this revision. The 1979 Book substantially en-
riches the material on the doctrine of the Eucharist, biblically and
patristically, in ways which parallel the enriched content of the
eucharistic prayers new to the Book. The first answer recalls the
historic forms of the anamnesis and of the memorial acclamation,
which stress the resurrection and the second coming as well as the
death of our Lord. The statement on the benefits of the sacrament
restores the patristic emphasis upon forgiveness as a benefit of the
sacrament rather than as a condition for receiving it, defines
the sacrament as a strengthening of our union not only with
Christ but also with one another, and depicts the sacrament as a
foretaste of the heavenly banquet.

Other Sacramental Rites (pp. 860–861)

The word "sacrament" (oath or pledge or earnest), sometimes used
as a translation of the Greek word "mysterion," became a part of the
Christian vocabulary probably at the end of the second century or the
beginning of the third, in relation to many rites or signs of spiritual
significance. Not until the twelfth century did Peter Lombard designate seven rites as the sacraments of the church, an enumeration
which was affirmed at the council of Florence (1439) and the council

of Trent. Various English Reformation formularies and the Elizabethan homilies speak of marriage or the reconciliation of a penitent, as well as Baptism and the Eucharist, as sacraments. Article XXV (p. 872) asserted that there are two sacraments ordained by our Lord, and that the five other rites "commonly called Sacraments," are partly "states of life" (for example, marriage or ordination) or arose in part from the "corrupt following of the Apostles" (for example, the unction for healing of the early church became the "Extreme Unction" of the late medieval period). The section on the sacraments, added to the catechism in 1604, asked the question "How many Sacraments hath Christ ordained in his Church?" The answer was "Two only, as generally necessary to salvation; that is to say, Baptism and the Supper of the Lord."

The present Book treats Baptism and the Eucharist as "the two great sacraments of the Gospel," "given by Christ to his Church" (p. 858). The "minor sacraments" of the late medieval enumeration are listed as "other sacramental rites" to be distinguished from the sacraments of the Gospel in that they are not necessary for all persons.

The answer to the first question on confirmation might be compared to the answer concerning confirmation included in the offices of instruction in the 1928 Book:

> The Church provides the Laying on of Hands, or Confirmation, wherein, after renewing the promises and vows of my Baptism, and declaring my loyalty and devotion to Christ as my Master, I receive the strengthening gifts of the Holy Spirit.

The answer to the question concerning the requirements for confirmation, and the definitions of the other sacramental rites, rely heavily on the English revised form of 1962. The two final questions and answers are new to this Book.

The Christian Hope (pp. 861–862)

In the English revised catechism of 1962 is a brief section on Christian hope which inspired this section of the 1979 Book. There is little verbal similarity in the answers, however, except in that to the final question.

582

Historical Documents
of the Church (*pp. 863-878*)

The Articles of Religion were bound in many editions of the 1662 Prayer Book. Sometimes other documents, such as the canons of 1604, were included. The American church revised and adopted the Articles in 1801, printing them between the psalter and the ordination rites. In 1886 the Articles were moved to the end of the Book.

During the controversy over the Athanasian Creed at the time of the first American revision it was suggested that the creed be included in the Book even though its use not be required. The recent Irish and Canadian revisions of the Prayer Book have followed that policy.

The preface of the 1549 Prayer Book, in a revised form printed under the title "Concerning the Service of the Church," appears in most Anglican revisions except those of the American church.

The 1979 Prayer Book retains the Articles of Religion, restores the Athanasian Creed and the preface to the 1549 Book—documents found in most Anglican Books—and includes two other important documents, the Chalcedonian definition and the Chicago-Lambeth Quadrilateral.

Definition of the Union of the Divine and Human Natures in the Person of Christ (p. 864)

The Council of Chalcedon (A.D. 451) affirmed the Nicene Creed of the Council of Constantinople (A.D. 381). It also adopted this definition which repudiates the errors of Nestorius and Eutyches. Nestorius, who had been condemned at the Council of Ephesus (A.D.

583

431), rejected the term Theotokos for the Virgin Mary, teaching that there are two separate persons in the Incarnate Christ, the divine and the human. In opposition to Nestorianism, the teaching of Eutyches confounds the two natures, denying that the manhood of Christ was consubstantial with ours. The definition adopted by the Council evolves from letters from Cyril of Alexandria to Nestorius and to John of Antioch, the Tome of Leo of Rome, and contributions by Theodoret of Antioch and Flavian of Constantinople. It is not a final or exact statement of a theological position, but a definition of limits of speculation. This Chalcedonian definition has been generally received both in the East and the West except among the Monophysite bodies.

The document is included for the first time in a Book of Common Prayer. The translation is from *Documents of the Christian Church*.[1]

Quicunque Vult, commonly called The Creed of Saint Athanasius (pp. 864–865)

The Quicunque Vult came to be called the Creed of Saint Athanasius not because it was written by him but because it was believed to express the faith which he taught. This rhythmic prose work is indebted to the writings of Augustine of Hippo and Vincent of Lerins. Most scholars believe it originated in southern Gaul late in the fifth century. Caesarius of Arles (502–542) used it as a test of orthodoxy and as an instructional aid. By the ninth century the Quicunque Vult was being said in some places at the office of Prime on Sundays, sometimes treated as a psalm, with an antiphon and the Gloria Patri. By the thirteenth century this statement was so commonly used in the Western church that people spoke of it as one of the three creeds of the church, along with the Apostles' Creed and the Nicene.

The 1549 Prayer Book printed it with a Gloria Patri for use after the Benedictus on six principal feasts: Christmas, Epiphany, Easter, Ascension, Pentecost, and Trinity Sunday. The 1552 revision required its use also on the feast days of Saint Matthias, Saint John the Baptist, Saint James, Saint Bartholomew, Saint Matthew, Saint Simon and Saint Jude, and Saint Andrew. These days were evidently chosen in order to ensure its use approximately once each month. The 1662 revision appointed it for use in place of the Apostles' Creed on those days.

In August of 1785 Bishop Samuel Seabury and a committee which he gathered proposed alterations to the 1662 Book. Among these was

---

[1] Ed. Henry Bettenson, New York: Oxford University Press, 1947, pp. 72–73.

the omission of the Athanasian Creed from the Book or the limiting of its use to Trinity Sunday only. A September convention of the other New England states recommended that it be "wholly disused." These were among the proposals sent from New England to the deputies from the states south of New England, meeting in convention in Philadelphia on September 27. The convention concurred with the recommendations from New England and omitted the Athanasian Creed from the Proposed Book of 1786. The English bishops, after having examined the Proposed Book, wrote the convention "we hope you . . . give [it] a place in your Book of Common Prayer, even though the use of [it] should be left discretional."

At the General Convention of 1789 Bishops Seabury and White proposed that the Athanasian Creed be included, but the deputies did not accept their recommendation. After the publication of the 1789 Book, Seabury wrote to Samuel Parker of Boston:

> With regard to the propriety of reading the Athanasian Creed in Church, I was never fully convinced. With regard to the impropriety of banishing it out of the Prayer-book I am clear. . . . And I do hope, though possibly I hope in vain, that Christian charity and love of union will one day bring that Creed into this book, were it only to stand as articles of faith stand; and to show that we do not renounce the Catholic doctrine of the Trinity as held in the Western Church.

Revisions of the Prayer Book for some other provinces of Anglicanism no longer require that the Athanasian Creed be used or else have reduced the number of occasions on which it is appointed to be used.

The present Book is the first American revision to include this creed. It is never appointed for liturgical use in the services of the church. The translation is that found in the 1662 English Book (with the addition of the word "both" in verse 18 as in other Anglican revisions). This is a slight revision of the 1549 translation which was based on that in Hilsey's Primer.

The first paragraph is devoted to the doctrine of the Trinity, the second to that of the Incarnation. The heresies condemned by the church councils in the fourth and fifth centuries are not mentioned by name; this creed, however, stands against the errors condemned by those councils.

Preface: The First Book of Common Prayer (1549) (pp. 866–867)

The preface of the first Book of Common Prayer is essentially a translation of the preface for one of Cranmer's two plans for revision of the daily office (see above, p. 94). That preface paraphrased a preface in the first recension (1535) of Cardinal Francisco de Quiñones' revised breviary, commissioned by Pope Clement VII in 1529. A rationale for the revision of the daily offices, this preface has been retained in the various editions of the English Prayer Book. (The revision of 1662 printed it under the title "Concerning the Service of the Church.") The revision of 1552 placed more stringent obligation upon the clergy to say the daily office and this was further stressed in the 1662 Book. In 1552 the following paragraphs were substituted for the last sentence of the 1549 preface:

> And all Priests and Deacons shall be bound to say daily the Morning and Evening Prayer, either privately or openly, except they be letted [prevented] by preaching, studying of divinity, or by some other urgent cause.
> And the Curate that ministereth in every Parish Church or Chapel, being at home, and not being otherwise reasonably letted, shall say the same in the Parish Church or Chapel where he ministereth, and shall toll a bell thereto, a convenient time before he begin, that such as be disposed may come to hear God's word and to pray with him.

The 1662 Book substituted "sickness" for both "preaching" and "studying of divinity" as the only sufficient excuse for failure to say the daily offices.

Articles of Religion (pp. 867–876)

The sixteenth century continental reformers developed various confessions in order to state clearly the principles of the Reformation, to repudiate errors of the Roman Church or of fellow reformers, and to serve as a basis for negotiations with other bodies of Christians. Two of these confessions, the Confession of Augsburg (1530) and the Württemberg Confession (1552), contributed substantially to the Articles of Religion for the Church of England. Neither confession was a systematic treatise on theology; both were statements of position on controversial issues.

In England, in 1536, a document commonly known as the Ten Articles was approved by convocation and issued by the king "to stablish Christian quietness and unity." A delegation from Germany in 1538 entered into negotiations with the English, producing a document known as the Thirteen Articles, which owed something to the Augsburg Confession. It was not published at the time, but became the source through which some parts of the Augsburg Confession influenced the Articles of Religion.

In 1553 the king signed the Forty-two Articles, largely the work of Cranmer. All beneficed clergy were ordered to sign them under penalty of deprivation. Issued to promote religious uniformity—"the establishment of a godly concord"—the Articles were aimed at the extremists of both sides, whether of Roman or Anabaptist persuasion. Otherwise the Articles are rather moderate. The extremes of some Lutheran statements on justification and of Calvinist statements on predestination are avoided. On the sacraments they take a middle course between Lutheranism and Zwinglianism.

After the accession of Elizabeth, Archbishop Matthew Parker and Bishop Edmund Guest of Rochester revised the Articles and presented them to convocation. In the process seven of the original forty-two were deleted, four new articles were added (V, XII, XXIX, and XXX), and seventeen were emended. This revision made use of material from the Württemberg Confession. Before publication in 1563, when they were considered by the queen in council, Article XXIX was deleted and the initial phrase added to Article XX. Parliament did not give sanction to the Articles until 1571, at which time Article XXIX was restored and a requirement of subscription approved.

From the time of Elizabeth Puritans resisted subscribing to the Articles just as Latitudinarians were later to oppose them after 1689. At the American convention in 1785 a revision of the Articles, based upon an anonymous work *Reasons Humbly Offered for Composing a New Set of Articles of Religion* (1751), was approved for the Proposed Book of 1786. At the convention of 1789 the bishops proposed to include the Articles, but the deputies postponed consideration. Despite pressure from the state conventions of New Jersey and New York, consideration was postponed again in 1792 and in 1795. Before the 1795 convention William White had prepared a proposal that the Articles, with "Notes explanatory of the 35th, the 36th & the 37th Articles," be "declared to be the Faith of this Church." At the 1799 convention a committee reported seventeen articles which drew upon those of the English Book and those of the Proposed Book of 1786. Consideration was again postponed, but their publication in the journal of the convention roused concern. In 1801, on the first day devoted to business at the convention, the bishops "agreed on a form and manner of setting forth the Articles of religion." Both houses approved a resolution that the Articles, "as in the Book of Common Prayer of the Church of England," be "set forth" with certain alterations and omissions. The alterations and omissions owed something to White's 1795 proposal. The substitution for Article XXXVII was that offered in 1799.[1] The convention of 1804 sought to require specific subscription to the Articles, but the journal records: "A proposed Canon, concerning subscription to the Articles of the Church, was negatived, under the impression that a sufficient subscription to the Articles is already required in the 7th Article of the Constitution."

The Chicago-Lambeth Quadrilateral 1886, 1888 (pp. 876–878)

The report of the Committee on Christian Unity to the House of Bishops at the General Convention of 1886, which introduced the resolution adopted by that body, traced the concern for Christian unity of that house to the Muhlenberg Memorial of 1853 (see above, p. 58). As a result of that memorial the House of Bishops had appointed a commission "empowered to confer with the several Christian Bodies in our land who were desirous of promoting godly union and concord among all who loved the Lord Jesus Christ in sincerity and truth."

The four essentials listed in the resolution were formulated by the Rev. Dr. William Reed Huntington and published in 1870 in his work, *The Church Idea:*

> The true Anglican position, like the City of God in the Apocalypse, may be said to lie foursquare. Honestly to accept that position is to accept,—
>
> 1st. The Holy Scriptures as the Word of God.
> 2nd. The Primitive Creeds as the Rule of Faith.
> 3rd. The two Sacraments ordained by Christ himself.
> 4th. The Episcopate as the key-stone of Governmental Unity.
>
> These four points, like the four famous fortresses of Lombardy, make the Quadrilateral of pure Anglicanism. Within them the Church of the Reconciliation may stand secure. . . . Only by a wise discrimination between what can and what cannot be conceded for the sake of unity, is unity attainable.

The preamble and the first two of the four points of the Quadrilateral adopted by the General Convention in 1886 were revised by the bishops of the Anglican Communion at the Lambeth Conference of 1888. The Quadrilateral was subsequently affirmed by the House of Deputies of the General Conventions of 1892 and 1895.

---

[1] The present Book notes the divergencies of the articles as approved in 1801 from those of 1571 in italics after each article which was altered.

Tables and Rules for Finding the Date of Easter Day (*pp. 879-885*)

For the history of tables of this type in the Prayer Book, see above, pp. 43–44.

As early as the second century, Christians of Asia Minor known as Quartodecimans observed Easter on the day of the Spring full moon, the fourteenth day of the month of Nisan on which the paschal lamb was slaughtered, regardless of the day of the week on which it occurred. Other churches throughout the world celebrated Easter on the following Sunday. At the council of Nicea in 325 it was decreed that Easter should be celebrated on the Sunday after the full moon occurring on or after the vernal equinox, March 21. If the full moon came on that date, however, the observance was to be transferred to the following Sunday to avoid having the celebration of Easter coincide with the Jewish Passover. The earliest possible date for the celebration of Easter, therefore, would be March 22, and the latest April 25. The last time that Easter fell on March 22 was 1818, and the last time that it fell on April 25 was 1943. It will not fall again on March 22 until 2285, or on April 25 until 2038.

By the use of the Golden Number and the Sunday Letter, which are explained on pages 880–881 of the Prayer Book, one can find the date of Easter for any particular year.

For convenience in planning ahead and as an aid in research a table is provided (pages 882–883) which gives the date of Easter Day for every year from 1900 to 2089. Another table (pages 884–885) indicates principal days of the church year which are determined by the date of Easter and shows the relationship between the title of the Sundays after Pentecost and the propers which are to be used on those days.

589

The Lectionary (pp. 887-931)

For background information on this lectionary, see above, pp. 324–326.

Concerning the Lectionary (p. 888)

The first paragraph explains how to find the cycle of the lectionary which is appointed for any year.

The second paragraph makes explicit the fact that this lectionary is to be used at all public services on a Sunday or major holy day, except for additional services which would be attended by persons who had been or would be present for a principal service at which this lectionary would be used. Through the use of this lectionary, a substantial amount of the Old Testament and almost all of the New Testament is read within a three year period. Vacillation between this lectionary and the daily office lectionary would result in crucial omissions.

When the congregation for a daily office on a Sunday is composed of people who have been or will be present for the Eucharist, the lessons for the daily office may be selected from among those appointed in the daily office lectionary (pp. 933–1001) or from one of the other years of the three-year Sunday cycle. The psalm from the Sunday cycle may be used, but those of the daily office are recommended because the creation and paschal deliverance themes found in them are traditionally associated with the Sunday offices.

The fourth paragraph points out that the selection from the psalter is frequently cited in a longer and shorter version; the longer is frequently more appropriate for use in the daily office, the shorter, between the first two lessons at the Eucharist. One case in point is the use of Psalm 95 or of Psalm 95:6–11 on the Third Sunday in Lent in

590

Year A. The use of the whole of the psalm would be quite appropriate at the daily office, when the final verses would introduce the reading of Exodus 17:1–7. On the other hand the use of the whole of that psalm after the reading at the Eucharist would separate the relevant portion of the psalm from the reading. The permission to lengthen or shorten the selection from the psalms may, on occasion, be desirable because of a particular musical setting or for other reasons.

The next paragraph is a caution, to those who are planning services, that the alternative lections are sometimes identical with those appointed in the daily office lectionary.

The medieval missals and earlier editions of the Prayer Book, for the sake of clarity, frequently substituted nouns for pronouns within lections or prefaced them with a phrase such as "Jesus said to his disciples." The reader is directed to omit initial conjunctions ("And" or "But"), to substitute nouns for pronouns for the sake of clarity, or to provide a clarifying introduction to identify who is speaking and, on occasion, to whom the person is speaking. At other times, for example the Fourth Sunday after the Epiphany in Year C, when the Gospel is Luke 4:21–32, a much fuller introduction may be needed.

The final paragraph gives permission for lessons to be lengthened at discretion. Suggestions for lengthening certain lessons are shown in parentheses; on occasion, particularly with transient congregations, the reader may be wise to bring a lection to a conclusion which would otherwise not be reached until the next Sunday, or to repeat a portion of the previous Sunday's lection to set the reading in context. To make use of the example cited above, in some situations it may be wise not to read only Luke 4:21–32 but to preface the reading with a repetition of the gospel of the prior Sunday, Luke 4:14–21, or to begin at Luke 4:16.

Though several translations of the Scriptures are authorized (see pp. 34–35), the chapter and verse divisions of the lectionary are based on the Revised Standard Version except for the psalms, which are those of the Prayer Book.

Daily Office Lectionary (*pp.* 933-1001)

For background information on this lectionary, see above, pp. 108–111.

Concerning the Daily Office Lectionary (pp. 934–935)

The first paragraph explains how to find the cycle of the lectionary which is appointed for any year.

The second and third paragraphs explain the distribution of the three readings appointed for each day. Ordinarily the Old Testament lesson will be used in the morning; one of the New Testament lessons (the Epistle in Year One and the Gospel in Year Two) will be read in the morning and the other in the evening. In situations where there is only one reading chosen for the morning office, the Old Testament lesson may be postponed until the evening. If only one office is read on any given day all three lections may be used. When it is appropriate to have an Old Testament reading at both offices, the reading for the alternate year is used at Evening Prayer.

One of the frequent criticisms of earlier lectionaries in the Prayer Book was that sequential readings were often interrupted by proper lections for saints' days and their eves, lections which contributed little or nothing to the congregation's knowledge of the saint being commemorated or of sainthood in general. The reading of John 11, the story of the raising of Lazarus, for example, was frequently interrupted by lessons for the feast day (and/or eve) of Saint Matthias; none of these lections mentioned Matthias. In the 1979 Book a general permission is given, when a major feast interrupts the sequence of readings, to lengthen, combine, or omit some of the appointed readings in order to secure continuity or avoid repetition.

The 1943 revision of the lectionary allowed the lengthening or shortening of readings. The present Book deletes permission to abbreviate a lesson, but retains the permission to lengthen. It may be wise, especially with a congregation which varies from day to day, to continue certain lections to a logical conclusion or to repeat a portion of the prior reading in order to provide the context, even though this may mean repetition for those who read the office daily.

The next four paragraphs deal with the use of psalms in the daily office. The first points out that, except for the periods from 4 Advent to 1 Epiphany and from Palm Sunday to 2 Easter, the psalms are arranged in a seven-week pattern, with appropriate variations for the seasons of Lent and Easter. Cranmer's sequential distribution of the psalms over the period of one month is retained as an alternative.[1]

Though in the lectionary psalms particularly appropriate to the morning are among those appointed for the morning office and psalms suited to the evening are among those for the evening office, the officiant may use the evening psalms in the morning or morning psalms in the evening. The psalms appointed for any day may be used on another day in the same week, except on a major feast day.

The use of the imprecatory psalms in public worship has been criticized for several centuries. The 1789, 1892, and 1928 revisions of the lectionary allowed the substitution of certain "selections" from the psalms at the discretion of the minister. The 1943 lectionary omitted eight psalms altogether. In the present revision the entire psalter is again included in the lectionary, but certain psalms or verses of psalms which may be omitted are indicated by brackets or parentheses.

This Book restores permission, for the first time since the Reformation, to use antiphons with the psalms. On occasion, antiphons may effectively highlight special themes or seasonal emphases. (See *The Prayer Book Office*, compiled and edited by Howard Galley, New York: The Seabury Press, 1980.)

The final paragraph permits the officiant to select suitable psalms and readings for special occasions (lessons for certain occasions are suggested on pp. 1000–1001). On the day of a momentous event, such as a baptism, a marriage, an ordination, the celebration of a new ministry, or the consecration of a church, it may be desirable to use at the daily office readings provided for the occasion which could not be used within the rite itself. At other times, when a group of people who do not say the office daily are gathered for some particular rea-

---

[1] For commentary see the material on the Psalter (pp. 551–553).

son, it may be suitable to have lections related to the purpose of the gathering in place of those appointed for the day.

Several translations of the scripture are authorized (see pp. 34–35), but the chapter and verse divisions of the lectionary are based on the Revised Standard Version, except for the psalms, which are those of the Prayer Book psalter.

Selected Bibliography

History and Meaning of Worship

Bouyer, L. *Liturgical Piety*. Notre Dame: University of Notre Dame Press, 1955.

Cope, G. *Symbolism in the Bible and the Church*. London: S. C. M. Press, 1959.

Davies, H. *Worship and Theology in England*. 5 vols. Princeton: Princeton University Press, 1961–1975.

Grainger, R. *The Language of the Rite*. London: Darton, Longman & Todd, 1974.

Hatchett, M. J. *Sanctifying Life, Time and Space: An Introduction to Liturgical Study*. New York: Seabury Press, 1976.

Hoon, P. W. *The Integrity of Worship: Ecumenical and Pastoral Studies in Liturgical Theology*. Nashville: Abingdon Press, 1971.

Jones, C., Wainwright, G., and Yarnold, E., ed. *The Study of Liturgy*. New York: Oxford University Press, 1978.

Micks, M. H. *The Future Present: The Phenomenon of Christian Worship*. New York: Seabury Press, 1970.

Schmemann, A. *Introduction to Liturgical Theology*. London: Faith Press, 1966.

von Allmen, J.-J. *Worship: Its Theology and Practice*. New York: Oxford University Press, 1965.

Wainwright, G. *Doxology: The Praise of God in Worship, Doctrine and Life: A Systematic Theology*. New York: Oxford University Press, 1980.

The Book of Common Prayer: *Texts and Commentaries*

Blunt, J. H. *The Annotated Book of Common Prayer: Being an Historical, Ritual, and Theological Commentary on the Devotional System of the Church of England*. London: Rivingtons, 1876.

Brightman, F. E. *The English Rite: Being a Synopsis of the Sources and Revisions of the Book of Common Prayer with an Introduction and an Appendix*. 2 vols. London: Rivingtons, 1915.

Cuming, G. J. *The Durham Book: Being the First Draft of the Revision of the Book of Common Prayer in 1661 Edited with an Introduction and Notes*. London: Oxford University Press, 1961.

Daniel, E. *The Prayer-Book: Its History, Language, and Contents.* 23d ed. London: Wells Gardner, Darton & Co., 1913.

McGarvey, W. *Liturgiae Americanae: or the Book of Common Prayer As Used in the United States of America Compared with the Proposed Book of 1786 and with the Prayer Book of the Church of England, and an Historical Account and Documents.* Philadelphia: Philadelphia Church Publishing Company, 1907.

Neil, C., and Willoughby, J. M. *The Tutorial Prayer Book for the Teacher, the Student, and the General Reader.* 3d Impression. London: Church Book Room Press, 1959.

Shepherd, M. H., Jr. *The Oxford American Prayer Book Commentary.* New York: Oxford University Press, 1950.

Warren, F. E., ed. *The Book of Common Prayer, with Commentary for Teachers and Students.* 2d ed. London: S. P. C. K., 1922.

Wheatly, C. *A Rational Illustration of the Book of Common Prayer of the Church of England, Being the Substance of Every Thing Liturgical in Bishop Sparrow, Mr. L'Estrange, Dr. Comber, Dr. Nichols, and All Former Ritualists, Commentators, or Others, upon the Same Subject; Collected and Reduced into One Continued and Regular Method, and Interspersed All Along with New Observations. By Charles Wheatly, A. M., Vicar of Brent and Furneux Pelham, in Hertfordshire. Improved by Additions and Notes Drawn from a Comparison with Shepherd and Other Writers on the Liturgy, Adapting This Edition to the Present State of the Protestant Episcopal Church in America, Without Any Alteration of the Original Text.* Boston: R. P. & C. Williams, 1825.

The Book of Common Prayer: *History and Rationale*

Brooks, S. *The Language of the Book of Common Prayer.* New York: Oxford University Press, 1965.

Cardwell, E. *A History of Conferences and Other Proceedings Connected with the Revision of the Book of Common Prayer; from the Year 1558 to the Year 1690.* 3d ed. Oxford: University Press, 1849.

Clarke, W. K. L., ed. *Liturgy and Worship: A Companion to the Prayer Books of the Anglican Communion.* London: S. P. C. K., 1932.

Cuming, G. J. *A History of Anglican Liturgy.* London: Macmillan and Co.; New York: St. Martin's Press, 1969.

Don, A. C. *The Scottish Book of Common Prayer 1929; Notes on Its Origin and Growth, with Illustrations from Original Documents.* London: S. P. C. K., 1949.

Donaldson, G. *The Making of the Scottish Prayer Book of 1637.* Edinburgh: University Press, 1954.

Hatchett, M. J. *A Manual of Ceremonial for the New Prayer Book.* Sewanee, Tennessee: St. Luke's Journal of Theology, 1977.

Hatchett, M. J. *A Manual for Clergy and Church Musicians.* Prepared for the Standing Commission on Church Music. New York: Church Hymnal Corporation, 1980.

Hatchett, M. J. "A Sunday Service in 1776 or Thereabouts." *Historical Magazine of the Protestant Episcopal Church,* XLV (December, 1976), 369–385.

Hatchett, M. J. "The First American Trial Liturgy." *The St. Luke's Journal of Theology,* XIV (September, 1971), 20–29.

Hatchett, M. J. "The Making of the First American Prayer Book." Unpublished Th. D. dissertation, General Theological Seminary, 1972.

Parsons, E. L., and Jones, B. H. *The American Prayer Book: Its Origins and Principles.* New York: Charles Scribner's Sons, 1937.

Prayer Book Studies. 29 vols. New York: Church Pension Fund, 1950–1976.

Price, C. P., and Weil, L. *Liturgy for Living.* New York: Seabury Press, 1979.

Proctor, F., and Frere, W. H. *A New History of the Book of Common Prayer with a Rationale of Its Offices.* London: Macmillan and Co., 1901.

Ratcliff, E. C. *The Booke of Common Prayer of the Churche of England: Its Making and Revisions M.D.xlix—M.D.clxi. Set Forth in Eighty Illustrations, with Introduction and Notes.* London: S. P. C. K., 1949.

Ratcliff, E. C. "The Savoy Conference and the Revision of the Book of Common Prayer." *From Uniformity to Unity 1662–1962.* Edited by Geoffrey F. Nuttall and Owen Chadwick. London: S. P. C. K., 1962, pp. 89–148.

Stevick, D. B. *Language in Worship: Reflections on a Crisis.* New York: Seabury Press, 1970.

Sydnor, W. *The REAL Prayer Book: 1549 to the Present.* Wilton, Connecticut: Morehouse-Barlow Co., 1978.

The English Prayer Book 1549–1662. London: S. P. C. K., 1963.

Woolverton, J. "W. R. Huntington: Liturgical Renewal and Church Unity in the 1880's." *Anglican Theological Review,* XLVIII (April, 1966), 175–199.

The Calendar of the Church Year

Denis-Boulet, N. M. *The Christian Calendar.* New York: Hawthorn Books, 1960.

Eliade, M. *Cosmos and History: The Myth of the Eternal Return.* New York: Harper & Row, 1959.

Gunstone, J. *Christmas and Epiphany.* London: Faith Press, 1967.

Gunstone, J. *The Feast of Pentecost: The Great Fifty Days in the Liturgy.* London: Faith Press, 1967.

Lesser Feasts and Fasts. 3d ed. New York: Church Pension Fund, 1980.

McArthur, A. A. *The Evolution of the Christian Year.* New York: Seabury Press, 1955.

Pieper, J. *In Tune with the World: A Theory of Festivity.* Chicago: Franciscan Herald Press, 1965.

Porter, H. B., Jr. *The Day of Light: The Biblical and Liturgical Meaning of Sunday.* Greenwich: Seabury Press, 1960.

Rordorf, W. *Sunday: The History of the Day of Rest and Worship in the Earliest Centuries of the Christian Church.* Philadelphia: Westminster Press, 1968.

The Daily Office

Grisbrooke, W. J. "A Contemporary Liturgical Problem: The Divine Office and Public Worship." *Studia Liturgica,* VIII (1971/1972), 129–168, IX (1973), 3–18, 81–106.

Levy, I. *The Synagogue: Its History and Function.* London: Valentine, Mitchell & Co., 1963.

Mateos, J. "The Morning and Evening Office." *Worship*, XLII (January, 1968), 31–47.

Mateos, J. "The Origin of the Divine Office." *Worship*, XLI (October, 1967), 477–485.

Porter, H. B., Jr. "What Does the Daily Office Do?" *Anglican Theological Review*, LVI (April, 1974), 170–181.

Salmon, P. *The Breviary through the Centuries.* Collegeville: Liturgical Press, 1962.

The Collects

Devereaux, J. A. "Reformed Doctrine in the Collects of the First Book of Common Prayer." *Harvard Theological Review*, LVIII (January, 1965), 49–68.

Goulburn, E. M. *The Collects of the Day: An Exposition Critical and Devotional of the Collects Appointed at the Communion.* 2 vols. London: Longmans, Green, and Co., 1880.

Proper Liturgies for Special Days

Davies, J. G. *Holy Week: A Short History.* Richmond: John Knox Press, 1963.

Tyrer, J. W. *Historical Survey of Holy Week: Its Services and Ceremonial.* London: Oxford University Press, 1932.

Wilkinson, J. *Egeria's Travels: Newly Translated with Supporting Documents and Notes.* London: S. P. C. K., 1971

Holy Baptism

Brock, S. "Studies in the Early History of the Syrian Orthodox Baptismal Liturgy." *The Journal of Theological Studies*, New Series, XXIII (April, 1972), 16–64.

Davies, J. G. *The Architectural Setting of Baptism.* London: Barrie and Rockliff, 1962.

Eliade, M. *Rites and Symbols of Initiation: The Mysteries of Birth and Rebirth.* New York: Harper & Row, 1965.

Fisher, J. D. C. *Christian Initiation: Baptism in the Medieval West.* London: S. P. C. K., 1965.

Fisher, J. D. C. *Christian Initiation: The Reformation Period.* London: S. P. C. K., 1970.

Hatchett, M. J. "The Rite of 'Confirmation' in the Book of Common Prayer and in Authorized Services 1973." *Anglican Theological Review*, LVI (July, 1974), 292–310.

Hatchett, M. J. "Thomas Cranmer and the Rites of Christian Initiation." Unpublished S. T. M. thesis, General Theological Seminary, 1967.

Holmes, U. T., III. *Confirmation: The Celebration of Maturity in Christ.* New York: Seabury Press, n. d.

Lampe, G. W. H. *The Seal of the Spirit.* rev. ed. London: S. P. C. K., 1967.

Mitchell, L. L. *Baptismal Anointing.* London: S. P. C. K., 1966.

Whitaker, E. C. *Documents of the Baptismal Liturgy.* 2d ed. London: S. P. C. K., 1970.

Yarnold, E. J. *The Awe-Inspiring Rites of Initiation: Baptismal Homilies of the Fourth Century.* Slough: St. Paul Publications, 1972.

The Holy Eucharist
Buchanan, C. O. *Further Anglican Liturgies 1968–1975.* Bramcote, Nottingham: Grove Books, 1975.
Buchanan, C. O. *Modern Anglican Liturgies 1958–1968.* London: Oxford University Press, 1968.
Buxton, R. G. *Eucharist and Institution Narrative: A Study in the Roman and Anglican Traditions of the Consecration of the Eucharist from the Eighth to the Twentieth Centuries.* Great Wakering: Mayhew-McCrimmon, 1976.
Dix, Gregory. *The Shape of the Liturgy.* Westminster: Dacre Press, 1945.
Grisbrooke, W. J. *Anglican Liturgies of the Seventeenth and Eighteenth Centuries.* London, S. P. C. K., 1958.
Hatchett, M. J. *The Eucharistic Liturgies of Historic Prayer Books: Historic Rites arranged for Contemporary Celebration.* Sewanee: St. Luke's Journal of Theology, 1980.
Hatchett, M. J. "Seven Pre-Reformation Eucharistic Liturgies: Historic Rites Arranged for Contemporary Celebration." Reprint from *The St. Luke's Journal of Theology,* XVI (June, 1973), 12–115. Sewanee: St. Luke's Bookstore.
Jasper, R. C. D., and Cuming, G. J. *Prayers of the Eucharist: Early and Reformed.* London: Collins, 1975.
Jungmann, J. A. *The Mass of the Roman Rite: Its Origins and Development.* 2 vols. New York: Benziger Brothers, 1950.
McKenna, J. H. *Eucharist and Holy Spirit: The Eucharistic Epiclesis in Twentieth Century Theology (1900–1966).* Great Wakering: Mayhew-McCrimmon, 1975.
Srawley, J. H. *The Early History of the Liturgy.* 2d ed. Cambridge: University Press, 1947.
Taft, R. F. *The Great Entrance: A History of the Transfer of Gifts and Other Preanaphoral Rites of the Liturgy of St. John Chrysostom,* Orientalia Christiana Analecta 200. Rome: Pontifical Oriental Institute, 1975.
Thompson, B. *Liturgies of the Western Church.* Cleveland: World Publishing Company, 1962.
Wainwright, G. *Eucharist and Eschatology.* London: Epworth Press, 1971.

Pastoral Offices
Marriage
Molina, J.-B., and Mutembe, P. *Le Rituel du Mariage en France du XIIᵉ au XVIᵉ siècle.* Paris: Beauchesne, 1974.
Ritzer, K. *Le mariage dans les Églises chrétiennes du Iᵉʳ au XIᵉ siècle,* Lex orandi 45. Paris: Les Éditions du Cerf, 1970.
Schillebeeckx, E. C. F. A. *Marriage: Secular Reality and Saving Mystery.* 2 vols. London: Sheed and Ward, 1965.
Penance
Gunstone, J. *The Liturgy of Penance.* London: Faith Press, 1966.
McNeill, J. T. *A History of the Cure of Souls.* New York: Harper & Row, 1965.
Poschmann, B. *Penance and the Anointing of the Sick.* New York: Herder and Herder, 1964.
Telfer, W. *The Forgiveness of Sins.* London: S. C. M. Press, 1959.

599

Thurian, M. *Confession*. London: S. C. M. Press, 1958.

Vogel, C. "Sin and Penance: A Survey of the Historical Evolution of the Penitential Discipline in the Latin Church." *Pastoral Treatment of Sin.* Edited by P. Delhaye. New York: Desclee Co., 1968, pp. 177–282.

Ministration to the Sick

Gusmer, C. W. *The Ministry of Healing in the Church of England: An Ecumenical-Liturgical Study.* Great Wakering: Mayhew-McCrimmon, 1974.

Porter, H. B., Jr. "The Origins of the Medieval Rite for Anointing." *Journal of Theological Studies,* New Series, VII (October, 1956), 211–225.

Puller, F. W. *The Anointing of the Sick in Scripture and Tradition.* London: S. P. C. K., 1910.

Burial

Rowell, G. *The Liturgy of Christian Burial: An Introductory Survey of the Historical Development of Christian Burial Rites.* London: S. P. C. K., 1977.

Rush, A. C. *Death and Burial in Christian Antiquity.* Washington: Catholic University of America Press, 1941.

Episcopal Services

Ordination Rites

Bradshaw, P. F. *The Anglican Ordinal: Its History and Development from the Reformation to the Present Day.* London: S. P. C. K., 1971.

Cope, G. "Vestments." *A Dictionary of Liturgy and Worship.* Edited by J. G. Davies. New York: Macmillan Company, 1972, pp. 365–383.

Porter, H. B., Jr. *The Ordination Prayers of the Ancient Western Churches.* London: S. P. C. K., 1967.

Porter, H. B., Jr. "The Theology of Ordination and the New Rites." *Anglican Theological Review,* LIV (April, 1972), 69–81.

Consecration of a Church

Addleshaw, G. W. O., and Etchells, F. *The Architectural Setting of Anglican Worship.* London: Faber and Faber, 1948

Bishops' Committee on the Liturgy. *Environment and Art in Catholic Worship.* Washington: Publications Office, United States Catholic Conference, 1978.

Clarke, B., and Betjeman, J. *English Churches.* London: Vista Books, 1964.

Davies, J. G. *The Origin and Development of Early Christian Church Architecture.* London: S. C. M. Press, 1952.

Davies, J. G. *The Secular Use of Church Buildings.* New York: Seabury Press, 1968.

DeBuyst, F. *Modern Architecture and Christian Celebration.* 2d ed. New York: Pueblo, 1980.

Krautheimer, R. *Early Christian and Byzantine Architecture.* Harmondsworth, Middlesex: Penguin Books, 1965.

Legg, J. W. *English Orders for Consecrating Churches,* Henry Bradshaw Society, Vol. XLI. London, 1911.

Sovik, E. A. *Architecture for Worship.* Minneapolis: Augsburg Publishing House, 1973.

White, J. F. *The Cambridge Movement: The Ecclesiologists and the Gothic Revival.* Cambridge: University Press, 1962.

Willis, G. G. "The Consecration of Churches down to the Ninth Century." *Further Essays in Early Roman Liturgy*. London: S. P. C. K., 1968.

The Psalter, or Psalms of David
Lamb, J. A. *The Psalms in Christian Worship*. London: Faith Press, 1962.
The Psalter: A New Version for Public Worship and Private Devotion Introduced by Charles Mortimer Guilbert. New York: Seabury Press, 1978.

An Outline of the Faith, or Catechism
Allen, A. J. C. *The Church Catechism: Its History and Contents*. London: Longmans, Green, and Co., 1892.

Historical Documents of the Church
Sellers, R. V. *The Council of Chalcedon: A Historical and Doctrinal Survey*. London: S. P. C. K., 1953.
Kelly, J. N. D. *The Athanasian Creed*. New York: Harper & Row, 1964.
Kelly, J. N. D. *Early Christian Creeds*. 3d ed. New York: David McKay Company, 1972.
Hardwick, C. *A History of the Articles of Religion: To Which Is Added a Series of Documents from A.D. 1536 to A.D. 1615*. Philadelphia: Herman Hooker, 1852.
Kidd, B. J. *The Thirty-nine Articles, Their History and Explanation*. 2 vols. 2d ed. New York: Edwin S. Gorham, 1903.
Bicknell, E. J. *A Theological Introduction to the Thirty-nine Articles of the Church of England*. London: Longmans, Green, and Co., 1919.

The Lectionary
Borsch, F. H. *Introducing the Lessons of the Church Year: A Guide for Lay Readers and Congregations*. New York: Seabury Press, 1978.
Bushong, A. B. *A Guide to the Lectionary*. New York: Seabury Press, 1978.
Fontaine, G. "The Ordo Lectionum Missae." *Notitiae*, Vol. 5, 1969, pp. 256–282.
Jones, B. H. *The American Lectionary*. New York: Morehouse-Gorham Co., 1944.

601

General Index

Alfred the Great, king 79
All baptized Christians, collect for 210
Allegorization 4, 152, 295, 307, 379, 527
Alleluia 31
    burial 478–479
    communion psalms 387
    daily office
        1549 Prayer Book 94
    dismissal 396
    Easter Vigil 249–250
    Eucharist 292, 298, 329–330
    fraction anthems 380
    Morning Prayer 103, 105–106
All Faithful Departed, commemoration
    of 80–81
All Martyrs 80
All Saints' Day 40, 44, 80, 81
    baptism 183, 268
    collects 206, 336, 408, 488
    in Lutheran orders 41
    Morning Prayer 99, 107
    prefaces 306, 398, 403
All Souls' Day 41–42, 94, 479
Alms 338, 347–349
Alphege, archbishop and martyr 59
Altar candles 137
Altar cloths 291, 347, 416–417, 540
Altar rail 384
Altars 293, 298, 301, 332, 342–343, 345,
    364–365
    candles, at Easter Vigil 249
    censing of 242
    in concelebration 313
    dedication and consecration of 540,
        542–543, 548–549
    elaboration of 295, 297
    marriage 429
    multiplication of 294
    relics 540
    separation from people 294
    stripping of 229–230
    symbolism of 548
    thanksgiving for birth or adoption of
        a child 444
    see also Table, eucharistic
Ambo 295, 327, 330, 332, 347, 418
Ambrose, bishop 72, 85–86, 117, 352
Ambrosian rite 39
    baptism 279
    canticles 119
    evening service 134
    Good Friday 234
    Holy Saturday 238
    litanies 155
    songs of praise 321
    Vespers 136

Amen 27, 293
    at baptism 278
    committal, in burial rites 493
    communion 385–386
    at declaration of marriage 437
    Eucharist 304
    eucharistic prayer 351, 359, 360–361,
        373, 414
    Jewish prayers 350
    ordination 527
    response to blessing 395
American liturgies 9
    see also Book of Common Prayer,
        American
American Prayer Books see Book of
    Common Prayer, American
Anabaptists 6, 259, 265, 505, 587
Anamnesis 242, 290, 297, 350, 351–352,
    356–357, 359–360, 365–369, 373–
    377, 391, 409, 415–416, 581
Anaphora 291, 360
Anaphora of Saint John the Evangelist
    350
Ancient Collects (Bright) 125–126, 141,
    143, 146, 167, 172, 174, 180–181, 191–
    192, 194, 201, 207, 208, 247–248, 468,
    474, 568–569
Andrew, Saint 78, 84, 165, 171, 196, 203,
    205, 584
Andrewes, Lancelot 7, 75, 135, 139, 151,
    541, 545
Angels 75–76
Anglican chant 553
    Gloria Patri 149
Anglican Church of the Province of New
    Zealand 405
Anglican Congress (1963) 12
Anglican monthly system (of reciting
    psalms) 107
Anne, mother of the Virgin Mary 69
Anniversary of the dedication of a
    church, collect on the 211
Announcement of a lesson 111, 326–
    327
Announcement of the Gospel 331–332,
    488
Announcements 304, 332, 396, 419
Annunciation 40, 46, 56–57, 71
    collects 200
    Morning Prayer 103, 107
    prefaces 306, 398–399
Anointing
    at baptism 240–241, 253, 256, 257–
        259, 261, 263–264, 266–267, 275–
        276, 278–281
    baptismal candidate 255

Barnabas, Saint 50, 59, 64, 72, 201, 208,
510, 512, 519
Bartholomew, Saint 72, 204, 584
Basil the Great 54, 61, 65, 130, 138, 261,
321, 323, 340, 353, 356–357, 367, 369–
370, 377, 382, 405, 407, 495
Bass, Edward 555, 567
Bassage, Harold 13
Bateman, Dupuy, Jr. 13
Baumstark's Law 235
Baxter, Richard 8
Baylay, Atwell M. Y. 169
Bede, the Venerable 42, 55, 62, 65, 79,
81, 183
Bells 95, 242, 249, 363, 533
Benedic, anima mea 112, 116
Benedicamus 131, 134, 147, 396
Benedicite 34, 94, 112, 113, 114
Benedictines 11
Benedictional 4, 395
Benediction of the Blessed Sacrament
297
Benedict of Aniane 3, 14, 61
Benedict of Nursia, abbot 67
Benedict of Nursia, rule of 90, 103, 114–
115, 117, 132, 144–145
Benedictus Dominus Deus 30, 91, 94,
96, 105, 112, 115–116, 121, 126, 138,
152, 163, 242, 321–323, 489, 491
Benedictus es, Domine 112–114
Benedictus qui venit 118, 293, 302, 331,
351, 353–354, 357, 363–365, 383
Benefee, Lee M. 13
Benson, Edward 125, 214
Berakoth 290, 292, 350
Bernard, abbot 72
Bersier, Eugene 236
Betrothal 428–429, 436
Bettenson, Henry 584
Bible 508, 529, 535, 538, 546, 577
translations 34–35, 591, 594
Bidding of the Bedes 123
Bidding to confession 304, 342–343, 382,
457, 466,
Evening Prayer 140
Bilikuddembe, Joseph Mkasa 63
Birney, James G. 563
Birth of child *see* Thanksgivings, for
birth or adoption of child
Bishops 3, 11, 28, 503
absolution 453
baptism 253, 256–258, 267–268,
278–281
blessing 394–395
blessing of oil 463
burial 484
catechism 573, 578

celebration of new ministry 533–539
confirmation 260, 271–272
consecration of chrism 276, 281, 286
Cyprian's teachings on 73
daily office 97
dedication and consecration of a
church 540–550
disciplinary rubrics 422
in early Christian liturgy 27
Easter Vigil 240–241, 243
episcopal services 501
Eucharist 312–313, 379
Eucharist following baptism 284
exorcism of baptismal candidates
253
extra-prayer book services 26
Good Friday 232, 237
Gospel reading 330
Ignatius' teachings on 78
liturgy of the presanctified gifts 421
marriage celebrations 428, 431
ministration of communion 385
ministration to the sick 459
ordination 504, 508, 510–530
permission for special observances
on Sundays 45
reaffirmation of baptismal commit-
ment 283
supplications for 158
vestments 527–528
visitation of 268—269, 276, 281, 424
baptism 183
Bishops' Book, The 5, 100, 572–573
Black letter days 6, 41–43, 46, 411
Agnes 49
Alban 65
Anne, mother of Mary 69
Augustine of Canterbury 62
Bede, the Venerable 62
Cyprian 73
Fabian 49
Holy Cross Day 74
Holy Name 47
Laurence, deacon 71
Martin of Tours 82
Mary Magdalene 68
Richard, bishop of Chichester 58
Transfiguration 70
Vincent 50
Visitation, feast of the
Black rubric 303, 305
Blandina, martyr 63
Blessing of light 135
see also Lucernarium
Blessings
1552 Prayer Book 41
of the ashes 173, 219

608

609

English (1552) 6
absolution 455
alms 348
Apostles' Creed 121
Ash Wednesday 219, 222
Athanasian Creed 121, 584
baptism 264–265, 270, 273, 275–277, 279–281, 284–285
burial 480–481, 487, 492–493, 495–496, 499
calendar of the church year 43
canticles 112–113, 115–116, 118
catechism 573
Clement 83
collects 165, 168–169, 181, 189, 196, 203, 407, 567–569
communion 383, 385–386
communion hymn 388
communion of the sick 410
confession of sin 144, 342–343
confirmation 282
daily office 95
Easter Day 491
entrance rites 315, 317–318, 320–322
Eucharist 301, 303–305, 308–309
conclusion of Eucharist 391
eucharistic bread 379
eucharistic prayer 357–358, 361, 363–365, 367–368, 370–372, 374
Evening Prayer 133, 139–141
exhortation 309
fast days 46
general confession 450
German church orders 282
Gloria in excelsis 321, 381, 393
Good Friday 234
Gospel and Epistle, reading of 331
kneeling and standing 122
Laurence, deacon 71
litanies 129, 158–159, 161
Lord's Prayer 123, 378
marriage rites 430, 435–436, 438
Mary Magdalene 68
Morning Prayer 97–99, 101–105
music 32
Nicene Creed 334
offertory 346
ordination 501, 511, 517, 529
penitential order 311
post-baptismal prayer 284
postcommunion prayer 393, 421
prayer for the whole state of
Christ's Church 355, 337–340
prayer of humble access 382

prayers 554–555, 565
preface of 1549 Prayer Book 586
prefaces 398–399, 401
private confession 451
proper liturgies 217
regular services 25
reserved sacrament 409
salutation 122, 322
sancta sanctis 383
sermon 332
table of contents 19
Ten Commandments 310, 417
thanksgiving of woman after child-birth 442–444
theology of consecration 389
title page 15
vestments 527
visitation of the sick 461, 464, 467–468
English (1559) 6–7
Ash Wednesday 220
calendar of the church year 43
communion 386
daily office 95
dismissal 131
Eucharist 303
eucharistic prayer 358
Grace, the 494
litanies 158
Morning Prayer 109
ordination 517–518
ornaments rubric 527–528
prayers 554, 558
table of contents 19
English (Latin version, 1560) 6
burial 481
calendar of the church year 42
collects 181
English (1604) 7
baptism 265, 288
calendar of the church year 43
catechism 573, 580, 582
collects 207
daily office 95
Eucharist 303–304
eucharistic prayer 358
feasts 42
occasional thanksgivings 158
table of contents 19
thanksgivings 130, 554
English (1662) 8, 10, 22, 491
absolution 455
Alban 65
announcement of lesson 327
announcements 419

612

Magnificat 141
Quiñones' revision 109
Breviarium Gothicum 137, 181
Bride and groom, presentation of, in
marriage 429–430, 434
Briggs, G. W. 209
Bright, William 125–126, 141, 143, 146,
167, 172, 174, 180–181, 191–192, 194,
201, 207–208, 247–248, 468, 474, 568–
569
Brightman F. E. 169
Brooks, Phillips 50
Bucer, Martin 5–6, 41, 222, 259–260, 263,
270, 301, 433, 496, 505, 508, 510, 520–
526
Burial 2, 32, 477–500
    1549 Prayer Book 19
    1928 Prayer Book 20
    of an adult 486
    anthems 106, 239, 329
    black garments for mourners 477–
    478
    blessings 396
    canticles 116
    of a child 482, 484, 486–487, 489,
    493, 498
    collects 142, 165, 180, 210, 324
    consecration of pavement beneath
    which bodies would be buried
    541
    entrance rites 316
    intercessions 372
    language 28
    music 32–33
    paschal candle 244
    prayer for the departed 341
    prayers 178, 403, 474–476
    prayers for vigil 475
    prefaces 404
    references in dedication of church
    540
    at sea 482, 492–493
    Trisagion 320
Bushong, Ann Brooke 565
Butler, Joseph 65
Byzantine rite 74, 120, 294, 452, 456–
457, 491

Caesarius of Arles, bishop 117, 584
Calendar (1561) 42
    Agnes 49
    Alphege 59
    Ambrose 86
    Anne, mother of Mary 69
    Augustine of Canterbury 62
    Chad, Bishop of Lichfield 54

Cyprian 73
David, Bishop of Menevia 54
Dunstan 61
Fabian 49
Gregory the Great 55
Hilary, bishop 48
Holy Cross Day 74
Holy Name 47
Hugh, bishop 83
Martin of Tours 82
Mary Magdalene 68
Nicholas 85
Perpetua and companions 54
Remigius 76
Richard, bishop of Chichester 58
Transfiguration 70
Vincent 50
Visitation, feast of 62
*Calendar and Lessons for the Church's
Year, The* 211
Calendar of the church year 36–68, 589
Callistus III, Pope 70
Calvin, John 5–6, 41, 222, 260, 297, 301,
311, 389, 393–394, 450
Cambridge Bede Book, The 169
Canadian Prayer Books *see* Book of
Common Prayer, Canadian
Candidates for baptism *see* Baptismal
candidates
Candlemas Day *see* Presentation of Our
Lord Jesus Christ in the Temple
Candles 442
    baptism 256, 286–287
    dedication and consecration of a
    church 544, 548
    at Easter Vigil 241–245, 249
    Eucharist 315
    Gospel procession 330
    Order of Worship for the Evening
    136–138
    see also Paschal candle
Canon *see* Eucharistic prayer
Canon law
    copies of canons given to new min-
    ister 534–535, 538
    consecration of a church 542, 550
    disciplinary rubrics 422
    marriage 431–433
    ministration of communion 385
    ordination 513–514, 516–518
Canons of 1604 280, 518, 583
Canons of Hippolytus 441
Cantate Domino 112, 115
Cantemus Domino (Song of Moses) 112,
119, 121, 247

615

616

624

Egyptian sacramentary 323
Eighth Day 37, 409
Eighth Sunday after Epiphany 172–173
Eighth Sunday after Trinity 186–187
Elders 503
    in early Church 27
Electoral Brandenberg 5
Eleona 223, 229
Elevations of the Sacrament 295, 297, 302, 356–357, 364, 368, 373, 383
Eleventh Sunday after Trinity 192
Elizabeth, mother of John the Baptist 65
    Visitation, feast of the 62–63
Elizabeth, princess of Hungary 83
Elizabeth I 6, 30, 95, 128, 130, 132, 135, 144, 147, 217, 231, 484, 587
Elizabethan calendar of 1561 see Calendar (1561)
Elizabethan homilies 559, 582
Elizabethan injunctions 160
Ember days 40, 47, 167, 174, 175, 184, 192–193
    1662 Prayer Book 46
    1928 Prayer Book 42, 44
    collects 173
    Holy Cross Day 74
    lessons 110
    ordination 513–514
    prayers 567
    prayers of the people 532
Ember vigil 167, 175
Ember weeks 212–213, 554
Emergency baptism 257, 265, 268, 285, 288
Encheiridion 432
English catechism (1962) see Revised catechism (Eng. 1962)
English Litany of 1544, 5, 19, 131
English non-jurors 359, 368
English Prayer Books see Book of Common Prayer, English
English Series Three (1973) 311, 382, 402, 406
English Series Two 406
Ennodius, bishop 245
Entrance of the ministers 33, 136
Entrance procession 27, 30–32, 261, 331
Entrance psalm 238, 298, 301, 315, 317–318, 387, 417
Entrance rites
    Eucharist 292, 308, 311–312, 315–324, 391–392, 411–412, 417–418
    litanies 335
    liturgies of Saint John Chrysostom and Saint Basil 130

    processional psalms 327–328, 552
Entrance song 317–318
    Ash Wednesday 219
    Eucharist 295–296
    Good Friday 233–234
Ephesus, Council of (431) 583
Ephrem of Edessa, deacon 64, 80
Epiclesis 297, 302, 304, 307, 313, 350–353, 355–360, 365, 369–371, 373, 375–377, 389–390, 415–416, 420, 466
Epiphany 38–39, 43–44, 48
    1928 Prayer Book 46
    precedence 44
    Athanasian Creed 584
    baptism 248
    baptismal references 256
    canticles 120
    collects 170, 336
    collects after 567–569
    confession of Saint Peter 49
    conversion of Saint Paul 50
    entrance rites 316–317, 320, 322
    eucharistic prayer 375
    Evening Prayer 99
    introit 316
    lessons 109
    Magna et mirabilia 121
    Morning Prayer 98, 103, 107, 109
    octave 325
    opening sentences 148
    Order of Worship for the Evening 137
    prefaces 306, 398–399
    songs of praise 322
    vigil 41
Episcopal
    included in name of church 16
Episcopal chair 530
Episcopal Church, The 16, 272
Episcopal services 20, 501–502
    language 29
    see also Celebration of a new ministry; Dedication and consecration of a church; Ordination
Epistles
    1549 Prayer Book 19
    1789 Prayer Book 28
    1892 Prayer Book 20
Erasmus, Desiderius 259, 263
Eschatological references
    of eucharistic prayer 351–352, 367, 375
Eschaton, 2, 37
Estill, Robert W. 13
Ethiopian liturgies 366, 375

625

629

Godparents 256, 259, 261, 263–266, 268–270, 277, 572
God the Father 575
God the Son 576
Golden Number 43, 47, 589
Golden Sequence, The see Veni Sancte Spiritus
Good Friday 43, 45–46
  1789 Prayer Book 46
  anthem 464
  collects 177–178, 194, 213, 217, 232–236, 246, 248, 324, 335, 394
  communion 387–388, 409–410, 421
  entrance rites 316
  Evening Prayer 99
  fasts 240
  Gallican rite 219
  Gospel 228
  Morning Prayer 98, 104, 106
  prayers 498
  proper liturgy 231–239
  reconciliation of penitents 229
  reserved sacrament 230
  Sext 177
  solemn collects 127
Gore, Charles 474
Gospel, in Eucharist 330–332
Gospel books 292, 294, 330, 504, 511, 529
  incense 152
  Palm Sunday 224
Gospel canticles 91, 112, 114–115
  daily office
    1549 Prayer Book 94
    1552 Prayer Book 95
    Morning Prayer 105
Gospel of the palms 226
Gospel procession 330–331
  music 32–33
  psalms 327
Gott, John
Grace, the 129, 131, 158–159, 161–162, 312, 361, 416, 481–482, 494
  1662 Prayer Book 95
  family and individual devotions 148
  Holy Saturday 239
Graces 556, 569
Gracious Light, O see Phos hilaron
Gradual 2, 31, 154, 227, 234, 298, 314, 326–328, 417, 494, 552
Gratias agamus 245
Grave, consecration of see Consecration of grave
Great Amen 27
Great Bible 113, 115, 116, 551–552

Great Compline 120
Great Entrance 293, 347
Great Fifty Days 24, 38, 40, 42, 46, 136, 184, 245, 256, 318, 380
Great Litany 154–162, 316–317, 342, 407, 417, 474, 476, 531–532, 566, 569
  Lord's Prayer 123, 150
  ordination 508, 510–512, 524
  special petitions 214
Great Offering 309
  see also Eucharist
Great Sunday 24, 38
Great Thanksgiving 286, 292, 349–378, 415
  celebration of new ministry 539
  Eucharist 151
Great Vigil of Easter 170, 180, 184, 239–250
Greenfield, Robert H. 13, 373, 437, 488, 574
Greeting of priest, at ordination 530
Gregorian sacramentary 3, 14, 40
  Advent prayer 165
  Christmas prayers 170
  collect for aid against perils 137
  collect for grace 126
  collects 142, 146, 161–163, 166–169, 171–180, 183–184, 188, 191, 193–194, 196–200, 202, 204–205, 211, 219–220, 226, 233, 235, 246, 382, 407, 489, 567
  Easter Vigil 242, 246–247
  Exaltation of the Holy Cross 74
  Good Friday 232
  litanies 162
  Mark, Saint 59
  Mary the Virgin, Saint 72
  Maundy Thursday 229
  nativity of John the Baptist 66
  Pentecost vigil,
    prayer from 236
  Peter and Paul, feast of 66
  postcommunion prayer 126
  prayers over the people 233, 394
  prefaces 398–402
  proper prefaces 352
  solemn collects for Good Friday 127
  Thomas, Saint 86
Gregorian sacramentary, supplement to 3, 14
  absolution 222
  baptism 260
  Bartholomew, Saint 72
  burial 480, 494
  collects, 170, 171, 175, 181–182,

632

Holy Name of Jesus, feast of the 41, 45, 47–48, 169–170
Holy Saturday 43
  collect 178
  entrance rite 316
  Eucharist 234
  fasts 231, 240
  Morning Prayer 104
  proper liturgy 238–239
  Psalm 95, 153
  Sext 177
  Trisagion 320
Holy Scriptures *see* Bible
Holy Sepulchre, Church of the, Jerusalem 74
Holy Spirit 209, 577
Holy Trinity 209
Holy water 224, 241, 442, 459–460
Holy Week, 11, 40, 43, 45, 224, 479
  1928 Prayer Book precedence 44
  collects 125, 176–178
  Cyril, bishop of Jerusalem 55
  Eucharist 228
  lessons 108
  Morning Prayer 109
  Order of Worship for the Evening 135
  prefaces 400
Homilies 5
  of 1547 217, 298, 332, 460, 573
  Ash Wednesday 219, 220–221
  burial 486, 488, 500
  in early Church 90
  Easter Vigil 248, 250
  Eucharist 293, 298, 301, 332
  marriage 429–430, 435
  Morning and Evening Prayer 150
  Order of Worship for the Evening 138
  for Whitsunday 212
  see also Preaching; Sermon
Honey
  mystery religions 252
Honorius III, Pope 71
Hooker, Richard 7, 57, 81
Hooper, John 6, 303
Hope 582
Hopkins, John 30
House of Bishops 271–272, 470, 588
House of Deputies 588
Hugh, bishop 83
Hugh of St. Victor 4
Human nature 574

Huntington, Frederick Dan 215, 563, 565
Huntington, William Reed 69–70, 125–126, 143, 176, 204, 560, 563, 588
Hymnal 2
Hymnal (1871) 20
Hymnal (1940) 149, 381
Hymns 2, 5, 10, 29–33
  1789 Prayer Book 20
  agapé meal 415
  Agnus Dei 381
  Ambrose 86
  Bernard 72
  baptism 286–287
  burial 478–479, 482, 485–486, 491, 500
  catechism 574
  celebration of new ministry 536–537
  communion 387–388
  Compline 144–145, 147
  conclusion of Eucharist 391
  daily office 128–129
  dedication and consecration of a church 545–547, 549
  in early Church 27, 90
  Easter Vigil 241, 244
  Ephrem of Edessa 64
  Eucharist 292–293, 296, 306, 315–317, 321, 328–329, 413
  Evening Prayer 140, 149–150
  family and individual devotions 148
  German 330
  Good Friday 232–233, 237
  between Gospel and sermon 332
  Herbert, George 53
  Jewish funerals 477
  John of Damascus 85
  Ken, Thomas 56
  litanies 154
  little offices 132
  Magna et mirabilia 121
  marriage 432, 434
  Maundy Thursday 229
  monastic office 90
  Morning Prayer 149–150
  Neale, John Mason 70
  offertory 347–349
  Order of service for noonday 132–133
  Order of Worship for the Evening 138
  ordination 504–505, 508, 516, 521–523, 530
  Palm Sunday 223, 227
  penitential order 311
  postcommunion prayer 393, 421

633

634

637

Martyrs of Uganda 63, 80
Mary, Saint, of Bethany 68–69
Maryland convention 359–360
    of 1780 16
Mary Magdalene, Saint 43, 45, 68, 203
Mary the Virgin, Saint 43, 45, 71–72
    Annunciation 56–57
    antiphons in honor of 128
    canticles 95, 114
    collects 204
    commemoration, in prayer for the
        whole state of Christ's Church 340
    litanies 156–157
    Luke, Saint 78
    Magnificat 114–115
    Marian feasts
        songs of praise 322
    parents of 69
    prefaces 398–399
    Presentation (Candlemas) 51
    purification 442
    Theotokos 584
    Visitation 43, 62–63
Mary Tudor 5–6, 128
Mass 3–5, 25, 308
    canticles 116
    Christmas Day 170
    collects 163–164
    confession of priest and server 100,
        102
    Gloria in excelsis 117
    harvest blessings 84
    Kyrie 155
    litanies 155
    multiplication of 294
    music 34
    prayers over the people 177
    procession 157
    vigil of Christmas 168
    weekday 91
    see also Eucharist
Massachusetts
    Thanksgiving Day 84
Massachusetts convention (1785) 555,
    567
Materia Ritualis (Huntington) 69, 125–
    126, 143, 176
Matins 485
    1549 Prayer Book 19, 41, 94–95, 97
    antiphons 103
    Ash Wednesday 219
    Athanasian Creed 121
    burial 478
    canticles 112, 115, 117, 153
    Christmas prayers 170
    collects 126

Easter Day 178, 217, 242
Easter Week 181
Good Friday 233
middle ages 91, 99–100
monastic office 90
opening versicle 133
readings 108
Venite 104
Matthew, Saint 75, 203, 205, 208, 584
Matthias, Saint 41, 53, 199, 512, 519,
    584, 592
Maundy Thursday 43, 219
    blessing of oil and chrism 463
    collects 177, 209, 310, 410
    Eucharist 308
    evening service of Light 135
    Gospel 228
    office prayers 177
    proper liturgy 228–231
    reconciliation of penitents 449
    reserved Sacrament 410, 421
Maurice, Frederick Denison 57
Maximinus 49
McCrady, James Waring 160
McNutt, F. B. 175
Meals, sacred 289–291
Meat
    sacrificial 289
Medieval uses 4
Memorial acclamations 27, 32, 351, 365–
    367, 374–376, 415, 581
Memorial collects 298
Memorial Day 497
Memorial of the cross 237–238, 498
Memorials 165, 173, 324
Memorials Upon Several Occasions (Mil-
    ner-White) 143
Merbecke, John 34, 485
Methodists 9, 54, 305, 414
Methodius, bishop 52
Metrical psalms, canticles, and hymns
    112, 138, 140, 149, 317, 328, 388
Metrical psalter 10, 20, 30–31, 128–129
Michael, Saint and All Angels 41, 75–76,
    107, 205, 209, 403
Migne, J. P. 404
Milk and honey 240
Millenary Petition 7
Milner-White, Eric 143, 209, 238, 498,
    564
Ministers see Bishops; Celebration of a
    new ministry; Deacons; Institution of
    a minister; Liturgical ministries; Ordi-
    nation; Priests
Ministers, rite for the institution
    of 10

640

647

collects 134
dedication and consecration of a church 548
Easter Vigil 240
ember days 532
Eucharist 152
Form 1 405
Form 2 405
Form 3 405–406
Form 4 406
Form 5 406, 531
Form 6 406–407
Good Friday 235
newly baptized 278
Order of Worship for the Evening 138
penitential supplications 342
Taizé liturgy 236
Prayers of the Spirit (Suter) 470–471
Prayers New and Old 561
Prayers over the people (super populum) 163, 177, 197, 226, 233, 390, 394, 396
Ash Wednesday 220
ordination 510–511, 526–527
post-baptismal 284
renewal of baptismal vows 248
Prayers We have in Common 29
Preaching 2, 521
at baptisms 268
in daily office
of reformed churches 91
in early Church 27
Eucharist 296, 332, 418
furniture for 547
see also Homilies; Sermon
Precedence 44–46, 424
Preces 217, 442, 452, 461–462, 480, 494
Preces Privatae (Andrewes) 135, 139, 217
Preface to 1549 Prayer Book 6, 583, 585–586
Preface to American Book of Common Prayer 23
Preface to ordination rites 511, 513–514, 524
Prefaces 42, 117, 274–275, 293, 297, 302, 306, 351–354, 358, 360–363, 371, 374–376, 378, 397–404
1552 Prayer Book 25
baptism 284
burial 490
celebration of new ministry 539
Christmas Day 168
dedication and consecration of a church 549
Easter Vigil 242

Gallican 245
marriage 439
Pentecost 184
seasonal 398–402
Sundays 398
Pre-Lent 40
1928 Prayer Book
precedence of Sundays 44
canticles 117, 153
Eucharist 298
lessons 108
tract 329
Preliminary epiclesis 369, 371
Prelude, musical 33
Preparation of the table *see* Table, eucharistic, preparation of
Presanctified Sacrament *see* Reserved Sacrament
Presbyterians 7, 511, 525
Presbyters 3, 304, 503–504
anointing of the sick 459
baptism 253, 257, 277–278, 280
in early Church 27
Eucharist 312–313
ministration of communion 420
ordination of 212, 508, 514–515, 524, 527
see also Priests
Presentation of candidates for ordination 508, 510, 516–517, 529
Presentation of instruments 538
Presentation of new minister to congregation 538
Presentation of Our Lord Jesus Christ in the Temple 40, 45, 51, 71, 199, 399, 442
Presentation of the gifts 388
Presentation of the oblation 327–328
Presiding Bishop 514, 529
Previously authorized texts 34
Price, Charles P. 13, 557, 561, 564, 566, 569–570
Priesthood of the laity 467, 503–504
Priests 4, 11, 15, 27–28, 301, 314, 504
1789 Prayer Book 28
absolution 100, 102, 222, 453
baptism 268, 279
baptism within Eucharistic context 284
blessing of oil for the sick 464
blessing of penitent 455
blessings 391, 395–396
bread and wine 303
breaking of the bread 379–380
burials 482, 479, 484
catechism 573, 578

654

661

Wardens 301, 303, 346, 443
  celebration of new ministry 534–535, 537–538
  dedication and consecration of a church 543, 547
Washing of feet
  at baptism 241, 255, 278
  on Maundy Thursday 229–231
Washington, George 560
Water
  baptismal 286–287
  blessing of, for the sick 459
  in celebration of Epiphany 48
  dedication and consecration of a church 540
  in dedication of font 546
  dilution of the wine 347–348
  Eucharist 419
  presentation to new minister 535
Watts, Isaac 31
Wedding see Marriage
Wednesday of Easter Week 180, 339, 376, 556
Wednesday of Holy Week 177–178, 226, 228, 230, 233, 394
Wednesdays
  1552 Prayer Book 41
  1928 Prayer Book 42
  autumn ember day 192
  canticles 114, 120
  ember days 47
  Eucharist 302
  fasts, early Christian 37
  in Jewish ritual 36
  litanies 19, 129, 154–155, 157–159, 200, 335
  Morning Prayer 100
  prayers 556
  in reformed churches 41
  rogation day 47
  spring ember day 174
  summer ember day 184
  winter ember day 167
  see also Ash Wednesday
Wee Bookies 8, 305, 359–360, 368, 370–372, 482
Week, Christian see Liturgical week
Weekdays 24
  1552 Prayer Book 25
  collects 125, 165, 169
  communion 307
  communion in the home 409
  communion in the home, in early Church 232
  Creed 150

daily office
  of reformed churches 91
  in early Church 37, 90
  in Jewish ritual 36, 89
  lessons 325–326
  liturgies, early Christian 291
  masses 91, 294
  Morning Prayer 104
  peace, exchange of 281
  Prayer of Saint Chrysostom 131
  prayer over the people 163
  prefaces 398–399
  in reformed churches 41
  sermon 332
Weil, Louis 274
Welsh, Clement W. 561
We Praise Thee, You are God see Te Deum
Wesley, Charles 31, 54
Wesley, John 9, 31, 54, 305–306, 390
Western rites see Gallican rites; Roman rite
Westminster Directory 370
Wheatly, Charles 305, 390
Whiston, William 305–306, 390
Whitby, council of (664) 56, 83
White, William 67, 220, 403, 478, 585, 587–588
White cloth, for eucharistic table 291, 347, 416
White garments, baptism 241, 261, 442, 527
Whitehead, Cortlandt 565
White robes 254–256
Whitsunday see Pentecost
Widows, in early Church 505
Wilberforce, William 69–70, 82
Wiles, Preston 13
Wilfrid, bishop 54
Wilkinson, J. D. 211
William I 49
William II 49
William III 148
William and Mary 56, 559
Williams, Channing Moore 85
Willibrord, archbishop 81
Wills 447
Wilson, Thomas 10, 468, 542, 567
Wine 289–290
  1549 Prayer Book 25
  agapé meals 415
  blessed, in marriage ceremony 428
  in celebration of Epiphany 48
  celebration of new ministry 535
  consecration of
    early Christian Eucharist 292

Index of Scripture Citations

666

667

668

669